In the
Fullness
of Time

In the Fullness of Time

The Memoirs of
PAUL H. DOUGLAS

Harcourt Brace Jovanovich, Inc.
New York

ISBN 0-15-144376-9
Library of Congress Catalog Card Number: 74-182327
Printed in the United States of America
A B C D E F

To Emily, *my dear wife*

Contents

Illustrations

Acknowledgments

I BEGAN THESE MEMOIRS ten years ago and have worked at them intermittently ever since. During the first part of this period, I was deeply involved in the political life of our country and devoted my energies to these tasks. After I left the Senate in 1966 came two intense and frustrating years as chairman of a Presidential Commission on Housing and Urban Problems. The last three years have been marked by partial but increasing disability. Through it all I have kept at work on this manuscript.

There have been gains in all this time. Personal animosities have softened, so that there is no one whom I regard as a foe, and my attitude toward issues has mellowed. During these years of contemplation, I have continually revised chapters and worked to produce final ones.

This has necessitated a great deal of typing and editorial work. Jane Carey Enger, during my years in the Senate, did the supervisory work. Rosemary Cribben, Mary Frances de La Pava, Patricia Gray, Irene Farrar, Ann Healy, Sarah Smith, Nancy Stewart, Betty Summers, and Virginia Carey De Simone assisted with the typing; Patty Auchincloss Tirana has been of invaluable help in correcting proof.

I have been greatly aided by friends who have read and criticized sections of the book, particularly Joseph L. Rauh, who went over the chapters on civil rights and civil liberties; Howard Shuman, on critical portions of the manuscript; Kenneth Gray, on the Indiana Dunes; Ezra Levin, on sickness and health; Jonathan Lindley, on the depressed areas; Walter Rybeck, on housing; and Paul Taylor, on land monopoly. I also benefited from suggestions of my friend S. McKee Rosen and my daughter Helen Douglas Klein. Any mistakes, however, are my own and not the fault of others.

I have profited much from the co-operation and advice of those at Harcourt Brace Jovanovich, notably William Jovanovich, Hiram Haydn, and Roberta Leighton.

Above all, as in everything I have done, I am chiefly indebted to my wife for help in the initial decisions I made both in private life and as a senator and in the final revisions of the manuscript.

PART ONE

Early Life

1

Boyhood in the Maine Woods

I GREW UP in a log cabin in the heart of the Maine woods. This may help to explain some of the weaknesses and the strengths of my character.

My father, James Douglas, came from a line of sailors, fishermen, and shipbuilders who, from 1700 on, lived along the coast of Maine. After failing twice in business, he had become a traveling salesman, with his home in Salem, Massachusetts. There I was born on March 26, 1892.

My mother, Annie Smith, was a New Brunswick woman whose uncle, Harry Tuck, was chief justice of that Canadian province and previously a leader in the Conservative party. Their families had, I am afraid, been New England Tories, who, like so many others, fled after the American Revolution to Saint John to start life afresh. My mother was evidently a woman of artistic talent; I have some seascapes and water colors which she painted before she took lessons, and these pictures, reminiscent of both Turner and Salvator Rosa, show much promise, as do her later still-life studies. In 1880 she made the hitherto untried venture for a Canadian girl of going to Vassar to study. Since her money gave out after one year, she, like many women of the time, turned to teaching, and found an opening in Maine.

In Bucksport, on the Penobscot, in the eastern part of the state, she met my father, then in his early thirties. In due course they were married, and in 1884 my elder brother, John, was born. But my father's venture into the drygoods business was already collapsing, and another effort, in the little city of Gardiner, was no more successful. He gave up, became a traveling salesman, or "drummer," for a Providence firm, and was assigned the territory of upper New York State, which he covered for over twenty years, until his death in 1912.

I have only the faintest memories of my mother, who died of tuberculosis when I was four. I can remember a sweet and smiling face bending down toward me. Her mother, who lived with us, died at almost the same time of the same dread disease. Tuberculosis, or consumption, as it was called, was the feared killer, and no one knew the slightest thing about reducing its dangers. My brother and I were put out to board with a distant cousin, about whom I have vague but unpleasant memories.

In 1897 my father married for the second time. My new stepmother was a young Maine woman by the name of Florence Young. During the winter of 1897–98, we lived at Saratoga Springs, New York. There I learned to read, from the bulletin boards that chronicled the outbreak and progress of the Spanish-American War, Admiral Dewey's victory at Manila Bay, and Teddy Roosevelt's well-advertised charge up San Juan Hill. Two other memories of that year stand out. With eyes of wonder, I saw a horseless carriage move slowly up a hill. And I watched with fascination the broad verandas of the old United States Hotel, then the center of summer fashion, where in dappled sunlight beautifully dressed women and fashionably clad men moved to and fro in the minuets of conventional flirtation.

My stepmother, whom I soon adored and who in turn lavished a mother's love upon me, gradually found life with my father impossible. Sometimes he came home drunk, and he was often in a bad temper. I became ashamed of him, although my stepmother tried her best to conceal her difficulties from her new sons and to make us respect our father. Then she came to an extraordinary and heroic decision. She determined not only to leave my father, but also to take us with her to her uncle and brother, who were just starting a summer camp, or hotel, in the Maine woods near Moosehead Lake. As she later said, she could not bear to live with my father, but similarly she could not bear to leave us with him, since she felt certain that he would not care properly for us. So when he was away on one of his trips, she fled with us to Boston by rail, then to Bangor by boat, and then by rail to Onawa.

As I think back over this crucial event, which I little understood at the time, I marvel at her courage in taking under her wing two boys to whom she had so slight an obligation. Having no children of her own, she heaped upon us all the tender and loving care a mother could possibly give. Her memory has always been one of the most precious in my life.

Her brother, Rodney Young, and her uncle, Rodney Buxton, must have been surprised at the little flock so suddenly dumped upon them. But they rallied in good spirits and warmly welcomed us. My stepmother quickly made herself invaluable to their enterprise as cook and waitress, although I am afraid we youngsters were of little help.

There I lived for the next eight years, until 1906. During that time my father gradually faded out of my life. Except for two brief visits, I did not see him again for ten years, and during this time I received letters from him only rarely, along with packages of clothing, which, with his blundering way, always consisted of undershirts and stockings, with no connecting links between the two and with no outer clothing. I soon knew what to expect when these occasional offerings arrived, and thought with bitterness how inadequately he equipped me to face the world and to endure the rigors of the Maine winters.

So it was natural that my dislike for my father should grow. This feeling was somewhat abated in later years. In 1908 I spent a week with him on a sales trip through the lake country of upper New York State, and in 1910 John and I spent a final summer with him, in Gloversville, New York. But I was repelled by his taste for low life. It was not until years later that I realized that the loneliness, the strain, and the temptations of a traveling salesman's life accounted for much of what had happened. In a sense he was a prototype for the Willie Loman whom Arthur Miller commemorated in his *Death of a Salesman*. Moreover, while my father did not contribute to my support, he did help John, who early showed extraordinary mathematical and scientific ability, first at a little Methodist preparatory school in Bucksport, and then at the Massachusetts Institute of Technology, where, despite poverty, he made a brilliant record. So time has softened my former harsh judgments, although I have always feared the emergence of some of my father's traits in me.

Our hotel in Maine was located on a pine-clad point, jutting out into a lake four miles long and a mile wide, that was surrounded on three sides by hills or mountains ranging from 800 to 3,000 feet in height. One of these, Borestone, was bold in its outline, and we climbed it several times a year and were thrilled by the beauty of the forested landscape dotted with lakes and rivers that stretched out below us. While the little hamlet of Onawa was the exact geographical center of the state, it was a dozen miles from the nearest town, and there was no connecting road. One could travel 150 miles north to the Canadian border without seeing a house or a person. Our one physical link with the outside world was the Canadian Pacific Railroad; we were on its main line running through northern Maine on the way from Montreal to Halifax, Nova Scotia. A combination freight-and-passenger train ran daily each way, and at either Greenville or Brownville we could make connections with a line taking us to Bangor and the outside world. At night an express would thunder through on its transcontinental route.

Our life was primitive. Maine is still a residual frontier, and at the turn of the century was more so. With the help of a cow and a sad horse, we produced nearly all that we consumed, and, even with the money from summer guests, our cash income was very small. Although poor, we never realized it. We built the cabins from spruce logs cut in the nearby forests and chinked them with moss. After clearing a scant acre of hillside, we planted potatoes and other vegetables, which we harvested in the fall and used both for the guests and to store for the winter.

But the cycle of the year really began in March, when, with the snow still heavy on the ground, the succession of sunshiny days and cold nights would make the sap rise in the maples and it was syrup time. We then built a rude lean-to in the nearest maple grove, tapped several hundred trees, and, on snowshoes, carried the sap in buckets to the "sugaring-off" place, where we poured it into huge pans over fires that were kept constantly burning. In this way we made many gallons of syrup for the use of the summer guests, and, going one stage further, boiled down large quantities of syrup to be molded into maple sugar. The special delight, dear to all children of the north country, was the maple taffy made by pouring syrup, before it had sugared, in thin trails on the snow. This was fatal to the teeth, but delicious to the taste.

All this time the snow, at least five feet deep, would be melting. Toward the end of April the ice would break up with a crash, and the lake would again be cleared. The spring "drive" would follow almost immediately. During the winter, a logger and his crew of French-Canadian lumberjacks would have been busy cutting spruce trees and hauling them to level spots near the lake. As the ice went out, the logs were rolled into the lake one by one, formed into a "boom," and, with the aid of wind or oars, brought to the river at the foot of the lake. The waters were high from the melting snow, and the little river became a rushing torrent. If the logs became stuck on rock or bank, men rushed into the icy water and pried them loose to continue on their downward way. This work went on around the clock, with tired men in soaked clothes snatching such scanty sleep as they could.

Downstream the roar of the drive passed into another lake, Sebec, thence into still another but broader stream, and finally into the Penobscot itself. There the logs were finally sorted at the sawmills lining the river from Orono to Bangor, where the men collected their wages for the winter and spring and then sought rest and relaxation. Sex-starved from their long winter in the woods, they burst upon Bangor like hordes of Goths upon Rome. They drank heavily in the grog shops found on almost every downtown street and cavorted with the young whores who gathered to help pluck them clean. After a few days of riotous debauchery, they disappeared, only to return the next fall when the cycle of lumbering began again.

In theory Maine had been a prohibition state ever since the 1850's, when Neal Dow led the crusade outlawing the sale of intoxicants. But Bangor had literally hundreds of saloons, and it was political suicide for any public official to interfere with the trade. The prosperity of the little city was built not only on lumber and "stumpage rights," the titles to which some of the leading citizens had stolen shortly after the Civil War, but also upon the exploitation of the ignorant French-Canadians through underpayment as well as from the profits derived from whiskey and women. For another reason, the saloons were a major source of revenue for the city. Every six months the saloonkeepers were arrested, solemnly brought before the local police magistrate, and fined heavily. This, of course, was equivalent to an annual license fee, which, in turn, helped to provide for the upkeep of the police and fire departments, the maintenance of the streets, and the schools. In short, the institutions of civilization in Bangor were chiefly financed by taking advantage of the moral, social, and economic weaknesses of the poor and ignorant. If any serious protest was made by the "good" citizens of Bangor (which had an excellent theological school), I was not aware of it as a youth. Years later, when a fire swept the city, destroying most of the twenty-five churches, it did not touch any of the 225 saloons. The sanctimonious marveled at the peculiar workings of Providence, while the cynics and atheists, of whom there were many, smiled sardonically and attributed the selection to the basic sympathies of the Lord.

I developed a strong sympathy for the men who toiled so long and hard for the scanty wage of a dollar a day. Nearly every year one of them would be drowned during the drive, and I gazed upon their bodies when they were shipped off in wooden boxes on the railroad. In those days there was no workmen's compensation for industrial accidents, and under the common law, the poor fellows were supposed to have assumed all the legal risks of the job when they took it.

When the section hands of the railroad struck during the early years of the century, I was passionately on their side. Feeling that the financial magnates of Montreal and Great Britain, led by Sir William Van Horne, were treating them unfairly, I wondered why the train crews who shouted encouragement to the section hands as they passed would not also go out on strike to help them. That would have settled the matter, particularly during the winter months, when the Saint Lawrence was frozen over and wheat from the Canadian prairie provinces poured eastward in long trains on the one-track line. It was gravely explained to me that each of the four train crafts had its own union, that each of these had agreements with the company that were still in force, and that they were therefore honor bound not to strike. When I asked why the railway workers did not join one union uniting the demands of all, my elders smiled sadly. This, they said, had been tried some years before in Chicago by a man named Debs, but it had not worked. Debs had wound up in jail and had come to a bad end.

In these ways social problems, including immigration and the question of craft or industrial unionism, penetrated even the depths of the Maine woods, causing me to feel, to question, and to wonder. During the summer, immigrant trains passed through with strange men and women on board waving timidly to us from the windows. I was told that they came from a section of Russia called the Ukraine and that they were trying to escape from the economic and political tyranny of the czars. They were bound for the prairie provinces from Manitoba west. I can still see the buxom young women with gaily colored handkerchiefs tied around their heads and with eyes at once sparkling and frightened at the unknown life ahead. Summer visitors told us of similar sights as ships unloaded their human cargo at Ellis Island in New York. There, however, the newcomers were mostly Jews, Poles, Italians, and Greeks.

For all this, life in the woods was largely a pageant of the seasons. As the roar of the drive abated, the spring flowers and vegetation appeared in great profusion. The painted trillium was everywhere, as was the trailing arbutus, or Mayflower, and now and then a lady's-slipper. The woods were alive to the thrill of spring and all of its delicious scents.

Spring was also the signal for our work. It was time to clean and repair the cabins, readying them for the summer guests who would soon stream in from Boston and New York, and who paid for their room and board at the luxurious rate of ten to fourteen dollars a week. As unofficial bellboy, I carried bags, firewood, and water, ran errands, and conversed with the strangers from that world of mystery so far away. Along with these duties, which I performed clumsily, summer meant swimming in the lake, fishing for trout and salmon, and weekly picnics on the mountains or at nearby lakes. My mother bore the brunt of the work as cook, waitress, and chambermaid.

With the coming of Labor Day the guests left, and we had the camp and lake to ourselves. The year was swinging in full cycle. In the golden days, as the maples reddened, the mountains looked like Oriental carpets, changing their texture and color with every day.

Further duties then crowded in on us. In clearings, a few miles away, we gathered apples from abandoned farms whose former occupants had given up and gone west. We cut, sawed, and split both hardwood and softwood trees for the winter's supply of fuel, and woe betide us if we did not cut enough.

My uncles would go deer hunting, but in this I resolutely refused to join them. I had once killed a porcupine with a club and had been struck with remorse when I saw its pained and accusing eyes. It seemed to be telling me, "I have the right to live also." More important, I had a close relationship with a pet fawn, which I will later describe.

From these and other sources I felt a deep repugnance at taking any form of life, and this repugnance has always stayed with me. I was not logical in this, for I never refused to eat the venison my uncles brought back from the hunt, or the occasional bear or moose that they shot. And I not only ate fish, but also caught them happily, whether by fly, by trolling, or by still-fishing in pools. Later in life I made some halfhearted

ventures in vegetarianism, but finally gave it up. Since men now control
the rate of increase of the animals, and since the animals probably have a
surplus of sentient pleasure over pain, I convinced myself that for mankind to give up eating meat would decrease the number of the beasts of
the field and, hence, diminish the total amount of animal pleasure. As
Benjamin Franklin once remarked, "So great a thing it is to be a reasonable creature, for then one can always find a reason for what one wants to
do."

As the winter deepened, we shoveled paths through drifted snow and
moved about on snowshoes. Struggling to keep warm, we kept the fire-
places and stoves always burning. But the little cabin where my stepmother and I slept was freezing cold. When we wakened, the ice in the
water pail was many inches thick.

During these winter months my mother organized a little school, not
only for me, but also for the children of the French-Canadian section
hands. All my early schooling probably did not amount to more than a
year and a half of classroom attendance.

We read and broadened our vocabulary from McGuffey's *Readers,* for
which I retain a sentimental fondness. Adapted to a rural and small-town
society, they were full of moral stories and snatches of good literature,
poems by Longfellow, Whittier, and Felicia Hemans. We learned our
arithmetic from George Albert ("Bull") Wentworth's text. Geography
came to us through maps and such important information as "Concord on
the Merrimack is the capital of New Hampshire" and "The French are a
gay, frivolous people, fond of dancing and light wines."

It was a set of Dickens that captured my imagination. My start with
Dombey and Son was not too promising, but I thrilled to *A Tale of
Two Cities, David Copperfield,* and *Nicholas Nickleby,* and laughed lust-
ily over *Pickwick Papers.* Of course I identified myself with Copperfield
and wondered if I also could overcome the hurdles of life and prosper.
From *Martin Chuzzlewit* and *American Notes* I learned that to foreign
eyes America had not always seemed sun-crowned.

Among the most pleasant features of my boyhood were visits to my
grandmother, Mary Douglas, in Bucksport. She lived where she had for a
half a century, a block from the Penobscot River and directly opposite the
shipyard where my grandfather had been foreman, and where the ship
that took Peary to the North Pole was built. Without knowing it when I
visited her, I was carried back to the America of 1850. We got our water
from an old oaken bucket which, as in the song, was moss-covered and
hung in the well. Each morning the old lady, crippled with dropsy,
sat in her garden, told me about the strange flowers she had planted
there, and directed me as I tried to weed. She held to the memories of how
the garden had looked half a century before, when, as a young bride, she
had come to Bucksport from Elijah Kellogg's Orrs Island and had started

her new life with her grave husband, who was rumored to be a free-thinker. The garden was almost a period piece out of *Godey's Lady's Book* and was full of strange and charming flowers which, at first, I could not identify. My grandmother introduced me to the musk roses, the delphiniums, the japonica, and, especially, the lavender and heliotrope, which seemed the acme of beauty. Years later the sight of a lavender-colored gown adorned with heliotropes set up a wave of nostalgia within me.

My grandmother, knowing her son, made it clear that she was sympathetic with my stepmother in her inability to live with my father. When my grandmother died around 1907, it was as if a section of the past had been allowed to slip away.

The great events of the day in Bucksport were the coming of the boats on the Bangor-Boston line. Early in the morning the side-wheeler from Boston would appear, discharge both freight and passengers, and then go on its way to Bangor, eighteen miles north. Then in the late afternoon it would reappear, bound this time for the open sea and for Boston, the trading and intellectual center for northern New England. The whole town would turn out to admire the skill of the captain and for the thrill of the foaming white water as the ship approached the dock. As the boats grew older, they necessarily weakened, until in severe storms they often broke up and sank, with all on board lost and drowned. Thereafter, communication with the "Hub of the Universe," as the residents of Boston modestly referred to their city, was confined to the railroad and, after 1925, the automobile. Then after another quarter of a century, the railway went the way of the steamers.

From a historical eulogy of the nineteenth century, I learned that everything that had happened during that century was good—from the development of the factory system to the war in the Sudan—and that, next to the United States, the British Empire was the noblest work of man. To this historian, Mr. Gladstone and Queen Victoria were the apotheosis of manhood and womanhood. Not until many years later, when I read John Morley and Lytton Strachey, did I discover how Gladstone and the Queen had heartily disliked each other.

I was by nature a bit of a rebel, and in this I was egged on by my stepmother's brother. Ill-health had forced him to give up his hopes of a medical career, and, to an extent which I did not realize at the time, he had found solace elsewhere. He would disappear into his cabin for days at a time; while I thought he was studying or meditating, he was drinking close to a quart of whiskey a day. Although his eyes might be bloodshot at night, his mind was always sharp and his tongue caustic. His uncle, Rodney Buxton, was a much superior character, who, with my mother, really kept our family together. He was also a devout and uncritical conservative, and his nephew and I took delight in criticizing—and, I am afraid, in ridiculing—his implicit trust in the Republican trinity of President McKinley, Mark Hanna, and John D. Rockefeller.

I found ammunition for this in the pages of the New York *World,* which came to us three times a week full of documented exposures. It became my Bible and chief contact with the outside world. Although it died in the 1930's, I still rank it as one of the most useful papers ever published in this country. I owe an incalculable debt to its publisher, Joseph Pulitzer, and to the brilliant group of writers and cartoonists he gathered about him. James Creelman and Homer Davenport were my boyhood heroes.

The summer guests brought copies of the current "muckraking" magazines, notably *McClure's,* with articles by Lincoln Steffens on "The Shame of the Cities" and by Ida M. Tarbell on the Standard Oil Company; while Tom Lawson was telling the story of his battles with Wall Street over Amalgamated Copper in *Everybody's,* and *Collier's* was exposing the frauds of patent medicines and paving the way for the Pure Food and Drug Act. Copies of the English magazine *The Strand* were also left behind, making the unfamiliar names of H. G. Wells, Arnold Bennett, W. W. Jacobs, and E. Nesbit household words.

So I became a sophisticated, if somewhat callow and remote, observer of the contemporary scene, with passionate convictions. I readily defended the Boers and the Irish against the British. I derided Sir Redvers Buller's periodic dispatch, "I regret to report," and gloried in the successes of the Boer generals Botha and Smuts. Joe Chamberlain, the British Colonial Secretary, with his ribboned eyeglass, was a special target. After the Boers, I soon took on the cause of the Filipinos. The *World* began to publish the revelations of Senator Edward W. Carmack, of Tennessee, about the American "water cure" for reluctant Filipinos on Mindanao. They would be tied to the ground and water would be poured through a funnel into their mouths until their stomachs burst. I gave half of the first dollar that I earned picking berries to the American Anti-Imperialist League, then headed by Moorfield Storey, the icy Boston Brahmin who later helped lead the opposition to the confirmation of Louis D. Brandeis for the Supreme Court. He marshaled the presidents of Eastern universities, along with other notables, in the League's cause.

Meanwhile, I recall an incident which took on enhanced interest many years later. A handsome young Army lieutenant, who had spent some months playing the horses at Saratoga, came to us to get back into shape. In the morning, after bringing his bucket of water, I would read to him the latest tidbit from the *World.* He grew purple with rage protesting the virtue of his father, a general in the Philippines, and that of James F. ("Hell-Roaring Jake") Smith, who commanded in Mindanao. We argued pungently about the comparative merits of imperialism and independence, and I reminded him that we had presumably fought the Spanish-

American War to set the Cubans and Filipinos free and not merely to give them a new set of masters. Neither of us convinced the other. After he departed, I thought no more about him for nearly forty years. Then, during the night of December 8, 1941, after Pearl Harbor and Manila had been attacked, I woke with a start. Could it be possible? That profile of the dashing officer seemed familiar. The young lieutenant's first name had been the same as my last, and his father's name was Arthur. I rushed to my copy of *Who's Who,* and, sure enough, there it was: Douglas MacArthur.

Another summer guest was Mae Greely, a beautiful white-haired widow and ardent feminist from Minneapolis. Determined to make a convert of me, she missed no opportunity to tell me how well woman suffrage was working in Wyoming and Colorado, Australia and New Zealand, and what a good job women doctors and lawyers were doing in their professions. I argued fiercely, urging the natural superiority of the male and the need for a separation of functions between the sexes. She replied with arguments drawn from Mary Wollstonecraft, Elizabeth Cady Stanton, and John Stuart Mill. As the days wore on, my arguments sounded ever a little more hollow, but I still conceded nothing. However, immediately after she left I realized that she was right, and I have ever since been a firm believer in equal rights and opportunities for women. This experience taught me that while reasoned arguments may not convince an opponent at the time, they may do so ultimately.

But nature taught me most. Lonely as I was, I gained a certain serenity of spirit from the woods and mountains, along with a basic faith in the goodness of the earth. This has stayed with me, making me want to preserve forever for the people as many places of natural beauty as possible. Wild areas are the beneficent healers of the tensions created by city life.

The life of the woods was, in a sense, an opiate. Days, externally so uneventful, merged with each other indistinguishably. Time seemed at once to vanish and to expand. Visitors from the outside world frequently fell under its rhythm and stayed with us until their relatives had to come and take them back to the world of affairs. I felt much the same magic at work within me, but knew that I must resist lest I end as a lumberjack. I knew I would not be a good lumberjack and that it was not my destiny.

Not until I read Thomas Mann's *The Magic Mountain,* years later in Switzerland, did I find the same mood put into words. It may be that the timelessness of the woods gave me the habit of putting off action, which has been a handicap all my life.

My faith in the goodness of nature was reinforced by two pets, a dog and a deer. The dog, Skinks, was my faithful and loyal friend until, stiff-legged with age and fatal sickness, he gave a deep groan one day and, without looking back at us, limped slowly away to die in a cave. I watched his parting with streaming tears. He wanted to die alone and with dignity.

The fawn I acquired when hunters shot its mother. I raised him and, fencing in a large area to house him, fed and watered him regularly. As he grew older he would break out of his pen, but he always came back. I finally fastened a cowbell around his neck so that if he again escaped, hunters might know that he was tame and, taking pity on him, would not shoot. As was inevitable, he broke out again. From time to time he would come to the edge of our little clearing and look at me with his liquid eyes, evidently wanting to keep some contact with me. But when I walked toward him, even with a carrot in my hand, he would wait until I had nearly reached him and then quietly slip off into the depths of the forest. At last I heard that a Sunday sportsman had killed Bucky as he walked confidently down a woods road with the cowbell tinkling at his throat. I could scarcely eat for several days while I brooded over the fact that our loving care had merely made our shy and noble friend more defenseless before the cruelty of man.

But I could not idealize all animals, because for a brief spell I kept a fox. Never have I seen a dirtier, more thieving, cunning, or basically false character, and as I read Æsop and Joel Chandler Harris, I felt they had been too generous to the fox.

There were two things that life in the woods stamped indelibly on my consciousness. These were the workings of the Malthusian theory of population and the cumulative nature of change. To beguile the winter hours and to keep down the inroads of mice, we adopted a cat, who performed her functions well. But, like all feminine felines, she loved to roam at night. Somewhere, somehow, she struck up a liaison with another rover of the woods. In due course she brought forth a litter of handsome kittens, whom I adored and tended. These grew into virile cats, and soon they, too, began to increase and multiply. Since neither my stepmother nor I would permit the men to drown any of these offspring, their numbers rose until, by an incomplete census, I counted over seventy. Inbreeding had produced some ill-favored specimens, and there was war between many of them. My mother and I finally realized that we had to reduce the cat population. So I was sent away for three days, leaving behind a list of those I wanted spared. I never tried to learn the full details of what happened during that time, which must indeed have resembled Herod's slaughter of the innocents. But when I returned, the tribe numbered only ten, and thereafter population control was strictly enforced. Long before I read either Malthus or Darwin, I had seen at first hand the tendency of life to outrun the means of subsistence and the hard choices this forces upon both nature and the sons of men.

Forest fires were the major drama of my youth, giving an insight that served well in later struggles. To fight one fire I journeyed in a railroad caboose beyond Jackman and nearly to the Canadian border. No one knew whether the fire had started from an ember from a locomotive or from a match thrown by a careless smoker. But it had spread until its front was nearly a mile long, and the raging hell, fanned by a heavy wind, was eating rapidly into new territory. The wind carried sparks for hundreds of yards, and we were in constant danger of being encircled.

With terror in my heart I fought the fire all that day and night. The heat was scorching, and at times it seemed as though all avenues of escape were being cut. The night was particularly bad, because the fire leaped from thicket to thicket and grew in intensity with every minute. Trees blazed and fell. We dug ditches, which the fire leaped over, we felled trees and tried to create a nonconducting zone, and we started backfires. At the second dawn the fire slackened. Then came a merciful, driving rain, which removed all danger. We climbed into the caboose for the return trip, dirty, singed, and hungry, but triumphant and humbled at the same time by what we had endured.

Fire fighting made me doubt the classical theories of equilibrium as applied to economics and to human history. I had seen how fires behave. As the initial spark spreads, a blaze is created. The blaze heats the air. Since hot air is lighter than ordinary air, it rises. This creates a vacuum into which other air rushes. But this in turn brings a wind that fans the flames and heats more air, creating a further vacuum into which the colder winds rush. And so it goes on in cumulative fashion. After that searing experience, I could never hold to the pendulum theory of history: that social events swing from right to left and back again with decreasing momentum until they come to rest at dead center. Rather, I became aware of impetuous forces that, once set in motion, release latent forces until a cumulative process of change takes place in which the final, unpredictable result is out of all proportion to the initial cause.

Years after, my observations were confirmed by an article in the *Monthly Weather Review* by William Storrs Franklin. In it, Professor Franklin described alternate layers of hot and cold air in the atmosphere —a condition of extremely unstable equilibrium. Under this condition the kicking of a fly's hind leg in Idaho might start a wind that would pass harmlessly out over the Gulf of Mexico, while that of another leg might initiate a storm center that could sweep out over the country and destroy New York City. These would be vastly differing end results flowing from infinitesimal differences in their initial cause.

It was the failure of businessmen, politicians, and orthodox economists to understand these simple concepts that made them ignore the dangers of the Great Depression of 1929 until it was almost too late. Thinking in terms of classical mechanics, they depended upon natural forces to right

matters speedily and, as the Harvard forecasters predicted, to bring revival and prosperity by the fall of 1930. Throughout the 1920's, as I remembered that woods fire, I found myself wondering whether there were
not unstable elements in the apparently prosperous economic system that
could lead to the cumulative breakdown of employment, demand, production, purchasing power, and price levels, and that in a vicious fashion
would feed upon and reinforce each other. And so I shocked my economic
colleagues of the 1920's and '30's by proposing the injection at critical
times of additional monetary purchasing power, through public works
and unemployment benefits. When the orthodox economists broke into
angry reproaches, I recalled the behavior of that Maine fire which had
threatened our lives so far away and long ago.

In the same way that the fire helped to shape my interpretation of
history, it also disabused me of any strict theory of determinism and emphasized, instead, the role of chance and of human will. The pistol shot at
Sarajevo in 1914 that killed Austrian Archduke Francis Ferdinand certainly unleashed unexpected and terrible results: the cumulative movement of the European nations into World War I and, hence, our own
ultimate entrance, the Bolshevik Revolution of 1917, and the development of Communism, which, in turn, gave rise to fascism in Italy and
Nazism in Germany. All this led to World War II and the present not-so-
cold war between the Communist states and the Free World. But it was
certainly not foreordained that the fanatical Serbian patriot would shoot
or that, if he did, he would fatally wound the Archduke. Had these things
not happened, there might not have been a world war, and the history of
the whole human race might have been different. Perhaps, therefore, in
our own place and time we can by our infinitesimal efforts help to determine the shape of things to come. So, from the fire, I derived not only a
deeper understanding of human history and of the impetuous forces of
potential breakdown that lie below the smiling surface of society, but also
a keener faith in the importance of human effort.

These thoughts were not in my mind as the caboose rattled and
swayed on its way back home and we talked of the coming fight for the
lightweight championship between Battling Nelson and Young Corbett.
Underneath, however, I may have pondered not only the behavior of the
fire, but also the refusal of men in the hamlets through which we had
passed to join us in the common effort to put out the flames. "It is still far
from us," some had said. "Probably it will stop before it reaches us, and
there are lots of others to help."

Most of the residents of the Indiana Dunes behaved in exactly the
same way in the late 1930's when a few of us tried to rally forces to check
another fire. To me there was a parallel between this complacence and
callousness to latent danger and the way the democracies were allowing

Hitler and Mussolini to stride on from conquest to conquest, first in Ethiopia, then in the Rhineland, then in Spain, Austria, and Czechoslovakia. And has the world yet learned its lesson?

But all this was in the future. In the meantime, the gawky woods boy was growing older and needed to decide what he was going to do. Along with the self-reliance and fortitude that the woods developed, it also drew to itself men who had either failed in life or were disgraced and wanted a place in which to hide. On one valley farm lived an old patriarch with flowing beard who had come to the woods forty years before to escape the draft during the Civil War. He finally owned much valuable wooded land, only to have a "city slicker" from Boston move in with him, seduce his daughter, tyrannize over the family, and wind up enjoying the stumpage rights to the timber.

A mile away lived his mortal enemy, "Doctor" Trustram Brown, a self-styled spiritualist and mental healer. Perhaps tragedy had turned the Doctor's thoughts to metaphysics, for he had undergone real trouble. After returning empty-handed from the California gold fields in the 1850's, he had seen his wife and children all carried away by diphtheria. In any case, he took to the woods, where he lived by trapping, fishing, and hunting. He punctuated his long spells of isolation with occasional trips to the little hamlet of Etna for spiritualist camp meetings that were also reputed to be free expressions of bodily affection. There he would celebrate in doggerel the powers of his fellow mediums and, in particular, those of Maude E. Lord.

He finally sold his farm and wood lot for $600 and spent his fortune mainly on his own curious sentimental journey back to the Sierras, where he had fruitlessly panned for gold over half a century before. He then used the residue to publish his poems and to buy one of the new phonographs, from whose cylindrical records, extolling the delights of "Cigarette, Sweet Cigarette," he derived endless pleasure. When his money was gone, he calmly moved in with us and after a time announced that in recompense, upon his death, we were to inherit his body, which was to be stuffed and mounted upon our mantelpiece. The good Doctor was deeply hurt when my elders, although glad to give him welcome, would never agree to make him the future lares and penates of our household.

One winter my mother's distant cousin made his entrance through the snow to stay with us until the ice melted. He had been a lawyer in Bangor, but for some reason that wild city had become too hot for him. I was never allowed to ask any questions about him, but one night my uncle took him to Greenville and put him, under an assumed name, in an upper berth. There he was to stay until the next morning found him safely in Boston. So he, too, vanished into the mist of the beyond.

A far more sinister character, J. Thomas Black, once descended upon us. With his wife he spent many months in our camp and periodically received the New York papers and the *Police Gazette,* which he studied avidly. Once, I caught a scurrilous reference to him in that journal, but it was quickly whisked away and my suspicions were pooh-poohed. Another time, I overheard his wife confiding to my mother that J. Thomas had threatened her with a dire fate if she ever told on him.

At length the man of mystery bought a remote woods farm. His wife disappeared, and eventually another woman was introduced as Mrs. Black. His farmhouse was guarded by fierce dogs, and any visitor who braved them advanced to find himself faced with the muzzle of a gun. Periodically the couple would vanish and then reappear after a few weeks. The only other time they left their mountain fortress was when the Monson basketball team played in that village. Then they journeyed to town to let Mrs. Black regale herself by screaming insults and profanity at the visiting players.

My kindly stepmother always explained away Black's actions as those of a remittance man. But after his death, the papers spread the story that he was a vital link in an international opium ring. Boxes of opium were said to have been smuggled from ships at Halifax onto a through Canadian Pacific train and then thrown off the baggage car at midnight as the train passed a remote and lonely crossing a few miles beyond Onawa. There in the shadows lurked J. Thomas Black, and after the train had passed he would come forward, put the boxes in his carriage, and drive off to his farmhouse. Some days later, it was said, he would take the train to New York, where, suitcase in hand, he was often seen on the Bowery.

Whether this account was accurate, I never knew. But there was always a sinister undertone to Black's otherwise courtly manners, which made me sense that he was a man to be avoided.

So in this lonely but lovely place where I grew up there were picturesque characters. Paraphrasing Ernest Renan, I can say in retrospect that the woods were also the home of lost people and the refuge of those beaten by life.

2

Adolescence, High School,
and College

EVENTS compelled a change in our way and place of life. Although my stepmother was steadfast in refusing to return to my father, she was equally steadfast in refusing to give me up. Finally, my father yielded, granting a divorce on the ground of desertion, and she had the burden of keeping me. Her brother had married a placid summer guest, and my stepmother no longer felt she was essential to the little hotel. Since she was determined that I should go to high school and, if possible, to college, like my brother, she resolved to resume her profession as a stenographer and went back to Bangor to study and renew her skills.

She was still young and attractive, and while in Bangor she changed her plans because she and a second cousin, Arthur Holbrook, fell in love. She married again, and we went to live on his grandfather's farm in Newport, where Arthur worked in a factory. I went to a little high school of some thirty pupils and received a slightly more systematic education.

For four years I studied Latin, working through the conventional texts of Caesar, Cicero, and Virgil, but missing the inner significance of each. In three years I learned to read French fluently, but spoke with such a New England accent that no Frenchman has ever understood me. I owe a great debt, intellectually and emotionally, to Emily Mitchell Merrill, who was my teacher in Latin and French. There was a year of chemistry and another of physics, both miserably taught and with only a sink for a laboratory. Algebra and geometry, which I studied from Wentworth's texts, came off much better, because of their inherent precision.

But my chief joys were history—ancient, English, American, and modern—and literature. I read everything I could get my hands on, and my happiest hours were on Saturday nights when I returned to the library my week's allowance of books and took out a new quota. Carlyle's *French Revolution* and Creasy's *Fifteen Decisive Battles of the World* were favorites.

At first I swallowed all sorts and varieties of books, but gradually I sifted out the better ones and concentrated on novels, histories, and poetry, notably the poems of Tennyson and Kipling. I read virtually all of Washington Irving and the poems of the New England elders—Longfellow, Lowell, Whittier, and Holmes.

Despite its two churches, Newport, like most Maine communities, was an essentially pagan town with few inner traces of Puritanism. Puritanism in fact never went farther north than Portsmouth, and the north countrymen were almost untouched by it. The emotional preoccupation of the boys was girl hunting, with the only restraint upon each sex being the fear of pregnancy. Every summer, remnants of the Grand Army of the Republic held a ten-day camp meeting at the village lake. There was a ball game every afternoon and a dance at night. Only recently had the outer tradition of Victorianism been modified by the coming of the waltz and the two-step to replace the former square dances such as the Virginia reel. While the GAR had retreated to rocking chairs, the younger generation was avid for adventure. A few girls were brought out from Bangor to each camp meeting and quartered in tents, where they did a thriving business.

The main industries of the town were a woolen mill, which used the fast-flowing waters of the Sebasticook River for its power, and a condensed-milk factory owned by the Borden Milk Company. In the latter Arthur Holbrook worked until he became the local agent for the express company. We then moved to town, where I helped in the express office by unloading and transferring the packages and boxes from the trains and sometimes delivering them. A good part of our business was from Boston liquor stores to citizens suffering from a thirst they had no mind to let the local bootlegger publicize. Since some of our patrons were church elders, I developed a contempt for the hypocrisy of many of the unco guid. I also learned that state action alone would not insure prohibition. Even though the protection of interstate commerce was ultimately withdrawn from such shipments into legally "dry" states, this did not stop truck and automobile traffic. These were factors that finally led to the passage of the Eighteenth Amendment and, in turn, raised the enforcement failures from localities and states to a national level.

Next to reading came the unfamiliar joy of games with my contemporaries, for which my lonely childhood in the woods had given me a great yearning. We organized a baseball team to play the nearby high schools, and I practiced mightily to acquire skill as a first baseman. In my senior year we formed a football team. I enjoyed the thrills of combat and earned the distinction of a broken nose.

The two great events of each year were town-meeting day, on the third Monday in March, and Memorial Day. School was let out for the former, and we youngsters gathered in the balcony of the little town hall to see our elders govern themselves. They chose a moderator, generally by acclamation, following which came the din of balloting for the three selectmen. This usually woke the town drunkard, lodged at this season in the basement jail, who would shake the bars of his cage and send up unearthly howls to mingle with the election cries of the free men. After the election of town officers came passage of the school budget.

The meeting adjourned for "dinner" downstairs, where the ladies' auxiliary of the library served a sumptuous banquet for the exorbitant charge of twenty-five cents. Forgetting the rivalries of the morning, the men pitched in with gusto and were plied by the beaming women with full platters of beans, meat, and vegetables together with pitchers of foaming milk and coffee. Then came a procession of pies, doughnuts, chocolate cake, and more coffee. Replete, the men staggered to their feet and, walking out into the March sunshine, announced that the women had done themselves proud, that the dinner was better than the last church supper, when the oysters in the stew had, as usual, been scanty. There followed talk about the decisions of the morning, and at two o'clock they filed upstairs to deal with the remaining pieces of business: how much was to be spent for roads and bridges, whether a new light was to be put in at Main and Maple streets, whether the town should continue the poor farm, what to do about the pound for stray dogs, and whether they should buy a new truck for the fire department. By five o'clock the meeting had adjourned until the next year.

It was all down-to-earth, with the decisions, on the whole, sound and wise. What was perhaps more important was that everyone enjoyed the process, feeling a sense of participation. The afterglow of discussion lasted for several days. Certainly the town burghers would have taken out their rifles to defend their institution had it ever been seriously threatened.

On the other hand, few resented the efforts of the manager of the woolen mill to sway the vote at Presidential elections. People still recalled that when Bryan seemed to be sweeping the country singlehandedly in 1896, Charley Jones warned his workmen that if the "anarchist" was elected, he would close down the mill and everyone would be out of work. When the solid William McKinley won, and the boy orator was sent safely back to the Platte, the factory whistle celebrated the news in steady triumph for twenty-four hours. Most of the men saw nothing wrong in this, believing that the mill was merely fighting for survival. If the Democrats had won, they would have lowered the tariff, and the cheap woolens of Europe might have swept all before them. Besides, who but the Republicans could be trusted to guarantee pensions to the Union veterans and their widows?

We Democrats, who saw our beloved hero defeated for the third time in 1908, felt a smarting sense of injustice at this use of naked power to coerce the judgments of free men. There were also independents and Republicans who admitted that Charley Jones had played a dirty trick. Later I learned that what had been done in Newport was standard procedure throughout New England.

Town-meeting day was full of excitement, but Memorial Day was marked by solemnity. The previous Sunday we all went to the Congregational church to hear the minister, John W. Webster, who had fought with the 20th Maine at Gettysburg, preach his memorial sermon. There was seldom a dry eye as he described the second day of the battle, when his regiment rushed up Little Round Top just in time to stop the Confederates from taking that hill and thereby turning the Union left flank. He told how Devil's Glen, below, had run with the mingled blood of the boys in blue and those in gray. On the third day, Lee had sent Pickett and his brave men with steady pace across the mile of open ground. By Hancock's artillery fire and the aim of our soldiers, this charge had been broken at close range, even as it reached its goal under the trees. Thus, we learned, the Union had been saved.

Spring comes late in northern Maine, but the apple blossoms and lilacs, always keeping faith, appeared for Memorial Day. We boys and girls, with arms filled with fragrant boughs, hurried to the town square, where the band was already playing "Marching Through Georgia" and "The Girl I Left Behind Me." The twenty or so remaining members of the GAR were reassembled in their misty but splendid glory. Many wore their faded uniforms and campaign hats with gold braid. These grizzled heroes of the day, with their battered looks, gave me the notion that the Civil War had been fought by old men. It was a shock when I learned later that the average age of the soldiers in Grant's army was less than twenty.

As the hour for the parade approached, the old soldiers sauntered into the alleys by twos and threes and secretly took a pull at the flasks that mysteriously appeared from hip pockets. When at last the command "Fall in" was sounded, the old soldiers formed at the head of the procession, right behind the band. Next came carriages for the elderly, the infirm, and the town leaders, then the young veterans of the Spanish-American War, followed by the Masons and the Odd Fellows and, at the end, we school children with our arms full of purple and white lilacs and pink and white apple blossoms. Democratic youngsters gradually discovered that they were always placed at the very end of the line, and this not by chance. Even on that day, as for most of the year, we were second-class citizens, allowed to exist only by the tolerance of the great republic.

As we marched the half-mile to the little cemetery, the band played the sad martial air "Tenting on the Old Camp Ground." Those lining the sidewalks whispered to each other that the veterans were feebler and fewer this year, and that the real political power in the town was passing out of their hands into those of the lodges, the fire company, and the mills. After we reached the cemetery, we placed our floral tributes on the graves of the Union veterans to the accompaniment of music as soft as a brass band could play. Then we gathered together to hear the high light of the day—the oration.

The speaker always seemed to be the same man, although his name changed with the years. His theme was the same, and so was the final sentence. Invariably, with uplifted arms and showing his gleaming white cuffs, he shouted, "I do not say that every Democrat poisoned our wells here in the North or starved our brave boys in Libby Prison. But I do say, my fellow countrymen, that everyone who did poison the wells and who did starve and abuse our prisoners was a Democrat."

In time, we Democratic boys, whose families had also fought on the Union side and who also loved our country, slipped away before the oration. In further protest, I finally stopped marching altogether and walked instead in the open fields as I heard the band play its familiar tunes. Only years later was I forced to admit that a large share of the Northern Democrats had, in sober fact, been opposed to the war and that many had been potential fifth columnists. This did not excuse visiting the errors of one generation upon the second or third. Nor did it justify its being used to perpetuate the errors of the tariffs and trusts. But it was a weapon that a self-righteous political party could not be expected to give up, and it was a powerful asset for the Republicans down nearly to the Depression of 1929.

After graduating from the Massachusetts Institute of Technology with high honors, my brother had spent several years as a junior assistant to the celebrated Charles P. Steinmetz, at the General Electric Company in Schenectady, and later was appointed to an instructorship in electrical engineering at Cornell University. At this time he generously offered to help me through college. In September, 1909, I was admitted to Bowdoin College, in Brunswick, Maine, only a few miles from the barren point at South Harpswell where a distant great-great-grandfather, after coming up the coast from Massachusetts, had settled in about 1725.

Brunswick was a mill town, as well as a college community, and had sharp class distinctions. The French-Canadians who came down from Quebec to man the paper mill were a separate and alien society. They lived in jerry-built, three-story tenements on unpaved back streets that were muddy in winter and clouded with dust in summer. They spoke English with difficulty, worshiped in the Catholic church, and were shunned by their Anglo-Saxon fellow townsmen, who profited from their labors and expenditures.

This cleavage between the native and the immigrant stocks was the spiritual Achilles' heel of New England. Irish lads were still being stoned by the native sons as they wended their way to parochial schools. The Irish fought back fiercely, although they could not cope with the glacial social exclusion practiced upon them. The French-Canadians, however, were a gentler people, who took their slights patiently. The whole situation was grossly unfair, and although I was an Anglo-Saxon Protestant, I resented it. As the newer races have come to maturity and position, the native stock in New England has begun to pay dearly for the snobbishness of its fathers and grandfathers. The latent hostility between Protestants and Catholics that still characterizes so much of New England is due in large part to this century of cleavage and to the resentments created by it.

Here, as elsewhere in the country, the Democratic party has performed a most valuable service in furnishing the political vehicle whereby some of these newer racial stocks can take part in public affairs, have their rights respected, rise to political prominence, and obtain an economic and social foothold in life. It has helped the Irish, but in northern New England it has been somewhat backward in according equal consideration to the French-Canadians and the Italians.

Bowdoin was a good college in the accepted New England tradition. Like so many others, it was Congregational in origin but, under the influence of Carnegie grants and theological liberalism, was becoming non-denominational. Conservative in politics and economics, it nevertheless had a broad tolerance and a willingness to consider new ideas. The president, William DeWitt Hyde, a free-trade Democrat, had openly supported Grover Cleveland for President in the campaign of 1888 and, by holding fast before a torrent of denunciation, had established at Bowdoin, once and for all, the principle of academic freedom.

In my first year I did not distinguish myself scholastically. My preparation had been faulty, and I was thrown off balance by the new world into which I plunged. But I was, nevertheless, elected president of my class. This was on the strength of my preventing our forces from being caught off guard by the sophomores in the opening class rush and of reversing the usual roles by leading a successful headlong attack on our tormentors. In my second year an ultimate blessing occurred in the form of an immediate misfortune. My father was taken ill, and my brother, who was now compelled to support him, could no longer help me.

The news came at Christmas, and I realized it was sink or swim. Although my stepmother, who had gone back to Onawa with her husband on the death of her uncle, helped as much as she could, the main responsibility was mine. I got a variety of odd jobs, such as waiting on table. By working hard at my studies, I also won a larger scholarship and several academic prizes. It was a Spartan life, but the bracing need for self-reliance stimulated me. In the summer I took to the road as a door-to-door salesman of extracts and somehow, with the aid of a meager inheritance from my father, who died in 1912, scraped up enough money to finish four years at Bowdoin.

Intellectually, I found the college placidly stimulating. I took naturally to history and political science and profited greatly from James Bryce's *American Commonwealth* and Abbott L. Lowell's *Governments and Parties in Continental Europe*. The labor struggles of the time greatly interested me, and one year I won the prize for excellence in political economy.

But economics became my consuming passion. I took every course offered and read everything I could find in the library. John Stuart Mill became an inspiration, and has remained so throughout my life. My teacher, Warren Catlin, a lonely bachelor who was badly overworked and miserably underpaid, took an interest in me, had me clip articles from the New York *Times,* and gave me the job of reading and marking some of his weekly quizzes. I owe a great debt to him, and we were fast friends for nearly sixty years, until he died in 1968. Then, to everyone's astonishment, his will disclosed that he had left his entire inheritance, of nearly $2 million, to the college. Unknown to all, he had been a highly successful speculator in the stock market. But this had never deadened his human sympathies.

The most thrilling experience of college life for me was football. From being a second-team scrub in my freshman year, I became a substitute center as a sophomore, and then, to my joy, made the first team as a junior and a senior. We played many of the smaller New England colleges and closed our season with games against the other three Maine colleges. One disastrous season we played Harvard, Dartmouth, and Brown on successive Saturdays. I still bear the results of the beatings we received. Out of that year I learned a certain degree of caution about putting myself too far out of my class. But this has not been a dominant influence. While I played center on the offense, I played halfback when the other team had the ball. Thus I had the thrill both of breaking up interference and of tackling the ball carrier. I also learned how the human body can absorb terrific punishment and yet come through it all if the spirit can be kept determined and aflame.

Years afterward, in Chicago, when I was in desperate straits in my struggles both with Samuel Insull and with political opponents, my old football habits helped give me courage to go on. I concluded that college football was excellent for the participants but poor for the spectators, and this conclusion has been reinforced through the years.

Later, when serving in the Marines with many former great football players and boxers, I learned how dangerous it is for the young to achieve fame. All too often this makes everything else an anticlimax, causing them to approach later tests looking back over their shoulders at the greater glories and achievements of the past. While it is true that poets, musicians, artists, mathematicians, and geniuses of all varieties develop quickly, it is better for the rest of us to ripen slowly, developing such talents as we have by prolonged exercise and trial and trusting to the fullness of time.

Twice I made the debating team. We argued the issues of the day, such as the popular election of senators, the direct primary, workmen's compensation, the minimum wage, the tariff, the income tax, and what to do about the trusts. I never defended a position in which I did not believe. Perhaps this decision was helped by the fact that the vast majority of my classmates always chose the other side. The practice of debating, accompanied as it was by written exercises, helped to develop not only logical sequences in exposition, but also a greater appreciation for opposing points of view, which later would sometimes modify or change my own opinions.

In my senior year I began to be a social reformer. College life was dominated by eight fraternities. Mine, Delta Upsilon, was close to the bottom in prestige. But the untouchables were the some forty or fifty nonfraternity men, who, by the cruelty of youth, were largely walled off from the social life of the college. They were unhappy and dogged by an inferiority complex. In that last year, when we played Wesleyan I found a former Bowdoin nonfraternity man playing opposite me at center. The eagerness and strength with which he straight-armed me awakened me to his pent-up resentments and those of his fellows. So as soon as the football season ended I started a movement to form a nonfraternity club. I got the college to buy and rent a house for it and organized the club. It was a bit too paternalistic, but it gave a home and fellowship to the disinherited and led to the formation of other fraternities. We at least enlarged the circle of the privileged, making even the lower social depths more endurable.

I took two courses that had a particularly enriching effect. The first was the year-long sequence in philosophy and ethics with which Hyde, like all presidents of similar colleges of his time, was supposed to round off the four years of study and prepare the seniors for the basic problems of life. I was never able to understand the technical issues posed by Leibnitz, Berkeley, and Kant. But Kant's categorical imperatives—"So act that the maxim of thy actions should become universal law" and "Treat humanity whether in thyself or in another, always as an end, never as a means"—made a deep and abiding impression upon me. While the first imperative may have been too sweeping, its basic command was similar to what later moved me in Walt Whitman: I will not ask for anything that others may not have on the same terms. The second imperative made me accept more readily John Ruskin's dictum "There is no Wealth but Life," and stirred an interest in him and in William Morris. This, in turn, led me to rebel later at the acquisitive and purely hedonistic bent of classical economics, to welcome John A. Hobson's *Work and Wealth: A Human Valuation* and Arthur C. Pigou's *Economics of Welfare,* and to want to devote myself to this field rather than to so-called business economics. I came to know also the magnificent sentence of Kant's which throughout my life has never failed to thrill me, "Two things there are which fill me with wonder, the starry heavens above and the moral law within."

Hyde was a Hegelian, who believed that his Oxford master, T. H. Green, had finally brought philosophy to its climax. I, however, was repelled by what seemed to be the wooliness of much of Hegel's thought and style. But the Hegelian dialectic, with its original thesis meeting its antithesis and with the two finally merging into a synthesis that would then serve as a new thesis and fresh starting place for an ensuing dialectic process, seemed not only to describe the processes of logic, but also to furnish at least a clue to the ceaseless change of human history. I did not know at the time that Marx had built his system upon the Hegelian dialectic, although in his system, instead of the ideal creating and becoming embodied in the material, technical change was made the transformer of economic classes and of ideologies, until, by inherent contradictions within one system of society, it became transformed into a newer and "higher" form. Thus feudalism was changed by commerce and machinery into capitalism, and the latter, according to Marx, into communism. But just as Hegel had the dialectic process cease when the supremacy of the Prussian state was established, so Marx believed that once a communist world had been born, history would thereafter stand still. The modern rulers of Russia and China seem to hold the same opinion.

The Hegelian and Marxian dialectic has bewitched millions by its fatalism. Fortunately, I have always had a built-in faith in indeterminism, based on my experience with that forest fire in the Maine woods, and consequently the belief that, within limits, men hold the future in their own hands.

In the course on ethics, which in New England fashion was designed as the climax of our education, we studied the ethical philosophies of the Epicureans and Stoics and of Plato, Aristotle, and Jesus. We progressed from the principle of tempered pleasure to that of noble fortitude and on to the Platonic sense of subordination and the Aristotelian doctrine of the balanced mean. All of these, though not submerged, were finally to be permeated by the superior principle of reconciling love as embodied in the life and teachings of Jesus. Although Hyde was not quite fair to the Epicureans and Stoics, his lectures and the attendant readings served as a scaffolding which in later years caused my wife and me to embark upon early-morning reading periods, not only in Epicurus, but even more in Epictetus, the Stoic slave, and, above all, in the meditations of the noble but sad Roman Emperor Marcus Aurelius. He belongs to the small company of the true immortals, one of the few men whom the possession of absolute power did not corrupt, but, rather, ennobled.

But even more of an eye-opener was the course in evolution, for which my experience with the fecundity of cats prepared me. From the Malthusian starting point that all forms of life tend to be reproduced in greater quantities than there are means of subsistence, Darwin, like Malthus, deduced that there was a struggle for existence. From his *Origin of Species* the story of evolution unfolded. Nature also produced variations within each species, and those individuals and species that survived had those features which were best adapted to endure in the environment in which they were placed. These, in turn, passed on their own attributes, but with enough variation so that in the continuing struggle for existence the less adapted were constantly discarded and the more adapted survived. Thus a slow change in the forms of life developed through the ages, and the tree of life was an organic whole. This truth is now so universally accepted that it is hard for the modern generation to realize the excitement it still created nearly sixty years ago. It unlocked many doors and suggested further questions. Mendel, as rediscovered by Hugo De Vries, had given an initial answer to the question of how variations arrived. And when I later went to Columbia University, I heard reports of how Thomas Hunt Morgan was pushing Mendelism still further with his experiments with fruit flies, whose lives are perhaps the most ephemeral of all. In recent years, the nature of the amazing coil of life has begun to unfold even more.

When I graduated from Bowdoin, I was awarded a graduate fellowship of $500 a year. With this and the remnants of my small inheritance, I went to New York in September, 1913, to enroll in the Graduate School of Economics and Political Science at Columbia. I was trembling with excitement when the Portland boat docked and as I made my way by subway up to Morningside Heights.

3

Graduate School: Columbia and Harvard

THE COLUMBIA GRADUATE SCHOOL was modeled on the University of Berlin, and virtually all its professors were German-trained. Since the instruction was by means of lectures, there was little give and take between teacher and student. Seminars were huge, and as a result one did not have to read a paper more than once a year. Students for the Ph.D. degree were not required to take examinations, and therefore everything depended on the final oral test and the dissertation. Often the supervision was cursory, and the student, in accordance with German practice, was largely thrown upon his own resources. Sometimes this led to ludicrous results. The perpetual student, "Daddy" Kemp, who dressed and looked like King Edward VII, was a familiar figure on the campus, although ignored by the faculty. In 1880 an aunt had given him an annuity of a few thousand dollars a year as long as he was in college. He never left. Once, when registering for a semester's work, I heard Daddy shouting ahead of me in line, "You can't fool me, Mr. Registrar. I took that course in 1889."

There was one mild-mannered Southerner in my seminar whom we all thought slightly feeble-minded. He was always taken ill when called on for a report, but because of his good manners and apparent need, kind-hearted Professor E. R. A. Seligman recommended him for a teaching job at a Midwestern university. Facing his classes, he sat at the table in front whispering so softly to himself that no one could hear a word. But his university was so large that months passed before his peculiarities became known to the head of his department.

The economics lectures at Columbia were competent, and the library facilities adequate. I learned a good deal from Seligman in public finance, Robert E. Chaddock in statistics, Henry R. Seager in labor problems, and John Bates Clark, then at the end of his career, in economic theory. Clark had been the American originator of the marginal-productivity theory as the determinant of the basic rates of wages and interest. I received a thorough drilling in this principle, which served me well a decade later when I started my own inductive work in the theory.

Across the water, Lloyd George had launched Britain upon a program of social insurance against sickness, unemployment, and old age. At home, states were beginning to adopt workmen's compensation for industrial accidents. Many were limiting the working hours for women, while a pitched battle was being fought over restrictions on child labor and the minimum wage. Most of this legislation dealing with adults was being reviewed by the courts and was commonly held to violate the Fourteenth Amendment to the Constitution, which prohibited a state from taking "life, liberty, or property, without due process of law." So there was much to study, in the fields of both legislation and constitutional law, and all of my generation were forced to consider how free, in fact, were penniless and hard-pressed men and women. Legal freedom was very different from effective freedom.

As is frequently the case, some of the best insights came by osmosis. I sometimes wandered into the classroom of Charles A. Beard, who was then at the height of his powers. I admired his scholarship and mordant wit as he lectured on constitutional history, and I shall never forget his comment on the Dred Scott decision: that free soil did not make free men.

Since John Dewey was lecturing in a nearby hall, I began to read about pragmatism and, after devouring the writings of William James, turned to Dewey's philosophical and educational essays. His seminal book *The School and Society,* written years before as a by-product of his work at the University of Chicago, opened with the bold assertion "The school is not a preparation for life. It is life itself." In this work Dewey laid down the principles of what was later to become "progressive education." His phrase "It is not we who think, rather it is thought which happens within us" illuminated the subconscious processes of the mind. It correctly described how after preparation the mind often painlessly solves its problems. Fifteen years later I became an intimate of Dewey in the League for Independent Political Action, and came to admire deeply his intellectual integrity, courage, and extraordinary personal modesty.

A course that was destined to have a great effect on American politics was that given by William A. Dunning on the Civil War and Reconstruction. A New York aristocrat who, like others of us, had been repelled in his youth by the corruption and indiscriminate "waving of the bloody shirt" by the Republicans, Dunning scarcely mentioned the evils of slavery. Instead, he stressed the excesses of Wendell Phillips, William Lloyd Garrison, and Horace Greeley. Reconstruction and the black legislatures of the South were the great crimes, and Thaddeus Stevens, Benjamin Wade, and the carpetbaggers were the ultimate villains. Almost nothing was said about the "black statutes" by which the deep South had tried to re-enslave the Negroes after the war. The moral basis for the civil-rights acts and the Fourteenth and Fifteenth amendments was down-graded.

In Dunning's seminars the more advanced of his Southern students were busy turning out master's theses and doctoral dissertations on the horrors of Reconstruction in their particular states and the delinquencies of Northern radicalism. These works, by James W. Garner, Joseph G. Hamilton, Walter L. Fleming, and others, which gave highly colored accounts of Reconstruction in every Southern state except Virginia and Louisiana, and the essays and books by Dunning himself furnished, in turn, the rationale for such books as G. F. Milton's *Age of Hate* and the denigration of Charles Sumner and William Lloyd Garrison. One of Dunning's students, Ulrich B. Phillips, later went so far as to write a two-volume history of slavery in the United States that pictured that institution as beneficent and one where the lash and auction block were virtually unknown.*

Dunning's motives were doubtless good in wanting to heal the bitterness between the North and the South. However, he bent the bow too far in the other direction, furnishing the South with an intellectual justification that not only pervaded that section, but also permeated the North. It morally disarmed those whose fathers had fought to save the union, to free the slaves, and to create a society where black men as well as white might have equal rights. Dunning and his followers helped to strengthen the Southern belief that they had suffered unforgivable wrongs. And they helped give the North—always self-scrutinizing, in accordance with its Protestant conscience—an uneasy moral inferiority complex which, although in the main unfounded, nevertheless operated to blunt concern for protecting the rights of Negroes, whether in the North or in the South. From 1876 on, therefore, the ideals of the white South began to infiltrate the North in increasing measure, until, in a certain sense, it could be said that they had won the psychological war.

* For those who are still influenced by these books and similar whitewashings of slavery, may I recommend Fanny A. Kemble, *A Journal of a Residence on a Georgian Plantation in 1838–1839;* Frederick Law Olmstead, *Journey in the Seaboard Slave States* and *Journey in the Back Country;* Hinton R. Helper, *Impending Crisis of the South: How to Meet It,* and *The Life and Times of Frederick Douglass.* It is worthwhile also to read Dickens' *American Notes.* Harriet Beecher Stowe's *Uncle Tom's Cabin* has been scored by generations of Southerners as being unfair to them. But Mrs. Stowe was careful to praise the good slaveowner, St. Clair, and to make the brutal supervisor, Simon Legree, a Yankee. Mrs. Stowe's later *Key to Uncle Tom's Cabin* is devastating, since it consists of excerpts from the news columns and advertisements of Southern newspapers themselves.

Only in the last quarter of a century has the tide begun to turn. Northern opinion has taken a more balanced view, realizing that the purposes of the Fourteenth and Fifteenth amendments are not yet fulfilled. But the rise of racism is now weakening much of this concern.

I learned more from living in New York than from listening to the lectures on Morningside Heights. The city was one of sharp contrasts. Fifth Avenue was probably the most opulent street in the world, but the Lower East Side was certainly one of the most abject areas. Before the day of the income tax, the yearly receipts of Andrew Carnegie were equal to the combined incomes of 50,000 families. And Carnegie was not the wealthiest among the thousands of millionaires who lived in New York. The brownstone palaces of the Vanderbilts dominated Fifth Avenue between 58th and 59th streets, and at teatime Peacock Alley in the Waldorf outshone the splendors of Solomon.

Intellectually, New York was in a ferment. The Triangle Waist Company fire, in which over 200 young women garment workers had been burned to death, had not only shocked the conscience of the city, but also had furthered the careers of three young politicians of widely different backgrounds: Alfred E. Smith, Robert F. Wagner, and Franklin D. Roosevelt. The *World* was thundering every day, while Franklin P. Adams' column was giving comfort to the lonely and isolated in the great city. The International Ladies' Garment Workers' Union was beginning its long and ultimately successful struggle against the sweatshops and was raising the economic level of the East Side jungle. As a result of the exposures of graft and of the murder of Herman Rosenthal, for which a powerful police lieutenant, Charles Becker, was finally executed, a revolt against Tammany and its boss, Charles F. Murphy, was in full swing.

Mayor William J. Gaynor, the bearded Epictetus-quoting Unitarian, who, in an anomalous fashion, had presided over the polyglot city, was shot; he died three years later. A young reform Irishman, John Purroy Mitchel, stepped forward to lead a fusion movement and became mayor.

Woodrow Wilson's New Freedom was rapidly taking shape in Washington with the lowering of the tariff, stronger antitrust laws, an income tax, and creation of the Federal Reserve System. A handsome and liberal young columnist by the name of David Lawrence was writing fiery articles every day in Oswald Garrison Villard's *Evening Post* defending Wilson's programs. Wall Street and the bankers, fighting back, denounced all this legislation as arrant socialism. They were especially bitter about the Federal Reserve System, although they now think they invented it. Carter Glass, who was so active in its foundation, was hissed at their meetings as a dangerous innovator.

On another front, the Armory Show had introduced modern European art, including the Cubists and post-Impressionists, to the American scene. The *New Republic* had been founded by Willard D. Straight and

Herbert Croly. Young Walter Lippmann had aroused us all with his brilliant *A Preface to Politics,* and we avidly read his weekly editorials in the *New Republic.* Young people moved into Greenwich Village, tasting the "new freedom" in a somewhat different fashion from that contemplated by Wilson. A brave young nurse, Margaret Sanger, was advocating and teaching birth control, for which she was repeatedly thrown into jail.

Looking back on that period evokes an echo of Wordsworth: "Bliss was it in that dawn to be alive, / But to be young was very heaven!"

Finding this strange life fascinating, I threw myself into it with full energy. I went to lectures and debates, heard Taft and Bryan speak, and every week attended studio gatherings in Greenwich Village where men and women argued all the issues of the day. From high up in the second gallery I came to know Shaw's plays as they were introduced to New York by Arnold Daly, Mrs. Patrick Campbell, Granville-Barker, and Grace George. I also became more familiar with Shakespeare through Forbes-Robertson and Sothern and Marlowe.

I enlisted in the campaign to help organize the shopgirls, all of whom worked long hours and most of whom were badly underpaid, many getting as little as $6.00 a week. Quite unexpectedly, my participation brought me into conflict with the police. While making an organization speech outside Stern's department store on 43rd Street to a group of about six persons, I was arrested on the charge of blocking traffic. Also quite unexpectedly, this arrest brought me into contact with Mrs. O. H. P. Belmont, leader of the Four Hundred. She had tired of social life and had become both a suffragette and a social reformer. With her worldly eyes and bearing, she strode into the police court and bailed me out.

When I came up for trial, the policeman solemnly and falsely testified that I had harangued a crowd of over a thousand and had cursed and pushed the police officers. For the first time, I saw how the law could be used to prevent the weak from peacefully trying to redress their grievances, and, having suffered in my own person, I realized the practical pressures being used against the organization of workmen into unions. I could also understand the feeling of the workers that the law and, indeed, government itself were hostile to them. Despite my testimony and that of those who accompanied me, the police magistrate found me guilty and levied a fine, which Mrs. Belmont kindly paid.

Toward the end of my first year at Columbia, my money gave out and for weeks I looked in vain for work. There was a minor depression, and though I tramped the streets in search of teaching, tutoring, factory, or longshoreman's work, I found nothing. I budgeted myself to thirty cents a day for food, taking advantage at times of the abundant free lunches in the corner saloons which then went with a nickel schooner of beer, and looked with envy upon anyone who had a job and an assured income. Then my luck improved. I was not only given the scholarly task of revising the articles on European history for the *International Encyclopedia,* but also a promotion job of selling tickets and writing publicity blurbs for the Charles Coburn Players' outdoor productions of Shakespeare and Euripides.

Then, just as the European war, contrary to all predictions, was erupting, I went to Indiana and Michigan to act as platform manager for the Lincoln Chautauqua. My real job was to get the contract for the next year, and I had an attendant immersion in small-town politics.

In these ways, and with loans from William J. Curtis, a Bowdoin man and a senior partner in the law firm of Sullivan and Cromwell, and Dr. A. T. Sanden, of electric-belt fame, who had a summer place at Onawa and had introduced me to the painter Albert Ryder, I raised enough money to get through my second year at Columbia.

To strengthen myself in economic theory, I went to Harvard for my final year of graduate school and studied under Professors F. W. Taussig, T. N. Carver, and C. J. Bullock. The last two were real disappointments. They had earlier done good theoretical work, but the years had narrowed and embittered them. In the field of social philosophy, Carver had become an emotional neo-Darwinian who believed that there were no values but survival values. Whatever made a nation or a people either economically or militarily strong was right, in his eyes, for he regarded material success as the standard by which individuals were to be judged. Bullock was supposed to teach a course in the history of economic theory prior to Adam Smith, but spent most of his time in virulent attacks on Woodrow Wilson, Jane Addams, and William S. U'ren, the Oregonian who was the father of the initiative and referendum and of direct popular government in the United States.

Taussig was a different sort of man. Professor Seligman had given me a letter of introduction to him, which was reputed to be the first communication in years between those two old enemies. Taussig took this as a challenge to demonstrate how little Seligman's favorite pupil really knew. From the sounding of the first bell, he set out to prove me ignorant, illogical, and intellectually ridiculous. He raised knotty questions in our reading of Francis A. Walker, Smith, Ricardo, and Mill, and then tried to get me to commit myself hastily. Once successful in this, he would lead me into contradictions, rubbing his hands with glee as he did so. This was accompanied by alternate bland enticements, sharp sarcasm, and stormy denunciations, which would have done credit to a prosecuting attorney. Of course I was no match for him, and each session ended with his triumph and my rout. This delighted the Harvard men, who were pleased to see Columbia shown up. As word spread, the gallery of spectators who came to see the slaughter increased. I left each session soaked with perspiration, and hurried back to my rooms to change my clothes and start studying for the next day. I kept at the texts until midnight and rose early each morning to begin again. In the process I learned David Ricardo's theory of distribution and some of the basic features of his views on international trade.

The daily rout continued for months. Then one day in a furious argument over John Stuart Mill, I felt that I had held my own, and I noticed that some of the supercilious students looked at me with a measure of curious respect as we filed out. The next day Taussig incautiously launched into an exposition of his own wage theory of discounted marginal productivity, which did not really explain how or why the marginal productivity of labor was discounted by the interest on capital. I had been waiting for this, and after a few minutes started to press my objections and to advocate Clark's marginal-productivity doctrine. As it became clear that Taussig could not really answer these points, I passed to the aggressive, imitating his manner. No student except Jacob Viner had dared do this. The gallery was now greatly disturbed by this totally unexpected turn of events. At our next meeting I continued to attack his position, urging the separate productivity of labor and capital and developing a position such as that which I later learned had been advanced by Knut Wicksell, in Sweden, and Philip H. Wicksteed, in England.

The following day, Taussig cordially shook hands with me at the end of the hour, and we then moved forward harmoniously through Alfred Marshall's principles. We also became fast friends for the rest of his life.

Trying as the experience was, it was the best thing that happened to me in my academic life. It forced me to master the reasoning of the great economic theorists and to stand my ground under verbal and logical bombardment.

There was one feature of Harvard life that I did not like. That was the deep-rooted provincialism and social snobbery that pervaded both the student body and many of the faculty. Though the university had given up rating students in the catalogue with numbers indicating their social standing, informally the practice was still followed. The poor were regarded with disdain by all but a few, while an air of effortless superiority exuded from the others. This has been a spiritual handicap to thousands of Harvard men. Nevertheless, for years Harvard also produced more intelligent rebels than any other college in the Ivy League.

4

Apprenticeship

Upon Taussig's recommendation and my winning an honorable mention for the Ricardo Prize in political economy, I was appointed for the next year to an instructorship at the University of Illinois. After that, I accepted an assistant professorship at Reed College, in Portland, Oregon, where I enjoyed a most stimulating year. Despite many obstacles, Reed has maintained as high academic standards as any college in the country for over half a century. This has made it one of the most worthwhile of American colleges, although it has always been troubled by the internal excesses and outer hostility to which such experimental colleges are prone.

During my first few years of teaching, I adopted Taussig's somewhat aggressive method, driving my students hard and trying to rule through fear. But I found these practices incompatible with my growing absorption in Quakerism and I could no longer be happy winning verbal battles in the classroom. I began to change my approach to try to bring out the best in students. This was harder and devoid of fireworks, but in the long run it was better. My students developed initiative and sometimes became friends, while I felt more at peace with myself. John R. Commons, then at the University of Wisconsin and perhaps the most magnificent economics teacher of my time, had arrived at a somewhat similar process, by which he encouraged scores of students to work with him and not merely for him. I became convinced that, in the field of learning, sympathy is more helpful than fear.

I had formed a close intellectual attachment with a brilliant fellow student, Dorothy Wolff, of a prominent New York family. Her father had died, but her mother and I developed a warm and enduring affection. Meanwhile, I found Dorothy's mind very stimulating, and, beyond that, she was the most generous and altruistic person I had ever met. With plans for a life of high academic endeavor and social crusading, we were married in 1915. Originally, we meant to live on my salary, while she used her income in support of worthy causes and individuals.

We did not long maintain such standards, in part because we both wanted a large family. In the next eleven years we had four fine children, Helen, John, Dorothea, and Paul. At the same time, Dorothy continued with her studies, full time, although she switched to economics from sociology, in which she had earned a Ph.D. The problem of finding congenial positions for both of us was to be a main reason for our later separation.

As the war drew ever closer to America, I, like many others in the liberal group to which I was drawn, went through internal agony trying to determine where my duty lay. I wanted to help my country, but at first the basic moral differences between the European contestants seemed unclear. Nor could I reconcile the teachings of religion with the taking of human life. Since I could not bring myself to kill an animal, how could I kill a fellow human being? Or how could I even indirectly help to kill? Something within me kept insisting that it was wrong to take the life of one's fellow men even in uniform. When war came in 1917, I made these scruples known to the proper authorities, where I suppose they are still on the record. After German aggressions persuaded me of a real difference between the belligerents, I tried to enlist in 1918. An Army doctor at a camp near Astoria, Oregon, rated my eyes at only 5–20, which prevented my acceptance. While I was considering whether or not to go north from Portland into British Columbia to enlist in the Canadian Army, which had lower physical standards, an offer came for me to help settle industrial disputes for the Emergency Fleet Corporation. I decided to accept and went to Philadelphia to work under that inspiring leader of men L. C. Marshall, of Chicago.

Just as the armistice was in the process of being signed, I experienced one of the turning points in my personal life. Quakerism had attracted me for some time, and there was a Quaker branch among the Maine Douglases. My wife and I one day walked the twelve miles from Bryn Mawr to the Quaker School at Westtown, where we spent the night. Before starting back the next day, I picked up a copy of Whittier's edition of John Woolman's *Journal* in the parlor of the little inn. The hours passed, but for me time stood still as I read the record of that pure life. When evening came, I walked back to Bryn Mawr in a state of exaltation. Every step seemed to be a part of a pilgrimage into a new life. I had learned the power of active love to melt opposition and transform opponents into friends.

John Woolman, a tailor from Mount Holly, in New Jersey, had devoted himself to following his inner light, or, as others would say, acting solely in obedience to his conscience. This meant plainness in dress and living so that he would not consume too much of this world's goods or make others labor unduly for him. Once, he embarked on a dangerous mission to a hostile Indian tribe and convinced them that he was their friend. His greatest work was an unceasing effort to free the slaves. He would not write any bill of sale for them, or eat sugar or any tropical product produced by their labor. Quietly he persuaded Quakers to free their own slaves. One by one the yearly meetings asked their members to set their slaves free and to do so without seeking compensation. Woolman was assigned the thankless task of visiting the slaveholding Friends and exhorting them to comply. He did so with such a sweet spirit that almost all did free their slaves. Those who refused were quietly dropped from membership. By 1776, the Quakers had repudiated the great curse of slavery, and later furnished the spiritual seed pods from which the nineteenth-century abolitionist movement largely sprang. The hardheaded Scot Adam Smith wrote in his *Wealth of Nations* that this proved that the Quakers could not have owned many slaves. But he was wrong. A large number were set free in what was a conspicuous case of moral principle proving stronger than economic interest.

Because the nation as a whole would not follow the way of John Woolman, it later had to follow that of John Brown, and Grant and Sherman to boot. Yet in the long run what person of his time had a better influence on mankind?

For months this vision of what an individual could accomplish if guided by a true and informed inner light obsessed me. From a negative repugnance to physical force and violence as instruments of coercion, I felt a mission to try to practice the principle of redemptive love. I failed more often than I succeeded, but felt my feet were on the right path and that I was trying to move in the light. This persuaded me to join the Society of Friends in 1920, one of the best steps I have ever taken. It led me to consider my own conduct more carefully and, though with much stumbling and many errors, to try at least to remedy some of the weaknesses in my own character. I wanted in some small manner to follow Woolman and "live in that spirit" which, as George Fox said, "taketh away the occasion for all war."

Fifty years have passed since then. Although I came in the middle 1930's to reject the doctrine of nonresistance, or spiritual superresistance, as ineffective in an age of aggressive dictatorships and police states, I am, by their sufferance, still a member of the Society of Friends. With all their imperfections, they are, I believe, the best corporate body of men and women with whom it has ever been my privilege to be associated. Over the years the mystic glow of Woolman has faded for me, but there remains a deep respect and a wistful desire that the Quakers, rather than I, may ultimately prove to be right. Certainly the world as a whole needs more, rather than less, of that spirit.

During this period, as I began to acquire through teaching and research an increasing mastery over the principles of economics, I became almost equally fascinated by literature and biography. I devoured the novels and essays of Wells, Galsworthy, and Chesterton and the plays of Shaw and Ibsen. Then I went back to the Victorians—Thackeray, Hardy, and Meredith. *The Oxford Book of English Verse* opened up a whole body of poetry. And after my interest in Quakerism had led me to George M. Trevelyan's *Life of John Bright,* I went on to John Morley's biographies of Cobden and Gladstone, and from there to Morley's own essays and other literary biographies.

But the eye opener came with Tolstoy and the Russians. After nearly half a century and many rereadings, I still regard *War and Peace* as the greatest novel ever written. My memories of Natasha, Pierre, and Bolkonsky remain poignant. The book so stirred me that I got hold of nearly everything Tolstoy had ever written, from his early *Childhood, Boyhood, Youth,* and *The Cossacks* to *Anna Karenina, Resurrection,* and the moving essays and stories on war, peace, and the Christian life.

The frankness with which Tolstoy discussed his inner conflicts and sins reinforced what I was learning from the writings of Sigmund Freud. Both had benefited from the work of the French neurologists J. M. Charcot and P. M. F. Janet, which William James discussed in his *The Principles of Psychology.* The life of the emotions was more than mere logic. The problem was to purify it, a function that for years Quakerism helped serve for me.

Tolstoy led me inevitably to Dostoevsky's *The Brothers Karamazov* and *Crime and Punishment* and from there to Turgenev's *Smoke* and *Fathers and Sons,* thence to Chekhov and Gorky. This was accompanied by excursions into the writings of those twin satirists Anatole France and Voltaire. The forest-bred youth was growing up and getting older, but the real work lay ahead.

I went back to the West Coast in 1919 and taught for a year at the University of Washington, in Seattle. The classes were huge and the work heavy, but I managed to write a series of articles on labor problems, the system of federal aid, and the relationship of the newly developing shop committees to unionism. On the side, I got acquainted with the aggressive labor movement of the Northwest by teaching at the Seattle Labor College.

While I was in Seattle I met a most unforgettable character—Sam Hill, the son-in-law of the railway empire builder James J. Hill. One evening while walking behind my hillside house, I saw moving toward me a huge gray-clad man with cloak and Quaker hat crowning a shock of white hair. "Can you tell me," he asked, "where Paul Douglas lives?" "I am he," I replied. "I thought so," he rejoined. "I am Samuel Hill." Prodding me majestically with his walking stick, he ordered me into his car. He wanted me to come home for a talk, which turned into an almost continuous monologue. In quick succession he told of his twenty-eight Atlantic crossings, explained where the best snails in Paris were served and the best seafood in Naples, told how he had picked out the site upon which Bryn Mawr College was built and how one morning at 10:14 A.M., in a three-minute conference with railway and shipping executives, he had cleared up the confusion on the Jersey City waterfront. Knowing my labor sympathies, he told me how, after graduating from Haverford, he had been one of the Northwest leaders of the Knights of Labor and after fighting James J. Hill had married his daughter and become his partner. During the depression of 1893, when they had to stop western construction of the Great Northern for lack of funds, he went to Europe to raise additional money, and there decided that the royal families were the only ones who were depression-proof. After studying the *Almanach de Gotha,* he concluded that King Leopold of Belgium was the key to his acquaintance with royalty. Leopold, with his swarm of feminine favorites, then held summer court at Ostend. By judicious flattery, Sam gained entrance to the court there, and not only sold a big block of Great Northern bonds, but obtained a letter to Queen Victoria, who also became a purchaser. She passed him on to her niece Marie, the Crown Princess of Rumania. After journeying to the Balkans, he made a big sale to the Rumanian royal house. "We built the line to the Pacific," concluded my host, "while I became the intimate of royalty. Not bad for a North Carolina Quaker."

Then, in rapid succession, he fired questions at me. "Who laid out the Columbia River Highway?" Sam Hill, of course. "Who had the corners of Seattle sidewalks made to slope gradually down to street level?" None other than Sam Hill. "Who made Herbert Putnam the librarian of Congress and the foremost librarian in the country?" Again it was Sam Hill. In the early '90's he had pointed out to his father-in-law that a seedy-looking Eastern lawyer named Putnam would make an excellent librarian. "Let's put him in charge of the Minneapolis Library," he said. "After two or three years we'll make him Congressional librarian." They did. "Who outwitted E. H. Harriman and Kuhn, Loeb in the Northern Pacific fight?" So the reminiscences flowed by the hour, with their inevitable answers.

As the self-styled modest Quaker really warmed up, he told how he and James J. Hill had fooled their banking ally, the mighty J. Pierpont Morgan. "Morgan thought he knew everything," said Sam. "He boasted that he could identify the hide of every animal that ever lived." So he and James J. left Morgan's Madison Avenue mansion once vowing that they would humble him. They went out to Montana and bred a bull moose to a cow. When the resulting offspring was a year old, they had it killed and its hide tanned. "We reappeared with this rug as a gift to J. Pierpont," Sam continued, "and asked him to identify it." After long scrutiny, Morgan confessed he could not. "Of course you can't, Mr. Morgan," said the irrepressible Sam. "There never before was such a creature!" James J. later boasted, "We Quakers are just as smart and perhaps a bit smarter than he is."

Hill's huge, four-story house had ivy reaching to the eaves. My host asked how old I thought his house was. I told him that it must have taken at least fifty years for ivy to climb so high. But I was mystified, because no house in Seattle was that old. "This house," said Sam, "is six months old." He explained that he was going to entertain royalty that summer. King Albert and Queen Elizabeth of Belgium and Queen Marie of Rumania were coming. They were going to dedicate his Peace Portal at the border between Washington and Canada. He needed a mansion covered with English ivy to make them feel at home. After scouring the Cascade and Olympic mountains, he finally found an abandoned log cabin over which ivy had been growing for half a century. He had the ivy dug up and fastened to wire netting and its roots planted in deep boxes. Then he had a trench dug around the house and had strong hooks coming out from the bricks. Dropping the ivy into the trench, he fastened the netting to the hooks and instantly had an ivy-clad mansion fit for royalty.

When we drove into the basement garage, I saw several trucks loaded with furniture. My host, surprised, remarked that he did not know that he was so well equipped. "Sometimes," he said, "the mood comes over me to travel. I get into my car and drive, with the trucks following me, night and day until we reach my first stopping place. Then, too, I address the legislatures of Washington, Oregon, and California, and indeed of other states as well, preaching the need for good roads and the need for conserving the scenic beauties of the Northwest."

Going up in the elevator, he said that there were no staircases; only elevators connected the floors. As we entered the darkness of the ground floor, a vivid likeness of the Columbia River Highway sprang out from the paneling. "That is my work," said Sam proudly—"modeled on the Dolomites." A moment later, where there had been darkness glowed the face of a horsy-looking woman wearing a crown. "My Queen Elizabeth," announced Sam. Darkness again, followed by a lighted photograph on glass of a modest man in soldier's uniform. "That, of course, is my friend King Albert."

There was a long period of darkness. Suddenly from the wall at my elbow there leaped out the portrait of an opulent beauty across whose largely bare bosom was written in glowing words, "To my darling Sam, Marie of Rumania." "All three of them are coming to help dedicate the Peace Portal I have built on the border of British Columbia. This commemorates one hundred years of friendship between us and Great Britain. I have written the words for the portal. They rival Lincoln's speech at Gettysburg."

We moved up to the second floor, where a library ran the full length of the house. Near the center table was a huge globe. "I make three of these every year for those of whom I am especially fond. You are going to get one," he continued. "Do you see something striking about this globe?" As usual, he answered his own question. "It shows that all the trade winds of the world go up the Columbia River and cross over my house at Mary Hill. I am at the real topographical center of the world."

So the monologue continued. At around four in the morning, Sam said that he wanted to found a Quaker college in Seattle, with me as its president. I told him I had already agreed to go to the University of Chicago, but that I hoped we could keep in touch with each other.

As his car started to take me home, a huge spout of water gushed through the pavement of his driveway, rising at least thirty feet in the air. I said to myself that it was another of Sam Hill's stunts. He had probably arranged this for his royal visitors and was trying it out on me. Since it was Saturday, I tumbled into bed to sleep until noon. When I opened the afternoon paper, I read that at 4:15 A.M. a bolt of lightning had struck the pavement in front of Hill's mansion, hitting a water main. Even nature had collaborated to heighten the drama at his house.

I never saw Sam again. In the fall, however, he was in the news when Queen Marie made her tour of the country. She stopped to dedicate what the press unkindly called Sam Hill's "empty museum" at Mary Hill. After that the Baltimore and Ohio Railroad, which acted as the Queen's impresario, pried her loose from her admirer. Sam set out after her and on his Chicago stopover called to assure me of his continued friendship. He sounded like a wounded King Lear, bereft of his daughter, but he was confident that he would finally win out, for, as he said of Queen Marie, "our ties are so close that we will surely be reunited." Alas for Sam, this was not to be.

I never heard from him again, but for years the reverberations of his picaresque adventures came from many quarters. There were stories of how he had made three successive killings in real estate by letting Everett, Tacoma, and Seattle each in turn believe that they were to be the western terminus of the Great Northern. He had an unfailing ability to buy land cheap and sell it dear. On a transatlantic steamer, a graduate-school classmate of Sam's at Harvard told how the latter had virtually kidnapped him on a trip to Alaska and had him treated as a visiting potentate. In the alumni reception room at Haverford I saw a large photograph of modest Sam, his chest covered with medals, while at the little Quaker meeting at Jordans in England, where William Penn lies buried, the members spoke incredulously of the railway magnate who burst into their meeting accompanied by Loie Fuller, the dancer. Unabashed at invading their quiet services, he took over the role of motion-picture director.

Some students of folklore ascribe the expression "What in Sam Hill" to the exploits of this Sam. Others claim that his mother, anticipating those exploits, tailored her son to the expression. I concluded that most of what he said about himself was true and that if the expression had not been derived from his actions, he had modeled his acts to live up to the expression.

In 1920, L. C. Marshall offered me an assistant professorship at the University of Chicago, and in the fall of that year I began my work on the Midway. I finished my dissertation on apprenticeship and received my doctor's degree from Columbia. My period of preparation and personal apprenticeship was over, and productive life had begun.

5

Chicago: University and City in the Early and Middle 1920's

THE UNIVERSITY OF CHICAGO was only as old as I. It had been founded by John D. Rockefeller in 1892, with William Rainey Harper as president. Harper had traveled over the country to find adventurous and able professors and had assembled a truly extraordinary faculty. He had almost stripped Clark University bare, prompting its president, G. Stanley Hall, to compare his tactics with those of the founder.

Although the momentum had slowed after Harper's death, it was still a fine university. The emphasis was upon scholarship, and the departments of physics, mathematics, and chemistry were perhaps the best in the country. During my years, seven Nobel Prize winners in physics worked in its laboratories: Albert A. Michelson, Robert A. Millikan, Arthur H. Compton, Harold C. Urey, Enrico Fermi, James Franck, and W. F. Libby. The social sciences were not as strong as the physical, but included Charles E. Merriam in political science and William E. Dodd, Andrew C. McLaughlin, and James Westfall Thompson in history. Economics was weaker, although Thorstein Veblen, James Laughlin, Herbert J. Davenport, and Harold Moulton had taught there. But with the coming of Jacob Viner, Frank Knight, Henry Schultz, John Nef, and others, by the end of the 1920's the department was second to none in the nation.

Best of all, men were encouraged at Chicago to think, study, and produce for themselves. There was complete academic freedom, to which both the faculty and the Rockefeller family were deeply committed. I never saw any personal competition in the social or teaching life, or any evidence of politics in academic affairs. Everyone, from the president down

43

to the janitors, was called "Mr.," and distinctions of rank were relatively unknown.

No wonder I fell in love with the university, and, although over twenty years have passed since I was a member of its staff, I still have a deep affection for it and for the values it has fostered.

Chicago itself, although horrible to some, was fascinating to me. Until the rise of São Paulo and Mexico City, it was the most rapidly growing city in the Americas. While there was a small aristocracy, based on two generations of wealth, in the main men were still judged on ability and effort. It was a vital place, well named, by Carl Sandburg, "City of the Big Shoulders." And yet, even as I came to it, Chicago was entering the most disgraceful decades that any American city has ever experienced. Prohibition had brought enormous profits from bootlegging, while powerful underworld gangs, headed by Al Capone and "Bugs" Moran, made millions and, with their retainers, waged war upon each other. At the same time, Samuel Insull ruled the upperworld of finance and business, running the electric and gas companies and the elevated lines. Through a fantastic cobweb of holding companies, he was reaching out for the utilities of a large portion of the nation.

True to the analysis of Lincoln Steffens, both the criminal syndicate of the underworld and the upperworld of industry and finance were aided and protected by the political "system," which they in turn supported. The buffoon William Hale ("Big Bill") Thompson, mayor for most of the time between 1915 and 1931, gave each group virtually all it wanted. Bribery was rampant in both political parties, and for eight years Illinois had, in Len Small, a governor who was more flagrantly corrupt than was Big Bill. The first generation of reformers had died, become tired, or gone over to the Insull group. Younger people, making money and rising in the world, did not want to "stick their necks out." If they did, they were likely to suffer. While the underworld fought with pistols and submachine guns, Insull and his associates fought with the equally lethal weapons of propaganda and financial pressure.

The literary renaissance that had burst upon Chicago around 1915 was fading. By the end of the '20's, William Vaughn Moody was dead, Sandburg had retired to the Michigan dunes, Edgar Lee Masters had gone to New York, and the *Little Review* of Margaret Anderson had made its inevitable journey to Paris. Stuart Walker and Ellen van Volkenburg, who had founded the Little Theater movement, had been divorced and moved on, and Vachel Lindsay, inadequately appreciated, was soon to commit suicide. Others, including Ben Hecht, developed but quickly packed up for New York. The city could not support a general publishing house, or any literary periodical aside from *Poetry*. Yet the *Daily News* developed a great string of foreign correspondents: the Mowrer brothers—Paul Scott and Edgar Ansel—Carroll Binder, Vincent

Sheean, and John Gunther. And the museums, the orchestra, and the universities kept the cultural life aglow.

Despite its manifold sins and weaknesses, I grew to love the city. Underneath the brutality that gave Chicago its global reputation, I found the overwhelming proportion of its people generous and without pretense.

It was my good fortune to become a friend of Jane Addams during the last fifteen years of her life. Born a Quaker, she had grown into a veritable saint. She was for her time what John Woolman had been for his. Devoting her early life to the bewildered immigrants of Chicago's teeming West Side, she was the vital force behind nearly every forward movement in the city and the state.

Appointed to the school board in 1906 by the liberal Mayor, Edward F. Dunne, she soon brought down on her head the wrath of the *Tribune*. She insisted that the paper pay an adequate rent for the land it leased from the school board at a fraction of its true value. Since her conscience made her a pacifist, the *Tribune* pursued her with a torrent of abuse during World War I, and forever after. Their lead encouraged irresponsible sections of the community to denounce and ridicule her. She bore these attacks with quiet dignity, and persevered through the '20's in her efforts for civic reform, protective legislation for women and children, and international peace. No award of the Nobel Prize was ever more fully merited than hers. She had attracted to Hull House a group of remarkable women, including the witty and wise Julia Lathrop, the first head of the Children's Bureau, and Grace and Edith Abbott, two keen and sharp-tongued sisters of whom I stood in fearsome awe. To Hull House came distinguished visitors from all parts of the world, to most of whom Jane Addams introduced me. In this way I met British journalists and politicians and fiery Indian nationalists.

But Jane Addams was more than a devoted social worker and helpful friend of all mankind. She was also a highly cultivated woman and a magnificent stylist and writer. Believing that the poor had a right to beauty as well as to bread, she had established a museum of textiles and a playhouse. She launched music classes and an orchestra, where Benny Goodman and James C. Petrillo were introduced to music. The autobiography of her early and middle periods, *Twenty Years at Hull-House,* is an American classic. *Democracy and Social Ethics, The Long Road of Women's Memory,* and *The Spirit of Youth and the City Streets* are some of the wisest and best of American writings.

With especial fondness I recall her subtle sense of humor and her lack of rancor toward those who abused her. Whenever I was with her, I felt strengthened, even purified. Her recommendations brought me the chance to give brief lecture courses at Hull House and before union study groups.

As I became better acquainted with the foreign-language groups and some of the struggling unions, I made friends with many kindred spirits who broadened and deepened my appreciation. The Amalgamated Clothing Workers and the International Ladies' Garment Workers, under Jewish leadership, were particularly compatible, and through the National Association for the Advancement of Colored People and the Brotherhood of Sleeping Car Porters I began to make friends in the rapidly growing Negro community. As a result, when chances came to teach elsewhere, the thought of leaving the city and the university was more than I could bear.

During this period I studied hard for my classes, averaging sixty to seventy hours of work a week. The subjects investigated ranged from labor problems and wage systems to proportional representation and the problem of incentives in economic life. I published several articles a year and a book nearly every other year. In 1924, I started a study of real wages, or the relative actual amounts that wage and salaried workers could buy, on a yearly, weekly, and hourly basis for each year from 1890 on. To carry out this work, I needed a staff of assistants, but could not finance their salaries from my meager research funds. That was why I started lecturing, at $25 and $50 a talk, first in Chicago and then throughout the Middle West, using the money I earned to pay my computers. The book, *Real Wages in the United States, 1890–1926*, finally appeared in 1930, and was well received.

By this time, I had embarked on my most ambitious project—a treatise on wages, which won a $5,000 international prize given by Hart, Schaffner and Marx. It began as an analysis of the relative elasticities of supply of both labor and capital and the effect of varying rates of change in these upon the distribution of the product. But without an adequate theory of production, elasticities of supply did not in themselves explain much.

One spring day in 1927, while lecturing at Amherst, I charted on a logarithmic scale three variables I had laboriously compiled for American manufacturing for the years 1889 to 1922: an index of total fixed capital corrected for changes in the cost of capital goods (C), an index of the total number of wage earners employed in manufacturing (L), and an index of physical production in manufacturing (P). I noticed that the index of production lay between those for capital and labor and that it was from one-third to one-quarter of the relative distance between the lower index of labor and the higher index of capital. After consulting with my friend Charles W. Cobb, the mathematician, we decided to try to find on the basis of these observations the relative contributions which each of the two factors of production (labor and capital) had upon production itself. We chose the Euler formula of a simple homogeneous function of the first degree, which that remarkable Englishman Philip Wicksteed had developed some years before ($P = b\ L^K\ C^{1-K}$). We found the values of K and $1-K$ by the method of least squares to be .75 and .25, and that b was merely 1.01.

The production values computed by this formula came close to the actual values with a very low average error. Furthermore, such deviations from the actual values as did occur were largely accounted for by known inaccuracies in the data themselves and by the business cycle. Thus, during depressions both the quantity of capital actually used and the relative amount of labor employed were overstated, with the result that this was reflected in the computed product. The opposite tendency prevailed in years of prosperity, when capital was used for more hours a day and workers would put in overtime. A final test was that the actual shares of the total product received by labor and capital according to the National Bureau of Economic Research were almost the same as their exponents, namely 74.1 per cent for labor.

Cobb and I presented a paper on this subject at the meeting of the American Economic Association in December of 1927 which touched off an animated discussion. The general response was unfavorable. In succeeding years I pushed this analysis further with different sets of data, and arrived at almost the same results. Conquering my usual haste, I revised the manuscript many times, financing the research both from the prize money and from outside lecture fees.

Finally, in 1934, eight years after I had submitted the original manuscript, the book, *The Theory of Wages,* was published. To this day it remains my chief claim to scholarly distinction, and I made many improvements in it during the next fifteen years. For example, in accordance with a suggestion made by David Durand, of Cornell, I freed the formula from the restriction that the sum of the exponents must equal unity (1.0), so that it was now $P = b\ L^K\ C^j$. The exponent for labor now tended to be .65 and that for capital .35. And this was fairly close to improved studies on the distribution of the product. I also pushed the analysis into many cross-section studies within specific years. Here the different industries served as the observations. Someday I hope to use plants within industries as the observations. The general results for the British Commonwealth countries of Australia, Canada, and New Zealand proved strikingly similar to those for the United States, as did the studies of specific industries.

In 1925 I was selected by the newspaper publishers and the printing unions to be the impartial chairman of the national board of arbitration for that industry. From these disputes, which were hard fought and well prepared, I learned a great deal. At that time neither side wanted stoppages that would be crippling for both. So if they could not settle their differences directly, they turned them over to an arbitration board, on which the neutral chairman held the balance of power. The national board was sometimes called to settle local disputes in different parts of the country and sometimes sat as an appeals board in either Indianapolis or Chicago.

The life of an arbitrator is usually brief, for all blame is shifted to his shoulders. It was gratifying to me, therefore, that my services were wanted for sixteen years, until World War II engaged me elsewhere. And the generous fees supplemented my meager salary and enabled me to make small savings. As an arbitrator I handed down scores of decisions on a wide range of questions and for many cities. Despite occasional grumblings, my judgments met with general approval. My faith in collective bargaining was deepened by this service.

An experience I never forgot occurred in Denver. Rivalry was intense between the Denver *Post* and the Scripps-Howard paper, the *Rocky Mountain News*. During the first period of negotiation and mediation between them and the union, one of the papers made an offer that the other refused to match. The case was then referred to me. Since it was a rule that these preliminary offers should not be admitted as evidence, I was ignorant of what had been offered. After studying the evidence, I handed down an award that, while giving a sizable increase, fixed it at a figure lower than that which had been offered—even lower than that the other paper would have granted. Here, lacking information, I had been led to violate another basic rule of arbitration, namely, an arbitrator should not set a lower minimum than that offered in mediation.

The union rose in anger, not only denouncing me, but also burning me in effigy. It demanded that the case be reargued. For a full year union and publishers vainly tried to agree upon a new arbitrator. Then the union sheepishly suggested that I be asked to rehear the case. "He probably meant well," it was said, "and after all it wasn't his fault that he didn't know what had been offered." I reheard the case and solemnly awarded the previous offer plus an allowance for the intervening increase in the cost of living and productivity. Peace returned to Denver.

In the winter of 1926 I was asked by the American Friends Service Committee to join a commission to investigate the American occupation of the Negro republic of Haiti. There I spent a fascinating month. Emily G. Balch, who was later awarded the Nobel peace prize, and I prepared a report that is credited with having helped bring about the later withdrawal of the Marines and the restoration of self-government. This self-government, I am sorry to say, has been a failure.

Miserably poor, the people of Haiti had been exploited by a mulatto aristocracy who held most of the offices of government. By levying an export tax on coffee, the rulers supported themselves both at home and abroad. The diplomatic service was, indeed, a form of subsidized foreign travel and residence for the so-called elite. Between 1908 and 1914 the country had fallen into an epidemic of revolutions. They started in the north, around Cap Haitien, and moved south to Port-au-Prince. When a president escaped, he usually went to nearby Jamaica and from there to Paris, where he lived a pleasant life on the boulevards. Meanwhile, the process recommenced under a new leader.

American capital had worsened the situation. It had financed a railroad ostensibly meant to run from Port-au-Prince to Cap Haitien, and had floated a bond issue guaranteed by the Haitian government under a scandalous concession. But the promoters had built only three disconnected sections of the railroad, which carefully avoided the mountains. With no through traffic, the line could not meet the interest on its bonds, and the government faced bankruptcy. Financial interests, headed by the National City Bank of New York, then clamored for United States intervention. Finally, when another revolution developed and the President, Vilbrun Guillaume Sam, was murdered, they convinced Secretary of State Bryan and President Wilson that we should send in the Marines to take over the country and restore order.

Once there, it was not easy to get out. When the commission arrived, the occupation had been in effect for eleven years. This occupation, together with like interventions in Santo Domingo and Nicaragua, had stirred up a deep Latin-American hostility toward the United States. While our record was mixed, it seemed wise to withdraw. Some of the effects of these interventions have remained to this day. Combined with the Mexican-American war of 1846–48 and Theodore Roosevelt's "seizure" of the Panama Canal Zone in 1903, they have led Latin Americans to distrust our motives and have embittered our relationships. As I described in an article published at the time in the *Nation,* insiders in both Haiti and Panama who bought bonds when they were low did very well for themselves in the final financial settlements. In the United States we have hastened to forget these incidents. It comes as a shock to most Americans that our neighbors to the south recall this history and that it feeds a substructure of anti-Americanism.

Another exciting offer came to me, during the spring of 1927, when I was asked to serve as an economic adviser to a trade-union delegation going to the Soviet Union. This group had been organized by Albert F. Coyle, editor of the *Journal* of the highly conservative Brotherhood of Locomotive Engineers. The two leading members of the delegation were James Maurer, president of the Pennsylvania Federation of Labor, and John Brophy, recently defeated by John L. Lewis for the presidency of the United Mine Workers. Among those who were attached to the delegation were Rexford Guy Tugwell, then a professor at Columbia, and Stuart Chase, the popular writer on economic subjects. I was assured that the expedition was to be independently financed, and I paid my own fare over and back and even made some contributions to the over-all expenses. As a condition for my going I asked that no Communist be included on this trip, but I found out some months later that a confirmed fellow traveler, not a party member, had joined the group at Coyle's invitation.

After ten years, the Soviet Union was starting to recover from civil war and famine. The low standard of living was improving. Trotsky was still present, and though his open feud with Stalin was approaching its final throes, the latter had not yet triumphed. Public discussion and criticism were still permitted within party circles, but not by the general public. The leaders of the movement still led rather austere lives. While there was a concentration of political power, this had not yet resulted in great economic inequality. The terrors of military communism, created by the civil war and Allied intervention, had abated, and private enterprise continued in farming, the handicrafts, and service trades, and over a large section of retailing. It was perhaps the most promising year in postrevolutionary Russia. There was, indeed, the possibility that the country might develop into a humane society freed from the tyranny of the czar without substituting a new tyranny. I spent some weeks studying the operation of factories, farms, and trade, and the economic and political agencies that governed them. It seemed possible that East and West, despite their differing economic systems, might yet exist peacefully side by side, competing to create a better society, rather than in military conquest.

Over the protests of Trotsky, Stalin had just abandoned the Chinese Communists to Chiang Kai-shek. The struggle between the two Soviet leaders was ostensibly being waged over whether socialism could be confined to one country, as Stalin contended, or whether it should be expanded into permanent world revolution, as Trotsky and his supporters argued. It was apparent that with the party bureaucracy behind him Stalin would win, and this strengthened my hope for peaceful coexistence. Within a decade, however, the roles would be reversed.

In the report of the delegation, *Russia After Ten Years,* we pointed out that the Russian government, after a decade of trial, was firmly established. We urged that the United States return to its historic policy, launched by Henry Clay, of recognizing governments even though we disagreed with their policies on crucial matters. Six years later this principle was applied by the Roosevelt administration. The Soviet government was recognized, and diplomatic missions were exchanged.

As one who must bear perhaps an infinitesimal share of responsibility for this decision, I have often wondered whether it was wise. Certainly recognition helped pave the way for Russia's combining with Great Britain and the United States to defeat the menace of monolithic Nazism. But Hitler's invasion of Russia in 1941 might have brought the same results without any such recognition.

But whether or not this decision was wise, I no longer believe in Clay's doctrine of always recognizing existent governments. When a nation is in fact reaching for your throat, it may not be wise to give it the facilities that recognition inevitably brings. An open and free society should not unduly handicap itself. My disillusioning experience with Russian recognition was one of the factors that led me to oppose the recognition of Communist China and its admission into the United Nations. Many of my liberal friends have disagreed. They believe that recognition need not connote approval, and that there is value in keeping lines of communication open.

Of one thing in Russia, we found, there could be no doubt. Differences of opinion on the basic economic and political structure of society were not tolerated. Instead, the Communist party, acting through the state, used the press, the schools, the radio, the churches, and the stage to inculcate what it termed "communism." It applied terror through imprisonment, exile, and death itself to those who persisted in differing. These tactics had been outlined by Lenin in his *The State and Revolution,* his blueprint for the assumption and use of power. They had been explained by Trotsky himself, in an exchange of pamphlets with Kautsky, the German Social Democrat; in his *Defense of Terrorism* he said that during a crisis period "imprisonment is an insufficient deterrent since people do not believe in its duration. It is this simple fact which explains the widespread recourse to shooting during a civil war."

One evening Stuart Chase and I were invited to visit an airplane factory during a night shift, and were asked to speak at the time allowed for a meal. When I had finished, some of the workers shouted, "Sacco and Vanzetti," and one who could speak English fairly well cried, "You Americans have no justice. You are unjustly putting Sacco and Vanzetti to death!" I decided that they should hear some unpleasant truths. Seizing the interpreter by the arm, I stepped to the edge of the platform. "Listen," I said. "I believe Sacco and Vanzetti to be innocent. I have signed petitions on their behalf and have contributed financially to their defense. But remember this: they received the full protection of the law. Their case was reviewed a number of times, and it is now seven years since they were arrested. I think those who administer the law have made a grave mistake, but it is the fault of men and not of our system of justice. We gave the accused the full right to be heard, to be represented by counsel, to be tried by a jury of their peers, and to appeal. You ask for justice for Sacco and Vanzetti; so do I.

"But what about yourselves? Two months ago a group of bank clerks were arrested at two o'clock in the morning." Here the interpreter stopped and refused to go on. I shook him and demanded that he continue to translate, and he did so, trembling in obvious fear: "They were tried at four o'clock and executed at six. Where was their right to assemble witnesses, to engage counsel, to argue their case, and if convicted, appeal? If you demand justice for those with whom you sympathize, you must be prepared to give justice to those whom you dislike. You cannot have a double standard either logically or morally." The crowd was now in an uproar. I saw some furtive nods of approval, but there were more loud screams of "Sacco and Vanzetti!" and the chairman hastily and with obvious relief adjourned the meeting.

As I stepped down from the platform, a handsome young woman said that she wanted to talk with me. She led the way to a table, where with great earnestness she lectured me in perfect English, which I later recorded in my notebook. "You talked only about individual justice," she said. "This is a bourgeois idea. We are interested in class justice and in ending the exploitation of man by man. To effect this we made the revolution which is still going on. We do not intend to sacrifice class justice in order to protect the individual justice of some petty bank clerk. It is important that you bourgeois should recognize this."

I replied, "You condemn your opponents when, in support of a class system which they believe to be just, they victimize some unfortunate person in your camp. But as you condemn them on the basis of justice and morality, you obviously have some standard of justice outside mere class advantage to which you appeal in your own behalf. If this is a universal principle, as I believe it is, then it should be applied universally. If you ask for justice for yourself, you must be willing to grant it to others. Furthermore, classes are composed of individuals. It is impossible to have class justice if the individuals who make up that class are treated unjustly. You are now denying a fair trial to your opponents. If you keep on doing this, you Communists will get into the habit of using blind force against each other and against innocent people who think differently from you. Even you, yourself, may come to be condemned and you will then want some of that individual justice which you now scorn."

The discussion continued for an hour or more. Finally she rose and, with a confident shake of her head, said with a superior smile, "History will prove us right and you wrong." Before going, she wrote her name, "Betty Glan," in my notebook.

Some ten years later I read a brief dispatch in the New York *Times* recording that a Trotskyite leader, Betty Glan, had been executed by the Russian secret police on the preceding day.

The high points of our trip were interviews with Trotsky and Stalin. Trotsky still had a minor post, that of commissar of Foreign Concessions. We were kept waiting in his conference room for a full half hour. Then the door at the end of the room flew open, and in strode the star of the production, dressed in an immaculate white linen suit. Trotsky picked up the list of questions we had prepared and commented, "A very nasty list." He replied rapidly in Russian and in great detail. His interpreter translated into English with an irreproachable Oxford accent.

Trotsky put on a brilliant performance, using many historical analyses and striking figures of speech. Though pretending to speak English poorly, he was really a complete master of the finer shadings of the language. When his interpreter said that it was "necessary" to do something, Trotsky immediately corrected him, with faultless pronunciation, "Nay, not 'necessary,' rather, 'imperative.'" I concluded that he was one of the ablest men I had ever met and that even under great difficulties he was every inch a consummate actor. I agreed with the saying of a contemporary that "Trotsky would have gladly died for the revolution, provided there were ten thousand men looking on!"

Our interview was published in both *Pravda* and *Isvestia;* this was the first time in many months that Trotsky had broken through the press barrier.

Some of us left for a week's trip in the Ukraine and upon our return were informed that Stalin, who had previously declined to see us, had changed his mind and would now grant an interview in the Kremlin. Evidently he had determined that Trotsky was not to monopolize the publicity in connection with the Americans. We took Louis Fischer, the American correspondent, along with us, and he has described the interview in one of his books, saying that it was significant, amongst other things, for the fact that it was the first time Stalin had publicly exchanged opinions with a non-Communist delegation.

Recalling the deeds of terror that had been committed throughout its history, I shivered inwardly as we entered Red Square and then went through the gates of the Kremlin. The very buildings were mysterious and strange. We were escorted to a small cloakroom on the second floor of a building to the right, where we were met by a short man with a heavy mustache and a pock-marked face. He wore the patched uniform of a private, and, because he shook hands timidly and hung up our raincoats, I assumed that he was an attendant. We were escorted into a medium-sized conference room and seated around a long table. The place at the head of the table was vacant. Our attendant entered the room and moved slowly to the vacant chair, presumably to prepare for Stalin's entrance. To my consternation, he sat down at the head place, and as he faced us his stature seemed to grow. It was Stalin himself.

For four hours, in a slow, calm, and didactic manner, he answered the questions we had sent over to him. Then big trays of meat sandwiches and tea were brought in. With elaborate and ironical politeness, Stalin said that if we were not too exhausted he would like to ask us some questions. Then for two more hours he did so, asking why the United States did not recognize the Soviet Union, why there was no labor party, why the American Federation of Labor opposed the recognition of the USSR, and so on. To these queries we made the best replies we could, which later the Communist press called inadequate. This six-hour interview was the longest ever held in the Kremlin until Hubert Humphrey tied it with his cele-brated go-around with Nikita Khrushchev in December of 1959.

As we were leaving, I noticed a bust of Karl Marx in a corner of the room, and went over to peer up at the profuse beard. Startled by a heavy hand on my shoulder, I turned to face Stalin, who wanted to know what I was up to. I said that H. G. Wells had raised the question whether Marx, like a bourgeois, had worn a necktie behind his beard, or whether he took advantage of his foliage to economize by not wearing a tie. And where, I asked, was there a better place to settle this question than in the office of the Secretary of the Soviet Communist party and the head of the Communist International. Laughing, Stalin turned away. (Incidentally, Marx did wear a tie—carefully knotted in front of a stand-up collar.)

For our report, I wrote a section strongly condemning the Soviet viola-tion of civil liberties, but when the report appeared these charges were greatly watered down, presumably by Coyle, who had read and corrected the proofs.

I concluded that Stalin, while less brilliant, was steadier than Trotsky, but that I would hate to be in front of his steam roller. Little did I foresee the program of slaughter upon which he embarked some years later with his purges and liquidations. His career well illustrated the truth of Lord Acton's dictum "Power tends to corrupt; absolute power corrupts abso-lutely."

6

Battles with Samuel Insull
and Entrance into Public Life

In 1929 Samuel Insull was the uncrowned king of both Chicago and Illinois. He controlled the two big electric companies, Commonwealth Edison and Public Service of Northern Illinois, the gas company, and the elevated lines. He had also bought up scores of utility companies over the country and had tied them together through a maze of holding companies that were, in turn, controlled at the top by two super holding companies, Insull Utility Investments and Corporation Securities.

In 1926 he had elected his man, Frank L. Smith, to the United States Senate, contributing over $125,000 to Smith's primary fund. At the same time, Smith, as chairman of the Illinois Commerce Commission, was sustaining Insull's utility rates in the face of reduced costs and increased profits. Through his lawyers, Daniel J. Schuyler and Samuel Ettleson, Insull could get anything he wanted from Mayor William H. Thompson, and he placated the Democratic party leaders, George E. Brennan and Anton Cermak, with smaller favors and donations.

All but one of the big banks were so anxious to stand in well with Insull that their fortunes were interwoven with his. Furthermore, he was the chief patron of the arts, as backer and promoter of the Chicago Civic Opera Company, for which he built, in 1929, a forty-two-story opera house intended also to house many of his corporations. This edifice resembled a gigantic throne, from which Insull could survey and rule his kingdom.

The owners of the surface transportation lines had agreed to a consolidation with Insull's elevated lines whereby the latter would assume the joint management. To do this he sought enabling legislation from the state that would permit him to obtain not only a so-called "indeterminate

franchise," but also a valuation of $264 million for the combined proper-
ties. After this legislation was passed, he sought such a franchise from the
City Council, and set up an imposing list of "front" organizations to
sponsor his measures. All but the Hearst newspapers were on his side, and
most of the leading law firms were tied up with him in one way or another. In a sense, he seemed to be a magnified reincarnation of Charles T.
Yerkes, who, during the 1890's, had corrupted the politics of Chicago and
Illinois in his quest for a fifty-year traction franchise and whose exploits
had been immortalized by Theodore Dreiser in his novel *The Titan*.

Early in 1929 a group of progressive real-estate men asked me to analyze Insull's proposals and to recommend a policy for them to follow. I
devoted most of my spare time during that winter and spring to investigating the valuation claims and other features of the proposed legislation.

I discovered some half-suppressed reports that Milo R. Maltbie, chairman of the New York Public Utility Commission, had prepared for
former Mayor William E. Dever. Finally, I was able to piece the story together. The valuation of $167 million claimed for the surface lines in-
cluded most of the cost of the original horsecar system, which had long
since gone the way of all flesh; the cost of the cable-car system that had
replaced the horsecars and had also been scrapped; the cost of the first
trolley system, which had already been largely obsolete when a twenty-
year franchise was granted in 1907; the cost of the second trolley system,
built under the 1907 franchise, plus an additional 15 per cent allowed
upon this cost, but with no deduction for the physical depreciation of the
properties incurred during their twenty-some years of use.

As far as the claims of $97 million as the current valuation of the
elevated lines were concerned, it appeared that the original cost of these
lines in the 1890's had not exceeded $45 million, and that after over
forty years of wear and tear both structures and rolling stock were badly
worn and relatively obsolete. This was clear to the viewer.

The traction companies, in other words, had been guilty of the greatest abuses in paying dividends instead of providing amortization funds to
meet the depreciation of these properties. Instead, as one traction system
was scrapped, the company kept its costs in the valuation account and
then floated a new bond issue to finance the costs of the new system, plus
the 15 per cent allowed for the improvements made after 1907. It was now
proposed to carry over all these past costs into the new value structure
instead of confining the valuation to property currently used and usable.

In the list of physical properties, we actually found horses itemized
that had departed this life many decades before, together with tracks and
cars that had long since disappeared. As Yerkes once said, "The car riders
pay the fares, but the straphangers pay the dividends."

It became clear that after allowing for depreciation the combined lines were not worth more than $125 million or $130 million, and that Insull's claims for a valuation of $264 million contained perhaps $135 million of water. It also was apparent that the so-called indeterminate franchise would, in reality, be a perpetual franchise, because the city would be unable to carry out its nominal right to purchase at the stated and excessive valuation. Long-term franchises had a malodorous history in Chicago, from post-Civil War days, when a corrupt City Council had granted a ninety-nine-year franchise to a horsecar company, to the 1890's, when Yerkes tried to jam through his fifty-year franchise for the remaining lines. This effort had first been stopped by a veto of Governor John P. Altgeld, who turned down a $500,000 bribe in so doing, and later by the opposition of an outraged citizenry led by Mayor Carter H. Harrison and John Maynard Harlan, son of the indomitable Supreme Court Justice John Marshall Harlan and father of the second Justice Harlan.

My group decided to fight the Insull proposals, and we formed the People's Traction League, headed by Harold L. Ickes, Charles E. Merriam, and William H. Holly (later a federal judge), all veterans of previous traction battles. I was given the role of economic expert, chief witness, and spokesman for the group. All that spring and summer, in the midst of other troubles, I was kept busy testifying before the state legislature and the City Council, speaking before civic groups, and preparing statements.

It was a baptism of fire. Insull, himself in some financial trouble, turned on his full power and besieged us both economically and socially. The independent professional and business men who had rallied in the '90's to defeat Yerkes had largely vanished and had been replaced by the new breed of organization men, who were either direct retainers of Insull or were afraid to risk their jobs. The Insull forces put heavy pressure on the university either to fire or to muzzle me. I was distinctly conscious of being followed. To the credit of the university authorities, no one interfered with me, and the new president, Robert M. Hutchins, was particularly firm in his stand for academic freedom.

Furthermore, we attracted some unexpected allies. One of these was William Randolph Hearst, who then owned two newspapers in Chicago, the morning *Herald and Examiner* and the afternoon *American*. In his early days, Hearst had been an economic radical, having fought the utilities in New York and in other cities. He had advocated municipal ownership of the traction lines in Chicago and had supported the reform mayor, Ed Dunne. However, his enthusiasm for popular causes had greatly abated. Vanity, always a strong trait, had largely pushed his earlier interests aside, and he was getting his satisfaction by building his fabulous estate at San Simeon, on the California coast. But as we began to oppose Insull, Hearst smelled battle, and the old, submerged feelings stirred within him. Jumping into the fight, he put his papers at our disposal and began running fiery editorials, for which I helped to provide the ammunition and sometimes wrote the whole piece.

Another unexpected and temporary ally in our traction fight was Fred Lundin, the former Republican boss of Chicago, and for some years of all Illinois. He had made Big Bill Thompson mayor in 1915, and had got him re-elected in 1919. He then proceeded, in 1920, to nominate Len Small for governor and get him elected. Both of these men had made disgraceful records, and Lundin was assumed to have shared in some of their worst actions.

But there was another side to him. In his youth, he had been a patent-medicine vendor, selling Indian remedies from the back of a wagon at night by the light of a kerosene torch. There remained a touch of his former profession in his dress and conduct. With tinted glasses, dark clothes, and a flowing white silk tie gleaming over a ruffled shirt, he made a striking, if slightly sinister, picture. From his rough-and-tumble beginnings, he had developed sympathy for underdogs, combined with contempt for their intelligence. He had served a term in Congress around 1908 and was proud to have introduced the first bill for federal old-age pensions. From time to time, therefore, he would persuade Mayor Thompson and Governor Small to take some liberal action. Thus, in 1917, he had insisted that Thompson permit the People's Councils to meet in Chicago to protest against the war. Their meetings had been broken up by Governor Frank O. Lowden's threat to send in troops.

But Lundin had broken with Thompson, because, he alleged, the latter had fallen under the influence of Insull. It was because of this, I believe, and the fact that his mortal enemy, the *Tribune*, was attacking me that he turned my way. We had several long conversations, and I was fascinated by him—half attracted, half repelled. He was certainly an unfamiliar type. From Lincoln Steffens and from my own observations I had assumed that corruptionists were economic conservatives. Here, however, was a probable corruptionist who was economically far more radical than I. He was, in fact, a blown-in-the-bottle Populist in his political and some of his economic views. The type was later to become familiar in Mexico and the Philippines.

When Ickes and I first went to see Lundin, at his invitation, he asked us to outline our plans for a public campaign. I suggested a program of mass meetings in various parts of the city at which we would present the true facts of valuation compared with Insull's claims and the meaning of this in terms of excessive fares and profits. We would also expose the evils of the indeterminate or perpetual franchise. Lundin listened carefully and then retorted, "Douglas, you are making too rational an argument. Don't you know that the Army intelligence tests in the World War showed that the average adult has the intelligence of only a fourteen-year-old? You can't appeal to him successfully by reason. You can only appeal through hate. Make them hate Insull. Make them hate the Mayor. That's the way to beat them." With all my Quaker faith, I protested, arguing that while these tactics might be temporarily successful, hatred once aroused would have side effects that would be disastrous. To use proper means was just as important as to work for correct ends, since in life the means used would ultimately dominate us and become our ends. Lundin, listening intently, smiled sympathetically but was not convinced. However, he offered to see us again, at his summer place at Fox Lake.

Ickes and I drove out there one Sunday afternoon and spent several hours with him. He was wary of a definite commitment, but talked frankly about his political experiences. He had served in Congress with Lowden and thought him far too conservative. He was proud that he had helped prevent Lowden from being nominated for President by swinging the Chicago delegates against him at the 1920 Republican convention. The fact that this had also led to the nomination of Warren G. Harding did not disturb him.

There were few politicians, either Republicans or Democrats, who escaped his scathing judgment. I reminded him that he had been telling us only about bad politicians and asked who was the best man he had ever known in politics. Without an instant's hesitation he replied, "George Norris, of course. You can't buy him, you can't bully him, you can't frighten him." He stopped for a minute, and I thought I saw tears in his eyes. "Douglas," he went on, "I would give anything to be just half as good a man as George Norris." Such a tribute from so hard-boiled a politician was eloquent testimony to Norris' real worth. It also convinced me that politicians often have inner standards that are high indeed. Basically, they respect nothing more than honesty.

From this time on I was a marked man. The financial interests on La Salle Street considered me dangerous because I had dared to stand up to Insull and to them. Some of these tycoons were trying to have me dropped by the university. While I did not develop a persecution complex, I was uncomfortably aware of what was going on. Through it all, Hutchins behaved like a thoroughbred and, whenever possible, publicly supported me. Although I made enemies among the powerful, the fight also brought me many friends among the men and women who rode the streetcars and who resented Insull's arbitrary use of power.

We were beaten in the legislature by four to one, after which Insull's franchise passed the City Council with only one dissenting vote. Finally, with newspaper support plus liberal financing of the precinct workers of both parties, the voters gave their approval in a referendum. John M. Lee, an honorable state senator from the Southwest Side who had stood

firmly with us, was punished by the Democratic organization by being
dropped from his position as deputy bailiff. Others also paid a heavy
price.

But fate began to catch up with Insull when the Depression burst
upon us. Travel on the traction lines fell off sharply. The Eastern bondholders, who had been relegated to a junior position in the reorganization, started suit. The lines were then thrown by a federal court into a
friendly receivership. The years dragged on with the lines continuously in
limbo, until the city eventually bought the properties for a net cost of $83
million. This was too high. The mills of the gods had indeed ground
slowly, but they had ground inexorably. The fight we had made helped to
squeeze out most of the water contained in Insull's original claims.

While the traction ordinance was being held up by the bondholders'
suit, our little group moved to probe both the rate structure and the
financial practices of the other Insull utility companies. We found that
while great operating economies had been made during the '20's in generating and transmitting electrical power, the Illinois Commerce Commission had not passed any appreciable share of these gains on to the
consumers in the form of rate reductions. Instead, the profits of Insull's
operating companies had soared. Elsewhere, his empire was crumbling. He
had erected a confusing pyramid of holding companies on top of his scattered operating companies, which permitted a comparatively small stock
ownership at the top to exercise multiplied control down through the
corporate pyramid. It also resulted, however, in a cumulative contraction
in earnings as they were distributed upward through the corporate structures. Moreover, Cyrus Eaton, the Cleveland industrialist who had tried
presumably to take control of Commonwealth Edison away from Insull in
the summer of 1929, had succeeded in unloading huge blocks of stock
upon him at exaggerated prices. Insull had badly overstrained himself
to meet the purchase price.

We believed that the Chicago operating companies were being milked
to support the increasingly shaky structure of the Insull empire. Obtaining the services of two able young attorneys, Joseph C. Swidler, who became chairman of the Federal Power Commission under President Kennedy and is now chairman of the New York commission under Nelson
Rockefeller, and Harry A. Booth, both former associates of David E. Lilienthal, we formed the Illinois Utility Consumers and Investors League,
and published a report that laid bare much of what had happened.
Joined by a handful of progressive downstate politicians of both parties,
we called upon the Commerce Commission to reduce rates in keeping
with the reduction in costs and to probe some of Insull's financial practices. This skirmish turned into an open battle when the commission, in
1932, without adequate notice or hearing, hastily approved a $40-million
bond issue that was not devoted to capital construction but merely to

intercorporate transfers from the operating to the holding companies. This pumped money into the weak Insull companies at the expense of diluting the equities of stockholders in Commonwealth Edison, and by increasing the fixed debt made rate reductions more difficult.

Swinging into action, we demanded that the Commerce Commission recall its hasty decision and hold hearings on the projected bond issue. Anticipating trouble at such a hearing, I asked Ickes and Holly to join us. It was a stormy session. The commission refused to go into the merits of our complaints, but, instead, tried to deflect the purpose of the hearing by asking irrelevant questions in latter-day Joe McCarthy style. The chairman insisted on calling Swidler "Swindler." After demanding to know if I was a Quaker, one member asked whether I had gone to Russia in 1927 and whether I had subsequently advocated the recognition of that country. I regarded these questions as immaterial and irrelevant to the issue at stake, namely, whether the $40-million bond issue was in the interests of the stockholders and the public. On the advice of Ickes and Holly, I therefore abstained from replying to the questions and insisted that the commission go into the merits of the complaint. The room was soon in an uproar, with the commissioners shouting at me and with Ickes declaring that the whole procedure was biased and unfair.

While these hearings were in process, Insull, in his lofty office high in the Opera House, was resigning from all his companies. That very night, he fled to Paris. I do not claim to be the cause of his downfall and flight, but it is possible that our action had something to do with his final collapse. A run on the banks started. Certainly the city had never seen a more dramatic reversal of roles than in the conclusion of the three-year struggle between the most powerful man in the Midwest and an impecunious college professor. But if I expected any public vindication, I was sadly disappointed. The financial community of the city, shaken but not broken by the turn of events, redoubled their hostility toward me for "rocking the boat." I was accused of shaking the confidence of the people in the utility companies and in the so-called "regulatory" process. The *Tribune,* of course, led the attack.

In the fall, further explosions occurred inside the Insull groupings. To avoid extradition on indictments charging him with malfeasance, Insull fled from Paris to Greece. Sometime later he left Greece and was picked up in a boat in the Aegean Sea grotesquely disguised as a woman. When he was ultimately tried, the prosecution was incompetent, perhaps intentionally so, and he escaped conviction. But he was broken, and died shortly afterward.

In the meantime, we had been able to publicize proof in the Hearst papers that leading politicians, in both parties, as well as business and financial magnates had been allowed to buy Insull stocks prior to issuance at greatly reduced prices. It was also shown that by giving away used equipment to a prominent Democratic politician, who was also a junk dealer, Insull had won the support of many elements in the Democratic party. It was then clear why we had been defeated in the traction fight and why we had been manhandled in the rate and security struggles.

Despite the opposition of the private utilities and La Salle Street, deep forces were moving underneath the surface. The landslide of 1932 not only elected Franklin D. Roosevelt as President, but also carried Henry Horner into the Illinois governor's chair. Horner was an honest and high-minded Chicago judge, who lived in the university neighborhood and with whom I had many friends in common. One evening in the spring of 1933 the telephone rang; it was Governor Horner, asking if I was still interested in the utilities question. When I assured him that I was, he replied, "Then I want you to draft a model utility bill and bring it down to me next Monday. I know you will do a good job and I think we can pass it." With the aid of my colleagues Booth and Swidler, a bill was drafted over the weekend, modeled on the New York law. On Monday I took it to the Governor.

For Illinois we made two chief improvements. First, we provided that the Commerce Commission could start rate actions and that it did not have to throw the full burden of preparing its case upon weak groups of consumers and localities. Hitherto, the commission had taken the position that its functions were purely judicial, and, while it would hear cases started by others, it would not initiate them. Firsthand experience had shown how uneven the struggle was under these conditions. For example, our Consumers and Investors League had been able to raise only $800 to carry on its battle, and out of a none-too-ample salary I had given half. Swidler was several times threatened with eviction by his landlord, and I had to bail him out so that he could continue his work. Meanwhile, Insull and the utilities had unlimited funds with which to fight our suits and, ironically, could charge their costs to the consumers as operating expense.

In order to redress these unfair odds, our draft bill would make it possible for the commission to take the initiative and set up a unit to represent the consumers, while the commission itself would then act in a judicial capacity. If the commission got out of line, its decisions were, of course, always subject to review by the courts.

Our second major change was to make it more possible for the commission to use "original cost," or "prudent investment," as a basis for valuing utility properties. This use had been upheld by the U.S. Supreme Court in the fall of 1929.

On that Monday I entered Horner's office with a certain degree of nervousness. He put me immediately at ease and told me why he had called on me. He said, "Last week I opened the World's Fair in Chicago, and I saw tens of thousands who, after suffering so severely during the

Depression and having been betrayed by those in high places, were never-theless law-abiding." He determined that he must do something for them and that probably the best thing he could do would be to help clean up the utility mess.

After my bill was introduced in the legislature, I was asked to testify before the Utilities Committee of the state Senate. The utility people were caught off balance, and despite a bitter attack on me by Senator Richard ("Slippery Dick") Barr, of Joliet, Horner, with the aid of the Hearst papers, pushed the bill through without amendment.

Although Booth was made an attorney for the new commission, that body was slow to act and was only galvanized by occasional threats from the Governor that if they did not move, he would appoint me chairman. I learned at this time how wide the gap was between legislation and en-forcement, and how insidious the influences that fasten themselves upon even a reform administration.

Meanwhile, when Hearst offered me an editorial position, we con-cluded an agreement whereby I was to write three signed columns a week on local issues, which Hearst and his editors could accept or reject, but which they could not alter. I was thus able to use the Hearst papers for the campaign to regulate the utilities and for local and state reforms. In the process I had the chance to watch the anarchism that underlay the top-side despotism of the Hearst chain. At one time there were three publish-ers—past, present, and future—on the payroll and two managing editors, one of whom was that extraordinary character Victor Watson. Watson had been the confidant of Hearst on the New York *American* and the *Journal* and had been responsible for the ultimate unmasking and con-viction of William J. Fallon, the "Great Mouthpiece" for Arnold Roth-stein and the New York criminal syndicate. For some peccadilloes, real or fancied, Hearst had sent Watson to Chicago to take over the *Examiner,* and Victor was determined to carry on in the slam-bang style of former years, as immortalized by Hecht and MacArthur in *The Front Page.* We had a lively time together going after the local tie-ups among crime, poli-tics, and business. This brought me many advisers and confidants, of whom one, Alexander Jamie, the real head of the Secret Six, was by far the most instructive. Jamie had informants on the inside of both the criminal "syn-dicate" and the political "system." Since he trusted me, he poured out his evidence to share a heavy psychic burden and perhaps also to provide, through Watson and me, a continuation of his efforts should he be killed. My ears still burn and my stomach turns over at what I was told by him, much of which was later confirmed.

We published authentic evidence that made many highly placed Chi-cagoans squirm. But while most of the material we gathered would not have held up in court without further corroboration, it did justify us in making general charges with little danger of libel suits. For a year we led exciting lives. But Hearst was rapidly tiring of reform; San Simeon was again engrossing his attention. The big advertisers were putting pressure on him to stop crusading, and so, by the time we parted company, my editorials had been frequently killed.

As Hearst turned against Roosevelt and the New Deal, he determined to go after college professors and he singled out the University of Chicago as his first victim. Watson got Charles Walgreen, of the drug-store chain, to sponsor charges against several professors for unorthodox views expressed in classes his niece attended. With this material, the Hearst papers staged a full-fledged witch hunt, which led to a legislative investigation of the university. I was scheduled to be pilloried, I was told, but the Hearst papers objected and their attorneys could not find enough evidence. The affair wound up paradoxically, with Walgreen giving the university a half-million dollars to make amends. Nevertheless, the university received a black eye in the process, and the hostility of the business community hardened. Throughout the uproar, the Rockefeller family behaved magnificently—increasing their contributions by millions of dollars and throwing their influence on the side of academic freedom.

My Illinois struggles had by now attracted a good deal of national attention. In the fall of 1933 I was appointed by the Roosevelt administration a member of the Consumers' Advisory Board of the National Recovery Administration. As we checked through the proposed "codes of fair competition," it became clear that in the vast majority of cases they were price-fixing and output-restricting in their nature. This meant that consumers would have to pay more and that the codes would check revival and re-employment. How could we increase the total national output by decreasing each and every portion of it?

The board began to oppose these features in the various codes, but our recommendations were always turned down. Businessmen were powerful, and the labor representatives were so absorbed in getting wage increases and some recognition of collective bargaining that they had no surplus energies for trying to protect consumers. We were disregarded because we had no organized constituency behind us and represented only the diffused interests of uninformed and otherwise occupied consumers. Like Mahomet's coffin, we were suspended in the air with no visible means of support.

To help remedy this situation, the board's chairman, Mary Harriman Rumsey, the public-spirited daughter of the railway magnate E. H. Harriman and sister of W. Averell Harriman, asked me to set up a chain of local consumers' councils over the country. I organized nearly a hundred of these bodies, but most went out of existence when the NRA was declared unconstitutional in 1935. However, the councils did help in some measure to arouse public interest in consumer problems and to bring about some legal improvements. Our requests for informative labeling of textiles and furs, so that shoddy goods could not be passed off as wool, synthetics as silk, and skunk as "Manchurian wolf," were immediately rejected, but they were put into effect twenty years later, when I was in the Senate. We are slowly replacing the old maxim of *"caveat emptor,"* or "let the buyer beware," with the better principle of "the consumer is entitled to the truth." Since sunlight is a great disinfectant, this trend is reducing the temptation for men to indulge in sharp practices. In this crusade, women's groups have been strong allies. And perhaps the Consumers' Advisory Board, despite its apparent impotence, sowed some of the seeds that are now beginning to bear fruit.

I had also become interested in consumer credit, which my friend Dr. William T. Foster, the former president of Reed, was probing. He had pointed out that interest was figured on amounts originally borrowed and not on amounts actually owed, and that it was commonly reckoned in monthly and not, as elsewhere, in yearly terms. The so-called "model" bill permitted up to 3½ per cent a month. Thus, the actual rate of 42 per cent a year was being covered up, and borrowers were also being charged interest in many cases on amounts they had already repaid. With an even retirement rate, this meant that the actual rate was approximately double the stated rate. I was appointed under the NRA as a member of the code authority for the consumer-finance industry. I can well remember our first meeting in 1934, when I timidly suggested that the interest should be computed only on the amounts actually owed and not on the amounts repaid, and that it should be expressed in yearly, rather than monthly, terms. Never did the temperature of a meeting drop more rapidly. We quickly adjourned, and a few days later I received a letter suggesting that I resign from the code authority. I was disillusioned with the NRA, which I felt was injuring consumers instead of promoting economic recovery.

It is with some shame that I confess that this was one time when I backed away from a fight. However, the experience remained vivid in my mind and led me, as a senator, a quarter of a century later, to introduce the truth-in-lending bill, based on the principle that borrowers and debtors are entitled to the truth about what are the real charges and rates they are being asked to pay.

7

The Struggle for Social Security
and Labor Legislation

IN 1923 I had a curious experience which illustrated John
Dewey's theory of how thought happens within us. I was due to begin
discussing in my class on labor problems the standard of the minimum
wage, which reformers and unionists had more or less agreed was the
amount necessary to maintain a family of five. After allowing for deaths
and sterile marriages, that number, it was felt, would be needed to provide a stationary population. I had accepted this standard, but as I entered Cobb Hall and started to climb to the second floor, doubts began to
assail and overwhelm me. To pay everyone this agreed-on sum was more
than the national income could then bear. Economic reality could not
stand what the idealists were demanding. Halfway up the first flight of
stairs, another objection swept in upon me. The standard family of five
was not the prevalent norm. Only about 10 per cent of U.S. families were
of that size. While another 10 per cent might have more than a husband,
wife, and three children, there was another 80 per cent who had fewer.
Single men certainly did not have families of five to support, nor did
childless couples and those with only one or two children. It was indeed
the necessity of paying for nonexistent wives and children that would
make the plan insupportable. The family of five was a phase through
which the average family passed, but it represented only a fraction of a
man's working life.

When I reached the second floor I was in profound despair. As I began
to go to the third floor, a thought came. Why not fix the basic minimum
needed at enough to support man and wife, and then make additional
payments for children? Then we would be supporting actual, and not

fictitious, dependents. A hasty calculation assured me that industry could pay these added allowances and have enough left over to meet all other charges. But this reassurance lasted for only a second. As I reached the third floor, an irrefutable objection took possession of me. If men of apparently equal abilities were to be paid different wages, then those with the greatest number of dependents would be the first to be unemployed. From not being paid enough to support their actual dependents, they would be transformed into a more or less permanent army of the unemployed, and it would not be the employers who would be responsible for the misery of these unemployed, but the reformers who had wished them well and done them ill. I could see no way out as I started up the final flight of stairs leading to my classroom on the fourth floor. I had to confess that under present conditions of productivity, the payment of the standard minimum was impossible and unwise. As I took my final steps upward, however, a possible solution shot into my mind. The basic wage could still be paid by the individual employers, on the basis of the amount needed to support man and wife, but the separate children's allowance would be paid by an industrial pool of employers. These pools would collect the necessary amount from the employers according to the total payroll for the covered employees or on some basis other than the number of dependents. Families could be paid a living wage with no discriminations against those with dependents. The basic problem was solved, and as I entered the room and went to my desk, a flood of happiness swept over me. I lectured for several days on the successive steps I had taken, and in the process ironed out some of the incidental problems.

During this time I thought that I was the discoverer of a system that would solve some of the ethical dilemmas of life. But on browsing through the files of the *International Labour Review,* I found that children's allowances were being paid under a pooled system in most of the countries of Western Europe and that any claim for originality was belied by an article Eleanor Rathbone had written for the *Hibbert Journal* and by the activities of a group of English Quakers. I could never tell whether I had been subconsciously influenced by these latter articles or whether it was a case, so familiar in the natural sciences, of a multiple independent discovery of an invention.

My role was to be the humbler one, not of discoverer, but of expositor and historian. I made an agreement with the International Labor Organization whereby they would collect material for me, and, marshaling arguments and details, I prepared a book, *Wages and the Family,* which for many years was the only American book on the subject. The plan did not, however, catch on in this country. As I became absorbed in the problems of old age and unemployment, being pushed into the foreground by the Depression, I let my advocacy of family allowances slip into the past.

I woke up about 1950 to find that family allowances had spread to every other Western country as a mandatory state system, rather than a voluntary private practice. It was adopted by Canada, and was advocated by many social workers and publicists, including my old friend Richard Strout, of the *Christian Science Monitor*. It became evident that it would meet the problem of the working poor far better than any other proposal, but in President Richard Nixon's 1969 plan it was rejected in favor of a variant of Milton Friedman's negative income tax.

I still think that with the increase in national productivity it is the best monetary answer to the problems of poverty among the employed population. It could be combined with the various programs for the aged and the unemployed. Then it could face the problems of human nature, namely, the tendency of some to give the least amount of work in return for a living, and the tendency to overpopulate. The latter danger could be minimized by paying only half the standard children's allowance for the third or fourth child and discontinuing it for all beyond that number. At the same time, propaganda for birth control could be widely distributed and the facilities for adequate help made available. Perhaps by such methods the external barriers to human development might be brushed aside.

Labor legislation was one of the fields in which I had specialized both as a student at Columbia and as a teacher in Chicago. I studied and later taught in considerable detail the social-insurance systems of Germany and Great Britain and the workings of the minimum-wage laws in Australia, New Zealand, Great Britain, and the United States. I also wrote numerous articles and one book about them. During the '20's I was active in the American Association for Labor Legislation, whose moving spirits were two disciples of Commons, John and Irene Andrews, with my old teacher Henry Seager as a benevolent patron. But the Andrewses had been more or less shell-shocked by the defeat after World War I of their efforts in behalf of health insurance and by the political and economic reaction of the '20's. They confined themselves, therefore, to relatively innocuous proposals such as the improvement of state laws on workmen's compensation and the extension of this principle to longshoremen. It was fortunate for me that in the latter part of the decade I made the acquaintance of two remarkable men who deepened my interests and turned them into more practical channels.

I. M. Rubinow was an actuary and economist who had started life as a physician and had then gone on to a distinguished career as an expert for the old U.S. Bureau of Labor. His books and articles on social insurance were acknowledged classics, but I learned at least as much from our frequent conversations as from them.

Abraham Epstein, a disciple of Rubinow's, was one of the most successful and constructive men of my generation. This was so despite the fact that he was hot-tempered, not prepossessing, and had a statistical blind spot and an accent that could be cut only with a hatchet. He was also chivalrous, devoted to the unfortunate, tireless, charming, and a shrewd judge of public and political opinion. Throughout the 1920's he carried on a one-man crusade to establish state systems of old-age pensions, which we then thought of in terms of a guaranteed total income of $7.00 a week for those over seventy. This was modest enough, and I increasingly worked with the activist Epstein for labor legislation, rather than with the slower-moving American Association. The opposition was strong, however, and the inertia of the public great.

As in the utility fights, we slowly picked up allies. One of these was the Fraternal Order of Eagles. Their rival order, the Moose, had for some years devoted itself to philanthropic work with children and had established a huge model home for the orphans of their members at Mooseheart, about thirty miles west of Chicago, on the Fox River. Not to be outdone in good works, the Eagles took up the cause of the aged and became sturdy advocates of modest state pension systems. This gave our movement a grass-roots strength we had not possessed. Legislators might smile disdainfully when reformers and professors, such as Epstein and I, appeared before them, but they were impressed when the earth-bound Eagles backed us. The saltier the testimony of our allies, the more our political stock rose in the committee rooms. This experience impressed me with the possibilities for good of the fraternal orders and "service clubs." For this reason I never joined in the bitter ridicule of them, begun by Sinclair Lewis in *Babbitt* and continued by H. L. Mencken in his *American Mercury*.

Other developments slowly strengthened our case. One was the rising proportion of old people in the nation and their increasing difficulty in finding jobs. In addition, there was the growing urbanization of the country, the decrease in self-employment, the loosening of family ties caused by the greater mobility of the population, and the universal hatred of the poorhouse as the refuge for the aged. Gradually our arguments made sufficient impression to cause a few states to make a cautious start by authorizing a county-option system. This permitted the counties to act, but gave them no revenue with which to do so.

The Depression gave the movement its final impetus. Men who had painfully saved a nest egg for their old age and who thought themselves secure lost everything. With the decline in the price of stocks, they had to turn to public relief, which was humiliating, inadequate, and uncertain.

In November, 1928, Epstein, who had been in Ohio waging a campaign for old-age pensions in a popular referendum, telegraphed me to meet him the next morning when he came to Chicago on the Cleveland train. There was a torrent of rain, and as Abe climbed down from the train I could see that his spirits were as damp as the weather. "Paul," he moaned, "we have just taken a terrible beating in Ohio. I traveled all over the state for a solid month and never had more than twenty people to hear me; I couldn't get any space in the newspapers, and for once in my life I am discouraged. We are through, and my life is a failure. Don't tell me how badly we were beaten; just try to cheer me up."

My answer was to show him the morning paper, which reported that old-age pensions had carried in the Ohio referendum by three to one. Public opinion had shifted so quickly that people did not bother to hear talks on the subject. They were already convinced.

From that morning I knew that the final victory would be ours. That winter, the AFL reversed its historic opposition and threw its full support behind old-age pensions. This was crucial in Illinois, as elsewhere. I was no longer alone in my advocacy. I was asked not only to help draft the Illinois AFL reports on the subject, but also to write the minority state reports. Despite the shortage of funds created by the Depression, one by one states passed our legislation, and I was exultant in 1935 when Illinois finally adopted the pension bill that I had drafted.

Long before this, the movement for old-age pensions had merged and largely been absorbed in the need for general social insurance, or, as it was finally called, "social security." My own part in this broader field began in 1930. I was invited by Frank Aydelotte, the president of Swarthmore College, to make a six-month study of the causes and possible cures of unemployment under a grant given to the college by S. S. Fels, the philanthropic Philadelphia soap manufacturer. I accepted. The salary was ample, and I had stored up academic credit for such a leave. Not only was the subject vital, but also I welcomed the chance to become better acquainted with Philadelphia Quakerism.

Paramount was a personal need. Dorothy and I had come to the end of the road in our marriage and had agreed on a divorce. Chicago itself had been an early source of friction. Although we had made our home there for four years, Dorothy did not like the city, or the university, which barred employment of faculty wives. When I received an offer from Amherst, she begged me to take it, which I finally did in order to keep the family together. But my heart already belonged to Chicago and so, I believed, did my future. Dorothy, meanwhile, found an opening at Smith, which she wanted to accept. We therefore agreed on a separation, which continued for most of five years.

Equally important, we were two people with some common interests but with strong wills and dissimilar temperaments. Each saw one side of the problem, although today I accept by far most of the blame for our failure. Never having known much family life, I had allowed my career and public concerns to crowd out family responsibilities. In later years I paid a heavy price for the tenuousness of my relations with the children. Probably all of the family suffered similar heartaches. In any case, I welcomed the Swarthmore assignment, which permitted me to lick my wounds in private, while I worked on a new set of problems.

The six months at Swarthmore were crowded with activity. With Clair Wilcox I drafted an appeal to President Herbert Hoover urging him to veto the Smoot-Hawley tariff, which raised duties to their highest level. In this we pointed out how the increase in duties on imports decreased the ability of other countries to buy goods from us. Also, it would provoke them to retaliatory tariffs. No fewer than 1,028 economists signed the appeal, and I think poor Hoover wanted to take our advice. His party was so strongly committed to protection, however, that he felt compelled to sign the bill, with the result that all our predictions came true. The Depression deepened and the Western democracies fell apart. Our letter did make it somewhat easier for Congress later to pass Cordell Hull's reciprocal-trade bill, and thus helped to lead the way to a reversal of our trade policy.

With Aaron Director I finished a book, *The Problem of Unemployment,* which appeared during 1931, and also found myself caught up in the efforts to deal with the huge and rising numbers of the unemployed. At the invitation of Henry Bruére, of the Bowery Savings Bank, and Frances Perkins, I served as secretary of Governor Franklin Roosevelt's New York Committee to Stabilize Employment. I helped with the hearings, drafted their report, and am credited by Frances Perkins with having converted Roosevelt to unemployment insurance. Later in the summer, Gifford Pinchot, running for governor of Pennsylvania on the Republican ticket, also pressed me into service as his adviser on unemployment. We co-operated on a program for the Pennsylvania legislature. Working simultaneously with the Democrats in New York and the reform Republicans in Pennsylvania, I had the chance to compare the two groups as well as the Governors, whom I found strikingly alike.

Both Roosevelt and Pinchot were Hudson Valley aristocrats with inherited wealth. They had broad estates on opposite sides of the river and were somewhat aloof from the pressures of the powerful industrial and financial interests of New York and Philadelphia. Both regarded the Wall Street millionaires as parvenus who had not proved their right to eminence. Both wanted to help people, but each was wary, realizing he could not move too far ahead of the procession. Each was willing to accept dubious allies to gain his ends. Joseph R. Grundy, the head of the Pennsylvania Manufacturers Association, had allied himself with Pinchot for reasons of his own and, though a coreligionist of mine, was insistent that Pinchot fire me. Roosevelt was still allied with Tammany and was fearful of breaking with them lest he thereby lose the New York delegation at the 1932 Democratic convention. It was clear to me from the outset that he had his eyes on the Presidential nomination, and after his triumphant and overwhelming re-election in the fall of 1930 this became a certainty.

I liked both men and enjoyed working with them. And my long-running fight with Insull made both of them my friends. Pinchot, in his sixties, was still an outdoorsman and a forester. He loved to tell me of his partnership with Teddy Roosevelt, how they had fought to conserve our natural resources and of their battles with Secretary of the Interior Richard A. Ballinger and President William Howard Taft. Teddy was his idol, and working with him had been the great experience in Pinchot's life. Mrs. Pinchot, a striking redhead and a gianthearted woman, became my fast friend and remained so until her death nearly thirty years later.

Teddy's distant cousin Franklin could no longer be physically active, like Pinchot, because of his polio attack. But his mind was vigorous, and he was always interested in new ideas. Both men opposed the power trusts and were proponents of public power. Roosevelt wanted to use the energies of Niagara to generate public power, while Pinchot, stimulated by my close friend Morris L. Cooke, wanted to distribute low-rate power to the farmers in the countryside. I believed that the programs should be combined. The state or the nation could generate and transport the power, while voluntary co-operatives could distribute it.

I was also pressed at this time into other activities such as testifying before Congressional committees (where Fiorello La Guardia protected me from the wolves) on a federal system of employment offices and trying to stabilize the women's clothing industry of Cleveland. It was a crowded and exciting year, which helped to assuage the unhappiness of my marital failure.

During the early summer of 1930, a sharp cleavage developed among those who believed in social insurance to meet some of the costs of unemployment.

John R. Commons, the fertile Wisconsin economist, had developed the theory some years earlier that unemployment should be treated like industrial accidents. "Lodge the cost of unemployment," he said, "upon the immediate employer and he will strive to reduce or abolish unemployment, just as making him pay under workmen's compensation for those injured in his plant has made him anxious to prevent industrial accidents." It was an attractive theory and found many adherents. It threw responsibility upon the employer, rather than upon the government, thus avoiding the label of "dole" and enabling the proposal to be called the "American plan." "Dole" was an unpopular term because of the high volume of unemployment that had continued in England through the 1920's and was blamed on the system, rather than on the decline in British exports. Commons' students, scattered over the country, had a deep affection for their inspiring teacher, which made them ardent propagandists for his theories. Mr. and Mrs. Andrews and others were active in the East. Elizabeth Brandeis Raushenbush, the daughter of the famous Supreme Court Justice, was another effective advocate of the Wisconsin idea, as was her father.

Despite all this, the more I studied the Commons plan, the more I became convinced that it was basically wrong. The analogy between unemployment and industrial accidents was faulty. Industrial accidents occur inside the work place and to a large degree are under the control of the employer. But unemployment is primarily caused by factors outside the work place over which the employer has little control. Seasonal unemployment can sometimes be reduced by producing for stock and by developing side lines as "fillers" for the off-seasons. But cyclical unemployment is different. It is caused by decreases in total demand, in the face of which the individual employer is almost as helpless as a Kansas farmer in the path of a tornado. Nor can an employer do a great deal when hit by a deep shift in consumer demand. In short, Commons and his friends placed too much liability upon the individual employer for losses that arose out of the obscure and impersonal workings of economic society.

Furthermore, to place responsibility upon the employers in those plants where high unemployment occurred would heap the heaviest burdens during a depression upon those who suffered the most. The producers of capital goods, such as steel and machinery, were, through no fault of their own, hit the hardest when a depression came, and their burdens under the Commons plan would be further increased. If a top limit was placed on the amount for which any employer would be liable, as was urged, then the industries that suffered the most would have to either reduce or cut off benefits to their unemployed, while others, in less stringent circumstances, would continue to draw larger amounts.

I concluded that a state pooled fund was far superior to the system of separate employer reserves. This would provide uniform benefits and would not overburden the industries that, through no fault of their own, suffered most during depressions. In July of 1930, a conference was called, at the Yale Club in New York, in an effort to find agreement on a common program. We argued all evening and into the early hours of the morning. The adherents of Commons finally carried an endorsement of their plan by a vote of 21 to 2. As I walked down Fifth Avenue at three in the morning I realized that unless the advantages of the pooled fund were vigorously stated, we were likely to blunder into a fatally weak and inadequate system that would ultimately break down. I immediately took a train to Cleveland, where a group of citizens under the leadership of Elizabeth Magee, of the Consumers' League, was planning to introduce a bill in the Ohio legislature. We spent a stimulating day together, and at its conclusion the Ohio group decided unanimously to espouse the idea of a state pooled fund.

In my work with Roosevelt and Pinchot, I tried to keep this conflict in the background. But as the Ohio plan gained ground, I spoke and wrote in its behalf, and Rubinow and Epstein were invaluable allies. Finally, the AFL, which had previously opposed even the idea of unemployment compensation, not only endorsed the general proposal, but also came increasingly to support the idea of a pooled fund.

It is noteworthy that at first few thought there was any possibility for federal legislation. This was my position, too, in my book *Standards of Unemployment Insurance*. We felt that we must confine ourselves to state action despite the inevitable fear that a pioneer state would be placed at a competitive disadvantage if other states did not act. Slowly, I became convinced that the unit of regulation must be as broad as the market itself, and that since the market for most products was national, a state was an inadequate agency for dealing with the problems of child labor, wage and hour legislation, old-age and unemployment insurance. Federal action was needed. But the psychology of the Supreme Court at that time and of Congress itself seemed an insurmountable barrier. Politically, we were stymied.

Much as I liked Roosevelt, I felt I could not support him, because neither he nor the Democratic party showed any inclination to use national power to cope with the problems neglected during the '20's. Failure to deal with these problems had brought the country to the brink of disaster; 16 million people were unemployed.

For several years I tried, with Oswald Villard and others, to help form a third party. Despite our efforts, and those of others in Wisconsin, Minnesota, and North Dakota, this movement never got far nationally. In the middle of 1935, when it was clear that Roosevelt had changed his views and after the passage of the National Labor Relations Act and the Social Security Act, I gave my full allegiance to the Democratic party. Roosevelt's change of policy was perhaps partially affected by our movement, but an even more potent factor was probably Huey P. Long and his Share-Our-Wealth movement.

When Roosevelt took office after his sweeping victory in 1932, I rejoiced to find that he was ready to use national power to deal with such economic problems as the collapse of the banking system, the halving of the national income, the 14 to 16 million unemployed, and the farm crisis created by thirty-cent wheat, twelve-cent corn, and three-cent hogs. Roosevelt used his first year, 1933–34, in an effort to restore business and protect property. He reopened the banks and guaranteed deposits up to $5,000. He halted the foreclosures of farms and homes and set up the Federal Housing Administration insurance system to stimulate the building of new homes by the middle class. He devised an agricultural program to restrict production and raise farm income, and launched the ill-fated National Recovery Administration.

My work on the Consumers' Advisory Board of the NRA, as well as my training as an economist, gave me no enthusiasm for trying to restore prosperity by restricting production. Convinced that we should build up total demand, whether of consumption or investment, and not allow the weight of the Depression to fall upon those least able to bear it, I helped file dissents to all the codes. Many others came to the same conclusion, and Roosevelt sensed the change. In the spring and summer of 1934 he began to move cautiously toward national action to provide protection against indigent old age and unemployment. At the same time, we started to draft legislation to make effective the legal right of workmen to join and be active in unions by protecting them from arbitrary discharge and discrimination. In the late winter of 1934 I was asked to be the lead-off witness for the government in hearings on the precursor of the Wagner Act of the following year. This set up the National Labor Relations Board. I was active, too, in testifying before Congress in behalf of a federal-state system of old-age pensions and in helping to popularize the idea of unemployment insurance.

The men whom Secretary of Labor Frances Perkins called in to help her with social security were ardent supporters of the Wisconsin Plan, led by Edwin Witte and Arthur J. Altmeyer. In turn, their staff was largely recruited from the followers of Commons. Since they had determined to promote the system of separate employer reserves, they wanted the services of those who agreed with that policy. It became apparent that my presence was not desired, and I was, therefore, free once more to return to my classes in Chicago.

As the administration's proposals for what they termed "unemployment compensation" took form, further errors appeared. Tax-offset inducements modeled on the federal inheritance tax were launched to stimulate state action. But no minimum standards of benefits were set up, and the states were given almost complete freedom to write their own tickets. Some of us vainly argued for a national system, or, at least, minimum national standards of benefits for both insurance and relief that would apply across the country, with a national reinsurance fund. The latter would guarantee insurance benefits in those states which, because of their types of industry, suffered most during a depression. Since these ideas were rejected by the administration's advisers, my participation in these matters also ended.

The weaknesses I had foreseen have since developed. Part of my efforts in the Senate later helped to cover those who had been deprived of protection during recessions under the inadequate state laws. States and employers now have a vested interest, so that it is almost impossible to put the insurance system on any sounder basis. It has been no consolation to hear that some of my early opponents, including Altmeyer, long ago admitted that they were wrong. The whole experience bears out the truth of the saying that the good is often the worst enemy of the best. I would add that imaginative, high-minded innovators such as Commons sometimes become so enamored with their own ideas that, deaf to reasoned criticism, they force through measures that ultimately prove grossly unworkable.

For my part, the rejection of my views on social security and my severance from the NRA turned into an advantage. It sent me back to Chicago and enabled me to concentrate once again on my researches and studies. In the course of the next years I finally brought out my *Theory of Wages*, and then, successively, *Controlling Depressions* and *Social Security in the United States*. Most important, from the standpoint of my future career, it encouraged me to take a renewed interest in the problems and politics of my city and state. It was a relief to have the freedom of a citizen and not experience the constraints of a consultant.

Meantime, in 1931 I had the good fortune to marry Emily Taft, the daughter of the sculptor Lorado Taft. After graduating from the University of Chicago, Emily had spent some time on the stage, in stock companies and on Broadway. But divided concerns led to work with the Illinois League of Women Voters. Our political views were congenial, and her love of the arts has greatly enriched my life. For forty years we have shared a happy and eventful life. Much more tactful than I, with a firm integrity and a gracious attitude toward people, she has been a perfect companion, counselor, and wife.

Out of the royalties from my books, we built a cottage in the Indiana Dunes, forty miles from Chicago. Here we spent our summers on Lake Michigan, watched our daughter, Jean, grow up, and enjoyed one of the happiest periods of our lives. Like Antaeus, I retouched the earth and became the stronger thereby. We had rare privacy, with mornings of quiet study and work, afternoons of swimming and walks along the magnificent beach and in the fascinating back country. The Dunes, built up over the course of 20,000 years, were a paradise for botanists, geologists, and nature lovers. Their blowouts were grim reminders of the desert. Before us was the lake and behind us marshes and more hills. All about us were flowers: the blue spring lupine, the yellow puccoon and fireweed, wild roses, columbine, and the prickly cactus blooming gloriously for one day every year. We were on the flyway for the north-south migration of birds, and many varieties would stop on their spring and fall flights. In 1920 the twenty-five miles from Gary to Michigan City had all been like this in its wild splendor. At that time it could have been purchased for around $15 million. Later, real-estate developments absorbed all but eight miles of the lake front, of which three were in a little Indiana state park. The rest was wild and owned by scattered interests.

What remained was idyllic and an ever-present source of physical and spiritual renewal. I seemed to live again in the simplicities of my boyhood. But hanging over our heads was the danger of further industrialization. We knew that the National Steel Company had bought a big tract there, and there were rumors that other companies were planning similar moves. Steel had already taken over and disfigured the waterfront from Chicago to Gary. I felt we were in the grip of an almost irreversible force, which would overrun those who loved the Dunes and sweep on to Michigan City and beyond. Then we would have a continuous jungle of asphalt and steel, with pollution of air and water, with no place for the millions of pent-up city folk to seek refuge, quiet, and renewal. It seemed impossible to stop this movement, but one moonlit evening I made a secret pledge that if I could help to do so I would. Twenty years later the way opened, and I followed it. The memories of my boyhood and of the idyllic years that the three of us had spent together in the Dunes were deeply rooted in me.

During the academic year, in addition to my research and public activities, I tried to develop close ties with my students. I set aside three hours a week for individual consultations, and we invited every student to our home at least once a quarter. In our hurried lives this was sometimes not easy, but we thought it important at a large, impersonal university.

I was fortunate in one of my classes to have three youngsters who promised to be among the country's best economists; they were Paul Samuelson, Gregg Lewis, and Jacob Mosak. Samuelson has, I think, become the ablest modern economist in the world. He has won a Nobel Prize, and his textbook, *Economics,* is mounting toward the 2-million mark in sales. The former needy student has become a millionaire. From talks with these three I think I learned more than they did, and my adherence to Alfred Marshall was further modified.

Every fall I went east to spend the brief week allotted to me with my children. Helen was growing up a handsome, able girl, who entered Vassar and was elected president of her class. John had a flair for both sports and scholarship, while ardent little Dorothea loved dancing and drawing. Young Paul early showed unusual aplomb and ability.

8

The Oncoming Storm

BY THE FALL OF 1935, I had finished my book on social security and was free to fulfill a cherished plan with Emily. Both of us had visited Europe several times, but only on my last trip had I discovered the world of the Renaissance. We decided to browse through Italy, visiting out-of-the-way towns and becoming better acquainted with our favorite artists. Having passed nearly four decades oblivious to painting and sculpture, now, under my wife's tutelage, I had fallen in love with both. So with much zeal and more delight than I had known in tracking down economic theories, I prepared to concentrate on art.

We renewed our acquaintance with the Sistine Chapel, the Uffizi, Assisi, Perugia, the Accademia and the churches in Venice. We broke new ground by studying the Sienese school and seeking out the austere paintings of Piero della Francesca. Evenings we read Burckhardt, Vasari, Berenson, and Symonds.

But as we came to Rome, the Abyssinian crisis was boiling. One sunny noon in October, the church bells summoned all citizens to an *adunata,* or assembly, in the square fronting the Palazzo Venezia. Here were Benito Mussolini's offices, overlooking the hideous Victor Emmanuel Monument. Hurrying there from our pension near the Castel Sant' Angelo, we joined the huge crowd that was swelling with every minute. Soon a regiment of black-shirted Fascists marched down the Via dei Fori Imperiali from the Colosseum and, goose-stepping, swung into the square. In an almost mesmerized fashion the crowd was chanting, "Duce, Duce, Duce." Mussolini then appeared on the little balcony overlooking the square. Thrusting forward his massive chin, he began his speech. "Italy's patience is exhausted. *Basta,*" he shouted. "Enough." Ethiopia's crowning provocation had been to withdraw its troops several kilometers *inside* its own frontiers. To avenge this "aggression," Mussolini had ordered his troops to invade Ethiopia. His armies, he disclosed, had already crossed the border and were proceeding triumphantly.

If anyone noticed the extraordinary contradictions in this statement, we did not detect it. Of course, the people were afraid of the secret police, but it is also true that there was a certain lightheartedness in the general bearing of the million who had gathered to hear the announcement.

When we journeyed north a few days later, we found that Fascist youth in Arezzo made sleep impossible by their constant singing of *"Giovinezza."* Black-shirted lads of eight to ten years drilled stoutly with wooden guns behind our pension in Siena. But it became evident that underneath the surface the war was unpopular with most Italians. Pension managers confided that it was a terrible mistake. Men wearing the lapel button of the Fascist party said that Mussolini was ruining the country and that he would squander lives and treasure in conquering Ethiopia, which was not worth the cost. Many spoke of a popular revolt should he lose, and others looked hopefully to the League of Nations. They asked if it might impose economic sanctions sufficient to deliver them from Mussolini.

So we hoped, but as we read the newspapers from London, Paris, and Geneva, we became skeptical. We noted that there was no embargo on oil and that the Suez Canal, under British control, was not closed either to Mussolini's troops or to his supplies. This was the acid test, for that passage was vital to Mussolini. If he could not use the canal, then he could not attack Ethiopia. But many of the leading journalists and politicians in France and Britain were openly pro-Fascist.

The final blow fell on a cold December day. In the mountain town of Urbino we were absorbed in the Renaissance with Raphael and Piero della Francesca, and we were prepared to retire further into the past at our next stop, Ravenna, with its Byzantine mosaics. The achievements as well as the struggles and problems of these earlier times had blurred our consciousness of contemporary events until we reached the railroad station at Pesaro and heard the newsboys proclaiming another crisis. Sir Samuel Hoare, the British Foreign Secretary, had just signed an agreement with the French Premier, Pierre Laval. The agreement, in effect, turned most of Ethiopia over to Italy. This was staggering news and a body blow both to the League of Nations and to the whole concept of collective security.

During the night, as our train raced north along the Adriatic, I became physically sick. I saw a preview of the future. The democracies would not resist aggression, fearing that it might set off a working-class revolt inside Italy. To prevent this, they would let Mussolini have his way. But matters would not end there. Because there was no will to resist aggression, Hitler would form an alliance with Mussolini and take the initiative himself. The movement would spread to Japan, where Army leaders were the natural allies of dictators. And within the democracies there were crypto-Fascists. "It can't happen here," we had thought, but when Sinclair Lewis wrote his novel by that name, he suggested that it might.

At midnight, in a chilling rain in Ravenna, we went to our unheated pension. Shivering in our beds, we discussed the probability that within five years we might be locked in a concentration camp. I thought we must make up our minds whether we would let the steam roller go over our country without protest or resist with all our strength. Without a moment's hesitation my wife said, "Of course, with all our strength." We then considered who among our friends would feel the same way. We were sure of only a half-dozen, and we have retained a lasting affection for those we named.

As the days wore on, the hypocrisy of the Hoare-Laval pact became more evident. Stanley Baldwin, the British Prime Minister, made absurd pretenses that he had known nothing about the pact and suggested that Sir Samuel had just stopped off to visit Laval in Paris on his way to a skating holiday in the Engadine. It was solemnly claimed that Sir Samuel had casually signed the agreement without telling anyone and, since he was then busy cutting figure eights in Switzerland, he should not be disturbed. The English Establishment and the press, except for the sturdy Manchester *Guardian,* agreed.

It was clear that the League of Nations as an instrument for collective security was dead. A few weeks later, when we journeyed from Milan to Geneva in a blinding snowstorm, our worst fears were confirmed. The disheartened supporters of the League now felt that it could not be revived. Moving on to Paris, we found that the pro-Fascist faction headed by Laval was so strong that a chain of subsidized journals was not only preaching the virtues of Mussolini, but also actually working for an accommodation with Hitler. This alliance brought about a rival union between Socialists, the conservative "Radical" Socialists, and the Communists. The shift in Communist tactics from bitter opposition to co-operation with the non-Communist parties of the left filled me with foreboding. I hoped that it might be confined to France and not become a world-wide policy.

In England we found Liberals and Labour dispirited by their second crushing defeat at the polls. Few wanted to face up to the danger of Fascist aggression, and for the first time I lost patience with my Quaker friends. They and other pacifists such as George Lansbury still argued that Christian love would melt the hearts of the Nazis; we should not try to check them by force.

Freedom itself was at stake and it, we decided, was more precious than peace. On the steamer back to New York, Emily and I decided that in our small way we must not only personally resist the spread of the police state but also try to strengthen the will of our country to do so. It was becoming a world struggle from which the United States could not be isolated. Whether or not we liked it, we would ultimately be involved. But did Americans recognize the purport of these events? I soon knew that most of them did not. In the future, wherever I spoke in Chicago and throughout the Midwest, I stressed the dangers of the situation and also the dangers of a united front with the Communists. At a labor rally in Springfield I even warned my friends about the newly formed American League Against War and Fascism, which under J. B. Matthews was one of the first Communist-directed fronts. Many audiences were incredulous and disagreed that there was any real danger for the United States.

Events abroad bore out my worst fears and predictions. In March, when Hitler sent his troops into the Rhineland in violation of the treaties of Versailles and Locarno, I stood on the rim of the Grand Canyon. That tremendous chasm, down to whose bottom I walked, seemed symbolic of the future. Today we know that Hitler had only two divisions ready. In case Britain and France resisted, his troops had orders to withdraw. The German generals would probably then have staged a revolution, which would have ousted Hitler and brought a less aggressive government to power. To its credit, France was ready to move. But Britain refused to give consent. Hitler had guessed right, just as Mussolini had about Ethiopia. The Hoare-Laval pact was no isolated occurrence. Basically, the British Conservative government did not want to check either the Nazis or the Fascists.

Hitler soon took the inevitable next step. He set his engineers to building a strong wall of trenches, pillboxes, and mine fields on the west bank of the Rhine, which was expressly forbidden under the Treaty of Locarno. His act was meant to immobilize France, so that he would have a free hand in Eastern Europe. If he attacked Czechoslovakia or Poland, the French could not effectively counterattack. A possible deterrent to Nazi aggression in this way was greatly blunted.

In the summer of 1936 came the Spanish revolution, or civil war. Using the appearance of anti-Communist slogans as an excuse, the Spanish Army rebelled against a republican government that did not include a single Communist in its cabinet and had only twenty Communists, out of nearly 400 members, in the Parliament. General Francisco Franco became the leader of invading Army forces, and was aided by Moorish mercenaries and by the big landlords, employers, and the feudal aristocracy. Hitler and Mussolini at once sent him munitions, airplanes, and pilots. They saw that if the revolution succeeded, France would be hemmed in from the south as well as from the east, and could not block Germany from taking over Austria, Czechoslovakia, and Poland.

It seemed clear to me that the Loyalist government, duly elected and democratic at the start, should be helped. I joined both the North American Committee to Aid Spanish Democracy and the Committee on Medical Aid to Spain, accepting the Chicago chairmanship of the latter body. We raised money for doctors, nurses, medical supplies, and blood plasma for the Loyalist troops. For this, I, along with many others, have been bitterly criticized. Yet the national committees of these bodies were headed by men and women of fine reputation, in no sense Communists. My friend W. W. Norton, the publisher, was treasurer of one, and the Bishop of eastern Oregon was chairman of another. Since no one in my local group was identified as a Communist, I took up the work with a clear conscience. However, disquieting developments came when volunteers showed up to run the mimeograph machine and I found that they were writing and circulating unauthorized copy. Once, I caught a huge issue of anti-Catholic literature, which was to be distributed in front of the Catholic churches the next Sunday. Only my threat to resign and denounce these tactics blocked the plan. I constantly urged that our funds be spent only on medical aid, whereas some of the workers cared only for propaganda. But, like others across the nation, I thought that I could restrain these questionable forces.

Meanwhile, unknown to us, events in Spain were taking a tragic turn. The democracies embargoed arms and supplies to the Loyalists, while Italy and Germany continued to help Franco. This compelled the Spanish government to take aid from Russia, for which they paid a heavy price. The moderate President Manuel Azaña was forced out of office, as was the prime minister, Democratic Socialist Francisco Largo Caballero. A new government took over which, we learned years later, handed the leadership to the Communists. The gold reserves were transferred to Russia; the Syndicalists and Catalonian nationalists of Barcelona were persecuted; and decent liberals and moderate socialists were ruthlessly purged from the Army and, in many cases, executed.

In 1938 the pace of disintegration in Europe quickened. After grabbing Austria in March, Hitler isolated Czechoslovakia. Since the Czechs were an important nationality group in Chicago, I began to speak at their meetings, in this way becoming better acquainted with their leaders. We struck up a deep and permanent friendship.

Once again that summer, Hitler showed his hand by threatening Czechoslovakia. From reading the London *Times* and the Manchester *Guardian*, I believed that the British government was preparing for another surrender. A mission headed by Walter Runciman sent by Prime Minister Neville Chamberlain to Czechoslovakia gave every evidence of being a put-up job. Hitler's demoniac harangue broadcast from the Nazi convention in Nuremberg shocked most of the world. Nuremberg, which we had visited, had previously meant the homes of Albrecht Dürer and

Hans Sachs and the site of Wagner's *gemütlich* opera, *Die Meistersinger*. Now we felt that Armageddon was near.

The November, 1938, elections were approaching, and because of the large German vote most of Chicago's political leaders were afraid to talk about foreign affairs. On the eve of Munich I was asked to be the main speaker at a gigantic Czechoslovak rally in the Chicago Stadium. I came in from the Indiana Dunes to find about 30,000 highly emotional people inside and an equal number outside waiting to hear through loudspeakers. I felt that the occasion called for the truth, and I spoke from the heart. I said that their ancient homeland was threatened by tyranny and that unless the democracies stood together in effective resistance it would soon be our turn. For the next three years I spoke not only before the Slavic nationality groups, but also for all those who favored more vigorous action by the democracies.

Munich came, and what I had predicted three years before, on that chilly night in Ravenna, was borne out. Not only did Britain and France refuse to defend Czechoslovakia, but also they served notice that if that country resisted, they would adjudge it the aggressor. President Eduard Beneš fled the country and, by a strange quirk of history, came to the University of Chicago to lecture on modern history, as his friend and teacher, Thomas G. Masaryk, had done some thirty years before. I had the pleasure of meeting Beneš, and while I admired his fine qualities, I thought he lacked the ultimate steel needed to resist. If the Czechs, with their excellent army, had refused to yield, Britain and France might have been shamed into coming to their defense.

In the spring of 1939 came the final partition of Czechoslovakia, after which it ceased to exist as an independent country until 1945. Thirteen million people, a strong fighting force, and the great Skoda munitions works now reinforced Hitler's empire and the swelling Nazi power. Next time Hitler moved it would be harder for the democracies to act.

Then, by the Molotov-Ribbentrop pact, Hitler and Stalin in August divided up Poland and the Baltic states. Russia thus gave Hitler the go-ahead signal for further aggression and, like a hyena, took its share of the spoils. Bad as the Hoare-Laval pact had been, it was nothing compared with the villainy of Stalin's agreement with Hitler. I attacked the whole proceeding, and when Russia invaded Finland in the late fall I rallied to the Finnish cause and presided at a big protest meeting held at the close of the year.

The worst had happened. Openly collaborating, the three dictators now made war on the weakest of the democracies. The abrupt switch of the Communists from an anti-Fascist to a pro-Fascist position should have disillusioned everybody. Those who had once defended the Soviet Union from now on should have known better. Personally, I welcomed the attacks of the Communist group in my ward. They passed out handbills denouncing me. The *Midwest Record,* a Communist daily, devoted an angry page to my defense of Poland and Finland. For years I had been attacked by the political and economic right; now I was being attacked by the extreme left.

9

The Chicago City Council
1939–1942

BROUGHT UP on the writings of the muckrakers, I had always felt that the major political challenge of the twentieth century was to clean up the big cities. I wanted to help do just that. The Fifth Ward, in which I lived, in Hyde Park, had long been known as the most independent political section of Chicago. From 1909 to 1917, it had elected Charles E. Merriam, a political scientist, to the City Council, where he made a magnificent record. In the 1920's the district had elected to the state legislature two noble women, Mrs. Flora Cheney and Mrs. Katherine Goode. I had canvassed precincts and watched at the polls for these women and felt more than repaid by their excellent performance.

But the ward, once Republican, had finally turned Democratic with the Depression. While this meant big pluralities for Roosevelt, it also meant dominance by City Hall and its two bosses, Mayor Edward J. Kelly and County Chairman Pat Nash. Horace Lindheimer was ward committeeman. Many of us felt that our ward should set an example by shaking off the Kelly-Nash control and returning to progressive leadership. With Professor Harold Gosnell, I helped to organize the independents in 1935, when we ran a Methodist minister for alderman. With only $900 to spend, of which I gave $400, we made a creditable showing and polled nearly 6,000 votes. At the same election, I turned down an invitation to run for mayor on an independent ticket, although my secret ambition was to be mayor of Chicago.

The Democratic party was split down the middle as the 1939 city elections approached. Thomas J. Courtney, the state's attorney, had long since broken with Kelly and Nash in order to run for mayor. Harold Ickes and I first tried to induce the President to intervene and to get both Kelly and Courtney to withdraw in favor of some third candidate, such as John Gutknecht, a liberal judge. Roosevelt was sufficiently interested to summon Kelly to Washington for a conference. But since neither Kelly nor Courtney would give way, there had to be a knockdown battle. Ickes, himself, I thought was the best possibility, and we then started a boom for him. He finally refused, and, so far as the mayoralty was concerned, we were left stranded.

Within the ward we were also looking for a candidate for alderman. We spent a hectic fortnight trying to find the right person, offering the nomination to at least a dozen men and women, only to be rebuffed by each. Some were too busy, some could not afford the race, and others felt unequipped for a rough-and-tumble campaign. When pressed, two men confided that there were skeletons in their closets which were certain to come out during the campaign and to which they could not expose their families. The time for filing was near, and we were in despair. Finally, the committee turned to me and insisted that I be the candidate. I refused on several grounds: I was too busy with teaching, research on the production function, and other activities to take on the job. Besides, I preferred working for others. The committee replied that since I had been trying to get others to run and was critical of their refusals, it was unfair for me to decline. They had already canvassed the independents, who agreed on my candidacy. Furthermore, since they must start circulating the nominating petitions the next day, I must give them their answer in a few hours. I said I would ask my wife; her reply was a second "No."

But she and I did not sleep that night. We rehearsed all the objections. It would mean a completely different life, with staggering new activities heaped upon an already crowded schedule. But we could not escape the question: If I had urged others to become a candidate, how could I refuse to take up the burden myself? So, on the next day, the independents ratified my candidacy, and I was in the race.

In addition to our independent group, there were three other political organizations in the ward: the Republicans, who had selected a young attorney, Noble Lee, as their candidate; the Courtney faction, which had taken Ward Committeeman Horace Lindheimer and the sitting Alderman, James Cusack; and the City Hall group, which had not yet selected its candidate. The prospects were that the Courtney group and Cusack would carry the ward and that I would run third.

Then I received an extraordinary message. Would I accept a City Hall endorsement? I protested vigorously that since I had always fought the Kelly-Nash organization, I could not now take its support. To my surprise, I found that most of the independents thought otherwise. We therefore arranged a meeting at City Hall, to consist of ten independents, an

equal number from the Kelly-Nash organization, and Mayor Kelly himself. These hitherto bitterly opposed groups then united in asking me to
run as a joint candidate. I urged that it would be inconsistent for me
to run under dual auspices and asked to be excused. I tried to get them to
endorse another candidate, but they refused. Both groups continued
to insist that I run. Finally, I asked for ten minutes in which to consider
the proposal, and after some meditation told the group that I would run
provided that it was understood that if elected, I would follow only my
conscience and would take orders from no one. At this, Kelly brought his
fist down on the table, shouting, "That's what I want!" He said the council was too one-sided and needed someone to stir it up. There would be
some fights, he admitted, but since he was Irish, that, too, was all right, for
the Irish loved a fight. In justice to Ed Kelly, it must be said that he kept
his word. Although later we often clashed, he never hit me below the belt,
and he kept his followers within the limits of moderation.

So the unlikely happened, and a few days after I filed as an independent, the City Hall group endorsed me. At first, I had the arrogance to
believe that my reputation as a professor and the combined backing of the
two groups would enable me to win without much effort. It took only one
day of campaigning to discover that I was in for a hard fight. There were
only ten university precincts in the ward's more than a hundred. The
west end of the ward, beyond Washington Park, which fifteen years before
had been the Irish-American locale for James T. Farrell's *Studs Lonigan,*
was now solidly Negro, and of uncertain allegiance. They had been Republicans, but Roosevelt and Kelly were making great inroads. Room-
ing houses had taken over Woodlawn, while the rest of the East Side
was about evenly divided between the university community, a well-to-do
and conservative Jewish population living in apartment hotels, and a
middle-class Irish Catholic group who disliked the university. I learned
quickly that outside the university precincts I was not widely known, and
that college professors were not a favored species.

The *Daily News,* owned by Frank Knox, which was backing Courtney
for mayor, immediately attacked me for having "sold out" to City Hall.
The *Tribune* was hostile. I may say here that for over thirty years the
Tribune has always been consistent in its opposition to me.

My first day of campaigning taught me that I could not "stand" for
office, as the British say. I must at least walk for it. So after my classes and
other university work, I started, on a systematic schedule, calling on the
small businessmen and ringing doorbells. I introduced myself and asked
for support. Then, from five o'clock to ten, I appeared at a series of teas
and meetings which friends organized. I spoke briefly and answered questions. With her League of Women Voters background, Emily master-
minded these house meetings.

Soon I found that I must step up the tempo of the campaign and "run" instead of walk for office. We badly needed money. We could not manage the campaign from our fourth-story walk-up apartment, so we rented a vacant store for our headquarters. As the bills for printing pamphlets and posters mounted, so did the telephone charges. Although we had many volunteers to canvass voters and distribute literature, some who were unemployed were paid a modest stipend to keep them going. I put in $2,000 of my own and later borrowed $3,000 from my wife's savings over the years from her household allowance. I regret that to this day I have never fully repaid her. Friends and supporters gave me another $2,000 in small contributions, and a wealthy former student came forward at a crucial moment with $3,000 more. In addition to the $10,000 which we independents spent in the ward, the City Hall organization probably put out at least twice this amount, while the Courtney-Lindheimer-Cusack faction was rumored to have spent up to $40,000. All this money was spent to get a job that paid only $5,000 a year and was subject to large expenses.

The campaign became a rip-roaring one, catching the attention of the whole city. It was drama to have a professor in the lion's pit with the professional politicians. Previously, I had been charged with being too uncompromising, but now I was attacked as an opportunist who had made an unholy deal with Kelly-Nash. Every day the *News* blasted me on the front page, while the *Tribune* joined in with its heavy artillery, along with whiffs of poison gas.

I could not have won without the unselfish support of scores of volunteers. During that cold, snowy winter they canvassed precincts, stuffed envelopes, addressed letters and postcards, made telephone calls, manned headquarters, arranged meetings, and did the myriad jobs involved in a campaign. Out of the struggle my wife and I formed many friendships that endure to this day. In all parts of the country I run into men and women who tell me that they helped elect me. And I am especially grateful that they still seem to be proud of the fact. One man, Michael Greenebaum, made unusual sacrifices. He gave up his business to take over the management of my campaign, contributing a degree of calm practicality that was invaluable. We have remained lifelong friends, and he has been of immeasurable help in the later political activities of the Douglas family.

Furthermore, the members of the City Hall organization were good allies. If they felt it odd to have a crusading professor as their candidate, they nobly concealed it, and as the weeks wore on they rather enjoyed the alliance. Since they were attacked as corruptionists, it was an asset to have their candidate a "reformer." We developed a mutual understanding, as well as a comradeship, which has lasted for thirty years. I always felt solidly rooted among the Fifth Ward Democrats. Gradually, I was also accepted in the Negro community, which had been added to the ward expressly to prevent another Merriam from being elected to the council. While distrustful of the promises of all white politicians, the Negroes learned that I was sincere in wanting to improve their educational and recreational opportunities and to open up more jobs for them. Perhaps, most of all, they sensed that I really liked them and had no racial prejudices.

The organization men became alarmed when it was rumored that I was a prohibitionist. This really hurt. To scotch this libel, I closed every evening by visiting three taverns on 63rd Street with a companion who knew his way around. I drank a half-beer at each, talked with voters brought up to meet me, and left after twenty minutes, with a liberal tip behind on the table. One tavern was run by a salt-water Irishman, related to James Connolly, who had been in the Easter uprising of 1916. We took to each other at once, exchanging our mutual appreciation of Lady Gregory, W. B. Yeats, and J. M. Synge. Quoting lines from *Riders to the Sea,* we pretended to be natives of the Aran Islands. The next night I took my half-glass of beer in a tavern run by a young Greek, where we recited Byron's lines about the Isles of Greece, from *Don Juan,* and the tavern keeper did better than I.

Invading a few mysterious precincts supposedly controlled by Republicans, I found them full of needy gentlefolk. With them, I read Carl Sandburg's *Chicago Poems* and Vachel Lindsay's *The Congo* and *General William Booth Enters into Heaven.* The precinct captains were flabbergasted at such a literary campaign.

Primary Day I visited every one of the 126 precincts in the ward. In fact, I went beyond my boundaries and mistakenly campaigned for a precious half hour in the Fourth Ward. As the returns came in, it was apparent that I was leading Cusack by a big margin, but that because of the Republican vote and four minor candidates I might not get a clear majority. Nor did I. Although I received over 16,000 votes, to Cusack's 11,000, I failed by a few hundreds to get the needed majority, and had, therefore, to go into a runoff. Those on the inside told me, and there was some evidence for it, that City Hall had held back pluralities in a few precincts to force me into this runoff. This meant a continuation, until the final election, of my alliance with Kelly, who had won the Democratic primary and had to face the Republican candidate, Dwight H. Green.

While the Kelly leaders would not publicly admit it, they privately conceded that their alliance with the independents had not only insured the Fifth Ward victory, but had also helped in other parts of the city. They wanted the alliance to continue.

The runoff moved slowly before bursting into intense activity in the last weeks. I kept up my schedule of visiting with the voters, canvassing precincts, and at the end I had personally shaken hands and talked with over 10,000 voters.

But my opponents did not give up. Sound trucks cruised the ward day and night attacking me. Emily and I had "adopted" a Spanish orphan and were paying for her maintenance through the Foster Parents organization. This was broadcast as proof that I was a Communist. So were the facts that I had favored the recognition of the Soviet Union, had tried to help the unemployed, and had opposed Franco. I was tempted to reply in kind but fortunately did not and finished the campaign with a clean taste in my mouth. This set a precedent for my later campaigns, in which I stuck to issues and neither threw any mud nor allowed others to throw it. It was a good lesson.

As the results of this second voting poured in, hundreds exulted at our headquarters. My majority was 25,000, to 16,000. I had just finished a little speech of thanks to our workers when Paul Scott Mowrer, the editor of the *Daily News,* telephoned. He said that his paper had finally become convinced that I was sincere and had not sold out. If I tackled the abuses that we both knew existed, they would support me in the oncoming struggle. I suppressed my impulse to tell him that his endorsement came rather late and, with unnatural diplomacy, said that I hoped we could work together for constructive purposes. For some years we were firm allies.

As alderman, I was introduced into a strange new world. Ed Kelly dominated the City Council. With great native intelligence, he had come up the hard way from Mr. Dooley's "Archey Road." This was in the section called Bridgeport, where Finley Peter Dunne had located both Mr. Dooley and Hennessey. This was the place in which most of the Democratic leaders had grown up and from whence they had gone out to rule over various sections of the city. Kelly once confided to me that as a boy he had thrown rocks at the federal troops during the Pullman strike of 1894. He got a job as rodman for the Sanitary District, studied nights, and became a protégé of Colonel Robert R. McCormick, who was then a member of the Sanitary Board. This close friendship lasted throughout their lives, so that the *Tribune,* archfoe of Roosevelt and most Democrats, was at the same time Kelly's patron and powerful supporter. In return, the Mayor gave crucial favors to the *Tribune.*

Kelly, who had cut some sharp corners in the Sanitary District, where he rose to be chief engineer, continued to have entangling alliances when he was chosen mayor, after the murder in Miami of his predecessor, Anton Cermak. Gambling was prevalent all over the city, and it was commonly known that City Hall, the ward organizations, and the police all shared in the payoffs. I never learned the ratios but I knew each captain had a man who picked up the tribute. The public schools were run by friends of the Mayor, with gross irregularities in the purchase of supplies. Appointments and promotions in many city departments were dependent on a price. The police and fire departments were run the same way.

But Kelly was shaking himself loose from some of his early associates and was becoming concerned with his final place in local history. He closed down most commercialized prostitution and tried to clean up some abuses in the collection of garbage. However, the city had not recovered from its moral debauch of the '20's, and both political and business ethics were on a relatively low level. There was no reforming zeal on the council. Even Kelly worried over the shakedown practices of many aldermen in granting driveway permits and zoning variations.

The ablest member of the council was Alderman Jacob M. Arvey, of the Twenty-fourth Ward, chairman of the all-powerful Finance Committee and Kelly's floor leader. Arvey was and is a fascinating man. He had come up the hard way, from the ghetto, and had made his ward the strongest Democratic center in the nation. It polled some 25,000 Democratic votes at each election, to not more than a thousand Republican votes. Arvey was polished, lucid, and conciliatory in manner, but underneath the surface he had a will of steel. His sympathies were basically on the side of the poor, and his acquaintance with the educated Jewish community had given him an insight into liberal movements that the average politician lacked. We were usually in conflict on the floor and in committee, but developed a healthy mutual respect. This grew through the years into a warm friendship and later became a significant factor in my own political career.

At the other extreme from Arvey were Michael ("Hinky Dink") Kenna, the boss of the First Ward, and Paddy Bauler, the leader of the Forty-third. These were rough, tough politicians of the old school, who had an open scorn for professors. Kenna owned a saloon that boasted the longest bar in the world, over which hung the motto "IN VINO VERITAS." One day a visitor asked him, "What does that mean?" Kenna's reply, in the best idiomatic tradition, showed that he was a man of parts. "It means," he said, "that when a man is drunk he gives his right name!"

Kenna never liked me, and one day when I was speaking about ghetto conditions and inadequate relief, he rose to his feet with a scornful grunt. "Housing, relief! 'Tain't seemly," he snorted. Clapping his ever-present derby on his head and with an ice-cold eye, he stalked out of the council chamber, never to return. Time had passed him by. He died a few months later, mourned by a dismally small funeral group. Hinky Dink had not liked funerals, and as a fellow alderman put it, "If you won't go to other people's funerals, they won't come to yours."

I also started badly with Paddy Bauler, whose doubtful victory was credited only to his own manipulations. I voted against reseating him, after which, whenever Paddy was high, he would come behind my chair to offer a "Mickey Finn" or threaten to have me beaten up. Later, when I resigned from the council to join the Marines, he shouted, "Good riddance!" After the war we became friends, and at election times in his ward we enjoyed singing loudly, but off key, duets of the Roosevelt theme songs, "Happy Days Are Here Again" and "Home on the Range."

There were other interesting characters in the council, including Roger Kiley, now a federal judge, who had been an All-American end at Notre Dame and who, after losing his voice, had become interested in philosophy and literature. Another, William T. Murphy, from the Southwest Side, later went to Congress and, on being placed on the Foreign Affairs Committee, astounded his fellow members with his intimate knowledge of the intricacies of African politics.

Two of my favorites were the old-timers Jim Bowler and Tom Keene. Jim had been a champion six-day bicycle racer and had the bowed legs of his profession. Tom had been literally mesmerized by Bryan's "Cross of Gold" speech at the 1896 convention. Both were complete organization men, but were personally friendly and in off moments told me stories of James A. ("Hot Stove" Jimmie) Quinn, the mighty Roger Sullivan, and the icy Carter Harrison. Not in the council, but on its outskirts was the little leprechaun Jimmie Denvir, of the Twenty-eighth Ward, who in later years poured out to me his total recall of a half-century of Chicago politics.

Aside from Murphy and Kiley, few of my new associates had ever gone to college. But in terms of innate intelligence most of them would have held their own with my colleagues on the Midway. I liked them and believed them better persons than most of the well-educated and wealthy utility lawyers who, living in the suburbs, looked down on those they helped to corrupt in the slum areas.

While I pushed vigorously for what I believed right, and was usually in conflict with the Kelly-Nash organization, I made it a rule never to attack a fellow member or to question his motives. Gradually, politicians build up personal friendships underneath sharp debates, and I eventually liked nearly all my colleagues.

While my education proceeded at City Hall, I also learned much in the ward. Most of my constituents were in deep trouble, as people were everywhere. They turned for help to their alderman, as the local representative of government.

After a decade of depression, physical misery was widespread and appalling. Scores of thousands were still out of work, with their savings long since exhausted. Many actually lacked food. Miserably clothed, they huddled together in crowded and unsanitary tenements. At this time, state and city relief were grossly inadequate. Food allowances were far less than 2,000 calories a day, not even up to subsistence standards. The amount seemed to be just enough to keep people docile and fearful that they might lose the little they received.

Taking over our campaign headquarters for an office, I engaged the brilliant young Sydney Hyman as secretary, for the ridiculous sum of $100 a month. Kate Sulzberger, later the wife of Edward H. Levi, now the able president of the university, volunteered her services, which she gave for the next three years. Without her, I could not have continued. The three of us interviewed constituents. For those in grave need, we made every effort to get them either work on a WPA project or some sort of relief. Many were in such straits that I gave them money from my own pocket for food or to prevent eviction. But as important as material help to some of the frightened and lonely who came to us, as to a wailing wall, was the chance to tell their misfortunes to a friendly ear.

The routine ward services had been erratic and inefficient. Now, with a new superintendent, garbage collections were soon on a regular schedule, and the streets were systematically swept every few days. The Superintendent and I also worked amicably together to reduce individual grievances and to improve the ward as best we could. I bought and distributed 250 garbage cans for families that could not afford them. We assigned able-bodied relief clients to clean up vacant lots, sow grass seed, and plant several hundred trees in the Negro section to replace those cut down for fuel during the Depression. I myself supplied some of the seed, the city gave the saplings, and there were donations from many public-spirited individuals.

The Friends Service Committee recruited a summer work group, first to turn vacant lots into recreation grounds for Negro children, and later to supervise them. With the aid of a Catholic priest, we transformed a vacant lot into an athletic field. It was exciting to find that as we organized softball teams, juvenile delinquency dropped. We planted vegetables in other lots, and tried to develop neighborhood groups to care for them. To stimulate these efforts, we organized two citizens' committees—one for the white east end and the other for the Negro west end—and encouraged the leaders of the two groups to meet together to discuss their common problems. Finally, we organized a gala week to commemorate the fiftieth anniversary of the founding of Hyde Park. For this we engaged the WPA Symphony for concerts and a WPA ballet to perform. These activities helped to build community spirit. In recent years, some of this effort might have been called an experiment in "ecology." But use of that word had not yet appeared.

After paying Sydney Hyman, the office rent, and the telephone bill, there was only $200 left from my monthly salary of $417. With this I had to meet a myriad of demands. Each month found me deeper in the red, the situation worsening through the requests of churches and charitable organizations to support their benefits. In great need themselves, and holding to the common belief that politicians were grafters who made lots of money, they expected my help. After two months, I awoke to the fact that I had not only given away my aldermanic salary, but $500 in addition. This could not continue. My academic work was suffering, for I was barely able to keep even with my university classes. I had been compelled to slow down on my research. My job as alderman kept me busy from noon until ten or eleven at night, when I began preparation for the next day's classes. To go on subsidizing my aldermanic job at the rate of $250 a month from a none-too-large university salary, on top of giving up my previous fees for outside lectures, was out of the question.

The last straw came when a solicitor for a church benefit demanded $50. I explained my problem, which did not impress her in the least. She repeated that she wanted the money, and if I didn't give it, the members of her church would be told and would act accordingly at the next election. I asked for a day to think it over. When she reappeared, grim and determined as ever, I gave her a typed document entitled "An Appeal to the Churches and Charitable Organizations of the Fifth Ward," with the subtitle, "Please Help Me to Be an Honest Alderman." In it, I described what I faced and closed with the sentence, "I do not think the churches and good people of the Ward will force me to be dishonest as the price of staying in politics and thus contribute to the delinquency of a politician whose moral lapses they will then denounce."

I shall never forget her look of concentrated fury as she read my appeal. Without a word she turned and stamped out of the office. My scouts reported that we must expect reprisals. However, when others approached for contributions, I chuckled inwardly at their change of expression while reading my mimeographed answer. What frustrated many was not just their failure to get the money, but that they, good, pious church people, were being given a lesson in ethics by a despised politician. My situation was not unique, for, talking to my colleagues, I found that they gave many thousands of dollars a year to churches and charities. Evidently, the so-called "good" people of the community contributed to the moral downfall of the politicians as much as did the "bad." The "bad" gave money to the politician; the "good" took most of it away.

In order to make people conscious of a politician's difficulties, I had my income and aldermanic expenses audited and published each year. This showed that in addition to giving my time, I had, except for one year, subsidized my aldermanic work by several hundred dollars. And yet I probably gave less money for civic causes than any alderman in the city. The publication of these figures was useful. It alerted many to the demands on their officials and helped Kelly put through an appropriation providing office space and a secretary for all members of the City Council. Even so, I was always forced to spend more than my salary.

At first, I wondered at the inconsistencies of people. For instance, during the campaign, a dear friend had been distressed because I had accepted Kelly's endorsement. She often called up in deep emotional concern about my integrity. Each time I repeated what I had told the Mayor, and her doubts would be momentarily lessened—only to flare up again.

Two days after the election she called in great excitement. She wanted me to ask Mayor Kelly right off for a job for the fiancé of her landlord's daughter. I replied that reciprocity was the law of politics as well as life. If I asked the Mayor for jobs and favors, he had the right to ask me for favors in return, and I would be under obligation to support him even though I disapproved of his policies. The only way I could maintain the independence she wanted me to show was not to ask him for favors. My friend was only temporarily silenced. In a few days, I received an appealing letter saying that her landlord's daughter was nearly forty and had been engaged for ten years to a man who was unable to marry her unless he got a well-paying job. The family and daughter suspected that his ardor might be cooling. Unless I could get Henry a job, she reiterated, "Susan will be an old maid for the rest of her life, and you will be responsible." I regretted poor Susan's plight and certainly had no desire to condemn her to a forlorn middle age, but I declined to put my head in the noose.

Every week brought similar requests and temptations from all kinds of people, including ardent reformers. I made enemies by reminding them of the political facts of life. I concluded that many people who want the general good, nevertheless put their own interests first. I felt that I must work hard for the legitimate needs of my constituents, giving them both attention and recognition, but at the same time refuse to sell out the larger interests of the community. I was told that after a time Kelly noticed this and remarked, "Well, at least the s.o.b. doesn't run with the hare and hunt with the hounds."

Soon after the election I started taking walks through the Negro slums in the South Side of the city. The East Side of New York had been bad enough, but at least it was brightened by vivacity, hope, and intellectual excitement. Chicago's Negro slums were sodden, dismal, depressing, and filthy beyond words. To see children playing in those miserable streets surrounded by man-made evils almost broke my heart, and I came home feeling both physically and mentally befouled. When my tours were publicized, I urged that the city, in conjunction with the state and federal governments, embark on a program of slum clearance and the construction of more public housing to provide decent quarters for poor families with many children. I argued that in the long run this would save money, because it would reduce fire, police, and hospital costs and curb juvenile delinquency, thus cutting the great and hidden costs of crime. I told some of my dubious neighbors in Hyde Park that the slums were rapidly spreading southward and that unless arrested by some such program, they would in a few years engulf our middle-class community. I persuaded many, but not the real-estate dealers and agents. To keep Negroes out, they put their trust in restrictive covenants and thought slum clearance and public housing not only dangerous but also vicious. Nevertheless, the city began to co-operate in the field of public housing, and sentiment developed in favor of slum clearance. We also started to enforce the building ordinances and to lessen the conversion of houses into overcrowded slum apartments. When I went to the Senate a decade later and began to work on housing legislation, I knew from personal experience what I was talking about.

Back of all this was the ever-present threat of an open and bloody race war. Since the Negro population was rapidly growing, the restrictive covenants and white pressures were increasingly hemming them in. While the city had one of the most beautiful lake fronts in the world, it lacked sufficient bathing beaches. Two beaches were in my ward, but Negroes living west of Washington Park were afraid to use them. They remembered the bloody race riots of 1919, triggered by a beach incident four miles to the north. Meanwhile, a little band of energetic Communists, who loved to fish in troubled waters, was urging Negro youngsters to make a mass descent upon these beaches. For months I slept uneasily, fearing that another race war would erupt under our windows. It was clear that we needed more beaches on the lake front and sufficient overpasses, above the Illinois Central Railroad and the high-speed automobile freeways, so that people could cross to them in safety. If there was enough space on the beaches for all, there would be less conflict about sharing. Eventually the many protests that summer did achieve the constructive ends of more beaches and overpasses. The patience and restraint of the Negroes were remarkable. These qualities of our deprived neighbors helped to avoid a bloody clash.

Not only were there no riots, but a better feeling between whites and blacks gradually developed. Hyde Park has been as successful in developing an interracial community as any place in this country. Some terrible incidents have occurred, but, on the whole, the public-spirited and generous people of the ward have maintained leadership and stability. It is one of the few neighborhoods where integration has been relatively permanent and not merely a transitional stage between a segregated white and a segregated black community. I hope it is not fantasy to believe that what we did back then has had some influence on the final result.

With hundreds of thousands of Chicagoans badly underfed and, indeed, not far from starvation, the city, facing a shortage of funds, cut the food budget by 40 per cent. Deciding to fight this, I took a market basket into the council chamber with a week's food ration for a family of five. This was scanty enough, but when I took away 40 per cent of the bread, milk, eggs, and pork, I showed that what was left was less than a starvation diet. Two fat aldermen tried to prove that this was the diet for a day rather than a week. Then they claimed it was for a person, not a family. After I had cleared up these attacks, a corpulent joker, having taken some of the food, gaily passed it around. This was treated as a joke by one of the reporters, who continued to refer to it as such for many years. Word sped up to the Mayor's office on the fifth floor. In a few minutes Kelly came hurrying in to announce that he had found a million dollars in the budget, which would be used to increase the food allowed relief clients. When I went back to my ward office, some gaunt fathers of many children wrung my hand and stammered their thanks.

The traction problem was still unsolved after ten years of litigation, but when Kelly tried to put through a new franchise, I proved that the surface and elevated lines were now not worth more than $100 million. I urged that the city purchase them for that figure so that they might be run by an independent public corporation or authority. The city had hired a well-known firm of engineers, which, on the basis of a long and costly appraisal, announced that their estimate of value was precisely the same as mine. This created something of a sensation and was a far cry from 1929, when Insull seemed to be successful in getting the lines valued at $264 million. Nevertheless, over the objections of a few of us, the lines were given a renewal of their franchise. Ten years after the war the competition of automobiles forced them to throw in the sponge for $100 million. Since this figure carried with it a cash reserve of $17 million accumulated for renewals, this reduced the actual price to $83 million, or less than a third of that which Insull had claimed at the height of his power.

When the time arrived for drawing up the new budget, Sydney Hyman and I made a minute study of city expenditures before I appeared at an open hearing with a detailed plan for saving over $3 million a year. We made four major proposals. The first was to eliminate some city agencies, including the Board of Local Improvements, that had once performed a useful function but, though now obsolete, still retained a large number of purely political employees.

Our second proposal was to reform the city garbage dumps. Abandoned stone quarries were used as open pits into which loose garbage was dumped at twenty-five cents a cubic yard. The odors were frightful, fires smoldered in the pits, and rats and health hazards multiplied. Moreover, since the garbage was loose, pressure compressed it into smaller bulk, so that the city paid for its space several times over. By the time the quarries were filled, the owners, with inside political connections, had received millions of dollars. They had also created many acres of valuable real estate that continued in their possession. There was gold in those dumps.

I proposed to cure this waste by having the city buy swampland to the south and, using the fill-and-cover method, cover each day's increment of dumped garbage with earth to reduce the odors and health hazards. The city would thus create hundreds of acres of land, which it could later either sell for industrial purposes or use for parks and playgrounds. I estimated that we could save a half-million dollars a year in this way, and, in the process, build up valuable assets.

When I presented this proposal as an amendment to the budget, I was voted down 48 to 2. Throughout my service in the council, garbage dumps continued to be a source of conflict with the City Hall organization. Within a decade, however, my proposal won out. Today the city has created a square mile of land at far lower costs and with less stench than formerly. Perhaps my greatest political achievement was garbage reform. I revel in the rumor that this garbage dump may be called Douglas Field.

The uproar over garbage was as nothing to that which I aroused with my proposal for bridge tenders. There were scores of bascule bridges over the Chicago River, which were raised and lowered when the bigger boats passed up and down. Every bridge had six tenders, one at each end for an eight-hour shift. This cost the city a million dollars a year. Some bridges, I found, on the upper reaches of the north branch of the Chicago River were almost never raised, and on even the busiest bridges the crews worked less than an hour a day. I proposed to reduce the numbers by having two or three crews move by auto in leapfrog fashion over large sections of the river, opening and lowering alternate bridges as they progressed. This would have saved another half-million dollars a year, but when the proposal came to a hearing, Michael ("Umbrella Mike") Boyle, the head of the International Brotherhood of Electrical Workers, marched into the room with fifty strapping bridge tenders, who glared at me throughout the hearing. When my amendment came to a vote in the small hours of the morning, I was the only one for it. As I was about to leave the chamber, numb and depressed, I felt a hand on my shoulder. There was the Mayor beside me. Did I really think my plan would work, he asked. "Why not?" I demanded. "Perhaps I can do something myself," he suggested. Slowly, over the years, he actually reduced the number of tenders, until many of the bridges were cared for by roving crews.

The electrical union, with its 25,000 members, was an especially determined and formidable opponent of mine until 1966, when, upon the intercession of Mayor Richard J. Daley and with a new business agent, they turned around and became my loyal friends and supporters.

My final major proposal for the budget was that new collective agreements be negotiated with the skilled crafts so that in return for the full 2,000 hours of work a year that they were guaranteed, the unions would agree to take a somewhat lower hourly rate. The high rates they had obtained in the open market were due not merely to their comparative skill, but also to the irregularity of employment and the time lost through unemployment. But since the city furnished steady work to all its men, it was not fair for the skilled to demand a big bonus for time that they did not lose. This argument made no impression upon either the building unions or the politicians. I later discovered that the business agents of the unions assigned these jobs to personal and political favorites who helped to keep them in control of the local unions and on the side of the city administration as well. It is small wonder that the leaders of the unions affected by my bridge-tender proposals and for compensation in yearly sums should have become my political opponents throughout the next quarter of a century.

During the first year, I stood alone in the council, and the votes were usually 49 to 1. As the second year opened, John Boyle, a Courtney man from the Sixteenth Ward, joined me. We formed an alliance on economy measures and on the traction and bus franchises. This friendship, lasting through the years, has given me great pleasure in seeing John first as state's attorney and finally as chief justice of the local courts. A few others occasionally joined us, and once our count rose to nine. The council was again becoming a deliberative body, and Kelly's professed desire for more fighting was satisfied. If Kelly regretted this, he gave no public sign.

As we went into 1940, the Mayor, under pressure from the White House, decided that he would break with James A. Farley, the Democratic national chairman, to support Roosevelt for a third term. When the national convention was brought to the Chicago Stadium, Kelly took charge of the arrangements, including the management of the loudspeakers. At opportune times they would blare out, "Illinois wants Roosevelt," "New York wants Roosevelt," "Alabama wants Roosevelt," "Texas wants Roosevelt" (which it didn't!), and so on. No one could tell where the cries came from, or whose voice it was. Later we discovered that Kelly had posted one of his trusted lieutenants, the Sewer Commissioner, in the basement, whence his voice was rotated to different parts of the huge hall. The "voice from the sewers" became famous.

But the enthusiasm for Roosevelt among the people was not synthetic. Despite Wendell Willkie's gallant campaign, Chicago went wild for FDR and, polling a tremendous vote, carried the state for him. Some were suspicious that Kelly did not want to win the governorship for an excellent downstater, Harry Hershey, and that he was also more than ready to let the *Tribune*'s favorite, C. Wayland ("Curly") Brooks, win the U.S. senatorship over Governor Horner's candidate, James Slattery, for the unexpired term of James Hamilton Lewis, who had died in 1939. As election night wore on, my friends and I gloried in Roosevelt's mounting victory even as we regretted the loss of the governorship to Dwight Green. The senatorial race was obviously close, and at two o'clock in the morning, Slattery was ahead by 20,000 votes but with the votes of 200 precincts in Chicago and 200 in the suburbs still not counted. Three of the missing precincts, in the west end of my ward, were the very ones that a year before had prevented me from winning the aldermanic election on the first ballot. The Ward Committeeman, David Eichner, and I made repeated visits during the night to these precincts to urge them to finish the count and report the results. One excuse after another delayed action. Finally, at six o'clock, with the precincts still out, I had to go home to shave, take a shower, and get ready for my eight o'clock class. On paper, Slattery should still win, for his majorities in the missing Chicago precincts should offset the majorities for Brooks in the suburbs. Nevertheless, I had forebodings and was not greatly surprised when the ten o'clock news reported that, with the 400 missing precincts in, Brooks had finally won, by 20,000 votes.

To this day, nobody knows precisely what happened, but many believe there was a deal between the Mayor and his old friend Colonel McCormick. We did know that there were about 200 precincts scattered over the city whose committeemen held especially well-paid jobs in the offices of the clerk and bailiff of the courts. The three precincts that behaved so badly in my ward were in this category. Insiders told me that the members of this group were under the ultimate control, not of their ward committeemen, but of the Mayor himself, and received their cryptic orders at the last minute from somewhere in City Hall.

10

Nazism Comes Closer

AFTER THE PASSAGE of a third of a century, it is almost impossible for the present generation to realize the dangers we faced as a nation during those years from 1937 to 1941. It is even hard for those who lived through those frightening times to remember vividly what happened. The Depression continued, although with reduced impetus. Despite Roosevelt's efforts to buttress the capitalist system, most men of property hated him bitterly. They still smarted from the Wagner Act, passed in 1935, which gave labor the effective right to organize and bargain collectively. The wealthy also opposed the Social Security Act, of the same year, which set up a national system of old-age insurance and a curiously complicated system of unemployment insurance. In trying to defeat Roosevelt in 1936, they had been overwhelmingly rebuked.

As business took a second downward dive in 1937, they were highly resentful. John L. Lewis was starting a drive, through his Committee for Industrial Organization, to unionize, on an industrial, and not a craft, basis, the great mass-production industries of steel, automobiles, rubber, oil, chemicals, textiles, and machinery. The new unions were using not only unconventional, but probably illegal tactics. Instead of walking out and "hitting the bricks," their members sat down inside the factories and refused to work or to permit others to replace them. While they were careful not to damage the machinery or the factories and, indeed, would often leave the plants in better condition than they had found them, and while they made all their demands negotiable, rather than nonnegotiable, in today's student fashion, they nevertheless frightened most employers. These sit-down strikes resembled the seizure of factories by the Italian unions in the fall of 1920. That had turned the big Italian employers toward Fascism and Mussolini, as a protection against labor and Communism. In the same way, a decade later, as depression deepened and labor became more militant, German employers formed an alliance behind Hitler. Events were creating similar attitudes in this country. The espionage agents of the employers reported Communists among the new organizers John L. Lewis had turned loose. This later proved to be true in some cases. Lewis defended the practice by saying that since industry had once hired these men, it could not complain if they then tried to organize their fellows.

Stocks were falling and values were again shrinking. The misdeeds of many business leaders were coming to light. Richard Whitney, the former head of the New York Stock Exchange, made his trip to Sing Sing prison. Insull, Howard Hopson, and Charles E. Mitchell, although escaping prison, lost prestige. All over the country were the scattered industrial and financial wrecks of the Great Depression, for which the past business leaders of the nation were blamed. This loss of face was perhaps what the majority of businessmen resented most. They were no longer at the centers of political power.

In the 1920's, the industrial tycoons had virtually ruled the nation. Presidents Harding, Coolidge, and Hoover had revered and consulted them. Now they were ignored and discredited. Roosevelt ended his final speech of the 1936 campaign, "I should like to have it said of my first Administration that in it the forces of selfishness and of lust for power met their match. . . . I should like to have it said of my second Administration that in it these forces met their master."

Despite rebuffs, much of the business community persevered in trying to reverse events. In some states, confusing social reform with Communism, they launched legislative inquiries, like a preview of McCarthyism. Some looked forward to a reversal by constitutional means; while others expected to use force, as in Italy and Germany.

In the middle 1930's, General Smedley Butler, of the Marines, twice winner of the Congressional Medal of Honor, testified before a Congressional committee that leading Wall Street personalities had urged him to organize an armed force and take over the government. Butler was eccentric and irascible, but was always regarded as a man of honor.

In the late spring and summer of 1937, open trouble erupted. The gentle Myron Taylor had signed a contract with John L. Lewis providing for the unionization of the United States Steel Corporation. But since the smaller companies refused to follow his example, a strike broke out in the Chicago area, involving Republic, Youngstown, and Inland Steel. When a group of strikers tried to parade on Memorial Day in front of the Republic plant in South Chicago, the police fired and, having routed them, then pursued them with clubs and revolvers. They killed ten and wounded many. Louis Ruppel, the vigorous managing editor of the Chicago *Times,* urged me to investigate the shooting. Reporters had told him that it was a massacre and that the police were to blame. The situation needed an impartial study and report. I tried to beg off on the grounds of having my hands full and that it would be impossible to learn the truth. Ruppel replied that there was a full record of what had happened, taken by a movie outfit. Mayor Kelly would not allow the film to be shown, because it would reflect on the police. Ruppel asked me to see it, and it was this photographic evidence that brought me into the controversy.

The first reel showed the strikers marching peacefully and apparently unarmed across a field toward the Republic Steel plant, where large numbers of police were drawn up in battle array. The second reel began with the police not only shooting directly at the strikers, now in flight, but clubbing the wounded on the ground. The photographs were so shocking that I asked for a rerun in order to take notes.

After twice seeing the film, I agreed to preside at a protest meeting at Insull's Opera House. My one stipulation was that no Communist should serve on the committee or take part in the meeting. This was so that the facts would be judged on their merits and the meeting not dismissed as a subversive plot.

To insure order, I arrived early at the hall, where admission to the stage was by invitation only. I had heard that a group might try to slip in by a back door. I personally bolted this door, just in time to prevent a mob of perhaps a hundred from entering. The meeting proceeded as scheduled, with testimony by onlookers that was both factual and to the point. Afterward I agreed to serve as chairman of a citizens' committee, which took more testimony in the next weeks. We recommended the dismissal of the two police captains who had given the orders. The *Times* redoubled its stories, and other papers published some of the photographs. Although the Mayor took no publicized action, for some years there were no further instances of mass brutality by the police.

At about the same time, Henry Ford's police, under Harry Bennett, made a similar attack on a group of pickets in front of a Ford plant. Many of the latter were beaten unmercifully, including a young man named Walter P. Reuther. This time public opinion was so revolted that "Little Steel" finally had to sign a contract with the new union. So in the end did Ford. This outcome infuriated many employers. In Chicago, demands were renewed that I be fired for my criticism of the Little Steel massacre. President Hutchins, as always, stood firm.

In the early fall, a high official of a big employers' organization came to see me. I scarcely knew him and was mystified when he carefully closed the door, explaining that his visit was confidential. A group of prominent industrialists, he said, planned to take power one way or another, and in preparation for this had prepared a list of 500,000 people whom they meant to take out of circulation by means of prison or otherwise. His implication was that my name was high on the list.

I knew such a blacklist had been prepared in New York, was sent west, and was presumably in the custody of Harry Jung, a Chicago antiunionist. Elizabeth Dilling, author of *The Red Network,* had used it for her blacklist.

While I was not able to verify my visitor's story, I never found any motive for his giving me false information. He was not a radical, but a conservative with a reputation for both accuracy and restraint. His connections were with the group of whose alleged plans he had warned me, because they disturbed him. For nearly a third of a century since then he has distinguished himself and shown no sign of paranoia. Certainly in this period numerous such groups flourished, modeled on fascist groups, notably the Silver Shirts and those led by Father Charles E. Coughlin, a Catholic priest in Detroit, and by Harry Jung.

Fortunately, the United States did not go the way of Italy and Germany, but the danger of its doing so was greater than most are now willing to admit. There were several deep-rooted deterrents. First, the democratic tradition was still strong among all classes in the population— farmers, workers, businessmen, intellectuals. Second, the Eastern bankers were more enlightened than their German counterparts and exercised a restraining influence. This was especially true of the Rockefeller family. Third, once the unions had won recognition, most of them acted responsibly, and the majority of employers found that life under collective bargaining was not as bad as they had feared. Fourth, business conditions improved; earnings rose, as did the price of stocks. This assuaged the anger of the mighty. Fifth, while the business groups were still bitterly opposed to Roosevelt, his third victory in 1940 forced on them the realization that he was more powerful than they had thought. Finally, the records of Hitler and Mussolini had so revolted the nation that few wanted to follow them.

In the new era of national radio broadcasts, the United States was also fortunate in having such men as Elmer Davis, with his cool, Midwestern twang and clear vision, Raymond Gram Swing, William L. Shirer, and Edward R. Murrow reporting the world crises. It became increasingly evident that even internal events were partially dependent on the fate of Europe.

The fall of France and the Low Countries in the spring of 1940, crowned by the disaster at Dunkirk, brought closer the physical danger of Nazism. As far back as 1935 I had become convinced that isolation was impossible and pacifism self-defeating against dictators. For this reason, I joined a volunteer military organization which drilled one night a week. I also became a member of William Allen White's Committee to Defend America by Aiding the Allies, working at that time to aid by way of giving our overage destroyers to Britain and later by Lend-Lease.

Chicago, with its large German population and its isolationist tradition, was, on the surface, deeply divided. The *Tribune* and the Hearst papers denounced all forms of aid to the Allies. The isolationist organization America First had its center in Chicago and was backed by most of the leading financiers and industrialists. Frank Knox had entered the Cabinet, as secretary of the Navy, and his *Daily News,* as well as the little *Times* under Richard J. Finnegan, was, on the whole, interventionist. But until Roosevelt swept the city, the state, and the country in the 1940 election, the weight of articulate opinion seemed to be on the other side. Chicago was always a Roosevelt city, and the more the *Tribune* reviled him and his wife, Eleanor, the more the people gave him their love. As in 1936, when Roosevelt came to town for his big meeting in the Stadium, hundreds of thousands booed the *Tribune* and the Hearst papers.

After Russia and Germany became allies, the local Communists formed an incongruous alliance with the pro-Nazis and circulated handbills throughout my ward calling me a "war-monger" and accusing my amateur military unit of being a tool to promote race and class warfare. They also made common cause with my old friends the honest pacifists, led by the followers of Norman Thomas, and gave wide currency to the slogan "The Yanks are *not* coming."

When, on June 22, 1941, Hitler invaded Russia, overnight the Communists reversed themselves once more. This time they changed from violent isolationists to equally aggressive interventionists. It was the second complete change of their position in two years, and it again showed that their hard-core members did not follow principle but, instead, had become moral automatons, twisting and reversing themselves with every change in the party line.

My first reaction was like that of the character in Dostoevsky's *Brothers Karamazov* who, when two members of his family plotted to kill each other, said, "Let one reptile devour the other." Luckily, this was not the decision of Winston Churchill. While hating Communism, he immediately accepted Communist Russia as an ally in the war against Hitler. Roosevelt followed suit, and Lend-Lease supplies soon flowed to Russia as well as to Britain.

As matters moved to a climax through the summer and fall of 1941, I tried to make amends for my sedentary years by swimming, exercising, and continuing my drills. In late summer, at the Dunes, I decided to test myself. On a slightly stormy day I swam two miles in a choppy sea and returned by a run up the beach. I felt fairly fresh at the end. A few days later, when I had a medical examination, I was pronounced in fine physical condition. Although on the edge of fifty, I found myself obsessed with a wish seemingly impossible of fulfillment. I wanted to do more than talk; I wanted to enlist in the armed forces.

However, there was something more immediate, related to democracy in the state, that I felt I must try to do. It was commonly thought that a deal between Colonel McCormick and Mayor Kelly had originally elected the Colonel's mouthpiece, Curly Brooks, to the United States Senate. Brooks was coming up for election again in 1942, and I thought that he should be blocked. Somewhat to my surprise, a large group of citizens petitioned me to run in the primaries for the Democratic nomination for this Senate seat. Although the Mayor had treated me fairly, and I had developed considerable respect for him, I had never doubted that we needed another type of leadership. Not only was it wrong to sacrifice the offices of governor and senator to Kelly's continued tenure of office, but Chicago itself had never had its chance at good government. In New York, La Guardia had proved what could be done with an effective and humane administration. Other cities, including Cincinnati and Cleveland, had been experimenting with reform governments, and it was time for a new deal in the second-largest city of the land. If I could beat the Democratic organization in the race for the Senate seat, it might spark a revolt that would clean out corruption from the schools to City Hall. To feel out the situation, I took off the fall quarter of 1941 for a tour of the state in support of President Roosevelt's foreign policy. Gradually, this effort evolved into a candidacy, speeded by Tom Courtney's decision not to make the venture.

In early December, 1941, the Chicago *Sun* was born. The grandson and heir of the original Marshall Field had left Chicago for New York and Long Island in the early 1920's, but, for many reasons, became basically unhappy there. Increasingly aware of the social obligations of a fabulously rich man, he wanted to do something significant for his native city. First, he built a housing project on the near North Side. Then, having become a supporter of Roosevelt and an interventionist, he decided that what the city needed most was a new morning paper. It would try to tell the truth, neither slanting its news columns nor indulging in character assassination. Field came back to Chicago to hire an enormous staff and launch the new paper. Frank Knox agreed to let him share the presses of the afternoon *Daily News*.

The date of birth was fixed for Thursday, December 4. The whole city was wildly excited over the coming battle between Field and the *Tribune*. The lines were sharply drawn, with the supporters of Roosevelt vigorously pro-Field while most of the Republicans rallied behind their leader, Colonel McCormick. The staff of the new paper was divided over its name. Some urged that the paper be called the Chicago *Truth,* so that the newsstand dealers could ask their patrons, "Do you want the *Truth* or the

Tribune?" But since it was a morning paper, and would come on the streets very early, it was finally called the *Sun*.

Some recalled the newspaper war between the *Tribune* and the Hearst papers three decades before, when sluggers operated on both sides. The possibility of another war depended upon whether the police would protect the distribution of the *Sun* or stand aside to allow the private battle to erupt. In the latter case, there was a chance that the newsstand operators might refuse to accept the *Sun*. The scheduled hour for delivery was 11:00 P.M.

Early that Wednesday afternoon, in order to protect the delivery of the *Sun,* I requested that a policeman be stationed at each newsstand in my ward. At that time there was no information as to what the police would do, nor was there when I made a second and third call to find out. But the Mayor had apparently decided to follow the President, rather than his old friend the Colonel. The presses started to roll in the *News* building. Crowds poured into the streets in all parts of the city. By eleven, as the trucks started to move out from downtown, there were probably close to a million excited people around the hundreds of newsstands, and in the background there lurked tough and suspicious-looking characters. Driving from one stand to another, I urged the police to see that the law was obeyed and no violence permitted. When the wagons delivered their cargoes, a mighty cheer usually went up as men and women rushed forward to get their new champion. This kept on all night, and by morning more than a million copies had been sold. There had never been such a first run in the history of the nation.

There should be a book about the tangled history of the *Sun* during the next thirty years. On the whole, it has been a constructive force, but, like all things human, it has not fulfilled early hopes. At the beginning it was overstaffed, with discards from the Hearst papers and the Saint Louis *Star-Times*. Its circulation steadily fell. Around 1945, when John S. Knight raised the rent for the *News* presses, the *Sun* bought the afternoon tabloid, the *Times,* and itself became a morning tabloid. For years the resultant *Sun-Times* probably operated in the red, but Field met the deficits without flinching. I came to know and admire him immensely. He had a sad and modest manner, and if there was ever a rich man who sought to enter Heaven through the eye of the proverbial needle, it was he. What happened after his death, when his son, Marshall Field IV, took over, is another story. Yet my political fortunes were for years intertwined with the *Sun* and with the shifts of policy and personnel that went on within that paper.

Three days after the *Sun* was born, the Japanese bombed Pearl Harbor. The political struggle shifted to another set of issues.

Meanwhile, the senatorial race moved into the open. As I expected, the Kelly-Nash organization came out against me, endorsing Congressman

Raymond S. McKeough, who had made an excellent record in the House of Representatives. However, he suffered from obvious disadvantages, for he was tarred with the Kelly-Nash brush, and his first act was to pay a glowing tribute to his sponsor, Pat Nash. While this was a loyal gesture, it was used later with deadly effect by the Republicans.

Furthermore, McKeough had voted against the renewal of the draft a few months previously, and was unknown downstate, which was strongly anti-Kelly-Nash. The *Daily News* immediately charged a sellout. McKeough would be sacrificed, it said, and in return the Republican leaders would give Kelly only token opposition in the mayoralty election of 1943. Since a big downstate rally was scheduled for Springfield on the day following the Kelly-Nash endorsement of McKeough, I had to decide at once whether I would throw down the gauntlet to Kelly-Nash. I decided to do so and spent the next few hours working on my speech.

It was after ten o'clock when I finished. Suddenly I realized that my only good suit of clothes was at the cleaner. I rushed to the shop but, of course, it was closed. I located the tailor's home, only to learn that he was out. Finally, I found him playing poker in the back room of a cigar store. Hurrying back with him to his store, I retrieved the suit and caught the last train to Springfield with only a minute to spare. Then, as I lay panting in my berth, I thought to myself, What a fool you are, Paul Douglas. Here you are challenging the most powerful political organization in the country without any money and with only one pair of pants.

The contest was utterly quixotic. Driblets of money came in, John Boyle and Spike McAdams came to my aid, and the *Daily News* went all out in my support. While the *Sun* gave me full publicity in its columns, as did the afternoon *Times*, they both withheld their editorial endorsement. I later learned that Roosevelt had sent Ickes to Chicago to persuade Field to keep the *Sun* neutral. He needed Kelly far more than he needed me.

As I went through the state, support began to develop. The old Horner and anti-Kelly-Nash forces moved toward me. Polls taken by the *Times* surprised everyone by showing me leading McKeough by a wide margin despite the fact that my staff's total expenditures amounted to slightly less than $20,000. But I was realist enough to be skeptical. The Kelly-Nash organization would marshal all its supporters to vote and could probably deliver 350,000 to 400,000 votes in Chicago's Cook County alone. The organization also had alliances with many Democratic leaders downstate, which would give them at least another 100,000. I had almost no precinct workers. To cap this, many of my supporters were independents, who could not take part in the Democratic primary. If there was bad weather, many more people would stay home, not wanting to get their feet wet.

Primary Day opened with a cold drizzle, which grew steadily worse. Some overoptimistic supporters had engaged the ballroom of the Congress

Hotel to celebrate my expected victory. So Emily and I went down to the hotel to await the returns, and, win or lose, to thank our supporters. The first reports were favorable, but then came the top-heavy totals from Chicago. While I carried downstate by a three to two ratio, my own Fifth Ward was the only one in Chicago that went for me. The final vote was 570,000 for McKeough to my 285,000. Never since then has the present *Sun-Times* taken a preprimary poll.

As the returns mounted, my supporters gradually disappeared, until at the end Emily and I were left practically alone in the huge, glittering, and deserted ballroom. When it was clear what had hit me, I made a brief speech over the radio thanking my supporters and congratulating McKeough. Then we went out into the rain, hailed a taxicab, and drove home. A feeling of relief surged up within me and, turning to my wife, I said, "Emily, I am free now. I want to enlist in the Marine Corps as a private and, with your consent, I would like to do so tomorrow." Although she did not want me to do this, Emily replied that she would not stand in my way.

The next morning I applied for enlistment in the Marine Corps. A week later, Secretary of the Navy Knox wired his permission, after my friend General Lorenzen had called on him. Knox had been in much the same position in World War I, when he had been accepted as an overage private. He knew what was going on in my mind and sympathized with me. He sent word that he knew I wanted to be put in an ordinary platoon with the young Marine "boots" and be subjected to their severe drill. Aside from a waiver on teeth and eyesight, I was to be given no favors and judged solely on my merits. Henceforth, I would be strictly on my own. I shall never cease to be grateful to that stouthearted patriot, as well as to Ralph Bard, his under secretary, and to General Thomas Holcomb, the commandant of the Marine Corps, for accepting me. It seemed a strange turn for a Quaker, but my conscience was clear. To this day many honest pacifists have never forgiven me.

It is natural to ask how the once-mystical Quaker could, twenty years after, try to become a Marine, seeking combat service. The answer, I think, was both logical and emotional. Logically, I had come to realize over the years the limited power of nonresistance to melt the hearts of mass oppressors. Germany, Italy, and Japan had become police states, governing by force and terror in the interest of the mighty. Russia was also a police state, using terror as an instrument of policy. If the democratic nations of the world allowed oppressors free rein, then sooner or later their ideals would be swallowed, and they, too, would become police states. Their citizens as a whole did not have sufficient love to overcome evil. I was quite sure that this was true of me.

If aggression was to be stopped, it would have to be by force. But unless good will was mixed with this, there was danger that the original purpose of resistance would be lost, and that we would become the new oppressors. There were risks in any such venture, but if we could retain political and cultural freedom, it could be done. Believing, therefore, in physical resistance to organized terror, I did not want to be exempted on account of age or other weaknesses and so I decided if possible to enlist in the Marines.

There were emotional forces at work, also. I was dissatisfied with my record in World War I, when I had waited too long. I had been deeply hurt by the charges that I was pro-Russian or pro-Communist when, in fact, I was loyal to the historic principles of freedom upon which this country was founded. I wanted to erase that stigma, and how better could I do that than by risking my life in defense of my country?

Since I knew that I would be accused of doing this for political effect, I tried to avoid publicity. I asked only for the chance to prove myself and be judged by results.

Such, I think, were the motives that I tried to live up to both during and after my service in the Marines. They did not satisfy many honest pacifists, any more than they did extreme conservatives, Communists, or political cynics. Now, toward the close of my life, I am ready to be judged both by men and by Him who sits in the great seat of supreme justice, if indeed there be such a One.

11

Service with the Marines

I WAS TO LEAVE for Parris Island, the basic Eastern training camp of the Marine Corps, on May 15. Many thought that my action was political. Others sorrowfully told me that I could not last a week under the severe Marine drill. I spent the intervening month not only trying to put my financial affairs in order so that Emily and Jean would be all right while I was in service, but also toughening myself for the ordeal. Each noon I spent an hour on Stagg Field in a physical-fitness class. The first time, I fainted after a rigorous set of exercises climaxed by a half-mile run. But I grew stronger, and on the final day I scaled a ten-foot concrete wall as a graduating exercise. I was still fearful, but my hopes were rising.

The day of departure came. After resigning from the City Council, I shook hands warmly with Ed Kelly and went home to spend the last hours with Emily and Jean. After we put Jean to bed and she had gone to sleep, we went down to Union Station, from which I would start the long trip to South Carolina. I still wondered if a man of fifty could keep up with the young boys, or if my decision might boomerang in grotesque failure. My wife's eyes reassured me. Just before I passed through the gates to the train, a delegation of Czechoslovaks, headed by Voijta Beneš, the brother of the former Czech President, arrived to bid me good-by. Strengthened by their handclasps and a hug from Emily, I swung on board the train.

A day and a half later we arrived at Yemassee, South Carolina. There we were joined by other recruits—tough young Italians from Brooklyn, freckle-faced Irish boys from Boston, lanky, drawling mountaineers from North Carolina, Tennessee, and Kentucky. Crowded into trucks, we were driven to the island and to the recruit depot. As we passed working parties of Marines, they greeted us with catcalls and jeers of "You'll be sorry!" When we were interviewed, the corporal shouted, "Pop, aren't your papers wrong? You are listed for active duty." I stoutly replied that there was no mistake and that I was going to do my best to make the grade.

I was assigned to Platoon 367, where I found myself among sixty youngsters whose average age was nineteen. They were probably as scared as I, but we were all determined not to show it. For a couple of days we went through the experience of all recruits: discarding civilian clothes, donning uniform, receiving the close-cropped haircut, proudly acquiring a rifle, taking tests—all the red tape of induction. Ever present were the tough drill instructors, swearing and shouting at us. Marine training was then based on the principle of mass humiliation, aimed at destroying individual conceit. The old type of drill instructor, prior to the war, had often used physical violence against recruits. Stories were told of platoons that had been marched off the docks into the bay or compelled to hold rifles above their heads until they fainted.

Marine training had been modeled in part on that of the French Foreign Legion, and many of its recruits had been like those who entered the Legion. Laurence Stallings' play *What Price Glory?* had been not far wrong. But the enlistment of masses of idealistic young men had compelled a change of tactics. The toughest DI's were leaving for newly formed combat divisions. Under the direction of a stern but humane commanding officer, Colonel Harry L. Smith, Parris Island was being stripped of many of its "hellhole" features and remodeled into a more efficient training camp for free citizens.

Never have I spent such physically strenuous weeks. Most of the time from reveille at 5:30 A.M. to taps at 10:00 P.M. we were kept busy under a broiling sun. Exhausted each night, I prayed that I might endure another day with credit. I woke up terrified by dreams that I was being "surveyed out" or ignominiously assigned to the school for cooks and bakers.

Gradually I realized that I could keep up and that I was not the worst Marine in the platoon. We soon gloried in the hardships heaped upon us and in our ability to endure them. We also developed a fierce loyalty to each other and pride in being members of a corps that asked for tough and dangerous duty. Platoon 367 became dearer to me than Bowdoin 1913. My young comrades treated me as an equal, and not as someone to be jeered. To my great pleasure, I was accepted as one of the boys.

The climax of "boot camp" was three weeks on the rifle range; the final test was firing for record. We used the old "03" bolt-operated rifle, and I could not overcome the conflict between the speed needed to operate the bolt and the care required to take aim and fire. This, along with my poor eyesight, was responsible for my making a score of only 186 out of a possible 250. This was a relatively good score by Army standards, but fell short by nine points of the Marine qualifying mark.

I was truly disconsolate when I marched back to the barracks that evening. I had failed in the test Marines valued above all. Back surged the visions of being relegated to the kitchen. Next morning, when I was ordered to appear before the commanding officer, I feared they were a certainty. But before this appointment I was ordered back to the range for test-firing of the new M-1 rifle. With a fatalistic sense that I must resign myself to the kitchen, I became strangely relaxed and, to my incredulous joy, made a very high score.

Terror-stricken and perspiring profusely, I then stood at attention before the desk of the Colonel. To my surprise, he spoke kindly, asking if I would like to be assigned to his office. Although this was a step up, I thought it was a polite way of telling me that I was too old and inept for field service. It looked as if I would be kept in rear echelons throughout the war. Summoning my courage, I stammered my thanks but said that, while it might seem ridiculous, my deepest wish was to be assigned as a rifleman in a combat unit. I hoped that this assignment would be given.

Colonel Smith listened gravely and said, in a noncommittal manner, that he would see. When the assignments were published, however, the vast majority were ordered to join the Third Division, forming at New River, North Carolina, while I was relegated to the garrison troops at Parris Island. As we marched in our final parade, we carried ourselves with a bit of swagger, but inside I felt that I had failed.

Colonel Smith kept me busy. He set me to work preparing a drill book, organizing a school for noncoms, and giving a daily orientation lecture to recruits. In these talks I stressed the causes of the war, what we were fighting for, and the superiority of democracy over dictatorship. To keep fit, I rose early to walk two miles before breakfast, and in the evening I swam for forty-five minutes. Also, I spent a half hour a day field-stripping various weapons and another hour studying books on military tactics. One by George C. Marshall seemed especially good. On Sunday afternoons I read Southern and South Carolina history.

Learning about these efforts, Colonel Smith urged me to take the examination for private first class. When my name appeared at the head of the promotion list, he was as pleased as I, and when he awarded the chevron for this exalted rank, I was far prouder than I had been in winning my Ph.D. or being promoted to a full professorship.

Parris Island during that summer and fall was broiling hot and teeming with recruits, who arrived frightened, were drilled hard and competently, and left proudly. I was promoted to corporal and then to sergeant.

Before the Colonel went once to Washington on Marine Corps business, he asked me if I still wanted to go overseas in a rifle company. I replied that I wanted this above everything else. On his return, he reported that the personnel section in Washington had ruled that I was altogether too old to go overseas as an enlisted man. On the other hand, they were considering making me an officer to head the newly established personnel section at the training center, and later they might send me to the Pacific as a staff officer. I protested that this promotion was far too rapid, that people would say it had been politically inspired, and that I would prefer to stay in the ranks. The good Colonel said that he would answer for the criticism and I should obey orders. "Besides," he added, "it is your only chance of getting overseas." I later found out that, with excessive generosity, he had called me the best recruit in the more than 200,000 who had passed through Parris Island. I went crimson with pleasure when I learned this.

I assembled a staff, and we tried to do a better and more scientific job of making assignments. On the side, as a captain, I was allowed to drill platoons and get field experience in military maneuvers and exercises. But as the winter of 1942–43 wore on, I was restive, and I finally asked the Colonel if I might write to Secretary Knox and ask for assignment to the Pacific and to a combat division if possible.

He agreed, and the Secretary gave instructions that I should have my way. My orders directed me to Camp Elliott, in California, and from there to a place designated by a code symbol. I spent three days, happy although tinged with sadness, with Emily and Jean in Chicago, one of which was in our beloved Dunes. Then, after ten days at Elliott, I shipped out in a replacement battalion.

On the long trip I was able to read a great deal about the Pacific, especially the novels and plays of Somerset Maugham. When we docked in the verdant harbor of Pago Pago—truly the most beautiful in the world—I walked up to the little hotel that was the scene of *Rain* and the unforgettable Sadie Thompson. At Tutuila, I looked up at the mountainside where Robert Louis Stevenson had lived, died, was buried, and which he commemorated with his familiar "Requiem":

> *This be the verse you 'grave for me:*
> *'Here he lies where he longed to be;*
> *Home is the sailor, home from the sea,*
> *And the hunter home from the hill.'*

The ship kept on, and "scuttlebutt" said we were bound for Nouméa, in New Caledonia. After some days, we came into that crowded harbor, which was full of Navy craft and cargo ships. The war in the Pacific was in the doldrums. The Allies had not advanced since the First Marine Division had taken Guadalcanal the preceding autumn.

I was assigned, as an assistant adjutant, to the staff of the First Amphibious Corps, another rear-echelon outfit, which did the paperwork for three Marine divisions, two in Australia and the other in New Zealand, a thousand miles to the south. I quickly found out that our hard-drinking commanding general was away, and no one knew when he would return.

Evans Carlson and James Roosevelt, who were the idols of their men, were being "busted out" of their Second Raider Battalion and sent home by the martinets and old-timers. I slowly discovered that the old noncoms who were supposed to be my assistants apparently hated reservists almost as much as they hated the Japanese and meant to prevent my doing a good job.

I spent some anxious weeks before General A. A. Vandegrift, the commander of the First Division, appeared suddenly with secret orders, took over the command of the corps, and sent home most of the former staff. Colonel Gerald Thomas came in as his chief of staff and was the embodiment of efficiency. My chief saboteur asked for and obtained a transfer. A new breeze began to blow. I felt more at ease in my work and, although difficulties continued in my unit, I could foresee them before they became fatal.

The tempo of activity heightened. Marine and Army units went into action successfully on New Georgia. The Third Marine Division attacked and took Bougainville; the Second, after a bloody struggle, in which Colonel David M. Shoup distinguished himself, captured Tarawa; the First took New Gloucester, on the western tip of New Britain. Corps headquarters was now too far in the rear and was moved to Guadalcanal. For a few weeks, I was held back in Nouméa and busied myself in finding out more about the island.

For many years, Nouméa had been a French penal colony, to which the Parisians who had taken part in the Commune of 1870–71 had been exiled, and where Henri Rochefort and Louise Michel had been imprisoned. It was among the descendants of these folk that the Gaullist movement had found its supporters, and they were proud of the fact that they had overthrown the wealthy Vichyites and had hoisted the Cross of Lorraine prior to the coming of the American troops in the fall of 1942. A Protestant church and streets in the working-class section named after Jaurès, Gambetta, and Zola testified to the independence of this stock. But we knew that our security officers were closely watching the big nickel company, the bank, and the leading merchants.

Rummaging one day behind the counters of a stationery store, I found paperback copies of two works I had always wanted to read: the famous encyclopedia edited by Diderot and the memoirs of the Comte de Saint-Simon, which described court life at Versailles under Louis XIV and Louis XV. For the next few weeks the academician in me reveled at night in eighteenth-century French literature, enjoying Molière but never quite warming up to Corneille and Racine. Saint-Simon's stories of monarchs and courtiers showed how absolute power bred arrogance in those at the top and destroyed self-respect in those below. It was a relief to turn to the rationalism of the emerging middle class as expressed by Voltaire,

Diderot, Montesquieu, and Rousseau. The Enlightenment was a healthy injection of science and common sense into an absurd and morally false tyranny.

In March, 1944, to my great delight, I received orders to join the First Division at New Gloucester, with the understanding that I was to become its adjutant. As I went to the dock to take ship for Oro Bay, on New Guinea, I noticed a paperback copy of Stephen Crane's *Red Badge of Courage* in the window of a nearby cutlery shop. This book had long been out of print, and I had never seen a copy. Here, providentially, was one with an introduction by my wife's uncle Hamlin Garland. On the trip, I read, with rapidly beating heart, of how the recruit was first confused under fire and then terror-stricken, but finally rallied and at the end was a tried veteran. This book seems to me one of the best pictures of the actual feelings and behavior of the soldier in the ranks. It is all the more remarkable because Crane, at the time he wrote it, had never heard a gun go off in anger. It has been surpassed only by a little-known novel of the Civil War, *The History of Rome Hanks,* by Joseph S. Pennell, which appeared in 1944.

I stayed a week at Oro Bay. The heat, always intense until three o'clock in the afternoon, drew moisture into sullen rain clouds a few thousand feet up on the Owen Stanley Range. Then the heavens opened, and rain came down in torrents. The average yearly rainfall was between 350 and 400 inches, or twelve times that of northern Illinois and about three times that of Samoa.

In the interval before the daily rain I followed a tempestuous stream up to a waterfall and swam in a translucent pool at its foot. The jungle was alive with orchids and butterflies. New Guinea is a lepidopterist's paradise. I can still see the huge butterflies with white dots on their celestial blue wings, looking exactly like polka-dot bow ties. I resolved to specialize in these ties when I got back into civilian clothes, and I did so for some years, always thinking when I put one on of that sodden and sullen land where the butterflies had given me some moments of pure beauty. Like the proverbial Eden, it was also full of snakes, and my heart froze in terror when, on emerging from the pool, I once saw a gigantic one glide by with its wicked eye on me. It looked like a python, but I may have exaggerated.

From Oro Bay, I took a coastal lighter to New Gloucester. This was a vessel with a deep draught, which the Navy had always used for coastal duty and for ship-to-shore operations. Indeed, the Bureau of Ships had at first greatly preferred it to the relatively flat-bottomed boats designed by Andrew Jackson Higgins, of New Orleans. It was not until Senator Harry S. Truman, as chairman of a Congressional investigating committee, had blasted down the stupid opposition of the Navy that the family of Higgins boats of the LCT and LST classes began to pour out of the shipyards.

These new craft made it possible to land troops and supplies on a wide variety of shallow beaches, instead of being limited to established harbors, and thereby increased mobility for the offense and made obsolete much of the old coastal artillery. Truman's victory on this point, one of his and his committee counsel Hugh Fulton's many contributions to the war, showed that the fresh eye of Congress can be more effective than the hidebound customs of the armed services.

The First Division was in good shape after its battles of December and January. I was sent for a month to be seasoned with the 7th Marines and went with them on scouting parties to the villages of the primitive tribes at Sag Sag. The natives had just emerged from the rough Stone Age and had only recently learned the uses of fire. They had a passion for cigarettes, and we won their hearts by giving them packages, which they shared with their youngest children. These unhappy boys and girls invariably had the swollen stomachs that are the mark of severe malnutrition. Since these people had no idea of sanitation or hygiene, they polluted their drinking water with perfect abandon.

Although my mission was military, I had the chance to see at first hand the basic needs of a primitive people. They were certainly not the noble and dignified savages pictured by Rousseau and Chateaubriand, but, instead, were fear-stricken and miserable. In the next decades, both the United States and the United Nations attempted to cope with some of their needs by a series of technical-assistance programs. These programs telescoped the trial-and-error progress of the millennia and gave to developing people certain standards of hygiene and nutrition to make their lives more tolerable.

Twenty-five years later my son Paul, acting as the agent for a consortium, successfully opened up a copper-rich but equally primitive area in western New Guinea. Like me, he was drawn to the natives, but, unlike me, he was probably able to do something to help them. Some idea of the need in both places can be gained from the fact that half of their population was and is under the age of four. There was a continuous stream of births and deaths.

One of the most graphic contrasts between innate ability and opportunity was impressed on me during a visit to Port Moresby. I went into the long house built by the Papuans on piles over the sea, as the lake dwellers of Switzerland had built theirs before the days of Rome. The villagers had been moved out; a forced-labor gang had then been moved in. They had left for work before daybreak and would not return until after dark, so the long house was empty. Beside each of the cots was a little locker for the scanty personal belongings of the conscripts. On top of one of these I noticed *The Oxford Book of Victorian Verse,* George Eliot's *The Mill on the Floss,* and Aldous Huxley's *Brave New World.* I remarked that this must be an extraordinary man. My Australian guide replied that, although he came from a primitive tribe, he had been more or less adopted by Methodist missionaries. They had sent him to their college in the Fiji Islands, where he did brilliantly. He then went to Australia and tried to practice law. But of course he had about as much chance as a Negro would in Mississippi. So he had to return home, and the only way he could keep from starving was to join the labor gang. When I commented that this man would be a natural leader of his people, my guide frowned. With something of a smirk, he replied that to avoid this they worked him so hard that he did not have any spare strength with which to cause trouble.

I never saw this Papuan, but I have often thought of him. Surrounded by hostility and harsh brutality, he tried in his few spare moments to keep his scanty contacts with European civilization alive.

The next morning, when I was to fly over the Owen Stanley Range, a group of Papuans, naked except for a breechcloth and with rods through their noses, huddled under the wings of the plane for temporary shelter from a torrential rain.

In May, I went to division headquarters to serve as adjutant and found myself the chief administrative officer. The division moved back into the Russell Islands, to the little island of Pavuvu, the seat of a coconut plantation owned by Lever Brothers, to ready itself for the next push. The tempo of the war was increasing. Pavuvu had been the Allies' most northerly point of advance only a year before, but by now they had partly broken through and partly bypassed the middle chain of Japanese defenses and were attacking Guam and Saipan, over a thousand miles to the north. I worked long days on the housekeeping problems of the division and for an hour each evening read the speeches, opinions, and other writings of Justice Oliver Wendell Holmes, a first edition of whose *Common Law* a fellow officer had picked up in Melbourne a few months previous.

From officers who flew in with orders we learned that the division was to attack an island we had never heard of: Peleliu, in the Carolines east of Mindanao. The war plans called for us to take the island in four days.

In September, as we steamed northward, approaching the island, the Navy proudly boasted that after only three days of bombardment they had run out of targets. By implication, it would be easy for the Marines to effect a landing. But as our amphibian tractors took off from the landing craft and neared the beach, they hit unexpected coral reefs and were exposed to a murderous fire from pillboxes just back of the beaches. There was also firing from a mysterious source gradually identified as the central mountain massif that dominated the island. Losses were heavy as the 5th Marines pushed up to the nearby airfield. The 1st Marines, to the north, suffered even more severely. Hundreds were killed on that first day, and many more were wounded or were evacuated because of heat exposure.

Nevertheless, under heavy fire, the 5th pushed across the airfield the next morning. As they did so, a mortar shell burst near their command post and knocked out most of the regimental staff. Their colonel sent word to division headquarters: "If that white-haired old s.o.b. who is your adjutant wants to come down and join us, tell him this is his chance." General O. P. Smith gave the word, and, with my gear in my pack, I took off for the command post of the 5th. Everything was confused, but I finally found the regimental headquarters at the edge of a wood.

Since there was need for a mobile regimental trouble shooter, I took charge of provisioning the Marines on the firing line with water and food, getting munitions and weapons to them, and seeing that the wounded were collected and treated and, if badly hit, evacuated. The quartermaster units, true to form, wanted to keep the orange juice and delicacies for themselves. I had to overpower them to get these supplies for the men who were bearing the brunt of the battle. These chores kept me busy throughout the day, and at night I prepared reports on the casualties and the effective strength of the units.

Nearly every day, rifle in hand, I went up for an hour to our advancing front lines to take part in the battle myself. At first the Marines did not know what to make of the white-haired staff officer who, as they said, was "rushing around like crazy." But they finally decided they liked the idea, and we developed a comradeship that was precious to me.

On Peleliu I had the good fortune to serve under Lieutenant Colonel Lewis W. Walt, who, as executive officer, really ran the 5th Marines. He was the finest officer I ever served under. Skilled, brave, and a born leader of men, he inspired us all. He had great moral, as well as physical, courage. Once, earlier, during a practice maneuver, the colonel of the 5th Marines became hopelessly confused. No one was willing to report this to General William H. Rupertus, because the two were close friends. But Walt calmly walked up to division headquarters to say that the regiment would be slaughtered if the colonel remained in command. This was an unheard-of act. Rupertus, threatening to arrest and confine Walt to his tent, sent him back to his regiment. But he soon thought better of his threat and told me to make out orders sending the 5th's colonel back to the States. He was to be accompanied by a second lieutenant to see that he did not commit suicide on the way. Later, the colonel had the grace to tell Walt he had been right.

In 1965, after Walt had commanded the Marines in Vietnam, I tried to persuade President Johnson to appoint him commandant of the Corps. Johnson did not do this, but he appointed him assistant commandant and, later, a four-star general. A hero in combat and stern in bearing, Walt is at heart gentle and kind. He was and is the favorite general of the Marine Corps. And as the main author of the genuine pacification program in Vietnam, he has helped to introduce the idea of informal and concrete friendliness as a military function. I cherish the fact that our friendship has endured and, indeed, grown with the years.

The 1st Marine Regiment, under the stubbornly brave "Chesty" Puller, had largely exhausted itself in attacking the northern part of the line, under conditions George P. Hunt, later managing editor of *Life,* described in *Coral Comes High,* the story of his company. The 5th was, therefore, given the job of taking most of the island. Never have I spent a more active month and never one in which I had fewer doubts as to the usefulness of what I was doing.

One day I went down into an area where two Marines had been killed on successive days, presumably by random shots from our own men. I found that they had been killed in precisely the same place. This suggested that there might be a Japanese sniper lurking in some foxhole or cave. As I explored the place, I found a cave about two feet high, with its entrance covered by strands of barbed wire. After cutting the wire, I had started to crawl into the cave when the sniper who was within opened fire on me. Why he did not hit me and kill me is something I can never understand, for I filled nearly all the cave and he was firing at close range. He was probably just as frightened and rattled as I was and fired over my head, rather than at me. Certain it is that no man ever backed out of a cave faster than I. The boys who saw me said I looked like a crab, with a greater backward speed than any forward gait I had ever shown.

It was his life against a constant loss of our own men. Millennia of civilization were stripped away in the elemental need for self-preservation. We found the other entrance to the cave, sealed it, and then threw in a charge of TNT and detonated it. I crawled in again to finish the awful job and heard the dying gasps of my antagonist. All my past feelings about the sacredness of life surged up within me, so that I could not use my knife. I withdrew again. As I came out, covered with mud and blood, the thought went through my head that perhaps the fellow was a professor of economics at the University of Tokyo. What a world it is that causes each of us to seek the other's life.

Quaker though I was, I saw no other course than that we followed. Our ultimate cause was just. Although the Japanese fought bravely and with great defensive skill, they had violated their agreement at Versailles in 1919. They had fortified the island in depth, and we had to take it back ridge after ridge. For years, while they prepared their fortifications, the Japanese had barred both tourists and inspectors of the League of Nations from the whole Central and South Pacific. Amelia Earhart had disappeared while flying over the area. At first hand I learned then that no disarmament agreement can be relied upon unless implemented by an adequate system of inspection. Because the Japanese had fortified the islands in violation of their pledge, they had successfully sealed off the Philippines after Pearl Harbor, were able to take that country, and then to hold off all the Allies for three years, making them painfully fight their way through the island chains.

During this operation, Walt continued to show qualities of physical and moral bravery. At one stage, General Rupertus ordered the regiment at dawn to attack straight up a barren mountain, where heavy Japanese fire would have cut it to pieces. We prepared with a sense of fatalism. Then, at midnight, Walt walked down to the divisional command post. He told the General that the order was plain slaughter, but that as executive officer he would lead the attack. The General shouted, "This time I will arrest you," and sent him back in disgrace. A half hour later, however, the order came through canceling the attack.

Instead of the expected four days, it was six weeks before we could leave Peleliu virtually secure in the hands of the Eighty-first Division. The day after we got back to Pavuvu, radio reports of the 1944 election began to trickle in. A friend had asked me some months previous if I knew that my wife "was at large . . . running for Congress." The fact was that Emily had been persuaded to run for congressman-at-large. I had marked my rain-soaked absentee ballot for her one stormy day right on the firing line. Now I was overjoyed to hear that she had won. Actually, she had run 50,000 votes ahead of Roosevelt. I was especially proud because she had campaigned solely on the issues, not referring to my being in service or slightly wounded at Peleliu. She was always a thoroughbred and never more so than in this campaign, when she worked politically for the same goals that I was trying to serve in another way.

The division's next attack was scheduled for Okinawa, in the Ryukyu Islands. We spent the next three months re-forming our regiments and assimilating the men who had been sent to take the place of those killed, hospitalized, or rotated home. In March, we went on board ship, made some practice landings, and then rendezvoused with the invasion fleet at the recently captured naval base of Ulithi. Then for five days we steamed northward while Okinawa was subjected to an intense bombardment from both air and sea.

As the sun rose on Easter Sunday, April 1, our invasion ships were stretched as far as the eye could see. We had 250,000 troops in the Army and Marine divisions and in the supply units. Though the flotilla had come from all parts of the Pacific, every one of the 1,200 ships was in precisely its right place at the right time. It was a triumph of planning and increased my respect for the painstaking staff work that is necessary but, since unseen, all too often unappreciated by the men in the ranks.

With awe I looked at the ships and forces about us, the embodiment of the power of our country. Four or five battleships were steaming slowly in a line between ourselves and the shore, bombarding the Japanese emplacements with great dignity. At precisely 0950 we got into our boats, transferred to amphibian tractors, and landed on time at Okinawa.

To our surprise, our landing on the west beaches was almost unopposed, and we crossed the island without much opposition. Our Sixth Division was sent north to clean up the small Japanese forces stationed there. The Army divisions headed south, where the main body of Japanese troops was firmly dug in. The Army, under Lieutenant General Simon Bolivar Buckner, wanted to make this their show. We marked time in the center. The Japanese fortifications were then subjected to a murderous bombardment from our massed artillery battalions, the first and only time that the war in the Pacific was conducted on the European scale.

After a week of this softening up, the Army divisions began their attack. Unfortunately, one of these divisions, which had done poorly in previous operations, made an even worse record here. After a few gains the men stopped moving forward, and their officers began leaving their troops on alleged missions to the rear. After a few days, the division was relieved, and the First Marine Division was given orders to replace it and move rapidly to make up for lost time.

For the next two weeks we fought our way slowly forward, losing many men as we progressed. Another Marine division came up to the line. I went to the front early, taking a squad of stretcher-bearers from division headquarters, and stayed on when these men returned to the division. I had taken off my major's oak leaves and was serving in the ranks as a private. Only the Marine Corps was unconventional enough to permit this. But the Marines have always encouraged eccentrics, and the spectacle of an adjutant serving as a rifleman appealed to the old-timers. I was, therefore, not recalled or court-martialed. Division headquarters knew that nothing improved morale more than to have staff officers expose themselves to danger. We had a commanding general whose sympathies had been with Mussolini and who hated Roosevelt. But he insisted on going forward and exposing himself to enemy fire for an hour each day. We admired him, for the staff is generally held in contempt by the men for keeping safe while the combat troops do the fighting, bleed, and die. If staff officers share the dangers, it inevitably diminishes the separation between them and their men. This sense of comradeship is further heightened if staff officers are wounded.

My contribution to morale occurred on May 9. During the attack on a hill just north of Naha and Suri Castle, we took cover for a minute and then started to move forward. I had been lying flat, with arms outstretched, but as I tried to get up by pushing down, I found myself repeatedly rolling onto my left side. Bewildered, I found blood pouring in a stream from my left arm. A bullet must have cut the artery, and probably some of the nerves. It had narrowly missed my heart. There was a heavy rain, but my company moved on and was soon near the top of the hill. I took a handkerchief and tried to tie a tourniquet on my upper arm to stop the blood flow. I could not tie an effective knot with one hand, however, and the flow continued.

A deep wave of exaltation swept through me that at my age I had shed blood in defense of my country. Since the shock had taken away all pain, I resolved not to go back down the hill to safety but to move forward to see if I could join those in the forward ranks. This resolution was rudely quashed by the appearance of four dirty and unshaven Marines who had learned that I had been hit and had come up the hill under fire to drag me out. I vainly protested; they carried me down to an amphibian tractor, which, plowing through the mud, bore me to a dressing station. After my wound was washed and bandaged, I was given an anesthetic, which put me in a philosophic mood. On the appearance of the Protestant chaplain, a high-church Episcopalian, I found myself conversing about the Eucharist. I discussed the light thrown upon this doctrine by Frazer's *Golden Bough,* and how primitive people thought they acquired strength by eating the body and drinking the blood of their god. As I cited the works of Cumont and Reinach, the rain kept pouring over us. It must surely have been one of the strangest discussions ever to occur on a battlefield.

Because of the absence of my officer's insignia, I had been put with the enlisted men, and I later awoke to find myself in their ward of the Army field hospital, about to have an operation.

Afterward, as I rested from it, I found that my duffel bag had been brought to me and in it was the Modern Library translation of Dante. I had finished *Inferno* a few days before while lying in a foxhole filled with icy water, and it had seemed most appropriate to read then of how the most infamous sinners were condemned, not to perpetual fire, but to being encased in eternal ice. Now, in a milder setting, I started on the *Paradiso,* which, I discovered to my delight, had been translated by one of my favorites, Philip H. Wicksteed, the brilliant economist and mathematician from whom I had learned the co-ordination of the laws of production and distribution. He was also the Unitarian minister who had taught Bernard Shaw marginal-utility economics and who was an illuminating scholar of the Italian Middle Ages and of the Icelandic sagas.

I came to Piccarda, who occupied the lowest rank among the blessed but could never rise higher. Dante, it will be remembered, asked her how she could be content with such a static position and whether she did not have an ambition to move up in the spiritual hierarchy. To this the placid saint replied that she was content, "For in His will is our peace."

Somehow this spoke to my condition, and it continued to do so on the long journey home on the hospital ship, as we successively passed Guam and Hawaii to reach the port of San Francisco in the middle of June. The penetrating fog was intense outside the Golden Gate, and my arm throbbed with the cold and pain. But my heart was beating rapidly. I was coming home. And as we entered that broad harbor, with its teeming cities enthroned in mountains, I found myself repeating familiar lines of Walter Scott that I had not recited since my school days.

> *Breathes there the man, with soul so dead,*
> *Who never to himself hath said,*
> *This is my own, my native land!*
> *Whose heart hath ne'er within him burn'd*
> *As home his footsteps he hath turn'd,*
> *From wandering on a foreign strand?*

12

Interlude: The Return
to Civilian Life

FROM SAN FRANCISCO, where the United Nations was being born, I was ordered to Norfolk and then sent to the Naval Hospital at Bethesda, just outside Washington.

Having received permission first to see my wife, I rushed to her office, only to find that she had been called to the floor of the House of Representatives to answer a roll call on the extension of the Fair Employment Practices Committee. At the family gallery I told the guard that I was Major Douglas, just returned from two years overseas, and that I wanted to see my wife, Congresswoman Douglas, who was on the floor. The guard scornfully replied, "Don't give me that story. Major Douglas, husband of Congresswoman Douglas, arrived five minutes ago and told me the same thing." This stranger-than-fiction fact came about because Melvyn Douglas, the actor, who had returned from two years in the Burma-India theater, had indeed just been admitted to see his wife, Congresswoman Helen Gahagan Douglas, of California. That we should have come from identical backgrounds at an identical moment amply justified the guard's skepticism.

Once this confusion had been cleared up, I was ushered into the gallery as the clerk was calling the roll in the middle of the D's. I heard him call, "Mrs. Douglas of Illinois," and then I heard Emily's clear voice answer, "Aye." When a great sob of happiness rose in my throat, people turned to look at me, but in my weakened condition I could not for a moment control my feelings.

I was at Bethesda for over a year. The skilled surgeons did their best in four operations to repair the nerves that had been shot away, and I worked hard at corrective exercises to recover the use of my left hand and lower arm. But these were largely unsuccessful, and I permanently lost the use of my left hand. Ever since, I have considered it only a good paperweight.

The long period in the hospital gave me the chance to see something of my children. Helen was a researcher with *Life,* and it was a stimulus to see her keen mind at work. In 1947, to my delight, she went to Chicago as a correspondent. Dorothea had just graduated from Bennington and was about to marry Robert John and join Martha Graham's dance company. Paul was leaving the Navy and his bell-bottom trousers behind to enter Princeton. John, who had graduated from Princeton after making a brilliant record both athletically and scholastically and had taken part in naval operations as a PT-boat skipper in the Mediterranean and the Philippines, had been fortunate to marry Mary St. John, the daughter of a fine New York surgeon. She has proved an ideal wife and mother. He went to Yale Law School in 1946, where he was an editor of the *Law Review* and from which he was graduated with honors. He then went off to Oxford as a Rhodes Scholar. Jean was growing up as a spirited teenager at Friends School in Washington and the Junior Putney in Vermont.

Emily was making a splendid record in Congress, and, although a freshman, carried a large part of the responsibility for getting the bills authorizing the United Nations Relief and Rehabilitation Agency through the House. Both she and I felt drawn to General Dwight D. Eisenhower when he accepted the invitation to be the lead-off witness in behalf of UNRRA. He gave up his Thanksgiving Day to do so, and when he entered the hearing room with perspiration pouring off his face, his uniform soaked, and his voice broken, it was obvious that he was trembling on the verge of pneumonia. He would not quit, however, and drew his prepared testimony from a briefcase. He looked it over, shook his head, and threw it aside. Then he started to talk informally, saying that his business as a soldier had been to defeat the enemy in battle, but that you could not permanently keep men down with bayonets. Ultimately, people could be reconciled only by love and good works. That was what UNRRA was doing. There had been every reason it should have failed. We had given it the worst of everything: supplies, trucks, quarters, and personnel. "I was fighting a war," he said, "and I had to give the troops the best. I unloaded a lot of eight balls on UNRRA. But instead of being a failure, it has been a great success. I ask you to support and continue it."

There could be no hostile questioning following that. After the General left the room, he went to the hospital. The opposition collapsed, and UNRRA was saved. Emily and I were happy, and I thought of the General's gentle pacifist mother, a member of an obscure sect, who during the conflict had taught and preached against war. She may have thought her teachings had fallen on rocky ground, but they bore fruit in the life of her son.

With Senator Lister Hill, of Alabama, Emily sponsored a bill to help the states provide traveling libraries on wheels for people in inaccessible places. Some years later, with a new Hill-Douglas partnership, I helped secure the passage of this bookmobile bill. Meanwhile, in 1946, those I talked to in Washington seemed confident that Emily would easily win re-election on the basis of personal popularity.

But in the winter and spring of 1946 we could both see breakers ahead. There was the usual postwar disillusionment. Parents and wives were demanding that the boys be brought home immediately. Emily refused to join the stampede to bring all the troops home. "How," she asked, "can we use our influence for collective security if we strip ourselves of our armed forces abroad?" Russia was reverting to its old intransigence and was acting like an enemy and not like a good ally. In the United States the Communists were trying to take over the new industrial unions and were infiltrating liberal organizations. All the frustrations of the war were recoiling on the heads of the Democratic party. Truman was doing his best, but he seemed inept after Roosevelt. Moreover, he was trying to continue price controls in order to keep down living costs. As a result, livestock dealers were holding cattle and hogs from the market, and there was a meat shortage. In the resultant "pork-chop election" my gallant wife, attacked by both left and right, went down to defeat, by no fewer than 300,000 votes, running, nevertheless, 150,000 votes ahead of the rest of the ticket.

By this time I was back at the University of Chicago, picking up the threads of my academic career. Teaching was enjoyable after all those years, and I was honored by election to the presidency of the American Economic Association—the highest distinction my profession could accord. Nonetheless, I was disconcerted to find that the economic and political conservatives had acquired an almost complete dominance over my department and taught that market decisions were always right and profit values the supreme ones. The doctrine of noninterference with the market meant, in practice, clear the track for big business. Inequalities of bargaining power, knowledge, and income were brushed aside, and the realities of monopoly, quasi monopoly, and imperfect competition were treated as either immaterial or nonexistent. Similarly, conflicts of interest between producers and consumers were also brushed aside, as were the possibilities of private firms unloading social costs upon the community and the environment. Polluted air and water and excessive noise seemed unimportant to the dominant conservatives. Furthermore, since market demand was based on the distribution of income, and really of surplus income above the minimum of subsistence, it reflected all the injustices of modern society and the thinking of Ruskin and Hobson.

I could not accept this as the complete gospel. The dislike of government, which was sound in the case of permanent price-fixing, was carried over into many fields where the state seemed to be a good agency for widely needed reforms, in health, housing, education, conservation, and recreation. The opinions of my colleagues would have confined government to the eighteenth-century functions of justice, police, and arms, which I thought had been insufficient even for that time and were certainly so for ours. These men would neither use statistical data to develop economic theory nor accept critical analysis of the economic system. Though expounded with intellectual subtlety, their unrealistic view did not furnish adequate answers to the problems that beset us. It was too much like the economics of the period prior to World War I. So I found myself increasingly out of tune with many of my faculty colleagues and was keenly aware of their impatience and disgust with me. The university I had loved so much seemed to be a different place. Schultz was dead, Viner was gone, Knight was now openly hostile, and his disciples seemed to be everywhere. If I stayed, it would be in an unfriendly environment. I felt stifled and did not think I could live in that atmosphere. My emotions turned outward and not inward.

Meanwhile, I helped to break the long hold of Ed Kelly over the Democratic party in Illinois by threatening to run as an independent candidate for mayor unless the Democrats nominated either Martin Kennelly, an honest businessman, or my old friend John Boyle. Jack Arvey, who had gone to war with the Army's Thirty-third Division, had come back a colonel. He was now the county chairman of the party, and was not only intelligent enough to see that Kelly's day was over, but also strong enough to get Kennelly nominated. My threat helped, as did the *Sun-Times*. Kelly went out like a gentleman, smiling, to become national committeeman. Kennelly was elected with the help of all but the *Tribune*. In my own ward, for my old office of alderman, young Robert E. Merriam, the son of my dear friend Charles, was elected. I hoped that we had launched another liberal Democrat on a promising political career.

Since politicians always have their eyes on the next election, they soon began to approach me about running for governor or senator in 1948. I doubted whether the Chicago organization would ever consent, but during 1947 I began to tour the state on weekends and on weekday evenings spoke at meetings in and near Chicago. After the party's crushing defeat in 1946, few thought it had a chance to win in 1948. Despite Kennelly's victory, the party was still discredited in Chicago and, after being out of power in Illinois for seven years, was disorganized and largely nonexistent downstate.

One reason some politicians wanted me to run was that they believed I would be badly beaten and thus be removed forever as a threat in local and state politics. Arvey was my sincere and constant friend, however, and while I went into the downstate counties he worked among his fellows to convince them that I would make a good race and would, at the least, strengthen the Cook County ticket, which in 1946 had lost by a big margin. Downstate there was strong support for me, as there was among the rank and file of the Slavic communities. The Berwyn group, under Frank Pavek, was especially vigorous.

At first, I have been told, I was scheduled to run for governor, and Adlai E. Stevenson was to get his wish to run for the Senate. But this was switched, perhaps because of the belief that as a fellow Marine I might be a stronger candidate against Senator Brooks, or because as governor I would be more obstinate to deal with on state patronage, if the unlikely were to happen and we were to win. I preferred to run for the Senate, and I thought that if I encouraged the contrary belief, that I wanted to run for governor, the Chicago organization, not wishing to tangle with me on the state level, would be more likely to select me for the Senate. Also, a junior senator had neither patronage nor political power. I guessed correctly, but Stevenson was unhappy about the arrangement, and this may have weakened his early collaboration with me. His followers, I think, held me responsible for thwarting his ambition.

Arvey notified me of the final choice of the state committee just as I was about to deliver my presidential address, on the theory of production, before the American Economic Association. This was the best piece of economic work I had ever done.* As we walked into the crowded room, I quoted to Emily the lines from *Othello,* "Oh, now forever / Farewell the tranquil mind!" It had not been tranquil, but would become less so. It was, indeed, the end of one life and the beginning of another.

* See *The American Economic Review,* March, 1948, pp. 1–41, and the opening chapter to the second edition of my *Theory of Wages.*

13

Election to the Senate

IF I WAS TO HAVE the slightest chance of winning, I knew that I must reach the people by a vigorous campaign. In addition to the organizational weakness of the Illinois Democratic party, there was an apparent nationwide reaction against both President Truman and his party, as well as a general distrust of liberals. I could count on the support of only a few newspapers, including the *Sun-Times* and the Saint Louis *Post-Dispatch*. The *Tribune* would wage heavy war on me, and the *Daily News*, under its new editor and publisher, John S. Knight, was editorially opposed.

Virtually all the big corporations and banks would throw their full support behind Brooks, as would the leaders of the American Legion. The labor movement, while favorable to me, was bitterly divided between the AFL and the CIO. Sections of the building trades were closely allied with the Republicans in crucial downstate counties; in Chicago and Cook County they were indifferent, and one or two were hostile.

In 1946 my wife, scheduled by the party managers, had followed the usual unprofitable campaign routine. This meant appearing before small groups of faithful workers in each of the courthouses of the 101 county seats. She had also made the rounds of the fifty ward meetings in Chicago and the thirty suburban townships, and although the crowds were good, they were made up of the precinct captains and their assistants. My plan was to break through the crust of professionals to reach the people where they lived and worked: outdoors, on village squares and on main streets, at factory gates and stores, and in the cities and towns and at street corners and traffic intersections. With the help of my friend Spike McAdams, I got a jeep station wagon equipped with a loud-speaker and a phonograph. I also got Sergeant Theodore Tierney a leave of absence from the

Police Department. In early 1948 we set out to carry the battle to the voters. Nobody thought I had a chance.

In February the whole state ticket joined forces for a month's get-acquainted tour of the Congressional districts. Adlai Stevenson already had a reputation for his concise, polished speeches before the Chicago Council on Foreign Relations and other prestigious groups. In the next few years he would become nationally admired for his felicitous and impressive oratory. But this winter tour was his first exposure to "the people." He was also disadvantaged because he had never studied state issues. In "Little Egypt," down in the southernmost tip of Illinois, he talked of *"noblesse oblige"* on the part of the privileged. This did not appeal to the miners and hard-scrabble farmers, who were having trouble getting enough to eat and to wear.

Once the primaries were over in early April, it was the Illinois custom to put the campaign on ice until after Labor Day. "You can't campaign in a straw hat" was the saying. Instead, I returned at once to southern Illinois to try out my strategy, upon which I staked all. For my first appearance I chose Tamaroa, a Democratic town in Perry County, where my advance man, Ed Kelly, distributed handbills, and, by radio and press notices, publicized my two o'clock meeting. At five minutes before the appointed hour, I drove to the crossroads that was the center of Tamaroa's activity. There was no one in sight. Somewhat crestfallen, I asked Ted Tierney to play the "Stars and Stripes Forever," but not even its stirring strains induced anyone to come out. We then drove around the little town announcing that in ten minutes I would speak at the crossroads on the issues of the campaign.

Despite all this ballyhoo, the streets remained empty. It was already hot in southern Illinois, and the sun was blazing. My heart started throbbing, and my stomach seemed to turn over. Here I am, I thought, starting my campaign in a Democratic town and not a soul will come out to hear me. What a fool I was to think of running for the Senate. I'll be clobbered. Why keep it up?

At this bleak moment the memory of an incident in Quaker history fortified me. An English Friend, visiting Norway, felt a "call" to testify when he was in the forest near Stavanger. As he spoke, men and women came out of the woods to gather about him. Following his example, I introduced myself, although to no visible audience, and, with a parched throat, launched upon a discussion of the issues. Then I noticed that in a nearby restaurant and poolroom there were a dozen young men, who had their backs to the street but who seemed to have their ears cocked. Perhaps they were listening, after all. I went on for a minute and then I glanced into a tavern, where the men seemed to be attentive. I looked across the street at Kelly's General Store. There, about twenty women, with market baskets, were not buying anything and seemed to be frozen into immobility. Perhaps I did have an audience. So I gathered my strength and went on to finish. Then I invited all who might have been listening to come out and shake hands. Unlike the incident in Norway, there was absolutely no response to my invitation. Not a soul ventured to greet me. My heart sank again, but I determined not to quit. I said I would like to meet them, and if they did not object, I would come into the stores to introduce myself. No one walked out when I entered, but I was greeted with long and steady looks as I went up to shake hands. I left somewhat discouraged but with the feeling that after facing that iceberg of indifference, nothing worse could happen to me during the campaign.

And so it went for four months. I spoke to more or less empty streets in virtually every town in the state that had a population of a thousand or more and in many that were smaller. I went into the mines, journeyed down into the shafts and near the working faces, and shook hands with the miners in the washhouses. I met the morning shifts as they entered the factories and covered the afternoon entrances and departures. I would often be on hand for the "graveyard shift" at midnight. I haunted county fairs. It was an eighteen-hour, and sometimes even a twenty-hour, day. In Chicago I spoke at every traffic intersection, at all the elevated and railway stations, in neighborhood shopping districts, and at factory gates. I ventured into the Republican suburbs and their shopping centers and supermarkets. Sewell Avery had me ordered out of the neighborhood of Montgomery Ward under threat of arrest. In Joliet I was also threatened with arrest; the chairman of the Republican County Committee is said to have told the chief of police that Democrats were not allowed to speak on the streets of that city. In Waukegan and in Elgin, workers in nonunion factories ostentatiously tore up my handbills and jumped on them, looking over their shoulders to see if their bosses were noticing their loyalty— which they were. But I kept doggedly on.

The most important event in the early part of the campaign occurred in July, and not in Illinois, but in Philadelphia, where the Democratic convention was being held. Truman was in full control of the convention, and Eisenhower, who had been refused nomination by the Republicans, also refused to consider the support that several Democratic groups offered him.

A fight broke out early on civil rights. We liberals started by protesting the seating of the Mississippi delegation, which had been chosen by star-chamber tactics and which would not agree to support the Democratic candidates. We moved to unseat them and, to the surprise of nearly everyone, we almost carried our motion. Many thought we actually had won and had been counted out only by some last-minute manipulations of the vote. We were inherently stronger than Truman's followers had believed. Perhaps we were even stronger than Truman himself.

This gave us courage to go on when the platform came to the floor. The overwhelming majority of the Resolutions Committee, under the direction of Truman's managers, wanted to cover up the cleavage on civil rights. They proposed an innocuous plank, acceptable to the South, and felt confident they could sweep the convention. Only four members of the committee had stood out for a strong civil-rights plank. They were the young Mayor of Minneapolis, Hubert H. Humphrey; Andrew J. Biemiller, of Wisconsin, Hugh Mitchell, of Washington, and Mrs. Esther Murray, of California. They were members of the newly formed Americans for Democratic Action (ADA) and were supported by the strong body of its members who had been attracted to Philadelphia for the convention.

The majority report was read with assurance. Then Humphrey stepped onto the platform to speak for the little minority. No braver Daniel ever faced a more powerful Goliath. I can see Hubert still, his face shining with an incandescent inner light as he told the suddenly hushed crowd that our party could no longer dally with the question of the civil rights of all Americans. We must advance, he said, to equal opportunities in the armed services, at the polls, and in the factories. He was using direct and moving words, the equal of any orator. As he reached his climax, I saw hard-boiled politicians dabbing their eyes with their handkerchiefs. Then came the magnificent last line: "We must move out from the shadow of states' rights into the bright sunshine of human rights."

Hubert has had a distinguished later career, carrying him close to the White House, but he never had a finer hour than this. To me, he will always be the orator of the dawn.

The convention exploded in a storm of cheers. I turned to Ed Kelly, who was by my side, and said, "Mr. Mayor, that was a great speech. It may possibly ruin the convention, but if Illinois will lead a parade, we can certainly break down the opposition and carry the day. You are the man to lead our delegation. We will fall in behind you."

Ed looked at his erstwhile opponent and smiled benevolently. "Paul," he said, "we ought to have a parade, and Illinois ought to lead it. I would like to do so. But I am getting old, my legs are tired, and I couldn't hold up under this terrible heat."

He paused for a moment and then said, "But, Paul, I want you to lead the parade." With a gleam in his eye, he lifted our standard from its socket and put it firmly in my hands and then, turning to the delegation, pointed to me and motioned to them to follow. We formed and started to march.

Then from underneath the chairman's stand came a uniformed band of forty pieces, led by none other than James Caesar Petrillo, the president of the American Federation of Musicians and one of the most vigorous drummers in his organization. Ed had brought them quietly to Philadelphia and had stationed them under the platform to be ready for just such an emergency. With martial music, we started down the center aisle. As we did so, the big California delegation, led by John F. Shelley, later a congressman and mayor of San Francisco, and Esther Murray, fell in behind us, and then New York, overcoming the caution of its Tammany leaders. As we moved to the back of the hall and then started around it, delegation after delegation joined us. The convention was in an uproar. Here and there groups of sullen Southerners and conservative Northerners remained stubbornly in their seats, but the main mass of Democrats was moving with jubilant feet toward a better and more equal America.

The forces of the Democratic Establishment would not give up, however. When Sam Rayburn, long-time speaker of the House, permanent chairman of the convention, and complete Texan, put the Humphrey amendment to a vote, he kept referring to it as the "Biemiller amendment." Few knew Biemiller, and Rayburn undoubtedly hoped that, on a confused voice vote, he could get a strong negative majority. Arvey and I had seen this coming. Jack was little more than five feet tall and weighed only about a hundred pounds. I lifted him to my shoulders, and, with his legs around my neck, we walked up directly under Rayburn. Jack politely asked, "Is this the Humphrey amendment?" Rayburn replied, "This is the Biemiller amendment." I have seldom seen Jack angry, but he now shouted, "Is this the Humphrey amendment?" Once more the reply came, "This is the amendment of Mr. Biemiller." Jack grabbed a microphone and yelled for a third time, "Is this the amendment Mayor Humphrey supported?" Rayburn decided he could no longer try to fool with the chairman of the Cook County Committee and, with a grim smile, said, "I believe this is what Mayor Humphrey was supporting." The convention understood now. And when the voice vote was called for, the verdict was overwhelming. No one, not even Rayburn, could dare to say before the assembled press and radio representatives that the amendment had been defeated.

This was how the Democratic party moved forward into a new era, so far as its public attitude toward civil rights was concerned. In his autobiography, Truman later claimed that he had originated the civil-rights plank and had pushed it through the convention. Great are the powers of self-deception. It was Humphrey and his supporters who, against the opposition of Truman's followers, carried the day. Those who took part in the struggle know what happened. We should not permit history to be rewritten.

The civil-rights plank proved to be a campaign aid, and not a detriment, as the Truman forces had feared. It breathed new life into the party and brought the Negro and sections of the liberal vote into our ranks. To Truman's credit, once the decision was made, he stood by it loyally, so far as the campaign was concerned. It helped him and us to win.

When the extreme opponents of civil rights from South Carolina, Louisiana, Alabama, Mississippi, and Georgia marched out of the convention, to nominate Strom Thurmond for President, Ed Kelly took a long look at them and said to me, "Paul, those fellows look just like the APA'ers [American Protective Association] who used to stone us Catholic kids when I was a boy. We can do without them." And so we could and did.

The long hot fight in a stifling hall that lacked air conditioning left me exhausted and dehydrated. My son John and his wife, Mary, took me to her parents' farm outside Albany, where for a few days I saw America as it had been in the 1890's, when her father had grown up. Then, after a brief rest at the beloved Dunes, I resumed my street-corner campaign.

In August I felt a subtle change in the atmosphere. The streets were not quite empty. People stopped to listen and even came up afterward to shake hands. Factory workers shouted encouragement. "Go to it, Paul," they would yell. And once in a while I would hear "We are with you." A druggist in Eldorado told his customers, "Come out and hear old Paul. He is giving them hell!" People no longer thought of me as a college professor.

Then in early September a Republican Congressman who was a leader in the American Legion made a speech at a closed meeting in Champaign in which he charged that I was a secret Communist and cited as part of his proof that I had been a premature antifascist and had been an opponent of Franco. He started next on a statewide speaking trip, and the *Tribune* broke into frenzied front-page headlines with his claims. At his next meeting, in Republican Du Page County, however, my brave wife challenged him publicly on his facts and asked for the chance to reply. This was denied her, and the meeting broke up in disorder. But since reporters and photographers were present, the meeting received favorable statewide publicity. I then went to Champaign-Urbana and, before a large audience, refuted his charges in great detail. He quietly called off his trip.

I went south on a final tour of that area. It rained almost constantly. The crowds were small. After contracting a heavy cold, which turned into a fever, I felt it was almost literally impossible to take another step, but somehow I forced myself through six to eight speeches a day and an incessant round of handshaking. The night at Carbondale, in a run-down and unheated old hotel, was the low point of the trip. Only the action of Ted Tierney in heaping blankets on me and giving me a liberal dose of aspirin and Kentucky's favorite lubricant pulled me through. Soaked with perspiration and barely able to stand, I yet made eight meetings the next day.

We were strapped for funds and had barely kept going. We had done so only by the sacrifices of friends and former students such as Robert Picken, who, when I did not want to take his initial gift of $500 promptly proceeded to double it. Now, when I got back to Chicago, I found that there was not a dollar in my campaign treasury, that the staff had not been paid for a month, and that one of the kingpins of my organization had not been around headquarters for six weeks. The newspaper attacks were continuing, and contributions had stopped. We did not have a billboard in the state and could not pay for an hour of radio time. Our supply of literature was exhausted, and the printer would not give us any more credit. It was the darkest hour of the campaign. With the election only six weeks off, my race seemed hopeless.

To add to our difficulties, the Bloomington *Pantagraph,* which was the leading paper in central Illinois and in which my running mate Adlai Stevenson and his sister owned 49 per cent of the stock, came out in opposition to my candidacy. Of course Stevenson was not behind this move, and he and his sister regretted it. Yet despite his letter of disavowal, many voters always thought that he had turned me down. The fact that he kept his campaign separate from mine and only referred to me before union audiences deepened this belief and cost me votes. No doubt his strategy was based on attracting Republican voters who would not support me.

Meanwhile, after much effort I succeeded in preventing the state Federation of Labor from endorsing the Republican candidate for governor, their friend Dwight Green. This helped keep the unions at least neutral on the governorship. I also made a point of praising Stevenson at every meeting.

Emily and I determined not to give up. Money was the immediate need. Without it we were completely immobilized. We mortgaged our cottage in the Dunes and borrowed on our small holdings of stocks and bonds. In this way we scraped together about $25,000. With this we paid the staff, ordered literature, and bought about $10,000 of radio time. A friend told me, half in jest and half in earnest, "Paul, you are about to lose your life, your fortune, and your sacred honor."

I redoubled my speaking engagements at factory gates and traffic centers, and in every speech I was careful to praise Stevenson. As we fought on, help began to arrive, and voluntary contributions came from men and women I had never known. The crowds became larger and warmer. Some of the West Side leaders who had hitherto been either inactive or secretly hostile put on extra steam and welcomed me into their wards. My wife was cheered to the echo wherever she appeared as the plucky woman who had dared to defend her husband in the face of his defamers. People began to smile and wave at me. I was so much the underdog that human sympathy moved in my direction.

I had challenged Brooks to a series of debates, which he had refused. So from September on, in my afternoon and evening meetings I placed him hypothetically in an empty chair. Then I debated the empty chair, and at intervals I would stop and take his part of the argument. Somehow, however, Brooks's replies, as I delivered them, never seemed to have the cogency and force of my attacks. It is always a great help to have the weight of the argument on one's own side. I emphasized his opposition to collective security and the United Nations, and to domestic humanitarian legislation as well. And I pledged myself to an exactly opposite course.

One evening, as I was speaking in the dusk to the workmen who were leaving the Crane factory on the Southwest Side, unbeknownst to me Ed Kelly drove by in a closed limousine. "My God," he is said to have told his secretary, "that man is a fighter. He deserves to win. We can't let him down." And going back to his headquarters, in the Morrison Hotel, he immediately issued orders to the ward organizations that under no conditions were they to cut Douglas, but, instead, were to do their very best. This helped tremendously.

The smears went on; a torrent of abusive leaflets was distributed throughout the state. But then came an unexpected turn. The *Tribune,* which for years had waged a bitter war against me and had highlighted the attacks, had the decency to run an editorial stating that I was personally loyal, although "mistaken." It admitted that as national chairman of the arbitration board for the newspaper industry I had been conspicuously fair in my awards over the whole sixteen-year period.

But though my crowds increased, the betting odds were still ten to one against me. At this time, too, I was harassed by two Republican plots involving members of unions that supported me. An Illinois Central conductor was such a zealous Republican that, on learning that I was to board his train at 63rd Street, he pulled the train out before I got on. To keep my appointment in Cairo, at the southern end of the state, I had to hire a private plane, which I could ill afford. In the other case, a letter carrier dumped 32,000 of my campaign letters into the lake.

Truman's appearance in Chicago a week before the election was a spur to victory. He had already visited the state three times and had been greeted by large and enthusiastic crowds, which were always understated by the newspapers. In early September I had introduced him at six o'clock on a Saturday morning in Rock Island as he opened his transcontinental speaking tour. To our amazement, a crowd of at least 6,000 swarmed around his car in the railroad yards, cheering wildly. In a factory town this was extraordinary for a Saturday morning. The newspapers and other news media downgraded the numbers by half.

On the following Monday, Thomas E. Dewey, the Republican candidate, tailing Truman like a shadow, also spoke in Rock Island, at noon, in the very center of the city. School children were encouraged to come out, as were the noon shoppers. Reliable eyewitnesses said that the total crowd did not exceed 4,000 and that within twenty minutes a full half had slipped away. The newspapers reported the meeting as huge and enthusiastic.

The news media not only were unanimous in describing the "failure" of Truman's campaign and predicting defeat, but also seemed determined to bring it about. To question their accuracy was to question three basic pillars of American life: the press, the radio, and the public-opinion pollsters. Only one reporter making the trip with Truman had the courage to tell his home office that Truman's crowds were both large and enthusiastic and that the so-called "experts" were wrong. Yet in view of Thurmond's candidacy in the South and that of Henry A. Wallace, on the Progressive party ticket, in the North and West, it did not seem possible for Truman to win.

I was with Truman in the central part of the state and I also accompanied him on his one-day swing through southern Illinois. At least 200,000 people crowded the squares of the towns and lined the roads. There was great applause, and there were constant shouts of "Give them hell, Harry." The newspapers were not impressed. Stevenson did not accompany us, nor had he been with us on Truman's previous trips.

The Chicago rally outdid all others. I had taken part in the great Roosevelt rallies of 1936 and 1940, which had seemed the ultimate in numbers and enthusiasm. But this was even more impressive. As Stevenson and I drove over early to start the meeting, we found at least a half-million people lining the twenty blocks nearest the Chicago Stadium. They were not cheering, but were sober, and I could see tears in many eyes. The newspapers had convinced them that Truman was going to lose, and they believed that the gains they had made under the New Deal were going to be taken away. They seemed to feel that something precious was about to be lost, and they wanted to come out and show their sympathy and support for the doughty little warrior who was doing battle for them against such great odds. At the stadium, there were about 100,000 outside and inside. The cheering was a continuous roar. Truman did not make a great speech, but a fighting one, and he was at home with the crowd. Throughout the campaign he was simple, unaffected, and determined. We were proud of him.

We could feel the upsurge of sentiment during the next week. My meetings were large. The crowds at the street corners and factory gates were now enthusiastic. Accompanied by a *Time* reporter who was sure of my defeat, I went down to Granite City. In spite of him, I found the sentiment as moving as it was in Chicago. The odds against me dropped to four to one. I was on the streets and before the factories from dawn until midnight. My loyal jeep began to break down, though, like its master, it was determined to go on.

I still expected to lose. The wiseacres were predicting my defeat by over 300,000 votes. But I was startled the Sunday before Election Day when a friend who was a professional pollster called me to say that he had a surprise for me. "You are going to carry Chicago by well over a half a million and Cook County by at least 425,000, and you will win the state by about 400,000." "Eddie," I replied, "for once you are greatly mistaken. I am not going to lose by as much as the newspapers say, but I think I will be about 50,000 behind." "No, Paul," he said. "You are going to win big, and I advise you to bet on yourself in a big way." I replied that I did not have a dollar left.

Election Day dawned cold, with a slight drizzle. Emily and I voted early, and then I toured four precincts in my own Fifth Ward and an equal number in each of the other ten South Side wards. Everywhere, I thanked the precinct workers, who, like valiant soldiers, were hustling through the rain to bring friendly voters to the polls.

Late in the afternoon, just as the polls were closing, I went home, completely exhausted, took a hot bath, and lay down to sleep. When I woke up, there was Helen with a cup of soup in her hand. She found Matthew Arnold's "Dover Beach" and read:

> *And we are here as on a darkling plain*
> *Swept with confused alarms of struggle and flight,*
> *Where ignorant armies clash by night.*

And, thinking how our precinct captains and their helpers were working so valiantly, I read, with deep appreciation, A. E. Housman's poem "Epitaph on an Army of Mercenaries," written when the Tommy Atkinses of the British Army were saving Great Britain from defeat in the Boer War:

> *These, in the day when heaven was falling,*
> *The hour when earth's foundations fled,*
> *Followed their mercenary calling*
> *And took their wages and are dead.*
>
> *Their shoulders held the sky suspended;*
> *They stood, and earth's foundations stay;*
> *What God abandoned, these defended,*
> *And saved the sum of things for pay.*

How much better are the professional politicians than those who criticize them so caustically from the side lines but who never lift a finger to help the causes in which they say they believe, I thought as I drifted off again to sleep.

I awoke with the radio announcing that I was leading by a big margin in Chicago and that Truman was also doing unexpectedly well. But the votes from the suburbs and downstate were still to come in, and I knew the danger of claiming victory too soon. Finally, as the news continued to be good, Emily, Helen, Jean, and I decided to go down to our headquarters. On the way, I picked up the first edition of the *Tribune*, with its headlines DEWEY SWAMPS TRUMAN and BROOKS AND GREEN WIN OVERWHELMINGLY.

Despite the *Tribune,* our headquarters was a bedlam. The reports seemed incredible, for I was piling up a big lead almost everywhere. But the Republican strongholds were still held out by their election officials, and I remembered past elections when they had mysteriously been used to reverse earlier results. After thanking all the helpers and volunteers, I refused to claim victory until Brooks himself had conceded defeat. This he did at about four o'clock the next morning.

The biggest upset in the political history both of the nation and of Illinois had occurred. To everyone's amazement, Truman not only had carried the country, but also had a majority of 31,000 in Illinois. My majority was 407,000; I carried Cook County by 435,000 and lost downstate by only 28,000. My pollster friend had been right. Only once in Illinois history had any senator obtained a larger majority. Stevenson did even better, winning by over 570,000. The solitary newsman who had tried to tell his boss what was really happening was called in and thanked profusely; then after a week he was fired.

The morning after the election Ted and I took the jeep to turn it in. It wheezed painfully through the streets and when it reached the doors of the garage, it stopped short, never to move on its own again. It had traveled over 50,000 miles in blinding heat, rain, and snow, and over its loudspeaker I had made 1,250 speeches. Its work was done. It had carried me to victory. And now it was ready to give up the ghost.

At headquarters we began to receive checks dated before Election Day but which had mysteriously been "delayed," either in the mails or by an "oversight" in mailing. All the world, it seems, loves a winner. We thanked our newly found friends, but we could not help contrasting this outpouring with the dead silence that had greeted my primary defeat in 1942 and my wife's defeat in 1946, and wondering just why there had been so many sudden oversights in mailing.

The professions of friendship continued. Daily, the expressman staggered up to our fourth-floor apartment heavily laden with mysterious packages. Most were from people we had never heard of but who affirmed their long-time devotion. The packages began to fill a small bedroom. We found boxes of candy, bottles of whiskey, potted plants galore, a bolt of Damascus silk for my wife, and offers of mink coats. We were urged to take a holiday trip to Miami, which would be underwritten by a mysterious admirer, and, to top all, a sixteen-volume set on the art and architecture of Italy appeared from an unknown source.

I was puzzled about what to do with these presents. In the main, they were not real gifts, but were attempted investments in good will. I suspected that my benefactors would later ask for reciprocal favors in the form of legislation, appointments, or timely intercessions. In the end, we tied the presents up again and sent them back collect. The flowers and other perishables were sent to hospitals after we thanked the donors and told them what we were doing. For the time being, the tide ceased, and we thought we had solved that problem.

I made a speaking trip to California, and, awed and humbled, went down again into the depths of the Grand Canyon. Then I went to Washington. Jean wanted to finish her school year in Chicago. So for the first six months of 1949 I was alone. It was not a pleasant life. Instead, it was full of worries, fears, and suspected enemies. I was afraid I might stumble, and tried to feel my way step by step. Every night I called Emily for advice. It was always good, which was reassuring and gave me courage. I look back upon this period as a nightmare. The only consolation came when Dorothea appeared in Washington with Martha Graham.

PART TWO

The Senate

14

The Days and Years
of a Senator's Life

THE POPULAR IMPRESSION of a senator's life is that he rises late, works little, but talks, smokes, and drinks too much. The reality is quite different. My schedule at that time, fairly typical, may help to correct the impression.

The Days

BECAUSE I was afflicted with insomnia, I usually started my day at 5:30 A.M., when I groped at the front door for the *Congressional Record,* the New York *Times,* and the Washington *Post.* It would take me nearly three-quarters of an hour to read the *Times* and find out what was happening in the world and the country, as well as get a sharpened sense of impending issues. The *Post* provided informed comment on administrative actions, and a glance at the women's section would reveal the social combinations that were forming. Then I would read the *Congressional Record,* a verbatim account of the proceedings in both houses of Congress on the preceding day. While there is a great deal of dross in the *Record,* it is also a mine of information and an invaluable account of the line-up of political forces, including the arguments advanced in support of various positions. Each issue has a summary of actions taken on the floor of both House and Senate and in committees, and the schedule for the day about to start.

With all its faults, the *Congressional Record* was in my day a marvel of editing and printing. Stenographers present in the chambers took down every word. After these notes had been corrected for style and possible errors, the revised copy was sent a few blocks away to the Government Printing Office, which in a few hours produced an issue of from 100 to 200 pages, closely printed in three columns to the page. Meanwhile, those who had spoken had a chance to correct the manuscript and edit out any errors. Some of us were suspected of being wittier with our pencils than we had been with our tongues. Richard Neuberger used to say that Congress was the only place in the world where a man could exclaim "I wish I had said that" and then say it.

During most of my service, the chief reporter for the Senate was James W. Murphy, a grizzled and corpulent veteran whose family had exercised a similar editorship for nearly a century. The integrity of the *Record* was Murphy's passion. He insisted on accuracy and he gently corrected mistakes made by members in quoting Shakespeare, poets, or preceding politicians. Buttressed by anthologies, he seemed to be omniscient. Even when nearing death, with face and body swollen almost beyond recognition, he insisted on coming to his desk and shepherding his beloved charge through publication. If there ever was a devoted public servant, it was James Murphy. Others caught his spirit, but there was an inevitable letdown after his death, and the *Record* is not as good as it was during the long reign of the Murphys. I have gained the impression that when an inattentive presiding officer has made either an ambiguous ruling or one not satisfactory to the senatorial Establishment, the *Record* has been subsequently edited to uphold its desires. Murphy would never have permitted that.

While the *Record* is extraordinary in the relative speed and accuracy of its printing, skeptics have at times questioned its value. I would say that it is invaluable. It gives the raw material of history upon which the newspapers, journals, contemporary historians, and others may draw, and it furnishes the basis for a better-informed and wiser public opinion. The social and political history of the country could not be written without it. It permits the voters to check on their Senators and Congressmen and, hence, makes political campaigns more informed. It also makes Senators and Congressmen more careful in their speeches, in the hope that they will be judged favorably by their constituents and by history.

While the total circulation of the *Record* probably does not exceed 50,000, it goes to the main libraries and opinion makers of the country. Many thoughtful attorneys and editors read it and discuss its contents. So its influence is multiplied many fold.

In 1945 my friends Nelson and Henrietta Poynter, of the Saint Petersburg *Times,* founded the efficient and accurate *Congressional Quarterly,* which gives a full record of all the roll calls, with individual members identified, and an impartial summary of the issues under consideration both on the floor and in committee. It is a pleasure to record that after a long period of subsidizing the *Quarterly,* the Poynters finally saw it operating in the black, a flourishing and presumably permanent institution. They succeeded where previously heroic and poorly financed pioneers found the burden too heavy. So far as I know, Robert M. La Follette was the first, between 1905 and 1910, to complete connected records of the votes of individual Senators. He published them in his magazine, the *Progressive,* and then recited them in his Chautauqua lectures, often to the embarrassment of his colleagues. When he was compelled to lay down the burden, Lynn and Dora Haines took it up, but it proved too much for their purse and strength. After a time Thomas R. Amlie, the progressive congressman from Wisconsin, assumed the task, and he also prepared a volume giving the historical record of the key votes in both House and Senate over a twenty-year period. All these pioneers deserve great credit for their unselfish drudgery. But the Poynters, with equal zeal, seem to have overcome the difficulties that were too much for the others. The *Congressional Quarterly* is a prime resource for newspapers, editorial writers, and students of public affairs.

All my early-morning reading was helpful, but it was not enough. I subscribed to many newspapers and magazines. One winter, a conceited young man came to quiz me on my reading, for his dissertation. He seemed unfavorably impressed at seeing all the Chicago papers and four Illinois downstate journals on a side table, and I was only slightly redeemed when he found the Saint Louis *Post-Dispatch,* the *Wall Street Journal,* and the *Christian Science Monitor* on another table. His caustic impression of Midwestern politicians was on the whole being confirmed. So, leading him to an alcove where I kept the current issues of the Manchester *Guardian,* the *New Statesman,* the *Economist,* the *Observer,* and *Le Monde,* I asked his critical appraisal of each. He knew little of them, or of the great journalists of the world, nor could he advise me as to whether I should subscribe to the *Corrière de la Sera.* I then showed him my technical journals: the *Federal Reserve Bulletin, Economic Indicators,* the *Monthly Labor Review,* the *Social Security Bulletin,* the *American Economic Review,* and the publications of the Monetary Fund. Beads of perspiration appeared on the young man's face as he offered inept answers to my cross-examination. Finally, almost in a rage, he fled. I have never seen his dissertation.

After my morning reading at home, I usually exercised for half an hour. In spring, summer, and early fall, I swam in a pool we built in 1956 to help me recover from undulant fever. I paid for the pool by cashing in on my life-insurance policy, since I thought that Emily would be better protected by my living for a few more years than by a bigger cash sum payable at death. In the winter, I depended on walking for exercise.

Shortly before 9:00 A.M., Emily drove me down to the office. This was the most rewarding half hour of the day, for I would tell her about impending decisions and get her sound advice. Emily combines idealism with a woman's sense of caution, and integrity with a politician's sense of timing, qualities that have saved me from many mistakes.

Arriving at my office about 9:30, I generally found a collection of "hot" letters, telegrams, and phone calls, which I tried to answer during the next half hour. At ten o'clock, there was usually a meeting of one of my Senate committees, which filled the next two hours. I went back to my office at noon, when the Senate convened, to answer more mail and meet a few visitors, whom I might take to lunch in the Senate restaurant. On the way there I generally stopped on the Senate floor, during the so-called "morning hour," which normally lasted until two o'clock in the afternoon. This was a time for submitting articles for publication in the *Congressional Record* or perhaps for giving a five-minute speech. I could also pick up word about the next measure to be considered.

After lunch, I went back to the floor if there was an important bill before the Senate. On those occasions when I wanted to make a formal speech, I normally spent the afternoon awaiting my turn and then speaking from notes my staff and I had prepared during the preceding days. After this, and earlier if there was no serious business on the floor, I took a brief nap, worked on correspondence, met visitors—generally constituents —and then, at around 6:00 P.M., I turned to the most time-consuming task of the day: the signing of the 200 to 300 letters prepared for my signature. Members of the staff came in as I signed to discuss issues involved in the letters. Sometimes we modified or decided to redraft a reply. This took at least an hour, added to which were other matters to be dealt with, including telephone calls. I seldom left the office before 7:30, and usually arrived home at around 8:00.

The Offices

I WANTED my offices to reflect and help create a spirit of tranquil strength. Until John F. Kennedy came along, I did not show a photograph of a contemporary politician. Instead, in the outer office, hung somewhat haphazardly, were reproductions of great works of art, most of which I had picked up abroad. In the reception room, Brueghel's *Kermesse,* which Helen had given me, covered half a wall. Across the room were photographs of national heroes: Washington, Jefferson, Jackson, Lincoln, Cleveland, Wilson, and Franklin Roosevelt. In the inner offices were works of Renaissance painters: Giovanni Bellini, Botticelli, Leonardo, Antonello da Messina, and Piero della Francesca. At the end of the suite, large sepia photographs of Michelangelo's Night and Day, Morning and Evening, from the Medici Chapel, hung over the door to my private office.

Facing me when I was at my desk were Holbein's portraits of two Reformation scholars: Thomas More, the man for all seasons who went into politics and lost his head in consequence, and Erasmus, who kept out of politics and therefore retained his head. I used to show these to young visitors and ask them which was the wiser. During the 1950's, the almost unanimous answer was Erasmus. Occasionally an imaginative youngster looked apprehensively at me, as if to see if the headsman's ax was about to take its toll.

In alcoves to the side of my desk, invisible to a frontal view of the desk, were personal memorabilia, including some studio pieces by my mother and the prayer of Saint Francis for peace, given to me by the nuns of Joliet. Directly behind the desk were the American flag and the colors of the Marine Corps. Once, a belligerent representative of a farm organization pointed his finger accusingly at the red field of the latter, hanging loosely from its staff, and in a loud voice demanded to know what it represented. As I silently unfolded the colors, I could not make out whether he was reassured or crestfallen because it bore the anchor and globe of the Corps instead of the hammer and sickle he had suspected.

Alone on the left wall were six large photographs, chosen with some care. At the center was a portrait by Hessler, which I prefer to all others, of the smooth-shaven Lincoln, taken immediately after his nomination. To his left were two other Illinoisans, belonging in his company: Jane Addams, saint of the bloody Twentieth Ward as well as of all the world, and Governor John Peter Altgeld, who passed the first eight-hour law for women, pardoned the Haymarket riot anarchists, and resisted President Cleveland's use of federal troops to break a railway strike. Directly under Lincoln was a marvelous photograph of my old friend Clarence Darrow, in no sense a saint, or, at best, a badly mud-bespattered one, but a virile and resourceful defender of the damned. At the right were pictures of the two Senators who, in the whole history of the Senate, I most admired: Robert M. La Follette, of Wisconsin, and George W. Norris, of Nebraska. Both were men of dauntless courage who stood out against the multitude in defense of what they believed right. Both were men of and for the people. I hung Norris above La Follette because he was less theatrical and had a homespun sense of humor. All six were from the soil of the Middle West and all carried with them more than a touch of greatness. I hoped that if I looked at them long enough, like the man in Hawthorne's story of the Great Stone Face, I might catch a little of their qualities. I wish I had added Thomas J. Walsh, of Montana, who broke open the Teapot Dome scandal and who, slightly sad but incorruptible, presided with complete fairness over the tempestuous Democratic convention of 1924. He was the man we should have nominated for the Presidency instead of J. P. Morgan's lawyer, John W. Davis.

My inner office was where I made the final decisions of which the recorded speeches and votes were merely the outer expressions. Looking at men who had faced equally hard questions and who in the larger sense had finally triumphed, I hoped to derive insight and courage.

In short, I wanted all the offices to give a sense of the permanent amidst the temporal, while adding a touch of the eternal to the crowded moments of the present.

The Mail

FEW REALIZE the difficulties of coping with a congressman's mail. When Congress was in session, from nine to nine and a half months a year, letters came in a deluge. This started for me at first with about 600, and, in the last twelve years, increased to about 1,000 to 1,200 letters a day. Colleagues from other large states who had served in the 1920's told me that their daily mail during that period did not amount to more than 100 pieces and could be easily handled by the small staff of clerks then provided.

Senators found the mail to be their hardest managerial problem. I knew of one Senator who started his term trying to read every letter he received and to dictate individual replies. Within two months he had a physical and mental breakdown. My mail was opened and sorted into two main groups: legislative matters and cases. The first, averaging from 750 to 800 letters a day, became the special care of four or five assistants. Whenever the number of legislative letters on a single issue reached fifteen or twenty, I replied with a form letter which we tried to individualize with a personal word. As automatic typewriters were developed, this became more possible. I tried to be definite in my replies, to give information and not be content—as one of my predecessors had been—with a mere acknowledgment. If I favored a given bill, I would normally say so and tell why. If I was definitely opposed, I would do the same. If I was uncertain or did not think it tactical to declare my position at the time, I would give a more guarded answer. This was sometimes necessary because a premature declaration might be obsolete because of the amending process by the time the vote was taken, leaving me open to the charge of voting otherwise than I had promised. While cautious, I tried to say the same thing to both proponents and opponents of a given measure, generally only softening the blow by a few conciliatory sentences.

I found it distressing that I had to use form letters. But with the time and staff available, there was literally no other way. They sometimes brought complaints, generally from businessmen who felt they were entitled to individual treatment. One millionaire head of a big company in northern Illinois made a practice of protesting. I replied that an individually dictated and signed letter would take at least five minutes of my time, and that with 1,000 letters coming in a day, answering the mail alone would take up 5,000 minutes, or over 83 hours, a day and require a staff of stenographers and typists several times greater than my personnel allowance would permit. Nevertheless, he insisted that in view of his importance he was entitled to a specially dictated private letter. He was never satisfied by my reply that I treated all citizens equally, notwithstanding their prominence in *Who's Who,* the *Social Register,* or the *Directory of Directors.* He renewed his complaints from time to time, finally forcing me to end the correspondence with another form letter. As was to be expected, he became a confirmed and vindictive opponent and was tireless in his antagonism.

On the whole, I received relatively few discourteous letters and was surprised by the consideration of those who corresponded. When I did receive an abusive letter, I was often tempted to follow the example of a later colleague, Stephen M. Young, of Ohio, who replied to such tirades with witty and sarcastic rejoinders. In so doing, he won both the admiration of most of the Ohio voters and, in 1964, re-election against heavy odds. Forgoing this emotional release, I followed the pedestrian policy of not answering the grossly abusive letters and of mailing firm but courteous replies to the others.

Letters concerning individual complaints or grievances against the government, although far fewer in number than the legislative mail, were much more difficult to answer. I personally reviewed and signed every reply. These cases usually involved complicated matters of military service and veterans' benefits, unemployment and education, immigration, and welfare and relief problems. They required investigation, with inquiries to the appropriate government departments, and prompt attention, since they involved pressing matters. The obvious solution to handling this mail was to develop assistants specializing in one or more different sets of allied problems and familiar with the administrative regulations and personnel. The most stubborn difficulties were brought to me for settlement.

Teachers of public administration have often insisted that a legislator should not concern himself with such matters, but should turn all complaints over to the administrative authorities. This is the general practice in Great Britain, where the civil service is the prototype upon which most American political scientists in the 1950's wanted to model our system. But on the basis of my experience as alderman and as senator, I disagreed. No doubt the great mass of public officials have good motives. Some are selfless and work themselves to death. One of my friends, Arnold Miles, did just that, and I literally saw him gasp his life away in the service of our country. It is also true that many senators and congressmen have been and are abusive and unreasonable in their contacts with officials of the administrative branch, and have subjected them to improper pressures.

But it is also true that administrators are not infallible. They are human. Some are careless, others are swollen by authority, a few are cruel, and an occasional one is corrupt. Most of all, they suffer from being at a physical and psychological distance from those affected by their rulings. It is hard for them to enter into the actual plight of those who petition them. Relatively secure and comfortable, some become indifferent. Since the administrators are generally swamped with work, they find it hard to deal swiftly with any matter. People become "cases" represented by sheets of bloodless paper. Delays are characteristic. Decisions are commonly made by rote, without regard to the individual circumstances. Once made, they are defended; it is almost impossible for a bureaucrat to admit that either he or a colleague has made a mistake. People cannot count on obtaining redress from the bureaucracy, and so they turn to their local legislators.

An alderman, a congressman, or a senator becomes, therefore, a people's representative, a kind of public defender, or, in the modern phrase, an "ombudsman." As such, he can perform a valuable function. He can reduce excessive delays and cause bureaucrats to find papers that have been lost or put aside. He can and often does rescue living, breathing human beings from the file of unanswered papers. The farther away an official is from the people, the greater are these delays. An overworked or unimaginative official who pays little attention to the complaints of an unknown and humble citizen will be more likely to act if the inquiry comes from someone who helps to make the laws under which the bureaucrat operates and who has at least some share, however slight, in determining the amounts his agency will be allowed to spend.

Just as every large organization needs expediters to see that work moves swiftly through an office, so does the administrative state. This I felt my office was able to accomplish. Of course, no administrator ever admitted that our inquiries had galvanized him into action. Usually, a negligent bureaucrat did not reply for some time and then wrote reprovingly that "action has already been taken" to correct the situation. This implied that our inquiry was unnecessary. Bureaucrats made this claim even if the correction had been prompted by our inquiry and had occurred just before they wrote to us.

There were also cases where a bureaucrat acted without enough information and where we could supply additional facts. The best administrators welcomed our doing this. The rest resented it. Sometimes officials had made patently wrong decisions or had been thoughtless or cruel. These cases were much harder to correct, as I shall relate later. Occasionally we were able to do so, and as our reputation for fair dealing improved, a few of the higher bureaucrats were more willing to modify earlier decisions by their subordinates. Moreover, the best way of discovering weaknesses and ambiguities in the laws themselves was through this process of finding out how they worked. Some of the needed changes in our immigration, social security, housing, and welfare laws grew out of such discoveries.

As a result of over twenty years' experience in local and national government, I became convinced that this casework was one of the most constructive services of a legislator, and that, contrary to the political scientists, the time spent in trying to deal humanely with the grievances of individuals was as productive as the writing of legislation itself. But it was toilsome work.

The whole staff and I got enormous satisfaction from the misery averted and the happiness we helped to create. To unite husbands and wives, children and parents, by obtaining a more flexible interpretation of the immigration laws and regulations was one of the most durable results we obtained. On occasion we could stay deportations by the introduction of special bills when no question of national security was involved. We prevented men from being taken from their families because of minor offenses committed long ago for which full atonement had been made. To relieve need by speeding up delayed benefits gave us a thrill of pleasure, and once in a while we remedied a gross injustice. In short, we could help to temper justice with mercy and to substitute right for wrong.

Dealing with Officialdom

IN DEALING with officials, there are certain standards a legislator should follow and to which I tried to conform. I never tried to influence any civil or criminal trial or prosecution. The judicial process should be left to the courts and to the Department of Justice. I kept away from tax cases involving either the Internal Revenue Service or the courts. Having seen how political influence broke down morale in the armed services, I never recommended promotions in the military service or tried to reduce penalties. When hardship discharges were sought, I transmitted the papers to the proper military authorities without recommendation and with the request that they be given "only such consideration as in the judgment of the service" they merited.

I tried not to assume that my constituents were always right. To the degree that time and circumstances permitted, my staff and I checked the alleged facts. If the grievance seemed ill-founded, we declined to present it and told the complainant why. Some complaints we merely passed on for consideration. In well-founded cases, I added a personal word saying that the request appeared justified. But I tried to observe the proper distinction between the legislative and executive branches of government and not to tell the administrators and quasi-judicial bodies what they should do.

Above all, I tried to be courteous in all my dealings, but I must admit that I sinned grievously at least twice. When a federal housing official, who had repeatedly postponed a badly needed and authorized public-housing project for Chicago, offered one more lame excuse for further delay, I found myself shouting that if he persisted, I would nail his hide to the door of City Hall. I still blush at the violence of those words, but they may have been effective. Work was started shortly thereafter.

The second time was when I compelled another housing official to stand before a public meeting and swear under oath with uplifted hand that he had no intention of bulldozing a self-respecting Chicago commu-nity. Instead of leveling it to the ground in the name of urban renewal, he promised to rehabilitate existing buildings and to preserve the com-munity. It was wrong of me to humiliate and coerce him in this way. Nevertheless, the audience was relieved to find that, because they had a spokesman ready to act tough in their defense, they were not wholly at the mercy of anonymous public officials.

One morning I had an unexpected visitor in my Washington office. It was William McChesney Martin, the chairman of the Federal Reserve Board, whose restrictive monetary policies I had been criticizing. He told me he had heard that I had attributed this to his desire to enable the big banks to receive more interest. He said he was sure I had not said it, but he wanted me to make a formal denial so that due publicity could be given to that fact. I searched my memory and truthfully replied that I could not recall a single instance in which I had mentioned that this was even a partial reason for the Reserve Board's high-interest-rate policy. Martin visibly began to beam at this. But, I went on, it was also true that I had often thought about it as a possible explanation, and that in view of this it would have been extraordinary if I had kept it to myself. So I supposed I must have said it, even though I could not remember doing so. Martin looked nonplused at this frank revelation of my inner thoughts, and soon withdrew. But my inability to conceal my conclusions was us-ually less fortunate than in this case. In the short run, my frankness caused me trouble. I do not know what the long-run effects were.

In general, legislators and administrators should neither ignore each other nor regard themselves as adversaries. Certainly they should work together on matters of national interest. Lawmakers should have the final decision in matters of legislation, but should welcome administrative ad-vice based on study and experience. The administrators should have the final decision in specific cases, but should, reciprocally, welcome advice. This policy of partnership is one that is still not accepted by many believ-ers in the administrative state; they exalt the bureaucrat and belittle the legislator. But it is important to realize that such an administrative state can be icily dehumanized and impersonal. In fact, it tends to be. Franz Kafka, in his chilling work *The Trial,* was not writing about the Nazis, who did not come to power for another decade, but about the supposedly easygoing Austrian and Czech bureaucracy in one of the gentlest of European cities, Prague, where the humanistic philosopher Thomas Masaryk was chief of state.

Sometimes we legislators discovered the same weaknesses in ourselves. Complaints came to me one fall that I was not answering my mail from southern Illinois, the most hard-pressed part of the state. The assistant responsible assured me that his correspondence was up to date, but a later inspection of his filing cabinet and desk disclosed hundreds of unanswered letters, from weeks back. Although a special squad was put to work cleaning up the backlog, and the negligent assistant promised reform, the same trouble recurred in another eighteen months. Apparently some persons cannot stand the strain of a steady tide of complaints and requests and, instead of keeping pace with it, gradually become swamped. Other Senators had the same trouble. I tried to correct it by requiring weekly statistical reports, by shifting the assignments of certain staff members, and, as a last resort, by firing them or, sometimes, having them transferred to another government office. If such neglect infected otherwise loyal workers who knew that my political fate and their jobs depended on how well my mail was answered, it is even truer for anonymous workers, shielded from public gaze in a giant bureaucracy, to be delinquent in their duties.

Leisure

MY WIFE AND I went out little in the evening, probably not more than once a week. Sometimes we played our favorite records—Beethoven being my chief enthusiasm; Mozart, Emily's—or we read together, and then went early to bed. At waking intervals during the night I often did more reading. Generally I would be able to read two books a week, the total number being divided almost equally between those on contemporary problems and those that were eternal. One winter I read all the speeches of Burke, and during another, Tocqueville and Aristotle.

There were two liberal salons in Washington to which we had the good fortune to be often invited. One was that of Mrs. Gifford Pinchot, the widow of my old boss the reform governor of Pennsylvania. She was a nominal Republican, but Gifford had been strong for the conservation of natural resources, public power, and protective legislation for women and children. With orange-dyed hair, she made a striking figure among her Renaissance furnishings.

The other salon was that of Mrs. J. Borden ("Daisy") Harriman, a New York blue blood and social leader who had been a member of Wilson's Commission on Federal Industrial Relations, had helped to form the Women's National Democratic Club, and had been Roosevelt's minister to Norway during the time of the Nazi invasion, when she had behaved magnificently. It was Mrs. Harriman's custom to invite twelve to fifteen persons each Saturday and to start general discussion upon some topic that she would draw from a leading guest. There would be differing points of view, but good humor and decent manners throughout. She represented the aristocracy at its best, and nearly everyone loved her. We saw her grow weaker with the years, until she died, in 1967, at well over the age of ninety.

Trips Home

I RETURNED to Illinois at least two weekends a month, spending one in and around Chicago and the other downstate. I would also go out during the week. In the fall, after Congress had adjourned, I usually spent six weeks back home. In the even-numbered years, when elections were held, I campaigned vigorously for Democratic candidates, visiting and speaking in at least two-thirds of the 102 counties and covering two or three counties a day. In the odd-numbered years, I visited about the same number of counties, but included the small and strongly Republican ones, which I had usually not visited the year before. In all, I never spent fewer than 100 days a year in Illinois, while in Presidential-election years and in those when I ran myself, I was there for at least 130 to 140 days.

Emily was with me for a full month in the fall, for occasional trips during the year, and joined me in campaigning for our county and state candidates. In Presidential years, we both did our best for the national ticket. It would have been only human if Emily had resented the way I had replaced her in the political arena, which she had filled so well. But she never showed a trace of any such feeling and devoted her full energies to promoting my career. Being a congresswoman, she admitted, was the most exciting chapter in her life, but she had always thought of herself as a political "sport." She had risen to an opportunity and found her stage experience helpful in campaigning, but she kept an inflated respect for my qualifications, which she claimed gave me a political background that she lacked. So, for years, like most wives, she did our housework, helped in emergencies, and scattered her efforts over worthy causes. Gradually she concentrated on her real love, writing. Her first book, *Appleseed Farm,* was a story for juveniles that came out as I launched my race for the Senate and whose sales have outlasted my political career.

I came to know every nook and cranny of my state and to love all of it. Although mistakenly regarded sometimes as a monotonous prairie, Illinois is a state of extraordinary variety. My own tempestuous city, Chicago, with its variegated population and burgeoning suburbs, is infinitely fascinating; as are the conservative northern and middle sections, with their good, black earth, abundant corn, soybeans, and excessive crops of Republicans. But in this same north country, at Cedarville, Jane Addams was born and returned home to be buried. Nearly every year I journeyed there to lay flowers on her simple Quaker grave and to pause for a few minutes of prayer and meditation. One spring I took with me a dear friend, Spike McAdams, who was a Chicago politician. After I had laid my handful of flowers on the grave and thought of specific acts of kindness she had done, I looked around for my companion. At first I could not see him; then there he was, kneeling by the stone. Getting up with misty eyes, he remarked, "Paul, we've been in the presence of eternity."

The other Illinois, south of Springfield, is mostly inhabited by folk from Kentucky, Tennessee, and Virginia—proud, friendly, and far more hospitable to Democrats. Since the party's main strength was in the cities and the south, I took pains to visit Rockford, a machine-tool city full of Swedes; the tri-cities of Rock Island, Moline, and East Moline, which formed the farm-implement capital of the world; Peoria, the home of the bulldozer and of bourbon whiskey and Colonel Robert G. Ingersoll; Decatur, a civilized city with an excellent newspaper; the many-sided Lincoln city of Springfield; and the great industrial complex just opposite Saint Louis which, with Chicago, was the Democratic stronghold of the state.

And I loved the gently flowing rivers: the mighty Mississippi, which formed the state's western limits; the Ohio, on the south; and the Wabash, which formed half of the eastern boundary with Indiana. The internal rivers flowed even more gently. The Rock, or Sinnissippi, is in the extreme northwest, and on its high cliffs, at Oregon, Emily's father had founded an artists' colony. In the early 1840's, Margaret Fuller had spent a summer there, and she wrote in her *Summer on the Lakes* about Eagles Nest Bluff: "The latter I visited one glorious morning; it was that of the Fourth of July and certainly I think I had never felt so happy that I was born in America. Woe to all country folk that never saw this spot, never swept an enraptured gaze over the prospect that stretched beneath. I do believe Rome and Florence are suburbs compared to this capital of nature's grace." Here, on this very bluff, with his own labor and at his own expense, Lorado Taft had constructed his simple and heroic fifty-foot statue of Black Hawk, with folded arms, bidding a dignified farewell to his country.

It was the state's central river, which bore the name of Illinois, that the explorers La Salle and Tonty had paddled down on their way to the Mississippi and the Gulf. In the southern part of the state is the Kaskaskia. In 1779, George Rogers Clark wended his way up this river from the Mississippi to capture by surprise the British fort at Vincennes, and by so doing enabled the new republic to acquire the Northwest Territory. True are the words of our little-sung state song: "Not without thy wondrous story, / Can be told the Nation's glory."

I especially enjoyed the farming counties around the bend of the lower Illinois River: Pike, whence came such dissimilar characters as Lincoln's secretaries and biographers John G. Nicolay and John Hay and, a half century later, Floyd Dell, of the *Masses;* and Scott, to which the rain-soaked twenty-year-old Stephen A. Douglas came in 1833, with a silver half-dollar in his pocket, to seek his fortune. Within the space of only fourteen years, he became, successively, state's attorney, state legislator, supervisor of public lands, Illinois Supreme Court justice, congressman, and, finally, United States senator. This was not only Douglas country, but also, and more important, Lincoln country, for Abe had flowered in little New Salem, in nearby Menard County, had successfully defended Duff Armstrong against a murder charge at Beardstown, had ridden the circuit and the prairie here, and had followed Douglas about in the great senatorial campaign of 1858, rising to true heights in the closing debates at Galesburg and Quincy and down the river at Alton. It was Edgar Lee Masters country, too, for his *Spoon River Anthology* was the inside story of many lives in Menard and in Fulton County, just across the Illinois River. Carl Sandburg grew up in this area, as did Vachel Lindsay. And my friend and older colleague in the Senate, Scott W. Lucas, the son of a tenant farmer, came from this region.

When I was in these counties, I seemed to be back in an older, simpler, and more heroic America. I would always have Sandburg's *Lincoln* or Lindsay's poetry or *Spoon River Anthology* in my bag, and nearly every year I would spend a night at New Salem with a Lincoln book and would walk for an hour on the hilltop where the rawboned prairie boy had passed through his prologue to glory. Usually I spent another half hour walking through the neighboring hillside cemetery at Petersburg where the embittered Masters was finally brought home to rest and where the remains of Lincoln's love, Ann Rutledge, are buried under Masters' lines:

> *I am Anne Rutledge who sleep beneath these weeds,*
> *Beloved in life of Abraham Lincoln,*
> *Wedded to him, not through union, but through separation.*
> *Bloom forever, O Republic*
> *From the dust of my bosom.*

I had a love affair with my state. I loved its people. And for eighteen years, until 1966, I was told that they rather liked me. The habitués of the diplomatic set in Washington used to belittle these trips back home as mere "fence-mending" and unworthy of the time and attention of a serious statesman. But to me they were one of the most interesting and important parts of my job.

Certainly the trips were essential for political survival. While voters occasionally asked why I was not in Washington tending to business, they would have objected even more strenuously had I not returned. They would have charged that I had forgotten the home folks and had become too "stuck-up" to visit with them. And they would have been believed.

Voters want to see their representative in the round, and not merely on television. They want to hear him talk, and not merely read what he said in the newspapers. They want to see if his gaze is still straightforward or whether, as a result of the compromises of political life, it has become shifty and uncertain. Even if not teetotalers themselves, they want to scrutinize his face to see if there are signs of excessive drinking or whether the flabbiness of his belly betrays a softness of life. Most of all, they want to know if he will talk sense to them, and not try to put on airs in a "high-falutin'" manner. All in all, they like to give him a close examination to see if he has any symptoms of Potomac fever, or of swelling without growing.

Many a Senator has found too late that his support at home has shrunk because he has neglected home visits. Robert M. ("Young Bob") La Follette, Jr., was one of the best of the modern Senators, but he was ultimately undone from this very cause, when in 1946 Joseph R. McCarthy defeated him in the Republican primary by only 5,400 votes. The colorful Henry F. Ashurst, of Arizona, became so enamored of Washington life and so overconfident about his prestige that he allowed his support to wither away from inattention. A well-established senator from a one-party state in the South may indeed coast along on the inertia of the voters, but this is fatal for a senator from a vigorous two-party state in the North and West. This is particularly true if he is a Democrat, because he is already compelled to swim upstream against the swift and powerful current of newspaper and financial influence.

But visits home fulfill a deeper purpose than mere political survival. They are the vital part of a continuing political dialogue between constituents and representatives that operates to the advantage of both. Each party to this dialogue learns from the other. I certainly learned a lot. Illinois history not only came alive, but so, too, did the problems the people faced. I saw at first hand the way people in southern Illinois were suffering from the closing down of the coal mines and the consolidation of small farms. As each shopping center rose, I noticed the following year that old friends who had previously run small, independent groceries or drugstores were no longer around, and no one could quite tell where they had gone. Occasionally, in the new centers, as I went about shaking hands and talking, I saw the familiar faces of some who had joined the trek from downstate or from city to suburb and heard how they were faring. I saw the offices of the consumer-finance companies multiply around traffic intersections in Chicago, and from the hard-toiling young lawyers in the legal-aid bureaus I learned how trying was the lot of the poor who got into debt and of how usurers had not changed through the ages. In the meager lives of old folks, I saw at first hand the loneliness of old age and the inadequacy of old-age security and assistance. Negroes occasionally told me of why they had come north from the deep South and what their hopes and frustrations were in their new homes. In the suburbs, as I met with my fellow Democrats they occasionally dropped a sentence that showed they had come out from the city not only to get more space for their children, but also to take refuge from the black tides that were engulfing their old neighborhoods.

In trade-union halls and offices, organizers and members sometimes told me of how well collective bargaining was working and at other times of how employers could defeat the purposes of the labor laws by interminable delays and subtle pressures. At the luncheons of the Rotary, Kiwanis, and Lions clubs, I met the representatives of the sturdy American middle class, with their emphasis upon the praiseworthy qualities of hard work, self-help, and individual initiative. These had been the dominant qualities of the small-town America in which I had grown up. They were still strong, and, while not all of life, were a necessary ingredient. Most of the members of Rotary and Kiwanis were uneasily aware of the criticisms that had been made of them decades before by Sinclair Lewis and H. L. Mencken. They were unfailingly courteous to their strange guest and anxious to let him know of their good works. The Lions were younger and more robust, and had a sprinkling of Democrats. We got on well together, without much reserve on either side.

Occasionally I was invited to an American Legion post or to one of the Veterans of Foreign Wars. In the 1930's, the leaders of the Illinois Legion had branded me, along with Clarence Darrow and Jane Addams, as one of the "ten most dangerous citizens of Illinois," and had wanted to drive me from the state. This fact was not forgotten, but it was beginning to be ignored. A number of the more ostentatious leaders of the Legion had never served outside the States during World War I and had perhaps developed a high degree of vocal patriotism to compensate for this lack. They kept a grudging silence when they finally saw, though I tried to conceal it, that my left arm hung limply at my side. The VFW members, like the Lions, were more outgoing and received me as one of their own.

Many of my Congressional bills originated from these contacts with actual life, rather than being derived secondhand from books and reports, as I tried to follow up on what I thought I had seen. The chief stimulus from which I learned was the turbulent flow of my experiences.

These exchanges between constituents and senator were not wholly one-sided. I found that thoughtful voters were far more numerous than cynics alleged. Most people wanted a straightforward discussion of such domestic issues as unemployment, housing, the cost of living, government expenditures and taxation, and how federal, state, and local governments could co-operate better, as well as such foreign-policy issues as tariffs, economic and military aid, and our stake in Europe, Latin America, and Asia.

I tried to be specific in my discussions and to deal with current issues. Emily, in her speeches to women's groups, was even more effective.

Perhaps the two of us helped raise the level of public discussion and understanding in the state. Possibly we may have made people feel like participants in the process of public decision, rather than passive witnesses of a political juggernaut which rolled by and over them.

I tried to keep up my connections in Illinois with both the Society of Friends and the Unitarians. The former I would say were good for my soul; the latter, for my mind. While I could not accept pacifism as a national policy and believed in armed resistance as the best deterrent to the aggression of a police state, I was humbled as I saw many of my fellow Quakers quietly adopt for themselves the commandment "Thou shalt not kill" and seek, instead, through deeds of kindness the reconciliation of people. I felt that society was less brutal because of this small remnant and less idolatrous because of them and the rationalism of the Unitarians. But as I sat silently in our little Quaker meeting, I could never recover that sense of exalted oneness with the Eternal Goodness that for a decade long ago I had thought was mine. The cares of the world or the realities of life had closed that avenue for me, perhaps forever. It was gone, and I could not recover it. I tried to console myself with the lines from the old evangelical hymn "Tasks in hours of insight willed / may be in hours of gloom fulfilled," and with the thought that it was practically impossible to be both a mystic and a practicing politician in a frostbitten world.

At the same time I also became much more appreciative of the solid virtues of the Catholic church and of the sense of historic communion it gives to its members. My acquaintanceship with many priests deepened. Some of the sisters at Rosary College took an especially protective interest in me, and I found that in the difficult moments of my political life they were actually praying for both my spiritual welfare and my temporal victory. I never met Sister Thomas Aquinas, who was the most concerned friend, but in some strange way I was constantly aware of her intercession, and it gave me reassurance that I should be thought worthy of her care.

Weekends I did not spend in Illinois were devoted to gardening, reading, swimming, and visiting. Since the Senate was shut down for ten days around Lincoln's birthday to permit the Republicans to hold their annual dinners back home, when they attacked the Democrats and all their works, I devoted this time to the lecture circuit. It kept me solvent, and in the process I became acquainted with all sections of the country and nearly every state. In the years when I was up for election, however, I had no time for lectures. Instead, I toured Illinois, gently suggesting that Lincoln was spiritually a Democrat, since he drew his inspiration from Thomas Jefferson, and that if he were alive, he would be a dues-paying, card-carrying member of my party.

Vacations

EMILY AND I spent one month annually away from both Washington and Illinois. In the 1950's we went to warmer climates within our own country or in Europe or the Middle East. In the 1960's we went to Latin America. In a sense, these were busman's holidays, for, in addition to the change of scene, we sought firsthand information on international relations and the problems of other countries. I also found time for study and writing. However useful these tours were to me as a senator, they were chiefly vacations, for which I never charged the government. Only when I was on official business and only for the time actually spent on such business was I reimbursed or did I use counterpart funds. There has, of course, been abuse in this matter, which has led to the suggestion that all Congressional travel at government expense should be banned. This would be a great mistake. With over $72 billion being spent on defense, and with the whole question of war and peace and, indeed, national survival depending on foreign relations, it is vital that legislators know at first hand about the people and countries with whom we deal. Senator William E. Borah, who for years, as head of the Foreign Relations Committee, helped make our foreign policy, was wrong to boast that he had never left the shores of the United States. Perhaps he would have been less isolationist had he known more of other nations.

On our European trips, I specialized in the problems of reciprocal trade and the Common Market—with which I had to deal on the Finance Committee. Emily looked into the work of our public-information libraries, which were unjustly attacked both at home and abroad. In Latin America we involved ourselves in studying the Alliance for Progress and the work of the Peace Corps, and in noting the contrast between the abject poverty of the masses and the great wealth and luxury of the few. We also observed the power of the military. Mexico and Puerto Rico were making demonstrable progress, although terrible poverty remained. Throughout Central America we saw the conflict between the need to relieve poverty and the stubborn resistance of the landlords.

Our personal pleasure was in plunging back through the centuries to the outcroppings of the mysterious civilizations of the Mayans, Aztecs, and Toltecs, as seen in Mexico, Guatemala, and elsewhere. Despite our travels and our visits to the museums of Mexico City and Mérida, and to those in Washington, we knew that we had only turned a page in the pre-Colombian history of the Americas.

Legislation and Staff

WHEN did I have time to do that for which legislators are sent to Washington, namely, to legislate? I had to fight to find it. In the afternoons there was a continuous struggle to choose between legislation coming up on the Senate floor and the visitors, telephone calls, and ever-present letters waiting in the office. There was always the danger that the immediate was crowding out the ultimate, that I was being dominated by the constituents who wanted me to be present on the floor all the time and yet wanted their letters and telegrams answered at once and expected me to receive them personally and show them around the Capitol if they came to Washington. Committee meetings were invaluable, for it is in committees that the major course and shape of legislation is planned. For this work, my outside reading helped; I also invited newspapermen and experts for lunch at least once a fortnight.

Most of all I was helped by my able and devoted staff. For twelve years I had the help of a brilliant saint, Frank McCulloch, as my administrative assistant. Never in our long association did I know him to do a wrong thing or say anything either untruthful or unkind. Having a fine legal mind, he could master the essentials of any proposal and prepare a thorough position paper. With it all, he had extraordinary patience, quiet industry, and devotion to the public interest, topped by a frosting of wry Scottish humor.

Besides McCulloch, I had an assistant to watch legislation, collect information, and help with speeches. Originally, I brought Robert A. Wallace from Chicago for this. A graduate student in political science at the university, he had been active in my 1948 campaign. He quickly and ably took up the work, and continued it until 1955, when he left to become staff director of the Banking and Currency Committee. From there he went with John F. Kennedy when the latter started to spread his wings toward the Presidency. In Kennedy's administration, Wallace became an assistant secretary of the Treasury, where he gave valuable service. He is now vice-chairman of a big Chicago bank. For more than twenty years, we have been warm friends.

To succeed Wallace as legislative assistant, I was fortunate in getting Howard Shuman, a young Illinoisan who was teaching at the University of Illinois. After graduating from that university, he had gone to Oxford for three years. There he had made a great success, achieving the unique honor of being the first American elected president of the Oxford Union. Having read about his debating exploits in the Manchester *Guardian*, I had been delighted in 1954 to find him at the University of Illinois and, as a Democratic precinct committeeman, active in my campaign. When I later persuaded Kennedy to appoint Frank McCulloch chairman of the National Labor Relations Board, Shuman moved up to his post as my administrative assistant. In his way, Shuman was as remarkable as McCulloch. He could turn out a large quantity of accurate work in short order. He was always on the side of the angels, despising sham and pretense. For many years he was my strong right arm, and he is now administrative assistant to my friend Senator William Proxmire, of Wisconsin.

When Shuman moved up, I got Kenneth Gray, from the University of Chicago, to replace him. Having a judicious temperament and a sharp eye for detail, Ken proved a good shepherd to my legislative interests and particularly showed his mettle in the long struggle to save the Dunes. In 1964 I loaned him to Hubert Humphrey to act as transport quartermaster on his plane trips around the country. I have never seen anyone develop more rapidly than Ken did under those responsibilities. He came back with a polished *savoir-faire* and skill in conciliating diverse views. Later he became a confidential assistant to Vice President Humphrey, and after working for Senator Joseph Tydings, returned to Humphrey as his administrative assistant.

Meanwhile, I needed a third man, to deal with relationships with local governments and corporations. In 1955 Harold Brown, from southern Illinois, filled this role, doing much to help get the Area Redevelopment Act passed. Taking his place came Kyran McGrath, who in turn was succeeded by Martin Gleason, a former Peace Corps volunteer. These men took the main brunt of the requests of local governments for water and sewer assistance, educational grants, and projects under the Area Redevelopment Act. They also handled the difficulties Illinois corporations had with departments of the federal government. We followed a policy of promoting competitive bidding on contracts and of awards for merit. When an Illinois firm was not particularly responsible or was a high bidder, we did not intervene. But when they were at once the low bidder and had a good reputation, we did our best to see that they got the contract. We saved much money for the taxpayers by this method and brought many jobs to Illinois.

Relations with Business

THE REACTION of business to this was interesting. Most industrialists heartily disliked me for my support of labor and consumer legislation. Furthermore, they were continually sprayed by propaganda from the extreme right wing. Only a few turned to me in despair when all seemed lost. In general, they were pleased at the way they were treated by me, and toward the end of my service came in greater numbers and with

friendlier feelings. The two crowning achievements in this direction occurred in 1965 and 1966.

In the former year Governor Otto Kerner and I succeeded in persuading Jones and Laughlin to build a new steel mill, at the cost of a half-
billion dollars, at the upper bend of the Illinois River. This was constructed at tiny Hennepin, in Putnam County, where one of the few
downstate Quaker meetings exists, having survived for over a century and
a quarter. In the days before the Civil War this group of farmers was a
highly cultivated nucleus and the backbone of the state's antislavery
movement. Among them was Benjamin Lundy, the editor of the *Genius
of Universal Emancipation* and the first employer of William Lloyd Garrison. I was active in getting satisfactory housing and water and sewer
facilities for the new town springing up in the wake of the mill, and this
was at the time when the president of the company, Admiral Ben Moreell,
who was also head of Americans for Conservative Action, was trying to
defeat me for what he called my "excessive" action to improve the lot of
the poor and the weak.

The second victory came when Kerner and I succeeded in getting the
Atomic Energy Commission to locate a half-billion-dollar nuclear accelerator at Weston, in the western part of Du Page County. It was a hard
battle because nearly every state wanted this accelerator. Finally, the
competition narrowed to six sites. We had some heartbreaking obstacles,
but we argued the merits of our location with both the commission and
President Lyndon B. Johnson. The happy verdict came right after the
1966 election, when I was retired to private life.

So far as I can tell, I did not reap direct political advantage from any
of my help to industry. The firms that disliked me continued to do so,
although perhaps less acridly. One Rock Island company, for which I had
helped to secure a big contract, later sent a policeman to arrest me when I
inadvertently let my station wagon trespass fifteen feet onto their property. Two firms to whom I had been especially helpful were always vigorous in trying to defeat me. Though the accelerator in Du Page County
will ultimately be of great benefit to the people who live in the surrounding towns, they voted three to one against me in 1966. Of course, an
elected official should try to be helpful and accept in good grace whatever
happens.

Sometimes, as counterbalance, one finds a degree of gratitude in the
young that is touching. I experienced this with a boy, Lawrence Loren-
sen, whom I had put through college by means of a patronage job in
Washington. He always came to see me with his family when I was near
his city. Although I did nothing more for him, he continued to work for
my interests, and I am always touched when I think of him braving the
political tides that rushed in upon us in 1966. He is now both a teacher
and a member of the city council of his city.

I felt some relief that the choice of the nuclear site came after, and not before, my final defeat. I could rejoice at the benefits I had helped to bring to the state without any thought of its effect upon my own fortunes. I was also pleased to see it accepted by many who would otherwise have rejected it because of what it might have done for me. Some now came forward to claim to be the fathers of the success.

Other Staff Members

TO RETURN to my staff, for briefer periods of time I had the services of two amazingly brilliant youngsters. One was an angular and reticent young Nebraskan, Theodore C. Sorensen, who wrote like a clearheaded angel and whom I later recommended to John Kennedy for the job of legislative assistant, thus forming a partnership that led to glory for both.

The other was Philip M. Stern, a grandson of Julius Rosenwald, who had built up Sears, Roebuck on the basis of an honest catalogue and excellent goods. Phil worked for me as a research assistant from 1950 to 1952. He had one of the quickest minds and most trenchant pens I have ever known, and, although he was destined to inherit a fortune, he put his great talents at the service of the underdogs of society. Phil left me to join the speech writers in the first Stevenson campaign. He has since had a brilliant and useful career. For some years he and Clayton Fritchey edited the uniquely satirical publications of the Democratic National Committee, and then the Arlington *Sun.* Finally, he settled down as an independent author and grubstaker of good but impoverished causes. His book on tax loopholes, *The Great Treasury Raid,* was our best reinforcement in the later battle for tax reform. With his wife he brought out one of the first picture books about poverty. More recently, he has written a scholarly history, *The Oppenheimer Case,* which is a partial rehabilitation of that gifted scientist's reputation.

My son John was often my effective and unpaid counselor. His advice was almost invariably sound, idealistic, and wise. On his return to the United States from Oxford, he became law clerk for a year to Supreme Court Justice Harold H. Burton. Later, he entered the law firm of Covington and Burling as a clerk, and is now a partner. For three and a half years he served under Kennedy and then Johnson as the assistant attorney general in charge of the Justice Department's Civil Division, where he ran one of the largest law offices in the nation with what his colleagues have told me was extraordinary efficiency. He resigned from that job in the summer of 1966 to help manage my last campaign, although he disagreed with my position on Vietnam. All through those trying weeks he was a tower of strength.

I always searched for the help of experts both in and out of government who had a public interest. One of these was Randolph Paul, formerly the general counsel of the Treasury and then the highest-paid private tax lawyer in the country. He earned enormous fees helping wealthy clients to take full advantage of every loophole in the tax laws and also devoted a large share of his spare time to instructing legislators on how best to close them. He died with his boots on, falling as he pleaded with the Joint Economic Committee to introduce a greater degree of justice in the tax system.

My office also had the unpaid help of three other experts: Mel Van Scoyoc, in the field of gas and electric rates, and Joseph L. Rauh, Jr., and Paul Sifton, in civil rights and civil liberties. Rauh, gifted with great legal acumen, is a most effective lawyer and citizen. Sifton, the cousin of the prominent and brilliant Canadian liberal Clifford Sifton, had an amazing ability to translate a complicated situation into pithy prose. I believe Paul Sifton was the real author of the phrase about old folks being "too old to work and too young to die," as well as many others that he put into the mouths of more famous persons. During the perennial battles on Rule XXII (the use of cloture) and on civil rights, Rauh and Sifton would daily plan strategy with us in my offices and then, with Clarence Mitchell, of the NAACP, sit high in a corner of the gallery watching the debate. Toward evening, like football coaches, they would hold a skull session in my office over what the day had brought forth.

There were other experts, whom we gradually learned to know and trust, who wanted to help and who did so both anonymously and unselfishly.

It was soon said that I had the best staff of aides and advisers on Capitol Hill. Nor was this true merely of my technical staff. Along with the administrative and legislative assistants, an important person on one's staff is one's personal secretary. Here I was amazingly lucky. Jeanette Raymond served splendidly for two years before she married William Foster and went off with him to the University of Wisconsin. Then came Jane Carey, later to be Jane Enger, who for sixteen years filled this position for me with peerless grace and efficiency. Unfailingly serene, she turned out huge amounts of work smoothly, and in the process made everyone happy. Without Jane, I would have estranged many more persons than I did.

None of my staff observed civil-service hours, but continued until I left at night and frequently far beyond. Most of the women on the staff were completely devoted, and it was also true that the abilities of many far exceeded those required by the jobs available. Daisy Warren broke all Capitol Hill records one day when she turned out 123 letters, while Patty Auchincloss produced peerless answers to the hardest correspondence. Perhaps with masculine obtuseness I did not give them sufficient appreciation.

The devotion of my staff involved me at times in peculiar difficulties. In the crucial summer of 1954, when my continuance in the Senate seemed more than doubtful, I found that a large group was coming back every night to answer the heavy mail and to get out the franked letters on several highly controversial matters pending in the Senate. While I was touched by their devotion, I knew that if they kept it up, some would fall ill from exhaustion. They were already suffering from low pay and too much work, caused by the scantiness of the office allowances in relation to the big volume of work that poured in upon me as a liberal senator from one of the largest states. Along with Humphrey, I had consequently earned the reputation of paying the lowest salaries in the Senate, far lower than our Southern colleagues, who had ample funds, both senatorial and committee-based, to handle a much smaller volume of mail. I was sensitive to this, but the country was disturbed again at that time over the Communist threat, and the mail, pro and con, was piling up. Somehow we had to answer it.

My staff, to meet this added strain, had voluntarily lengthened their work span by three or four hours. I tried to dissuade them, but this had no effect. Finally, I posted a notice saying that work must stop at ten o'clock in the evening, and that those who worked beyond that would be escorted out of the building by the Senate police. The staff took this as a joke and kept on working.

The next night I came back at 10:15, and the staff was still there. Picking up the telephone, I foolishly called the Senate security force and asked for their help. They were at the door in five minutes. Seizing each frightened girl by the elbow, they rapidly hurried the staff out of the building, leaving me somewhat ruefully behind. Since nothing on Capitol Hill can escape the notice of the press, the papers on the following afternoon had a somewhat satirical account. No one would believe that government employees, particularly senatorial, would voluntarily work overtime. So various other explanations were offered. By the next day, it was hinted that the police had come to quell a revolt, and some reporters offered more derogatory explanations. My heavy-handed efforts to protect my devoted staff had redounded to their further injury. They nevertheless forgave me, and when I went out to do battle in Illinois, they resumed their long evenings of toil.

Another instance of staff devotion, but of a different nature, involved a genteel widow whom Frank McCulloch had hired as a receptionist. On her first morning, Walter Reuther came to the office just before he was to testify before a Senate committee, and asked to see me. The flustered receptionist, not knowing who he was, turned him away, saying that I was telephoning and could not be disturbed. Reuther smiled, left his card, and told her where he was going. A couple of minutes afterward, Frank came into the office and asked what had happened on her first morning.

"Nothing," said she, "except that a man named Reuther tried to see Mr. Douglas. But," she added triumphantly, "I got rid of him by telling him that Mr. Douglas was telephoning and was too busy to see him." The usually calm Frank blanched a little and told her who Reuther was and that he was one of my best personal and political friends. She let out a terrified shriek and rushed out of the office and up the stairs to the hearing room. Reuther was about to take the stand when she seized him and gasped out that she was going to lose her job unless he followed her and came back to meet me. Reuther smiled, patted her shoulder, and said that she had nothing to fear. Asking to be excused, he walked briskly back to my office and told me what was on his mind. Then he shook hands and said as he left, "Paul, please don't scold her. She was trying to protect you." The novice, who, with her upper-class background, had previously regarded all labor leaders as denizens of the deep, looked at the departing Reuther and remarked in an awe-struck tone, "He is the most perfect gentleman I have ever seen." That quarter of an hour made a new woman out of her.

This episode was completely typical of Walter Reuther. Eloquent, combative, and shrewd, he was also forgiving. In 1937 he had been beaten nearly to death by thugs whom Harry Bennett had recruited for Henry Ford. In 1948 he was nearly killed by a shotgun blast fired by a hired killer at close range. But in the late '40's and early '50's, no one could have been more gentlemanly than he in dealing with the representatives of the Ford Motor Company. His equal will not be seen for a long time.

Beginning in the late 1950's, I took into my office selected college students as apprentices in politics. I paid most of them $90 a month for twenty hours of routine work a week. In the remainder of their time they were supposed to attend committee meetings, listen to important debates, and prepare a research paper. Those who were hard up were given an extra allowance. The Republican newspapers at home sometimes criticized me for having so many persons on my payroll, and I was never quite successful in explaining to them that a considerable number were really on scholarships. This was praised when practiced by my Republican colleagues but was somehow treated in my case as political padding of the payroll.

From the first, I had one or more Negroes on my staff; in fact, I was the first on Capitol Hill to have any. Some of these did splendidly, but one was a catastrophe who went wrong in every way, including criminal assaults.

My Illinois staff, with offices in the Federal Building in Chicago, was headed by Douglas Anderson, a former Methodist minister who had turned labor organizer. Had he been a crook, he could have become rich at the expense of my reputation; but, scrupulously honest and humane, he served with great integrity for all of our eighteen years together. And he kept the lines of friendly communication open with all groups, political and nonpolitical. To help him, I had the assistance of Marguerite Ingram, who became especially skilled in immigration and welfare cases, and the efficient services of Ed Kelly and his successor, Frank Burkey, who specialized in veterans' affairs and in helping me make the appointments to West Point, Annapolis, and the Air Force Academy. Since most "service cases" involved dealing with the local and regional offices of the federal agencies, such as immigration, welfare, and Social Security, I tried to decentralize their handling as much as possible and to have the Chicago office carry the brunt of the load. I was increasingly successful in doing this, although we did go through the difficulties that always occur between headquarters and field staff.

In all, during my eighteen years, 200 people worked with me. I would like to itemize the special gifts and kindnesses of each, but it would take another book to do so. Some have subsequently won public recognition on their own, and perhaps others will in time. But all have my abiding thanks for loyalty, hard work, and good fellowship. Certainly the friendships formed and kept with this alumni association have been some of the most pleasant of my later years.

Postmasters

IN HIS SPARE TIME, Anderson carried out a first sifting of candidates for political appointment. These were mostly for the job of postmaster. One of the most important jobs of Congressmen and Senators whose party was in power was to recommend to the Post Office Department candidates for the various postmasterships and rural carriers, of which there were in Illinois well over a thousand of the first and many hundreds of the latter. There was keen competition for these well-paid posts, and there were often many applicants.

The department conducted an examination based largely on character and experience and graded the applicants accordingly. The postmaster was supposed to be selected from among the top three. It was the task of the county committees to see that properly qualified party members took the examination. In each district, if the Congressman was of the same political party as the President, he recommended one of the top three for appointment, and it was made unless some grave fault of character was discovered. If the Congressman was not of the President's party, the Senator of that party, if there was one, had the right to recommend. Sometimes there would be no one from the dominant party among the top three candidates. In this case, the Congressman or Senator could ask for a second set of examinations. He would then urge the county committee to put up some properly qualified candidates. Veterans automatically had a five-point credit, and ten points if they had been wounded in combat. In fact, if a wounded veteran was among the first three, he automatically went to the head of the list.

As a result of all this curious jockeying and combination of politics and civil service, those successful were nearly always of the dominant national party. That is the way the Republicans conducted affairs during the eight years Eisenhower was President, and the Democrats followed the same course under Truman, Kennedy, and Johnson. Since the vast majority of the downstate Illinois Congressmen were Republicans, I was in charge of most of the post-office appointments in 1951 and 1952 and again from 1961 to 1966.

I placed most of the responsibility upon the county chairmen, urging them to set up patronage committees representing the different sections and factions of the counties. They were told that those selected should have given real service to the party and that I would not recognize any interparty deals. No one was to pay for his job.

Anderson made an independent check to see if those recommended conformed to our standards and then passed on his recommendations to me. For the more important posts, we took the initiative in seeking out possibilities, always trying to get the assent of the local and, if necessary, the state political leaders.

Purists who believe that all appointments should be completely divorced from politics and made under a supposedly impartial civil service will undoubtedly criticize these arrangements. I believe that the vast majority of appointments in federal employment should be made under civil service, but not all. Civil-service politics can be as bad as or worse than political politics. Furthermore, in order to protect government employees from political discrimination, such a high degree of job security has been built around them that it is almost impossible to discharge anyone for inefficiency except in the grossest of cases. All too often, civil-service workers become routineers whose security lessens both their efforts and their desire to be of service.

The Postal Act of 1970 aims to take politics out of the service. It remains to be seen if it does or if Presidential politics merely replaces Congressional.

The injection of fresh blood into government employment is often healthy. I found that most of the political appointees felt the necessity of justifying their appointments and worked hard to win public favor. They also had an uneasy fear that having been appointed by political means, they might perish by the same means.

Anderson and I periodically assembled each group of prospective postmasters and rural carriers to instruct them in what was expected. Under no conditions were they ever to pay anybody for getting their appointment, and if we ever found that they had, the chairman or precinct committeeman who had received the money would be shut off from all future patronage. If a postal employee was guilty, we would try to have him dropped.

This had a good effect. In one case, after we became convinced that the county chairman had been personally shaking down applicants, we refused to accept any further recommendations from him, and he was later deposed from his office, though only after he had been successful in preventing Emily and me from speaking in his county and had helped to pile up a big majority against me in 1966.

Another requirement we made was that the men recommended must be of good character and ability. By checking the actual records of those recommended, we weeded out a number who clearly did not meet this standard. In each of these cases, the county chairman was told that he should submit a second name. This second man was invariably better than the first.

We also told the aspirants that our first desire was for them to be obliging, honest, and efficient postmasters and that there was to be no discrimination in the conduct of their office. Because they would become government employees, they would not cease to be citizens. The Hatch Act, it was true, forbade them to be party workers, and they should not be. We pointed out, however, that it was equally important for them to realize that they were legally permitted to attend political meetings and to contribute voluntarily to the party and to its campaigns. Had it not been for the party, we told them, they could never have been appointed. The opposing party had the advantage of being financed by the big corporations and by most men of wealth. It was therefore right for them to help the party that had done so much for them. We emphasized that other members of their families could be party workers, and that in our judgment they should be. There had been a tendency among postmasters, once appointed, to hide behind the Hatch Act and refuse to contribute to the party. This I wanted to correct.

But I insisted that inside the post offices nonpartisanship should prevail. During the Eisenhower administration, postal inspectors had been turned loose on Democratic postmasters, and many were discharged for the most trivial reasons, such as not putting up all of the criminal "wanted" notices in the lobbies of the post offices. In those cases where the injustices had been most striking, as in one southern Illinois district, I refused to permit the new appointees to be confirmed; they were given "acting" appointments. When Kennedy became President, I had the original postmasters reappointed and ultimately confirmed. Though I was urged to give the Republicans a dose of their own medicine, I refused. As long as the Republican postmasters appointed under Eisenhower were giving decent service and were not guilty of gross improprieties, I protected them.

Civil-service advocates generally do not realize the importance of political parties, and because they are usually members of the middle and upper economic classes, look with especial disfavor upon the Democrats. If they can cut away a taproot of that party's strength in the name of civic virtue, they have the double pleasure of simultaneously serving God and Mammon, always a pleasing combination.

While the Republicans use patronage as much as the Democrats, the latter have an especial need for it. The newspapers of the country, with some honorable exceptions, are overwhelmingly Republican and highly conservative. They are the most effective precinct captains of the Republican party, and they enter the home every morning and evening. The Republican party in the North and the West also has the local power structure—employers, bankers, doctors, lawyers, big merchants, and large farmers—on its side, radiating prestige and strength. It is an advantage to be in their good graces. This creates a great gravitational pull toward the Republican party.

Democrats in the North and West have to spread their doctrines by word of mouth. However, men and women are so constituted that it is exceedingly hard to find voluntary workers who will canvass homes and apartments to retain those who incline in their party's favor and to make converts among the neutrals. Not many will at present come forward to carry out this necessary drudgery if all hope of material advantage is removed. Once appointed to federal office, and assured of security by the Hatch and Civil Service acts, they may pass into the ranks of the politically inert. But before they are appointed, the prospect of future preferment will spur them on to greater effort. This helps to keep the two-party system alive in towns and counties that otherwise would become completely monolithic.

In comparing our Democratic postmasters with their colleagues, I found that the Democrats generally were superior in both energy and ability. This was due, I believe, to the fact that most Democrats, because of family, race, politics, and religion, had a much harder job in rising in the business and financial worlds. A larger proportion of the more able turned, therefore, to politics. Politics has, indeed, been the initial channel through which many of the talented among the immigrant stocks have entered business and the professions.

For all these reasons, I felt justified in having only Democrats appointed to those offices over which I had some control. I did not attempt to build up a personal machine, as some Senators have, but based the appointments solidly on merit and the party structure. As long as those endorsed were able and honest, I recommended them. It is a pleasure to record that the Cook County Democratic party under Jack Arvey and Dick Daley never asked me to endorse a man who did not conform to these standards. They were as anxious as I to keep our record clean.

In 1966 I had a hard decision to make on the appointment of a post-master in Chicago. The previous postmaster, Harry Semrow, had resigned to run for president of the County Board on the Democratic ticket. For generations, under Republicans and Democrats alike, this postmaster had been drawn from the German community. I had slightly altered this prec-edent with Semrow. Although he had a German father, he had a Polish mother and was accepted by the Polish-Americans as at least partially theirs. But when I looked over those eligible in 1966, one man stood out over all others. This was Henry W. McGee. He had entered the postal service forty years before as a substitute carrier and clerk. After a decade, he became a regular clerk. Moving up to supervisor, he was put in charge of a substation and handled large sums of money with complete integrity. Next he became personnel officer for the Chicago Post Office, and in 1961 took on similar duties for the Illinois-Michigan region. At each stage, he had received the highest fitness reports, and, a year or two before, had been decorated as the most efficient member of the some 60,000 federal employees in the Chicago region. He was an active member of civic organ-izations, including the Hyde Park co-operative. He had put himself through college after hours and had earned a master's degree in public administration. He helped his wife to get an A.B. and then got his chil-dren through college. His son was an attorney, and his daughter, along with her mother, was a respected teacher in the public schools.

The more I learned about McGee, the more enthusiastic I became about him. If appointed, he would be the first postmaster of a major me-tropolis to be chosen from the ranks. But McGee was a Negro and had been president of the local branch of the NAACP. I had already been criticized for being biased in favor of Negroes. The Germans, Poles, and Italians were all pushing forward strong candidates, and the white back-lash against me was gathering strength in the campaign.

But there seemed to be only one right thing to do. I tried to prepare the ground. Mayor Daley was favorable. So was the Postmaster General, Lawrence F. O'Brien. I met with the fifty ward committeemen in groups of ten and laid my cards on the table. There was a good deal of early grumbling, but McGee's record was such that he was finally accepted with good grace. With all objectors I stressed that, while it would be wrong to discriminate in favor of a man because he was a Negro, it was even worse to discriminate against him because of his color. At the same time I tried to placate all the nationality groups by helping to find advantageous openings for some of the best of their members.

When McGee was finally appointed in midsummer, there was little open criticism, but the underground fires of discontent and racism were growing.

Effect of the Hatch Act

THE MEMBERS of the House and Senate had passed the Hatch Act, in 1939, as a means of getting back at President Franklin D. Roosevelt. He had aroused the conservative Democrats when he had tried to purge Senators Walter George and Millard Tydings and Congressman John O'Connor in the 1938 primaries. The anti-Roosevelt forces charged that federal employees had been induced or coerced to join in this attempt. In retaliation, they passed the act that bars federal employees from participating in any kind of politics.

For this they were applauded by the Republicans, who had made great gains in the 1938 elections, by civil-service advocates, and by the conservative press. But in so doing they unwittingly helped to cut off their own political noses. Formerly, because of their power over not only appointment but also retention, Senators and Congressmen had powerful political machines of their own. At national conventions they were figures in their own right. Now, with no hold over men once they were appointed and with their followers actually barred from taking part in politics, their direct political power was largely a thing of the past. Power in the national conventions and within the states now passed to the governors and mayors, and the receding tide left the members of Congress stranded like crustaceans on the political beach.

Realizing this, and seeing my function in the Senate as far different, I had made no effort to become a political power. But I was amused by venerable Senators at national conventions trying to pretend they were still political power bosses and not recognizing that a new generation had arisen which knew them not. The shade of Franklin Roosevelt must have laughed heartily to see his old enemies so hoist by their own petard.

If a group of devoted precinct workers can be developed who will work voluntarily, for the love of it, further experiment in reducing political influence upon original appointments can be made. I have always felt that those who would abolish all political influence have a moral obligation to devote equal energy to building up such a volunteer force within both political parties. If the professional politicians are merely disarmed, without providing for their more altruistic equivalents, the parties will be compelled to turn to organized pressure groups, which are all too anxious to step into the arena. Republicans will lean increasingly on the well-dressed younger members of the managerial class, while the Democrats will be driven to recruit their precinct committeemen from union activists. This is already happening to a large degree. I am not opposed to this development, for it introduces a greater degree of relevance into political battles. But it also sharpens political conflicts between economic classes and weakens the reconciling influence that the professional politicians can still exercise unseen by the public and scorned by many purists. If that should happen, then the purists may come to mourn the old times.

The Foreign Service and the Military

INSIDE the great federal departments, the self-perpetuating bureaucracy is infinitely more important than individual politicians or either of the political parties. In the State Department, the Foreign Service holds sway. When I went to the Senate, this was dominated by wealthy graduates of Eastern colleges who had gone to the proper preparatory schools and belonged to the proper clubs. If not wealthy, they were attractive to daughters of rich families and therefore frequently married money. Secretaries of State came and had their little hour and went. The Foreign Service stayed on and, by conducting the daily activities of the department, largely shaped the foreign policy of the nation. Walter Lippmann was the most prominent open defender of this system. It was the "experts," he declared, who should run foreign affairs.

Most of the Foreign Service members viewed diplomacy as consisting of relationships between governments and were cold to the idea that it also involved intercourse between peoples. They were often like characters out of the novels of Henry James. The garden party, with tea in the prewar days and cocktails in the following and more raucous years, was their habitat and Anthony Eden their model. Living most of their professional lives away from the United States, they tended to become expatriates. In the democratic and anticolonialist world that they saw arising around them, they felt uneasy, being largely alienated by birth, upbringing, and tradition from the parties of the people. Usually they were hostile to Democrats at home and wary of labor parties or socialists abroad. Few were either Communists or Communist sympathizers, as McCarthy had charged, and they were essentially patriotic. But their natural affinities were with the rich and well-born of all countries. With many honorable exceptions, they seemed to be aristocratic anachronisms for a country supposedly dedicated to "government of the people, by the people, for the people." And yet, through their control over the conduct of foreign affairs, American youth might be called upon to die because of the emotional parochialism of the Foreign Service.

With the passage of time, such criticisms began to have some effect. The service was opened to include agricultural and labor attachés and information officers. Efforts were made to recruit young men from the state universities of the Middle West as well as from Harvard, Yale, and Princeton. All this was well meant, and it helped. But too often the youngsters from the Midwest soon came to talk and feel like the gilded youths from the East.

We Democrats always felt that we were entering a strange and somewhat hostile world when we ventured to visit U.S. embassies abroad. Emily and I will never forget our ambassador to a Latin-American country who thought it entertaining to play a record for us that savagely satirized John F. Kennedy, who had just completed a triumphant tour through the same area during which he had been tumultuously greeted by millions of ordinary people.

Yet the Foreign Service itself, though operating with its own brand of internal politics, remained aloof from political politics. In this connection it is interesting to note that during Lyndon Johnson's administration, the higher ranks of the diplomatic service, which had previously been selected from leading industrialists and political statesmen, were largely filled from the Foreign Service itself. Thus, the supposedly most political of Presidents for some years made the fewest political appointments.

Military men, too, were outside direct political influence, and properly so. Here the difficulty was that those we sent to the service academies from the grass roots of the country began to consider themselves the allies of those industrialists who also had the power of command. Like members of the Foreign Service, they were usually anti-Democratic and opposed to the liberal democracy of the North and West. I tried to appoint able and poor boys to the academies, but they soon vanished into the ranks of the officer class and took on the feelings of their fellows. Marine officers always seemed the most democratic in their sympathies.

Voting

THE MOST EXCITING moments in Congress came when important measures were on the floor, when the debate was lively and roll calls imperative. I tried to be informed on these issues, through briefings by my assistants and advisers and by the study of relevant books and reports. If I felt that I could contribute anything, I would take part in the debate. Sometimes there was a lively passage at arms and volleying at close range.

When there was an important roll call, a hush fell over the chamber and its galleries. We all felt that the shuttle of the roll call was swiftly weaving the fabric of history. When the issue was crucial, I would look up into the galleries for reinforcement. Emily was often there. But at times I fancied that I saw the faces of those with whom I had worked and struggled in Illinois. There would be the devoted schoolteacher Lillian Herstein, who had been the inspiration of so many poor boys and girls, one of whom rose to the Supreme Court of the United States, and who always fought for everything generous and kind. Sometimes there would loom the sturdy oaken figure of a downstate farmer whose life was bound up in his REA co-operative and what it stood for. When labor bills were being voted on, I thought I saw the faces of pickets who had been beaten up and shot by police. At other times I would see the bearing of some suburban housewife faithful to the principles of the League of Women Voters amidst the derision of Philistine neighbors, or young idealists in pulpit and pew sighing for the Kingdom of Heaven to manifest itself in Illinois and America. I would often see idealistic party workers like Genevieve Watson, of Peoria, Alice Spear, of Washington County, and Betty Keegan, of Rockford, who also believed in the Democratic party as an instrument of social reform. All these and many others, at great sacrifice to themselves, had helped to put me in the Senate, and in a sense they were there in the chamber with me. They were bone of my bone and flesh of my flesh. I could not let them down or disappoint them. So by the time the clerk called my name, all doubts and fears had fallen away, and I could answer "Aye" or "No" in a steady voice and with a clear conscience.

And that was the way it had to be. We could not answer "Maybe" or "I want to think it over." It was the moment of truth. It had to be yes or no. We had to stake our future and possibly that of the republic upon some faith based upon imperfect knowledge.

It was always fascinating to see this weaving of history. One could predict in advance how most Senators would vote. Some from both sides of the aisle, from the South and the Midwest, would always vote against every measure designed to help the poor and weak and for every bill intended to aid the rich and powerful. From the tautness of their expressions, I knew that their reactions were visceral as well as coldly calculating. And yet commonly these men not only were kind to their families and friends, but also would put themselves out to help individuals who were in trouble. Indeed, they were often kinder in their private lives than those of us who always voted for the downtrodden.

There were some who followed no ideological line, but who voted according to the relative pressures in their states and in the country. Some, especially from the Southwest, were deliberate "switch-hitters," batting from both right and left sides of the plate. One, Senator William Langer, of North Dakota, was the last blown-in-the-bottle Populist, although there were tinges of Populism in many of us. The newspapers always rated him as unpredictable. I always knew exactly how, and why, he would vote. Whenever people were in trouble, with their backs against the wall, Bill would be on their side, swinging both arms and pouring out a stream of violent language. For all his rough talk, he had the warmest of hearts. Yet on any proposal for co-operation with other nations, he would fancy that it was a device of the British and Wall Street bankers to seduce the farmers and workers of America. He would be just as vehement and equally sincere.

Another Senator puzzled many. Guy Gillette, handsome, kindly, and deeply religious in his personal life, continually dashed my group's hopes by his voting. Before most of the crucial roll calls, he would sweetly tell us that he had been wrestling with his conscience and could not vote with us. I was tempted to reply, "Yes, you always wrestle with your conscience, but your conscience always loses."

Analyzing the reasons for the votes often seemed like an exercise in vector analysis, where the position of a point in space is determined by a complex of forces from different directions and distances and with varying intensities. But the result was not always mechanical. Some unexpected turn of friendship, hatred, or conscience would introduce a surprise. Those occasions were like a story by Dostoevsky in which it becomes clear that consciousness is not additive and that results cannot be predicted with the precision of a mathematical equation.

The Years

AND so those busy years went by. My brown hairs changed to gray and then to white. Jean grew from teen-ager to young woman, a student and practitioner of social work, and then left us to form her own household. John became an able and experienced lawyer, Helen an imaginative public-relations woman, Paul a rising executive in industry, and Dorothea a dancer in the Martha Graham tradition and then a devoted teacher. Trials and threatened disasters loomed, but somehow never quite overwhelmed us. Life went on.

15

On Guard against Temptation

FROM MY YEARS as an alderman and my experience in the 1942 primary, I knew at the beginning of my Congressional career that my greatest difficulties would be internal and personal, not merely external. I had seen many men destroy themselves. These lines of George Meredith had always seemed true:

> . . . In tragic life, God wot,
> No villain need be! Passions spin the plot:
> We are betray'd by what is false within.

Although I did not have a persecution complex, I knew that I had enemies, ranging from the extreme right to the far left. I had to protect myself against flank attacks from these quarters, which soon began—with a broadcast from the far right by Fulton Lewis and in articles by conservative commentators.

But I felt that if I did my best, in time I could overcome these attacks. The ultimate answer must be my own life. Tests do not always come in open conflicts between what is right or wrong, but over shadings, where it is hard to find guiding principles. They can emerge when one is tired and off guard, or in the soft requests of a friend. But the wrong road can lead you farther and farther from the true path, and to ultimate ruin. The downfall of President Harding had happened this way. I, too, was impulsive and made quick decisions without regard to the consequences. This could be my undoing.

Another difficulty for me at the start was money. The heavy campaign debts of 1948 had not been paid, and were not until I entered my second race and had contracted new ones. My scanty assets were still pledged at the bank. Since Jean was finishing her school year in Chicago, I had the expense of a double household. My room at the Congressional Hotel in Washington was expensive as well as lonely. With the strictest economy, I could just barely get through each month.

Two other problems immediately came up: what to do about gifts and about my wartime disability pension. I had hoped that the first problem would disappear when I went to Washington. It did not. Presents continued to pour in, and I was spending an inordinate amount of time dealing with them. I kept asking myself why various people sent me gifts. Would I incur an obligation if I accepted some and would I be expected to repay them with future favors? My days were eaten up by such queries, when I needed all my time and energy for my mail and for study of the Taft-Hartley law and the new budget. Sometimes I decided one way and sometimes another, until I realized that I must make a general rule. I would fix the dividing line between the acceptable and the unacceptable at $2.50. Gifts of greater value I would not accept, but if perishable, I would give them away to veterans' hospitals. In order to lessen the explanations, I let the press know what I was doing.

This, of course, excited some derision. Any mechanical principle arouses laughter, as Henri Bergson had pointed out a half-century before in his little book on laughter. A few writers said that I evidently felt that I could resist $2.49 of temptation but not $2.51. My reply was that, although this limit might be humorous, it saved time, which I could then devote to my duties. At any rate, I have followed this rule ever since. My secretary made the appraisals and wrote the necessary letters. After a few years, as the word spread, gifts stopped coming, and the rule was almost self-enforcing. This saved me from some of the obvious forms of trouble that have engulfed many hard-pressed legislators and administrators. But there were other rocks and shoals.

There were constant efforts to trap me. For example, my friends once found out that I was charged with having a very expensive limousine assigned to me by one of the big auto companies for which a grossly inadequate rent was paid. I had never seen this car and was quite happy to ride in my own bedraggled Chevrolet. Immediately launching an inquiry, I found that the company had wanted to assign the car to me but had been told that I probably would not accept it. The company then gave it to another but kept its books in such a way as to show me as the recipient. I protested publicly just as one of the newspapers was launching an inquiry into the general practice, which would have branded me as a chief offender. I managed to clear my name, to the disappointment of some elements of the Democratic leadership, but I could never find out who had authorized the false bookkeeping.

My disability pension, awarded for battle wounds on Okinawa, amounted to about $250 a month. I had been classified as 75 per cent disabled and had accepted these checks. During the long-drawn-out campaign of 1947–48, they had in fact helped to finance my out-of-pocket expenses and had made it possible for me to pursue my political career.

But I was uneasy about continuing to receive this pension. Though my left arm hung limp, I was not truly disabled, for I could still earn my living as a teacher. Now I was a senator, and, while I was legally entitled to the benefits, it was certainly not true that I was 75 per cent disabled, nor in fact could I properly claim any disability at all. Not wanting to receive double payment from the government, I began sending the monthly checks back to the paymaster of the Marine Corps.

He returned them, saying that he had no power to stop them, that I was entitled to the money, and that he must send it. We played battledore and shuttlecock in this way for several months, until we worked out a legal and acceptable solution. Perhaps I should have followed the example of Charles E. Bennett, a congressman from Florida much more badly wounded than I, who accepted the money and then quietly gave it to deserving charities. In July, 1971, I finally followed Bennett's example.

Instead, my money was put into a separate account, upon which I was not to draw during my service in Congress and which was to stop when it reached a given maximum. I then added a memorandum to my will saying that the interest on this could be used for the benefit of Emily and Jean after my death, but that after they died it was to revert to the United States of America with the hope that it would purchase badly needed recreational land for Chicago. It ceased to accumulate in the early 1960's, and I never drew upon it. In order not to seem too self-righteous, I had directed that no publicity be given to my rejection of the funds. I was largely successful in this, although word got around among many in the Marine Corps and became public in 1967, after my final political defeat.

I felt that I had successfully breasted the second wave of temptation. Then came the third. A lecture that I was to give before a group of independent bankers caused me concern. They had sent me a check in advance. Although this was unusual, I gave it no thought until I discovered that they were sponsoring legislation to limit chain banking. Their bill, which I heartily approved of, would soon come before me in the Banking and Currency Committee. I suddenly realized that, if publicized, the facts would look bad. Senators were rightly criticized for appearing before trade groups to deliver speeches allegedly written to order for them. To outsiders, my case would look the same. With regret, I returned the check.

Under different guises the same problem came up recurrently. The Federal Reserve Bank of Minneapolis once invited me to speak at a seminar, but when they paid me I realized that they were not neutral. On the contrary, they were vitally interested in legislation before Congress. Back went their check. After my visit to Israel in 1956, I was invited to speak to many meetings of the United Jewish Appeal for charity and for the Israel bond drives. Sizable fees were attached to these appearances. But since these organizations backed policies favoring Israel, there was another conflict of interests. While I wanted to help that little nation, my loyalties were to my own country. Generally the two purposes were compatible, but some of the Zionists urged a unilateral guarantee of the borders of Israel. I favored a multilateral guarantee through the United Nations or with Great Britain and France; I did not believe the United States should be saddled with the sole responsibility for the defense of that country. So I turned down their fees, although I continued to speak before Jewish gatherings, on an unpaid basis. Following the same policy with the unions, I spoke to their conventions without pay, even during campaign times, when I was hard pressed for funds.

These decisions soon hardened into a general policy. I would accept no fee from any organization backing legislation, administrative orders, or foreign policies involving the government of the United States. Since such matters concerned national welfare, I must have no tentacles of past obligations enfolding me in an octopus embrace. So I confined my paid lectures to colleges, public forums, and bodies that took no stand on public issues. But I charged no fees for such addresses in Illinois. They were part of my job.

There was an exception once, when I accepted a moderate fee from the rock-ribbed and highly conservative Republican Union League Club of Chicago. Although I paid an income tax on the fee, I split this money among three hard-pressed and progressive Republicans facing primary campaigns, thereby helping Republicans to finance their superior representatives.

Despite all these restrictions, which at first I feared would sink me, I managed to do all right. My fees from lecturing and writing amounted to between $7,500 and $10,000 a year. They kept my head above water and enabled me to make small savings by acquiring an added equity in my house.

Then came the fourth wave of temptation. During the fight Russell Long and I made against the basing point system, a pillar of monopoly prices, I asked myself what effect our victory would have on my investments. Certainly it would decrease the price of the shares of U.S. Steel I had bought in 1929. Although I did not allow this thought to hinder our fight, the fact that it had occurred to me suggested that I should divest myself of the shares. This I did, reinvesting the proceeds in a number of mutual-investment trusts whose holdings were so widely diffused and unknown to me that they could have no influence on my actions. Thus I think I surmounted the fourth wave.

But there was present a subtler danger. Most of the men and women who backed me did so without hope of personal recompense. Some, however, had been brought up in a different school. They saw politicians who parlayed their positions into lucrative contracts, concessions, high-paying jobs, and success in the worlds of construction, utilities, and finance. They, too, wanted a piece of the tenderloin and felt that I should help them get it.

Many of these were genuine friends and had proved this in hard-fought political battles. I liked them and wanted to help them, if I could do so legitimately. But what was legitimate? The test often came unexpectedly during the course of a long conversation when I was near exhaustion and swamped with other matters: "Would you call up the Treasury to deal with X's tax case?" "Poor lawyer Y is having trouble with the Justice Department. Would you go over to see the Assistant Attorney General and straighten him out?" "Z wants a defense contract and was only a few thousand dollars above the next bidder. He is reliable; the other man isn't. Couldn't this be taken into account?" I would gently repeat my rule about not interfering in tax and criminal cases and in contract matters only when a firm was both reliable and the low, not the high, bidder.

There were also the legal friends who wanted to be made federal masters in chancery, with consequent high legal fees, or to be designated lawyers and receivers for bankrupt companies. Once or twice, from sources that surprised me, there were requests that I talk with some federal judge whom I had helped get appointed about a case that was before him.

These requests shocked me at first, but I learned to shrug them off with a courteous disclaimer. Usually the requests were verbally justified on the ground that it was a common practice in the so-called "Establishment." The wealthy and socially impeccable had a thousand social approaches to the judiciary and to leading federal officials. They met them in their clubs, at church, and on the golf course. They entertained each other at dinner. They could easily but surely get in their word. Those of the lower economic strata did not have such advantages. They could not meet the Establishment socially. Politics was their only access, and it was unfair, so they argued, to close it to them.

Once, I asked the most respected judge on the federal bench, Learned Hand, of the Second Circuit, whether he was ever approached in this fashion. I added that he was probably too much revered to have had such an experience. "Douglas," he replied sadly, "this happens more often than you would think." Then he enumerated some of the subtle ways in which it was tried.

But the most heart-racking trial came when close friends suggested themselves or had others suggest them for the federal bench. In some cases men of whom I was deeply fond and to whom I was personally indebted were by temperament, training, and background not qualified for appointment. But to tell them so would turn friends into mortal enemies.

How to parry these requests without estranging the candidates was a problem I never really solved.

It is a pleasure to record that neither Jack Arvey nor Dick Daley ever asked for an improper appointment or favor. They seemed as anxious as I that we recruit good men. Once, in the early years, when I was pressed on many matters, my secretary told me that Colonel Arvey was on the phone. I said to myself, "Here it comes at last." Then I heard Jack's voice. "Paul, I know you are making a fight for economy, but do you mind my speaking to you about a matter which is coming up on the floor this afternoon?" I told him that the right of petition was inherent in our system of government and was guaranteed by the First Amendment to the Constitution. He explained that Senator Claude Pepper was trying to increase the appropriations for tuberculosis and cancer research. Of course I should do as I thought best, but would I bear in mind that a lot of people had died from those diseases, and that research into their causes and cures would be both humane and productive. I told him that I would swallow my scruples, overcome my Scotch penuriousness, and vote as he would on this matter. I did so with no twinge of conscience. That was the only time in our long years of association that Jack ever tried to influence my vote.

In some degree I helped to raise the former low level of the federal bench in Illinois. There were no bad appointments made on my recommendation, and there were some very good ones. On the whole, I did not do as well as I had hoped, but I consoled myself with the thought that I had probably done as well as I could in the world that surrounded me.

Having refused to intercede before the federal courts, I naturally took the same position with the quasi-judicial bodies. These have multiplied since the creation of the Interstate Commerce Commission in 1887. After a long interlude came the current Tariff Commission, the Federal Trade Commission, the Federal Power Commission, the Federal Communications Commission, and the Federal Aviation Agency, the Federal Maritime Commission, and the National Labor Relations Board. Strongly political, and mixed creations, partly administrative, partly judicial, they were struggling to become more of the latter and less of the former. In all administrations, political influences were strong in choosing the commissioners, and there were ugly rumors about outside pressures on specific decisions. Membership on the Senate's Committee on Interstate and Foreign Commerce, which handled all legislation for most of those bodies, was second only to the Appropriations Committee for those wanting raw power. With special eagerness, the commissioners generally toadied to these men. One Senator represented the airlines, a few the railroads, some the power companies, while nearly everyone was concerned with the franchises doled out gratuitously for radio and television stations. Legislators were constantly begged to intercede on behalf of some special interest.

Republican firms hired Democratic lawyers and "lame-duck" men of influence to represent them. It was commonly said that Republicans did not mind letting Democrats have 10 per cent of the plunder if they could keep the remaining 90 per cent. Some of those who objected publicly to such practices possessed subterranean channels of influence into the very bodies which they did not want to have the politicians intrude upon.

My efforts to bring about a more impartial status for the regulatory commissions were chiefly negative. I would not take part in the scramble, and would make no recommendations, either verbal or written, on any individual case. The most I ever did was to ask that there be no undue delay in dealing with a case and that it be settled on its merits. This partially placated the business groups, many of whom really desired just that but were suspicious that their competitors would take an unfair advantage over them. Since a large part of the influence was exerted informally, at cocktail parties, I kept away from them. Though an increasing part of the Washington scene, they were, in fact, a general waste of time.

I did make one concession. I appeared publicly before the Federal Aviation Agency to urge that an airline be granted a franchise to serve the depressed areas of southern Illinois. I was helping the effort to build up this section to compensate for the loss of the coal mines and the decline in subsistence farming. The lack of air connections discouraged corporations from locating badly needed plants there.

Advocates of the administrative state, including nearly all professors of political science, insisted that legislators keep their hands off administrative matters. While recognizing the evils that ignorant, corrupt, and brutal legislators can wreak upon high-minded and conscientious administrators, I did not and do not agree that administrators are all-knowing, all-competent, untiring, and incorruptible. Moreover, while professors of public administration denied that legislators should interfere with or advise administrators, they were equally certain that it was the privilege and duty of the latter to advise legislators. Who knew as much about a given subject as the pure-minded administrators? The Depression, the war, and the universities had all strengthened this attitude. There was some truth to the complaint that a largely irresponsible bureaucracy was developing.

I felt that the relationship between administrators and legislators should be mutually reinforcing. We legislators could learn a great deal from the administrators, but they could learn from us, too. We could remove delays, bring new facts to the attention of the executives, and be a deterrent to the arbitrary and occasionally corrupt bureaucrat. I took the position that neither the complaining constituent nor the bureaucrat was necessarily right. It depended on the circumstances, and these were frequently mixed. My staff and I tried to investigate the complaints that came to us in both Washington and Chicago, and if they were justified we would get in touch with the appropriate group.

A political-science student who believed in the relative infallibility of the administrative process spent a year studying this aspect of our work. We threw everything open to him. He not only read the correspondence, but he also listened to conversations with constituents and administrators. He came to scoff and criticize, but he was largely converted and is now one of the most useful servants of the legislative branch. This was also the experience of other interns in my office.

In dealings with the administrative agencies we generally made it clear that theirs was to be the final decision and we merely presented facts and hoped there would be no delay. A few times, when convinced that an earlier ruling had been wrong, we argued the case vigorously and sometimes pressed for appeal.

We tried to be courteous, but as I recounted earlier, housing delays triggered my anger on two occasions. Since I had been instrumental in getting the Housing Act passed in 1949 and wanted Chicago to receive an adequate slice of the authorized 810,000 units, I had been emotionally deeply involved. My anger naturally embittered the housing bureaucracy, and later handicapped me. Their feelings were intensified in the '50's and '60's by the way I barred housing officials from being present when the Banking and Currency Committee marked up the housing bills. Holding to the doctrine that experts should be on tap but not on top, I did not want the bureaucracy to exercise pressure over the Congress when the crucial decisions were being made. If complex questions arose, we could invite them into the inner room and ask for information or advice, and individual members could go into the side room at any time and get similar help. But the supremacy of the Congress was to be just as much protected from administrative pressure as is that of a jury. I am happy to say that this procedure is increasingly followed.

In 1950–51, I helped Senator J. William Fulbright conduct an investigation of the Reconstruction Finance Corporation, which had fallen on evil times. Loans were being made to dubious companies, and then almost immediately the officials who had approved the loans would resign and become officers in those firms. As we probed the matter, it became clear that there was a ring operating through a little Missourian named E. Merl Young, who looked like Harry Truman and at times traded on this resemblance. We suspected that there was also a set of attorneys masterminding operations outside the RFC, but, although we were on the verge of clear proof several times, we never definitely established the connection.

We did, however, find out that Young's wife, who was a White House stenographer, had been given a "royal pastel" mink coat worth over $8,000 by a New York firm that utilized her husband's services in getting an RFC loan. When this was questioned, and answered, in committee, a hush fell over the hearing room, and I realized that here was something the public could grasp. Graft in the tens of millions of dollars in the disposal of surplus property and even bigger sums in gas rates might be too huge and complicated to make an impression, but an $8,000 mink coat was tailored to public understanding. The mink-coat case was followed by the disclosure of other gifts, such as refrigerators. Senators and White House aides whose offices had interceded for a Miami Beach hotel were revealed to have been among the freeloaders.

Other committees began spading up similar material. A former Kansas City bootblack, John Maragon, who had followed Truman to Washington, was found to be a professional influence peddler, as was the ineffable but personally loyal Harry Vaughn. A number of high officials in the Internal Revenue Service had taken bribes in return for fixing taxes. Many of the guilty went to jail, but others escaped.

Although Truman himself was incorruptible, over his administration settled a black cloud known as "the mess in Washington." The atmosphere grew murkier with Joe McCarthy's charges of widespread Communist infiltration. Both the Democratic party and wartime ideals seemed to be going out "not with a bang but a whimper."

In the midst of this I was asked to head a Senate committee to investigate ethics in government. Wanting to make the inquiry constructive, the members listed practical suggestions, partially drawn from my experience. Our first rule was that officials should not accept costly gifts or entertainment. I tried to have my $2.50 limit specified, but this was too Spartan. We did propose that an official coming into government from private industry should disqualify himself for two years from determining any matter affecting his former firm, and that on leaving government service there should be a similar "delousing" period before he could approach the government department with which he had been affiliated. Most important of all, I advocated the detailed disclosure by public officials of the sources and amounts of their income. This seemed the best deterrent to improper conduct. I elaborated on these matters in the Godkin Lectures at Harvard in the early winter of 1952, which were published that summer.

While these proposals had a good press, action to carry them out was very slow. Here and there a government agency accepted some of them, and finally a few states, notably New York, adopted a similar code of ethics. The Kennedy administration put most of the provisions into effect for its administrative officials.

Meanwhile, there were tragedies in this area. Under Eisenhower, a Secretary of the Air Force who had made a bad slip as a young man sought business for his private consulting firm from companies doing business with his department. Also, Eisenhower's most trusted assistant, Sherman Adams, the outward epitome of frosty integrity, was found to have accepted costly gifts and accommodations from a shady New England operator while helping him in his complicated dealings with government departments.

Perhaps worst of all, I found that swarms of high-ranking military officers, on retiring from the service, joined firms doing a huge volume of work for the government. In their new capacity they dealt with their former subordinates and associates.

None of this work made me popular with either the civilian or the military bureaucracy. All of it increased my need to walk a strict and narrow path, since the slightest slip would be seized upon for exposure by those I had offended. This was one reason why I returned to my aldermanic practice of making a full disclosure of my income and expenses of office. If I had done this as an official of local government, why should I refrain as a national legislator? I had introduced bills requiring this for top-ranking administrators and for members of the Senate. Should I postpone action until it became mandatory? Perhaps my best argument for disclosure would be to do so, voluntarily, myself.

Nevertheless, I delayed for a few years because of two worries: I would probably be thought a sanctimonious publicity seeker and be offensive to my colleagues, and I was like the man with a meager wardrobe who did not want his few possessions laid bare to the world. But I finally summoned my courage and, with Jane Enger's skilled help, made a detailed statement of the Douglas sources of joint income and of the amount of stock which we held in the mutual-investment funds and deposits in banks. I also listed the extra expenses of holding office, or what can be called "political expenses of a noncampaign nature." These ran, for me, around $15,000 a year. Having inserted this statement in the *Congressional Record*, I distributed it to those on my mailing list and offered to make my files and income-tax records available for inspection. I was glad that one newspaper reporter took me up on this offer and pronounced himself satisfied.

The public report I made for 1966 is fairly typical of later years and illustrates some of the problems legislators face. By that time the salary of a senator or congressman had increased from $22,500 to $30,000. It had been only $15,000 during my first years.

First, there were my political expenses, which did not include any of the direct costs of the campaign and which were fairly representative of other years. Travel to and from Illinois and Washington came to $3,569.69. The government paid for a total of only six trips ($864.56), leaving a net travel cost of $2,705.13. My radio and television programs cost $3,413.31. I wish to repeat that this did not include direct campaign broadcasting, but merely periodic reports. The fifty-two radio stations and eight television stations that carried the programs did so without charge, as a public service, but I had to pay for the cost of the tapes. Only WGN, the station owned by my most vigorous opponent, the *Tribune*, met the cost of its tapes. The entertainment of constituents came to a minimum of $2,156.47. In reality, it was more, because I charged off only half of the bills submitted by the Senate dining room, whereas probably two-thirds and a total of $2,900 would have been closer figures. Contributions to other candidates and to Democratic organizations came to $1,505. This was about typical. It did not include my expenses, but because I had troubles of my own that year I did not give as much to others as I would in other even-numbered years. On the other hand, it was more than I would give in the odd-numbered years. Incidentals, such as telegrams and telephone bills in excess of senatorial allowances, and including gifts to charities that would not otherwise have been made and subscriptions to newspapers and journals, came to $1,172.06. Finally, petty-cash outlays for office and other incidental expenses amounted to $566.25.

These totaled $11,518.22. But this was really not all. It did not include the expenses of travel through the state, or hotel and motel accommodations. In 1966 these were charged to campaign expenses. In other years I paid for them myself. There were always two of us, and more commonly three or four. Estimating that at least fifty to sixty days were spent downstate at a daily cost of not less than $50 or $60 a day, these came to a total, outside Chicago, of between $2,500 and $3,000. The expenditures in Chicago were free from taxation up to $3,000, but they amounted to from $25 to $30 a day more than in Washington. This was an added cost of at least $1,500.

It was safe to estimate out-of-pocket expenses at $15,000 to $16,000 a year. They may have amounted to more.

In addition, the federal income tax on my basic salary came to $5,472.80. Local property taxes in Washington and Chicago amounted to another $1,000. While my tangible possessions in Illinois were scanty, I was next to the highest payer of personal property taxes in the Hyde Park–Kenwood community. The contribution of 7½ per cent to the retirement annuity for Congress came to another $2,250. These additional deductions totaled, in round numbers, nearly $9,000.

My take-home pay even in this year when my official salary was at its height was, therefore, about $5,000. Prior to 1965, it was much less, and in some years was probably nonexistent. At times I was out of pocket so far as my salary was concerned.

Of course, I was saved by income from annuities and investments, which amounted in 1966 to about $7,500, and from lectures and royalties for books and articles, $8,285. All in all, 1966 was a prosperous financial year. In other years Emily and I had a hard time. On the whole, we lived on about the same scale as we had when I was a college professor. This was satisfactory to us. But I often wondered what would have happened to me if, like Senator Thomas Dodd, I had had six children to support and educate or if I had not been able to earn more money by my pen and tongue.

As for property, we owned our house and adjoining lots in Washington, valued at not far from $50,000, and shares in the investment trusts of $68,501. The government bonds we owned came to $10,500, with $500 more in miscellaneous institutions. Our bank deposits were $7,984, and the value of our credits in the Marine Corps account came to $32,390.66. The principal of the latter will, as I have said, ultimately revert to the United States for the purchase of recreational land in or near Chicago. I have not counted the withdrawal value of my pension rights. These sums have been accumulated over our lifetimes by my wife and me from savings and small inheritances. I do not feel that I have endangered the fortunes of my family by my strictness. When I die, my wife will benefit from insurance payments in the Marine Corps and Senate accounts.

To conciliate my colleagues, I added, with my public report, that although this practice of reporting seemed right to me, I did not prescribe it for others. They might see it as an unjustifiable invasion of privacy, and if they so believed, it should not be held against them. This did reduce the opposition of some Senators, who chose to regard the disclosure as a peculiarity of mine. Others saw the point. I had never forgotten Confucius' maxim that the most important act of a lawmaker was the example he set. There are signs that matters are working my way. A number of Senators have made similar disclosures, and someday the practice may be adopted as a rule of the Senate.

One of the backbreaking tasks upon which my continuance in the Senate depended was that of raising money for the periodic campaigns.

A candidate for the Senate is limited by federal law to a campaign expenditure of $25,000, regardless of the size of his state. In a small one-party state like Vermont this may be enough, but only when the candidate is widely and favorably known. In a state such as Illinois, where from 4½ to 5 million votes are cast, it is a ludicrously small sum. A candidate who confined himself to this amount would, in race-track language, be left at the post. He could not have television or radio time or any wide distribution of literature. And yet by federal law he must swear on his final report that he does not know of any other expenditures made for him. If he had to live up to the strict letter of the law, it would be better for an aspirant not to run, but, rather, to quit national politics.

Starting with Wendell Willkie's campaign of 1940, nearly every candidate has avoided and in a sense evaded this requirement. The usual way is to have trusted friends organize one or more independent committees. There may be a general citizens committee, and frequently ethnic, labor, and business groups. These raise and spend money, while the candidate tries to keep himself technically ignorant of their receipts and expenditures. Even so, he has to be consulted frequently, because sources of support involve the very essence of the campaign. How to allow this and yet not commit perjury is a constant problem. In my case it was complicated because many large contributors insisted on giving the money to me in person, so that I would know whence came my help and be properly grateful. My efforts to deflect them to the appropriate committee were at times laughable and commonly unsuccessful. As a safety device, I made it a practice always to have a trusted counselor with me, who could take the money without my seeing it pass. At the conclusion of a campaign I made a technically correct disclaimer, which I could defend in a court of law, but about which I felt unhappy. My managers then gave me a list of those who had been personally "most helpful," and I wrote letters of general thanks.

But there was also a personal fund, which we could report. Douglas Anderson handled this, and I put into it all sums given to me personally that the donors were willing to have reported. This was spent for travel, personal expenses, mailing, and other smaller items.

I never learned precisely how much my elections cost, but I was always told how big was the deficit. Although not supposed to know how much money was raised or how it was expended, the candidate is expected as a matter of honor to make good any deficit. After the 1948 election, I found that the outstanding bills came to $20,000, and I was already in debt to my bank. By lectures, articles, and two books published in 1952, and with added contributions from friends, I managed to pay them just as I entered the 1954 campaign. That time the debt was $25,000. It took several years more to work this down, and it was finally removed by a personal loan of $15,000, from a wealthy good Samaritan, who later canceled the debt.

In 1960 my managers had a surplus of $760, which we promptly spent on a spaghetti dinner for 200 of our most active workers. In the last campaign, in 1966, after months of meeting new bills, we gave the final surplus of $2,000 to an organization of independent Democrats for future research. The next year we also gave the net proceeds of a dinner given in my honor to the same group. In short, I succeeded fairly well in insulating myself from the expenditures and surpluses of the campaign funds, while assuming personal responsibility for deficits.

In all these campaigns, my opponents spent vastly larger sums of money and apparently used many of the same devices. My final opponent went so far as not to file any statement at all, saying that all his campaign expenses had been met by sundry independent committees.

The whole experience convinced me that we must reform our election procedures by providing new sources of revenue, rather than by increasing penalties. I became converted to the idea that the basic costs of elections should be met out of taxes and that private contributions, while not prohibited, should be limited. A subsidy of fifteen cents a registered voter for each of the major candidates for federal office seems adequate. This could give about $750,000 in a state like Illinois, which should be enough for anyone.

The gravity of this problem has increased with the years as election costs have skyrocketed. Television has shown the greatest increase. Thus, in 1966 twenty seconds of prime time on the most important television station in Chicago already cost $1,900 on the barrelhead. Of this time, six seconds had to be used for the station disclaimer that the views expressed were not necessarily theirs. So the net time was only fourteen seconds.

With millions spent by candidates for governor and senator in many states, it is almost impossible for a poor man or one of moderate means to run or be elected to office unless he agrees to be the servant of great wealth. The United States is fast becoming a plutocracy, or a government by the wealthy, instead of a government by the people. Political power has in part always followed economic power, and this is increasingly the case today.

I regard a solution to the problem of campaign expenditures as the most needed governmental reform. Russell Long and Albert Gore, former colleagues on the Senate Finance Committee, have developed ingenious plans for getting more funds, and their proposals, if accepted, would represent a substantial improvement. If this incomplete account of the experience of one politician helps to awaken voters to this crucial weakness in our political system, my frankness may be justified.

Perhaps it is appropriate at this point to mention my own casual experience with the political disease or temptation known as "Presidentitis," which has overpowered many public servants.

I had been warned by friendly New Yorkers as early as December, 1948, that the Tammany Hall group and other Eastern leaders, alarmed at the way the recent election had thrust forward Humphrey, Stevenson, Chester Bowles, and me, had decided they would try to disrupt us by encouraging each of us to think of himself as the Presidential candidate for 1952. I told Stevenson about this, stressing my desire to work with him and not at cross-purposes. I told him that he need not fear or distrust me.

Although I still supported social legislation on the domestic front and collective security on the international scene, my stand for economy and a higher ethical code had apparently caught on with the public. When the Democratic leaders gathered at Denver in the early spring of 1951, the New York *Times* reported that if Truman withdrew from the race, the consensus overwhelmingly favored me. Leslie Biffle, the secretary of the Senate, who had won a reputation as a prophet in 1948, told me the same thing.

All this frightened me. In the first place, not believing that I could be either nominated or elected, I shrank from the terrible and futile ordeal.

Even if by some wild chance the improbable happened, I dreaded the consequences and the portentous decisions I would have to make.

Nevertheless, the New York Establishment wanted to look me over, and they had me speak to a curious audience at the Waldorf Astoria, after which I was given a series of luncheons. One of these was under the auspices of a mysterious character who specialized in "building up" public figures. Privately, I poured cold water on all these efforts. I turned away the enthusiasm of one wealthy group by telling of my boyhood admiration for Eugene V. Debs. And at the end of 1951 I issued a statement modeled on the celebrated refusal of General William Tecumseh Sherman in 1884.

An undercurrent of pressure persisted, however, for in early 1952 an intermediary for a well-known leader appeared with an offer that he would set aside a million dollars for a preconvention campaign on my behalf. I rejected the idea. I continued to fear that if I allowed the fever really to enter my blood, it would divert my efforts from being a good senator. My basic desire was to be a people's representative like George Norris, and not to be seduced by other ambitions.

The Presidential fever faded, although some leaders in the Michigan delegation insisted that if a deadlock developed in the 1952 convention they would bring me out as a compromise candidate. Rumors of this movement did not help me with Truman and may have contributed to a cleavage with Stevenson.

A busy man does not have much time in which to worry about his soul. During vacations, Emily and I read to each other passages from the Bible, Epictetus, Marcus Aurelius, Schweitzer, and others. But the rush of life and the need to find out what was right in matters of legislative conduct absorbed my energies. I consoled myself by saying that these matters were not apart from, but in fact were the essence of, the ethical life. But I knew I had lost something from those days when Quakerism and the doctrine of all-conquering love had seemed the very foundation of life.

At this time, I was shocked to learn that critics accused me of smugness, a quality I have always disliked in others. I tried to dismiss this criticism as politically inspired, but it continued, culminating in an extraordinary column by a conservative writer, Holmes Alexander. He probed my inner depths and, despite a few misconceptions, analyzed me in a way Freud would have envied. Although not unfriendly, his analysis hurt me more than any former criticism. In fact, I literally gasped with pain. After reading the piece, Emily said that he had made a point. Sometimes I did seem self-righteous. Nevertheless, if I took this criticism to heart, she said, it could be the best thing that had ever happened to me.

Thereafter, I tried to be on guard against this weakness. Although I avoided Alexander, I felt that he was watching me closely. Years later I told him that, while his article had hurt me more than anything that had ever been published about me, it had also helped me more. Eying me quizzically, he shook hands. Shortly afterward he went on vacation and had to discontinue his column temporarily. At his request I stepped into the breach to write an article, contrary to his views, on current issues. Candid friends tell me that I am not yet cured of an occasional look of smugness. But perhaps the events of 1966 have helped.

The political life is by its nature a competitive one. To stay in the swing requires effort; to make one's ideas prevail requires more. With huge electorates, it is vital to make news and to have it published.

Sometimes this is done crudely, as in the slogan "He who tooteth not his own horn, the same will not be tooted." Yet there have been many public figures who have ultimately destroyed themselves by a tasteless pursuit of publicity. Benjamin Jowett, the old master of Balliol, expressed this with refinement when advising unduly ambitious graduates: "In this world it is important to be pushing. But it is equally important not to seem so." Good manners gild the pill, but do not alter its contents.

Perhaps worse was a growing tendency to be suspicious of new acquaintances. There were so many people trying to get favors when I was off guard that I began to build up a crust of suspicion. I became chary of confidences except with a handful of old friends whose fidelity had been proven under fire. Probably this was necessary to protect me from my undiscriminating tendency to like everyone. It saved me from some errors, but it also hardened my personality. While maintaining a surface affability, I began to look for selfish motives and too often found them. Gone was the boyish trust of the 1920's and '30's, but the new sophistication inhibited the growing points of friendship. This may be one of the reasons why older politicians make fewer friends and ultimately are defeated.

I had seen my friend Secretary of the Interior Harold Ickes increasingly poison himself with this virus of suspicion, until there was almost no one in the world whom he trusted. The one exception, I had thought, was his old fellow crusader and my friend Charlie Merriam. But Merriam once told me that Ickes at times distrusted even him.

I was fortunate in my wife and family, a sterling staff, and a group of loyal friends who saved me from becoming a misanthrope. In later years, some lines from Marcus Aurelius were a good antidote:

Say to thyself at daybreak: I shall come across the busybody, the thankless, the overbearing, the treacherous, the envious, the unneighborly . . . but I can neither be injured by any of them nor could I be wrathful with my kinsman and hate him. For we are made for cooperation like the feet, the hands, the eyelids, like the rows of the upper and lower teeth.

16

The Composition and Power Structure of the Senate

FROM 1949 TO 1966, we Democrats had a nominal majority in the Senate during all but two years (1953–54), although there was a Republican President during eight of them. We had a margin of 54 to 42 votes in 1949–50, which was reduced by the elections in the latter year. We lost both Congress and the Presidency in 1952. In 1954 we regained a majority of the Senate by one vote. Then in 1958 came the great break-through, when we increased our representation to 64. This was increased to 65 in 1960, and as a result of the Johnson landslide in 1964 we increased our strength to 67, or two to one.

In Great Britain this would have enabled us to have our will during most of these years, particularly since a similar movement occurred in the House. But the American system is different. Members divided on strict party lines only on the opening day, when the Senate was organizing and the president pro tem being elected. This was done so that the selection of committees could proceed and the majority could hold its position. But this was also the last time during the session there would be such party cohesion. While there would be fairly sharp differences between the majority of Democrats and the majority of Republicans, there were minorities within both parties, which led to combinations across party lines. There was also a great deal of independent voting. There were, in fact, only a handful of roll calls during every session in which there would be a straight party vote. This blurred the distinction between the parties that was stressed every four years in the Presidential elections and that still existed between the respective majorities.

Yet the real issues and cleavages in this country are by no means identical with party lines, but to some degree run across them. During the Depression, from 1930 to 1938, the differences had been largely based on what the government should do in connection with the economic collapse. Then for seven years the center of discussion switched to foreign affairs and the war.

When Emily and I came on the Washington scene, there were two main sources of cleavage in the Senate, which in turn were affected by two parliamentary institutions. The cleavages were economic and racial; the peculiar Congressional institutions were the seniority system and the filibuster.

The sympathies and interests of one group were largely identified with the possessors of wealth and power or the economically successful. Those of another group were more attached in their sympathies to the less successful elements in society, the small farmers and businessmen, the lower middle class, the wage earners, and the poor.

The second source of division was the question of white supremacy. Nearly all the Southerners were openly, or secretly, committed to this principle and were opposed to enlarging the rights of Negroes or other racial minorities, such as the Mexican-Americans. This was the evil heritage of the system of slavery. The sympathies of the other group were primarily with these very minorities.

To a large degree, these groups were mutually reinforcing. Those who were strong supporters of white supremacy generally lined up in defense of wealth and privilege, while those who defended the racial underdogs supported the less powerful. This was not, however, an invariable rule. For example, Olin D. Johnston, of South Carolina, was a defender of the small farmers and mill hands against the owners of the big plantations and cotton mills. He was the political heir of the semi-Populist movement led in former times by Benjamin R. ("Pitchfork Ben") Tillman and Coleman Blease. But, though a kindly and slow-moving giant, he could be aroused, like his predecessors, to deep passions against the Negro. These slumbered in his breast, as they did in most of his "poor white" supporters.

Those who lacked power had no direct representative of their own in Congress. There were no propertyless workers, or what Marx called the "proletariat," among us. I do not know that there are such in many countries. Elections cost too much and political life is too precarious for those who live on the ragged edge. There was no Negro in the Senate during the eighteen years I was there. The highly cultivated, intelligent, and honorable Senator Edward W. Brooke, of Massachusetts, who entered as I left, is a moderate and not in any sense a militant, and he represents a state in which the proportion of Negroes is relatively small. The defenders of the economically depressed came in the main from the middle class of professionals, primarily lawyers and teachers, with here and there a successful businessman.

Nor did the division on economic issues conform rigidly to what a strict economic interpretation of history would have predicted. Some of our wealthiest members were defenders of the underdogs. The most conspicuous of these was Herbert Lehman, of New York. He was enormously wealthy and a member of a powerful family banking house. He was also our most militant defender of the poor and the weak. He always voted against his direct economic interest. James E. Murray, of Montana, also on the side of the poor, was quietly wealthy, as was the aged and cynical Theodore F. Green, of Rhode Island. There have been others, such as the three Kennedys, whose sympathies and votes did not follow their personal economic interests and who increasingly defended the less fortunate.

Some of the main defenders of wealth and economic power actually possessed it, as was the case with Robert S. Kerr, of Oklahoma, James O. Eastland, of Mississippi, Peter H. Dominick, of Colorado, and Prescott S. Bush, of Connecticut. But the Senate in my time was no longer the millionaires' club so vigorously satirized by David Graham Phillips in the days of Nelson Aldrich and Tom Platt. Most of those who served in the armies of power were either moderately wealthy or were the attorneys and political representatives of the wealthy.

There was a third group of Senators, who occupied an intermediate position on both sets of issues and who were allied sometimes with one economic group and sometimes with the other. Some solicited the support of both groups, getting campaign contributions from the wealthy and votes from the mass of voters on the pretext of protecting each from the other. They played the part of mediators, giving favors to both sides in an effort to avoid being classed as the firm adherents of a single group.

Some would make alliances with subgroups whose ideologies were different but whose immediate interests did not conflict. There were strong supporters of unions who also defended the interests of shipping and lumber firms. Some were for the poor but also for the big oil and gas interests. None of us who sided with the less powerful were antibusiness or opponents of the wealthy as such. There was little of the class struggle on our side, although we sometimes felt that the same could not be said of the hard-core business bloc.

To the untutored public, however, the important division was between Democrats and Republicans. Since the Democrats had a majority in all the years except 1953–54, the public held us responsible for all that happened.

Such a classification is superficial. There were not two, but really three —or perhaps, more accurately, three and a half—parties in the Senate, and three and a quarter parties in the House. These were the conservative

Republicans, who comprised from four-fifths to nine-tenths of the Republican Senators; the liberal Democrats, comprising most but not all of the Northern and Western representatives of the party; the Southern Democrats, a group unto themselves, coming from the eleven states of the old Confederacy and from former slave states such as Maryland and Delaware which, though tempted, did not secede during the Civil War, plus a group from the Southwest, along the old Santa Fe trail, over which the Southerners had moved westward. Finally, there was a small but gallant body of liberal Republicans, who took the tradition of Abraham Lincoln seriously. When I entered the Senate, this handful came primarily from the three states north of Boston, and was led by the admirable George D. Aiken, of Vermont, flanked by his two warm friends Charles W. Tobey, of New Hampshire, and Margaret Chase Smith, of Maine. North Dakota's Bill Langer often voted with them. Later the group was reinforced by the coming of Thomas Kuchel, of California, Clifford P. Case, of New Jersey, John Sherman Cooper, of Kentucky, and the brilliant Jacob Javits, of New York. I found the members of this group personally attractive and among the best in the Senate. My only regret was that there were so few of them. This was also true of liberal Southern Democrats. They, too, were few but choice.

In the House there were three Democratic parties. The third consisted of the followers of the big-city machines, who pursued a double policy. They voted mostly with the liberals on issues but with the South on organization.

Visitors from Britain always marvel at the differences that exist inside our parties, and in particular at the sharp cleavages among the Democrats. Their parliamentary system is highly concentrated nationally along party lines; ours is highly decentralized. Their campaigns are largely financed centrally through their national committees; ours are primarily financed locally. Their candidates must be approved centrally as well as by the closed club of local party members; our party candidates are almost universally selected by the direct primary, which is really a preliminary election. Their candidates are, therefore, creatures of their national party; to a far greater degree, ours run on their own.

These differences are heightened in Congress by the procedure of voting, the relative roles of executive and legislature, the committee system, and even by the layout of the chambers. In England, the parties face each other from opposite sides of the House. Due probably to the influence of Jefferson and Madison, we adopted the French system of seating the members in a semicircle in front of the presiding officer. The Republicans are on his left and the Democrats on his right, with a center aisle between them. When one party has a distinct majority, the middle aisle seems to shrivel. When the majority is overwhelming, as after the 1936 election, when the Republicans had only seventeen senators out of ninety-six,

Democrats have to sit on the nominally Republican side. So there is not the same physical separation there is in the House of Commons.

In Britain, moreover, there are no individually recorded roll calls. Members file out between tellers and are counted as so many sheep passing between turnstiles. With us, upon demand of one-fifth of a quorum, a roll call must be held. By persistence, any sizable group can force such a call and compel each member to go on record. This can be done by the device of incessant quorum calls after nominally new business occurs, which can in practice be devised and continued until a roll call is agreed upon. Sometimes by more or less mutual consent or by acquiescence, a roll call is not insisted on, and voting takes place by voice, by a show of hands, or by division in the form of a standing count. In the first case it is almost impossible for the press and lobbyists to identify the voters, and it is not always easy in the last two. The 1970 change in the rules of the House provided for identification. In the House, teller votes are generally taken during the time that body is meeting as a committee of the whole and is perfecting action on important amendments. Even with these exceptions, roll calls are generally held in the Senate for most of the important votes. We never had fewer than 200 roll calls in a year, and sometimes there were well over 300. In my eighteen years I probably answered around 4,000 roll calls. Thus an inescapable record is built up, which becomes the most important criterion by which the press and public can judge representatives.

This is much truer today than it was at the turn of the century, when it was hard for voters to find out just how their representatives had voted. Bob La Follette was the man who began to let the daylight in upon this process, when he insisted on Senate roll calls, and published them, and took them to the people in the summer through his Chautauqua lectures all over the country. It was frequently embarrassing for Senators to have La Follette ruthlessly read their record back home. In his autobiography, La Follette tells a grimly amusing story of how Senator James A. Hemenway, of Indiana, came out to his tent meeting in Indianapolis to make a flowery introduction, only to flee in terror and anger as La Follette proceeded to read Hemenway's voting record. The tradition of La Follette has now been perfected by the *Congressional Quarterly*.

With the wire services and newspapers also giving far more attention to roll calls than before, the publication of the results is often immediate. I remember calling on the editor of a small afternoon newspaper in a town just north of Danville during my first campaign. It was 2:30 in the afternoon, and the details of an important roll call were coming in over the ticker. Twenty minutes later I held my rival's recorded vote in my hand as I stood in the town square excoriating him.

American legislators are held much more responsible for their votes than are their counterparts in Britain, who are protected by the anonymity of the tellers. Our system, encouraging a greater degree of independence on the part of both legislators and voters, still further weakens the power of political parties, for a senator may defy his party's policies and be re-elected on the strength of his own popularity. Even if the voters disagree with him on many matters, they generally want someone who expresses his own beliefs and is not a puppet in the hands of party bosses. This feeling is particularly strong in Wisconsin and Oregon, largely because of the La Follette tradition in the former state and that of the Popular Government League and W. S. U'ren in the latter. It enabled the highly independent Senators William Proxmire and Wayne Morse to win successive elections.

The weakness of our national party organizations also contributes to the independence of senators. In Britain the consent of the central party is necessary for a candidate to stand for Parliament, and the refusal of continued support is almost fatal for his chances of re-election. At the time of the Suez crisis this was seen in the punishment of Anthony Nutting, who had objected to the policies of Anthony Eden.

Local financing also makes American legislators more independent than the British. In England centralized financing usually prevails. Our House and Senatorial Campaign committees do furnish funds, but the novice is foolish to rely on them. Except in rare instances, they provide only a small fraction of a campaign's total cost. In my case, where the Democratic Senatorial Campaign Committee contributed less than its average, the amount never exceeded 2 per cent of what my local committees spent. A state organization, however, if strong and cohesive, can discipline mavericks and ultimately defeat those who defy it. This happened in California to Kuchel in 1968, and in Texas in 1970 to Ralph Yarborough.

Our system affords much more opportunity for individual expression and activity than the British. A backbencher in the House of Commons has little chance to distinguish himself. He is dominated by the administrative arm of government, denied the advantages of the committee system, confronted with the supremacy of national over local avenues of communication. In the words of Gilbert and Sullivan:

> *When in that House M.P.'s divide,*
> *If they've a brain and cerebellum, too,*
> *They've got to leave that brain outside,*
> *And vote just as their leaders tell 'em to.*

Under our system a new member has several ways to make himself known. He can make insertions in the *Congressional Record* during the morning hour and then send inexpensive reprints to constituents. By taking up important issues, even a freshman can make a name for himself. While it is hard for a novice to be heard in the big full committees of either house, there are subcommittees where he can distinguish himself. He can also take part briefly in floor debates. On television there is still a chance for local and state news, and the alert legislator can take advantage of this. He can prepare periodic television programs, recorded at cost, which most stations are willing to carry free as a public service. Local radio stations are especially glad to carry such programs. Some newspapers run occasional columns written by members and use their releases.

Many students of political science have flirted with the idea that we should adopt the British parliamentary system. My reply is twofold. It cannot be done and it would be wasted motion. We elect our President. In Britain the Members of Parliament choose their leaders, and the leader of the majority becomes prime minister. He selects the cabinet, which runs both the party and the Parliament. Even if it were practicable, I do not believe such a conversion would be desirable for us. It would weaken the relationship between legislators and their constituents and add to the voters' growing sense of alienation from government.

Admittedly, the weakness of our system is that our parties often become loose and conflicting associations of geographic and economic groups representing no coherent national policy. The prime example, of course, is the behavior of most Southern legislators, so much at odds with their party platform as to justify their being called a third political party.

The Southern Senators and Congressmen have represented largely the same economic and social classes as the Republicans from the Middle West and the East. They have served the owners of the big plantations, the private utilities and banks, and the fast-developing textile, chemical, and tobacco factories. On economic questions, after their support of the New Deal declined, they went overwhelmingly to the side of the propertied and powerful, with here and there one whose sympathies lay with the poor. Pepper, Olin Johnston, Estes Kefauver, Gore, and Yarborough have been notable exceptions to the general rule. Russell Long's dominant sympathies were of this kind during his early years in the Senate.

It was easy for the Republicans and Southerners, therefore, to form an undercover alliance on economic matters. They were the same breed. In the past they had been divided by slavery, Reconstruction, and the tariff. When I came to the Senate, the memories of the first two, though fading, were still sufficiently strong among Southern voters to prevent their candidates from joining the Republican party or openly supporting its Presidential nominee. James Thomas Heflin, of Alabama, had done that in 1928 out of opposition to the Catholicism of Al Smith, and had paid the price in banishment from political life. If they went too far, they might lose Presidential patronage or their committee-assignment priorities. Since the Democratic party was still dominant in county and state elections, Congressional candidates would not surrender the party label lest they lose state and local control. Yet to them it was not only acceptable, but praiseworthy, to oppose the policies and persons of the Northerners in the Democratic party. Something of the aura of the lost cause would then attach itself to those who raised the Stars and Bars.

This conservative alliance on domestic issues accounted for the fact that even when we Democrats had a paper majority in both houses, we were seldom able to pass the program to which we were pledged. During the period of the Great Depression and the successive cumulative land-slides of 1932, '34, and '36, the sheer weight of numbers and the gravity of the economic situation had enabled us to pass a series of long-delayed and badly needed measures, culminating in the Wages and Hours law of 1938. If we had not done this, we might not have survived the Depression. But from the fall of 1938 through the next decade, the political tide steadily receded. The paper majorities shrank as the party lost heavily in the North and West. Losses were particularly heavy in the Mississippi Valley. By 1947 Scott Lucas was the only Democratic senator from the states north of the Ohio River and between the Alleghenies and the Rockies. During and after the war, Southerners and Republicans found it increasingly easy to work together and perfected the technique of interparty co-operation. While neither had a majority alone, when united they did. This conservative coalition dominated Congress during these years. Its members always showed up for roll calls, and its power was occasionally openly flaunted, as when Harry F. Byrd and Robert A. Taft sat together on the floor checking the list of Senators and sending out for the absent or the few recalcitrants.

Opposition to national action for dealing with economic and social problems on behalf of the less fortunate was the common faith of the two components of the conservative alliance. Their visceral reactions were to use governmental power to help the well-to-do, but to oppose such action for the poor and the weak.

A second column in the structure of the alliance was the tacit protection the Northern Republicans gave the Southern Democrats on racial matters. They did not openly espouse white supremacy or denounce efforts to improve the position of blacks. This would have been politically fatal in many parts of the North. In the Senate they did it by protecting the Southerners' right to filibuster. If the many civil-rights measures could ever have been brought to a vote during this period, they would have been passed. Even the conservative Republicans would not have dared to vote against them. Only the Southerners and their fringe adherents from the border and Southwestern states would have actually voted "No." Up to 1964, the Southerners could, however, kill civil-rights bills by not permitting them to come to a vote. They would do this by use of the filibuster, as I will later explain. This practice was the chief barrier to legislation throughout my service in the Senate, and it remains so, although to a lesser degree.

In my time, the South could not by itself muster the votes required to defeat cloture, which limits the filibuster. Their maximum strength with the border and Southwestern states did not exceed 30 per cent of the Senate. They needed some of the Northern Republicans for the necessary margin. This was the other consideration in the implicit bargain. The Republicans not only furnished the margin, but also did so in full measure, pressed down and running over.

Of course, in doing this, the Republicans did not avow any open opposition to civil rights as such. On the contrary, they protested their devotion to these rights. Their opposition to cloture, they insisted, was due to their deep faith in freedom of debate; it was the foundation of all our liberties. Even if debate had already gone on for days and weeks, it must not be interfered with.

In effect, the Republicans held the Senate passive, so that the Southerners could anesthetize and put the civil-rights measures to death. For many years the Republican party was shielded from the public opinion of its constituents by this complicated parliamentary process and by the weakness of the pro-Negro sympathies of the North. Only our repeated efforts disclosed the nature of the filibuster, so that with the increase in civil-rights sentiment we were temporarily able to overcome it during the years from 1964 to 1966.

The underdogs in both the Senate and the House were the Northern liberals. We were disliked by the conservative Republicans because we supported the cause of the weak and less privileged. We were rejected by most of the Southern Democrats because we wanted to help the Negroes. And of all the Northern liberals, those of us from the big industrial states were the most despised. Those from the mountain and Western states could be tolerated by the conservative coalition because, while they frequently voted with us, they did not initiate vexatious measures on civil rights. Westerners and Southerners had learned to live with each other. In return for help on silver, wool, and appropriations for irrigation, the Westerners did not provoke the South. There were few Negroes in their states, and the question of civil rights was not a burning local issue.

The Democrats from the border states and the Southwest were usually allies of the South. In some cases, as in those of the venerable Carl Hayden, of Arizona, and his colleague, Ernest W. McFarland, this alliance was transparent. In others it was concealed. Alben W. Barkley, of Kentucky, the best of the "pros," attempted, however, to be an honest mediator between the North, South, and West. For a full quarter of a century he was deservedly the best-loved Senator.

Separated thus from the Democrats of the South and differentiated from those of the West and the border, we Democrats from the Northern states were at the bottom of the totem pole of prestige. Of all these, Douglas, Humphrey, and Lehman were at first the very lowest. It was suspected that we not only advocated liberal causes, but also actually believed in them. This was the unforgivable sin. In time, with Johnson's help, Humphrey crawled up the totem pole without sacrificing his principle on roll calls. Lehman and I never tried.

We wanted to represent with all our strength the causes in which we believed. And we looked to our constituents, rather than to our colleagues, for approval. On the surface, the Southerners treated us with the formal courtesy that is the regional characteristic. But there was always the ineradicable belief in the air that we and our ancestors had perpetrated the unpardonable wrong of freeing the slaves, winning the Civil War, and carrying out Reconstruction. Now we were espousing the cause of the Negroes and the other mudsills of society against the natural aristocracy, of which they were the finest flower.

There was, therefore, little or no social relationship between us and the Southerners, except with two or three kindly souls who in their hearts desired reconciliation. We recognized this exclusion but did not resent it. We were busy and sought our friends among those with kindred ideals, whether in Congress or members of the press or the public.

But while the big industrial states were weak in the Senate, their support was necessary for the election of a Democratic President. The eight largest states of the North and West had only one-sixth of the membership of the Senate, but they contained nearly half the total population of the country and, hence, had approximately that proportion in the House. They comprised about two-fifths of the Electoral College. It was a constant source of irritation to the Southerners, therefore, that our Presidential candidates had to be satisfactory to the North and West and particularly to the big states, with their cities and industrial populations. No Democrat could win without us. If we needed the South to pass legislation, they needed the North to elect a President and to gain a legislative majority, which would reward them under the seniority system. Some of their plans to revise the Electoral College, such as splitting the electoral vote of each state proportionately, were designed to overcome this power.

From General George B. McClellan in 1864 to Harry Truman in 1948, our candidates (with the exception of the Bryan interlude) had almost invariably come from either New York or New Jersey. Even when the President was from a border state, as in the case of Truman, he had to adopt policies that would command the support of the industrial workers. We liberal Democrats were glad that this was so, and we were the strongest supporters of the Democratic Presidents. There was clear evidence, however, that while Truman depended on us for support, he did not like us personally. Indeed, judging by his statements both before and after his Presidency, I doubt whether he had much actual stomach for the racial reforms that he had to adopt. Since he was more Southern than Northern in his upbringing, I believe he did not like them. Certainly he disliked those who espoused the principles he proclaimed. I often felt that our position was like that of the antislavery Democrats such as Salmon P. Chase and John P. Hale in the decade prior to 1856.

Standing alone gave us moral strength, as Ibsen had observed it could in *The Enemy of the People*. While at first we were a relatively despised minority in the Senate, we believed that we represented an ever-growing proportion both of the public and of our national party. It was this fact that most alarmed the leaders of the South. They were determined to control the party and the legislative machinery in both houses. They did not intend to let the modern mudsills win.

The chief device they used for effecting this control was the seniority system, whereby men moved up on committees according to their relative length of service. Seniority was also supposed to determine the order in which men were designated to serve on the important committees. This worked almost invariably in the case of the South, but was frequently breached in the case of the North. This also gave the inside track to the Democratic Senators from the one-party states of the South and the mountains. On the Republican side, it rewarded those from the Middle West. The bipartisan alliance was, therefore, practiced in committee as well as on the floor, as was abundantly demonstrated in the committees on which I served.

The importance of seniority caused Southern Senators, once chosen, to have little or no opposition for their renomination and re-election. The Southern voters knew that the incumbents could get more for them than could a newcomer, who would have to start at the bottom. So they could serve as long as their health held out—and indeed longer, as did Carter Glass. A by-product of the seniority system in the South was that the governorship became largely a "dead-end" job; promotion to the Senate was largely blocked off.

The big states from which we liberal Democrats came were decidedly two-party states. After supporting the Democrats from 1930 to 1938, they had switched for ten years to the Republicans. This was particularly true of the Middle West. When this occurred, out went most of the sitting Senators and many Representatives. Changes also occurred in individual states due to the popularity or unpopularity of the incumbent and the importance of more or less local issues. It was rare when a Democrat from a "swing" state served more than two terms, and few went beyond a third term.

When our party came back in 1948 and carried Truman with it, we found the Southerners ensconced in the seats of power by means of the seniority system. That group, repudiated by the national convention and having tried, but failed, to defeat our Presidential candidate, now appeared in the legislative driver's seat. Of the fourteen Senate committees, no fewer than ten had Southern or pro-Southern chairmen. These included such all-important committees as Finance, Appropriations, Armed Services, Foreign Relations, and Judiciary. The Westerners were allowed complete control over the Interior Committee, the committee that most concerned them. Since the new Northerners had to be given some committees, they were relegated to those of secondary importance. The two subcellar or ghetto committees were those for the District of Columbia and the Post Office and Civil Service. These were stuffed with liberals. But control over the Post Office Committee was kept in Southern hands by its chairman, while Northern control over the District of Columbia Committee was offset by the fact that the Southerners always obtained complete dominance over the corresponding House committee. They could thus checkmate any Northern move to improve the legal status or facilities of the fast-swelling Negro population of the District.

There were two somewhat minor committees upon which the Southern overlords permitted the Northerners to sit: Labor and Public Welfare, and Banking and Currency. The former was a reluctant concession to the power of organized labor; the latter during my eighteen years always had a Southern chairman. Nor did the Southerners content themselves with only the top positions. They stacked the important committees with dominance in depth. For example, on Appropriations when I entered the Senate ten of the thirteen Democrats, including the five top-ranking members, were either Southern or pro-Southern. Moreover, two of the remaining three members were ambivalent in their attitudes and frequently traded with the Southerners. Since the senior members of the Appropriations Committee served as chairmen of the various subcommittees, the work of the committee as a whole was kept in Southern hands. If the majority of Congress did pass progressive legislation, the Appropriations committees could so reduce actual expenditures as to lessen its effectiveness. While our Southern friends were loud in their denunciation of the federal government as such, and were opposed to the national regulatory power being exercised under the commerce clause of the Constitution for the benefit of wage earners and Negroes, they were avid for federal expenditures. These were paid for by the income and corporation taxes levied on the Northern industrial states. Thus, the vast preponderance of the military installations was carefully located in the South, buoying up its economy with their ample payrolls, and the rivers and harbors of the South received an extraordinary amount of solicitous attention. Within the Appropriations Committee, a large proportion of the subcommittee chairmen were also chairmen of legislative committees. These constituted the real inner Sanhedrin at the heart of the so-called "Senate Establishment." Commonly, they were in charge of the appropriations for the same departments over whose legislation they presided.

Georgia was especially favored in this respect. Throughout most of my three terms, Richard Russell was chairman of both Armed Services and the corresponding Appropriations subcommittee. His fellow Georgian Carl Vinson similarly dominated military affairs in the House. Georgia was so heavily weighted down with military installations, it was said, that it could never blow away. Sometimes this form of double service had benign results, as in the hands of the humane Lister Hill, of Alabama.

When one looked over to the House side of the Capitol, one saw a similar Southern dominance of the Appropriations Committee. In 1949, of the eleven top Democrats on that committee, eight were Southerners and one strongly pro-Southern.

Southern dominance in depth extended to other committees. Four of the top six members of Finance, including its chairman, Walter George, were Southerners. Right under George was Tom Connally, of Texas, and Byrd, of Virginia. To protect the cotton, tobacco, and rice industries, which were still the basic foundations of the Southern agricultural economy, four of the six Democratic members of the Agriculture Committee were Southerners. In return for Republican help, the Southerners gave aid also to wheat and corn. There was a reciprocal tendency for the wheat Senators from beyond the Mississippi River to help the South on racial matters. Since the all-important conference committees were chosen from the senior members of the respective House and Senate committees, these, too, were generally controlled by the conservative coalition.

This Southern dominance of the Senate was based on seniority and was maintained by the cohesiveness of the Southerners, the undemocratic organization of our party, and the inability of the Northern liberals to form a comparable power bloc. For many years the Democrats met, once in two years, for only a brief hour prior to the opening of Congress. We elected our leaders—a perfunctory ceremony, since the Southerners had already made their choices, and their candidates, including the assistant leader, or whip, and some administrative officials, could not be defeated. Then we adjourned. The majority leader quietly appointed two committees, the so-called "Steering Committee," which determined membership on other committees and was in reality the powerful Committee on Committees, and the Policy Committee, which, with the leader, determined the priority of business on the floor and, in fact although not in name, was the actual steering committee. The membership of these committees was not published and was unknown to the public and, indeed, to many Senators. But it wielded great power. The important Committee on Committees was inevitably dominated by Southerners. Until 1961 it had from seven to nine members, nearly all from below the Mason-Dixon Line, or else "tame" Northerners. Newcomers were advised to see the members of this group, and especially the leader, Dick Russell, if they wanted a particular committee assignment.

Committee designations were held back until after the biennial struggle over the filibuster. The Senators were then rewarded or punished on the basis of their behavior on this crucial issue. Joseph S. Clark, Jr., of Pennsylvania, and I demonstrated this on the floor of the Senate in February, 1963. We showed what had happened to those who had tried to change Rule XXII and to those who defended it.* If they had voted against restricting the filibuster and against a change in Rule XXII, they were given good committee assignments and, later, generous appropriations, together with favorable legislation for their states. It is only on this basis that I can explain the otherwise inexplicable votes of Alaska and Hawaii on Rule XXII. Those who voted with us were pushed off into the least desirable committee posts. Thus Frank E. Moss, of Utah, a man of the highest character, was systematically deprived of a post on the Appropriations Committee largely because he always voted for modifying Rule XXII.

Things improved slightly after 1960, when Mike Mansfield, of Montana, became majority leader. A few more party caucuses were held, largely due to the efforts of Proxmire and Clark. One or two Midwesterners were added to the Steering Committee. It was from this section of the country that we Democrats had largely staged the party's senatorial comeback. The solitary committee senator of 1947 had now been replaced by a full fifteen. But for years Humphrey was the sole representative of the Midwest on the Steering Committee. He did his best, I am sure, but his lone voice was relatively ineffective.

Many of my friends asked me why the Northerners did not put up more opposition to the seniority rule. That is precisely what I tried to do for a full fifteen years. I sought to consolidate the North and the Midwest, to reach for support from the far West and Southwest, and to welcome stray liberals from the South. I spent thousands of dollars on luncheons in my office and dinners in my home. I formed personal friendships that I cherished, but so far as a tight political alliance was concerned, it was like trying to weave a rope from sand. We developed a certain cohesion on specific pieces of legislation, and this ability increased during the 1960's. But we could not carry through any concerted action to storm the seats of senatorial power or change the seniority rule. For years I kept a speech on the seniority rule and a resolution on how to change it in a drawer of my desk, but after an informal nose count each year I put it aside, convinced that in any open show of strength it would be overwhelmingly defeated. We could not maintain a united front even on legislative matters when the Southerners and Senate leaders were opposed. They had much to give; we had little or nothing. They parceled out committee memberships, appropriations for pet projects, backing for minor pieces of legislation,

* See the *Congressional Record* for February 19, 20, and 21, 1963. Also, Clark and Other Senators, *The Senate Establishment,* New York: Hill and Wang, 1963.

trips abroad for special senatorial committees, and a foothold on the totem pole of status. We could offer only the rewards of good conscience and an appeal to the voters back home, many of whom were either ignorant or indifferent about the issues involved. The Establishment made constant efforts to detach Northerners and Westerners from us, and these were often successful, especially with members from the smaller and the mountain states.

The other side was tightly organized and cohesive. In the beginning, all the Southerners but Kefauver attended their secret conferences, presided over by Russell. Their decisions were rigidly followed. Later, Gore and Yarborough also stayed away. But the leaders could almost always deliver nineteen or twenty straight Southern votes plus four to six more from the border, the Southwest, and the mountains. Holding the vantage points on the committees, they were unbeatable within the Democratic caucus.

The important staffs of the committees were selected by the chairmen, and hence were Southern in origin and sympathy. This meant that we Northerners could not obtain the same degree of help as our Southern colleagues. During a filibuster, committee work was set aside so that the aides might turn out interminable speeches for the talkathon participants, the time having passed when filibustering Senators read telephone books and recipes, as Huey Long had done in the 1930's.

In the Senate chamber, both parliamentarians were from south of the Mason-Dixon Line, as were most of the clerks. The floor aides were headed by Robert G. ("Bobby") Baker, of South Carolina, who became the efficient and trusted lieutenant of Lyndon Johnson when he was majority leader. The Northerners were seldom informed of the real plans of the leadership, and often declined important invitations back home only to find that Johnson had returned to Texas, and we could not do anything in his absence. At other times, when we risked going home, we were caught flat-footed by an unannounced important vote. This happened to both Humphrey and me on crucial amendments to the Landrum-Griffin Act. Johnson once sprang an oil-depletion vote when no fewer than fifteen of our supporters were in Canada at an international conference.

Our objections were not personal, but to the system. It was not in the public interest that such great power should be given to a group of men who opposed the program of the national party and were chosen by a narrow segment of the electorate. Not only were most of their states relatively small, but also, because, through the poll tax and other devices, Negroes, Mexicans, and poor whites were kept from voting, Southern senators were actually elected by only a small percentage of their constituents. Under pressure from us Northern liberals, who were about to pass legislation ending the poll tax, Senator Spessard Holland, of Florida, finally got through a constitutional amendment abolishing the poll tax, but only in federal elections.*

With the passage of time, the control of the Southern oligarchy has been slightly eroded because the electoral base within their states has been broadened. Although efforts to limit the filibuster are still regularly defeated, prudence has made the Southern leaders more chary in its use.

The earlier hold of the Southern oligarchy was further strengthened by their control over such central campaign funds as did exist. Except in those cases where the Democratic candidates in the North and West were millionaires, they were generally without adequate funds and had to face well-heeled opponents who had the overwhelming weight of the press plus the corporations, banks, and utilities against them. To help offset this, the Senatorial Campaign Committee was set up, but the chairman and members were appointed by the leader. For years it was well known that this committee secured the major portion of its funds from the oil and gas crowd and from special business interests, such as mailers of advertising matter, which wanted Congressional protection. This money was primarily doled out to candidates with a good chance of winning who were amenable to the special interests. Bobby Baker was the field director of this work. In this way several who started out as defenders of the people were subverted at crucial periods into becoming workers for special privilege. These men were the real tragedies of Congressional life, and nothing was more painful than to see this erosion of character.

There *were* candidates made of sturdier stuff. One was Utah's Frank E. Moss. At first he was overlooked in 1958 by the committee. But when he gained ground during the last month of the campaign, a trusted lieutenant was sent out to look over the situation. He called Moss by telephone and asked if he would like to have $10,000. The reply was, "Of course!" Moss was hard up and badly needed money for printing and television and radio time. Then the emissary explained the catch: "The money is yours if you agree that if elected you will protect the 27½-percent depletion allowance on oil and gas." Moss was silent for a minute, after which his voice came over the telephone clear and strong. "I don't know much about that issue. We have oil in our state, and if I had time to go into it, I might decide as you suggest. But if the price for getting the $10,000 is to pledge myself in advance to support something which I am not sure is right, then I cannot pay that price." The agent came out of the telephone booth with tears in his eyes, convinced that here was an honest man going down to defeat because he would not sell out. Being a decent fellow, he subsequently told the story to a liberal contributor in the East. Quick as a flash, she said that she would send a major part of the $10,000,

---

* In the 1930's Louisiana, through Huey Long's efforts, and North Carolina, which was the most liberal of the Southern states, had abolished the poll tax by state action.

with no strings attached. Her gift turned the tide, and Ted always voted his conscience on every roll call.

Despite my opposition to the depletion allowance, I did not suffer for it inside our party when I came up for re-election in 1954. Earle C. Clements was then the whip and he was of great help at a crucial time. But in 1960, although from the fourth-largest state in the union, I received only $5,000 from the committee, $3,000 of which I had raised for them. At the same time, they poured enormous sums into a tiny state to help a Senator who voted against most of Truman's program when the latter was President and later in opposition to the national program of our party.

Joe Clark used to say that we Northern liberals would outlast the Southerners and would ultimately take over even under the seniority rule. The Southerners were getting old and would soon pass from the scene, but "we have held on from 1948 and 1956 through, 1964." He seemed confident of the future. I was not so sure. But the elections of 1966, 1968, and 1970 have in fact reduced the relative strength of the Northern Democrats. Both Joe and I have gone. The party's total strength has decreased by thirteen—nearly all from the North or the West —while our Southern friends have mostly shown a ruggedness that defies time. When a few are replaced by Republicans, the newcomers are generally even more conservative.

The Southerners, therefore, still hold the citadels of power. They still control the Committee on Committees, and up to now no one has been elected majority leader or secretary without their approval. The committees are almost as much under their control as formerly. Indeed, in 1967–68 they seemed to be slightly more so; no Northerner was chairman of any committee. Southerners headed no fewer than eleven committees, with a friend in charge of at least one more. Seven of the top eight members of the Appropriations Committee were Southerners, as were four of the top six on Armed Services. Well might the cynic say, *"Plus ça change, plus c'est la même chose."* Nevertheless, in 1969 we gained, and there were four Northern or Western chairmen.

Perhaps I should not further belabor the point, but the Southerners have yet another strength in their journalistic outriders. Just as the Scottish have sent their ablest administrators to London and the Sicilians their brightest lawyers north to Rome and Milan, so the Southerners send their ablest journalists to the North. There is a gravitational pull that brings them to Washington. Most of them are delightful fellows who have come north, in part, because as intellectually emancipated people they had found themselves uneasy under the rigid doctrine of white supremacy. There were none better than these men, of whom perhaps the best examples were the columnist Tom Stokes and, today, Tom Wicker. But some come north with a chip on their shoulder. They still believe that the

Negro should be kept down, and they yearn for the Southern society of pre-Civil War days.

Actually theirs was a false picture, as shown by such works as Fanny Kemble's account of a year on the Georgia plantation of her husband, Pierce Butler. But it was romantic and cherished. These scriveners gloried in the Southern domination of the Capitol and turned the full force of their ridicule and ire on those who tried to improve the status of the Negroes and Mexican-Americans, and who advocated majority rule. Perhaps the most talented was a Texan, William S. White, who had celebrated the ways of the Senate hierarchy in his widely read book *Citadel*. For many years he was the journalistic hatchet man for Lyndon Johnson, who, in turn, presented the book to each incoming Senate member for his guidance. It was White who, in a burst of frankness, referred to the Senate as "the South's revenge for Gettysburg." Truer words were never written. White and his friends lost no chance to satirize our little group of Northern liberals. We certainly had our weaknesses, but I hardly think we deserved the stream of abuse he poured on us. He invented the phrase "knee-jerk liberals," and claimed that our beliefs were derived from passion and prejudice. On top of this he berated our ineffectiveness as compared to the practical politicians Johnson, Dirksen, and Nixon, who "knew how to get things done." As the alliance between Johnson and Humphrey hardened, Hubert alone was promoted to the ranks of the redeemed.

This constant drumfire of syndicated criticism weakened us at home, especially since it was taken up in an antiphonal chorus by most of the Republican papers. I remembered a brave Southern comrade on Peleliu who, when his tongue was loosened by a few drinks in the evening, spoke of his real inner desires. He wanted one more war—this time a renewal of the conflict of 1861–65. He saw himself at the end of this second struggle leading a regiment of cavalry up Pennsylvania Avenue to take possession of the Capitol, from which he would hoist the Stars and Bars. Many times during my service in the Senate I thought of sending a telegram to this comrade: "Dear Walter, Relax. The Confederates have already moved on the Capitol and are in full possession. Hoisting the Stars and Bars would be only a formality."

I do not quite know how we kept on during the 1950's. Negroes in Alabama were no more isolated than we Northern liberals in Washington. But, pushing ahead, we survived to see a Texas President, swayed partially by opportunism, help us achieve many of the reforms for which we had worked for fifteen years and against which he, as a Senator, had striven. Is it not possible that some of the current arson and bloodshed might have been averted had the advice of the "knee-jerk liberals" been taken earlier?

In addition to the seniority system, the second, and reserve, weapon of the South was the filibuster, the practice of interminable debate and other delaying tactics by a minority. This was used to prevent a vote, and was, therefore, a device for balking the will of the majority.

Between 1815 and 1917 there had been no parliamentary rule that could be used in the Senate to limit debate, which could go on as long as Senators could stand and talk. There was no way to close debate, as the House did, by moving the "previous question." In the winter of 1917, when the Germans announced the opening of unrestricted submarine warfare to prevent us from supplying the Allied armies, President Wilson responded by asking for legislation to arm our merchantmen to repel these attacks. This was opposed by an antiwar bloc led by La Follette and Norris, who feared that it would accelerate the drift toward war. They were badly outnumbered, but they prevented action by a round-the-clock filibuster in the closing days of the lame-duck Congress, which at that time lasted until noon of March 4.

Popular indignation rose against those who filibustered, and there was great pressure to end the possibility of future filibusters. Wilson called the new Congress into session immediately. While the details of the negotiations are not fully known, it seems probable that Wilson's Congressional leaders used the threat of establishing the "previous question" as an approved parliamentary practice. This had been done in Jefferson's time and then allowed to lapse. Such a motion, like that of tabling, is not subject to debate and can immediately stop discussion to compel a vote without further talk. Unlike tabling, which kills a proposal, the motion can be used to brush aside all delays and thus to expedite a vote on the motion itself. If a motion to table an amendment is defeated, filibustering by those who are still hostile can continue unabated. To retain "tabling" and reject the "previous question" as parliamentary devices is, therefore, to provide a minority of objectors with a "heads I win, tails you lose" situation. But while the "previous question" is logically the affirmative analogue for the negative tabling motion, it is a very severe device. It is the parliamentary guillotine, and can be used by a majority to shut off all discussion by a minority. And yet so great was the indignation at the tactics of La Follette and Norris, and so deep the feeling against Germany, that had a motion been introduced to establish the "previous question," it would probably have carried.

Wilson's men finally persuaded the Senate recalcitrants to compromise, by accepting a way of limiting debate. This was the device of cloture, and it was embodied in the celebrated Rule XXII. Upon a petition of sixteen Senators, a vote must be held upon cloture after an intervening day. If two-thirds of those then voting are for cloture, subsequent debate is limited, each Senator being allowed to speak one hour and no more. This time is not transferable. At the expiration of this time a vote on the pending motion has to be taken. In the Senate of ninety-six members, the negative votes of thirty-three could, therefore, prevent debate from being limited and permit it to go on.

Various attempts had been made to invoke cloture in the third of a century between 1917 and 1949. These had commonly, though not exclusively, been on civil-rights issues. All but one had failed. It was hard enough to get favorable action on civil rights from the Judiciary Committee, which generally had a pro-Southern chairman. But even if such a measure successfully ran that gauntlet, there were three further barriers that it might be forced to surmount on the floor of the Senate itself.

One of these was invoked in 1946, when my wife was serving in the House and I was in the Naval Hospital in Bethesda. In amazement, I read in the newspapers of the Southerners objecting to the reading of the Journal for the preceding day. I had never heard of the Journal, as distinguished from the *Congressional Record*. It was apparently the bare but official record of action taken on the preceding day. It was now revealed to the public that it had to be approved before the Senate could proceed. This approval had always been taken for granted or given by unanimous consent. Now the Southerners professed such grave religious and ethical scruples as to forbid this granting of approval. After scrutinizing the little-known Journal, the Southerners had found that it lacked a proper prayer; there was no reference to a Supreme Being or one satisfactory to the religious sentiments of the South. This, they sanctimoniously proclaimed, was sacrilegious. Since the record was wanting in proper respect for God, the Senate could not proceed to consider civil rights until this error was corrected. The discussion went on day after day *ad nauseam*. To prevent civil rights from even being discussed by an obviously staged use of the Deity seemed to most people the real sacrilege, but it was effective. So much time was taken up in this foolishness, and the prospect of overcoming the obvious filibuster was so slight, that finally the civil-rights activists accepted defeat. The name of God had been successfully used to defeat civil rights. While this device was never again used to the full extent of this display, it was always there, and once or twice it was used as a delaying tactic to prolong discussion and to increase the effectiveness of a filibuster.

Another parliamentary obstacle the South could set up was the formal motion to take up the bill, a required first step for all legislation normally granted to the majority leader as a matter of course. After it has once been granted, the bill can be presented for consideration. The Southerners could always delay consideration of a civil-rights bill by debating this motion.

Once in a while in my time the main thrust of the filibuster would be staged against this very point. In general, however, after an intervening period of nonessential debate, Russell, with a magnanimous air, would withdraw his objections and in a condescending way permit debate to proceed on the motion itself. But the intervening delay set back the legislative schedule and, hence, strengthened the tactical position of the filibusterers. Then a tug of war began.

There was an elaborate display of courtesy by both sides, each pretending that logic and ethics, rather than force, would determine the final result. Arguments in support of the legislation were presented. The Southerners argued against it. This went on for a few days, and then the burden of debate was thrown upon the Southerners. They were ready, with long speeches stockpiled for just such occasions; they never ran out of material. This their speech writers had amply provided, and over the years we recognized the rerun of old favorites. Just as ministers occasionally repeat their sermons or swap them with colleagues, so did the Southern members of Congress.

The Majority Leader, wanting to give the impression that he was in earnest, would then take some steps to break the filibuster. He would begin by lengthening the hours of debate from noon to 6:00 or 8:00 P.M. Then the Senate would be called into session at 10:00 A.M. instead of at noon; this would be followed, or accompanied, by prolonging the parliamentary day to 10:00 P.M. or midnight. The Senate would then be on a twelve- to fourteen-hour day.

Meanwhile, the pressure of other work never let up. The daily quota of letters continued to pour into our offices, demanding answers. The telephone brought allegedly urgent messages. Large numbers of visitors called, who had to be greeted not only with courtesy but also with friendliness.

The group supporting civil rights faced a tactical choice: to proceed directly to the test by filing a cloture petition or to make one last, desperate effort to break the will of the Southerners by round-the-clock sessions. We were in a dilemma. If we decided to try the cloture route immediately and failed, as we probably would, we could be charged with neglecting the one method that, it was said, might have brought the South to its knees—namely, forcing the filibusterers into complete physical exhaustion.

My sympathy for the party leadership in this case was ironic, because the leaders did not really want their own motions to prevail. They had been elected to the leadership by Southern votes and held office at the pleasure of the South. They were active allies of the South in seeing to it that committee vacancies were so filled as to keep the Southerners in control of the strategic spots. Often they were forced into the effort to break a filibuster only by pressure from a Democratic President or a national party leader who had to deal with a nation and not a state and who sometimes did not actually believe in what he was doing. If ever trumpets gave an uncertain sound, theirs did. This in itself discouraged the less committed from following into battle with alacrity. The mountain states in particular displayed no enthusiasm for breaking a filibuster.

It was soon discovered, moreover, that the long—and especially the continuous—sessions tired us out far more than they did the filibusterers. They could count on a hard-core "battalion of death" of from eighteen to twenty. One such specialist was barrel-chested Allen J. Ellender, of Louisiana, known affectionately as the "Little Bull" or, to the classicists, the "Minotaur," who had the endurance of a marathon runner. He beamed happily once as he finished a solo stint of fifteen hours. But as Russell assumed greater control over Southern efforts, he introduced strict military discipline. A confidential schedule was drawn up apportioning the time in blocks of four hours. Two Southerners were assigned to each block —one to speak and the other as assistant or lookout. If the orator grew tired, his alter ego relieved him by asking ceremoniously, "Mr. President, I ask unanimous consent that the speaker may yield to me for a question." To this the speaker would carefully reply, with even greater ceremony, "I yield for a question only provided it is understood that I do not lose my right to the floor."

This was the chance for the Northern lookout, also in attendance, to object and force the speaker to continue. But this ungentlemanly practice was used only by those whom Mr. White called confirmed "knee-jerk liberals." Although theoretically the speaker could be compelled to stand erect at his desk, forcing compliance was held by the Sanhedrin not to be cricket.

Most Southerners, with one or two like-minded colleagues present, could last their four hours by reading slowly from a prepared text. Although Huey Long's model for a filibuster had been full of irrelevancies, such as his recipes for pot liquor, the Southerners of the 1950's spoke in relatively germane terms. Like medieval theologians, they could spin out their case to interminable lengths. When they finished, they called for a quorum but, in true military fashion, obeyed Russell's order not to quit until properly relieved.

Since there were eight two-man shifts of four hours each, any one speaker, when he finished his stint, would not have to talk again for at least three days, although he would stand watch. But he had to be on the floor only eight hours in all, or less than three hours a day. Only two to four of the Southerners answered any quorum.

But the opposition had to be on hand at every quorum call. During the call, all proceedings stopped. Unless we could muster a majority to answer the quorum, the clerk notified the absentees, and if a quorum was still not obtained, the sergeant at arms would be sent out to round up the others. Since that post was always filled by a Southerner, he would, of course, concentrate on the Northerners and be unable to find his fellow Southerners.

We wanted the quorums to be answered quickly, since this would deprive the South of these bonus periods of rest. And we did not want to see any of our members dragged in and shown to be one of those who had fallen asleep on duty. But it was hard to get and hold a quorum. The Southerners, with their allies from the border states and, quite commonly, from the mountains and the Southwest, would of course stay away. They did not want the quorum completed; the longer it took, the more their filibuster was strengthened. This meant a minimum loss of thirty members and gave us only a possible sixty-six to seventy from which to get the required forty-nine, or, after the admission of Alaska and Hawaii, fifty-one. The absentees, aided by fifth columnists within the ranks of both parties, were always more than thirty.

Every liberal had to be in constant readiness to go to the floor and also to appeal for co-operation to the indifferent. This was bad enough, but Russell, with the ingenuity of a Torquemada, frequently gave another turn to the screw. Instead of having his soldiers hold forth for a four-hour stretch, he reduced them to two hours. As each speaker yielded the floor, he called for a quorum, and the bells sounded. It was hard enough to sleep on the cots set up in the adjoining marble room, but it became impossible when there were at least twelve daily quorum calls. Sometimes, feeling their strength, the Southerners called for a quorum every hour. We, of course, did not get any help from Southern members of the Senate staff. During one continuous session of seventy-two hours, I was able to sleep only three. Flesh and blood cannot stand such a strain for long. But I take some pride in the fact that, though I was the oldest man in the civil-rights group, my record in answering quorum calls was equaled only by that of Bill Proxmire, who, of all Senators past and present, best deserves the title "Iron Man."

Finally we would give up the effort. We would file a cloture petition, catch some rest in the intervening day, and then, red-eyed, haggard, and weary, stagger into the chamber for the final showdown. The Southerners, on the other hand, would appear sleek, well-dressed, and have sparkling eyes and rosy cheeks. Visitors in the galleries could only conclude that they were superior beings. This impression would be heightened when Russell took the floor to denounce in terms of purest liberalism this nefarious attempt to impose "gag rule" upon "the greatest deliberative body in the world." Doggedly answering to our names, we would wait for the inevitable discouraging tally. The Democratic party leader usually made some comments in which he congratulated the Southerners for their sterling part in the debate. Back we would go to our offices to catch up on our mail and to our homes to sleep.

It seemed futile; we couldn't win. But in a few days some of us would repeat the motto Andrew Furuseth always carried on the masthead of his paper when he fought for seamen's rights: "Tomorrow is also a day." Our votes mounted over the years, and the absurdity of the most powerful democracy conducting its business in this way was not lost on the newspapers of the country. Many Americans abroad hung their heads in shame at the taunts of critics. Even the iron-willed Russell was said to have told his intimates that he did not know how many more tests they could make. Finally, in 1963, we broke through this barrier, and other victories came in 1964, 1965, and 1968.

In the background there were intellectual subtleties connected with the whole question of extended debate. We always believed in full discussion as a necessary prelude for wise action. This was especially true when the Senate or the public was either indifferent or ill-informed on an important issue. But when did extended debate cease and filibuster start? It was not easy to draw the dividing line.

This question came up continually during my period of service. We would find ourselves confronted by some bill supported by the bipartisan coalition that upon examination we would find to be gravely defective. The coalition would want to rush it through. Certainly it should be discussed and analyzed. But for how long? Since all Senators are busy, they try to concentrate on their own affairs and those of their special committees; on other matters they are likely to agree with those whom they trust. Yet in a popular argument repetition is essential. Busy men are not convinced by a glancing reference or a subtle allusion. The argument has to be ample, well-documented, and sustained. It has to be more than an individual venture and must have mass support among the voters to be seriously considered by the majority of the members.

It takes a hard core of at least ten to keep a discussion going for days in the Senate. When we could find allies to share the burden we sometimes, for a crucial matter, took on the task of trying to educate both the Senate and the public by extended debate. If we did so, some Southerners would accuse us of hypocrisy. But there was always a basic distinction between our tactics and those of the Southern filibusterers. They wanted to prevent a vote. We wanted only to delay it until the appropriate time.

In 1954 when Clinton P. Anderson and others filibustered over the atomic-energy bill being fostered by the Republicans and Johnson, I remained on the side lines. I even voted for cloture, lest I seem to be giving aid and comfort to the filibusterers. On the whole, I had come to believe that a debate should not run for more than a month, and that it should not be continued if the discussion had, for a considerable period of time, ceased to be educational and had become merely delaying. But during my last three years in the Senate I came much closer to Wayne Morse's position. Morse, who loved to filibuster and was a prima donna in his solo flights, acknowledged that he was filibustering but pointed out that he always supported measures to make cloture easier and would continue to do so. Moreover, since the Southerners maintained the filibuster for their own purposes, they could not properly object if he used it for his.

In 1963 the administration, with the help of Senators Mansfield and John O. Pastore, insisted on the passage of the so-called Comsat bill, giving monopoly control over the newly successful communications satellite to a mixed public-private corporation. Long, Kefauver, and Gore believed that the new corporation would be merely a front for the American Telephone and Telegraph Company, and they favored establishing something like the Tennessee Valley Authority or the Atomic Energy Commission, whereby the government would own the satellite but could lease it to a private corporation. Although slightly skeptical, I inclined to their views. I agreed to help by asking a dozen hitherto unanswered questions of Gore, which took him two hours to answer. There were not more than seven or eight of us in the delaying group, not enough to stage an effective filibuster, and to break it Mansfield ordered a continuous session and denounced the objectors. The contrast between the benign way in which he had always treated the Southern filibusterers against human rights and the way he was throwing the book at Kefauver and Gore because they were filibustering against A.T. & T. made me angry. I determined not to be a party to breaking the filibuster, and one day, along with a few others, absented myself from the floor. We had learned that a considerable number of the Senate would also be absent, and we believed that our failure to appear would prevent a quorum and so gain another day. Mansfield and Bobby Baker were furious that we had adopted Southern tactics. An assistant sergeant at arms was sent to hunt me down and bring me back. Leaving my house early, I went to the home of a friend who had an excellent swimming pool. Then, as the bloodhounds drew near, Emily and I drove out of the city and enjoyed a box lunch under the trees, reading poetry together. We came back to the city only after the Senate had recessed for lack of a quorum. As I moved about, I felt like a fugitive, and next morning returned with the rest to receive Mansfield's tongue-lashing. Most of the Southerners swallowed their dislike of cloture and either voted for it or did not oppose it. Mansfield then really applied the gag rule, moving to table without debate every amendment, no matter how sensible. It was like a legislative lynching bee.

During a final day of that debate, Estes Kefauver quietly asked if he might be excused, because he was having trouble breathing. He went home, and the next day his heart broke. A true soldier of the people and a steadfast friend, he died on the field of battle. We who loved him went to Tennessee to help bury him. A deluge of rain broke out as his coffin was lowered, drenching his wife, Nancy, and his children as they bravely stood by the open grave. Back in Washington the next day, the men who had helped to drive him to his death heaped fulsome tributes on his memory. Their hypocrisy so sickened me that I determined to leave word that if I died in office no word of praise was to be offered.

17

Some Political and Congressional Personalities

A President

FROM THE START, my relations with President Truman were unfortunate. As I look back at the magnitude of his tasks and the courage and wisdom with which he met crises, I sincerely regret our differences. Nevertheless, my academic background seems to have been a real liability in his eyes.

Not having gone beyond high school, Harry Truman spent his young manhood as a none-too-successful Missouri farmer. As President, he still felt uncomfortable with so-called intellectuals and preferred poker-playing intimates such as Major General Harry H. Vaughn, his military aide and court jester; Matthew J. Connelly, his appointments secretary; William M. Boyle, Jr., his Kansas City associate, whom he had made chairman of the National Committee; and Donald S. Dawson, an administrative assistant. After the 1948 election, they all journeyed together to Key West, where his associates apparently perfected their plans to take over the Reconstruction Finance Corporation. In the process, they naturally wanted to discredit potential roadblocks. William Fulbright, an Oxford graduate and Rhodes Scholar, and I were easy game. It was rumored that the President, in his characteristically pungent fashion, had referred to us both as "overeducated s.o.b.'s."

It is true that I had unwittingly given the President ample cause for offense. First, I had supported Eisenhower for the Democratic nomination at the Philadelphia convention. And when my campaign was at its most desperate period, Truman had written, in his own hand, congratulating me on my New York *Times Magazine* article on campaigning. One of my campaign contributors, a manuscript collector and dealer, asked for the letter, and I let him have it. I thought matters would end there, but he, in good faith, advertised it for sale. Truman found out about this and properly resented it. I do not think he ever forgave me, even though I recovered the letter and returned it to him with an apology.

In 1951 other strains developed. One stemmed from my work on the subcommittee that investigated the RFC, which I have described earlier. As our findings helped to uncover scandal, involving the administration, in government agencies, the White House coterie determined to counterattack. One afternoon while our committee was meeting in executive session, a secretary came in to tell our beloved Republican member, Charles Tobey, that the White House wanted to talk to him on the telephone. Tobey came back within ten minutes with a solemn pale face. "That was the President," he said. "He told me that the real crooks and influence peddlers were members of this committee, as we might soon find out." I asked if he interpreted this as a threat to open up on us if we went on with our investigation. Tobey confirmed this. "Then there is only one thing for us to do," I said. "We must go ahead full tilt and summon the crucial administration witnesses to the stand." Fulbright and Tobey agreed, so we sent out our summons for the following morning.

The RFC had already engaged a discredited publicity man, and false rumors started through the grapevine that Fulbright was deeply involved with the notorious gangster Frank Costello in a Hot Springs motel. Realizing that I would probably be next, I immediately ordered all my correspondence with the RFC to be reviewed. My files were not in good order, but by working all night my staff found three cases where I had recommended a loan. At the next morning's hearings I read all three letters into the record and stated that I had probably gone too far and should have recommended only "proper attention." The faces of the RFC representatives fell visibly as I made this statement, and their counterattack ceased abruptly.

Shortly afterward an Internal Revenue agent called to say that he wanted to investigate my income tax returns. I welcomed him, gave him all my major financial records, assigned him a desk in my secretary's office, and answered all questions. I asked him to go to Chicago and check on me there, too. He did, and combed the city thoroughly. After a month he returned, rather shamefacedly, to say that everything was in order and I owed the government nothing. "Is that all?" I asked. "No," he reluctantly replied. "We find you overpaid the government by $41.12." I told him to write me a letter saying that after examination he had found that instead of my owing the government money, it owed me that sum. His face whitened. "I can't do that," he said. I told him that he must. He had been running all over Chicago and Washington and in his inquiries had aroused the suspicions of many. Those had now been proved false. But the public did not know it. If nothing was said, people, with their readiness to believe the worst, would still think I was guilty. The agent grew more confused. Finally he said that he must take this up with higher authority, he had no power to do it on his own. In two days he was back again to say that he hoped I would not make any request about publicity.

By this time I was very angry. "Tell your principal, whoever he may be, high or low, that if such a statement is not made, I will issue a press release and indeed may take the floor of the Senate to say that during the RFC investigation the Bureau of Internal Revenue investigated me and, after a prolonged inquiry, found that I had not only paid every cent I owed the government, but had actually overpaid by $41.12. I will also state that upon my requesting that they send me a letter to that effect in order to clear my name, they refused." I thought I saw some beads of perspiration on his brow as he replied that he would have to go back and consult his principal.

He was there the next day with the statement and a check. I gave the letter to the press without comment. I was not further harassed by the Bureau, but, of course, always had my books ready for their inspection.

When asked about the incident, the Bureau tossed the matter off by saying that it was just a routine examination and had no relation to my investigation of the RFC. Perhaps this was true—but the experience gave me a glimpse of how those in power within the bureaucracy can punish and intimidate those who fall out of their favor. He who quarrels with them must not only have an impeccable record, but courage as well. How many are fortunate enough to be in that position?

At one point during the investigation of the RFC, Fulbright and I sought a conference with the President to urge him to clean house in the RFC and to allow Dawson to come before us to testify instead of pleading "executive privilege," as it was rumored he intended to do. I felt moved to tell him that he had been loyal to friends who had not been loyal to him. Now he was bearing the brunt of their falsity. We were in the Oval Room at the White House, and I recall his momentary silence as he sadly looked out at the slanting rain. "I guess you are right," he murmured. Then he rose, shook hands warmly, and the interview was over. But he made no changes in the RFC or in his personal staff, although he did direct Dawson to appear before us for questioning. Carefully coached by the able White House counsel, Clark Clifford, Dawson made a good showing, and only minor peccadilloes were proved against him.

These events were high-lighted by the Republican press, and the so-called "mess in Washington" played a considerable part in the Democratic defeat in 1952.

In 1950 I was chairman of the Senate committee to investigate and report on ethical standards in government. While I believe the report based on our hearings has exerted a long-run influence for good on both state and national government, it did not further endear me to the President. He subsequently sent me a handwritten letter telling me I should keep hands off the affairs of his public servants. I replied that I had been directed by Congress to do precisely what I was doing and could not default on my duty. Later, Newbold Morris was dismissed after having been summoned from New York by Truman ostensibly to do the same thing that I was doing.

My final clash with the President came over the filling of two vacancies on the federal bench for northern Illinois. After some negotiation, the Democratic leaders of Chicago agreed to accept my man, William H. King, a highly respected leader of the bar, and I accepted their suggestion of an able local judge, Benjamin Epstein. But there were dissident elements in the Cook County party who had other ideas and who convinced Truman that he should reject both these nominees and name two others, of their choice. Without consulting me, he sent these alternative names to the Senate in July, 1951. I then had the choice of meekly giving in or of fighting. Sparring for time, I asked the Bar Association to take an advisory poll of its members as to their preference. The result was an overwhelming victory for my men, which was confirmed by an independent poll of all Illinois lawyers conducted by the *Sun-Times*. Feeling more certain of my ground, I objected to the President's nominees, being careful to state that while they were not personally objectionable to me, the "manner and method" of their appointment was. The Senate, anxious not to surrender its prerogative in such matters, refused to confirm them. Jack Arvey and I then made efforts in the fall to come to an agreement with the President, but he was adamant. It had to be his way. So the judgeships remained vacant and were later filled by Republicans when Eisenhower took office. This experience strengthened the belief of the general public in my independence, but it did not help me with the Democratic ward leaders. In fact, it created some bitter cleavages, which not only hurt me in my race for re-election in 1954, but also endured long afterward.

In spite of these experiences, I never allowed my differences with Truman the man to interfere with my support of Truman the President. I worked hard for the passage of his legislation on housing, taxation, labor problems, and civil rights, in which I believed more strongly than he. And I was one of the leaders in defending the North Atlantic Treaty Organization alliance and building up NATO armed forces. I also took the lead in defending his action in coming to the defense of Korea against the Communist attack, and I energetically supported rearmament. In 1951 I became the Democrat who was usually pitted against Robert Taft on such matters. None of this softened Truman's personal dislike and opposition.

Looking back over these years, however, one must admire the bravery and the wisdom with which the untried and relatively untrained man from Missouri, catapulted into an awesome place of responsibility by the death of Franklin D. Roosevelt, faced and made some of the most important decisions in the history of the republic. Consider some of these: the use of the atomic bomb, a decision made on the basis of Army Intelligence estimates that a frontal attack on Japan by conventional forces would cost us 250,000 deaths and a million other casualties, with Japanese losses four or five times greater; the warning to Russia that it must live up to its agreement to get out of Iran; the stopping of Russian penetration of the eastern Aegean with its threat to Turkey; the provision of military and economic aid to Greece when the British laid down that burden, which prevented the Communists from taking over that country; the drafting and successful carrying out of the Marshall Plan, which saved Western Europe from economic collapse and Communism; the launching of Point Four, the "bold new program" to bring technical aid to the underdeveloped countries of the world; the development of the hydrogen bomb, which helped to prevent the Russians from dominating the world; the dispatch of immediate military aid to Korea when it was attacked, a decision made in desolate loneliness as Truman flew back from his mother's funeral; the dismissal of General Douglas MacArthur for disobeying orders issued by the President, as commander in chief, who feared that bombing beyond the Yalu River would bring China and Russia into the war and create a nuclear holocaust.

There were other great decisions, but these were perhaps the most important. As he made them, the little former artillery captain put aside his prejudices and his love of Missouri-style politics to act on the basis of what he thought was best for the United States of America. At such times the pettiness in Truman's character was burned away and he became a true and wise patriot who was not afraid to make a decision and who fully realized the truth of the slangy slogan that he put on his desk, "The buck stops here."

Truman did all this, moreover, without yielding to domestic reaction, striving all the while to help build a more tolerant and more humane America. Compared with his great decisions, his little personal animosities and vendettas were minor. It is one of the vindications of time that historians and the general public have started to realize this and to rate him while still living as one of our near-great Presidents. I have had the pleasure of personally telling him this several times, but I am sure that he continued to cherish his dislike.

The Southerners

BY THE TIME I reached the Senate, the most blatant Dixiecrats, or exponents of white supremacy, had disappeared from the scene. E. D. ("Cotton Ed") Smith and Theodore Bilbo had died, and W. Lee ("Pappy") O'Daniel had retired in high dudgeon. Only James Eastland remained, and he was personally far more temperate in manner, if not in speech, and far more courteous in his personal relations.

But the determination of the Southerners to preserve their supremacy, while more suavely expressed, was as strong as ever. The glove might be silken, but inside remained the fist of steel. Richard Russell, of Georgia, was the intellectual leader of the Southern hierarchy. Son of a distinguished family and one of sixteen children, he had been the youngest governor ever to rule in Georgia. To his credit, he had fought Eugene Talmadge, as a supporter of Franklin Roosevelt, and came to the Senate in the early 1930's at a young age. He quickly became more conservative. A reserved bachelor with no apparent social interests, he mastered the rules and procedures of the Senate and used them to defeat and emasculate any proposal aimed at improving the status of Negroes. Although in no sense a military veteran, he devoted himself to building a strong national defense and on military affairs was the best-informed and most influential man in the Senate. In this he complemented Carl Vinson, a fellow Georgian in the House. In their foreign-policy and military decisions both men were true patriots swayed by conventional wisdom. Russell spoke seldom, but when he came into the chamber with his nose tilted haughtily in the air, we knew we were in for trouble. We found that the higher his nose, the more coldly sarcastic he would be. I worked out a fairly accurate weather vane to measure his moods by the elevation he gave to his proboscis.

In tight parliamentary situations, a gentler and more lovable character would sit by his side. This was Lister Hill, of Alabama, still looking young and fine despite his thirty years of service in House and Senate. He had come to the Senate in 1938 as a liberal New Dealer whose victory, with that of Claude Pepper, had temporarily broken the back of Congressional opposition to the Fair Labor Standards Act and had enabled it to be passed. He had nominated Roosevelt at the 1940 Chicago convention with ringing old-style Southern oratory. With the passage of time and the pressure of his environment, Hill's liberalism had become muted. But his spirit remained humane, and he sought an expression for his true impulses in the way of his Quaker godfather, the founder of antiseptic surgery, Joseph Lister, under whom his father had studied. Hill promoted the widest variety of public-health measures, and was the real author of the Hill-Burton Act, which, by providing federal aid for the construction of hospitals, has added hundreds of thousands of much needed beds for the care of the sick. He was also the staunch defender of the National Institutes of Health, and, indeed, commonly insisted on stuffing them with more funds than they could properly spend. He would support the just claims of labor to the limit of political practicality, and federal aid to education to the degree that the passionate beliefs of his constituents would permit. We fought side by side to save the offshore oil for the nation. He was always a charming and civilized man, who not only refrained from racial ranting, but, I am convinced, had not the slightest touch of racial prejudice in his heart. The racial passions of his constituents required him, in order to survive politically, to join in resisting civil-rights measures. At such times he would put his keen, though largely concealed, parliamentary talents at the service of Russell, and act as navigator to the latter's pilot. Then, when the chamber was empty, he would rise and make a conventional and largely nongermane speech on behalf of the Southern position. He was the best of the conservative Southerners, and we of the North respected and loved him. We never urged him to take a more advanced position and often tempered our timing to make his political burden back home more bearable. He reminded me of Matthew Arnold's lines describing those who lived "between two worlds, one dead,/ The other powerless to be born."

His colleague John Sparkman was another excellent senator. He was really interested in helping the poor and, as chairman of the Subcommittee on Housing and later of the Banking and Currency Committee, did yeoman service in promoting federally insured housing and public housing.

John Stennis, of Mississippi, was a Southerner who steadily grew in the estimation of all his fellows. A country judge, he had won the senatorial nomination in 1946 over John Rankin, who had made a typical race-baiting campaign. Stennis was a conspicuously fair man. He believed in white supremacy, but without hatred. We differed on this and many other subjects, but I have often said that if ever on trial for my life I would rest content with receiving justice from his hands. He handled the censure of Joseph McCarthy in 1954 in the best traditions of the Senate and the South, and his region can well be proud of him. There is no finer representative of the conservative and white Southern tradition.

The most respected Southerner in Northern industrial and financial circles was Harry Byrd, of Virginia. The world's largest apple grower, with cheeks as ruddy as his pippins, he was the very embodiment of fiscal and political conservatism. He hated public debt with a holy passion and insisted on annually balanced budgets in bad times as well as good. Despite his highly articulate advocacy of economy, he saw to it that Virginia was profusely provided with public works and military installations. With little or no sympathy for poor people, and instinctively on the side of the rich and powerful, of whom he was one, he nevertheless had a certain rugged personal honesty and a genial air of courtesy toward his opponents, except when severely pressed. I served for many years on the Finance Committee with him and, although we commonly differed on matters of policy, I developed a real respect for him.

Most of the Southerners in the Senate followed the example of Russell and Byrd; even Fulbright, one of the most highly cultivated members of the Senate and in his beliefs essentially an eighteenth-century Whig, nearly always agreed with them.

There were, of course, variants from the general mold. The speech of Burnet R. Maybank, of South Carolina, a Charleston aristocrat, was so compounded of the deep South, the Gullah dialect, and cotton-broker stridency as to be almost incomprehensible. He was a tough-looking and warmhearted man who, remembering that his first wife had died of spinal meningitis which she had contracted from a Negro servant whom she was nursing in a pestilence-ridden Charleston slum, was a shrewd and devoted supporter of public housing for blacks as well as whites.

Florida's Pepper and Tennessee's Kefauver were the first two Southerners to break with conventional tradition and become truly national senators. The former was a fiery liberal who, like Humphrey, had an instant co-ordination of mind and tongue. He was defeated for a third term by his erstwhile protégé, George Smathers. After having been advanced by Pepper, Smathers turned against him in 1950 and was supported by the groups who opposed Pepper's liberalism. For a decade, Pepper waited in the political wilderness, and then returned to Congress as a representative from the liberal city of Miami.

Kefauver was less showy, but developed into one of the most doggedly useful legislators and campaigners of modern times. His example helped to inspire Albert Gore to take a similar course, and in 1958 they were both joined by Ralph Yarborough, of Texas, who fought his way to the Senate after repeated defeats for the governorship and over the opposition of Lyndon Johnson. While Gore and Yarborough are loyal to the best Southern traditions, they are men of whom the whole nation can be proud. Their defeat in 1970 was a great loss to the country.

My Fellow Democratic Liberals

MOST DEMOCRATIC CONGRESSMEN from the North and the West are termed "modern liberals." We believed in using the national powers under the Constitution to promote the general welfare, whether directly by the taxing and spending powers of Congress or indirectly through the commerce clause. In no sense socialists, we realized fully the stimulus that individual initiative gives and the dangers to human freedom of an all-powerful state. But we were equally aware of the abuses that private monopoly and the concentration of vast wealth and power in the hands of the relatively few can bring. Perhaps we could best be classified as "distributivists," or as favoring such a broad diffusion of economic and political power that all may have enough to be relatively secure, and none so much as to threaten the liberties of others. Believing in the essential dignity of all men regardless of race or color, we felt that this should be recognized and promoted by government. We believed in the Fourteenth and Fifteenth amendments to the Constitution. Among other doctrinal features was our faith in the power of truth ultimately to establish itself in the arena of public opinion. This led to our advocacy of education and freedom of thought, speech, political action, and religion as being the best means of winnowing out truth from error. We were, therefore, unyielding in our opposition to all dictatorships and totalitarian governments, whether of the extreme right or the extreme left, and, as a result, were equally unpopular with both.

Suffice it to say that we thought ourselves in the mainstream of the American tradition starting with the Mayflower Compact, including the Preamble to the Declaration of Independence, and reinforced by the Articles of Confederation and the Constitution for the promotion of the general welfare as one of the basic purposes of our republic. Our American heroes were Jefferson and Lincoln, with Jackson, Wilson, and Franklin Roosevelt standing just below them in the pantheon of our history. In the field of political thought we took our inspiration from John Locke, the early Burke, Jefferson, Franklin, Madison, and the noble English liberal John Stuart Mill—with a touch of Plato and Aristotle thrown in for good measure.

Naturally these beliefs were not shared with equal fervor by all the members of our group. Few thought through each position as carefully as did the great inspirers of our faith. But even the most superficial of our number had a yearning to make this kind of society a greater reality. It so happens that these basic beliefs are best adapted for a democratic and pluralistic nation such as ours, with its wide variety of races and classes seeking to live together fruitfully in an increasingly urban, industrial, and interdependent society. Our credo had, therefore, not only survival value, but also powers of attraction and inspiration, which made us think that it was and is the basic faith of the majority of Americans. This is probably why we were generally victorious during the third of a century from 1932 to 1966.

The three most picturesque senatorial exponents of this philosophy during my career were Hubert Humphrey, Estes Kefauver, and Wayne Morse. Humphrey and I came to the Senate at the same time, he at the age of thirty-seven, after a meteoric career as mayor of Minneapolis, where he helped fuse the Democratic and Farmer-Labor parties of his state. With more physical and nervous energy than any man I have ever known in political life, he could simultaneously push scores of measures, tend to the personal and political chores of his office, do his committee work, and speak wisely and almost incessantly both in and out of the Senate. In itself this would exhaust any ordinary man. During these years he was also the best rough-and-tumble debater in our whole political arena. Once, in a diatribe against the British, Senator Styles Bridges shouted, "What have the British got that we haven't?" Almost before Bridges could finish his sentence, Hubert shouted back, "Westminster Abbey." His reply brought down the house.

Hubert and I have been friends and associates for many years now. This relationship was particularly close during the early years, when he was anathema to both the conservatives and the racists, and during the tragic election of 1968.

In 1953 Humphrey and Johnson started to move toward each other. Hubert was useful in persuading some of the Northern liberals not to oppose Johnson's election as majority leader, and Johnson knew Humphrey's value as a bridge to the liberals when we took back the control of the Senate in 1955. And yet while Hubert co-operated frequently with Johnson on parliamentary tactics, he never sold us out on the substantive issues and continued to be a leader in the liberal ranks. He influenced Johnson for the good, and in the long stretch of history may well be vindicated for the decision he made to co-operate with the shrewd Texan, rather than oppose him. After ten years of fruitful association, it was natural that Johnson should select Humphrey as his Vice Presidential running mate in 1964.

Wayne Morse was one of the ablest men ever to sit in the Senate. On any intelligence test he would probably have ranked at the top with Kerr, Humphrey, and Javits. In addition, he was a master of constitutional law and parliamentary procedure. His mind was independent, he had the proverbial courage of a tiger, and his heart was on the side of the people. I have seen him repeatedly and almost singlehandedly defy the Senate and show complete composure as he marshaled his arguments without a single note before him. For many years, before he became embittered over Vietnam, I regarded him as one of the most useful members of the Senate, and I am proud of having fought by his side in most of his battles.

Wayne, like the rest of us, carried his treasures in an earthen vessel, and his detractors have magnified his weaknesses. Perhaps he had a morbid compulsion to differ from others and to stand alone. On such occasions, no one was more denunciatory of his fellow liberals than he. Indeed, he would turn on long-time friends and allies with searing denunciations and do it all in the name of high principle. But though I often felt the whiplash of his tongue, I always believed that he was a valuable force, and I was glad to campaign for him in both 1956 and 1962. He was unique in making the switch from one party to another when in the years between 1952 and 1956 he changed from Republican to liberal Democrat. Strom Thurmond has since switched in exactly the opposite direction.

Estes Kefauver was one of the Senators who were least appreciated by Eastern writers and sophisticates. Newspaper reporters loved to picture him as a shambling hillbilly politician. His long-tailed coonskin cap, which he had worn in his 1948 campaign to defeat Edward H. ("Boss") Crump, of Memphis, seemed a hammy affectation. A poor speaker, with a limp and ineffective style, he had no gift for striking utterance. The men around Stevenson looked down on him.

But he was a true people's senator. Against great opposition in 1950 and 1951 he exposed criminal and gambling rings and let daylight in on many sordid places. He attacked monopoly and cartels and showed how prices were kept up in the steel, cement, electrical machinery, and other industries. He exposed the practices of the drug industry and in the process revealed how the Food and Drug Administration sided with the manufacturers against the public. With Gore and Russell Long, he fought the plan of the political and financial Establishments to turn over the communication satellite to a mixed, but suspect, corporation. And he did something better. With Gore, he raised the level of politics in Tennessee, though temporarily, and, indeed, throughout the South.

Behind Kefauver's casual manner there was a keen mind, a disarming power of penetrating cross-examination, and, with the exception of Proxmire, the most tireless zest for handshaking and personal greetings of any recent politician. It nearly carried him to a Presidential nomination. He deserves to be rated as one of the best Senators of the last half-century.

In the late 1950's, the ranks of liberal Democrats were enriched by the coming of the able patrician Joseph Clark, of Philadelphia, modest and devoted Philip A. Hart, of Michigan, fiery Stephen M. Young, of Ohio, Stuart Symington, of Missouri, Edmund S. Muskie, of Maine, Thomas J. McIntyre, of New Hampshire, and William Proxmire, of Wisconsin, together with the sturdy Westerners Quentin Burdick, of North Dakota, George McGovern, of South Dakota, Lee Metcalf, of Montana, Frank Moss, of Utah, Frank Church, of Idaho, Henry M. ("Scoop") Jackson, of Washington, and my friend of a half-century Ernest Gruening, of Alaska. Later came Fritz Mondale, of Minnesota, Birch Bayh, of Indiana, Joseph Tydings, of Maryland, Fred R. Harris, of Oklahoma, Thomas Eagleton, of Missouri, Alan Cranston, of California, and the Kennedy brothers, of New York and Massachusetts. All these, and others, have been honorable tribunes of the people, who, on the whole, are better served now than when Humphrey, Kefauver, and I first entered the Senate in 1949.-

Two Democratic Senate Leaders

HAD I BEEN TOLD in 1956 that ten years later I would be one of Lyndon Johnson's strongest supporters, I would have thought the seer was out of his mind, for I was then locked in mortal combat with him as I tried to pass civil-rights legislation, abolish the filibuster, plug tax loopholes, and prevent the oil and gas industry from getting special favors. Our differences seemed irreconcilable. While I understood that as a senator from Texas he might feel compelled to act as he did, I objected to having the leadership of our party in the hands of one opposed to the national platforms we had repeatedly adopted and in which I believed.

Johnson had begun his political career as a New Dealer and special protégé of Franklin Roosevelt. He was a supporter of rural electrification and of work relief for the unemployed. After serving two terms in Congress, he was beaten for the Senate in 1942 by "Pappy" O'Daniel. He returned to the House in 1944, after a short period of service in the Navy, and then won the senatorial primary in 1948 by eighty-seven votes, in an election characterized by many irregularities. In the Senate, he subordinated his early New Deal causes to adapt himself to the power structure of Texas political and economic life. His wife's inheritance was multiplying through her monopoly of Austin radio and television stations, and he became more and more a champion of the rich contractors, the big oil and gas millionaires, and the cattle aristocracy of Texas so well described by Edna Ferber in *Giant*. And yet even in the mid-'50's it would have been a great mistake to label Johnson a reactionary. He still kept much of the Rooseveltian philosophy, which made old colleagues, including Thomas Corcoran and Benjamin Cohen, his close friends and advisers. In fact, Johnson was then neither a liberal nor a reactionary, but, rather, a skilled political opportunist with an adroit mastery of parliamentary tactics, partly native and partly learned from his mentor, Speaker of the House Sam Rayburn. There was a touch of native populism in his make-up, derived from both his father and the spirit of the High Plains.

Upon the defeat of McFarland in 1952, Johnson convinced Russell and the Southerners that he was in their camp, quieted Northern opposition, with the help of Humphrey, and became Democratic floor leader. He continued in that office for eight years, until his election as Vice President in 1960. Not a persuasive speaker, he disliked to have measures debated on the floor. Instead, he preferred private deals and arrangements through cloakroom compromises. With Southern backing and an uncanny knowledge of the desires and weaknesses of individuals, he could usually put together a shaky majority for his measures. We always believed that he had a concealed and shifting coterie of about ten or twelve Senators, mainly from the Southwest and mountain states, which he could muster in varying degrees to help the Southerners and the conservative Republicans when the occasion demanded it. His strategy was to close off debate.

To Johnson, the Senate was a circus and he was the ringmaster, putting the animals through their paces by the lure of the carrot and the sharp crack of the whip. He seldom called party conferences. The party line was supposed to emerge from the Southern-dominated Policy Committee as interpreted by Johnson.

As a deliberative body, the Senate degenerated under Johnson's leadership. The bases of our political faith, as evidenced in our national platforms of 1952 and 1956, were largely disregarded and muted. Johnson refused to lift a finger to help Stevenson in either of his campaigns, and was always seeking accommodation with the Eisenhower administration and the Republican leadership. Thus, in the atomic-energy battle of 1954 he finally entered the battle on their side, and not on ours.

And yet, in justice to Johnson as Senate leader, I must also chronicle his good deeds. Perhaps the most important was his mustering of a solid Democratic vote for the censure of Joseph McCarthy. This, combined with the even Republican split on the question, produced a margin of nearly three to one and marked the turning point in McCarthy's effectiveness. In addition, Johnson always helped with my depressed-areas bill and with our minimum-wage and housing measures.

Not realizing that he was distrusted in the industrial North and West, Johnson came to believe in 1959 that he could be nominated and elected President in his newly acquired role as a Westerner. He was balked only by John Kennedy's vigorous campaigning. Even so, had Kennedy not obtained a narrow majority on the first convention ballot with the vote of Wyoming, Johnson might have won the nomination, because some delegations, including Indiana, were ready to break away from Kennedy, and the party pros from the smaller and Western states were ready to join the South in Johnson's support. But if he had been nominated, he would, in my judgment, have been badly defeated and would not have carried a single important Northern or Midwestern state.

When he became President upon Kennedy's tragic assassination, I feared the worst. But to my surprise and delight, he then militantly championed the cause of civil rights and pushed a far-flung program to help the poor and disadvantaged. Saddled with an unpopular struggle to prevent Communist aggressors from taking over not only Southeast Asia, but perhaps ultimately all of Asia, as well, he nevertheless stood firm while always holding the door open for peace. I never felt that I should inquire whether this welcome change of direction came from his recognition that liberal-minded people in the industrial states of the North, Midwest, and far West must be won over in order for him to carry the 1964 election, or whether it was due to the inevitable broadening of viewpoint that comes to any prescient man upon reaching the Presidency. Believing that one should judge men primarily by their acts, without attempting too searching a probe of their motives, I tried to help accomplish the many features of his program with which I agreed. Yet the secretive tactics he had early adopted as majority leader helped to destroy popular confidence in him during the later days of his Presidency. The voters felt that he was never frank with them about the facts of the war in Vietnam and that he always had something up his sleeve. In a sense, he outsmarted himself.

The uncrowned king of the Senate for some years was Robert S. Kerr. This son of a Baptist preacher early fused piety with great wealth, which came from the oil business; he was head of Kerr-McGee. With a touch of populism from his Southwestern background, Kerr became the New Deal governor of Oklahoma and, in 1944, the thundering liberal keynote speaker at the Democratic national convention. But these qualities became vestigial under the erosion of enormously increased wealth. Entering the Senate with an estimated $15 to $20 million, he so increased his holdings that when he died in 1962 rumor said they amounted to from $40 to $200 million. In the main this wealth was acquired by shrewdness and good management, but Bob was not one to worry about ethical implications and conflicts of interest. He made large profits from his holdings in uranium and other materials needed for the atomic-energy and space programs. As chairman of the Joint Congressional Committee on Space, he controlled the latter programs. He even placed his former chief of operations at Kerr-McGee as the administrative head of the new agency. He also became the chief legislative representative of the oil, gas, lead, and zinc industries. The most powerful figure on the Public Works Committee, he dotted Oklahoma with dams and lakes and spoke of the time when he would transform the shriveled Arkansas River into a great artery of commerce, with steel mills and basic industries lining its banks.

Stating that he was opposed only "to any deal I am not in on," and acting on this philosophy in the Finance Committee, he was a keen and remorseless bargainer, who usually won the lion's share of any spoils that were divided. He was formidable in counsel and terrified many of his colleagues in debate. Although able to argue logically, when deeply stirred he discarded reason to pour out a stream of cutting and witty ridicule or fiery denunciation, like a prosecuting attorney and frontier evangelist, backed by enormous wealth, a gigantic body, and a thunderous voice. He was more feared than liked, and the vast majority, not caring to tangle with him, preferred to go along, lest they excite his anger. In the Senate, as among his constituents, it was hard to quarrel with such material success. I clashed with him early, and we were frequently at swords' points in the Finance Committee and on the floor of the Senate itself. When Johnson became Vice President, Bobby Baker became Kerr's right-hand man, making a formidable combination. What Bobby did then carried him, after a long delay, to a federal penitentiary.

The Saints

POLITICS produces few saints. At best, it requires a large degree of personal striving to arrive and survive, and this encourages egotism. Modesty is one of the first virtues eroded and is an especial handicap in large states, where it is hard for a man to become known. A notable exception to this rule is Philip Hart, an effective senator who has consistently sought to conceal his many virtues. He and Congressman Neal Smith, of Iowa, are rare examples.

Moreover, the need to hold together a majority in a pluralistic society produces a willingness to compromise on vital matters to win either an election or a petty advance. This practice is defended by many newspaper commentators as not only a necessity of modern political life, but also the supreme virtue. To this contemporary school, moderation, as in the 1850's, is the most praised quality, while idealism looms, surprisingly, as the real enemy of attainable good. There is a degree of truth in this. Compromises must be made to attain the possible, but they should be such as to reduce the danger of divisive race and class warfare. In practice, this pragmatic approach sometimes becomes essentially negative and devalues all issues, so that mere agreement is made more important than any positive good. Leadership becomes a matter of adjustment and not of initiating needed reforms. Even in a world such as this, idealists are still needed to raise the standards higher. Politics needs the much maligned idealists and saints.

In my experience and that of my wife, we have known at least three men who could be called "political saints." These were Jerry Voorhis, Congressman for ten years from California, Frank P. Graham, and Herbert Lehman, Senators, respectively, from North Carolina and New York.

I first met Voorhis in 1936 when I was on a lecture trip to California. Young and handsome, he had inherited a fortune from his father, but instead of using his wealth to launch himself on a conventional career, he displayed aspirations that to the Philistines seemed quixotic. After graduating from Yale, he spent two years working as a common laborer, and then, with the help of his beautiful wife, Louise, opened a school for orphans near Pomona which his father donated to the state. In passing on to fatherless children the good fortune that had come to him, he tried to make the school a luminous experience.

He had become actively interested in the Democratic party in Upton Sinclair's campaign of 1934, and in 1936 he was elected to Congress. After his father gave the school to the State of California, Jerry endowed it with the remainder of his legacy. Then he came east with his family in a secondhand car and set himself to work on a daily schedule of sixteen to eighteen hours. Many nights he snatched only a few hours' sleep on his office couch. Driven by conscience, he had a compulsion to master every subject that came before the House, and having mastered it, he spoke his mind. Press cynics nicknamed him "Kid Atlas." But as the years went by, their satire turned to reverential awe, and the House members voted him its "most conscientious" member.

One of the most important achievements of the last quarter-century— forcing the Federal Reserve to turn its net earnings over to the govern- ment—was accomplished with his help. These earnings come from the interest on government bonds purchased by the various Federal Reserve banks. As deposits, they serve as a fractional reserve for the numerous banks against the credit they create. Backed by the redoubtable Wright Patman, Voorhis proposed that the ownership of the Reserve banks be federalized, so that the earnings would not go to the stockholders, which were, nominally, the member banks. In fright, the Reserve promised that it would turn over most of the net earnings to the government if the nominal ownership could be retained by the member banks. Their shares now became like bonds. By this move Voorhis helped save over a billion dollars a year for the people. Seldom has a saint achieved such practical results, although many so-called economic experts have forgot- ten this.

The year 1946 was a bad year for many liberal Democrats besides my wife. It was particularly so for Jerry, for his opponent was a vigorous young man by the name of Richard M. Nixon. Jerry was an anti- Communist and had, indeed, been a member of the House Un-American Activities Committee, where, without shielding the guilty, he had labored to protect the innocent. But the Nixon forces accused him of being the candidate of the Communists. And during the week before election, tele- phones began to ring through his district. Many housewives told him that they heard a silky voice say, "Good morning, Mrs. ——, did you know Jerry Voorhis was a Communist?" "No, I didn't" was the standard reply. "Who are you?" "Just a friend who thought you ought to know." And the anonymous character assassin would hang up. When Jerry's workers real- ized that this was an organized and wholesale campaign, it was too late to do anything effective about it. On Election Day the character assassins triumphed. Jerry was defeated, and Nixon was launched on a career that has now taken him to the White House.

With characteristic forgiveness, Jerry offered the victor help in getting settled in Washington, and while Nixon accepted some of his advice, he never apologized for the type of campaign waged on his behalf. Those who knew the deep wounds inflicted by the slander, especially upon Jerry's young son, found it hard to forgive Nixon. In 1950, in his Senate race, the followers of Nixon used much the same formula for his successful campaign against Helen Gahagan Douglas, one of whose managers was a radical young movie actor named Ronald Reagan. In 1960 thousands worked with redoubled vigor for John Kennedy because of memories of those former campaigns. The same motives steeled other thousands to help defeat Nixon when he ran for governor of California in 1962. Nixon's friends claimed that what the liberals resented was his role in the Alger Hiss affair. This may be true of some, but in my opinion Nixon played a necessary role in the exposure of Hiss. In the future, history will judge Nixon chiefly on his Presidential record. Great responsibility often calls out the best in men, as in the case of Harry Truman. Nevertheless, one would feel more confidence if Nixon broke with his old campaign manager, Murray Chotiner.

Upon retiring from Congress, Jerry Voorhis wrote a valuable book, *Confessions of a Congressman.* He then went to Chicago and for over twenty years gave his indomitable energies to the Cooperative League of the USA and, later, to the cause of co-operative housing. I believe he is truly one of the saints of the earth.

Frank Graham was the beloved president of the University of North Carolina, which he helped to make the foremost university of the South. By warm personal interest and determination to preserve academic freedom, he won the passionate devotion of the students. At the same time, he defended the right of trade unions to organize in the rapidly growing textile centers, fought child labor, and helped those who were trying to protect the users of electrical power. The Negroes of the state knew that he was their friend; through sociologist Howard Odum, he sponsored a path-breaking series of studies of the social structure and the racial and industrial problems of the South. For these reasons the state textile and power hierarchy came to hate him as the devil is reputed to hate holy water. But they never could oust him or materially injure his university, because both alumni and students were solidly behind him.

"Dr. Frank" came to the Senate in early 1949 when a liberal governor, W. Kerr Scott, appointed him to fill a Senate vacancy. Because I had known and admired him since the days of the NRA, I was delighted, but also concerned.

When Senator John W. Bricker made some slighting remarks about Frank before he took his seat, I saw the breakers ahead and tried to warn him. I told him that his old enemies would do their best to defeat him when he came up for election in 1950. He and his friends should start at once to organize and to raise a campaign fund. "Don't worry, Paul" was Frank's reply. "My wife and I have saved up $11,000, and we have decided to put that into the campaign." That was chicken feed compared to what he really needed. I told him the textile and power groups would spend from a half-million to a million dollars to beat him and that we must start work in both South and North to secure a minimum of $200,-000.

Because I made little headway in this direction, I tried another tack. I asked him to look over his budget for clerical hire. He would find money enough to hire an assistant who would stay in North Carolina to handle requests from constituents in matters of veterans' affairs, social security, and farm problems, and, in the late afternoons and evenings, promote the Senator's political fortunes and organize Graham clubs throughout the state. Somewhat shocked, Frank asked if I meant that he should use a man paid by the taxpayers for his own political benefit. I admitted that this was what everyone did to some degree. In any event, the representative could do it largely on his own time, once he was assured of a living. This was the price one had to pay for political survival. "Well, if it is," said Frank, "it is a price which I shall not pay."

Although disheartened, I made still another effort. The alumni office at the university, I pointed out, undoubtedly classified its graduates by county and town. Frank should get that list from the alumni secretary and ask a few of his devoted admirers to go over the state on a voluntary basis organizing Graham clubs in every important town, city, and county. This should be done at once, to build up a momentum his opponents could not overcome. "Paul, you surprise me," said Frank. "Here you are proposing that I use my former position as president to obtain from the university a list which does not belong to me and should not be used for my purposes. I could never ask for such a thing." In despair I replied that he did not have to ask for anything. A friend could ask for him and copy off the list. But Frank would not budge. "I cannot ask others to do for me what it would be improper for me to do for myself."

I was torn between irritation and admiration. "If you keep on this way, that pack of powerful and bloodthirsty wolves who are after you will surely defeat you." I told him that I and others would do everything we could to help him, but that unless he could be tougher, he would not survive. Decent government would then lose a crucial vote; and the Senate, an A-1 member.

And so it proved. After a notable year, during which Frank forced the State Department to adopt a more friendly attitude toward Indonesia, he entered the Democratic primaries of 1950. The political and economic hierarchy of North Carolina ran Willis Smith, a successful corporation lawyer and former president of the American Bar Association. I raised several thousand dollars for Frank and impressed upon him how much all the liberals wanted him back and that he should not be too stiff-necked in the positions he took. In the first primary, the Smith forces called Frank a Communist. Since no one really believed this smear, Frank led Smith by a small margin. But he did not obtain an outright majority because of the additional candidacy of former Senator Robert R. Reynolds.

Frank came up to Washington for an important roll call with a touch of apprehension in his clear blue eyes. I told him that he had beaten off the first attack. They had failed by calling him a Communist; in the runoff they would try something worse. They would call him a "nigger lover," and he must be ready for it. I suspected that it would be harder than before, since he really did like Negroes and wanted to help them.

"What shall I do?" asked Frank. I told him that there was only one thing he could do. Of course he should not respond by race-baiting, as some Southern liberals had done. But since the Truman administration had served notice that it would again try to modify the stringent Rule XXII, the cloture rule, my advice was that upon his return to North Carolina he should issue a statement saying that on the coming vote he would stand with his fellow Southerners in upholding the right of free and unlimited debate in the Senate and that he would vote against any attempt by us Northerners to modify Rule XXII. He should put it all in the name of high principle, as Lister Hill did.

"Paul," replied Frank, "I don't quite know how I stand on Rule XXII. There is a lot to be said on both sides, and for me to come out for it now would indirectly inject the Negro issue into the campaign, where it does not belong."

"Frank, can't you realize that it is already in the campaign and that defamatory literature and photographs are already being circulated in your state? They have you shaking hands with Negroes. They may find photographs of you dancing the Virginia reel with a mixed group. Unless you take some such mild step as this, your enemies are going to win by default." I pointed out that we Northerners understood the position liberal Southerners were in. We believed in civil rights and that to get them we would probably have to change Rule XXII. But this was not heroic on our part, since public sentiment in our states was for the present behind us. On the other hand, white public opinion in the South strongly opposed the change. It would be fatal for a Southern politician either to advocate or to keep silent about our proposal to change Rule XXII. He would do the nation more good by coming back to the Senate than by trying to ignore the issue.

Frank squared his shoulders, turned away, and went back to North Carolina. As he did so, I realized that civic and political courage is rarer and more admirable than the military courage I had seen so many of my Marine comrades display under fire.

The campaign was even worse than I had expected. Pamphlets flooded the state with photographs showing Frank shaking hands with Negroes. When he or his followers appeared in public they were greeted by taunts of "nigger lover." At last Frank came down with influenza. Twice during the closing days of the campaign he called me at night from his sickbed to ask, in an agonized voice, what he should do. Each time I repeated my counsel about Rule XXII, telling him that every liberal as well as every thoughtful Negro in the country would understand and on the whole approve of such a statement. "If you do this," I told him, "you can still pull this election out of the fire. If you don't, the racists and private-power boys will triumph."

But Frank, unable to compromise his beliefs, went down to defeat, although not by any huge margin.

Stopping only to congratulate Smith in person, Frank hastened back to Washington, where the vote to modify Rule XXII was pending. I watched him as the clerk neared his name, and was not unduly surprised when his gentle voice answered, "No." A wave of anger swept over me, and I did something I have made a practice of never doing. I walked over to his desk and said to him, "Frank, in God's name, why couldn't you have told the voters of North Carolina what you were going to do?"

"I was not fully sure of my stand," he replied, "and in any case to do so would have been for me to inject the racial issue into my campaign."

Willis Smith came to Washington and was a conventional senator for the few years before he died. He seemed a bit remorseful, and was quoted as saying that he "felt he had been running against Jesus Christ himself." Upon his death, the New York *Times* published a column-long obituary. It was factual and fair, but it devoted two-thirds of the space to an account of how he had won his Senate seat. What price glory, I thought, to go down in history under such a judgment.

Herbert Lehman came from a very different background from Jerry and Frank. The son of extremely wealthy Jewish parents, Herbert entered the family banking house and for years was immersed in finance and philanthropy. He and his family were long-time supporters of the Democratic party, so when Al Smith, in running for the Presidency in 1928, wanted a "balanced ticket" in New York to offset his Catholicism, he slated Herbert for lieutenant governor and the Protestant Franklin Roosevelt for governor. Although Smith was defeated, Roosevelt and Lehman carried the state and went on to a much bigger victory in 1930. Lehman became Roosevelt's "good right arm" and was the man who actually carried out many of FDR's state programs. When Roosevelt was nominated for the Presidency in 1932, Herbert, over strong Tammany opposition, moved up to the governorship, where he remained for a full ten years. He was elected more times than any governor in the history of New York, and became the Empire State's best-loved politician. Starting as a moderate conservative, he became steadily more liberal and courageously humanitarian. Upon retiring as governor, he went to the United Nations Relief and Rehabilitation Administration, which he administered without pay, meeting all personal expenses out of his own pocket. Under his direction,

UNRRA, despite manifold difficulties both outside and inside the organization, saved tens of millions of people from starvation and Europe from immediate collapse.

Herbert came to the Senate in 1949, after beating John Foster Dulles in a special election. He voluntarily retired in 1957, at the age of seventy-eight.

An indomitable and rugged senator, he would take on anyone, even the dreaded Joe McCarthy, who was then at the height of his power. McCarthy and Kerr did not hesitate to ridicule and cast aspersions on Herbert, who never flinched and bore the attacks with a flashing eye and a quiet dignity. Generous in deed and hospitality, with purse and heart open to every unfortunate, Herbert was the very embodiment of friendly and hopeful compassion.

No man could have been more scrupulous in separating his private concerns from his political action. Again and again he voted against his own interests and those of his family, even when millions of dollars were involved. I remember when we were debating the removal of the punitive ten-cent tax on colored oleomargarine. I favored this removal because the studies of nutritionists had convinced me that oleo was nearly as nutritious as butter, and I believed that it should be allowed to compete in the open market if it was clearly labeled. Consumers would thereby save ten cents a pound and also force down the price of butter. But Herbert, although his political support was weakest among the New York dairy farmers, and Lehman Brothers had the controlling interest in big margarine companies, unhesitatingly voted against removing the punitive tax, because he believed in the unique qualities of butter. He was outvoted, but, as an economist, I rejoiced that Herbert's action had helped to weaken the dogma of the economic interpretation of politics as an all-governing force.

Herbert was the most indomitable of all the battlers for civil rights and civil liberties. Never yielding ground and always pushing forward, he was an inspiration to us and a source of irritation and anger to the Southerners and conservatives. As debate on the floor waxed hot toward the end of the day, Herbert would stand at the head of the center aisle and then walk slowly down it, making his points as he progressed and shaking his forefinger at the recalcitrant ones on either side of the aisle. His lovely and noble wife, Edith, was always in the gallery to give him courage and support.

Herbert did not retire to a life of inactivity. Instead, he set himself the herculean task of ousting Carmine De Sapio, the leader of Tammany, and of reforming the Democratic party of New York City. None of us gave him or the independents a chance, but with Eleanor Roosevelt at his side and with the support of Mayor Robert F. Wagner, Jr., he and his allies won a striking victory and gained their immediate objectives. I recall the appealing sight of eighty-three-year-old Herbert, in his shirt sleeves in the heat of summer, campaigning vigorously for Wagner on the sidewalks of New York. And I am sorry that the Reform Democrats have not fully lived up to his ideals.

Since the days of the Antonines and Marcus Aurelius, there have not been three public men with greater purity of motive or whose every political act was governed by greater fidelity to principle than Jerry Voorhis, Frank Graham, and Herbert Lehman. In the words of little Pompilia in Browning's *The Ring and the Book:*

> *Through such souls alone*
> *God stooping shows sufficient of his light*
> *For us i' the dark to rise by.*

The Republicans

THERE WAS A PERIOD when Republican leadership did not demand great exertion or ability. The party's doctrine was opposition to what was new. In addition to a tendency to identify with the prosperous, this has been the chief psychological basis for modern Republicanism. Although this position is tough-minded, not much intellectual ingenuity is needed to defend it. It is instinctive, rather than logical. Since the solid core of Republican strength during the twenty years after the New Deal lay in one-party districts and states, where nomination insured election, party candidates did not have to display much energy. Once they had won the approval of the chief financial, industrial, and newspaper leaders of their districts, their way to nomination and election was almost assured. This discouraged bold, able, and warmhearted men. Moreover, for many years the outstanding men in the dominant economic classes of the North and West turned their energies toward business, finance, and the law, rather than to politics. Regarding politics as somewhat beneath them, they preferred to direct the strategy of the politicians they controlled, rather than practice the lowly and erratic art themselves.

By the process of natural selection, most Democrats had to be abler than Republicans in order to get elected. In the first place, most Democrats, lacking money and influential connections, found the upper reaches of the business and legal worlds closed to them. Since the political door was open, however, politics attracted many of the abler members of the "lower" and "middle" economic groups. Furthermore, they had to display greater energy in the North and West to get elected, since, with rare exception, they had to swim against the current of newspaper and financial opposition.

The Democrats also attracted far more humanitarians, both wealthy and nonwealthy, who wanted to use the government as an instrument to promote human welfare. This doctrine favored those with an outgoing nature, a quality more attractive to voters than the often cold self-centeredness of Republicans.

But if most of the Republican Senators and Congressmen were not distinguished, there were in my day a number who stood out intellectually.

First of these, of course, was Robert A. Taft, of Ohio, an honorable man with a first-rate mind. Unlike his brother, Charles, however, he lacked broad human sympathy. Rumor said that he admitted to not liking the poor, and in his social attitude toward members of labor unions he resembled the British Tories. But he was intellectually honest and never knowingly twisted facts to suit his purpose. Although partisan, he was logical in debate, temperate in expression, and amenable to compromise. In 1946, after eight years in the Senate, he came out for the expenditure of a billion dollars a year on each of the three programs of public housing, education, and health. (The Republicans had a hard time dealing with this statement.) At first he seemed indifferent to foreign affairs, but upon the death of Arthur H. Vandenberg he assumed the lead in this field as well. Here, he was in the main an isolationist.

Increasingly, I was pitted against Taft, both on the floor of the Senate and in public discussion. I always thought him formidable and fair. Although I did not really like him, I respected him. One matter on which we agreed was the need for thorough public discussion, and we believed that Congress was the primary institution through which this discussion should be conducted. In this he was the direct opposite of Lyndon Johnson, who dominated the Senate for six years after Taft's death.

Although Taft was universally regarded as "Mr. Republican," the men who pulled the strings of the Eastern branch of the Republican party always felt he was too forthright and put too much asperity in his statements to be a strong Presidential candidate. That is why they defeated him with the expansive Willkie in 1940, the efficient and skilled public-relations figure Dewey in 1944 and 1948, and Eisenhower, father figure and superb soldier, in 1952. Like Daniel Webster, Taft was always shunted aside at the critical moments.

Shortly after the Senate convened in 1953, when Taft for the first time sat at the majority leader's desk, he learned he had cancer. Yet he went on with his Senate work with complete and cheerful composure. That year he won the admiration of us all. No one ever faced death with more gallant courage.

Eugene D. Millikin, of Colorado, was another extraordinarily able man. With a huge and towering body, he seemed like one of the black bears of his native Rocky Mountains. An unabashed champion of entrenched wealth and special privilege, he reserved most of his wiles for the

Finance Committee, where he was an expert in protecting the old tax loopholes and in opening new ones. In the Senate chamber itself he would lounge indifferently at an aisle desk in the last row. But if the debate took an adverse turn or was exceptionally interesting, he would rise, stretch himself, and lumber down the aisle pouring out a stream of questions, sarcasm, and acute—if somewhat ill-founded—criticism. I had the distinction of rousing him a number of times and never felt as hard pressed as when under his fire. He was valuable to the interests he represented, but he failed to become a national figure because of his natural indolence and the narrowness of his concerns.

The third Republican leader of the 1950's and early '60's was Styles Bridges, of New Hampshire. Born in Maine, he went to his adopted state as a county agent. He temporarily joined forces with the progressive governor, John G. Winant, and succeeded him when the latter became the first chairman of the Social Security Board. Bridges went to Washington as a senator in 1936, and it seemed at first that he might join the progressive bloc led by Norris and La Follette. But he took the opposite course and became a strong conservative. Backed by William Loeb, publisher of the Manchester *Union Leader,* he was invincible in his home state, and as the older Republican Senators died, he became the senior member on his side of the aisle. He spoke on the floor only to deliver a witty or cynical diatribe against the Democrats, preferring to operate by telephone from his confidential hide-out. From there he exercised remote control over many crucial matters.

In 1950 it was finally revealed that, by the grace of John L. Lewis, Bridges had also been the $35,000-a-year chairman of the coal miners' welfare fund. From time to time also he had formed tax connections with Charles Oliphant, the chief attorney of the Internal Revenue Service, who, having a large family, was forced by later scandal to clerk in a chain store. Ultimately Oliphant committed suicide.

Bridges was seemingly a man of iron nerves, but during his final years of service he had what must have been a nervous breakdown, from which he apparently never recovered. Altogether, he was a most mysterious person, whom few of us could fathom.

A group much more attractive to me was the small but gallant band of Republican progressives. When I arrived, the most prominent of these was George D. Aiken, of Vermont. Aiken started out as a dirt farmer and became a collector and dealer in wild flowers, at which time he wrote a classic piece on the flowering crab tree. He came from Putney, in southern Vermont, where there was a strong liberal nucleus, and he was elected to the legislature, in which each town is guaranteed one and only one representative in the lower house. Resenting the high utility rates charged to farmers and townspeople by the power companies, he led the fight for lower rates and for rural electrification. He was sympathetic to the workers in the marble quarries of Barre and in the mills and factories. With their help and that of the farmers, he was elected governor in 1934 and again in 1936. The dominant financial Establishment in his state always opposed Aiken, but he was widely trusted by the people, who sent him to the Senate in 1940. There he sought membership on the Agriculture and Labor committees, where he was a humane and effective worker. He became the staunch defender of the dairy interests, and of the American cow, which could not have had an abler spokesman for her interests. While some of George's early fire has been dampened by time and he is perhaps slightly more partisan than he was, he is still the best example of the old-fashioned Yankee in politics. In 1968 he was nominated by the Democrats as well as by the Republicans.

His companion for many years, Charles W. Tobey, was of a like breed. Starting as a legislator from a tiny New Hampshire hamlet, he was elected to Congress in the early 1930's, and was elected to the Senate as an honorable conservative in the same year as was Aiken. His sympathies steadily broadened and deepened; his warm heart responded to all forms of injustice and against dishonesty of any kind. I found him refreshing, and we became warm comrades. After his death, his wife, Lillian, became one of our dearest and closest friends.

The third progressive Yankee Republican was Margaret Chase Smith, a resident of Skowhegan, Maine, only a few miles from Newport, where I had gone to high school. Margaret had been a store clerk and country schoolteacher. After marrying the sheriff of Somerset County, she came with him to Washington when he was elected to Congress and became his secretary. When he was dying, he urged her to run for his seat and carry on his liberal interests. This she did with great effectiveness, displaying real independence. Emily served with her in the House, and they became friends and agreed on many basic issues.

In 1948 she set her cap for the Senate, and in her race was opposed by nearly all the Republican organization leaders in Maine. Few gave her a chance, but the alleged cold hearts of the down-Easters warmed at the sight of this beautiful, slender, white-haired woman battling the Republican power structure. When she slipped and broke her arm on an icy sidewalk in Bangor and yet pluckily continued her campaigning through slush and snow, her accident became a major asset, and her battle was won. Yankees may be cold, but they love a fighter, and her gallant struggle brought tears to many eyes. She has been in the Senate ever since, the only woman there through most of her service, and a national institution.

Margaret's finest hour, and one of the finest of the Senate itself, came when she delivered her Declaration of Conscience. This was a rebuke to McCarthyism when that disease was at its height. Her liberalism, like that of Aiken's, has abated a bit with the years, and, like him, she is now acceptable to the Republican Establishment.

She prides herself on her record of answering consecutive roll calls, which now totals more than 2,000. Many of us suspected that Lyndon Johnson, a friend in the House and later in the Senate, had a secret but decorous political alliance with her. He gave her inside information on expected roll calls so that she could arrange her schedule accordingly. In cases of serious conflict, we noted that Johnson would always postpone the roll call until she was in attendance. In return, she helped him on a few crucial roll calls that did not interfere with her conscience. When she voted with us to reject Eisenhower's nominee, Rear Admiral Lewis L. Strauss, for secretary of Commerce, we felt we had seen her *quid* for his *quo.*

During the 1950's a new group of Republican progressives came to the Senate, led by Thomas Kuchel, who was followed by John Sherman Cooper, Clifford Case, and Jacob Javits. They decided that they could not support the negative positions of the Republican party and that they should represent wider interests.

Kuchel was a protégé of Earl Warren. When the latter was governor of California, he appointed Kuchel to the Senate to replace Nixon, who had ascended to the Vice Presidency in 1953. Tom's first vote was to modify Rule XXII. At once this brought down on his head the wrath of the Republican leadership, which recurrently reacted against his independence. But he was deservedly popular with the voters and won election in 1956 and 1962 by wide margins. He had discovered that many progressive-minded voters preferred a Republican to a Democrat with similar beliefs. Once he had the nomination, he was assured of the election. Like Margaret Chase Smith, who threw down the gauntlet to McCarthy, Tom made open war on the John Birch Society. When a foul libel was circulated against him by wealthy California opponents, he took them on openly and forced them to confess and retract. While usually sunny in disposition, his face flushed when he became indignant, and he would thrust out his lower jaw like a bantam English bulldog. As Republican whip he was respected by all but the most bitter reactionaries. Since he refused to campaign for Barry Goldwater and George Murphy in 1964 or for Reagan in 1966, he consciously put his nomination in 1968 in danger, and, to the nation's loss, was defeated.

Case, who underwent his own baptism of fire, came to the Senate in 1954. He had served several terms with real distinction in the House, but his first senatorial race was threatened by Republican McCarthyites who tried to smear him. His progressive and pro-labor voting record, however, and his general attractiveness won him deserved re-election by enormous majorities in 1960 and 1966. During my later years he was perhaps the best-liked member of the Senate. Someone once defined him as being "winsome, but tough."

Cooper was a singularly courtly and generous man from eastern Kentucky, an area of strong Republican sympathies, which date back to the Civil War. He was twice elected to unexpired terms before he won a full Senate term in 1956. An able politician, he is keenly aware of the importance of tobacco to the farmers of his state, but he is a man of conscience, and when grave matters of ethics and national interest are involved, his response is sturdy and unfailingly true to his own beliefs.

Like Humphrey, the extremely intelligent Jacob Javits can handle a multitude of subjects at the same time and do so effectively. He can flip the pages of a complicated bill and immediately point out its strong points and its theoretical and technical weaknesses. Never at a loss in any circumstances, he had, when I served with him, a genius for hitting the front page of the New York *Times* and the *Herald Tribune* every morning. The rivalry for newspaper attention between Jack and his Republican colleague, Kenneth Keating, was both intense and amusing. When one would make a brief and catching statement on the floor during the morning hour, the other would soon rush in to deliver another speech on the same topic, but with a different twist. Both were good senators, but it was Keating's misfortune in 1964 to have Robert Kennedy enter the race against him and put an end to his senatorial career. In the next year the voters elected him by an enormous majority to the Court of Appeals, the highest judicial body in New York State. They did this as an evidence of their good will and personal liking and apparently out of a desire to atone for their rebuke.

I have the distinct impression that, on the whole, the caliber of Republican senators, in both ability and sympathy, has markedly improved over the years. I believe this is due to the fact that increasing Democratic strength in what were once one-party Republican states has forced the party to put up abler and more attractive candidates than previously. The improvement in the House has been less obvious, except from the districts in and around New York City, where a group of liberal Republicans, including Seymour Halpern and Ogden Reid, has come forward.

Some of the Less Desirable

I HAVE MET few evil men in politics. The public generally senses real malevolence and rejects it for high office. If a man is dominated by hatred, he may win support and do much damage for a time, but ultimately the voters will turn away. There is, however, a tendency for power to sweep men off their feet and cause them to do unworthy acts. While I have suspected only a few of my Senate colleagues of actual personal corruption, some have become bullies toward those who would not co-operate with them.

When I came to the Senate, three names, soon to be known as the

"Wrecking Crew," followed each other when the clerk intoned the roll call: McCarran, McCarthy, McKellar.

Pat McCarran was the florid-faced Senator from Nevada. The son of an Irish immigrant, he hated all other immigrant stocks, which he would periodically accuse of "polluting the bloodstream of America." He was a skillful politician and held his little state in the hollow of his hand.

He had first come to office through the help of the powerful gambling interests of Reno, and later worked for every pressure group in his state. He led the silver and wool blocs, was an active defender of the transcontinental railways, befriended the railway unions (the only strongly organized labor group in his state), and, though a devout Catholic, was the leading divorce lawyer in Nevada. In foreign affairs he was a red-hot supporter of Spanish dictator Franco and the friend of all the Latin-American dictators. Though he tried to shut the doors on immigrants from southern and eastern Europe, he was always sponsoring special bills to bring in more Basque shepherds to tend the flocks of the big wool growers back in the Nevada mountains. He viewed me as an enemy when I held up one of his Basque bills until he had accepted a more liberal general immigration bill.

The first Americans, the Indians, were the only Nevadans upon whom McCarran made bitter war. Being wards of the nation during most of his membership, they were defenseless because they could not vote.

As chairman of the Judiciary Committee he terrified the Department of Justice, whether Republican or Democratic, and as a powerful member of the Appropriations Committee he threw fear into many government agencies. Exercising his power like a despot, he could imperil any witness who came before his committees. As I watched him at work, I often recalled the lines from *Measure for Measure:*

> *Oh, it is excellent*
> *To have a giant's strength, but it is tyrannous*
> *To use it like a giant.*

During my service, Joseph R. McCarthy was the most controversial member of our body. Though starting life as a Democrat, he saw that he could not get ahead that way in the Wisconsin of the late 1930's. He switched to the Republican party and, with the surprising aid of the Communists, who had been rebuffed by the incumbent, Robert La Follette, Jr., he defeated that outstanding Senator in the 1946 primary and then easily overcame the Democratic candidate. Although a gambler for high stakes and a plunger in the stock market, McCarthy was quiet and little noticed during his first three years. In 1949 he took up the cause of the German SS troops who had shot large numbers of American prisoners during the Battle of the Bulge. Joe insisted that the trial of the SS troopers had been unfair, and he denounced his Republican colleague, the highly respected Raymond Baldwin, of Connecticut, who had investigated the whole affair and had refuted Joe's charges. Seldom has a senator used such language toward a colleague as Joe let loose on Baldwin. These diatribes may have gained a few votes among the German-American citizens of Wisconsin, but they brought general indignation from the public, and Joe therefore needed a new cause for his 1952 election.

Being a hunter, not a legislator, he looked around for something to investigate. There was material close at hand. Alger Hiss had just been convicted at a second trial, where the evidence against him seemed overwhelming to most who followed the case. For all its virtues, the Roosevelt administration had failed to detect and weed out the Communists and their sympathizers who had undoubtedly planted themselves in certain branches of the government. These men had posed as sincere democrats and antifascists, and while Hitler was the common enemy they had been hard to identify. Several Communist cells were active and during the war, when Russia was an ally, had doubtless transmitted confidential information to the Russians. By 1950 Truman's administration had removed virtually all of these men from government service and had started prosecutions against the worst offenders. But the take-over of China by the Communists, joined with Stalin's attack upon the West and the revelations of Stalin's widespread terror, had created an atmosphere of pervasive insecurity.

McCarthy capitalized on this. Unlike Nixon, he never succeeded in exposing any subversives, although at various meetings he claimed to know that there were scores of card-carrying Communists in the State Department alone. The numbers he variously stated were 205, 81, and 57. He also promised to rest his case on a few whose names he publicized, although he was never able to justify his charges.

In the next months, innocent as well as guilty were brought before his committee. The fact that many confirmed fellow travelers took refuge in the Fifth Amendment instead of defending themselves increased the general air of suspicion. But the only fault of some, like Bishop Bromley Oxnam, was to have joined anti-Nazi organizations in the days of the Nazi menace and not to have become aware of infiltration when the organizations became Communist fronts. Some in the diplomatic service were pilloried because they had criticized Chiang Kai-shek and his greedy entourage or had subscribed to the mistaken theory that the Chinese Communists were only "agrarian reformers."

McCarthy's malevolent contribution was to switch the pursuit of genuine subversives—of whom there were some—to that of liberal humanitarians. He ruined many honorable careers, and, even worse, he spread a pall of fear over large sections of the nation. Men and women became afraid to take a stand on controversial matters lest they be branded by the

Grand Inquisitor. The young, especially in the rising technical and managerial class, thought it dangerous to commit themselves to any but orthodox opinions. They played it cool. If this prevented association with those who might later become suspect, it also stifled youth's finest gift for heroic and humanitarian action.

McCarthy and his followers were in reality carrying through a purge somewhat like the revolutionary tribunals and mass trials that characterized the French, Russian, and Chinese revolutions. It was on a retail, rather than a wholesale, basis, and the punishment was not death or exile to a prison camp, but public disgrace. It was, thus, a more civilized procedure than those practiced by Joe's Communist critics. But it produced dangerous cleavages in the country and encouraged mutual distrust between basically good citizens.

Occasionally I heard rumors that McCarthy was about to attack me, but I tried not to be influenced by these reports. In 1954, when I was running for re-election, I was one of only a handful to vote for Senator Flanders' resolution calling for immediate action on McCarthy. Right after the vote, as I went out to Illinois, the press announced that McCarthy would campaign against me in the strongly Republican and conservative county of Du Page. I awaited his coming with interest, but a few days before the scheduled meeting Joe, for some unexplained reason, canceled his appearance.

On the Sunday before Election Day I was asked on "Meet the Press" what I would do in the McCarthy case. I said I would naturally wait until I had seen the report of the committee that was studying the charges. But I reminded the panel that I was one of the few who had voted for immediate action on Flanders' charges. The next day Joe responded in the press by denouncing me and asking for my defeat. After the election, the Senate was called into special session to consider action on the recommendations for censure made by the committee. The first to greet me was McCarthy. Rushing up, he shook hands heartily and assured me that he was delighted by my re-election. Joe was that kind of fellow. He was like a mongrel dog, fawning on you one moment and the next moment trying to bite your leg off.

The most courageous opposition to McCarthy had come from Lehman, Tydings, Margaret Chase Smith, Fulbright, Benton, and Flanders. McCarthy helped defeat Tydings in 1950 by falsely associating him with Earl Browder, the head of the Communist party. But as long as McCarthy concentrated his fire on Democrats, few opposed him, for he was a party asset to the Republicans. Many who would not have copied his tactics wanted him to continue and even encouraged him to do so. Meanwhile, the public watched, with horrified fascination, the televised hearings of his committee. His brutal treatment of witnesses brought about his ultimate downfall.

When McCarthy began to attack the Eisenhower administration and the Department of Defense, his Republican support began to erode. His contemptuous defiance of the Senate subcommittee investigating some of his financial dealings and his abuse of a hero of the Battle of the Bulge turned the tide against him. The final vote for censure was 67 to 22. While the Republicans split evenly on the roll call, the Democrats were unanimous for censure. Even Jim Eastland voted with us.

The man I saw deteriorate most during his senatorial career was Kenneth D. McKellar, of Tennessee. I recalled a photograph of him standing beside Woodrow Wilson that had been taken shortly after the latter's first inauguration. McKellar was then young, vigorous, black-haired, and he seemed a fitting representative of the New South. It was, therefore, a shock thirty-five years later to see a bleary-eyed old codger with a swollen face come limping with a cane onto the Senate floor. He was identified as Kenneth McKellar. By sheer survival he had become the senior member of the Senate, its president pro tempore and chairman of the all-powerful Appropriations Committee.

An inveterate spoilsman, he had feuded with David Lilienthal, chairman of the TVA, because the latter would not let him control the staff appointments for that body. In one of his public cross-examinations of Lilienthal he had questioned his patriotism. Lilienthal replied with a thrilling definition of true Americanism and a cutting rebuke to his assailant. Each year McKellar's great hour came when he brought up his Rivers and Harbors Appropriations bill, universally known as "the pork barrel." At such times he would gleefully pull out tasty bits for his favorites and, with an indignant leer, deny them to those whom he disliked.

I clashed with him at once. After studying a wide variety of the projects in his bill, I concluded that at least twenty were extremely wasteful. So with trembling knees I rose to oppose the bill by trying to cut it back by several millions. Furious, McKellar retorted that I had appeared before his committee urging the deepening and widening of the Cal-Sag canal, connecting Lake Michigan and the Illinois River. This was true, and in self-defense I said that it was right for a senator to represent his state before a committee but equally right for him to represent the nation on the floor of the Senate.

This was but the prelude to clashes between us which grew more fiery with every year. In our last encounter, McKellar started up the aisle toward me with his eyes blazing and his cane raised. I was conscious of a stir in the press gallery as the newsmen crowded to the railing. McKellar's fame as a feudist suggested the possibility of high drama. I stepped into the aisle to face him, with my hands clasped behind my back. Suddenly the old man stopped, turned on his heel, and walked away. Perhaps he had decided not to repeat Preston Brooks's famous attack upon Senator Charles Sumner.

By 1952 McKellar had served forty-one years in the Congress, of which thirty-six had been in the Senate. As it happens to all aging wild animals, so it happened to him: he was challenged by a young and virile rival, Congressman Albert Gore, from Cordell Hull's old district. McKellar started his campaign confidently, stressing his long service and saying that he could do more for Tennessee than his photogenic opponent. In the middle of the campaign, he plastered every highway in Tennessee with the slogan:

> *Thinking feller*
> *Vote for McKellar.*

The Gore forces, equal to the challenge, replied with two more lines, pasted immediately below every McKellar sign:

> *Think some more*
> *And vote for Gore.*

That did it. The substitution of Gore for McKellar turned out to be a great boon, not only for Tennessee, but also for the nation.

18

The Kennedys—Jack, Bob, and Ted, Too

JOHN F. KENNEDY was elected to Congress in 1946 from an Irish-American district in Boston. I saw almost nothing of him until 1952, when he challenged Henry Cabot Lodge for the Senate. In a strongly Republican year, he defeated that formidable opponent by dint of strenuous campaigning through every Massachusetts city and town, aided by the charm of his mother and sisters.

We served together for several years on the Labor Committee. Although he was reservedly friendly, I was not sure how able he was or what direction his life would take. Perhaps he did not know himself. But from his association with Ted Sorensen he began to develop rapidly. A severe spinal weakness laid him up for a year, and brought him at one time to the point of death. During that period he read widely about public figures who had overcome heavy difficulties, and in 1956 he brought out his Pulitzer Prize winner and best seller, *Profiles in Courage,* a truly remarkable book, which rescued many half-forgotten heroes from oblivion. He had been a war hero himself, and it was a pleasure to see him value civic courage on an equal or even higher plane. But I always thought he was too undiscriminating in rating the courage to compromise as highly as he did, and in putting the corrupt Daniel Webster upon so high a pedestal.

At the 1956 convention he was the favorite for Vice President, not only of Stevenson, but also of most of the party leaders, who were again determined to sidetrack Kefauver. Kefauver's colleague, Albert Gore, was also an aspirant and had won the majority of the Tennessee delegation. When the vote was nearly completed, and Kennedy and Kefauver were running neck to neck, with the former gaining, it seemed clear that Gore had no chance. Under pressure from Silliman Evans, the publisher of the Nashville *Tennessean,* he withdrew in favor of Kefauver. As delegations were scrambling for recognition, to alter their vote, and when it looked as though Kennedy would win, a Tennessee stalwart rushed to the platform. Knowing that the chairman, Sam Rayburn, hated Kefauver and would recognize only a delegation that he knew was switching to Kennedy, he shouted, "Mr. Speaker, Tennessee is switching to Kennedy. This will clinch it. Please recognize us." Rayburn prided himself on being completely impassive, but a gleam of delight illumined his face. This would do it. Kefauver could not survive this repudiation by his own state. Down came the gavel, and in his bull-like voice Rayburn roared, "I recognize the gentleman from Tennessee." Up from the floor came the startling response, "Tennessee shifts its entire vote from Albert Gore to its famous and beloved son Estes Kefauver."

That did it, indeed, but in a way opposite from what Rayburn had intended. Missouri, which had been hanging in the balance, joined in. So did other states. It was all over in a couple of minutes. Probably for the only time in his long career as chairman of the Democratic national conventions, Rayburn had been defeated by his own methods.

As matters turned out, it was an unforeseen godsend to Kennedy. Kefauver went down with Stevenson to a crushing defeat in the fall elections. He continued as an extremely useful senator, but he was through as a Presidential possibility. No one is more politically shopworn than a badly defeated candidate for Vice President. Who remembers William Miller, Goldwater's running mate in 1964? Meanwhile, Kennedy, projected on the national scene, had made a favorable impression but did not have to bear the stigma of defeat.

In the civil-rights struggle of 1957, Kennedy kept aloof from the caucuses of the Northern and Western liberals, which I organized. He was anxious not to offend the Southerners more than necessary, and he voted in favor of an unlimited use of jury trials in all civil-rights cases. While this could be justified on abstract grounds, it was obvious that Southern juries would almost never convict a violator of the Negroes' right to vote and that in practice this would have emasculated the law. Fortunately, the House amended it in a satisfactory fashion.

When Kennedy came up for his second term, in 1958, he was determined not only to win, but also to do so by a huge majority. That was the best way to put himself in the forefront of Presidential possibilities for 1960. The Republicans nominated an extremely weak candidate, but Kennedy did not let up. He campaigned through his state as thoroughly as he had six years before. He had one weakness, however. The Negroes and civil-rights advocates suspected him of not really being on their side. Sorensen and Mike Feldman urged him to invite me into the state to speak for him. Since he had supported civil rights in his way, and perhaps could be encouraged to be more active, I went to Boston, where I made a speech noting his civil-rights votes but not mentioning the jury-trial votes or difficulties in dealing with him.

Our relationship warmed up, and as 1959 progressed I noticed that his supporters stressed a closer historical connection between us than had existed. I wrote a widely read article that argued that the Democrats should not be afraid to nominate a Catholic and that they should not be deterred by the result of the Al Smith campaign of 1928.

In that year Kennedy first showed his real ability. The excesses of James Hoffa, the president of the Teamsters Union, and a few other union leaders led to a widespread popular demand for reforms in union procedures and practices. This had been further developed by a Senate committee headed by John L. McClellan, of Arkansas, whose chief counsel was John's brother Robert. With his usual acumen, Lister Hill, chairman of the Labor Committee, had put John Kennedy in charge of the proposed bill, and they reported out a comparatively good measure. Kennedy had got Archibald Cox, of Harvard Law School, to coach him on the intricacies of labor law. So, for several days on the Senate floor, and on his feet for hours, he answered the most difficult questions, never making a slip. Issues connected with the forms of the secondary boycott are most complicated, varying according to the ends sought, the means employed, and the degree of common interest between the participants. I had once developed a circular slide rule to help judges classify and rule on these cases. New to the field, Kennedy treated each point with the precision of a skilled surgeon. After that no one could doubt his ability.

When Congress adjourned, Kennedy took to the skies in the plane given him by his father and, swooping from state to state, made excellent speeches and met the working Democrats. I introduced him at Springfield, where he made a good impression. He came back to Illinois at least twice more—once to Chicago and once downstate. The younger generation identified with him, and the Catholics were enormously proud that one of their number was rising so high in the political firmament.

Meanwhile, Humphrey and Symington had quickly become open candidates for the Presidency, while Johnson and Stevenson were concealed aspirants. Neither of the latter wanted to surface politically, so they carefully kept out of the spring Presidential primaries. Stevenson's moneyed friends grubstaked Humphrey in the hopes that he would defeat Kennedy in some of the primaries and thus put him out of the running. They believed that in a divided convention the delegates, in desperation, might turn to Stevenson for a third time. Johnson thought that he, too, might have a chance in this situation.

But the money given to Humphrey was small indeed compared to that which the Kennedy family poured out for its own. With his brother Bob as manager, Kennedy won a qualified victory in Wisconsin, and then went on to battle in West Virginia, a poverty-stricken and strongly Protestant state. There, all the surface indications favored Humphrey. But Kennedy campaigned hard and, moved by the abject poverty he saw, made sincere pledges, if elected, to help the depressed areas. Someone in his entourage got Franklin D. Roosevelt, Jr., to come into the state and make an attack on Humphrey's war record. This shocked the fastidious, but probably helped Kennedy. When the ballots were counted, Kennedy had swept the state and had become the front runner.

Humphrey now fell into the background, and the Johnson and Stevenson forces came into the open. Johnson operated as he did in the Senate, tying up his fellow Senators—to whom he attached undue importance—and wooing party leaders, but eschewing any appeal to the mass of voters. Stevenson remained indecisive. He wanted to have the nomination offered to him, but would not struggle for it.

The crucial question of the convention was whether Kennedy could win on the first ballot. If he did not, several state delegations—notably Indiana, under a Johnson ally, Senator Vance Hartke—although bound initially to Kennedy, meant to switch to Johnson. This, in my judgment, would have meant Johnson's ultimate nomination, and also the probable victory of Nixon and the Republican party. And this would have happened had it not been for a group of progressive young Democrats from the mountain states, led by Congressman Stewart Udall, of Arizona, and the former football star Byron White. They managed to overturn Johnson's coterie of Senators and party leaders and round up a majority of the delegates from these small states for Kennedy. These were just enough to turn the tide, and it was the votes of the last state, Wyoming, that put Kennedy over the top.

Because I was running for a third term that year, I wanted to stay as far away from the contest for the Presidential nomination as possible. So I told the Illinois party leaders, Daley and Arvey, that, although a delegate, I would not go to the convention. Humphrey was my personal choice, but he had ceased to be a real contender. The Stevenson forces insisted that I help him, but I thought that Kennedy, with his youth and freshness, and unhandicapped by two crushing defeats, would be the stronger candidate in Illinois. Daley, who was a close friend and associate of Kennedy's father, evidently agreed, for despite a last-minute plea by Stevenson, Illinois cast an almost solid vote for Kennedy, as did most of the big-city states.

Kennedy was soon in trouble in Illinois. Beneath the surface, anti-Catholic sentiment was strong, and there were pockets of disaffection among some of the ethnic groups, including the Poles. Therefore, feeling that I was ahead in my own campaign, I gave my chief efforts in the last six weeks to working for Kennedy. I went into southern Illinois and carried his battle into the heart of the so-called Bible belt. Prospects were bleak, but a turning point came after Kennedy's first debate with Nixon.

My audiences immediately snowballed. The morning after Kennedy's fine performance, I found a breakfast meeting jammed with a hundred hopeful Democrats, and the big turnouts continued all day and every day thereafter. Back in Chicago, I spoke on street corners, concentrating on the Negro, Czech, Lithuanian, and Polish sections of the city. In the suburbs I worked with young Catholic couples recently migrated from the city, who felt somewhat isolated.

I rode with Kennedy during the four tumultuous days in which he campaigned in my state, and I admired his extraordinary composure under strain. Although the election hung in the balance, he never showed the slightest worry, and the one time in those hot fall days that he did perspire, he did so symmetrically, with one tiny drop appearing simultaneously over each eyebrow. Enduring a seventeen-hour day without tension, he made apt speeches, shook hands with dignified friendliness, and accepted applause gracefully. In between, we talked of how we could get the Federal Reserve Board to be more lenient on interest rates, which we both believed were a cause for the economic slowdown. To my surprise, I found him knowledgeable about international finance and the inner workings of the gold standard. From time to time as we rode, we would be surrounded by thick crowds of frenetic youngsters shouting "Mr. Kennedy," with the shrill cries of the Valkyries. Then came the characteristic stamp of a greeting to Kennedy: a number of the girls would leap into the air like rockets, but they always landed on their feet when they came down.

Kennedy showed his composure in a more trying situation in 1962. When Congressman Sidney Yates was running for the Senate against Everett M. Dirksen, Kennedy came for a day to campaign for him in Springfield and Chicago, in order to offset the well-founded rumor that he was secretly in favor of Dirksen. At the big dinner for Yates in Chicago he greeted everyone with exquisite courtesy. Only three days afterward did we learn that he had just seen the final photographs of the Russian missile emplacements in Cuba and was in the process of deciding what to do about them. On the verge of a possible nuclear war he was steeling his nerves for the brave decision to resist this nuclear blackmail, but he never showed the slightest sign of inner turmoil. If there ever was a thoroughbred demonstrating grace under pressure, it was he.

Franklin D. Roosevelt had much the same quality, and I have often wondered if the fact that they had ample means and high social position, giving them self-assurance, saved them from the fears and doubts of average men. If true, it is an argument for a genuine aristocracy harnessed to public service, but not for a plutocracy mistaking flabby opulence for excellence.

The Saturday before Election Day, the *Sun-Times* poll showed Kennedy carrying the state by a full 100,000 votes and me winning by at least

half a million. Over the weekend, however, a vicious anti-Catholic campaign was waged in many of the downstate counties, so that, while I carried the state by 420,000, Kennedy won by only 8,000. The Republicans
immediately raised charges of fraud in the Chicago voting, which were
unsupported. They were silent about their own irregularities downstate.
Had they been successful in throwing out the Illinois results, a sufficient
number of electors from the deep South might have broken away to throw
the final election into the House of Representatives. The deep South
would then, by demanding a soft-pedaling of civil rights, have controlled
the final decision. Fortunately this was not to be. We held Illinois, and
only a few of the Southerners bolted.

Some students of the Illinois election results have said that I pulled
Kennedy through. I have never claimed this. The real truth is that there
were a number of factors, of which my sweeping victory was only one, that
combined to win for him his narrow majority. If any ingredient had been
absent, the results might have been different. In the main, it was John F.
Kennedy himself who won the election and who deserved the credit.

Because he won by a narrow margin, Kennedy was cautious in choosing his Cabinet and in adopting economic policies. Dean Rusk was made
secretary of State, rather than Stevenson, who, probably in punishment
for his efforts at the convention, was relegated to the post of ambassador
to the United Nations. Stevenson was able, however, to obtain the appointment of many associates, most of whom, like Willard Wirtz, were
excellent.

No one who was present will ever forget Kennedy's Inaugural. It had
snowed for thirty-six hours, as *The Farmer's Almanack* had predicted
months before, putting the Weather Bureau prophets to shame. Traffic
was jammed. The air was biting cold. Suddenly, after the formal procession, down the steps came running the bareheaded young President. After
Chief Justice Earl Warren had administered the oath of office, Kennedy
stepped forward to deliver the best of modern inaugural addresses. The
magic of the Kennedy-Sorensen collaboration was in full flower: "Let us
never negotiate out of fear, but let us never fear to negotiate . . . ask not
what your country can do for you; ask what you can do for your country."

It was a perfect address, but a slight shadow was cast over me by one of
the sonorous sentences. "Let the word go forth from this time and place,
to friend and foe alike, that the torch has been passed to a new generation
. . . born in this century. . . ." Did this mean that I, born in 1892 and
now sixty-eight and who felt in the full flush of vigor, was no longer
young? It seemed impossible. Did this mean the inevitable succession of
the generations? Perhaps, I thought, but I have six full years in which to
prove that I can not only keep up with but also surpass the youngsters.

Almost immediately after the election, Kennedy had appointed me
chairman of a task force to recommend ways of helping the needy in the

depressed areas of the country, most notably those in West Virginia. We held hearings, visited West Virginia, and made a series of recommendations, which were adopted. The first were emergency measures to deal with hunger, requiring more nutritious foods among the surplus farm commodities and a revival of the food-stamp system on an experimental basis, in order to improve diets and avoid the humiliation that the provision of surplus foods can create. At Shawneetown, in Illinois, I had seen emaciated families come out from the underbrush to get their scanty quota of pork, flour, and corn meal. And I had decided then to help wage war on hunger. This I thought might be the beginning of our assuming greater national responsibility for the poor.

On the whole, the food-stamp venture proved successful, and by 1970 was used in 1,800 counties for almost 6 million persons. New York City adopted it for a million more. But, based, as it is, on state welfare rolls, the system has many weaknesses. Many who should be included are not. Since the food stamps have as their ceiling a quarter of the welfare allowance, where this is not enough, the food stamps are also not enough, and have to be augmented by the unsatisfactory food-supplement system. Thus, in Mississippi, where the average welfare allowance is less than $9.00 per month, the food stamps amount to about $2.25. No one can pretend that this is enough.

My task force also recommended the main outlines of my depressed-areas bill, which I had been vainly pushing since 1954, and which was aimed at bringing private industry into regions with high and persistent unemployment. We urged special treatment for Appalachia, although I was more doubtful than were many of the local sponsors that new highways were the cure. I evaded an outright endorsement of that proposal. Kennedy, who had helped me in 1955 with this bill, now immediately made it Senate bill number one. With his backing, it soon became law.

For his major measure, Kennedy chose to emphasize broadening international trade, with special emphasis on co-operation with the Common Market of Western Europe. Tariffs would be cut 50 per cent by international agreement. They would be completely removed on those commodities of which the United States and the Common Market provided 75 per cent of the world's exports and where our own tariff was less than 5 per cent. As an old free trader, I was enthusiastic about this bill and, with Gore, became its strongest supporter in the Finance Committee. Our efforts succeeded in 1962.

During this time Kennedy had suffered a crushing defeat in the ill-advised attempt to invade Castro's Cuba. This plan had been prepared by the Eisenhower administration, and Kennedy, on finding out about it, felt committed to it. It was not only morally wrong, but also miserably planned and executed. Every conceivable mistake was made, some by Kennedy himself, and the ill-fated expedition was quickly overpowered.

Kennedy took this humiliation in manly fashion. Instead of shifting the blame to the Central Intelligence Agency, where it chiefly belonged, he took it all upon himself. But internally he vowed to subordinate the CIA to the White House and the State Department, and to make our ambassador in each country the representative to whom the CIA was to report.

As the months wore on, Kennedy and I found ourselves in even closer unison on public policies. I understood when political considerations prevented him from following through on some of the tax reforms I advocated and which I believed he really approved.

He knew me to be one of a tiny religious group who were both Quakers and Unitarians. One day he asked quizzically if it was true that I did not believe in the Trinity. I replied that it was, since I had never known of a satisfactory description of the Holy Ghost as a separate being. There was a momentary silence and a slight flicker in one eye, a distant cousin to a wink, before he asked urbanely, "Isn't that going pretty far, Paul?"

On the memory of people of my generation are etched like hot coals three places and dates: where we were when we learned of Pearl Harbor, of Franklin Roosevelt's death, and of John Kennedy's murder. On the last, I happened to be in his home town, Boston, holding a public hearing on truth in lending. Then, and ever since, I felt that something of grace and charm had gone out of political life. Soon a revisionist school of historians will probably try, as they have even with Lincoln, to strip away some of the mystique that attaches itself to his name and memory. They may be right. He was not superhuman and he had many faults, as he would have been the first to acknowledge. But he had an excellence rare among mortals. He gave something genuine to build on for legend and hero worship.

The Kennedy mystique was, of course, an enormous help to his two brothers, Robert and Edward. They started public life with an aura around them. This is something unique among politicians. But the brothers also have had solid qualities underneath their glamour. Bob got good training as a counsel for the McClellan committee on labor racketeering, where he was, perhaps, too rough on hostile witnesses. He was the efficient manager of Jack's Presidential campaign, both for the nomination and for the election, and he was a good attorney general. My son John, who served under him as assistant attorney general in charge of the Civil Division, says that he was an incorruptible, able, and considerate chief. What is more, he found Bob to be sympathetic and to really want to help those who were poor and unfortunate. This showed in a warmth that appealed to the young and the powerless.

My first personal experience with Bob was when he called me to the Justice Department to inform me that he would soon appoint two Republicans to the federal bench in Chicago. If he expected me to acquiesce, he was mistaken. I told him that this was intolerable. We Democrats in Illinois had won the state for John Kennedy against heavy odds, and by so doing we had probably saved the election for him. To repudiate us now would be base ingratitude. Besides, we could furnish him with judges as good as, if not better than, the Republicans, who already were overrepresented on the federal bench in our area. If he wanted to court favor with the Republican-oriented American Bar Association, I said, he should do so in some state like Kansas or Nebraska where the Republicans were overpoweringly strong and where we had little or no organization. And if he wanted to conciliate Dirksen, let him ask himself who had done more for the Kennedys—Dirksen, or Daley and Douglas. Then I gently reminded him that while the President had the power to appoint, the Senate had the power to confirm, and that Truman had found in 1952 that I was no pushover when he had tried to nominate two judges without even consulting me. Being a college professor did not make me a softy.

We parted with some degree of hostility, but with a touch of mutual respect. Bob's department continued to harass my honorable and efficient U.S. marshal, Joseph Tierney, although it finally allowed Daley and me to name good judges for the next vacancies. In one case, Daley and I differed. I wanted Walter Cummings for the Appellate Court, but Kennedy turned me down.

The nationwide outpouring of sorrow over the tragic murder of President Kennedy made the public anxious to express its regard by perpetuating his name and memory against the erosion of time. Streets, bridges, and public squares were hurriedly and properly named for him. Everyone who bore his name shone in a beneficent and reflected light. What happened was inevitable. His youngest brother, Edward, had already moved to Boston, and he was elected to the Senate in 1962. Johnson, who was fearful of the popularity of the Kennedys, served notice that he would not have Robert for his Vice Presidential candidate. The latter, who had hitherto held his residence in Virginia, now suddenly executed an end run. He moved to New York and announced his candidacy for the Senate from that state. Despite the wounded cries of "carpetbagger" from the Republicans, he swept to victory in November by a million votes. But out in California a backlash against these hasty changes of residence carried John Kennedy's press secretary, Pierre Salinger, down to defeat at the hands of actor George Murphy. We were moving toward the British system of not requiring national legislators to live in the districts they represented. But we were by no means there, and perhaps we should not be.

But the two younger Kennedys in the Senate immediately became national figures and made excellent records as hard-working, liberal-minded, and conscientious members. A Kennedy party began to form, which was popularly presumed to have as its nucleus not only the brothers, but also two attractive young Senators, Birch Bayh, of Indiana, and Joseph Tydings, of Maryland.

In 1966 the Kennedy brothers did something for me that I shall always cherish. I had told President Johnson in early October that I would probably be defeated and that while I would deeply appreciate his coming into Illinois to help me, I did not want him to lose Presidential prestige by espousing a losing candidate—particularly in view of the great strains to which he was being subjected because of Vietnam. Even so, he was scheduled to appear in Chicago during the last weekend of the campaign. But he found it impossible to come, because of alleged "health reasons," and our big noon parade was held without him. Bob and Ted, however, insisted on coming. Bob spent one day touring Chicago with me and another in East Saint Louis. The crowds went wild over him. Ted made a triumphant trip with me from Chicago in the morning through Du Page County into Joliet and then from La Salle to big evening rallies at Peoria and Rock Island. The crowds of youngsters shouting "Senator Kennedy" and skyrocketing into the air were again evident, and for a few hours it seemed like 1960 again. Although Ted was in deep pain from a flare-up of the back injury caused by his airplane accident, he ignored it and was imperturbably gracious throughout. Early the next morning, before he flew east, he even took the trouble to send me a handwritten note.

The Kennedys had not only grace, along with their inner toughness, but also courage. Bob would climb Alaskan snow peaks and canoe down the white waters of the Grand Canyon when there was nothing else to do. Ted had shown his mettle many times, notably when campaigning for John in 1960 in Wisconsin, when he buckled on skis for the first time and took a seventy-five-foot jump, which frightened everyone, and yet landed far below on his feet.

When men stand beside you in hours of peril and imminent defeat, your heart goes out in gratitude to them. Ted has had his difficulties, and has not always surmounted his crises, but I still feel drawn to the man who in great pain came west to help me in my hour of need. In addition, he has turned out to be a very good senator.

PART THREE

The Issues in the Senate 1948–1966

19

Legislative Beginnings

I BEGAN my senatorial career by becoming involved in no fewer than five struggles: to change Rule XXII, to provide good housing, to repeal or modify the Taft-Hartley Act, to preserve and protect legitimate competition, and my own war on the pork barrel of the Rivers and Harbors bill. This did not make me popular with the elders of the Senate, who demanded decorous silence from newcomers during their first year of service and allowed only muted murmurs during the second. But these struggles, largely forced on me, helped to set the pattern for my later activities in the Senate.

In 1947, Truman's Committee on Civil Rights had recommended thoroughgoing national legislation to provide equal rights for Negroes in both employment and voting, and this had been affirmed by the successful revolt of Humphrey and our liberal bloc at the Philadelphia convention. Truman, really a Southerner at heart, basically did not like either the Negroes or their defenders. But he had come to realize that something must be done, and he started with an executive order to integrate the armed services down to platoon level. I had feared that this would create trouble, especially in the Southern-oriented Marine Corps. But my former comrades, including those from the South, assured me that it was working out well and were loud in their praise of the Negro enlisted men.

Truman then felt obligated to move toward employment and voting-rights legislation. But Rule XXII stood in the way. The Southerners and their allies did not have an open majority of the Senate, but they did comprise much more than a third, and also had secret sympathizers within both parties. They could probably defeat by interminable discussion any substantive effort to use the national power to protect Negroes, and then, in the name of freedom of discussion, prevent any limitation of debate.

Truman decided, therefore, to try to remove this roadblock before pressing a specific civil-rights bill. So, Majority Leader Scott Lucas proposed that a majority of the Senate, instead of two-thirds, be empowered to limit debate and proceed to a vote. But this motion was itself subject to a filibuster. After a few days, in which both sides discussed the question on its merits, the Southerners started a genuine filibuster. One obvious way to check this was to hold the Senate in continuous session around the clock, day after day. Lucas refused to try this, on the ground that it might kill elderly Senators, such as Walter George, who was thought to have a weak heart. The Senate recessed at 10:00 P.M. or midnight, to let the Southerners recuperate. They then continued their filibuster refreshed, while their secret allies looked on with benevolent satisfaction.

My contribution to the discussion, my maiden speech, pointed out that Rule XXII increased the existing control of the Senate by a minority. The constitutional provision that each state, however small, had equal representation in the Senate with other states, however large, gave a majority of the Senate votes to states with only a fifth of the nation's population. Nevada and Illinois, for instance, had an equal vote. This provision had been firmly embedded in the Constitution by the Great Compromise of 1787, and could not be amended. It was the price the big states had to pay to achieve union. Senators from these states might clank their chains from time to time to call attention to their plight, but they would not sabotage the legislative process because of their helplessness. However, to permit only one more than one-third of the members of the Senate to prevent a strong majority from working their will seemed too much. The seventeen smallest states in the union, with only 8 per cent of the population, could tie up the Senate and defeat the representatives of the remaining 92 per cent. I suggested that, because Negroes were barred from voting in most parts of the South and the poll tax disqualified many others, the ultimate veto power actually resided in a still-smaller section of the population. Furthermore, in eleven of the fourteen Southern state legislatures, debate could be ended by the vote of a *majority* of the members. The South, therefore, was demanding of the nation a restriction it would not impose upon itself. Across the haze of more than twenty years, I still think this was a good speech, although it had no effect upon the immediate results.

One evening a counterrevolution was sprung. Millard Tydings and Carl Hayden had been negotiating with the Southerners, the Republicans, and the border and Southwestern Democrats. Now, they proposed to make cloture *more,* rather than less, difficult. Instead of two-thirds of those who voted being required for limitation of debate, which was the 1917 provision, their new requirement would raise this to two-thirds of the entire membership of the Senate, or "those elected and sworn." All absentees on a cloture motion would be presumed, however unlikely, to have voted "No." Since in those days a certain number of the secret allies of the South made a practice of hiding out on cloture votes by absenting themselves, while protesting their general support of civil rights, an added hurdle would thus be raised for those of us who favored cloture to jump in order to win. We would have to get sixty-four affirmative votes to limit debate, even if the outright and open opponents only numbered from twenty-two to twenty-five.

In the final vote on changing Rule XXII those supporting Lucas were badly beaten, and so was the will of the Democratic national convention. We realized that we had a long struggle ahead. There was much inertia about civil rights among both whites and blacks. Few recognized the prior need for a procedural change in Rule XXII, and it was hard to arouse the general public to a realization that the walls of Jericho could not be leveled by a mere blast of senatorial trumpets. The Senate was not like the Democratic convention. So we began to stress to Negro, civil-rights, labor, and religious groups the effect of Rule XXII. A necessary education of the American people was begun.

The Truman administration next decided to attempt to get the repeal of the Taft-Hartley Labor Act, which a Republican Congress had passed over his veto in 1947. Many features of the act were distinctly unfair, such as the discrimination against the union shop, the failure to recognize that workers, through boycotts, had a right to use their buying power as well as their work, and the undue legal delays that played into the hands of employers. On the other hand, if it had been repealed outright, there would have been no provision to deal with national emergency strikes or with secondary boycotts, which could be used to force recognition of unions rejected in fair elections. I favored a thorough series of amendments, rather than complete repeal, and urged speed. But neither the AFL nor the CIO agreed, nor did the administration. Hearings before the Labor Committee, of which I was a member, were therefore delayed. By the time they began, much of the impetus of the fall election had been lost, and an employer-stimulated backlash was in full force. Discussion was heated when a new bill was brought to the Senate floor, but we lost the crucial vote, in late June, by 50 to 40. Instead of repealing or modifying Taft-Hartley, the act was reaffirmed. The House finally killed the whole bill.

I refrained from saying "I told you so," but felt relieved when several labor leaders came to me quietly during the next year to tell me that they had been wrong on tactics and I had been right. They admitted that if they had confined themselves to working for repeal of the worst features of the act, they could have obtained that quickly; by trying to get too much they had obtained nothing. This experience taught me that moderation is sometimes the wisest policy.

The battle over the famous Rivers and Harbors bill, in which every

state with a seaport or a river was given something in the name of navigation, was one into which I injected myself. This bill was the pride and joy
of Senator Kenneth McKellar, who delighted in playing the part of Santa
Claus, taking down from the Christmas tree juicy appropriations for his
followers and repulsing in the name of economy and "lack of feasibility"
those who had incurred his disfavor. Some projects were indeed desirable,
but others served no useful purpose and were a waste of public funds.

This bill seemed to me a prize example of how local interests could
triumph over national. Freshman though I was, I decided to make war on
it. I introduced an amendment to cut the total appropriation by several
million, giving the administration the power to determine where to make
the cuts. Carl Hayden was managing the bill, and I guessed what his
counterattack would be: he would ask me blandly what were the specific
items with which I disagreed and why. If I could not adequately take
issue with any one, then he could dismiss my whole indictment. So Bob
Wallace and I made a list of the most horrible projects, and I was ready
when the smooth query was launched. I first asked Hayden if he could
justify the appropriation of $33,000 for deepening the Josias River in
Maine. Carl, not expecting this, began to stall. He did not know where
the Josias River was, but of course could not admit that. Pressing my
advantage, I said that I had grown up in Maine but had never heard of it.
Wallace carried an atlas to my desk. I pulled a big magnifying glass from
my pocket and searched zealously for the Josias, but, as I knew, it just was
not there. Moreover, the National Geographic Society had also pleaded
ignorance. Though I blandly offered Carl the magnifying glass to see for
himself, he was too wary to fall for this, and we moved on to other subjects. Later, Margaret Smith and Owen Brewster came rushing to the floor
to defend the honor of the noble Josias. Brewster, a fellow Bowdoin graduate, lectured me on my pronunciation of Josias and of Cape Porpoise,
told us that the river ran into the ocean at the summer resort of Ogunquit,
and declared that the project was highly important. I had once spent a
week in that area in the 1930's and now remembered an insignificant
stream on which some summer residents anchored their boats. This, I
argued, did not seem to be a matter for national attention, since the
wealthy summer visitors could provide for themselves.

Of course I lost on the final vote. Most of the negative votes came from
states that did not have navigable streams and had no ambitions in that
direction. But some newspaper columnists had fun with the incident, and
the pork barrel became a little more discredited.

The battle for a housing program was far more successful. Stimulated
by the election results, the administration plucked up courage to ask for
half a billion dollars as an initial grant for slum clearance and a binding
authorization to build for the poor 135,000 housing units a year for six
years, or a total of 810,000 units. There were about 170,000 public-

housing units already built, under a 1937 act. Together this would provide accommodations for a million families and for almost 4 million of the poor.

Robert Taft had come out the year before for a big housing program costing $1 billion a year. As the intellectual leader of the Republicans and their prospective candidate for the Presidency, his support was a welcome reinforcement in the fight for this bill. The chairman of the Banking and Currency Committee, Burnet Maybank, had the courage to defy the prejudices of the planter aristocracy of which by birth and possessions he was an integral member. By the warmth of his personality, he carried with him some of his fellow Southerners, who would otherwise have been opposed.

I worked hard in the committee hearings to understand the scope of the housing proposals. The able sponsors of the bill (I suspect that they were David Krooth, James Fitzpatrick, and Nathaniel Keith) had devised an extraordinarily clever way of stimulating a maximum of construction with a minimum of initial expense. The federal government would meet the interest and amortization charges on approved municipal-bond issues for the construction of the public housing. These local bond issues, which would be exempted from federal income taxation, would sell at an interest rate from 1½ to 2 per cent lower than federal financing would provide. By removing the interest and amortization charges as local expenditures, the localities were left with only the burden of operating costs, which had to be met out of rentals. After forty years, the units would be debt-free and would belong to the communities. The half-billion authorized for slum clearance was to be funded out of future federal budgets and was to be matched by local contributions of at least half that of the national government. However, the local payments did not have to be in cash; they could be, in whole or in part, in the form of improvements of streets, sewers, water, parks, schools, and so on. In practice this has been the predominant form of the local contribution.

Without serious amendment, the bill passed the Banking and Currency Committee, of which I was also a member. We were insistent that the slum-clearance section be a part of the program designed to help house the poor, and not a mere real-estate transaction or simply a device for beautifying cities. This was referred to in the report of the committee, and in view of current contentions that this was never a part of the original purpose, I emphasize it here.

I was given the job of floor manager for Title I, the slum-clearance section, of the bill. I got Lee Johnson, of the National Housing Conference, to take and enlarge photographs of some of the worst slums in the major cities of the nation. These were mounted and hung around the Senate chamber. Since they spoke more eloquently than any words, the section carried without significant change.

The public-housing sections of the bill, however, faced a powerful and subtle move by John Bricker and Homer Capehart. Although they were confirmed opponents of both public housing and national action in the field of civil rights, they introduced an amendment that would have required municipalities to integrate all their public-housing projects. This was purely a wrecking proposal, designed to defeat public housing, not to promote integration. They knew that we Northern liberals not only were in favor of integration, but also had received a large share of our support from the Negroes. They hoped that through both conviction and political self-interest we would have to vote with them for the amendment. This combination, they believed, would be enough to carry it. But compulsory integration would necessarily lose us the support of Maybank and Sparkman and all their Southern followers, to the number of about a dozen.

I spent an agonizing weekend on tactics. Opposing racial discrimination as I did, I found insufferable the thought of voting against an amendment that on the surface outlawed segregation. Moreover, to do so would, I was told, endanger my whole political future; I would lose the Negro and liberal votes. And yet to vote for the amendment would probably kill the housing bill, which seemed the most promising attack on slums that had ever been proposed.

I did not reach a decision to oppose the amendment until just before the vote. I then obtained recognition and said that the amendment was obviously intended to defeat the bill by losing the ten or twelve Southern votes needed to pass it. Once defeated, there would be no public housing to integrate, so we would not have advanced that cause. I said that a victory would be as insubstantial as the smile of the Cheshire Cat, which was said to have been visible long after the cat itself had disappeared from sight. Yet, if we allowed the municipalities to decide this question for themselves, most of the Northern and Western cities would doubtless desegregate. If we defeated the amendment, there would still be hundreds of thousands of new houses which would be desegregated, and the general cause of integration would be furthered. I sat down with a parched mouth, thinking that I had cut my political throat. I was greatly pleased, however, that every Northern and Western liberal followed my example. With the aid of the Southerners and the Taft Republicans, the Bricker-Capehart amendment was defeated, and the bill was passed.

I spent a large part of that spring, summer, and fall trying to explain my vote to Negroes and doctrinaire liberals. I am not certain I would have succeeded had it not been for Mrs. Mary McLeod Bethune, the head of the National Council of Negro Women, who worked like a tiger to defend me before every group she could reach. Mrs. Bethune would not usually have been called handsome, but as I saw her face shining with courage and good will, I thought it the most beautiful I had ever seen.

When my first Congressional session was over, I had set my course. I was committed to a dual program: social reform to help the weak, and opposition to waste in public expenditures. Many conservatives doubted my sincerity; some liberals, made flabby by years of big budgets, could not believe that a practitioner of economy could be a supporter of public welfare. Neither group liked what it saw, and each suspected me of hypocrisy. But I felt that my feet were on firm ground. To be a liberal, I argued, one does not have to be a wastrel. Monetary resources were precious. They should not be thrown away for trivial purposes, in graft, or in excessive administrative costs. Americans had outgrown the idea that the state should concern itself only with courtroom justice, police, and arms. The improvement of human life was the most important function of the state. Some thoughtful observers believed mine was the proper reconciliation. I hoped their numbers would increase.

20

Civil Rights—Years of Effort

JUST AS slavery dominated political thought and action in the quarter-century from 1840 to 1865, so the treatment of the Negro has taken the center of the national stage during the last quarter of a century.

While the Civil War resulted in the abolition of chattel slavery, which was a great step forward, the Negroes were turned loose to shift for themselves without property or education. They did not get their forty acres and a mule, which some Northerners had promised them. They therefore gravitated into the control of the white planters who owned the land. For ten years after 1865, the federal government did try to protect the Southern Negroes through federal legislation and state governments that were supported by the bayonets of an army of occupation. The Fourteenth and Fifteenth amendments to the Constitution were passed to help protect the voting and economic rights of the Negroes. They were made national citizens, and steps were taken to override the Black Codes passed by many Southern states to keep the Negroes in subjection. While denounced by most of the South, these steps were, on the whole, beneficial. The Republicans deserve full credit for passing them.

But in 1876, in one of the most cynical political bargains in our nation's history, the South allowed the Republicans to deprive the Democratic candidate, Samuel J. Tilden, of the Presidency by miscounting the vote of Florida and probably of South Carolina and Louisiana. This enabled Rutherford B. Hayes, the Republican, to win the Presidency by the wafer-thin margin of one electoral vote. In return, Hayes agreed to withdraw federal troops from the South. Under overt pressure from the Ku Klux Klan and the white population, the so-called "carpetbag" and "scalawag" state and local governments then collapsed and were succeeded by vigorous believers in white supremacy. During the next half-century, Negroes in the South were progressively stripped of most of their short-lived political rights and reduced to something approaching economic serfdom. Only a pretense of educating them was made, and the relatively miserable schools set up for them were completely segregated. Northern churches and philanthropists tried to fill the gap by establishing private schools and colleges. These despised enclaves helped many Negroes to come north in search of greater opportunity, but they were of limited direct help in the South itself.

The white South went further. Segregation laws were passed requiring the races to be separated on all means of public transportation, in the schools, and in all public places. Churches teaching the brotherhood of men and the Christian doctrine of love closed their doors to those of darker skin. In at least one Southern city, Negroes were not allowed to take an oath on any Bible used by whites. It was a grievous violation of the social code for whites to invite Negroes to social gatherings or to do them the courtesy of addressing them as Mr., Mrs., or Miss. Instead, they were hailed with a false familiarity as "Joe," "Hattie," or "boy," and referred to as "niggers."

Since Southern Negroes had no political rights or power, they lacked judicial rights. They did not sit on juries, nor were they judges. They were excluded from most police and fire departments. Crimes by Negroes against whites were severely punished, while those by whites against Negroes were virtually ignored. Moreover, the protection of the law was not fully extended to Negroes assaulted by other Negroes. Instead, the white community adopted a do-nothing attitude, keeping hands off antisocial acts and institutions inside the Negro community. During the years from 1885 to 1910 there were over a hundred lynchings a year of Negroes by whites.

The better jobs were of course closed to Negroes. Their role was restricted to hoeing, picking cotton and tobacco, and doing unskilled labor and domestic and personal service.

The original purposes of the Fourteenth and Fifteenth amendments were ignored or forgotten. The Fourteenth Amendment, ratified in 1868, had declared that all persons born or naturalized in the United States were citizens of the national government as well as of the state in which they resided. As such, they were entitled to the "equal protection of the laws." No state could pass or enforce "any law which shall abridge the privileges or immunities" of any citizen, nor should any state "deprive any person of life, liberty, or property, without due process of law." The Fifteenth Amendment, ratified in 1870, concerned itself with the right of citizens to vote. It said that this right should not be "denied or abridged" either by the national or by any state government "on account of race, color, or previous condition of servitude." Since the Negroes were now national citizens, all these rights were intended to be theirs.

But the Supreme Court in 1883 declared, in the Civil Rights Cases, that it was constitutional for railways, hotels, theaters, and other places of public accommodation to segregate customers on the basis of color. The only dissenter to this reversal of the Fourteenth Amendment was the Southerner John Marshall Harlan. A decade and a half later, in 1896, the same court, in *Plessy* v. *Ferguson,* took the next step against the Fourteenth Amendment when it affirmed that the amendment did not prevent Louisiana from enacting racial segregation for passenger trains. Thus was born the "separate but equal" doctrine. Harlan once again was the lone dissenter, and uttered his famous passage saying that "our Constitution is color blind and neither knows nor tolerates classes among its citizens."

In addition to the general denial of the Fourteenth and Fifteenth amendments, these decisions invalidated much of the protective legislation passed between 1868 and 1876. Such legislation was often not enforced and was allowed to slip into public forgetfulness. Some of it was actually repealed by the Democrats during Cleveland's first administration. The South had lost the war, but in spirit it had largely conquered the North.

Wearied by the tremendous expenditure of life and energy in the Civil War, the North lost interest in the welfare of the Negro. The abolitionists died or lost their zeal. A new generation arose that was absorbed in the material progress of the country and in the settlement of the lands beyond the Mississippi and Missouri rivers. So, for over half a century, as the social position of the Southern Negro worsened, that of the Northern Negro did not advance.

It came as a shock to me when I found that my hero Woodrow Wilson, a Southerner, had relentlessly harried every Negro he could find out of any decent position in the civil service. And when I was a student at Columbia, "Dixie" was sung at public gatherings with more enthusiasm than any other air.

The Negro population in the North began to stir slightly in the late 1920's and '30's. Faced with the Great Depression, Franklin Roosevelt and his relief administrator, Harry Hopkins, strove to provide needy and unemployed Negroes as well as whites with food and work. This helped to bring down on Roosevelt's head the opposition of the conservative sections of the South, and, after 1937, helped to form the bipartisan conservative coalition, even as it attracted Northern Negroes to the Democratic party. An example was the able and forceful William Dawson, who had been the Republican alderman and ward committeeman of Chicago's Second Ward, but who in 1940 switched parties and for nearly thirty years served as the Democratic congressman from the First District.

The migration of Negroes to the North continued to increase, and reached a flood during World War II. Many served well in the armed forces, although virtually always in segregated units assigned to service, rather than combat, duties. At home many others found a place in war and war-related industries. A wartime Fair Employment Practice code, put into effect under pressure from the great Negro leader A. Philip Randolph, was partially enforced and led to their increased employment. In sheer numbers, they became a political power in many Northern and border states and in the cities. Soon Adam Clayton Powell joined Dawson in the House of Representatives.

We of the small civil-rights group in Congress realized that we had a pressing obligation to fulfill our pledges. Although a majority within our party, we were a very small minority within the Senate. We decided to base our program on the findings and recommendations of Truman's Committee on Civil Rights, issued, as *To Secure These Rights,* by a distinguished group of Americans toward the end of 1947. This report had inspired our successful battle at the Democratic convention in 1948.

We stressed equality of treatment in the armed services and in federal employment, and nondiscrimination in interstate transportation. We laid especial stress, however, on preventing discrimination in the right to vote and in the enactment of a federal fair employment practice act. But at first we did not go so far as to recommend federal legislation providing desegregation in the public schools, federal action to guarantee equal access to public accommodations, or the prevention by federal action of discrimination in the field of housing; nor had the committee. While condemning racial discrimination, the report asked only for state action against it. We had enough to do in working for federal action on voting and employment, and we knew that few of our goals could be realized without liberalizing the cloture provisions of Rule XXII.

We introduced bills and tried to stir public opinion. We stressed first the right to vote and then fair employment practices, and at every new Congress we would try to change Rule XXII so that a majority vote might limit debate after an adequate period for full discussion. These fights brought me close to NAACP leaders Walter White, Roy Wilkins, and Clarence Mitchell, whose friendships have been among the most satisfying of my life. I also became acquainted with church leaders of all denominations, and with those three sterling battlers Joe Rauh, Walter Reuther, and Paul Sifton. Frank McCulloch was as much committed to the cause as I, and we were taken into the inner circle of the planners and helped to lay out the legislation, the strategy, and the day-to-day tactics. But we had to move outside the Democratic leadership in the Senate and House, which was really opposed to our raising any of these thorny questions. We seemed to have returned to the 1850's, when Whigs and Democrats alike did not want to stir up the South by espousing the cause of the Negro.

After the conservative coalition succeeded in making cloture more difficult, and our 1949 effort to change Rule XXII was beaten, our 1951 proposal was also crushed, by the bipartisan alliance. In 1953 we not only had a Republican President, but also a slight Republican majority in both houses of Congress. The parliamentary situation was, therefore, more complicated.

After consultation with experts, our civil-rights group decided that before the Senate was fully organized we should move for consideration of the Senate rules. The South wanted the existing Rule XXII to carry over during this period so that a two-thirds vote would be required to stop a filibuster on any motion to change the rules. We believed, instead, that the incoming Senate had the innate right to adopt its own rules by majority vote. I was ready to make the motion to consider the Senate rules when Sifton told me that there were three or four Senators who would support the motion if it were made by Clinton Anderson, of New Mexico, but who would not do so if I were the mover. I stepped aside, and after some hesitation Anderson became the leader in this first move. If it carried, I was then to introduce my proposal for a change in Rule XXII. This would permit a majority of the Senators "elected and sworn," or the so-called "Constitutional majority," to enforce a limitation of debate, instead of two-thirds, and would reduce the needed number from sixty-seven to fifty-one. Anderson was opposed to the majority feature and announced that he would vote against it. I pointed out that if it were defeated, as was probable, I would then vote for his substitute, which provided for limitation of debate by a three-fifths vote.

Taft, who had just become the majority leader, stated that after a decent period of discussion he would move to table Anderson's motion. Since this put him and his party publicly on the side of the South, I admired his frankness. The former Republican policy was to protect the Southerners' power to filibuster but to justify themselves by saying that, while they were for civil rights, they believed even more in unlimited debate. This policy had, of course, permitted the South to defeat any civil-rights legislation. It reminded me of Arthur Clough's parody on the Ten Commandments: "Thou shalt not kill; But need'st not strive / Officiously to keep alive." Johnson had just become the minority leader, under the Southern-dominated circumstances earlier described, and he voted with Taft. We were beaten 70 to 21.

But we took the battle to the country, and public opinion began to stir in our favor. In the next year, 1954, came the epoch-making decision of the Supreme Court in the *Brown* v. *The Board of Education of Topeka* case.

Previously, the court had ruled against the establishment of a few segregated schools on the ground that they were manifestly unequal to those provided for the whites in the same community and thus violated the equal protection of the laws supposedly guaranteed by the Fourteenth Amendment. This had speeded the building of better schools in the South and getting better pay for qualified Negro teachers. In this way the moderate Southerners hoped they could avoid a decision holding segregation itself unconstitutional. Perhaps the members of the Supreme Court also had this hope. Always refusing to rule on this basic point, they had, instead, confined themselves to the question of physical, tangible inferiority or equality. They did not lay down any general principle. Obviously they did not want to challenge the "separate but equal" doctrine. They should have been intellectually strengthened, however, by Judge Henry W. Edgerton's brilliant dissenting opinion in 1951 in a District of Columbia Court of Appeals case. I think Judge Edgerton has been unequaled for honor, hard work, courage, scholarship, and compassion.

Meanwhile the NAACP and its able attorney Thurgood Marshall were closing in on the top court. They found their issue in naked form in Topeka, Kansas—in the state where during the 1850's the abolitionists had physically contended with the proslavery forces and in a city that was supposedly strong in the abolitionist faith. Yet even the good citizens of Topeka could not bring themselves to go all the way. They had segregated their schools, but had honestly tried and virtually succeeded in making those for Negroes equal, externally, to those for whites. When I had lectured in Topeka, I had inspected the Negro high school and found it to be identical with that for whites.

The chosen case came up on appeal from a lower court ruling. The Supreme Court, with an almost audible sigh, could no longer deny jurisdiction and agreed to hear it. Marshall was never in better form than when he argued in quiet tones, interspersed with an occasional rumble of distant thunder, that segregation was in itself unequal, and hence unconstitutional under the Fourteenth Amendment.

The Chief Justice, Earl Warren, long since convinced that segregation was both morally wrong and unconstitutional, now faced the crisis of his career, and made his decision like a hero. He wrote a brief majority opinion declaring that segregation helped to plant and encourage feelings of inferiority in members of a racial minority. Thus it gravely handicapped Negroes in the competitive struggle of life. He made it clear that the *Plessy* decision had been reversed and that John Marshall Harlan had been upheld. In this opinion he shocked many lawyers by referring to Gunnar Myrdal and to cultural anthropologists rather than to jurists. But what made the decision most impressive was the fact that it was delivered by a unanimous court. The two Southerners, the liberal Hugo Black, of Alabama, and the conservative Stanley Reed, of Kentucky, joined in the opinion with the others, economic conservatives and liberals alike.

The news was almost too good to be true. We hailed the verdict, but we tried to do so in terms that would not deepen sectional prejudice. We hoped that the South would accept it, and that there might be a relatively painless adoption of the principle of equal rights. At first this seemed possible. While a few extremists came forward with violent attacks on Warren and Black, the border states began to desegregate. The District of Columbia moved immediately. Maryland and West Virginia followed soon after, as did eastern and central Kentucky and all of Missouri except its southeastern tip. Sections of west Texas where Negroes were few also began to move. The South was cooling off along its edges. The so-called "moderate" Southern leaders kept silent and took their own counsel. We did not want to disturb their twinges of conscience; we hoped the process would spread. For a year we held our breath while the Court pondered its precise directives.

Then, as Congress opened in January of 1955, we had another chance for a significant step forward. The Democrats had gained sufficient seats to resume nominal control of both houses of Congress. Our little liberal group held a hurried caucus on the eve of the opening day to determine whether to push for a revision of Rule XXII. Lehman was insistent that we should; Humphrey was more insistent that we should not. The latter argued that since Johnson had recently become majority leader, we should give him a chance to see what he could do with the South. Lehman countered by pointing out that Johnson had already shown his hand by his support for Taft's motion in 1953 to table Anderson's motion to consider the Senate rules, and that we should push ahead. It was not clear what Humphrey would do if I carried a motion in our caucus to go ahead. He might have split our little group. In order to keep some degree of unity in the liberal camp, and to see if Johnson would perform as Humphrey hoped, I finally decided to support Humphrey's position. Lehman reluctantly acquiesced. Dick Neuberger, who had just come to the Senate, did not object, although he was later extremely critical of our decision.

Humphrey's role in this matter sealed his alliance with Johnson. This had begun in 1953 when our opposition to Johnson's election as party leader had crumbled. From then on Humphrey was at once publicly active as a civil-rights and liberal leader and also a quiet supporter of Johnson. He saw nothing inconsistent in these roles.

I soon felt that he and he we had made a bad mistake. There was no change in Johnson's opposition to civil rights and not the slightest softening in the attitude of the South. On the contrary, the South sharply stiffened its opposition. This came in response to the Supreme Court's decision, in a 1955 supplementary opinion, that, in language reminiscent of Francis Thompson's poem "The Hound of Heaven," desegregation should proceed "with all deliberate speed." While there was a certain ambiguity about the choice of the word "deliberate," there could be no mistaking the meaning of "speed."

The Southern moderates now made up their minds. Senator Walter George decided to oppose the court decision. He was, at the time, being challenged by a younger rival, Governor Herman Talmadge. He was joined by Senator Harry Byrd, the party boss and political dictator of Virginia. They and their advisers drew up a "Southern Manifesto," which pledged massive resistance to the decisions of the Court and asked all Southern members of Congress to sign. Only a few refused. Among these brave men were Senators Gore and Kefauver and Congressmen Charles B. Deane, Harold D. Cooley, and Thurmond Chatham from North Carolina. It became hard for the nonsigners to survive, and several were retired from public life.

Prince Edward County, in southern Virginia, closed down its public schools in order to avoid desegregating. Since Virginia was regarded as the intellectual and social leader of the South, its program of massive resistance won over large numbers of erstwhile moderates, and the South went into active and open opposition. The ruling of the Court was often simply disobeyed. There was no "speed."

After this there was no longer any point in keeping silent in order to encourage the less rabid Southerners. In view of my error in consenting to shelve the motion on Rule XXII, I felt a special need to strengthen the fight for changing it by removing the two-thirds requirement. In 1956 our group drafted a model civil-rights bill, encompassing a whole battery of proposals, from voting rights to an effective FEPC law. We went much further than our past attempts, since we could no longer place any hopes in state action. Direct federal action was required. This bill became the quarry from which much civil-rights legislation was later taken.

The House, then, to everyone's surprise, took up and passed a very good bill in the closing days of that session, in July, 1956. This bill had to come over to the Senate, but no one could tell when. I knew that the South would make every effort to conceal it physically, on the clerk's desk, until a time when the liberal group was not on the floor and it could be quietly brought up and referred to the Judiciary Committee. Under the chairmanship of Eastland, that committee would then simply stall, and the bill would thus perish, since Congress was scheduled to adjourn in a few days for the Democratic convention. In fact, by this time there were few Democratic liberals about. My attempts to build a liberal caucus had utterly failed. I could depend on only one man, whose attendance was extremely irregular, and on Lehman, who was overworked and ill. Most of the Westerners would vote with us, but would not come to our caucuses lest they endanger their understanding with the Southerners.

When word came that the roll call in the House was halfway through, and that the civil-rights bill would soon pass, I made a tactical mistake. I resolved to rush over to the House and get there before the roll call was completed. Then I would insist on accompanying the bill when it was countersigned over to the Senate. There I would announce that I would file a motion not to refer the bill to the Judiciary Committee, but to have it brought up directly for Senate action. As I look back, I see that this was a foolish idea. With almost no assistance, I was trying to cover too many bases. But that day there was no one to help me. When I reached the clerk's desk in the House, I found out that the bill had been passed only a minute before. I asked where it was, and the clerk feigned ignorance. When I insisted on an answer, the truth came out: it had been sent to the Senate. This was the fastest work in the history of the House, I thought as I sped up the center aisle to get back to the Senate before the bill arrived. The Southern staff in the House had been tipped off by their compatriots in the Senate that I was coming and had outwitted me. I rushed back at full speed through the corridors, colliding headlong with tourists. When the benign Lister Hill, who was in the chair, saw me burst into the chamber, a half-suppressed smile crept over his face. Then I knew the worst. I asked what he had done with the House-passed bill, and he blithely replied that it had just been referred to the Judiciary Committee. I protested that he should have known I was going to oppose that motion and asked why he had not waited until I could come to the floor to object. "Paul, my dear boy," he replied, "we move in accordance with the time-honored rules and procedures of the Senate." As I sputtered, the Southern parliamentarian and the clerk looked up with the air of grave and impassive disapproval they always presented to civil-rights liberals.

As soon as I could, I told the Senate what had happened and moved to recall the bill from the Judiciary Committee for consideration by the whole Senate. A point of order was made against this motion on the ground that it could not be made on the same legislative day as the original referral. Hill, who had probably devised the strategy with Russell, upheld the point of order, and his ruling, which was technically correct, was supported by the Senate.

I was seething. I felt that most of my liberal friends had deserted me and that in being forced to do too much I had been badly outwitted. Some of the newspapermen sent out stories that I had been in on the hoax and was really in cahoots with the South to stifle consideration of the bill. In view of our unfortunate decision not to press the antifilibuster fight during the preceding year, this version found credence both in Washington and over the country.

I consoled myself with the thought that I could bring up my motion the next day. Then I learned by the grapevine that it was the intention of Johnson not to "adjourn" the Senate that night, but, instead, to "recess." The next day would thus be the same "legislative day." As such, my motion to call back the bill would still be out of order. The leadership could keep this up until the Senate adjourned for the national conventions, and thus avoid a showdown vote.

In due time, Johnson again moved to recess, and I immediately moved to substitute a motion to adjourn. Everyone knew that I would be beaten in thus defying the technical leadership of my party, which in turn was violating the spirit of our national platform. Johnson determined to crush me, and he got Karl Mundt to ask for a roll call on my motion. I was certainly crushed. The vote was 76 to 6. Three Republicans, Langer, Irving Ives, and George Bender, and only two Democrats, Lehman and Thomas Hennings, joined me. Even my friend and ally Humphrey voted "No."

I tried to walk out of the chamber with my head high, and as I passed Muriel Humphrey, who had a concerned look in her eyes, I stopped to kiss her. As we waited for the elevator, I remarked to Howard Shuman, "Let us punch the bell three times and pretend that I am a senator." Then, closing the door to my office, I shed tears for the first time in years. How many Senators really care about civil rights, I asked myself. How could we ever reverse the tide, and what an imperfect and erring human instrument I was to fail in so crucial a moment.

In justice to the men who voted against me, it should be realized that the session was nearing its end and that the Southerners would have filibustered and prevented action. The Democratic party would have been revealed as badly divided on the eve of the national convention. It was only human for some of the civil-rights liberals to say, "We will wait for another day." I believed, however, that even if every battle was unsuccessful, constant but peaceful struggle would hasten the ultimate coming of needed reforms.

The next morning I went back on the floor to describe for the public what had happened the day before. I showed how the rules and procedures of the Senate, from the principle of seniority to Rule XXII to the "recess" instead of "adjourn" motion, were cunning traps to protect the practice of white supremacy and to prevent the granting of equal civil rights to Negroes and other racial minorities.

Throughout this long fight, Johnson had been most unpleasant in his treatment of Lehman and me. Both parties, led by Johnson and William Knowland, had prevented the question of civil rights from formally coming before the Senate.

After a day's rest, Emily and I went to the Chicago convention and then into the fall campaign. Truman had again killed Kefauver's chances for the nomination by his open opposition, and the main convention fight was over the civil-rights plank. Though a minority member of the Resolutions Committee, Robert Short, who was the Kefauver leader in Minnesota and had defeated the Stevenson slate of delegates in the Democratic primary, brought in a strong plank in place of the weaker one proposed by the party leaders and by the Stevenson forces led by the national chairman, Stephen A. Mitchell. I went from one delegation caucus to another urging support for Short's plan; Mitchell generally followed me urging the opposite. Because we knew that with a voice vote, Rayburn would resolve all doubts in favor of the negative, I closed the debate with a plea for a roll-call vote on Short's alternative. I had been led to believe that enough states (eight) would support me for a roll call. That way the delegations could no longer conceal their positions; they would have to face the music, with the whole country watching them on television. I was sure we would then win. However, G. Mennen Williams, the pro-civil-rights governor of Michigan, whispered to me that a roll call would not take place. I do not know how he learned this, or who had made the decision. It is a fact, however, that the Stevenson forces did not want an open fight on the issue. Since the required eight state standards were not raised to second my motion, Rayburn called for a voice vote. We got a respectable response, but the weight of the poll was against us. The anonymity of the vote had permitted those who would publicly have voted otherwise to express their inner desires to keep the civil-rights question muted. This was the leadership's compromise with reality; namely, not to face it.

Stevenson tried hard in the ensuing campaign, but the fire had gone out of his speeches, and the benign father image of Eisenhower triumphed overwhelmingly. I campaigned vigorously for Stevenson throughout Illinois and in the Middle West, but long before Election Day the results were obvious. We Democrats did well in the Congressional elections, however, and retained nominal control of both houses. In Illinois our last-minute candidate for governor lost by only 30,000 votes to his scandal-scarred opponent.

Immediately after the election I left for Europe with Bob Wallace to study the proposals for a European Common Market and to see the results of the half-successful attack of the French, British, and Israeli forces upon the Egyptians.

When I returned, I was plunged immediately into preparations for the next battle over Rule XXII. This time our liberal group was determined not to be deflected. Instead of arguing that the Senate was a continuing body, we stressed the fact that at the start of a session every legislative body has the right to adopt its own rules and that this should not be denied by the filibuster tradition. This was the long-established practice in the House. We aimed to create a parliamentary situation in which Vice President Nixon would be forced to rule on whether our motion was in order. If he decided in our favor—as we thought he would be forced to do—and the Southerners appealed from his ruling, we could force a vote directly on Rule XXII. We believed we could do this under general parliamentary law by moving, after a brief discussion, "the previous question" on any such appeal. Such a motion automatically ends debate and requires an immediate vote. Since the rules of the Senate had not yet been adopted, and did not provide for the previous question, we would maintain, and we believed successfully, that we could force a vote during this transitional period according to the general principles of parliamentary law.

Nixon, however, cleverly dealt with the whole situation. Declaring that he personally agreed that the Senate did have the right freely to adopt its own rules by a majority vote at the start of the session, he declined to rule on the matter and, instead, referred the motion to the Senate for its decision. If it voted against tabling, he would treat the failure as proof that the Senate wanted to go ahead "under whatever procedures the majority of the Senate approve."

We obtained the necessary signatures for a cloture petition and forced a vote. Johnson again lined up with the Southerners, as did his personal followers, together with Knowland and most of the Republicans. We were beaten 55 to 28. Then on their motion to table we got no fewer than 38 negative votes, plus three more who announced they were against tabling.

Although some of the conservative columnists jeered at our lack of success, we drafted a still-better omnibus civil-rights bill. It seemed that the public was becoming aroused. The spectacle of the Senate tying itself up for days in an effort to prevent a vote was so basically absurd that people finally caught the point. The nation moreover was putting itself in a bad light before the world by refusing to do anything about the civil rights of Negroes. I tried to hammer home the plain fact that whites were a relatively small proportion of the world's population, that the brown, yellow, and black races were the vast numerical majority. Continuing to neglect them was arousing world opposition.

The moderate section of the Republican party did not like the way it was being used as the tail to the Southerners' kite. Attorney General Herbert Brownell therefore started work on a Republican civil-rights bill. This was introduced in March of 1957. It would give the Department of Justice the right to intervene on behalf of a private suit to obtain the right to register and seek an injunction to restrain private individuals from later interfering with the right to vote.

At its best, this bill had vital weaknesses. Private suits would have to be started before the government could intervene, and, with this uncertainty, would be long, drawn-out, and costly. This meant that the relatively poor and disadvantaged would have the heavy burden of initial costs and the grave danger of losing their jobs and their incomes at the hands of the white rulers of their communities. If the NAACP, through its legal fund, helped, the financial burden would be lightened, but local pressures against litigants would still be heavy.

Even if a court finally ruled in favor of the plaintiff, the remedy would be slow. It would apply only to the individual litigant or to the locality in which he lived. It was a typical lawyers' device—using a retail remedy to cure a wholesale evil. Judging by the lack of progress in school desegregation, it promised to be equally ineffective in promoting the purposes of the Fifteenth Amendment, which was a voting-rights measure.

Nevertheless, the bill would have a limited beneficial effect and would end the federal government's neutrality when citizens were deprived of the right to vote. We therefore supported it. For the first time, the Republicans were now our allies, instead of covert opponents.

The liberal Democrats in the House immediately lined up in support of the Brownell bill. Since the rules of the House do not give the Southerners the filibuster weapon, the new coalition passed the bill in the House by a big margin.

This time we in the Senate were ready. I had been working for days, conferring with Knowland and my Republican friends and trying to rally as many liberal Democrats as possible to co-operate with them. The immediate decision was whether to let the House bill go first to the Judiciary Committee, which would be the normal procedure, or to try to bypass the committee by bringing it directly before the Senate for a vote. After the experience of the last summer, which weighed heavily on both the consciences and the public images of many, there was only one answer. Everyone knew that if the bill was sent to Eastland's committee, he would put it to death. There was strong opposition to our preventing this, however, from the Johnson Democrats. Although they had co-operated for years with the Republicans to defeat civil-rights legislation, they now argued that we should not let the Republicans have the credit for such legislation. Anderson held to this view, and so did Warren Magnuson and others from Western states where civil rights, due to the relative absence of Negroes were not a local issue.

At a series of luncheons for the liberals, I stressed the importance of the legislation itself. Who received the credit was merely incidental. The Democratic leadership had always been against us, but now that the Republicans were willing to co-operate with the civil-rights group, we should not spurn them. At length, seventeen of us signed a statement that we would support a Knowland motion to bypass the Judiciary Committee and we stated why. If we hung together, we would give Knowland a good majority and remove one roadblock to action. Our statement aroused such interest that Johnson and the South immediately tried to detach some of our number.

The next day, when I went to the floor of the Senate, I was astonished to find Wayne Morse, who had signed the statement, vigorously attacking our proposal. He declared that he was for proper parliamentary procedures and would not abandon his lifelong defense of them. Looking at Russell, I saw a broad and happy smile dissolve his usual somber expression. The Southerners were gleeful. "The Democratic liberals are breaking up" was the word that went out over the wires.

I called another meeting of the Northerners and Westerners and I told Morse to his face that his action was unpardonable. If he had experienced an honest conversion from his earlier position, he should have informed me before taking the floor. Morse left the room in anger. The break was complete, and we were down to sixteen votes.

I thought we would probably lose more, but the rest of our number held firm. After more maneuvering, with Knowland's help, we finally rescued the bill from the clutches of Eastland's committee. We had taken the first hurdle, but the threat of a filibuster on the bill remained.

During a controlled pause in this effort, Johnson reciprocated Morse's favor by bringing up a bill that would authorize the government to construct a big power dam at Hell's Canyon on the Snake River, between Idaho and Oregon. This was to furnish power to Idaho and eastern Oregon, and could also be used to process the area's rich phosphate deposits. I had been for this project for nearly a decade and had become even more enthusiastic after flying up into the deep canyon itself; I was in fact for Hell's Canyon before I knew that there was a canyon there. The proposal was being fought by the private-power interests, which wanted to check public power in the Northwest. The press galleries watched in amazement as four Southerners who had always fought public power calmly provided the margin by which the Hell's Canyon bill was passed. Morse was exultant, the galleries were dumbfounded, and I was mystified. Then I saw what seemed a great light. I turned to Frank Church, of Idaho, who was a fellow supporter of the dam, and said, "Frank, I am afraid you Hell's Canyon folk have been given some counterfeit money." I predicted that the private-power boys would beat the bill in the House, either in committee or on the floor. That is precisely what happened. By a close vote, the House Interior Committee turned down the public dam, and a few years later a smaller and less adequate private dam was substituted.

If this was the price Morse exacted for his reversal, he did not finally gain by it. His switch also touched off a fateful feud between him and his colleague, Dick Neuberger. Dick had been Morse's greatest booster in the Senate. He had written articles suggesting that Morse, who had just publicly switched from the Republican party to the Democratic, should be the Democratic candidate for President in 1960. But now the Morse supporters began to attack Neuberger for having been somehow wrong in opposing Morse on the bypassing of the Judiciary Committee. To help Dick, I offered to write to 100 Oregon advocates of civil rights praising his help in our struggle. I made no reference to Morse in my letter, but he took it as an affront and redoubled his attack on Dick. He never forgave him, and until Dick died of cancer, nearly three years later, Morse pursued him with his full strength. Watching that vendetta, an attendant christened Morse "the tiger of the Senate," the title of the later biography by A. Robert Smith.

The question of segregation, meanwhile, became a live issue when Governor Orval E. Faubus, of Arkansas, resisted the admission of a few

Negro children into a Little Rock high school. President Eisenhower finally and courageously sent federal troops there to enforce the decision of the Supreme Court. The gentle, manly Brooks Hays, congressman from Little Rock, had attempted to mediate the dispute. He was eliminated from Congress in favor of a rabid segregationist. This was a great loss to the South and the country.

To return to the Brownell bill, there was a mysterious Part III, which had been virtually ignored in all the House discussion. Brownell, who deserves credit for the substance of this provision, although his method of operation was lamentable, had never explained it, nor had others. On the surface it seemed merely to give the federal government injunctional power to try to restrain illegal acts. This seemed innocent enough, although I wondered why it was put in the bill. Of all the newspapermen, only James Marlowe, in a little-noticed column, saw its real significance. But Dick Russell knew what it meant. One day he walked into the Senate chamber with his nose pointing almost straight up to the ceiling and proceeded to give his interpretation. He said it referred to an ignored and never-used act of 1873 that made the violation of the civil rights of individuals an offense. Now, the injunctive remedy was to be applied so that the federal government itself could deal with these general violations in advance of their being committed. Its use did not have to depend on prior individual suits. Russell then refought the Reconstruction period and brandished the possibility of bayonet government.

His speech made a deep impression, and a motion to strike Part III was quickly made. The Democratic advocates of civil rights had not been taken into Brownell's confidence, and I do not think Knowland had been either. Although feeling that we had been dealt with unfairly, I prepared nevertheless to support Part III against the pending motion to strike it. It strengthened the bill and was at least a beginning. The federal government could use the sword of justice and would not be confined to being the tribunal where unequally matched litigants would contend for supremacy. The poor could get "equal justice under the law," once they got before the Supreme Court, as the motto on its building stated. But to get there was almost impossible for weak and despised racial minorities. Despite my work at Columbia, I did not know much about the details of civil-rights legislation of the decade from 1865, but I was certainly going to support our new allies, even though they had committed us to fight on an unexpected and unknown front.

I was on my feet defending Brownell and Eisenhower when Anderson, with a triumphant expression, walked into the Senate and read a news item from the teletype. Eisenhower had just said that he had not known what Part III was about, and that if it meant what it was said to mean, he was against it. That settled it. We were sunk. We now lost four more of our sixteen, and they were gone for good. Part III was stricken from the bill.

The opponents then opened up on the injunction features of the bill, the enforcement of which would lie solely in the discretion of a judge. The court could impose a fine or imprisonment for violation of an injunction. For half a century labor had regarded the injunction as the most evil of legal instruments. I myself had written and spoken on its use in avoiding jury trials, and Norris and La Guardia had limited its use in labor cases. Now, Brownell was proposing to use it as the enforcement device for his voting-rights bill, and I was Brownell's ally. Lister Hill and Sam Ervin moved in, with great unction, to the attack. In the name of liberty and the rights of the individual, they demanded the retention of trial by jury, and argued that some Northern liberals insisted on keeping jury trial in labor cases but not in cases of civil rights. The implication was that we were hypocrites, and certain columnists elaborated on this theme.

Disturbed, I spent several sleepless nights trying to reconcile these points. The facts then became clear. A typical Southern jury was carefully selected to exclude Negroes. In those rare cases where a Negro served, he was almost always an "Uncle Tom," who could not stand up against prevailing white sentiment. No such jury would ever convict a white Southern official of interfering with the voting rights of Negroes. Moreover, even if any members of the jury did have an urge for impartial justice, they knew that they would have to face their friends and neighbors, so few would actually vote to enforce the law. The federal judges were on the whole prejudiced against labor in the pre-1930 courts of the land, but in the South they were not as prejudiced against Negroes as were the main mass of the population and of jury members. Moreover, they had permanence of tenure. And yet, as a class, the judges were overwhelmingly Southern-born and -trained, and were not prejudiced against their fellow white Southerners. A closer, although still imperfect, approach to justice would be obtained without—rather than with—a jury trial. This I believed, and this I argued.

But our group lost four more members on this issue. Church took John Kennedy with him on his amendment requiring a jury trial if an injunction was violated. I told Knowland we could now rely on only eight votes, and this turned out to be the case. Russell had decided not to stage a filibuster if Part III and the injunction features were eliminated. He had won these two important points and believed that the bill's passage did not justify stirring up further opposition by another discredited filibuster. He correctly reasoned that while the South was winning all the legislative battles by the filibuster, it was losing the war—arousing public opinion against itself by this tactic. Our constant pressure was therefore beginning to pay off. It became known that Russell and his followers would vote against the bill but would not filibuster against passage in its final form.

This, however, did not satisfy Strom Thurmond, who would not passively accept *any* of the bill. In splendid physical condition, he thereupon staged a one-man filibuster, which ran for twenty-four hours and thirty-two minutes. His Southern colleagues gave him no help by relieving him with questions and looked on disgustedly as he outdid them in his zeal to maintain white supremacy. Because he was being deserted by his fellow Southerners, and to show good sportsmanship, I brought him a pitcher of orange juice at midnight to relieve his thirst. Suspicious at first, wondering if it was spiked, he finally drank it, and it helped carry him through the night.

His action brought in Wayne Morse. Not wanting to lose the title of filibuster champion, he took the floor early one evening, with a red rose in his buttonhole. He attacked the bill as a sellout that was opposed by all true believers in civil rights. Hour after hour his voice went on. Most of the time he was lyrical and spoke—though repetitiously—to the point, but there were many extraneous insertions, as when he discussed some of his gastronomic difficulties. Through it all ran the theme that he was the only true liberal, the only one concerned with procedural as well as substantive rights.

I decided not to follow his lead. The bill was indeed weak, and it would be hard to get the injunction to work in time to head off the deprivation of voting rights. But it gave the possibility of federal aid to hard-pressed Negroes who, lacking money and at the bottom of the social totem pole, could not adequately defend their rights through expensive suits after the offense had been committed. This measure would permit the federal government to help furnish the sword as well as the tribunal of justice and to head off some of the abuses before they occurred. Other Northern liberals adopted a similar position.

I was handicapped during the days we worked on the bill by the continued absence of the man we had informally designated as our floor leader. He was a lovable, able, and liberal lawyer and a tower of strength on the otherwise hostile Judiciary Committee, but he was unfortunately a confirmed alcoholic, and would be seized by attacks whenever he was under great strain. This was one of those times. He had disappeared weeks before. I tried to get word to him to return, or at least to tell me whether I was on the right course. But no one could tell me where he was. Perhaps they did not really know, although mysterious rumors kept coming back about his alleged doings. I was left with dubious credentials and a melting set of followers.

Johnson now emerged from the shadows of opposition as the great apostle of civil rights. He, a Southerner, had pruned away the excrescences, it was said, and was bringing to passage the first civil-rights bill in eighty-five years. It was a triumph, so he said, for his policy of moderation over the extremists, who would have prevented action by their wild talk. Some of his favorite columnists, including William S. White, burst into a chorus of antiphonal praise. Somehow I now became the man who had impeded progress. Johnson, our opponent, became, in their version, the great hero.

The bill was finally passed, by a vote of 71 to 18, and it went to the House. There, largely due to Richard Bolling and Joe Rauh, a surprising and sensible decision was made. While the jury-trial amendment was retained, it was restricted to those cases where the judge imposed a sentence of more than thirty days or a fine of more than $300. This was just what we had desired, since we did not want a severely punitive bill but, instead, one that would put the more gentle pressure of the law behind civil rights. The final result was confirmed by an exhausted Senate.

Morse confirmed his malediction when we adjourned, taking the stump to denounce liberals who, according to him, had voted for a sellout on civil rights.

At the request of the *Atlantic Monthly,* I wrote an article explaining the bill. In it I pointed out that the measure should help the Negroes to acquire some political power. Local courts and police departments would treat them more justly. Negro streets would gradually be paved and lighted, and water and sewage facilities would be brought into Negro quarters. Once they possessed greater political power, the Negroes would be treated with greater respect by whites. Other legislation, such as that dealing with schools and employment, would be made easier.

After returning from a month's study of the Common Market, which had just come into being and which I foresaw would require us to adopt a more liberal trade policy, I toured Illinois for six weeks, explaining what I had tried to do on the Brownell bill and defending my support for civil rights even in the supposedly anti-Negro counties of Little Egypt. Never was I treated with greater warmth and affection.

The civil-rights question continued to simmer. The bus boycott in Montgomery, Alabama, led by the young minister Martin Luther King, Jr., brought Gandhi's doctrine of passive resistance, or nonviolent coercion, for the first time to this country as an organized movement. The Negroes in Little Rock, under a courageous mother, Mrs. Daisy Bates, of the NAACP, were rallying to support the Negro children attending the high school. Church forces in the North were stirring, and Negro voter registration rose slowly.

We fought again to change Rule XXII when the Senate opened in 1959. Because of our great gains in the 1958 elections, we did better than ever before, but, after an exhausting filibuster, we failed to get the necessary two-thirds to enforce cloture, and were defeated, 60 to 36.

However, I had introduced another civil-rights bill in 1958, which embodied the "stick-and-carrot" approach. It authorized federal funds to assist school districts that were willing to desegregate and provided injunctive powers for the federal government when dealing with school districts that would not act without government suit. While this bill did not get anywhere in 1958, it became Part IV of the 1964 Civil Rights Act. Both the stick and the carrot have since proved to be powerful forces for desegregation.

21

Civil Rights—Years of Success

THE 1957 Civil Rights Act proved ineffective. It threw too much of the burden on the poor, the weak, and the frightened. The Republican Department of Justice, moreover, seemed uninterested in its enforcement. By 1960 even the most placid recognized that something more must be done to protect voting rights.

In that year a new movement started, not in Congress, but throughout the country, to desegregate public facilities such as restaurants, hotels, theaters, toilets, and public parks. A group of gentlemanly but determined young Negroes in Greensboro, North Carolina, staged a sit-in at a restaurant that refused to serve them hamburgers. As the idea spread, two more civil-rights organizations developed. The first was the Congress of Racial Equality (CORE), and the second, more radical, was the Student Nonviolent Coordinating Committee (SNCC). "Snick" began to recruit both black and white volunteers who wanted to take an active part in the struggle. The noninvolvement practiced by the young in the 1950's, which had been partially induced by the fear of McCarthyism, was being replaced by a desire to participate by becoming an "activist."

With the Presidential election coming up, the leaders of both parties wanted to do something to appease this growing strength of the civil-rights movement, but at the same time they did not want to inflame anti-Negro sentiment in either the South or the North. Therefore the official party leadership confined itself to further tinkering with the 1957 act. The liberals were not opposed to this, but thought the procedure too complicated. The judicially appointed referees to be set up under it, we felt, could stall interminably and would impose far more severe literacy tests on blacks than on whites.

An off-the-record conversation with a Southern segregationist confirmed an idea that had been simmering in my mind for years. "Douglas," he said in an unexpected burst of frankness, "you are never going to get anywhere on this tack. We will tie you up by the delays of the law and wear you out. The only way you are ever going to break through our defense is to give the federal government the power to send in marshals or legal officers who will directly register the voters themselves. They should also see to it that no rough stuff occurs in the election proper." My strange opponent, smiling as he spoke, added, "Of course, I am opposed to all this; I will fight it with all the strength I have. But you damn-fool innocents should wake up if you are really in earnest." Walking away, he said, "What I have been saying is confidential. I don't think you will repeat it, but if you do, I will deny it."

I was never sure whether he was a secret supporter of ours or just a strangely frank man. Whatever his motive, since I thought he was right I moved an amendment to give the President the powers he mentioned, by providing for the appointment of temporary federal registrars and for voting referees. This angered the two party leaders, Johnson and Dirksen, who, with intense indignation, jointly moved to table my motion. In turn, this shut off further debate, and we were beaten, 53 to 24. Five years later I had the happy experience of seeing the identical proposal embodied in the Voting Rights Act. It was highly praised by the same two men who had condemned and sidetracked it earlier, supposedly forever. They even posed as its originators.

Events had moved rapidly in the intervening years, and so had public opinion. Dr. King grew in both stature and influence, as did the NAACP and the Urban League. CORE and SNCC were still nonviolent organizations, but many Southern whites were becoming quite violent. Police broke up peaceful civil-rights parades in Birmingham, Alabama, in May, 1963, clubbing women and children and turning their dogs loose on them.

In sharp contrast, the civil-rights March on Washington in August of 1963 was a triumph of dignified concern. My son John with Bayard Rustin directed the logistics, and the needs of a quarter of a million people were quietly and efficiently cared for. Emily and I marched with a Catholic group from Chicago down the Mall to the Lincoln Memorial, where the people gathered. No one spoke a harsh word, and nothing could have been more peaceful. Martin Luther King made the most moving speech of the civil-rights movement. "I have a dream," he declared, "that my four little children will one day live in a nation where they will not be judged by the color of their skin but by the content of their character . . . that day when all of God's children, black men and white men, Jews and Gentiles, Protestants and Catholics, will be able to join hands and sing in the words of the old Negro spiritual, 'Free at last, Free at last,

Great God Almighty, We are free at last.' " There was a religious sense of fellowship throughout the enormous gathering.

Much as I admired John Kennedy, I regretted his delay when he assumed the Presidency in proposing effective civil-rights legislation. In 1961 and 1963 we liberals made our perennial fight to change Rule XXII without his help, and possibly even despite his quiet opposition. For two and a half years no legislation was proposed by the White House.

Kennedy was acutely aware that he had won by only a wafer-thin margin. His immediate objectives were a mutual lowering of tariffs and a tax cut as a business stimulant, sprinkled with mild proposals for tax reform. Wanting Southern support for these measures, he tried to avoid a divisive struggle over civil rights. He also tried to keep the civil-rights groups contented by individual kindnesses and executive orders, such as the appointment of Negroes to high positions in the government. Robert C. Weaver was raised to Cabinet rank and several Negroes were appointed as judges, federal attorneys, and marshals. I got an eloquent Negro appointed to the federal district court in Chicago, who soon declared that divine hands had elevated him, and God alone should be praised.

If Kennedy had lived, I believe he would have come out more strongly for civil rights. During the last few months of his Presidency, he sponsored a very good civil-rights bill, which began mildly, but steadily became more inclusive.

It remained for Lyndon Johnson, who as senator had been the most subtle and determined opponent of all civil-rights legislation, to become, as President, the evangelist for the movement. As I have said, I had been in despair when he succeeded Kennedy. I thought the tragic turn of events had elevated our adversary to the leadership of the country. It had been bad enough to have him operate in the Senate; it would be infinitely worse for him to operate from the White House. But Johnson as President was a different man.

The first sign of change came quickly. Herbert Lehman had died, and New York, which had held him in affectionate awe, prepared a hero's funeral. Johnson announced that he would be there, and he took with him not only Joe Rauh, brain truster of the civil-rights movement, but a planeful of us. I sat behind the President in Temple Emanu-El and observed his grief-stricken bearing. Having attacked Lehman in life, he paid him full homage in death.

The acid test came in the winter of 1964. Johnson took Kennedy's civil-rights bill and asked Attorney General Nicholas Katzenbach to revise it. In this version, the Department of Justice was given the power to seek general rules that would make it an offense for adults to be discriminated against in voting and employment, and for children to be segregated in their schooling. When necessary the department could thus move directly against major units of government in these areas. This was what we had vainly urged for years. Johnson and Katzenbach earnestly wooed Dirksen, and he began to shift his position. But the chief force for strengthening the bill and working to get it passed was the lobby headed by the churches and the Democratic Study Group, the organization of progressive Northern and Western Congressmen, which had steadily gained influence since the death of Rayburn. The churches aroused wide public support, which the Study Group helped translate into votes in the House. They demanded two strengthening steps: first, the guaranteed right for all people to be served in places of "public accommodation," and, second, the use of federal funds as an enforcing device. Katzenbach may not have welcomed this independence of the progressive wing of the party, but the members of the Study Group knew better than he and Johnson what the Negroes and the public wanted. The right of all persons to obtain non-discriminatory service in restaurants, hotels, motels, stores, toilets, and other places of public accommodation had become a fourth demand, with schooling, voting, and jobs. The administration finally accepted these proposals of its rank-and-file supporters. It could no longer dilute the popular will.

Together, all these forces enabled us in the Senate to overcome the filibuster and to pass the great Civil Rights Act of 1964. The South was stripped of most of its allies, although Goldwater stayed with them and voted against the bill on final passage.

In the winter of 1965, there was another brutal attack upon a peaceful group of marchers, in Selma, Alabama. Blood ran and heads were broken. Thousands of Northerners were outraged, and some traveled to Selma in protest. Lillian Tobey decided to go, and Emily told me that she could not conscientiously remain aloof and safe while Lillian, who was a decade older, was putting herself in such great danger. Jane Ickes, the widow of my old friend Harold, would also join them. I told Emily that I hoped she would not go, because the Southern mobs were bitter, and no one could tell what they might do. It would be unendurable for me if she were killed or injured. But, I added, the decision was hers; if she decided to go I would be at the airport to see her off.

The women were determined, and, proud of Emily, I saw them off with a rapidly beating heart. The next thirty-six hours were frightening. Would the sheriff dare to turn loose his clubs and dogs on defenseless women? In my office, I could see the worried faces of my staff. Finally the news came on the radio that the procession had started, and that Emily and Dr. King were leading it. The reports were that Emily was apparently unconcerned as she marched firmly along near the head of the procession, with Lillian and Jane right behind. As the two sides faced each other on the bridge, the police kept their clubs in their belts and the dogs on the leash. No violence occurred, and Dr. King, to our relief, turned back. Perhaps the Southerners did not want to beat up the wife of a senator and her two widowed friends. It was rumored that the Alabama authorities had promised that a procession to Montgomery would be allowed a day or two later. The civil-rights groups had won, and my wife had helped.

But that night brought tragedy. A Unitarian minister, the Reverend James J. Reeb, also a marcher, was beaten to death by the clubs of white Alabamans. The movement for effective civil-rights legislation now became irresistible.

After the 1964 elections, in which Johnson and the Democrats won a decisive victory, Johnson's pace did not slacken. He moved on voting rights. On March 15, 1965, he summoned Congress to a special session at which he delivered a fiery speech, which was nationally televised. The former opponent of civil and political rights for Negroes and other minorities had now become their ardent supporter and gave every evidence of deep, if delayed, sincerity. He concluded with the title of Dr. King's theme song, "We Shall Overcome." Dick Russell's nose went up almost parallel to the ceiling, and Johnson's Southern friends remained stonily silent. We advocates of civil rights greeted every sentence with applause, intensified by surprise, as did the galleries. In front of me, ruddy-faced Earl Warren so far forgot his prescribed neutrality as to applaud the conclusion with a fervor that was nonjudicial.

In the new proposed bill, Johnson struck at the core of Southern resistance. Up from the ashes of obscurity came our 1960 proposal for federal voting registrars. In addition, the government was to be given broad injunctive powers, and there was to be strict limitation on the use of literacy tests to qualify for voting. This would be particularly effective in the five states of the deep South. With big majorities in House and Senate, both the attempt to filibuster and all opposition were overpowered. So the Voting Rights bill of 1965 became law.

As a sop to the South, the act was to have effect for five years only, after which Congress would decide whether to renew it. Although unhappy about this, we supporters did not regard it as a serious defect. During that time large numbers of new voters would be enfranchised, and in a modern democracy an enfranchised minority never allows itself to be stripped of such rights; nor does a political party dare to take the vote away. This has been borne out by the facts, for in 1970 Congress renewed the law for five years more.

Johnson's political turnabout was one of the most striking in the history of American politics. Cynics have charged that it was done solely to catch the Negro and liberal vote of the North and Midwest. This was certainly a factor in his decision. He would not have acted as he did had it not been to his political advantage. Mrs. Johnson once told me in his defense that he had gained a broader view of what the country needed. In any case, having decided that it was to his advantage to promote civil rights, he welcomed both the arguments and the groups he had once attacked. He even got far more emotional satisfaction from working for civil rights than he had from intriguing against them. The old fires of his early populism still burned within him. On our side, once he had committed himself, we buried the hatchet.

There remain the questions of how and why public opinion changed. In 1948, when we began our struggle, the North was tepidly in favor of civil rights for Negroes. But it did not realize how deeply rooted the abuses were. The churches contented themselves with adopting resolutions at their national conventions and allowing their leaders to make a formal appearance for them before Congress. But the widely publicized brutality of Southern segregationists in 1963–65 and the superior behavior of the Negroes had touched the consciences of millions. In Washington, we were deluged by letters in favor of action and by concerned delegations, with the result that both houses had banned racial discrimination in employment, schooling, voting, and, finally, in public accommodations, and had provided effective means of enforcement.

The commerce clause of the Constitution was now brought in to strengthen the Fourteenth Amendment. The most effective device, however, was Part VI of the 1964 act. This shut off federal funds from state and local agencies practicing segregation on federally aided projects such as education, air transportation, hospitals, agricultural and vocational extension. Senator Javits had been introducing amendments to this effect for several years, and I had always broken away from the Democratic leadership to support them. These federally aided projects were so widely established in the South that such an enforcement of desegregation meant that few states would refuse to conform. It had now become possible to do what had been impossible in 1949.

I had marveled for years at the self-restraint of the Negroes. It was not only right, but also prudent. Southern whites, like the British in India a quarter of a century before, had an almost complete monopoly of the instruments of force and violence, and had the will to use them. I had doubted that any group that had suffered such cruelties as the Negroes had experienced could be expected to maintain a pacifist position for long. I had repeatedly warned my colleagues that if they persisted in defeating adequate civil-rights bills, they would arouse an armed revolt by the Negroes that would ultimately result in slaughter and divide the nation. Now, for a brief moment, it seemed as if the hopes and tenets of my Quaker friends were coming true. Perhaps love and good will could triumph, after all. The dream of the Swedenborgian poet William Blake, and of Edward Hicks, the Quaker painter, might be realized; the lion and the lamb might indeed lie down together in a peaceable kingdom. The future seemed more hopeful than it had in 1954–55. The country was catching up with the Supreme Court.

The Congressional civil-rights group had laid the basis for victory. By keeping the issue before Congress year after year despite political defeats, we had finally helped to arouse the conscience of the country. We had forced the Congressional leadership of the Democratic party to turn from bitter hostility to studied indifference and finally to ardent advocacy. We had been the whipping boys at every stage of the conflict and had been shunted aside at the conclusion. But we did not care. That was the law of life. The cause had won.

The real heroes of the struggle, however, were the relatively ignored participants in the battle—both black and white, men and women, Northerners and Southerners, who were killed, beaten, discharged, and black-listed. They made the real sacrifice and deserve the major share of the credit.

Tired from the long struggle, we hoped the task might now be the enforcement of the 1964 and 1965 acts. But neither the times nor the President would let us rest.

In the late spring of 1963, a group of SNCC youngsters, going South to promote desegregation, sought a conference with me. They filed into my office glowering. Half of them wore heavy beards, reminding me of the students I had seen thirty years or more before along the Boulevard Saint-Michel in Paris. The beards were then alien to American practices, particularly in the South. After some pleasantries, they asked if I had any advice. I told them to shave their beards and go south with smooth faces. They were not crusading for the right to wear beards, I told them, but for the right of Negroes to vote, to eat hamburgers in a white restaurant, and to go to a public toilet. Their beards would set them apart from the native Southerners and identify them unfavorably. This would be a powerful force against them. If treated politely, most Southerners are friendly people. Northerners should be careful not to create unnecessary dissension. There was no response. Their eyes smoldered, and I thought their beards bristled. Nevertheless, I gave them a second bit of advice: to guard their mimeograph machines carefully and to control what went out from them. There might be people seeking to infiltrate their ranks who wanted conflict between whites and Negroes more than they wanted to remedy the wrongs suffered by blacks. Some of these people would probably be Communists, though it would be difficult to prove. They would work hard, they would expose themselves to danger, and they would seem good comrades. But they would gravitate toward the mimeograph machine as the needle of a compass points to the magnetic pole. Then a lot of material would be issued that would unnecessarily stir up trouble. "This will hurt both you and your cause, and it will also hurt the country." I watched the group closely, waiting for a response. There was not a word. I thought I saw agreement in perhaps two pairs of eyes. But most of the faces became more truculent. After a few moments the meeting broke up.

I formed the conclusion that while there were many unselfish idealists in SNCC, it was largely run by men who wanted to provoke, rather than abate, a violent confrontation with Southern whites. Such a confrontation, they believed, would weaken the moral authority of the economic and political order, which they regarded as essentially immoral. I was, therefore, prepared intellectually for the change that came in SNCC and for its abandonment of the ideal of nonviolence, and I was not surprised by the birth in 1964 of a third group, Students for a Democratic Society (SDS), which began at the University of Michigan and spread rapidly in the following years.

Civil-rights agitation and its attendant disorders now began to spread from the South to the North. There was ample ground here for potential trouble. Many Northerners who had been for civil rights for Southern Negroes wanted to isolate the Negroes in the North. There was some justification, therefore, for the Southerners' charge that the Northerners were hypocrites wanting to set standards for others that they would not observe themselves.

Northerners protested that, unlike the South, they had no laws or ordinances enforcing segregation. Negroes voted freely in the North and held office, and they could eat in any restaurant and sleep in any hotel. Employers seldom openly discriminated against them. Some unions, especially those organized on industrial rather than craft lines, were having a change of heart. Nevertheless, the public schools of most Northern cities were, in practice, segregated. Those in Chicago were among the most so. This had developed not by law, but out of the segregated nature of the neighborhoods, which in turn led to *de facto* segregation in the schools.

The tractor and the mechanical cotton picker were displacing millions of Southern laborers and tenant farmers, who in growing numbers were coming north into the cities. By 1960 there were more than a million Negroes in Chicago, 30 per cent of the population. In East Saint Louis they were approaching a majority, as they were in the steel city of Gary, Indiana.

As the Negroes moved into a neighborhood, many of the whites moved out. When Negroes reached a "critical percentage," most whites left, however liberal their theoretical views. This percentage varied from 10 to 25, but nearly always when Negroes exceeded 50 per cent, there would be an outright exodus of whites. The integrated neighborhood in which so many said they believed was usually only a transitional stage as a community moved from segregated white to segregated black. This white exodus was generally accompanied and partially caused by an increase in crime as the Negroes became more numerous. Only a few communities could resist these tendencies. I was proud that my own neighborhood in Chicago maintained a precarious balance amidst many trials and difficulties.

Since most schools are neighborhood institutions serving areas where the distances are short enough for children to walk, neighborhood segregation leads to *de facto* segregation of the schools. It was also true that where a school served two or more neighborhoods, both black and white or partially white, the school authorities nearly always redrew the school-district boundaries so that each school was confined to the children of one race.

An illiterate Chicago Negro summed up the difference between the Northern and Southern attitudes as follows: "In the South, the white man lets us come up close to him but always at a lower level. Up north, the white man lets us stand on his level but he won't let us come near him." Any sociologist would have envied this succinct definition of "social distance."

The situation was made to order for trouble. And the fuels for a fire were increased by the lack of jobs for Negro youth, the decay of their housing, and the increasing number of crimes among the recent comers. Furthermore, the slum-dwelling Negroes were taken advantage of by many white merchants, moneylenders, and landlords. Recalling long oppression and faced by hostile police, thousands of blacks felt like aliens. Moreover, television brought this disparity into every home.

The legislative situation was actually improving when, like a clap of thunder, trouble broke out in Watts, a Negro slum of Los Angeles, in the summer of 1965. When the smoke cleared after a few days, many stores were in ruins and there had been widespread violence and destruction. In 1966 and 1967 more cities went up in flames and disorder. Newark and Detroit were the worst, but were not unique.

As SNCC moved from nonviolence to mass resistance, CORE with some reluctance followed suit. Both groups joined Dr. King in shifting their emphasis from the South to the North, and became more provocative in their tactics. Possibly they thought liberal opinion would restrain both the police and the white community from such brutality as the South would have unleashed if similarly treated.

Further trouble was coming in an army of militant Negro youth. Many had never found jobs in Northern cities. Some had dropped out of the labor force. Others, in frustration, became black nationalists and wanted to separate themselves completely from the white community. Still others followed Dr. King in attacking residential segregation and promoting integration in housing as well as in other branches of life. Since as a practical matter school segregation followed residential segregation, what was needed was more integrated housing for Negroes. On the one hand, middle-class Negro families, wanting to move out of the slums, insisted on freedom of residence. On the other hand, the whites felt that their neighborhoods were only an extension of their homes; they did not invite people to whom they objected into their homes or clubs, and they did not mean to do so in their communities.

My mind went back to the days when the liberals of Western Europe broke down the tightly segregated Jewish ghettos and brought the Jews into the mainstream of European life, to the benefit of all. Should we not do for our Negro ghettos in the last third of the twentieth century what our spiritual forebears had done for the Jews in the first third of the nineteenth?

The administration decided in 1966 to charge this last redoubt of prejudice, but this time the leaders did not care to sponsor the legislation. I was to have that unwelcome honor. The administration drafted and I introduced what we called an "open occupancy" bill. This would make it illegal to discriminate in the sale or leasing of housing on the ground of race. There was no requirement to rent or sell to a Negro because he was a Negro. If he was of bad character or slovenly in person or in the care of property, the applicant could be refused. But if in other ways he was satisfactory, he should not be excluded because he was a Negro.

Of course, such a general principle would be hard to enforce, but we hoped that we might prevent the worst cases of discrimination. Furthermore, we might build a climate of opinion that would make it easier for the less brave to abandon their past practices. In their hearts, many did not believe in racial discrimination, but they lacked the courage to break away from conventional standards and either hire Negroes or rent or sell to them. With discrimination made illegal, these people could tell their neighbors that they had to obey the law even though they did not believe in it. As people lost the habit of discrimination, they might change their feelings. Let them begin to act in a more fraternal way and they would gradually come to feel more fraternal. Thus legislation could help raise the level of conduct, as it has in the lessening of prostitution.

In the late spring of 1966, I led off, in the Senate Judiciary Committee, with these arguments. But while Senators Eastland and Ervin kept the bill bottled up, the House passed a modified bill, which applied open occupancy only to multiple dwellings of more than four units. This, in effect, exempted the suburbs and the residential wards, where the chief difficulties existed, and confined the act to the inner cities. The liberals were disappointed, but it was better than nothing.

We then bypassed the Judiciary Committee and brought the issue before the Senate as a whole. A poll showed that we had a small but comfortable margin if we could bring the measure to a vote. But that "if" was the real obstacle. The filibusterers started, and were joined and led by my colleague Everett Dirksen. Although his attitude on civil rights had often shifted, he had belonged until 1963 to the Dixiecrat-Republican coalition. Then for two years he had been most helpful in supporting the pathbreaking civil-rights acts of 1964 and 1965. Now, with his weather-vane sensitivity, he came out in violent opposition to our fair housing legislation. Thundering that the bill was an invasion of property rights, which should be supreme, he turned the full force of his oratory and influence not only against the bill, but also against letting the Senate vote on it. We tried to break the filibuster, but while we won by a slight majority—diminished by the unaccountable absence of some of those upon whom we relied—we fell far short of the necessary two-thirds.

I then hurried to Illinois, where the freedom-of-residence proposal was rapidly becoming the dominant issue in my own campaign for re-election. The results of that election, particularly for the House, where the Democrats lost forty-seven seats, combined with the many outbreaks of Negro rioting in the North, turned such a volume of white opinion against the proposal as seemingly to prevent it from becoming an immediate political possibility. We had tried to reduce racial cleavages and hatred. Despite our efforts, they had become sharper and more embittered.

Two years later, in 1968, however, under the able generalship of Senator Walter F. Mondale, of Minnesota, freedom of residence became law in the Housing and Urban Development Act.

22

The Struggle to Defend Civil
Liberties and the Supreme Court

SINCE ITS FOUNDATION IN 1920, I had been an active member of
the American Civil Liberties Union. In Chicago there was abundant work
for us to do. The police were vigorous in putting down public dissenters
with their clubs, and in getting those arrested to confess by "working
them over." They seemed to be ignorant of the First Amendment to the
Constitution. Frequently, when we tried to protect some poor devil from
them, they would move him about from station to station to prevent our
getting him out on bail. During the process he would be repeatedly
beaten up. Sometimes it seemed that few people believed in the old American doctrine that those arrested were presumed to be innocent until
proven guilty and were entitled to a fair trial, or took seriously their
constitutional right to assemble peaceably and to petition for redress of
their grievances.

But our troubles were not confined to the police. The Communists
were in constant trouble with the city administration and kept running to
the ACLU for protection. Sometimes their cases were good, and as citizens
they deserved aid. But sometimes they overstepped the "peaceable" limits,
and they, not the police, were at fault. Their own accounts could not be
depended on to give a truthful record of what actually happened. Commonly, the situation was mixed, and both sides were at fault.

Our troubles were intensified by the way the Communists tried to infiltrate the liberal organizations and the unions. Sometimes apparently
ardent defenders of civil liberties would turn out to be defenders of those
principles only for Communists, but not for others, and thought rough

tactics should be applied to profascists. These people were unmasked by the Stalin-Hitler alliance of 1939 and the reversal of June, 1941.

It was hard to keep the civil-liberties group pure, especially when some of the local executives gave every evidence of having been corrupted by the Communists. Fortunately, the national organization largely purged its ranks, and this gave us help locally.

Yet the principle we were trying to defend was, I think, fundamental. It permitted suggested changes to be considered on their merits and was an alternative to violence. Defending the rights of extremists also served to prevent suppression from being extended to moderates. But it required restraints that seemed excessively difficult for most men to apply, and its defenders not only were few, but also lacked ample resources.

Communists had infiltrated the ranks of government employees both before and after Hitler's invasion of Russia. As long as the war continued, immediate danger from them was not great. Russia was our ally; men who wanted to help Russia would not be hostile to the United States. But when Russia adopted an unfriendly attitude toward us after the war, the danger became acute. Truman was successful in getting the overwhelming majority of these people eliminated from government employ by the end of 1948, and in the process probably hurt many who were innocent. The CIO had ousted many Communists and expelled unions that had clung to them. Henry Wallace's candidacy for President had flushed many of these Communists into the open.

After the danger had largely passed, there were repercussions, which gave extreme conservatives an almost irresistible temptation to exploit what had happened. Alger Hiss was probed, and was convicted of having given false testimony to a grand jury. Many similar cases developed, and there was a discouraging tendency for those brought before the various Congressional committees to use the Fifth Amendment as the ground for refusal to answer embarrassing questions. This device was defended on principle, as being rooted in the Bill of Rights. But to the public its use seemed to indicate illegitimate connections and activities of men who were afraid to have these known. This helped produce the real danger that the country would swing to the other extreme and become some form of police state.

Into this situation Joe McCarthy rushed, with his inflated figures of Communists in the government. Many he attacked had been imprudent, but not disloyal to the United States. There were others who probably were indeed Communists, or at least confirmed and conscious fellow travelers. McCarthy seemed to avoid these, and to concentrate instead on the imprudent. He wrecked lives, created panic, and fostered paranoia. The Congress was faced with a conflict between the legitimate demands of both freedom and security.

Mundt and Nixon then introduced a bill in the Senate that was certain of passage by the House. It aimed to make Communist activity illegal, to force Communists to register with the government, and to authorize the public branding of members of Communist-front organizations. Truman wanted to keep this bill off the Senate floor in 1950 in order to kill it by inaction. Scott Lucas made the parliamentary mistake, however, of failing, as the session was drawing to a close, to schedule another bill for action after we had passed a relatively unimportant one. So there was an apparently unnoticed parliamentary vacuum on the floor. Late that night Mundt arose with a smile and introduced the Nixon bill. Since Lucas had left the floor to me while he took some much-needed rest, I at once called for a quorum, but it was too late. The motion was in order, and the Senate had to deal with the issue.

Our progressive group immediately asked Joe Rauh and Frank McCulloch to draft an alternative. We did not want to take a purely negative position when some real danger to the nation was involved. The alternative we devised was a compulsory-detention law based on the system adopted by Great Britain in World War II, under which Sir Oswald Mosley had been taken out of circulation.

Although there were dangers in this approach, we thought we might derail the Mundt-Nixon-McCarran steamroller with an affirmative substitute. Second, we hoped to change the focus of public attention from Communist speech and association (which were not the greatest dangers) to the genuine problems of sabotage and espionage. Third, and equally high in our thinking, was the fact that J. Edgar Hoover had just made clear that the Federal Bureau of Investigation was ready to seize some 12,000 dangerous persons in case of war with Russia. We thought there should be procedures for their release where there was no danger of sabotage or espionage.

We wrote in our alternative that forcible detention was to be practiced only during war, and not during domestic emergencies, and that action by both Congress and the President was required for it to be put into effect. Either one of these bodies could discontinue it. We also provided for judicial writs of habeas corpus to free persons unjustly detained. The bill guarded against conscious saboteurs and yet preserved legal freedoms. It was far more restrained than the system likely to be adopted in its stead in time of war, as had been evidenced by our detention of 130,-000 Japanese-Americans during World War II.

When we proposed this bill as a substitute, we were overwhelmingly defeated, 50 to 23. Lucas immediately moved to add our forcible-detention features to Title II of the Mundt-Nixon bill. But McCarran now became the chief sponsor and substituted his version. He eliminated many, indeed most, of our safeguards in the process.

The administration forces decided to give in and accept the revised

bill. They would thus escape being branded as pro-Communists and opponents of internal security. To oppose the bill would mean being labeled pro-Communist. It was with heavy hearts that Humphrey and I
conferred together just before the roll call and decided that as a practical
matter we would vote for the bill. Only seven voted "No." After twenty
years I have come to feel that their names should be inscribed on a roll of
honor, and that I had done the wrong thing. They were Frank Graham,
Theodore Green, Estes Kefauver, Edward Leahy, Herbert Lehman, James
Murray, and Glen Taylor. There were several liberal-minded Republicans
who stayed away during the entire round of votes. I think they could not
bring themselves to vote for the bill, and did not wish to be recorded as
formally voting against it.

That evening I found my sons, John and Paul, dispirited by what I
had done. I somehow felt, despite my excuses, that I had failed morally.
For the next two nights I could not sleep as I pictured the persecution of
the innocent that might come at the hands of the new Subversive Activities Control Board, and of a new reign of terror settling over the country.
Irving Ives evidently knew what I was feeling; he came up to me and said
that he had been through a similar experience in New York and that it
had not turned out as badly as he had feared. But I was inconsolable.

It was a relief when Truman vetoed the bill, with a most able message,
which not only stressed the bill's weakness as an enforcement device, but
also took a bold stand on the toleration of dissent. On the afternoon that
he did this, Truman called me on the telephone to tell me what he was
doing and ask for my support in voting to uphold his veto. He said it was
the greatest threat yet offered against the civil liberties of the American
people. I breathed with relief at this chance to redeem myself at least
partially, and pledged to uphold his veto.

Truman went on to say that an effort would be made to organize the
opposition, so if we would keep discussion going throughout the night,
public opinion might have time to rally. I agreed to this and hurried to
the floor to help organize our forces. Due to repairs being made on the
ceiling of the Senate chamber, we were meeting in the so-called Old Supreme Court room, where that body had met from 1850 to 1935, and,
before that, for thirty years the Senate itself had sat there. We quickly
made out an order of speakers and assembled documents and briefs to
assist them. The leaders of the administration forces—Barkley, Lucas, and
Francis J. Myers—had decided not to support Truman's veto and were
pushing for a quick and decisive vote to override it. They wanted to get
the issue out of the way.

Warmhearted Bill Langer had joined us, and it was his turn to speak
at about two o'clock in the morning. When he rose, he had a deathly
pallor, and it was evident that he was very weak. To give him a chance to
rest, I kept requesting him to yield, so that I might ask him a long ques-

tion. With characteristic impish perversity, he always refused, saying that he "did not have time," when that was one of the few things we did have. At about five in the morning he stopped, swayed slightly, and then fell with a crash to the floor. The *Congressional Record* for this tempestuous night is quite defective in recording what really happened, but Ellender, who was in the chair, immediately called for a vote; Humphrey called instead for a quorum; and I asked for recognition, which was somewhat reluctantly granted. I had to step over Bill's prostrate body in order to get to the front of the crowded chamber. I could not hear him breathe, and he seemed to be dead. A surge of sympathy and of admiration went through me.

I spoke for about four hours, and emphasized both the ineffective and delaying nature of the security features and the dangers to freedom contained in the proposed measure. Finally, at about ten o'clock, a storm of telegraphic protests began to pour into senatorial offices. Few, if any, votes were changed, however. The final vote came about midafternoon, and it was 57 to 10 in favor of overriding the veto. Dennis Chavez, Harley M. Kilgore, Humphrey, and I were the only ones who changed our votes. Taylor was absent this time, as, of course, was Langer.

I went to my office feeling a little better, dictated replies to the messages of protest, and went home to enjoy my first good sleep in many days. The next day, with flowers filling my arms, I went to the hospital to call on our fallen friend. He was not going to die, after all, but with rest and care was going to live. I threw my arms around him, and he responded in kind. Bill had many faults, which made national commentators quite caustic in their criticism of him. But when the chips were down, he was always on the side of the weak. That quality is easy for the strong to undervalue.

The following day, when I went to Chicago to start the fall campaign, I found far less interest in the McCarran Act than there had been in Washington. Since most of the Chicago Democrats in the House had voted to uphold the veto, there was no party cleavage because of my stand.

Now, after twenty years have passed, it can be seen that the actual damage from the act has been far less than we feared. The appointments by Truman, Eisenhower, Kennedy, and Johnson to the board have been of relatively decent men and women who did not launch any broad witch hunts involving large numbers of innocent people. The Supreme Court has protected the innocent, and perhaps even some of those who were tainted, and has declared much of the law unconstitutional. As we had predicted, there were so many built-in delays in the basic law that it has also been comparatively ineffective.

Moreover, those who wanted punitive action had more convenient agencies close at hand. The House Un-American Activities Committee

and the Senate Subcommittee on Internal Security under Senator East-
land were vigorous enough to please the most ardent opponents of the
Communists. This decreased the use of the Subversive Activities Control
Board. The emergency detention provisions were ultimately repealed in
September, 1971.

Although many people who were basically decent were badly damaged, there is little doubt that many were also deterred from engaging in
genuinely subversive activity. As with so many other measures, the final
results are mixed. Perhaps because of my earlier training, I still regret my
initial vote in favor of the McCarran Act and feel consoled by having
been one of ten to uphold Truman's veto. I think our final opposition
may have helped to moderate the administration of the act and to protect
some who might otherwise have been persecuted.

The contrast between the despondent way I felt after voting in favor
of the act and the purified feeling after voting to uphold Truman's veto
was so sharp that I resolved always to follow my conscience, though sometimes it was hard to determine what was right. To the best of my knowledge, I did that throughout my remaining years in the Senate.

Opposition to the Supreme Court had risen to such a high point by
1958 that the House of Representatives could and had passed a number of
measures reversing specific decisions of the court, notably those limiting
the federal security program to sensitive jobs, preventing the use in evidence of confessions resulting from delays in the arraignment of suspects,
keeping the states out of fields reserved by the Constitution and the courts
for federal action, and reaffirming the long-standing practice of federal
review by habeas corpus of state criminal laws and trials.

In addition to these House bills before the Senate for action, the Senate Judiciary Committee had reported out the Butler-Jenner bill, which
would have reversed a whole series of pro-civil-liberties decisions by the
Court. The Southern conservatives were seething with opposition to the
1954 and 1955 decisions outlawing segregation in the schools.* It was not
clear precisely what Majority Leader Lyndon Johnson intended to do
about all of this legislation, but it finally became evident that under the
prompting of Dick Russell he would try to pass most of it.

Humphrey and I conferred with John Carroll, the progressive senator
from Colorado, and we all determined that, so far as we were concerned,
we would pass none of it. We were going to defend the Court and its
opinions, and we were favored by the fact that it was near the end of the
session and the Senators wanted to go home to rest and then campaign.

* The only satisfactory treatment of this tremendously important struggle, now virtually
forgotten, is Joseph L. Rauh, Jr.'s article "The Truth About Congress and the Court,"
The Progressive, Nov., 1958, pp. 3–34.

After two days of skirmishing and debate, on August 20 we defeated the Butler-Jenner bill, 49 to 41.

I then determined to take the offensive. With Morse and Humphrey, I introduced an amendment giving the support of Congress to the Court, especially for its desegregation decisions. I wanted to reverse the license given critics of the Court to heap censure upon it, and to make the Senate decide whether or not it approved of the Court's work. If the Senate could consider reversals, it certainly could consider approvals. Johnson was highly displeased by my motion, which seemed to break up his program. He sent Bobby Baker to tell his followers that he intended to displace my amendment with another. McClellan thereupon added a House measure to the latter which would have opened the field to a whole range of so-called "antisubversive" laws including anti-civil-rights measures. Our effort to table this form of the amendment was defeated, 46 to 39.

We were faced, therefore, with this highly dangerous amendment. This was more than Johnson and a few of his followers wanted. We moved to recommit, and won by a wafer-thin margin: 41 to 40. Then, by threatening prolonged debate, we defeated the other House measures overruling the Court. The session ended with the slate clean and the Court unchallenged. Our overwhelming victories in the 1958 Congressional elections then removed the danger for some years.

A scurrilous campaign against Chief Justice Warren and the majority of the Court was mounted in the late 1950's. Billboards bearing the slogan "Impeach Earl Warren" appeared along highways in many parts of the country. However, the coming of William J. Brennan, Jr., and Arthur Goldberg reinforced Warren, Hugo Black, and William O. Douglas and gave us for some years a progressive court. It was a great change from the conditions prevailing a half-century before, when the Court was highly illiberal and when Holmes and Louis D. Brandeis were the great dissenters. More than any other factor, the composition of the Court was what has enabled us to move ahead to become a more democratic nation. The Frankfurter school may regret this action as nonjudicial, but I welcomed it.

I adopted the policy of speaking in defense of Earl Warren and the Supreme Court's decisions and of inserting favorable material about them into the *Congressional Record*. I tried to give the widest possible circulation to these statements. Through Drew Pearson I became personally acquainted with Warren, and liked him very much. He was a man who steadily improved with time and trials. To me, during the last quarter of a century the Court has far surpassed the other two branches of government. Trusted friends in whom I ordinarily have confidence go so far as to say that it has been a better body than articulate Americans deserve. What it will be in the future is uncertain. We may be in for a period of retrogression.

23

Waste and the Economy

WHILE the appropriation of money for public purposes is one of the most important of legislative functions, it is one to which progressive-spirited men have not given adequate attention. Two questions are involved: How large should the total spent by the government be? How should this total be distributed among the various purposes?

Instead of discussing the over-all actions of Congress in these matters, I shall tell the story from the standpoint of an individual senator who had to work his way through the claims of diverse and conflicting groups.

General Considerations

I CAME TO THE SENATE with a firsthand knowledge of the built-in tendency of administrative officials to expand their functions and personnel and to resist any reduction that might be threatened. I did not need the later promulgation of Parkinson's Law to convince me of this. I had also seen full evidence of it in the military service during the four and a half years from 1942 to 1946, and in the Labor Department in the summer of 1945. Friends in government service had told me of it in many departments and agencies.

Its existence was only natural. Administrators usually believe in the importance of what they are doing and see new work they think should be assumed. Unlike the officers in private industry, they do not have to pay the bills. Self-interest also operates in the direction of expansion. While officials will deny it, there is a tendency for the grade and salary of an administrator to increase along with the size of his staff. There is therefore a constant upward pressure from within the bureaucracy to expand activities, personnel, and expenditures. This involves not merely the top officials, but also almost the whole staff. Since most agencies also have an outside group of citizens who are economically and emotionally attached to each, the pressure for upping appropriations is both deep-rooted and widespread.

Furthermore, whatever might be the attitude of a senator or congressman toward total expenditures, there are tremendous pressures on him to support certain specific outlays. The most conspicuous of these in the period from 1945 to 1960 were appropriations for rivers and harbors, and in the West for irrigation. Highways, space, and military outlays came high, and are now probably the most notable.

And yet, all these appropriations must be paid for. There was no adequate counterforce on the part of the taxpayers to check these expansive tendencies. Some better sorting of priorities was effected by the Budget Bureau, which, though seldom critical of military appropriations, was in the main competent and public-spirited. But it, too, could be influenced or overruled.

Since Congress has the constitutional duty of appropriating money, I believed that this should be done wisely. I do not agree with most writers on public administration who urge that the President be given the power of an item veto. To me, it seems that the defects of democracy are not to be cured by taking such power away from the representatives of the people, but, rather, by persuading Congress and the people to make wiser decisions.

Of course it is true that the Congressional Establishment usually appropriates less money than is needed to protect the weak and restrain the strong. Thus the Securities and Exchange Commission, the National Labor Relations Board, the Federal Trade Commission, the Rural Electrification Administration, and other regulatory and service bodies are always handicapped, when they defend the public, by inadequate appropriations for their needs. Even if the inner circle of Congress has been forced to yield on matters of legislation and authorization, it can always stymie these measures by a failure to appropriate the money to carry them out. This erodes the devotion of conscientious administrators.

While liberals will fight to provide funds for agencies that advance the public interest, they seldom exert themselves to reduce outlays that are wasteful. Except for Senator Proxmire, they are generally oblivious to influences leading to expansion of the budget. Indeed, like their conservative colleagues, their concern is to add to other appropriations. Hard pressed as they are on the welfare front, they seek to conciliate other groups by voting for all projects. One of my closest associates never voted against any appropriation for any purpose, no matter how extravagant or foolish it was. This never hurt him politically. In fact, I think it helped him.

Whether the conservatives were really sincere in their talk of economy, or just wanted to save at the expense of the poor, the weak, the sick, and the unfortunate, was never really tested. They were allowed to become the "economizers" and to win the support of a large section of the taxpayers. While throwing the onus of extravagance on the liberals, the conservatives made welfare the whipping boy that consumed the taxpayers' dollar. Of course this was ridiculous. Before the 1964–65 legislation, welfare and regulatory activities formed a small fraction of total expenditures. Defense always took the major share of government outlays. When I entered the Senate this amounted to one-third, but it rose rapidly with the Korean War to one-half and later to the present figure of about 60 per cent. Adding the interest on the national debt created in time of war, military pensions, and the service of the Veterans Administration, the total was at least three-quarters of the budget. It was the warfare world, therefore, and not the welfare state that was chiefly responsible for high public expenditures. But it was hard to make the public realize this, and the progressive group was not effective in driving the fact home.

Toward the end of April in 1949 I had to make a crucial decision. When the appropriations bill for the Labor Department came to the Senate floor, the Republicans, led by Styles Bridges and Homer Ferguson, proposed a cut of 5 per cent in the total appropriated. As a supporter of nearly all the programs the department administered, I was personally friendly with its staff. But I had firsthand memories of the overstaffing and loose conduct of the department in 1945. The conditions had not changed. I knew that if I voted for the cut, many of my best friends and supporters would think that I had betrayed them, and the Truman administration would feel deeply aggrieved. Yet my duty seemed clear. There *was* waste, and that 5-per-cent cut could be taken out of the overhead, without damaging the substantive work of the department, simply by not filling vacancies as they developed. So when my name was called, I voted "Aye." This caused a stir. William E. Jenner, of Indiana, jumped out of his seat over on the Republican side and rushed to a fellow conservative to ask the meaning of my vote. Lucas and our whip, Frank Myers, looked disgusted. I had suffered a conflict of emotions during the previous quarter of an hour, but was now satisfied that I had made the right decision. As I went back to my office, reporters asked me to explain my vote. I refused to justify it, saying that they should look up my record in the Chicago City Council.

Realizing that this was merely the start, I knew that I must justify myself by keeping on with my program of rational, yet humane, economy. I must make my position clear and be specific in defending it.

Rivers, Harbors, Irrigation

THE NEXT big appropriations bill came four months later. It was the Rivers and Harbors bill, the favorite of congressmen because it included their pet projects. There was nothing that could make me more unpopular with my colleagues than trying to reduce sums in this bill. And yet this also must be done. As I have recounted earlier, I challenged McKellar, and the debate over the Josias River and the Cal-Sag canal followed. Though I lost that time, Bob Wallace and I prepared for the next battle on rivers and harbors.

Now we had allies, for conscientious members of the Budget Bureau secretly told us of weaknesses in many projects that either had been included by the "upstairs" administrators in their own bureau or had been added by the Appropriations Committee of the House or the Senate. On the eve of the debate we were even given a copy of the secret justifications compiled for members of the Appropriations Committee. So we knew the Establishment's case as well as our own. Loaded for bear when Millard Tydings brought out his bill, we fought a whole series of specific appropriations, including one or two for Illinois.

I remember two projects that were especially laughable. One was to deepen the entrance from a harbor to the open sea so that the revolutions of the propellers on motorboats would not stir up so much mud as to "roil the crabs." I argued that while I might favor the welfare state for people, I did not favor its extension to the world of crustacean life. It would be strange, indeed, for Congress to concern itself with the health of crabs while largely ignoring that of man. The proponents solemnly explained that they were not concerned with crabs, but with those who fished for them. The second case was an appropriation for a harbor six miles from Annapolis to provide the naval cadets with a place of refuge in time of storm. This would cut in half the existing distance from the Naval Academy to the nearest harbor. I asked if they wanted to dot the Atlantic Coast with ports every six miles for the benefit of sailors? Did they need to shield our future admirals from rough water? Tydings took this in good humor, but other members of the committee glowered at my attempts at ridicule.

In any event, I did not get the necessary one-fifth vote for a roll call on specific amendments, and on my final proposal to cut the appropriation I was defeated overwhelmingly. From the discussion it was plain that the Senate did not want any cuts, and certainly would not delegate its authority to others.

Ideally, one should oppose logrolling by one's own state as well as by others. The Cal-Sag project would have cost upward of $100 million, and this could never be repaid. No tolls could be levied, and special charges would be almost impossible to maintain. So I came out explicitly against the Cal-Sag appropriation. Because of this, I came under fire from the business leaders of both South Chicago and downtown, and I determined to carry the battle into the enemy's country. I hired a hall in South Chicago, and there one Sunday I defended my position. After reviewing the costs, and the present and future deficits, I urged that the necessary economies be made on those items that would cause the least human suffering. However, business interests resisted any attempts to hold down their appropriations. Only a few national reporters grasped the significance of my efforts, which I continued and which were always voted down.

Republicans did not want reductions any more than Democrats. This was an issue on which they united with a happy sense of fraternal comradeship. While conservative Republicans were slightly shamefaced about opposing a New Dealer's appeals for economy in this area, it never modified their stern demands to cut the welfare program.

Political scientists usually blamed Congress for these departures from sound procedure, but they ignored the real motivation. When a group of local businessmen became convinced that the deepening of a harbor or river or some other internal improvement would benefit their community, they began to pressure their congressmen. If Republicans, the latter agreed, since they were dependent for support on the business groups. If Democrats, they also probably agreed, for although the local power structure in the North and West seldom supported Democrats, they always hoped it would. The result was that congressmen felt obligated to support local projects, as at first I had, too. Moreover, they soon found that nearly all congressmen had a favorite project, and they were linked in mutual back-scratching or logrolling. As a boy along the tributaries of the Penobscot, I had seen the farmer-woodsman drag his own logs to the banks of the rivers, where he along with his neighbors would then help each other roll them into the water. The slogan there was "I'll roll your logs if you will help roll mine."

Once the Appropriations Committee had made its decisions, its members stuck together and were always present on the floor during debate on their bills. If there was trouble such as I was causing, they also brought in the chairmen and ranking members of the other committees, who were joined with them in an informal mutual-assistance pact. Other members of the Senate had little to gain and everything to lose by supporting a specific cut, and so they had no incentive to stay on the floor to vote. As a result, although I tried for ten years to make cuts, always with a thorough case, I was constantly beaten. Often I failed to get the necessary one-fifth for a quorum roll call, and even if I did, I was overwhelmingly defeated. I finally concluded that this was one fight I could not win. Furthermore, my own position in my state was weakened by the demands of business and farm groups who supported these improvements. The hoped-for toot of a steamboat whistle had a mesmeric effect, bringing visions of steamboats moving through cornfields to far-off and romantic shores.

Yet there were solid economic motives behind these romantic illusions. In one case, there was a 100-mile canal, dug around 1905, between the Mississippi, at Rock Island, and the Illinois River, at Hennepin. No steamboat, barge, or perhaps even canoe had ever traveled on it. But its existence had enabled a neighboring steel mill to force the railroads to reduce their freight rates on steel under the threat of potential water competition. A spur to the canal, linking a town with the system, also maintained the level of a lake around which members of the local Establishment had elaborate summer homes. These men, fervid Republicans, fancied themselves sincere economizers. One day I received a telegram from twenty of them demanding irately that I cut the federal budget by $2 billion. I was then trying to reduce it by $3 billion. The next day many of the same people sent me another telegram, demanding that I get an added appropriation for "widening and deepening" the Mississippi-Illinois Canal. This would have cost at least $70 million. They would not admit to any inconsistency between their two telegrams.

Work on rivers was also designed to reduce floods and to promote navigation on the upper as well as lower sections. This often meant that levees were constructed to wall off adjoining swampland so that the river could be both deeper and narrower. Farseeing speculators bought the adjacent land or its owners borrowed money to improve it. In either case bulldozers went to work, revealing the basic fertility of the soil, enriched by centuries of alluvial deposits washed down from the upper river. Under the plow, yields were high, and the land skyrocketed in value.

In the name of flood control, there soon emerged what I considered economic crimes. For instance, levees erected on the west side of the Illinois River to protect several thousand acres of land threw an extra amount of water, deluging Beardstown and the people on the other side. A similar one-sided levee, protecting Vincennes, Indiana, made life worse for Lawrence County, Illinois, opposite Vincennes on the Wabash. The Indiana delegation to Congress, aided by some Illinoisans with river-front land, tried to do the same thing in the 1960's to Mount Carmel, an Illinois town on the Wabash. Of course this was to be financed by federal funds in the name of flood control. I had protected Beardstown by getting a belated levee of equal height erected around it, and I now insisted on the same treatment for Mount Carmel. Senator Ellender finally agreed that to protect the town and its farmlands there should be a levee on its side of the river of about the same height as the one opposite.

Since they gave only temporary relief, I was not satisfied with levees as a permanent answer to floods. Instead, I favored upstream control, as prescribed by soil conservationists, with contour plowing, protective cover, such as nitrogen-fixing legumes, and small dams on minor streams. The Army Engineers preferred levees, big dams, big reservoirs, and navigation projects. They were supported by wealthy farmers and land speculators, and their work was dignified by the title "Civil Functions of the Army."

At the end of the 1950's President Eisenhower vetoed one bill because of several unsound projects. I was one of the few to uphold his veto, but he was overruled, even by his own party. This was the "last hurrah" on rivers and harbors as far as I was concerned. I turned my attention to irrigation.

In November, 1948, on a lecture trip to the Central Valley of California, I saw the good effects of water on low-altitude land, as I did again in 1951 on a visit to Bill Benton's home in Phoenix. There the water was held in reserve by the last of the stone dams, the Roosevelt. But such sites were almost exhausted, and irrigation groups were turning to the high-altitude lands, far up in the mountains. The growing season in this area was short; the chief crops were hay, potatoes, and apples. The normal value of the land after irrigation seldom exceeded $200 an acre, and often was less than $100. But the direct outlay for dams and distribution systems was seldom less than $700 an acre. If the interest forgiven on this investment, during the many years in which the principal was amortized, was counted, the total cost sometimes ran as high as $1,200 an acre, and in a few instances as much as $2,000. This certainly was paying too much.

Irrigation groups insisted that they repaid the government for the cost of the projects, but they neglected to mention that they paid no interest and that most of the principal was repaid out of power rather than from irrigation revenues. They also never mentioned that, upon the motion of a senator from an irrigation state, and with the support of his fellows, Congress had provided that the repayment of the principal should not return to the general funds of the Treasury but, instead, was to be diverted into a fund for financing more irrigation projects. The government was therefore committed to a continuing program of irrigation regardless of the comparative merits of new projects.

In 1955 the Eisenhower administration launched its program to develop the upper Colorado River. The altitudes there reached 5,000 feet, the growing season was very short, and the value of the irrigated land was very low. On the other hand, the costs, including interest, ranged from $1,200 to $2,000 an acre. Since it would supply Denver with water and power, I did not attack the dam and reservoir at Glen Canyon, but the dams higher up seemed, to me, superfluous.

In opening my fight against them, I first lamented the esthetic loss of the white water down which Major John Wesley Powell had made his historic trip. If we were going to put more water on farmland to increase production, which seemed strange when we were spending hundreds of millions to decrease farm output, I urged that it be applied in the Midwest, from the Ohio, Mississippi, and Missouri rivers. Once again I was beaten, by the power of the seventeen irrigation states (including not only the eight mountain and three Pacific Coast states, but also those of the high plains west of the Missouri River, beginning with the Dakotas and running south) and the massed strength of the Eisenhower administration. At first I was surprised at this stand, since Eisenhower was supposed to support economy. Friends explained that he recalled the parched soil of his native Kansas; critics said that it was payment to Senator Arthur Watkins, of Utah, for signing the report urging the censure of McCarthy.

With this crumbling of support from the administration, I slackened my efforts to economize on irrigation. Like rivers and harbors, it seemed untouchable. In the past I had used the supporters of each against the other, but this tactic was ended by the public-works bill of 1958, which consolidated both sets of measures into a single bill. The two sets of sponsors were now tied together as allies, instead of competing as rivals. Bob Kerr became the champion of both kinds of projects. Although I made occasional forays in support of Proxmire and other Senators, after the years of beating my head against a stone wall, I turned my initiative elsewhere.

Vacation Credits and Sick Leave

ONE JUSTIFIABLE ECONOMY I effected was to reduce the excessive vacation allowances for federal employees. To my surprise, I had found that the classified and wage-board federal personnel were entitled to a $5\frac{1}{5}$-week paid vacation each year plus three weeks of sick leave. This was far more than workers in private industry received. Indeed, a study by the National Industrial Conference Board showed that in 1951 less than 1 per cent of industrial wage earners and only $1\frac{1}{2}$ per cent of salaried employees had more than four weeks of paid vacation.

I was puzzled by the fact that classified employees received almost twice as much vacation credit as workers in the postal service, who had three weeks of vacation and two of sick leave. As I studied the history of the vacation provisions, it became clear that this excess was due to mere chance. In 1898 Congress had tried to equalize the leave of civilian employees with that of the Army and Navy by granting everyone thirty days' leave a year. This meant, according to a Civil Service Commission ruling in 1900, working days, not calendar days. Since the government was then on a six-day week, this gave a five-week vacation. To correct this, in 1937 civilian leave was fixed at twenty-six working days. The purpose was to restore once again the liberal vacation allowance of a month. But immediately after World War II, the federal service was put on a five-day week. This meant that the vacation period was now 5⅕ weeks, with additional sick leave of three weeks a year.

While I wanted the government to set a good example for private industry, as I said on the floor of the Senate, these allowances were excessive. In 1951 we reduced vacation leave, as a result of my motion, to twenty working days, or four weeks, and applied it to postal, wage-board, and classified employees. This saved six working days, or 1⅕ weeks. This was soon changed to a system of vacations on a graduated basis. Those with fewer than three years' service were given thirteen days' leave, with roughly a day allowed for every four weeks of work; those with between three and fifteen years, 19½ days, or three-quarters of a day for each fortnight in the year; the previous allowance of twenty-six days was continued for all those with over fifteen years of service. Sick leave was cut from fifteen to thirteen days a year, but the postal employees were raised to this level.

The economies so effected saved, at the time, $200 million a year; today they are at least double that amount. The changes of course infuriated most civil-service employees. I was told that there were over 100,000 of them waiting in Illinois for my 1954 campaign. They might have defeated me had it not been for the postal workers. Previously these had been badly discriminated against. I had raised them to an equality with other federal employees. While there were more civil-service and wage-board employees than postal workers in Illinois, as it turned out, the carriers, both urban and rural, were far more effective politically than the members of civil service. A carrier talked to fifty times as many people as a government clerk. So I always believed that in this case I had gained politically while saving money for the taxpayers, which was a rare occurrence. Horace Walpole would have called it a case of serendipity, or the unexpected benefits of a good deed.

Military Expenditures

THE MOST OBVIOUS FIELD for economy was military expenditures. My wartime experiences had disclosed great waste, and when I got to the Senate I found that 86 to 87 per cent of contracts for the purchase of supplies and equipment was negotiated with a single supplier, and hence was not subject to competitive bidding, and that fifty large contractors had obtained 64 per cent of all defense contracts. Waste was also created by the fact that the four branches of the military, as well as the medical and hospital corps, each maintained a separate supply service. In addition, there were extravagant bonuses in the Air Force for four-hours-a-month flight time for "passengers."

On another aspect of the military problem, I urged a cut in the ratio of noncombatant to combat troops. When Joseph C. O'Mahoney, of Wyoming, brought in a military appropriation bill in 1951 for $61 billion, I gave a detailed speech outlining specific cuts of about $1 billion. Very angry, O'Mahoney made a sarcastic reply. Though he later corrected some of his remarks for the *Record,* he implied that my speech gave aid and comfort to the Russians. In fact, he said that I was stabbing the armed forces in the back. Because I was exhausted, his words seemed to stab me, and I hurried toward an exit. But I did not get there in time; nor could I stifle a cry of pain. Later I realized that I had broken one of the unwritten rules of politics: to show no emotion in the face of any aspersion. After a few minutes of rest, I returned to the chamber. Although the newspaper comment was unfavorable, I received a thousand letters of sympathy, and O'Mahoney made a qualified personal apology the next day. The experience was humiliating, however, and was always used against me, but I did not let it deter me from pushing ahead with proposals for economy and for increasing the combat effectiveness of the armed forces.

In 1952 I worked for the continuance of the Marine Corps as a fighting unit and tried at the same time to lessen the unearned bonus given to desk officers who were taken up for four hours a month as passengers in a plane. The Air Force followed the usual bureaucratic practice of first denying that there was any abuse in granting flight pay and then, to avoid any legislative action, appointing a controlled committee to study the subject. They finally reduced the abuse by administrative action. This saved millions of dollars a year, and insiders told me that it would never have been done had I not raised the alarm. But the administrative officers in the Air Force and some of the fliers never forgot.

During the next eight years, I urged the centralized procurement of common-use items for the armed services and the pooling of reserve supplies. I wanted closer control over the "excess" stock sold at auction for about two cents on the dollar, which later often showed up at private "Army and Navy" stores at a handsome markup. Furthermore, I saw no reason why Army and Marine boots should differ—the former being generally superior—and I saw no virtue in differentiated underclothing. Perhaps most important, I urged competitive bidding for a much larger proportion of the contracts for soft goods and common-use items, which amounted to less than 15 per cent of the total dollar volume of military contracts.

I found allies in this in the General Accounting Office, headed by Joseph Campbell, whom Eisenhower had brought with him from Columbia University, and also in a remarkable crusader, Ray Ward, who had been working on these problems for years. They briefed me in these matters and helped me to stand up under criticism.

Nevertheless, I made no headway on any of these common-sense suggestions. All branches of the military were opposed. The Republican secretaries of Defense would not move, nor would the White House under Eisenhower. I was forced to conclude that the much-touted Republican desire for economy was mostly verbal, and, in practice, the party did not want to tangle with the vested interests of the military or of other government services.

I was increasingly disturbed by the fact that high-ranking officers, on retirement, entered the service of big suppliers to the military and dealt with their former colleagues serving as procurement officers. With contracts so negotiated, it seemed inevitable that there would be abuses and that the net result would be higher prices than those prevailing under competition. In 1958–59, I launched an investigation, asking for the names and numbers of high-ranking retired officers—Army colonels, Navy captains, and above—who were in the employ of the hundred biggest suppliers. This inquiry disclosed that there were 721 such officers, of which the ten biggest companies employed 372. These facts created such a stir that Representative Carl Vinson felt compelled to come charging into the fight. I was in favor of a legislative restriction, but this was headed off in favor of administrative regulations to curb the more flagrant abuses.

Ten years later, in 1969, Proxmire launched a parallel investigation. He found that there were then 2,072 such officers in the employ of the hundred largest firms. The top ten companies employed 1,065 former high-ranking officers, and the nine companies that produced antiballistic missiles had 465 retired officers in their service. The administrative regulations had obviously not worked.

In June, 1960, I broke the case open with definite proof of gross overcharges made for common-use items under negotiated contracts. The military was supposed to give the states first chance at obtaining surplus property. They made the mistake of accompanying one shipment with detailed invoices listing the respective prices they had paid for each item. The state authorities were so shocked that they turned these over to me and temporarily lent me an adequate supply of the items in question. I had these articles priced in local stores. You would expect the prices to be higher, at retail, than the government purchases cost wholesale. But the facts were the exact opposite. The prices the government paid were many times the competitive retail prices. The comparison of items bought by the Defense Department by negotiated contract and similar or identical items purchased at retail, as read into the *Congressional Record*, was as follows.

Item	Cost to Defense Department Wholesale	Retail Price of Similar or Identical Item
1. Cable operated headset	$10.67	$1.50
2. Wrench set with case	$29.00	$3.89 to $4.50
3. Lamp socket	$21.00	$ .25
4. Electric relay line	$250.00	$24.00 wholesale $40.00 retail
5. Blower, Bull Model	$50.00	
6. Aluminum gauge blades	$10.00	$ .50
7. Locating plug, steel ½ inch	$11.00	$ .25 to .50
8. Small Transfer punches	$ 8.18	$ .25
9. Dial Bushings	$ 9.65	$ .25 to .50
10. Assorted wrenches	$ 1.84	$ .10 to .15

I exhibited these items on the floor of the Senate, quoting my retail price on each and asking a fellow Senator to read the government's price from the invoice. The comparisons were at once tragic and laughable.

This made the problem of military waste understandable to the average citizen. Finding out that lamp sockets that they bought at any hardware store for a quarter had cost Uncle Sam $21.00 finally convinced them that there was something quite wrong with military procurement. Furthermore, the millions of men who had served in the military during World War II and the Korean War had personal knowledge of gross waste, which lent support to my evidence.

But the military unfortunately stood firm. They would not acknowledge that anything was wrong, and my appeals to the Secretary of Defense fell on deaf ears. Then they wanted the invoice numbers, and I of course gave them. After silence for a few weeks, the supply service of the branch in question asked for an appointment for its chief. When I went to the door to welcome him, to my surprise a whole squad of bemedaled and extra-stout officers filed impassively into the room. I was surrounded by fifteen or more hostile and frowning men determined to put me on trial. "Where did you obtain the invoices?" "Do you know that you have done a disservice to the armed forces and the national defense?"

I was tempted to answer that the supply services had done the combat troops the disservice. But, for once holding my tongue, I merely asked if my statements were true. No one answered. I then told them that they had been given ample time to check my statements, and if they found an error, I would be happy to correct it on the floor of the Senate. There was still no reply. Then I said, "I shall have to assume, therefore, that you admit my comparisons are accurate. I am not going to tell you who my informants were because that would permit you to use great pressure against them. But I am not going to retract my statements."

While my exposé had few tangible results, it did have an unexpected by-product. Malcolm Moos, of Eisenhower's staff, watched these developments closely, and three days before the General left office, Moos persuaded him to issue a farewell statement warning the public against the "military-industrial complex," which might threaten the liberties and resources of the country. Perhaps the battle had not, after all, been useless.

The Illinois Republicans were furious. Waste was supposed to be a Democratic sin, and they regarded themselves as the economizers. To have the roles reversed was more than they could bear. They accused me of diverting the energies of the Defense Department from important tasks to defending minor purchases. I replied that these were merely examples of the overcharges created by negotiated contracts and were proof of the savings that could be effected by competitive bidding. I pointed out that I had also inserted in the *Congressional Record* scores of reports by the General Accounting Office of overcharges made in the negotiated contracts they had audited, showing the waste to run into the hundreds of millions and probably billions of dollars. I had the worst examples mounted on a panel and took it on tour when I campaigned for re-election. Once seen, these exhibits told their own story and contributed to my big majority in November.

Shortly after his election, President Kennedy announced that he would appoint Robert S. McNamara as secretary of Defense. McNamara had been one of the so-called "whiz kids" under Secretary Henry L. Stimson and Under Secretary Robert Patterson during World War II and had just been made president of the Ford Motor Company. I confess that I had never heard of him, but friends assured me that he was an open-minded man who would not become a tool of the military bureaucracy. I decided to write him a personal letter telling what I had found and urging a number of reforms, such as the consolidation of supply functions for items other than weapons and a consolidated balance of stores to eliminate unnecessary purchases. I urged him to substitute competitive bidding for the negotiated contracts with a single supplier to a much larger degree than the prevailing 13 per cent, to close down many unneeded military installations inside the country, and to make other reforms. I did not go into the question of weapons systems or bases abroad, because I did not feel competent from either a military or a diplomatic standpoint to offer any authoritative advice on these topics.

I scarcely expected any action on my letter, but was greatly pleased by a prompt answer. On the whole, McNamara agreed with me, and he asked me to serve on an informal committee to review these problems. Shortly after he took office, he created this committee, which met with him four times a year. It included Thomas B. Curtis, a Republican representative from Missouri who had been an advocate of centralized procurement, and Representative Edward Hèbert, of Louisiana, who later became a violent critic of McNamara. We quickly agreed on a centralized supply agency.

This not only resulted in a saving in the quantities purchased, and later scrapped, but also diminished the total personnel in all the supply services. For some reason, which I could never understand, McNamara did not increase the proportion of competitive advertised bids beyond 15 per cent, although he admitted that where this was done an average of 25 per cent in price was saved. He did greatly increase the proportion of competitively negotiated contracts, where bids were invited not from a single supplier as before but from a number of the leading suppliers. Here the savings were estimated to average from 10 to 15 per cent.

McNamara also followed our advice to move away from the usual method of cost plus fixed fee to a fixed price plus a sharing of savings. This made large economies, and, reassured by our Congressional support, he began to sell and otherwise dispose of surplus plants, installations, and bases. The Portsmouth and Brooklyn Navy yards were slowly closed down. Many small Army posts in the West, a heritage of the Indian wars, were also discontinued. From these and other economies, he later claimed to have saved around $6 billion a year. While this figure may have been somewhat inflated, there is no doubt that at the least several billion dollars were saved annually.

These actions created problems for McNamara's backers, since the economies often hit constituents and communities, which protested loudly. I faced this myself when McNamara closed down a supply center in Decatur employing 1,500 people and transferred its operations to Louisville, where costs were lower. Trying to be consistent, I supported the move. The Republican mayor of the city then issued a statement denouncing me for not defending Decatur, and there was a movement to burn me in effigy. McNamara tried to soften the impact of the closing: those who wanted to move were in a minority and hence could be guaranteed a job if they did; liberal layoff allowances were granted to those who stayed. Luckily the installation was soon sold to a big automobile company, which hired more men than the government had previously employed. Besides, the new owners paid large local property taxes on property that had formerly been tax-exempt. Citizens later admitted that the whole transaction was one of the best things that had ever happened to the city. But of course no apology ever came from the mayor or his supporters.

Once in a while McNamara's advisers made a mistake. The headquarters of the Sixth Army had been moved after World War II from Fort Sheridan, in the wealthy suburb of Lake Forest, Illinois, to the South Side of Chicago. This had taken away much needed civilian housing. The Army now insisted that it must move back again. Although not stated, the probable reason was the rapidly growing Negro population in the South Side, which the officers and their families found unpleasant. What McNamara apparently did not realize was that there were about 600 Negro civilians employed in the offices of the Sixth Army who because of costs and social pressure could not be housed in or near Lake Forest, and for whom the daily journey from their Chicago enclaves to Lake Forest was both excessively time-consuming and costly. I tried to call this to his attention and to that of his subordinates, but without avail.

At the same time, the military, having been urged by the Massachusetts delegation, was carrying through the transfer of the food-research laboratories from Chicago, the food center of the nation, where it was handsomely housed near the stockyards, to Natick, outside Boston, which was far distant from the farm belt. I suspected that the Army was running away from the so-called "Negro problem."

On the whole, McNamara performed splendidly, especially in his handling of the common-use items, and I supported him in the face of mounting criticism from the military, who rebelled against the increasing civilian control over the armed services. He was ultimately undone on two counts. The first was his failure to check mistakes in the development of new systems of weapons and planes. With his civilian advisers, he insisted on developing the TFX, or F-111, a multipurpose plane, both bomber and fighter, which on the surface seemed to reduce costs. The Air Force opposed it, declaring it unworkable, and they were proved right when the rechristened plane failed in experimental tests and minor combats, and had to be scrapped. The costs ran into the hundreds of millions of dollars.

McNamara's confidence in himself was apparently shaken by his deepening realization that the TFX was a failure and that there seemed no end to the Vietnamese war. Then the military ran wild promoting costly new weapons systems, which had to be replaced almost immediately by newer and more expensive ones. Its mistakes were not publicized, as had been McNamara's, by McClellan and Hèbert. They did not come to the attention of the public until Proxmire exposed them in March, 1969, in an able but little-noticed speech. There is a real problem here. The military always cites Russian developments as a reason for needing improved American systems. These newer and more costly systems are then cited by the Russian military as justifying an increase in their weapons. The competition continues, with ever-increasing destructive powers, although ultimately there is no gain in relative security. In fact, history shows that the reverse is true, as in the dreadnought race between Germany and England prior to World War I, when the competition helped to precipitate the war. Yet today mutual disarmament or even the limitation of arms has been thwarted largely because of Russia's refusal to co-operate. Proxmire is right in saying that the qualitative arms race is likely not only to beggar us, but also to divert precious resources needed for the improvement of American life.

McNamara's second catastrophe was the unending war in Vietnam. In 1963 and 1964 he took the highly respected General Maxwell Taylor, chairman of the Joint Chiefs of Staff, with him every few months on inspection trips to South Vietnam. They were briefed by the U.S. military command and by the South Vietnamese government and invariably came back with optimistic accounts of progress. The North Vietnamese were always said to be close to collapse, which would come after a little more effort on our part. In spite of these repeated predictions of victory, Presidents Kennedy and Johnson were induced to increase the number of our armed "advisers."

Then in February of 1965 the military advice was suddenly reversed. It was South Vietnam that was about to fall apart unless we poured in more troops and stepped up our attacks on North Vietnam. Swept off his feet by this reversal, Johnson ordered more troops rushed to Vietnam and the systematic bombing of military targets in North Vietnam. We became more deeply involved, until by the start of 1969 we had over half a million troops in that small country. Nevertheless, it looked as though military victory might continue to elude us. As the number of our dead soared to 30,000 and beyond, it became clear that the American public wanted to end the war on almost any terms. Understandably, they could not bear to have 10,000 of our youth killed a year in a far-off tropical country in a war dimly understood and waged with allies of dubious virtue.

By this time, McNamara was himself evidently besieged by doubts and ready to leave. An honorable place was found for him as the head of the World Bank, which he is now administering with personal credit and public benefit. But he is through as a public figure and is one of the tragedies of the past decade.

In summary, from my experience I would say that legislators need to analyze the built-in tendency of both the civilian and the military bureaucracies to expand into unneeded fields. Furthermore, they should be reinforced with skilled assistants. The General Accounting Office could help significantly by making an appraisal of projected expenditures before their approval by Congress. Some will say that this is the function of the Budget Bureau, but, while this bureau does excellent work, it is the agent of the President. Congress needs a body of its own, which, despite past efforts to control it, the GAO most certainly is. The staffs of the two appropriations committees in Congress should also be enlarged.

Most of all we need a vigilant public to oppose government waste and expenditures for private interests, and to steer the country's resources properly, to fields of general benefit.

Subsidies

IN THE SENATE I soon became aware of the big subsidies paid to users of second-, third-, and fourth-class mail. The total postal deficit in 1950–51 was $625 million, and none of this came from first-class mail, which actually produced a surplus of about $80 million. In contrast, second-class mail, consisting of newspapers and magazines, caused a deficit of at least $180 million. Third-class mail, the unsealed advertising matter, or so-called "junk mail," cost Uncle Sam about $136 million. Fourth-class, or parcel post, had a net loss of $77 million.* These losses increased with the years, until, in the early 1960's, with liberal bookkeeping deductions for "public service" outlays, they probably amounted to over $300 million for both second- and third-class, or a total of over $600 million. Some readjustments had been made on parcel post, but this was also still a deficit operation. Third-class mail met only two-thirds of its cost, and second-class about 30 per cent.

By 1965, the total excess of costs over revenue amounted to $837 million.† First-class mail yielded a surplus of $148 million. The losses on the other types of mail therefore amounted to nearly a billion dollars. Various adjustments of costs, amounting to $400 million, were carried out, not all of which were logical, but even with them the net loss on second-class amounted to $227 million, on third-class $303 million, and on parcel post $107 million. At least 65 per cent of the losses could be charged to commercial interests. These were sums by which the taxpayers and users of first-class mail subsidized advertisers who increasingly used the third-class rate to sell magazines and to distribute samples of toothpaste, hair oil, cosmetics, and so on.

The publishing and direct-mail-advertising industries received the big subsidies. National magazines denounced government waste and inveighed against farm subsidies but themselves received indirect subsidies running into the millions. When Congressman George M. Rhodes, of Pennsylvania, bravely tried to increase their rates, they unleashed a high-powered lobby upon both House and Senate. They argued that we should compute costs on an incremental and not an average basis and that the post office should become more efficient. As a matter of fact, while it was not markedly efficient, it did not do badly considering all its difficulties, and it tried to lessen the cost of duplicate handling of mail by its adoption of the "zip code" system.

* See my treatment of these subjects in my *Economy in the National Government,* Chicago: University of Chicago Press, 1952, pp. 123–32. Transportation costs were averaged on the pound; handling costs, by the unit.
† Total costs were $5,275 million and total receipts $4,438 million. This excludes military mail. See *Cost Ascertainment Report 1965,* U.S. Post Office Department, pp. 10–18.

But the real evil was influence. Congressmen and senators hesitated to offend powerful newspapers, weeklies, and mail-order concerns. This made it hard for me because Chicago was the national center of the mail-order business, with Sears, Roebuck and Montgomery Ward, and, perhaps more than any other city, it also was the source of direct-mail advertising. Despite my efforts, the taxpayers continued to pay the excessive bill while the advertising clubs at once denounced the deficits and contributed to their size. Naturally, the press gave no publicity to the facts, although in justice to the *Tribune,* I must say that it did express mild disapproval.

With the wholesale avenues of publicity closed, I tried to spread the word by retail. Since I usually dedicated many small post offices each year, I used those occasions to stress postal subsidies. Still having faith in the parable of the sower and the seed, I hoped that some of the facts might take root. For many years, they had not, and my feeble efforts were like whispers in the face of a whirlwind. President Nixon has reorganized the post office, with the avowed purpose of taking politics out of it. The acid test will be whether rates on second-, third-, and fourth-class mail are materially increased to meet their real costs. That is where most of the trouble lies, and business is the culprit. A beginning has been made.

I also found that large subsidies were paid to shipbuilders and ship operators, which by 1966 amounted to about $200 million a year. The shipping subsidies on the ocean transportation of farm products alone came to nearly $160 million in 1966. These were supposed to compensate for the higher cost of building ships in this country rather than abroad, and of operating them under the American flag. As a measure of national defense, perhaps they were justified. But they certainly encouraged inefficiency.

George Aiken had crusaded against these subsidies for years, and when he moved on to other things, I tried to take up his interest and profited from his friendly advice.

In trying to reduce these subsidies, I was especially revolted to discover that shipping subsidies were used to hold American ships as members of international shipping cartels. Under these cartels, all lines charged more for U.S. exports than for U.S. imports of identical articles between similar ports. This directly injured our export business and helped to contribute to an unfavorable balance of payments and hence to the depletion of our gold reserves. For several years I tried to correct these injustices and, with the help of Rear Admiral John Harllee, of the Maritime Commission, and Nicholas Johnson, Maritime administrator, made some improvements. The American-owned lines were in a sense prisoners of their cartels, which were controlled by foreign-owned lines. Nevertheless, they stood by these cartels in trying to prevent any change in rates. There was evidence that at least on some routes there was a secret pooling of earnings, so that the American lines shared in the excess earnings of the for-

eign. In 1968 Harllee finally persuaded the Supreme Court that the differential rates used were illegal. With his departure from office, however, it is
uncertain whether the Court's decision will be carried out, though some
suits by the Department of Justice have been successful. The shipping
companies and the British and Japanese governments show few signs of
change.

Heavy subsidies were also paid to foreign producers of coffee and
sugar. In the case of sugar, a tariff, plus quotas for imports of cane sugar,
was imposed to maintain a price of between six and seven cents a pound
for domestic beet and cane sugar. Many European countries followed the
same practices, with Great Britain paying bonuses to the producers of
cane sugar in its tropical colonies and dependencies. There was a small
free-world market of countries where the market price was far less than
the world price. I tried to transfer this differential from the foreign planters to American consumers, or at least to American taxpayers. In 1963,
when I began, this amounted to two cents a pound, or $40 a ton. By 1966
the differential was twice as much, and was paid to foreign producers.
Thus, by the time I left the Senate we were paying on sugar in excess of
$100 million a year to the prosperous planters of Latin America and of
other favored countries.* Coffee presented similar problems.

The biggest domestic subsidies were paid to the producers of farm
products, including cotton, sugar, wool, wheat, and feed grains. This was
done to reduce production so that the price per unit could be raised.
Started during the Depression, after cotton on the farm had fallen to
three cents a pound, corn to twelve cents, and wheat to thirty cents a
bushel, the farm program's original purpose was to protect small producers from the disastrously low prices caused by the collapse of urban
buying power and the inelastic nature of the demand for food and fiber.

After 1950 the small farmers increasingly left the land, and the high
price of farm machinery was helping to drive out the homesteader. The
number of farms decreased, and the control of the land drifted into the
hands of a small number of big landowners. From 1940 to 1969 the number of farms was halved, from 6 to 3 million, while the average number of
acres per unit was doubled. Only about a million of these farms could be
called "commercial." The others were either subsistence or small-scale,
producing little for the market. The result was that the subsidies were
going to a minority of rich farmers, who lapped the cream meant for the
poor.

Secretary of Agriculture Charles F. Brannan in 1949 had tried to allow
farmers to produce without restrictions, with flexible prices, and for the
free market. Later they would receive a subsidy per unit, which would
bring their income up to a decent one, although no farmer was to receive

* See my *America in the Market Place*, New York: Holt, Rinehart and Winston, 1966,
pp. 185-94.

more than $25,000. In other words, his proposal was really for income, rather than for price support. Looking back, I think it was the most sensible farm plan ever proposed. At the time, the $25,000 upper limit seemed too much, but later we all would have felt fortunate to have obtained this limit.

In 1959–60, I urged what was really a modified Brannan plan, with subsidies limited to $5,000. This aroused the opposition of well-to-do Illinois farmers, who insisted that such a limitation was impossible in central and northern Illinois. In vain I pointed out that the vast majority of farmers, even in our prosperous state, had a net income of far less than $5,000. Yet even the poorer farmers in the southern part of the state were too apathetic to rally behind me. To broaden my appeal, I then proposed an upper limit of $10,000, but had no better luck. During my last years in the Senate, Senator Daniel Brewster, of Maryland, twice proposed that no farmer should receive a subsidy in excess of $25,000. Even this modest proposal was beaten, by a vote of 56 to 38. To make matters worse, when John Williams, of Delaware, raised the limit to $50,000, we were beaten 49 to 42, and as a crowning indignity the Senate refused to stop payments of over $100,000.

In 1970 a $53,000 limit on each crop finally passed both the House and the Senate, and became law. The big plantation owners are still complaining bitterly about their restriction to this subsidy and have subdivided their farms to avoid it.

Furthermore, there are now statistics on direct subsidies and on who gets them. The Department of Agriculture has given the names and addresses of all farm owners who in 1966 received $5,000 or more in direct subsidies. Listed by county and state, the 87,257 names filled a volume of 1,283 pages. The total direct subsidies to owners, excluding all "price support loans and purchases," amounted to $3.28 billion. Of this, $1.02 billion, or 31 per cent, went to those who received $5,000 or more. There were 48,524 who received upward of $10,000, and the sums they received amounted to $619.2 million. There were 5,306 who received $25,000 and more, and the amounts they received came to $276 million. There were eighteen farm owners who received between $500,000 and $1 million, and nine who received over a million and around a total of $16 million.

Congressman Paul Findley, of Illinois, in 1969 showed that in 1967 there were 16,430 farm owners who received a total of $518.5 million in sums of over $20,000 apiece. He filled thirty-seven pages of the *Congressional Record* with the names of those who in 1968 received subsidies in excess of $25,000. The subsidies were particularly large in the case of cotton and sugar, more modest in the case of corn and feed grains. This increased the hope that a limit of $5,000 or $10,000 might not create as much opposition as I had aroused in my efforts a decade earlier.

The spectacle of these huge sums being paid to a few in order to reduce farm production at a time when at least 10 or 15 million Americans are undernourished and go to bed hungry is intolerable. To pay lavishly for the reduction of output under present conditions is indefensible. What needs to be done is to allocate and finance a larger share of the farm surplus for the hungry, both here and abroad.

A hidden subsidy, seldom identified, is the widespread use of publicly supported airfields by private planes, for which no adequate payment is made. I learned about this from observation, rather than from books.

In northern Illinois there is a city where the business and political leaders oppose most forms of federal aid. They have sanctimoniously refused government money for urban renewal and for Head Start, on the ground that they do not want to undermine the independence of the poor. Nearly every year that I was in the Senate, however, I was visited by a delegation of these civic leaders asking support for additional appropriations to improve their airport. When I joked about their inconsistency, they earnestly replied that since Ozark Air Lines was scheduling more stops, the airport must keep pace. I always helped them. After two or three years, though, I took a closer look at their problem. I found that traffic on the scheduled public planes was only a small part of the activity at the field. The area reserved for private planes of the two-engine type was jammed. It turned out that nearly every nearby company had at least one plane. Many prosperous citizens were also plane owners. In fact, to own a plane, there, was a status symbol for the affluent, and the expense could be written off for tax purposes. When I tried to find out how much these owners paid for the use of the airport, for receiving traffic advice and control, and so on, the answers were ambiguous.

I learned of another instance of airport subsidies while at lunch with the mayor of a town opposite Saint Louis, where I met several officials of a big company whose head was a conservative Republican, "Mr. P.," high up in the affairs of his national party. I knew that he had been a big contributor to the campaigns of my opponents and was known as a stern advocate of government economy. With some interest, I waited to learn the real purpose of the meeting. They wanted federal funds to improve a local airport, which I did not know existed. No scheduled airline had ever used it. It was devoted entirely to private planes, mostly those of Mr. P.'s company, which maintained a fleet, charging them off as a business expense. Mr. P. was shrewd enough not to come to the lunch himself. The mayor, a strong supporter of mine, had made his peace with P.'s company and was genuinely anxious that I should do the same, thus removing a powerful opponent. But it was hard to justify a large public expenditure for private use, especially for one well able to take care of himself. The argument was heated. Not liking to end a conversation this way, I suggested that if Mr. P., whose absence I regretted, would make his proposal over his signature, asking for this large amount of public money for what was in effect his airport, I would recommend that the appropriation be made. The assembled vice-presidents could not object, and my friend the mayor permitted himself a sly smile. The letter never came; I never expected that it would. How could P., the steel-blue economizer and opponent of subsidies for the poor, reveal himself as an anxious feeder at the public trough?

When I saw even the big airports filled with private planes, I thought that the time had come to increase their fees. They should at least pay their share of operating costs, even if they were not charged for a portion of the original capital cost of the airfields and associated equipment.

Toward the end of 1965, the highly responsible newspaper journalist Marquis Childs revealed in his column that the Federal Aviation Agency estimated that the amount of these hidden subsidies came to over $100 million a year. To do something about this, I was ready to move on the next appropriation bill. But I was overtaken by events and found myself on the outside looking in. Making private owners pay their share would not only help the Treasury, but also reduce the overcrowding of the airports, which increasingly has become a national hazard and has stimulated the slowdowns of the air controllers.

Pegging the Interest Rate and the Price of Government Bonds

MY DIFFICULTIES with Truman were early increased by my opposition to his policy of pressuring the Federal Reserve to buy large quantities of government bonds at par on the open market and at low rates of interest. This did keep the interest rate low, but it required large purchases of bonds. It also added to the reserves of the commercial banks and, since they wanted to maximize their profits and avoid having unused reserves, it made them greatly expand their commercial loans. When these exceeded the rate of growth of the national product, the inevitable result was an increase in the price level. That happened immediately after World War II and during the first year or two of the Korean War. To me, this seemed a vindication of the quantity theory of money, supposedly known to every student of elementary economics.*

---

* In simple algebraic form, this can be stated by the following equation:

$$P = \frac{MV \ \& \ M'V'}{T}$$

where P = General Price Level; T = Volume of Transactions or Production, also Real Gross National Product (GNP); M = Quantity of Cash; V = Velocity or Turnover of Cash; M' = Quantity of Commercial Credit; V' = Velocity or Turnover of Commercial Credit. Forty years before, Irving Fisher, one of the few American economists of the first rank, emphasized M and assumed that M' (except during the business cycle) would bear a constant relation to it. He proposed to stabilize prices by varying the price at the mint

I wanted to guard against inflation and to do so by restricting the growth in the quantity of bank credit to that of the production of goods and services. This could not be done if the Federal Reserve had to buy an indefinite quantity of government bonds at par to keep interest rates low. The interest rate on these bonds was then below the marginal postwar productivity of capital. Truman and his followers wanted to stabilize the interest rate at this level, while I wanted to stabilize the price level and allow the rate of interest to fluctuate largely in accordance with the private market rate. I thought the price level more important than the interest rate, and in a speech in February, 1951, I took the floor of the Senate to expound this point of view.

Shortly afterward, the Treasury and the Reserve agreed to an "accord," removing from the Reserve the need to buy such an unlimited quantity of government bonds as would maintain a low and constant interest rate. But Truman did not accept this conclusion, either emotionally or intellectually. He appointed his fellow Missourian William McChesney Martin, from the Treasury, as chairman of the Federal Reserve Board in the hope or, as some of his friends said, the belief that in practice Martin would reverse the accord. Once in office, however, Martin became far more restrictive and more orthodox than I.

My friend Wright Patman has never forgiven me for the accord and has consistently denounced it as an infamous agreement. I have told him that while his knowledge of the mechanics of the Federal Reserve System is unequaled, he is being stubborn in refusing to admit the truth of the quantity theory. He comes from the exact location (Texarkana) where interest rates used to be the highest in the nation and has a justifiable abhorrence of them. I once suggested that he should cultivate an equal abhorrence of rising prices. Other people opposed the accord because they believed that rising prices would stimulate economic growth by forcing a fuller utilization of the labor supply and of capital equipment.

Looking back on the issue after twenty years, I still think I was substantially correct. But I was not wholly so. Some of the increase in general prices was due to an increase in the effective demand for specific goods. Thus, after the war, the pent-up demand for clothing and durable consumer goods was financed by the accumulated savings of wartime, and in 1950–51 by the purchase of materiel with which to fight the Korean War.

---

of the amount of gold in each dollar. He would then have regulated the quantity of money so that it would bear a constant relationship to T. In 1933 the gold standard had been replaced with a managed internal currency based on bank credit and a gold-exchange standard for international payments. This of course greatly increased the importance of M' and probably justified for ordinary use a still-simpler equation:

$$P = \frac{M'V'}{T}$$

where M' now represented the total of both cash and commercial deposits and V' the average circulation of both.

Individual prices helped to set general prices, as the former head of the University of Chicago's department of political economy, J. Laurence Laughlin, had contended in his debates with Irving Fisher forty years before. Laughlin had been laughed out of court by the monetary experts, but over the years I developed a greater faith in his ideas and even less reliance on the rigid quantity theory as the sole factor in the general price level.

In any event, my attitude had a curious effect on my political stock. The New York bankers suddenly developed an interest in and an approval of me. Although this puzzled me at first, the reason was soon evident. The slowing down of bond purchases would raise the interest rate, and interest was the price of the credit they sold and the investments they channeled. They thought the public policy sound, but their belief stemmed from economic self-interest. This was one of the factors in the brief interest in me for the Presidential candidacy in 1951.

Some Qualifications

IN MAKING LEGISLATION, there is always a danger of dealing with specific issues in an isolated way. Some believed that I was guilty of just this error. How could I be in favor of increased expenditures for education, health, housing, and welfare and yet try to reduce waste and balance the budget? If I was opposed to subsidizing the rich, should I not also be opposed to subsidizing the poor? Was I not trying to reconcile opposites with an eye to winning votes from groups whose interests were really opposed?

In my view, to cut waste was justifiable in itself, since it would release resources for greater needs, either personal or collective. But it would also either reduce or eliminate the budgetary deficit and so help to check the artificial creation of bank credit. Within the confines of a balanced budget and a more just system of taxation, the price level could be stabilized and at the same time more funds be provided for human welfare. And should not human welfare be the primary aim of any civilized society, and in itself lead ultimately to greater national prosperity? Man was both the end and the means of a just and strong society, and if divergent groups could be reconciled to such a common policy, was not this commendable?

There were two modifications to conventional arguments for a balanced budget, which became more apparent with the years. First, they should apply mostly to the operating budget, but not necessarily to capital investments made by the government. This is the practice followed by private corporations. New investments in plant are financed out of bond issues instead of from current income. The interest charges that arise are presumed to be paid out of future increased productivity, while the capital debt is amortized by payments that do not extend beyond the physical life of the property. Public investments in such institutions as TVA should have been charged in a similar way. Operating costs, such as those of the Justice and Labor departments, should, however, be met out of current income. There are, of course, borderline cases. What should we do, for example, in the cases of irrigation and public housing?

Increasingly, I stressed these points in my defense of TVA and of public power, as well as in the attempts at budgetary reform launched by the Joint Economic Committee, which for a time bore partial fruit. If the example of corporations had been followed, the published deficit for most years would have disappeared, and the conservative argument would have been correspondingly weakened.

The second modification grew out of monetary policy itself. Through the efforts of Jerry Voorhis and Wright Patman, the Federal Reserve System had been forced to turn over to the government most of the net profits on its operations. The major source of its income came from interest on government bonds purchased in the open market to increase the bank reserves and hence the lending powers of its member banks. It had paid for these bonds not by offering cash, but by creating the reserves credited to the member banks. The increase in the supply of active bank credit was therefore largely dependent on an increase in the public debt. If there were no further increase in the debt, it would be harder to increase the supply of bank credit. And yet in order to stabilize the price level, it was often necessary to increase bank credit in nearly the same ratio as the increase in production, since the production of physical goods and services was showing both a total and a per-capita increase. (Of course, the same effect could also be obtained by the Reserve buying government bonds from the public and crediting the transferred amounts to the accounts of the member banks.) The result is the apparently paradoxical view that in order to stabilize the price level and prevent its fall, the public debt might have to be increased by running an unbalanced budget. Instead of using an arbitrary ratio, I preferred to have the increase in the supply of money in years of prosperity nearly parallel the increase in the real gross national product during the preceding quarter, but always lagging a little. I wanted to have public expenditures in depression years increase moderately and to have the government buy some of the bonds that would be issued.

The justification for certain public expenditures was stronger when these sophisticated considerations were taken into account. But in public arguments one could not get too sophisticated. The Congress and the public could perhaps absorb a course in basic economics, but I could not expect them to pass an examination for the Ph.D. Waste was not justifiable; only expenditures of a high priority should be made.

24

Bureaucracy and the
Insolence of Office

ON COMING TO THE SENATE I was on the whole prejudiced in favor
of the federal civil service. Many of my academic friends at Chicago had
been enthusiastic about public administration. They believed that the
city-manager movement would redeem our cities from spoils politics and
that the extension of civil service was raising the level of public performance in both state and nation. Public officials could now be selected on
the basis of merit, rather than of political influence. By gaining relative
security, they would be free to do their best.

With funds furnished by the Rockefeller Foundation, associations of
public administrators were housed in a building on Chicago's Midway
which soon acquired the title "1313." The members were high-minded
and rapidly became experts in their separate fields, ranging from municipal finance to police administration.

In Washington at the same time, numbers of young men and a sprinkling of women flocked into the government under the mesmeric spell of
Franklin D. Roosevelt's New Deal. They, too, were dominated by a desire
to serve the public interest, and they worked long and hard. Through an
educated and devoted group of civil servants comparable to Plato's guardians, perhaps American political life might be redeemed. Some of my colleagues, with an eye on Great Britain's civil servants, wrote admiringly of
the "administrative state." Myopically, they discounted the class domination of Britain's bureaucracy by the well-to-do graduates of Oxford and
Cambridge, and ignored the less tolerable faults of Germany's system. My
friends Charles Merriam and Louis Brownlow, as advisers to Roosevelt,
were largely responsible for building up the Budget Bureau, which was to

be the agency for the general supervision and control of government by the executive.

When I talked confidentially with public administrators, they usually viewed politicians as their common enemies. Politicians were always trying to get jobs for their favorites instead of letting the positions be filled by qualified Ph.D.'s from the Ivy League and the Midwestern universities. They held lawmakers guilty of trying to interpret, as well as write, legislation, and of refusing to step aside to let their superiors run the state.

My experience as an alderman gave me a different outlook. In addition, when I was asked after the war, by Truman and Secretary of Labor Lewis B. Schwellenbach, to try to negotiate an agreement between labor and capital for national labor peace, my contacts with the overstaffed Department of Labor added to my disenchantment. No work could be done after two o'clock, and a large number ate breakfast on government time. Yet I resented the wholesale attacks on the bureaucracy as thinly veiled attacks on the New Deal. Many who had not dared to attack Roosevelt sought to discredit him by attacking his appointees. Rex Tugwell had been unjustifiably made such a whipping boy. I relished Alben Barkley's version of the situation, given at the 1948 Democratic convention. "To Republicans," he thundered, "a bureaucrat is a Democrat whose job is wanted by a Republican."

In the Senate I meant to be the defender of these men and women, who were not appreciated for their merits. The agency that above all others seemed to embody the public conscience was the Food and Drug Administration. It was started by a great scientist and reformer, Dr. Harvey W. Wiley, when the American public had been stirred by Upton Sinclair's exposé of the stockyards in *The Jungle* and by *Collier's Weekly,* with Norman Hapgood's assault on Lydia Pinkham's Vegetable Compound and other patent medicines. My skepticism was first aroused by information that the FDA was discriminating against a new bread that had a wheat-germ-and-soybean reinforcement far superior in nutrition to the usual tasteless and starchy product. This new bread, developed by a Cornell professor, was baked by the consumers' co-operative at Ithaca, New York. But the FDA would not permit it to be called "bread." It was different and better than ordinary bread, but it would be unfair, they reasoned, to allow the newcomer to share the name, even though a new name would not have the same appeal. This ruling seemed particularly strange because the Food and Drug Act was meant to provide minimum standards of quality, rather than to fix ceilings above which quality could not go. My letters, polite at first, but increasingly irate, were brushed aside. I was treated as being another politician trying to interfere with conscientious scientists.

The news of my interest must have spread, for it brought to my door a fellow Chicagoan, Daniel Brown. He had a process for milling wheat without damage to the wheat germ. He had produced this flour for a brief time, and my friend the great physiologist Anton J. Carlson had pronounced it to be of high quality. Dan lost control of his little mill in Grundy County, where his successors, without his formula, produced a poorer flour that the Department of Agriculture incorrectly confused with Dan's original product, perhaps in order to condemn his flour. I could not get them to recognize their error.

I tried demonstrations. Brown milled a small run of flour, which the Senate cook baked into bread as delicious as the best newly baked French loaf. At a lunch to which I had invited him, I fed Secretary of Agriculture Brannan some of the bread. Much impressed, he promised to consult his scientists. They turned their thumbs down. When Eisenhower came into office and made Ezra Taft Benson secretary of Agriculture, I tried again but made no headway at all. With the arrival of Orville Freeman, my hopes rose.

I told him the story. When wheat had been milled by stone grinders, turned by water from local rivers, the irregularities in the grinders permitted the wheat germs to pass into the flour without being crushed. When the big metal grinders of the Minneapolis mills moved into nationwide mass production, the wheat germs were crushed and the oil contained within them went into the flour, where it rancified. This spoiled the flour. To counteract it, the big millers developed a process to take out the wheat germs before the wheat was ground. What was left was largely starch. This process accounted for the fact that bread was often tasteless and lacking in nutrition. The vitamin-rich wheat germs were then either thrown away or sold as hog food, which meant that hogs were better fed than humans. I felt that men were entitled to at least equal treatment.

If Brown's new process proved popular, people would, moreover, eat more bread. Not only would this new bread be good for them, but also it would lead to an increased demand for wheat. This would benefit both farmers and millers. I thought this argument might turn the tide. But no. After fifteen more years of effort, I retired from the Senate and the fight. Brown is still balked in his efforts. Scientific reports on the shoddy quality of white bread are still produced without having any effect on the Department of Agriculture.

Nothing discredits a politician more than to be thought a crank, especially about diet, and I fast gained the reputation of being a food faddist. My friend Irving Fisher had been ridiculed for his interest in nutrition as well as in the compensated dollar. I did not want that stigma, but I was learning that malnutrition was often caused by too much starch and fat and not enough proteins and vitamins. So periodically I gave lunches and served bread made from stone-ground flour, some of it sent me from Bloomington by Mrs. Carl Vrooman, whose husband had been Under Secretary of Agriculture for Woodrow Wilson. Although my guests en-

Paul H. Douglas

Emily Taft Douglas

Helen Douglas Klein

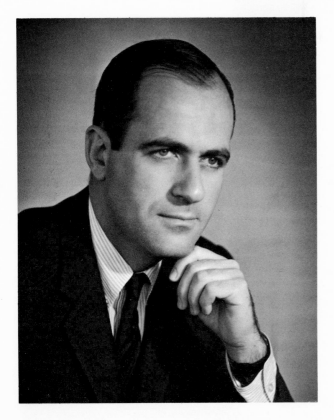

Paul W. Douglas

John W. Douglas

Dorothea Douglas John

Jean Douglas Bandler

Emily Douglas shortly after her marriage

With daughter Jean
in 1934

Newport, Maine, High School basketball team, 1909
(second from right, front row)

Bowdoin College football team, 1912
(third from left, back row)

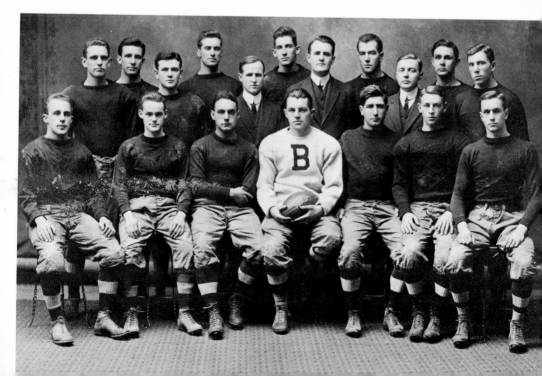

Receiving the Bronze Star for service on Peleliu during World War II

Campaigning in Decatur, Illinois, 1950

ith Helen, Jean, and Emily on election night, 1954

With President Harry S. Truman, Steve Bailey,
and Frank Annunzio at a labor meeting in Chicago,
about 1950

George Pollard

cob M. Arvey

Emily with Martin Luther King, Jr., after the protest march
in Selma, Alabama, 1965

With John F. Kennedy,
St. Charles, Illinois, 1960:
the end of a strenuous day
of campaigning

With President Lyndon B. Johnson, at the signing of the
Truth-in-Lending Act, May 29, 1968

Frank W. McCulloch

Jane Carey Enger

Herbert H. Lehman

Jerry Voorhis

Frank P. Graham

With Hubert H. Humphrey in the Senate antechamber, 1964

William Proxmire

lbert A. Gore

At a Housing Subcommittee hearing in Washington, with Milton Semer, Jack Carter, and Robert A. Wallace, mid-1950's

Paul Simon   Howard E. Shuman

las Anderson

Kenneth E. Gray

vieve Alloy Watson

Michael Greenebaum

Cecil Layne

Clarence M. Mitchell, Jr. and Roy Wilkins

Paul F. Sifton   Joseph L. Rauh, Jr.

Mrs. J. H. Buell

Richard L. Strout ("T.R.B.")

With the Save the Dunes delegation, 1959

Speaking in Chicago during the last week of the 1966 campaign

joyed the bread, nothing came of the demonstrations. Finally I concluded that the underofficials and scientists in both the Department of Agriculture and the FDA wanted to protect the millers from the expense of putting in new machinery and processes. I was growing tired of the struggle when another product offered new possibilities.

Ezra Levin, a nutritionist from the University of Michigan, was operating a small plant in Monticello, Illinois, where he produced Viobin, wheat-germ oil. Levin insisted that I take some, and it had a beneficial effect. My acquaintance with him led to many requests for his pills from people trying to improve either their own health or that of their pets. Sometimes they seemed more concerned with their dogs than with themselves. But, in either case, their reports were always good. Levin was making a small fortune for himself, and, as an inveterate idealist, was eager for a broader attack on nutrition.

Since the usual weakness in the diets of the poor, in both the United States and the hot countries, was a lack of protein and vitamins, Levin developed a fish flour that was 80 to 85 per cent protein and rich in vitamins. This could have been manufactured at about twelve cents a pound; and with the fish taste removed, at a total of fourteen cents. Since many dark-skinned children cannot tolerate milk because they lack the enzyme that makes milk sugar physiologically available, fish flour could be an essential aid to life.

As an additive to rice it was found to be excellent. I tried to popularize it among the personnel of the embassies of the tropical countries at luncheons for their cultural attachés and officers. The fish flour was concealed in the soup, the rolls, the vegetables, and even tucked away in ice cream. During the luncheon, we discussed the need for more protein in their countries and how fish flour was produced. But they were not told that they were eating it until the end of the meal. Then rice was served. The fish flour was brought out in its powdered form, and the guests were invited to sprinkle it on the rice. I thought it a successful demonstration. In the tropics, the seas abound in fish, but due to the great heat and lack of refrigeration, neither meat, fish, nor milk can be transported or kept long. In powdered form, immune to heat and time, fish flour might be the answer. For about one cent, a family would get as much protein from fish flour as from eight ounces of beefsteak. While the diplomats professed interest, I aroused no real response from them. "Malnutrition," "hunger," "protein" were as alien to their diplomatic concerns as they were to members of our own foreign service.

In another effort to make his point, Levin gave away large quantities of fish flour to children's hospitals in Peru and Mexico. In return he got them to make statistical reports on the results. Peru, which had an abundance of fish just off its coast, showed special interest, and in the next years a fish-flour plant materialized.

Our approach to the American market was to the hungry folks with low incomes in all states, but especially the poor whites and Negroes of the South and the Anglo-Saxons of the Appalachian highlands. Levin was ready to forgo all profit just to get his fish flour used. But the Food and Drug Administration barred the way. It pronounced fish flour "loathsome" and "unfit" for human use. Although the powder was made from whole fish, including both head and entrails, these had been subject to eight washings in water and the same number in alcohol, as well as being both boiled and baked in great heat. The FDA finally admitted that the flour was hygienic and beneficial, that there was nothing wrong with the final product except that it raised "unesthetic thoughts." I had never thought that their jurisdiction extended to intellectual esthetics.

Having no effective alternative, I delivered a series of speeches on the floor of Congress. After stressing the positive case for the fish flour, I gave the final arguments of the FDA. Displaying some of the powder and inviting members to taste it, I asked if it aroused "unesthetic thoughts" in the members of the Senate. Nobody claimed that it did. Then I brought out of a suitcase some products the FDA did permit to be sold. There were candied ants and bees, cross sections of rattlesnakes, clams and oysters that retained their digestive systems and that had not been subjected to the washing, cleaning, boiling, and baking processes Levin had devised for his fish flour. In my mind, these products did raise "unesthetic thoughts," but their sale was permitted with no restrictions. Although the FDA made no reply, my attacks intensified its hostility.

Nevertheless, still hopeful, I asked George P. Larrick, the head of the FDA, and Abraham Ribicoff, then Secretary of Health, Education, and Welfare, to lunch with me in my office. Ribicoff was genial and expansive, Larrick tight-lipped and sullen. At the close, I asked in an offhand manner if they had enjoyed their lunch. When they politely said they had, I brashly told them that they had eaten large quantities of fish flour in nearly every dish. Livid with anger, Larrick took his departure, never to be seen by me again. Ribicoff remained pleasant but was nonco-operative.

The FDA at last offered what seemed to be a concession. They would permit the manufacture of fish flour for sale abroad, but not for consumption in this country. Levin and I replied that this would play right into the hands of the Communists, who would charge that in the name of philanthropy we were sending abroad products thought too loathsome to be consumed by Americans. Certainly if fish flour was unfit for us to use, it was unfit for foreigners. We demanded authoritative findings on the product by a reputable group of scientists.

We were by this time gaining some popular support. The fishing industries of New England and of the Pacific Northwest, which had been in the doldrums for years, scented a new market. Levin had sunk part of his fortune in building and equipping a factory in New Bedford, which currently produced coarse fish meal for animal consumption. The fishermen found the prospect of human consumption of a new fish product most attractive. Increasing numbers of Senators supported us. Newspapers ridiculed Larrick's defenses. We softened the opposition of the wheat belt by rechristening Levin's product Fish Protein Concentrate (FPC).

Interior Secretary Udall finally referred the question to a committee from the National Academy of Sciences. After a year's study, the members brought out a highly favorable report, praising the product and finding no harmful side effects. However, instead of opening the way for Levin, the Interior Department announced that it would ask for $5 million with which to finance the Bureau of Fisheries in setting up plants for the manufacture of a government-sponsored fish-flour product. The lonely private innovator who had devised the method and had made the solitary fight was to be shunted aside and the work given to a government agency. This strategy would save face for the bureaucracy.

As it turned out, the Bureau of Fisheries' method did not produce a satisfactory product. A pilot plant has not yet been erected. For foreign aid, the government had to turn back to Levin for its supplies for Indonesia and Southeast Asia. I still hope for the clearance of Levin's product, so that the many millions of hungry and undernourished Americans may benefit from it, but the Food and Drug Administration is still hostile. It has widened the opposition to fish flour by insisting that it must be sold in one-pound packages and confined to hake. I cannot see how the size of the package affects the safety of its contents, or why other fish than hake are barred. The wheat interests and processors are determined to prevent fish protein from coming on the market, and they apparently control FDA in this matter.

My experience with the Food and Drug Administration made me especially interested in the work of my colleague Estes Kefauver. He had found that the big commercial drug firms made huge profits on many products by charging varying prices in different countries depending on the competition they faced. He wanted drugs to be sold under their generic, rather than their trade, names, and to have their side effects more thoroughly probed. The FDA always opposed him, and he received no help from the personnel at the National Institutes of Health.

Then two events played into his hands. It came to light that Dr. Henry Welch, in charge of licensing new antibiotics, was receiving a large income from advertisements by the drug companies in an allegedly scientific journal that he edited.* Although FDA officials must have known this, they had allowed this conflict of interest to continue. Only when it was publicized did they accept Dr. Welch's quiet resignation.

The second event was a near tragedy. The industry was pushing Dr.

* See *Administered Prices*, Hearings before the Senate Subcommittee on Antitrust and Monopoly, 86th Congress, Part 22, May 18, 1960, pp. 11948 *et seq.*

Frances Kelsey, of the FDA, to approve the new drug thalidomide. Without further evidence, she was reluctant to do this, and she was morally supported by Dr. Barbara Moulton, who had left FDA to work for its reorganization and a stronger drug law. During this delay, it was discovered that expectant mothers in Europe who took this drug frequently produced babies with malformed arms or legs or none. When this became publicized, thalidomide was of course dropped.

After that, a Kefauver bill was passed in truncated form, and Larrick eventually retired. A new and superior man, Dr. James L. Goddard, succeeded him and helped clean up some of his bureaucracy.

One feature of the Kefauver bill is still causing trouble, however. Products that were "ineffective" could be barred as well as those that were harmful. There is some evidence that the FDA is using this provision to outlaw natural products, such as vegetables. They are not the cure for everything, of course, but for some difficulties they can be helpful.

The worst case of bureaucratic injustice I encountered occurred in my own beloved Marine Corps. One day in 1956 my legislative assistant, Howard Shuman, and my office manager, Mary Nolan, informed me of a former Marine Corps master sergeant, Carl Buck, who had been given a dishonorable discharge and had served time in a naval prison for the alleged theft of $500 worth of chevrons. Having called at my office, he had convinced them of his innocence. They found him honest and frank. Since I had tried, as a sort of defendant's lawyer at Noumea thirteen years before, to protect boys who had an honest mien but later had been proved obviously guilty, I was now cautious about such cases. But I was aroused by their next point. After a long appeal, Buck had been offered a pardon, but one that did not reverse the findings of the court-martial. He was being offered mercy because of his previous eighteen-year spotless record in the Corps, but would still be adjudged guilty. He had declined that offer. He said that, being innocent, he did not want to have his wife and son hang their heads in shame over the false findings of the court. He wanted a pardon on the ground of innocence. I blanched at the thought of that. Only the President can grant such a pardon, and, in my memory, it had not been done during the current century. Buck's desire was certainly creditable, and it strengthened Shuman's and Mary's belief that he was innocent. But it was almost impossible to fight one's way up through the military bureaucracy. However, I agreed to talk to Buck before turning him down.

Buck was brought in, and I was impressed. Immediately we got down to the evidence. The theft had been committed at the post exchange at Camp Pendleton, which was two miles inside the main gate. Buck had been arrested twenty-three minutes later at a point over twenty miles down the road. There had been a steady downpour of rain, and the road was not only crowded but also full of many junctions punctuated by traffic lights. He was supposed to have gotten rid of the chevrons on the way and to have received his pay-off. It seemed impossible that he could have covered such a distance under such conditions in so short a time. Furthermore, he had parked his car directly behind one from the state police. A guilty man would most likely not have done that.

Buck had been convicted largely because his secondhand car was a yellow Studebaker, which was the color given as that of the car in which the thief had made his getaway. But no check had been made of those in the camp who might own similar-colored cars. I became more and more convinced that there had been a miscarriage of justice.

Buck had no personal claims on me. Although he had entered the Marine Corps a score of years before from Granite City, Illinois, his Illinois connections had long ago been dissolved. He was a stateless person, with closer connections to his wife's home in South Dakota than to any other. But the Senators from South Dakota had prudently refused to accept any jurisdiction. Now, as so often in Noumea, I told him that he had a good case, that someone ought to represent him. But since I was swamped with a thousand jobs, I could not devote the time needed for the preparation of the case. However, I said, if Howard Shuman cared to do so, I would release his time and I would meet all incidental expenses.

By now, Howard was so convinced of Buck's innocence that he jumped at the chance. I kept in touch with his work and signed the numerous memoranda and appeals to the military authorities. As we began the long journey to the White House, Howard kept finding new evidence. He discovered that the defense counsel at the court-martial had not really represented Buck, but had given testimony that seemed adverse to him. New suspicions appeared when we got a list from the Marines of those in the camp who at the time owned yellow cars.

When we finally secured an official review, the board was badly biased. It even included some who had taken part in the earlier miscarriage of justice. After trying the Justice Department, with no luck, we finally got the case referred to the White House itself. There were indications that Eisenhower, always a kindly man, was disturbed over the matter. But his aides would not let him act, insisting that the case must go back to the Navy Department.

Our case was strengthened by Howard's more precise computation of the distance of the trip, and the fact that Buck's secondhand car could scarcely have made it in the limited time. People around the White House were now talking about Buck as though he might become an American Dreyfus case without any racial animus.

Lee White, the President's counsel, suggested that the case be submitted to Charles Horsky for a recommendation. We jumped at the chance. Horsky was a highly respected partner in Covington and Burling, one of Washington's most prominent law firms. He had a strong public spirit, but a lawyer's caution. He was impressed with our case, but he did not think it was a closed one, and nothing else would justify such unprecedented Presidential action. He asked Shuman to go out to California and dig up more evidence.

Shuman, at my expense, had a most productive week. Traveling the road himself, he checked the distances, which were longer than reported. Furthermore, the ninety street intersections were punctuated by nineteen traffic lights, which slowed down speed from the gate at Camp Pendleton to the place of arrest. How could a secondhand car travel at more than seventy miles an hour, thread its way through this maze on a crowded highway in a driving rain, and have time to dispose of the stolen goods? Howard's crowning achievement was to find in official documents that the $100 in Buck's pocket, presumed to be the pay-off, was in two $50 bills, for which Buck had given a different, and verified, accounting. This and other material swept away the last shadow of doubt. As supplementary evidence, we found that the man we had long suspected of being the real culprit had, as the inquiry drew closer, committed suicide, and that another man, who had given crucial evidence against Buck, had literally run away from Shuman when the latter tried to talk to him.

The cautious Horsky recommended to President Johnson that he issue a full and unconditional pardon to Buck on the ground of "proved innocence." The President courageously agreed. We brought Buck and his wife from Seattle for the formal signing of the pardon. As we went into the President's office, Johnson greeted the couple warmly and kissed Mrs. Buck. He asked a few offhand questions, obviously designed to test Buck's sincerity and motives. Then he signed the full pardon. We next took the Bucks to see the Commandant of the Marine Corps, General Wallace M. Greene, Jr. Like a thoroughbred, he apologized for what had happened, gave them presents and a letter clearing Buck's record. Back at the Senate Office Building, we had a combination press conference and cocktail party to herald the news. Buck stood straighter than ever before, and the eyes of his brave wife sparkled. We saw to it that the news, by radio, television, and print, went immediately to Seattle and to the other places where the Bucks had lived.

This kind of pardon had not happened in over sixty-four years, and had taken eight years of effort to effect. So a senator, given an airtight case and a tireless, able, and indomitable assistant, *could* penetrate the citadels of the military in behalf of the poor, the weak, or the disinherited. Perhaps the full meaning of democracy became more evident to some people that night and in the days that followed.

The attorneys in the Justice and Defense departments were bitter at the way we had finally taken the appeal to the President, instead of going for the third time "through channels." Admitting that Buck was innocent, they condemned us for the unconventional route of his clearance.

The whole affair, they said, might besmirch military justice and increase the number of appeals from courts-martial. I answered that the remedy should be to observe justice more faithfully and not to punish the innocent in an effort to protect the institution.

The bureaucracy had lost, but they took a final revenge. Buck had lost pay, promotion, and pension because of his imprisonment. He now asked for compensation. The government paymasters and lawyers denied it. At first I was concerned only in the vindication of Buck's good name. But he had lost much income, and he was now in trouble because his Seattle bakery was not doing well. So I took the liberty of writing to the Under Secretary of the Navy, Paul Nitze. I reviewed the case and asked whether our government could not be generous to those it had wronged. Nitze, himself an outsider to the military bureaucracy, reviewed the case and made an ample and generous settlement with Buck. The financial damage had finally been made good, but not the tears and sleepless nights which Mrs. Buck, the children, and Carl Buck himself had been compelled to go through. The corrective truth seldom catches up with the initial calumny. As the old saying goes, "A lie can go around the world before truth can put on its boots."

Perhaps the military bureaucracy will be a little more careful in the future because of this pardon. I know of nothing that more became President Johnson.

For years thereafter at Christmastime, Howard and I have each received a large holiday cake with gay icing from Master Sergeant Carl Buck. Despite my rule of not allowing favors from those I have tried to help, I must report that we have accepted these cakes, and have shared them with many as we retold the story.

One thought is worth pondering. If all this could happen in the legislative experience of a comparatively minor member of the Senate, are there not a myriad of other cases which go either unrecorded or uncorrected? Should the presumption of the "administrative state" be ever again as easily accepted as it was a generation ago? The bureaucracy should not be worshipped as infallible, nor be indiscriminately denounced. Its members should be treated as are other men. But they need humility as well.

25

Saving the Marine Corps

IN 1948–49, the Army, with the approval and support of General Eisenhower, and under the command of General J. Lawton Collins, had drawn up a plan for the virtual elimination of the Marine Corps as a combat organization. Under the Collins plan, the Marines were to be confined to longshore work on the beaches, used as naval police and for ceremonial duties, but were no longer to fight in organized units.

Earlier, the separate departments of the Army and the Navy had been federated under a common Department of Defense, although they retained their autonomy for combat purposes. This was a forward step, as was the creation of a similar third department for the Air Force. To the armchair strategists of the Pentagon and to some military reporters in Washington, the Marine Corps seemed an unnecessary anomaly. It was, in a sense, a second army, specializing in amphibious landings, but, if necessary, fighting on foot far inland. It even had a separate air force. Those who thought in terms of organization charts found it simpler to eliminate the Marines, retaining only the three conventional services.

This move was strengthened by some members of the Army. They accused the Marines of being publicity hounds, and of attracting attention away from the Army. If the Marines were praised, it was thought that the Army was thereby downgraded. The Collins plan therefore won wide support among the military specialists on a number of newspapers and among the retired officers and men of the Regular Army. President Truman had been a strong supporter of this plan. His dislike for the Marine Corps came to the surface in a handwritten letter saying that the Marines had a publicity corps "as big as Stalin's." At first, I could not believe he had written it, but a telephone call to William D. Hasset, Truman's secretary, at the White House confirmed that it was authentic. Shortly afterward he made a belated apology at a meeting of the Marine Corps League. Although he was applauded, it was obvious where his heart was. He still remembered his animosities as an artillery captain in World War I.

Along with hundreds of thousands of Marines, I felt deeply wounded by the proposal. Over the years, the Marines had built up a deserved reputation for bravery, devotion to duty, and never striking their colors. This was part of the living tradition of the Corps, which even the rawest recruit cherished as an inspiration. There is more to life than an organization chart. Men are not merely wooden units to be moved about as some aloof chess player decrees. Young men in particular need some group smaller than the nation or a mass army, but not conflicting with it, to which they can pledge their devotion and which will call upon them for unselfish performance of duty. This was the peculiar contribution of the Marine Corps. The country needed a corps that sought danger not safety, hardship not ease, and service not privilege. Such, despite the excessive conceit of some of our younger members, was our Corps. It had proved itself in both World Wars and in many minor engagements. If the Army suffered by comparison, its remedy was to raise its own standards of performance, or exalt such historic units as the First Infantry Division and the First Cavalry. But, instead, the Corps was to be legislated or administered out of existence.

I did not feel that this was deserved. I therefore drafted a bill to put a mandatory floor under the Marine Corps, so that it would consist of at least four divisions, and to provide that when amphibious operations were under consideration, the commandant of the Marine Corps would be a member of the Joint Chiefs of Staff. Some forty-six Senators flocked to sign the bill as cosponsors, but that ended the effort. To insure victory, the bill's supporters needed a majority, or forty-nine, to act as cosponsors. The lobbyists for the Army were quite exultant at this failure.

I noticed that Joe McCarthy and several of his followers had not signed, although Joe had served with the Marines in World War II. I asked one of the retired reserve officers who was helping us what was wrong. After a few days of inquiry, he suggested that if I sat beside McCarthy on the floor of the Senate in full view of the press gallery, talked to him amiably, shook hands, and then asked for his help, I would get not only his signature but also that of several others, which would put us over the top. I told him that was a high price to pay, but that my love for the Corps was such that I would do even that. So I walked over to shake hands with Joe. We chatted for a while before I asked if he would serve as a sponsor. This seemed to please him immensely, and he gladly agreed. There was another handshake and smiles on both sides while spectators and the press looked on in wonder. Within ten minutes four other signatures were obtained, and I filed the bill with fifty-one cosponsors, two more than a majority. I never knew why Joe wanted this public recognition from me in view of his known feelings about me. But apparently he did, and that ultimately saved the Corps.

After an interesting set of hearings, we got the bill through the Senate, with three divisions as the minimum number for the Corps. I brought out the fact that a Marine regiment had many more combat infantrymen than a comparable Army unit. The greater proportion of fighting men extended all the way up through the divisional and corps levels. While there were also too many supply and administrative personnel in the Corps, it was not as top-heavy as the Army was. Moreover, although the Army had some excellent divisions, the Marines prided themselves on a higher proportion of Presidential unit citations, Congressional Medals of Honor, and on the ratio of men killed and wounded in action. In the Pacific they had been called on for the hardest and most dangerous tasks. They wanted to continue in the same tradition, and I was pleased to find that officers assigned to "soft" posts at headquarters would later struggle to get reassigned to troops in the field. It was an honor, not a punishment, to be assigned to the "boondocks," or, in Pentagon language, "trooped," and a double honor to be sent into combat.

The House passed the bill with some changes, and these required a conference in the spring of 1952 between the committees on the Armed Services of both houses. The Army took this as a chance to defeat the whole proposal. They succeeded in getting the backing of almost half of the conferees. Kefauver was for the bill, but he was so busy campaigning for the Presidential nomination that it was not certain that he could come to the crucial meeting. I followed him one afternoon from one meeting to another on the streets of Washington until he could think of nothing else and was limp with exhaustion. I finally won his promise to be there, and he came. When the group gathered, they asked me to state the case for the bill again. I tried to do so briefly and respectfully. The Army fought hard. John Stennis was the swing man, and he was deeply troubled. Just before the vote, he looked questioningly at me. After a pause that seemed an eternity, he nodded and then voted with me. Truman did not dare to veto the bill. The Corps was granted a reprieve.

From all that I can learn, our action has been justified and many fears and prejudices refuted. The Corps has done extremely well in both Korea and Vietnam. Under Lew Walt it started a three-pronged program in Vietnam to win the loyalty of the people by furnishing food and medical care, providing farm implements, seed, and work animals, and setting up schools. No disgraceful atrocities of the sort that happened at My Lai have, to my knowledge, occurred.

The relations between the Marine Corps and the Army have distinctly improved with time. The Corps is perhaps less bumptious and offensively egotistical. Since it no longer has to fight for its life, the behavior of both parties has improved. The Army, no longer hoping to do away with the Corps, is more disposed to accept it as a fact of life. And both sides have been helped to grow up emotionally by men like Walt and Omar Bradley.

The Corps has improved in other matters. It was formerly a tightly segregated service run primarily by brave Southerners, with their traditional attitudes. Negroes were reluctantly accepted during World War II, but only as longshore troops. However, Truman's desegregation order was loyally and even enthusiastically carried out down to platoon and squad level. The racial problem is certainly not solved, but relationships have improved. Negroes are in fact proving to be excellent Marines. Perhaps in time, as Marines, both black and white, go out into civilian life, they may mitigate some of the existing racial hatreds and help produce that justice for which so many patriots have yearned. For the present, the four military services are doing better in the way of relations between the races than is civil society.

26

Preserving and Strengthening Competition

It always seemed strange that those trying to preserve ethical competition from the inroads of private monopoly should be called opponents of the "American system of free enterprise." To the group of liberal Senators, "free enterprise" did not mean monopolistic enterprise, since that shut off potential producers from the market and resulted in higher prices to consumers. It was not free. We also saw that higher prices reduced the quantity of goods that were demanded and hence produced, and resulted in restricted employment. This in turn increased unemployment and forced labor into overcrowded and poorly paid industries. Labor was then divided into two groups: those in the monopolized or imperfectly competitive industries and those outside. Those inside might become a favored class sharing the monopoly advantages. Those outside would be in far worse straits and would include most of the Negroes, Puerto Ricans, Indians, and Mexican-Americans of the working force. The result would be sharp class cleavages, with a racist tinge. Jack London had forecast most of this in his somber novel *The Iron Heel*.

Along with most progressives, I favored measures increasing ethical competition and opposed those lessening it. My stand covered a wide range of business practices, the concentration of bank ownership, and even included the membership of and appropriations for the regulatory commissions.

To me it was a source of wonder that the self-styled defenders of the capitalist system should zealously defend what was threatening the very vitals of capitalism. They opposed any government action to reduce monopoly or protect competition.* In urging *laissez faire*, they really supported monopoly capitalism, and they tried to shift the blame for unemployment to the unions and government. Silent about private monopolies, they ignored the imperfect competition that Joan Robinson had so elegantly analyzed in the early 1930's.† According to them, government should stand aside to let the big companies gobble up their smaller rivals. Any interference excited their anger, which was, of course, focused on those of us trying to defend a purified capitalism.

With lowered prices and increased production, jobs were expanded. But when monopoly restraints could not be removed, the basic needs of those out of work could be met by government projects to enhance the common good. We were ready to make a permanent mixture of some state ownership in those utilities that were natural monopolies, but we vastly preferred ethical competition in other lines. This would decentralize both ownership and control, lessen the danger of economic and political tyranny, and at the same time give a greater stimulus to effort and invention than either private or government monopoly offered. I cannot remember that many of the "market economists" or politicians took a similar point of view. They were quiet on these subjects.

In the Senate in my time Estes Kefauver was perhaps the most effective champion of free enterprise. His House counterparts were Emanuel Celler and Wright Patman.

The Basing Point System

ONE OF THE FIRST measures that came before the Senate when I was a member was the so-called "basing point system." This was the prevailing practice in many heavy industries, such as steel, cement, copper, tin, and in others such as corn products. Under it, a basing point—Pittsburgh for example—would be chosen. Prices over the country would then be fixed at the market price there plus the freight rate from Pittsburgh to the place in question. This was done regardless of where the article was actually produced or the freight actually paid. Thus, if a company in City X, located 500 miles west of Pittsburgh, wanted to sell in its own city, it would charge the Pittsburgh price plus phantom freight costs from Pitts-

---

* As exceptions, Cyrus Eaton and Harry Stuart urged that the bond issues of publicly regulated companies, such as railroads and utilities, should be sold under competitive bidding, instead of being given to favored underwriters through private negotiation.

† I was strongly influenced by Joan Robinson's *The Economics of Imperfect Competition*. She was one of Keynes's favorite pupils, but I think she was on sounder ground than Keynes in his *The General Theory of Employment, Interest, and Money*. After nearly forty years I still think Mrs. Robinson's book was the best in my generation. I do not agree with some of her later positions, but in this work she was superb.

burgh to X. If these were $80 plus $20 respectively, or $100, and if the firm sold to a city, Y, halfway between X and Pittsburgh, the delivered price would be the Pittsburgh price of $80 plus a freight charge of $10. This would make the delivered price $10 less than sales in the home city. Furthermore, the producer would have to pay the eastward freight from X to Y, or $10 more, and hence would net only $80.

This was in fact a delivered price system, in which buyers were not allowed to purchase at the mill, and then pay actual freight costs themselves, but had to accept delivery with the price fixed at an artificially selected basing point plus freight from it to a given place, regardless of where the goods were produced or the freight paid. It was a handy instrument for monopoly control of price. In steel, the United States Steel Corporation would lead off by quoting its price in Pittsburgh. Then all companies in the agreement would take this price and, applying the freight charges from the rate books, would arrive at a uniform price in a given city regardless of where the product was produced or under what costs and irrespective of the freight actually paid. Prices in a given city were identical, although varying between cities. If a company got out of line and charged less, it was subject to reprisals and "discipline." The result was the abolition of price competition. Not only did consumers suffer, but also the development of regional producers in the South, West, and New England, who were denied the advantages of their location, was held back.

I had become acquainted with this system during the early and middle 1920's, when the Middle West was exercised over what it called "Pittsburgh plus." Once, I had spent an enthralling evening listening to John R. Commons analyze its full import. A quarter of a century later, in the United States Senate, I witnessed an effort to legitimize the basing point system. In a series of decisions, the Supreme Court had declared it to be a violation of the antitrust laws, but the big basing point industries were trying to overturn these decisions. As I entered the battle I was happy to find an able ally in Russell Long, who had just been elected to the Senate at the age of thirty. He had the antimonopoly sentiments of his father, Huey, and I found him to be a kindred soul on at least this issue.

In 1924, the Federal Trade Commission had ruled that the Pittsburgh-plus system was a violation of the antitrust statutes. Then the steel industry substituted a multiple basing point system for the single basing point of Pittsburgh. This reduced, but did not eliminate, the phantom freight charged to buyers, who could still be denied the chance to buy at the gates of the producing plants or of accepting shipments billed to them f.o.b. (free on board), when they would pay for the freight themselves. While the multiple basing point system introduced complexities, prices could still be fixed by the leader for the several basing points. Each firm had a book of freight rates and quoted prices in a community at the base price for that zone plus the freight from the zonal basing point to the place of purchase. Firms that got out of line and charged less in a given city could be subjected to price competition by the big firms and either crippled or put out of business. The system was a masquerade for monopoly. Successive decisions by the Supreme Court finally outlawed both the single and multiple systems in cement, glucose, and steel conduits.

Then in the summer of 1948 the basing point industries began their campaign for legislation to reverse these decisions and legitimize the practice. Senators Frank Myers, of Pennsylvania, and Herbert R. O'Conor, of Maryland, tried to compromise by introducing a bill that would have suspended the Supreme Court decisions for two years and made the practice legal during that period. Long and I, assisted by Langer and Kefauver, vigorously objected. Then, on June 1, O'Mahoney, hitherto a strong antitrust advocate, sprang a great surprise. In effect, he proposed a permanent change in the antitrust law which would legalize delivered prices under virtually all conditions. There was a brief and confused debate of less than an hour on this substitute bill, which O'Mahoney represented as being antitrust, and there was little or no chance to scrutinize the proposal, which contained much high-sounding language. In view of O'Mahoney's previous excellent antitrust record, we were reluctant to challenge him. Without a roll call, we allowed the bill to be passed by a voice vote.*

After we had the chance to study it, we regretted our negligence. Long decided that we should move to reconsider the vote, which we did in early August. We were careful not to attack O'Mahoney's motives; in fact, we eulogized him. But we pointed out that his bill did put the stamp of sanctity on the full basing point system. I cited the example of the Tucumcari dam in New Mexico, for which eleven cement companies had submitted sealed and allegedly competitive bids which were identical to the sixth decimal place. Regardless of where the cement was produced or the cost of production, the delivered price quoted by every company was $3.286854 for each barrel. That was the sum of the basic price plus the freight from one place. An eminent mathematician certified that the chance that such a coincidence was a natural occurrence was one out of a quintillion, or one followed by eighteen zeros. I also quoted figures from my own state. There, in 1947, the Highway Department had asked for bids on 50,000 barrels of cement to be delivered inside each of the 102 counties in the state. Eight firms submitted identical bids inside each of the counties. In other words, there were 816 identical bids. I asked the head of the mathematics department at Haverford College what chance there was that this was accidental. He replied that it would be more diffi-

---

* I have never been able to determine the motives for O'Mahoney's surprising change of position. His friend John D. Clark, of the Council of Economic Advisers, made the same shift. I think it accounted in part for O'Mahoney's later attitude toward me.

cult "than picking out at random a single predetermined electron in the total universe"! Despite our struggle, our motion to reconsider the bill was defeated, 49 to 28. A great many Senators had followed the time-honored practice of always speaking against monopoly but always voting for it.

The bill then went to a conference committee. The result was an even worse bill. Instead of giving the government and the courts the opportunity to declare price practices illegal if they could presumably lead to a consent agreement, the bill's language was changed so that positive proof would have to be supplied in advance showing that the practice would result in such combinations and conspiracies. Since this would have been almost impossible, I urged that we adopt instead Justice Holmes's standard of probable effects rather than presumed intent.

On October 15, toward the end of the session, when we were meeting in the crowded and historic Old Senate Chamber, Long told me that an attempt would probably be made to railroad the conference report through. As a Southerner, he fraternized with the Establishment and was generally informed as to what was in the wind. There was a good deal of disorder in the chamber when we went up to confer with the presiding officer, Senator McCarran. We stood below and on either side of him. Very softly and quickly he brought up the conference report and then declared it had been agreed to. Although standing next to him, I could not hear what had been said, nor could Long, but, being suspicious, I shouted out, "What motion did we vote on just now?" The presiding officer said, "The question was on agreeing to the conference report." I asked for the yeas and nays, because we had not been informed as to what the vote was about. The President Pro Tem tried to prevent this by insisting that the decision had already been made. Long and I began to sputter, while Scott Lucas, the majority leader, almost immediately said, "Let us be a little fair about this situation. After all, this report went through pretty fast." With their tactics exposed, the proponents backed down and moved to reconsider. Debate was fixed for October 17. At that time, Long and I led off. I finally moved to postpone further action until January 20, 1950. A motion to table this motion was defeated by a tie vote, and the bill went over to the date I had suggested. Thus the attempt to slip the bill through boomeranged.

When debate was resumed in January, we drove home added weaknesses in the conference report, although it was finally adopted by a vote of 42 to 27. But the public was making up its mind in our favor. We were pleased, but not surprised, when President Truman vetoed the bill on June 16. In view of the votes in both House and Senate, the sponsors gave up hope and made no effort to override his veto. They knew they could not get the necessary two-thirds. We had prevented the effort to legalize the basing point system and to reverse the courts. The future would depend on the degree to which the Federal Trade Commission and the Department of Justice continued to enforce the law. Since these battles are never finally won, it would be a continuing struggle.

Resale Price Maintenance or Vertical Price-Fixing

IN THE SPRING OF 1952 word spread that the Maguire bill, which had passed the House, would be approved by the Senate. This was a measure that allowed the producer of a trade-marked or branded product to fix the price at which it was to be sold at retail, and that made it illegal for any retailer to sell such a product for less. It gave federal legal enforcement for private price-fixing. Upon agreement of the producer with one or more retailers, the price fixed became binding on all retailers within a state. The price would have the force of law whether or not a retailer had himself signed the agreement.

The chief public sponsors of the act were the independent druggists. They complained that the big drugstore chains sometimes sold as "loss leaders" well-known branded or trade-marked products. The cut-rate prices were well advertised and drew large numbers of people into the chain stores, where they usually bought other articles, upon which the chains made a big profit. In turn, the independents said, they were forced to lower their prices on the branded products, with the result that their survival was threatened. They demanded legal protection not only providing that the producers of branded goods be allowed to name the retail price at which the goods were to be sold, but also making the national government the agent to see to it that these price schedules were enforced. Most states already had similar laws, but they were somewhat ineffective because they could not cover out-of-state shipments, which were increasing.

There were interesting side lights on these practices and on the Maguire bill itself. Some drug firms packaged an unbranded or differently branded product almost identical to their well-known branded one, which would sell at a lower price to chain and cut-rate stores. Yet they insisted that the standard retailers continue to sell the branded product at the higher fixed price. This meant double-crossing their own distributors in order to reach a lower-income market. But on their advertised brands, selling to more prosperous customers, the higher price was charged. In this way the monopoly advantages of a class price on advertised products were realized. Behind the retail druggists were the drug wholesalers and drug manufacturers. They feared that if a price war on the trade-marked goods got under way at the retail level, then they would be put under heavy pressure from the retailers to lower their prices. To protect themselves, they felt it important to suppress price competition among the retailers.

Comparisons of drug prices in neighboring states showed that the state laws had raised prices appreciably. In Missouri, which did not have such a state law, prices on selected products were 12 per cent lower than those across the Mississippi River in Illinois, which did have a pricing law. Identical products cost 20 per cent less in the District of Columbia, which had no law, than in Maryland and Virginia, which did. Evidence given before the House Judiciary Committee had shown that the cost of fixed-price items had increased from 10 to 25 per cent after a previous retail-price-maintenance bill (the Miller-Tydings bill) was passed. That bill had been declared unconstitutional by the Supreme Court on the ground that such an agreement could not be enforced against nonsigners. The Maguire bill was an effort to replace it.

While on the surface the struggle seemed to be confined to the drug trade, it soon became clear that the liquor and possibly the tobacco interests were involved in the price wars and wanted protection, too. Some retail bookstores and publications were curiously allied, because they resented the price-cutting of some department stores on certain best sellers, such as *Anthony Adverse* and *Gone With the Wind*. But the retail druggists were kept in the forefront and made an emotional appeal that the aim of the Maguire bill was only to protect small business from the unfair competition of the huge retail chains and stores. Since drugstores had largely succeeded the general stores of my boyhood as centers of neighborhood conversation and gossip, the druggists had a political influence out of all proportion to their numbers.

Some of my political friends and allies believed sincerely in their arguments. Hubert Humphrey's father had run a drugstore in Huron, South Dakota, and Hubert was himself a registered pharmacist. He had seen his father nearly put out of business by a chain drugstore on a neighboring corner. He remembered his whole family on the verge of ruin, and he wanted to put greater security underneath the hard-pressed retailers. To those of us who deplored the movement to decrease competition and increase prices, the supporters of the Maguire bill had a ready answer. There would still be competition between products where comparative prices were a factor. Two products might be largely identical, but the one with the lower price would get the business. Thus the consumer would be protected.

This defense ignored the purpose of the sponsors of nationally advertised and branded products. Their object was to lift these articles out of price competition by insisting on their alleged uniqueness. The economist E. H. Chamberlin had long since pointed this out. Two headache powders might be almost identical, but their sponsors insisted in the newspapers and over the airwaves that each was uniquely beneficial. The effort was made to attract a wide clientele demanding a given product, regardless of its price. The Maguire bill would prevent the consumer from being swayed by such motives as thrift. With faith in real competition, I had always reacted unfavorably to price-maintenance plans, and was especially opposed to the government's role as an enforcing agent. I found myself swamped by the sophistry of professors of marketing and business who became willing exponents of industry's point of view. Those in favor of the market as the sole determinant of prices kept relatively silent.

After the Maguire bill had passed the House, a drive began for Senate passage. The bill was on my desk late one afternoon, and the more I learned about its history, the more I marveled. If the Committee on Interstate and Foreign Commerce had held any hearings, this was not evident, for they had sent it to the Senate without a report.

Shortly after the dinner hour on July 1, Vice President Barkley, who generally was an impartial presiding officer, took the chair with a determined look, banged his gavel, and announced that H.R. 5767 (the Maguire bill) was the order of business. I expected that Edwin C. Johnson, of Colorado, the chairman of the committee, would take the floor and explain the bill, but he sat silent. Barkley, like Rayburn, was a fast man with his gavel, and he had started to shout "Without objection, the bill is passed" when I jumped to my feet.

"Mr. President," I shouted back, "will there be no discussion of this bill? Is it to go through with supersonic speed?" There was no answer. "Where is the published record of the hearings?" I then asked. Still no answer. "Will someone tell us what the bill is about and what it does," I insisted. Ed Johnson sat silent. Trying to keep cool, I pointed out that we were faced with a most unusual and improper proceeding. We were being asked to pass a bill on which no hearings had been held and no report made and which no one wanted to explain. "Well, Mr. President," I summed up, "if its sponsors won't tell the Senate what this bill is about, I shall have to do so. I will first explain what its contents are, and if I make any errors in doing so, I hope its backers will correct me." I spent the next few minutes explaining the bill, and at the conclusion nobody rose to correct me.

"Now, let me tell you why I think the bill is a bad one." I then launched into a discussion of its probable effect on prices and how it put the government in the position of enforcing, rather than opposing, monopoly. I pointed out from testimony given before the House committee that the selling price of 208 articles subject to retail-price maintenance came to $945 in the forty-five states that had permission laws, but came to only $741 in the four jurisdictions that did not have them (Texas, Vermont, Missouri, the District of Columbia). I thought it a fair conclusion to say that the state laws had cost consumers around 17 per cent on the items covered. *Fortune,* an organ for businessmen rather than consumers, had estimated that three-quarters of a billion dollars a year was at stake.

I offered a compromise outlawing "loss leaders" where the retail price was fixed lower than the wholesale, and even went so far as to permit a small retail markup, not to exceed 6 per cent. This last concession was probably a philosophical error, and I understand that certain economists who sat quietly on the side lines during the battle have properly taken me to task for it. I was fighting alone, with my back to the wall, against the bipartisan Senate Establishment and was trying to prevent big and un-needed markups from being put into effect. My motion was defeated, 69 to 12.

All concessions were spurned, and when the roll was called on the Maguire bill, it was passed by a vote of 64 to 16. One of its strong support-ers told me afterward that I was right. He wanted to vote against the bill but had already committed himself and could not break his word. I was also right, he said, about the extraordinary proceedings. In his long expe-rience he had never seen anything like this. I thanked him and thought of Tennyson's line in *Idylls of the King* of how ". . . faith unfaithful kept him falsely true."

Congress soon adjourned for the conventions, and during the two weeks before that I went on a speaking trip through southern Illinois in blistering heat. The retail druggists were waiting for me, and at Harris-burg the leading town druggist nearly broke up an outdoor meeting with a bitter assault on my opposition to the Maguire bill. I tried to defend myself, and I suppose this was just the sort of issue that should be threshed out before the voters. But the heat and the strain of the trip on top of a long hard session caused me to enter the Chicago convention in a state of near exhaustion, which led to some unfortunate consequences.

The country was saved from the effects of the Maguire Act by the Supreme Court, which stepped in to declare it unconstitutional, and thus helped to protect competition from those who in its name would have weakened it still further. Perhaps the fight we made gave the Court added courage and insight. By slowing down the progress of retail-price mainte-nance, we helped to maintain competition.

Branch Banking, Chain Banking, and Bank Holding Companies

THERE CANNOT BE a competitive industrial system if finance is closely concentrated. The financial monoliths in the U.S. had wanted to deal with as few industrial counterparts as possible. J. P. Morgan & Com-pany had therefore been the organizing promoter of the U.S. Steel Corpo-ration and was responsible for many other mergers in the period from 1900 to 1912 that aimed to substitute monopoly for competition.

On coming to the Senate, I found that the Clayton Anti-Trust Act of 1914 had been held not to apply to banks and bank mergers, and that financial concentration was proceeding apace. When I had lectured at Berkeley during the summer of 1923, the Bank of Italy already dominated the banking business of the state. By now it had changed its name to Bank of America and had spread into a controlling position in several of the Western states. There were two great banking chains, based in Minneapolis, dominating the Northwest, while the Marine-Midland chain was increasingly taking over the banking business in upstate New York. In states that permitted branch banking, the big banks were growing rapidly, and in a number of large cities two or three of them controlled from 60 to 65 per cent of commercial loans.

As a student I had of course read Walter Bagehot's *Lombard Street,* a classic on the English banking system of the third quarter of the nineteenth century. In it, Bagehot had described at great length the role of the "country" or "provincial" bankers, who made most of the actual loans and who sent their paper on to London to be discounted. I had identified many of these country bankers, including the Gilletts and Hoares, as being coreligionists of mine, but when I spent the summer of 1928 in England I found that the independent country bankers had vanished. Currently, the banking business of England and Wales was in the hands of five giant banks (Barclays, Lloyds, National Provincial, London, and Westminster), each of which had a multitude of branches. They had absorbed the independent bankers, the most important of whom had gone on the boards of the "Big Five," and many of the old Quaker families had now become communicants of the Established Church.

I also discovered that England, the country where competition had been extolled by its economists from Adam Smith to Alfred Marshall, was in practice dominated by monopolies and by a relatively few big companies. Imperial Chemicals ruled that industry. Three companies, soon reduced to two, controlled cocoa and candy. Liquor was in the hands of a few giants. Tobacco was a monopoly of two companies. Keynes and others were busy organizing cartels for textiles and steel—measures that, I think, lengthened and intensified the depression from which Britain suffered for nearly two decades. The financial concentration helped to make possible the concentration of all industry.

Years later I asked a prominent English economist who believed that trade unions and government, rather than employers, were responsible for monopoly practices how it was that the concentration of banking had occurred without public action or even protest. With a slightly apologetic air, he replied that it had all happened so quietly that they did not know it was happening until they awoke about 1920 to find only the Big Five.

Then I looked north to Canada, where branch banking was permitted and where two great banks, the Bank of Montreal and the Bank of Canada, controlled financial affairs. I found a monograph by an anonymous group of Canadian economists and publicists who pointed out that this had been accompanied by a corresponding concentration in industry.

I decided that I did not favor branch banking, or chain banking, where one group controlled a chain of separate banks through a given corporation or by any form of holding company. I also opposed bank mergers where these would significantly reduce competition. The one exception was where one bank was losing heavily and its failure would throw a great burden on its depositors and the community or upon the Federal Deposit Insurance Corporation.

Since Celler and Patman, in the House, and Kefauver, in the Senate, shared much the same views, we had an informal partnership in efforts to control branch and chain banking. We were helped by the Independent Bankers Association, whose members were struggling to survive in the face of the movement toward concentration. On these issues we waged almost continuous battles for many years inside the Banking and Currency Committee. We were always finding new infringements and trying to plug holes in the ship of competition. A. Willis Robertson, of Virginia, a high-ranking Democrat, was nearly always against us, as were most of the Republicans except the generous-spirited Tobey. Our liberal group was stronger here than on most committees, though, and we frequently carried our points.

After a series of struggles, we finally brought banking, bank mergers, and chain banking under the antitrust laws, by an act that gave to the Department of Justice the right to declare mergers and chains illegal and to obtain orders for their dissolution. Kefauver, Patman, and Celler deserve great credit for this. This law has already been of some help and if faithfully administered may do even more.

Between the time of its passage and its going into effect, however, two chains arranged some frantic acquisitions, so that we were faced with unpleasant accomplished facts. We were also taken in by a fellow Senator who urged us not to outlaw one-bank holding companies. We were told by him that it would apply only to the Du Pont trust in Florida, which was devoted to charity. Too late we found this was not true. Nor did we foresee that a bank, by becoming a holding company, could control various businesses and thus commingle its functions. Presumably, banking facilities should not be financially interested in the companies or ventures to which they made loans; they should not have this conflict of interest. But failing to foresee this, and having won the major point, we conceded far too much to the pleadings of those whom we thought we had overcome. Now, years afterward, bank holding companies have become a major issue.

Competition and the Militarized State

As MILITARY EXPENDITURES increased, the reality of the military-industrial complex was heightened. The big companies continued to get most of the government contracts. In the field of heavy weapons they were perhaps the best qualified. But, along with others, I tried to protect the little firms where possible. We had set up Small Business committees in both House and Senate, which would take up complaints of discrimination and occasionally be able to correct them. The more we could get truly competitive bidding, the greater the competition would be. In some cases we succeeded in obtaining compulsory set-asides for small business.

In general we felt we were swimming against the tide, because the procurement officers liked to deal with the giants. It was not only easier, but also more comradely, since they knew that the representatives of industry were often former colleagues and superiors.

Remembering how the big German industries had swung in behind the Nazis, forming an alliance from 1932 to 1945, I recognized some of the dangers in this. In a brutal world, with a police state as our avowed enemy, we had to be armed, but we should not accept monopoly as an inevitable accompaniment.

Toward a Breaking-up of the Giants

In OUR STRUGGLE to preserve competition, we seemed always on the defensive. The forces of monopoly were forever attacking, while we were trying desperately to hold what we had. It was not an inspiring contest. Thanks to President Truman and the Supreme Court, we had been saved twice. But it was unsafe to rely on them. The Court might change, and a servant of big business might become President. I wanted to move forward in obtaining more competition, and not merely prevent takeovers.

Obviously one way was to compel some of the giant companies to divest themselves of subsidiaries or actually to be subdivided, as the Supreme Court had done with the Standard Oil Company in 1911, when it was split into a series of somewhat independent companies. Around 1960 I launched a proposal that General Motors and U.S. Steel should also be subdivided into smaller companies, although each should be large enough not to lose the economics of large-scale production within a plant. In the case of General Motors, the separate corporate units would be the major makes of automobiles—Chevrolet, Buick, Oldsmobile, Cadillac, et cetera. The company could also have the same suppliers, if these were devoted only to furnishing parts and basic materials. The advantages of vertical combination and of the integration of production would thus remain. Yet the combination of horizontal units, turning out more or less the same product, when they had a total number of employees exceeding a given number would be banned. In this book *The Limitist,* Fred Raymond, father of my first secretary, Jeanette, had suggested this.

Daniel De Simone, in his able study of inventions, showed that small and medium-size businesses tended to be more inventive than the giants. The latter were apt to be complacent and not given to innovations. The development of the basic oxygen furnace and continuous casting in the steel industry, for example, came not from U.S. Steel, but from a relatively small mill in Linz, Austria.

The leadership was too often divorced from production, making the corporate bureaucracy as topheavy as that of the government. A superintendent of one of the Gary mills of U.S. Steel once told me about an inspection trip made by Myron Taylor, head of the company for many years. After explaining the blast furnaces and other processes, the superintendent said that they would now enter "the pickling mill." "That," exclaimed Taylor, "shows how out of touch I have been in New York. I didn't know we were making pickles." Moments later, when Taylor actually saw the pickling process with molten steel, he did in fact realize how out of touch he had been.

The advantages of the giants were not in the field of production, but, rather, in the field of finance, through an interlocking of personnel in the seats of power. But if finance could be democratized, the medium-sized companies could more than hold their own. Big Steel would do better if split into three or four moderate-sized concerns, than as one giant enterprise. The successors to Myron Taylor would then know what was going on.

This was in harmony with Joan Robinson's conclusions in her pathbreaking *The Economics of Imperfect Competition.* She found from her analysis that the larger the proportion of the output controlled by one company, the greater the fall in price, or in average revenue, caused by an increase in output. The increase in the added total revenue decreased even more rapidly, and the ultimate equilibrium of production was at a lower level if there was concentration of industry, because the reduction in price would affect all the units produced and not merely the last unit. The effects upon both production and employment were more restrictive even if net profits were greater. Decentralization would therefore have an expansive effect on output and the numbers employed.

My proposal for the breakup of the two industrial giants fell on deaf ears. The Supreme Court was the more effective agent when it ordered Du Pont to divest itself of its controlling interest in General Motors. I tried to uphold that decision while helping the public get its fair share of the capital gains.

The nation will sometime have to cope with the problem of size. We need not split an industry into a thousand parts, but some decentralization not only would be more economic but also would encourage diffusion of political power and intellectual innovation. In part these rest on the economic basis of who controls the sources of economic power.

Fostering Co-operatives

FOR over half a century I have supported co-operatives. If well conceived and administered, they help to reconcile the conflict between egoism and altruism. Where they cut costs and sell quality goods, the members help themselves as individuals as well as their fellow members. In a consumers' co-operative, the net profits are distributed according to the relative amounts the members buy; in a marketing co-operative, according to the relative amounts each member sells. Unlike corporations, control is exercised by those who use the service, rather than by the owners. So it is in the interests of everyone that a co-operative should succeed, since all will share in the success.*

I was a humble participant in the formation of the Cooperative League of the U.S.A., and in the early 1930's my wife and I helped to organize a consumers' co-operative in our community of Hyde Park. Emily served on its board for many years. After making many mistakes, it settled down under able management and today has over 13,000 members and does a business of more than $7 million a year. The Berkeley Cooperative is three times as large, and there is a scattering of similar co-operatives in the fields of health and consumer goods. But co-operative grocery stores have not grown as we had hoped and expected in the days of our youth. The chain stores have beaten them.

Co-operation is doing better in housing and in various other fields. These are: the rural electrical co-operatives (REA's) together with the telephone co-operatives, of which there are over a thousand, with 5½ million members; the credit unions, which were originally fostered by a noble philanthropist, E. A. Filene, and which have now grown so that they have 20 million members organized in over 23,000 units and with $12 billion of assets; and the farm marketing co-operatives, which sell about $15 billion of products a year and which in 1967 distributed a half-billion dollars in savings, roughly 30 per cent of the farm sales. All of these have proved

*·I have developed these points at greater length in the Weinstock Lecture, which I gave at the University of California in November, 1968, and which has been published by that institution as *The Protection of Consumers and Investors.*

their worth in the struggle to survive. All have been helped by the government, and all have been violently attacked by private rivals and by economic and political conservatives. In my senatorial career I tried to defend all of them, and indeed all forms of co-operative enterprise.

One battle has been over tax policy. Opponents have sought to tax co-operatives as though they were corporations, with a tax of 52 (and later 48) per cent on net earnings followed by an income tax on amounts distributed to individual members. Powerful economic interests battled for this. With other progressives, I believed this unjust. A co-operative is not a corporation run by owners seeking profits to be divided among stockholders in proportion to the stock held. Instead, it is an organization to serve the users, either consumers or sellers. It is controlled by them and financed by their savings. Voting is not in proportion to the stock held, but to the degree to which the services are used. The corporate tax should therefore not be applied to the savings of the co-operatives. When distributed, they should be taxed as income to the individuals. I was willing to have the corporate tax, or at least the capital-gains tax, applied to savings that were neither distributed nor invested in a general account, however. After a series of hard fights, both within and without the Finance Committee, this, in the main, was done, The answer may not be perfect, but it is on the right road.

Up to 1940, county agents helped organize the co-operative marketing organizations, which today operate mostly by themselves. The farm co-operative credit agencies, originally financed and run by the government, are now being bought out and managed by the farmers themselves.

In 1933 I had helped to bring Morris L. Cooke and Harold Ickes together, and they had worked out a plan for co-operatives to handle the distribution of electrical power to farmers in the countryside. The private power companies had balked at going into this field because of the scattered nature of the farms and the low ratio of connections and power consumed per mile of line. Power was not being brought to the farms, and a heavy burden of toil therefore rested upon the farmers and their families, with the result that farm women soon lost the roses in their cheeks. Instead of wanting the government to do either nothing or everything, Ickes and Cooke decided that it should follow the intermediate policy of helping to organize distributive co-operatives and to advance capital for the necessary lines and equipment. This capital, advanced originally by the federal government, was later to be repaid, and the interest rate was to be kept low.

Elsewhere the REA's bought power generated by the private companies at agreed rates. In the case of the Tennessee Valley and the Pacific Northwest, generating and transmission facilities were provided under the same general provisions, but with varying interest rates. As I journeyed over Illinois it was heartening to find the REA's flourishing in the southern and western parts of the state, although in the north the private companies were wise enough to venture out into the country themselves. Although the REA's were still being fought by the private power interests, I welcomed the opportunity to defend them. I helped obtain loans for generating and transmission purposes, to make them more independent of the private companies. It was a great satisfaction to see a modern power plant develop in Little Egypt, which, utilizing the coal of the region, brought low-cost power to hard-pressed farmers and rural folk. In the process, another lake was created, which added to the recreational opportunities of the region. In western Illinois the REA co-operatives have launched a central power plant on the Illinois River and have connected it with several successful municipal power plants in the central portion of the state.

In one respect the REA's were apparently subsidized. They were charged only 2 per cent interest. This was always below the rate on the long-term borrowings of the federal government, although for some years it was slightly above the combined rate on short- and long-term borrowings. But after 1950, as the short-term rate rose, it was much below the combined rate, and the difference was definitely a subsidy. This excited the conservatives, and there were periodic efforts to increase the interest rate on the loans to the REA's. Senator Frank Lausche, of Ohio, the northern Harry Byrd, moved in the early 1960's to increase it to the rate on long-term government bonds. I took him on, saying that while it was a subsidy in one sense, it had been granted in return for an important consideration, namely, that the REA's would cover the area and bring service to all farms in their territory regardless of their location. Perhaps from an accounting point of view, it might have been better to make this payment in the form of an outright subsidy, but it was a convenient way of extending service to those who needed cheap and available power. It was like the rural free delivery of mail, also carried at a loss and at first attacked after Cleveland had installed it in 1896. This had finally been accepted because it brought to the farming population the advantages that existed in the crowded urban centers where costs of collections and delivery were less. Money accounting was not the only measurement. Bringing isolated farmers mechanical power, including radio, television, and help with their chores, was, from a social point of view, more than worth the cost. Lausche's motion was beaten by a good margin. I did not feel inconsistent.

The government also helped to organize the credit unions, about half of which took out federal charters. They have become a strong force for good and have lessened the exactions of loan sharks. Interest rates are kept low, never above 12 per cent a year, and families are helped to tide over personal emergencies and to make needed purchases that are more than they can manage from current earnings. Self-government is the basic form here, as it is in the other co-operatives. I do not know whether the market economists approve of co-operatives. Certainly they have not been active supporters.

The 160-Acre Limitation on Water to Irrigated Lands

THE HOMESTEAD ACT of Civil War days established the 160-acre family farm as the dominant agricultural unit in the Middle West. This applied both east and west of the Mississippi River. This act, for which Lincoln and the Republican party deserve full credit, was admirably adapted to a farm economy where horsepower and human labor were the predominant forms of energy. The work on a farm of this size could best be done by a family group consisting of the farmer and his sons as outside laborers, while the women of the family worked equally hard on the inside. The whole stimulus was upon individual initiative, hard work, and family solidarity. This helped form the farm ethic, which dominated the agricultural sections of the country for so many years. Politically it also meant a fundamental loyalty to the Republican party, which had given them the soil and professed to the same principles. City dwellers, whose lives were much more individualistically conducted, were not moved by these values, and their number was swelled by the sons and daughters of the farm families who, attracted by the economic and cultural advantages of urban life, left the farms for the cities. The urban intellectuals, therefore, came to deride the farm culture as "hick," and this theme dominated much of journalistic and literary writing from 1890 on.

But rural values also emphasized government by substantially equal property owners. The farmers disliked seeing a few men accumulate excessive wealth and power, and they were opposed to private monopoly. In 1892, their candidate for the Presidency, General James B. Weaver, received over a million popular votes and twenty-two electoral ballots. The principles of the People's (Populist) party were the direct election of senators, the income tax, public ownership of the railways, and numerous other reforms bitterly denounced at the time, but since largely accepted. Bryan and Altgeld carried their principles into the Democratic party, and La Follette and Norris were Republican embodiments of the same spirit.

But there was one section of the country where the 160-acre farm was not dominant—that was the Southwest, and, in particular, the interior valleys of California. There, huge landed estates were the rule.* These

---

* For other cases of huge landholdings by American corporations, see Mason Gaffney in Daniel M. Holland, *The Assessment of Land Value*, published for the Committee on Taxation, Resources, and Economic Development, Madison: University of Wisconsin Press, 1970, pp. 160–167.

had been created by the Spanish-Mexican governments before the war of 1846–47, and were not disturbed after the United States took over the territory. A large part of the big railroad grants in this area after the Civil War had the same effects. Some idea of the concentration of land ownership of the 4 million acres involved in the joint federal-state San Luis project is given by the following table, whose accuracy was not challenged by our opponents when presented in the Senate:

Owner	Acres Owned	Per Cent of Total
Standard Oil Co.	218,485.6	5.5
Other oil companies	264,678.5	6.6
Kern County Land Co.	348,026.5	8.7
Southern Pacific R.R.*	201,851.7	5.1
Tejon Ranch	168,531.0	4.2
Boston Ranch	37,555.6	.9
U.S. government	192,762.1	4.8
Other private holdings over 1,000 acres for each owner	1,323,821.6	33.1
Private holdings under 1,000 acres, including all state, county, and municipal land	1,240,648.2	31.1

* Given by the U.S. government in return for a promise to build a railroad which was never built.

Over 68 per cent of the land was held by individuals and groups that owned more than a thousand acres.

I had become acquainted with these facts during the 1930's through my friend Paul Taylor, of the University of California, who had become a tireless student of and campaigner on the subject. On a trip to California after my election in 1948, he took me on a three-day journey through the interior San Joaquin Valley from San Francisco to Santa Barbara. There I saw the extraordinary fertility of the soil when given water, as well as the social structure that grew out of large-scale landlordism. I well remember a settlement on the west side of the river that we came into at sundown. It was peopled entirely by Mexican farm laborers who seemed to be single. They were quartered in bunkhouses, which reminded me of the Maine logging camps of my boyhood. They wore rough jackets, high boots, and overalls, which, in California style, were called "Levis." They were spending their leisure in a grogshop, drinking beer and whiskey. There was a general store opposite the saloon, which sold shoddy clothing and a few toilet articles and drugs. That was all there was for a camp of several hundred men. No books or newspapers were in sight. The unpaved street was thick with mud. I was told that this place was typical of life on the big estates. No one knew where the owners lived or what they did.

The next afternoon we crossed the river to the east and came to a typical American town. The main street, with its many stores, had no beauty, but it had variety, enterprise, and cordiality. The people were all well dressed; the men wore clean shirts and neckties, while the women looked immaculate. It was obviously a family town, since there were several hundred single-family dwellings. Most of these were attractive, well painted, and had close-cropped lawns. There were two churches and a school with an adjoining baseball diamond. One building was marked "Library," and we saw youngsters coming out of it with books under their arms. Like the other town, it was based on farming. But, unlike the first, there were no large estates. Farms did not exceed 160 acres, and many, particularly in the orange and lemon groves, were appreciably less. All seemed to be comfortable.

No sharper contrast between the two systems of farming could be found. They told their own story and pointed the moral.

"But how could this be changed?" I asked. The owners of the big estates had, at first sight, legal title, and it would cost too much to buy them out at current prices. Taylor mentioned the Newlands Act and briefly described it. Back in Washington, I looked it up.

At the turn of the century, when the Senate was presumably the rich man's instrument, Francis Newlands, of Nevada, under stimulus from Republican President Theodore Roosevelt, was able to get that body and the House to agree that reclamation water should only be turned on for farms that did not exceed 160 acres. Taylor had told me that the estates would soon want that water. With not more than five inches of rainfall a year, they were getting the needed minimum from pumping the interior pools that lay below the surface of the semiarid land. The water table was, therefore, falling quite rapidly, and the time would come when added water from the Reclamation Bureau, drawn either from the Sierras to the west or from the rain surplus in the north, would be required. Then, in order to apply the Newlands Act, smaller farms would replace the big estates, and southern California would begin to look like the rest of the United States, instead of like Sicily and Latin America. I checked Taylor's figures and statements and found them to be true.

It was ten years before I could put this information to practical use other than to defend the Bureau of Reclamation from the attacks of the land monopolists, and to sound warnings from time to time. Then in 1959 my chance came.

For over twenty years Paul Taylor had faithfully worked at the subject and had early won the support of the AFL, the Veterans of Foreign Wars, the Farmers' Union, the Grange, and the progressive wing of the Democratic party. Events had happened as he had prophesied. The waters of Mount Shasta and the northern Sierras, which had formerly flowed turgidly down the Sacramento River to the Pacific Ocean, were now partially deployed by a series of canals to the parched lands to the south. But the popular ardor for limitation had cooled. The big estates thought it was safe to move and began to work on the leaders of both political parties. The Republicans were their historic allies, but a section of the Democrats, having wearied of unavailing reforms, was now willing to make peace.

One day in the summer of 1959 there suddenly emerged from the Interior Committee a bill to give "home rule" to California in handling the irrigation waters. It was backed by California's two Senators, Tom Kuchel, the Republican, and Clair Engle, the Democrat. They were good men and in general liberal. Those who had fought the old battles for the Bureau of Reclamation had either died or left the Congress. Bob La Follette and Helen Gahagan Douglas were no longer present. Even the memory of the struggles of the 1940's had vanished. Remembering my trip of ten years before, I sprang to arms and telephoned Taylor and men who knew California politics. My suspicions were confirmed. The Newlands Act would be repealed by Section 6A of the new bill, for California's great Central Valley and the big estates would get the water and reap a profit of hundreds of millions and perhaps billions of dollars. Agrarian reform would be prevented.

The debate began, and, under questioning, Engle and Kuchel could not deny that probability. The Senate then began to be interested, and I pushed on to tell the story of the Newlands Act, why it was passed and its importance for the future. The limit of 160 acres was not enough in the high-altitude areas where the growing season was short and the value per acre low. But it was more than ample in the lush lands of the Central Valley, where oranges, lemons, grapes, nuts, lettuce, celery, once given water, would grow in profusion. A family could earn a good living on far less than the acreage limit Congress had imposed in setting up the wheat, corn, and dairy farms of the Middle West. But even here it was an improvement over no limit at all, and once the principle was established, perhaps more democratic methods of assignment of the waters and cultivation could be worked out. Certainly the great Central Valley should not remain or become another Sicily. The Senate, I could see, was impressed, and Wayne Morse joined my group with a powerful and cogent speech. Over on the House side, Albert C. Ullman, the progressive Democrat from eastern Oregon for whom I had campaigned in 1956, and Jeffery Cohelan, from California and a former student of Taylor's, took up the battle and made a strong fight. We could see also that Kuchel and Engle did not like what they were doing.

To everyone's surprise, we won decisively, defeating the repeal on a division vote to eliminate Section 6A. The House, under the leadership of Ullman and Cohelan, acted similarly. We thought that we had certainly defeated the efforts to repeal the 160-acre limitation embodied in the Newlands Act.

But the big landlords would not give up. Having so unexpectedly failed, they now sought the same end administratively. Governor Edmund G. ("Pat") Brown, an otherwise liberal Democrat, proposed that California appropriate a large sum of money to raise the height of the basic dams in the mountains to the east and north, as well as in the valley, and to provide added canals to help carry water to the parched lands in the south of the San Joaquin Valley. The added water would be divided into two parts, federal and state. The Newlands Act might apply to the federal water, but California was to be free not to apply the 160-acre limitation to its. Moreover, he proposed to do this administratively, between the state and the Department of the Interior, and get away from the danger of being balked for a third time by Congress. I am sorry to say that Secretary Udall agreed to this, and his solicitor, Frank Barry, issued an extraordinary opinion, saying that our 1959 action of eliminating Section 6A was not necessarily an affirmation of the 160-acre limitation. One has only to read the debates and the fact of the voice vote to see that this claim was essentially false. The Interior Committee, under the promptings of Kuchel and Engle, declined in 1962 to disapprove the contract, and gave a thin patina of Congressional approval. Morse, Proxmire, and I strongly disagreed. Morse was especially vigorous. We argued that the claimed separation of water into state and federal parts was as false as Solomon's proposed test of the two mothers who each claimed a child. The water was a joint product, and we could not have a state second story unless it rested on a first story already federally built and paid for by the national government, which had spent almost a billion dollars on the project. We argued, I think correctly, that granting a federal subsidy carried with it the right to impose conditions governing the use of the federal monies. Congress had acted under this power by refusing to alter the 160-acre limitation, and until this was done it would apply on federally subsidized projects as well as on those completely paid for by the federal government. With the leadership of both the Republican and Democratic parties in California and Washington supporting the ingenious device of using an administrative ruling by the Secretary of the Interior to overturn Congressional action in the late 1940's and in 1959, and with the extreme legal and political difficulty of penetrating the legal shield that had been thrown around this action, we who favored the continuation of the 160-acre limitation were finally unsuccessful. The Governor of California was coming up for re-election against Richard M. Nixon and did not want the issue raised in his campaign. Those who would benefit materially from limitation were conjectural citizens of the future. Those who would lose by it were powerful supermillionaires in the present. In the conflict the powerful materialists won over the idealists and insubstantial future distributivists. Our forces were, moreover, tired out by the long struggle and discouraged by the final behavior of our leaders.

The whole experience gave me reverence for idealists like Paul Taylor, who with tireless energy has kept up the struggle for a third of a century, and for men like Angus McDonald, of the Farmers' Union, as well as for the humble foot soldiers of the army for the common good. Their personal and political graves have lined the highways of our history. But I must confess I became increasingly disheartened over the inability of many of our leaders to withstand the strains and temptations of political life.

For some years I have hoped that the courts might reverse the executive, as the executive had been used to reverse the Congress. But the expense and difficulties seemed to be too great. Now, however, the legality of exempting the California Water Project from acreage limitation is under challenge in the federal courts. A public-spirited San Francisco clothing manufacturer, Alvin Duskin, aided by public contributions, is financing the challenge, with James D. Lorenz as attorney. With a new cast of characters I hope the practical outcome of the struggle may be reversed.

27

Labor Legislation and
Social Security

My chief goal in domestic affairs was to try to better the conditions of life for the common people of America through sound collective bargaining, improved labor-management relations, an adequate minimum wage, and a better system of social insurance. These were causes for which I had always worked. I had campaigned for them, and most of my support came from voters with like sympathies. Back of them was the desire to use the power of the state on behalf of the weak, the middle class, and those outside unions as well as within them. In the minds of many members of the Establishment in my home state, this was the unforgivable sin, and it created a solid and formidable core of opposition. The advocates of a market economy also condemned such efforts.

Taft-Hartley and Section 14 (b)

I have already described efforts to repeal or modify the Taft-Hartley Act and their failure in 1949 at the hands of the bipartisan coalition. During the rest of my Senate service, my group made periodic attempts to change specific portions of the act, notably Section 14 (b).

The 1935 Wagner Act had tried to protect union workers from being discriminated against, and had provided for collective bargaining if the majority in a bargaining unit so desired. Employers were not then compelled to reach an agreement, but they had to make an honest effort to do so, and to take the negotiating sessions seriously. The Taft-Hartley Act had retained the principle of national rules, but had outlawed the closed shop, where a worker had to be a union member before he could be hired. Even if an employer approved of the closed shop, he could not sign an agreement to provide for it.

The union shop, under which the employer could hire anyone he wished, although the worker had to join the union within a given time, removed many of the objections made to the closed shop. It could not, for example, effect a labor monopoly, since the employer retained control over the hiring process. But Taft-Hartley threw many barriers in the way of the unions. At first it required that a majority of the workers, not merely a majority of those voting, must vote for the union shop. This meant that all those who did not vote were counted as voting "No." This threw the full weight of the nonvoters against collective bargaining, thus conflicting with democratic procedures. In practice it was, therefore, both unfair and ineffective, and was ultimately eliminated.

But there was no such luck with Section 14 (b). This gave to the states the legal right to declare the union shop illegal even if a majority of the workers wanted it and the employer agreed to accept it. In other words, the principle of national regulation was used to outlaw the closed shop even if the employers and the states were favorable. But the states were given the power to outlaw the union shop even though the workers and employers were both favorable to such an arrangement.

All but one of the twelve Southern states took advantage of this option to make the union shop illegal, as did a few states west of the Mississippi, making a total of nineteen. Since the unions found it hard to get a foot-hold in these states, they could not establish themselves in such industries as textiles, tobacco, and chemicals. As a result, the wage scales were lower there than in the rest of the country. But the goods produced in these states competed with those produced elsewhere under union-shop and higher-wage conditions. This situation operated as a restraining force upon both unionism and Northern wage scales.

By their sponsors, these state regulations were called "right-to-work" laws, although they gave no one the effective right to work. What they did was to make it more possible for antiunion employers to prevent the unions from being effective and to permit the "free riders" amongst the workers to accept the benefits of union organization without making any contribution to the group that protected them. Most of those refusing to be bound by a majority vote for union representation probably did so because they did not want to pay union dues or accept the responsibilities of union membership. And yet here and there were genuine conscientious objectors to union membership and associated activity, especially among members of German pietistic sects such as the Mennonites, the Amish, some branches of the Brethren, and the Adventists.

Labor was constantly thrown on the defensive by state proposals to pass right-to-work laws. This absorbed much energy and prevented other progress. The leaders of most state Republican parties and their business backers favored these laws. This sometimes produced unexpected results. When the Ohio Republican party endorsed a referendum proposal for such a law in 1958, it helped to defeat the Republican Senator, John Bricker, and to elect peppery Stephen Young.

The steelworkers in Gary and the two big clothing unions worked out an arrangement that largely reconciled the genuine considerations on both sides. This became known as the "agency shop." The unions did not require membership of those who for religious or genuinely ethical motives could not bring themselves to join. But in order to prevent this privilege from being abused, it was provided that the nonmembers should pay an amount equal to the union dues either to the union itself or to some mutually approved charity. There was also an understanding, not always stated, that in the event of a strike, the nonmember was not to scab on his associates. The whole arrangement was similar to the one that developed for religious and ethical objectors to military service. The principle of alternate service became the test of sincerity.

It was not a perfect solution. Probably no complete reconciliation is possible. But it was about as close as one could come in an imperfect world. This proviso was adopted in our proposals for amendment of Taft-Hartley, but it did not appreciably weaken the opposition to the repeal of Section 14 (b). Nor did it assuage the scruples of those law firms who represented employers and yet were also strong for an "integrated bar," or a closed shop for lawyers, under which all attorneys had to be members of the private bar association. That was a different story.

Try as we might, we were not able to get a majority to repeal 14 (b). The antiunion elements for their part could not get a majority in additional states to pass further right-to-work laws. The political guerrilla warfare therefore sputtered to a temporary, informal truce.

Efforts to change the general provisions governing national-emergency strikes have also failed. Although few were satisfied with the "cooling-off" provisions of the law, it was impossible to get a majority to agree to any substitute except to deal with threatened railway strikes as they came up.

The Minimum Wage

THE MINIMUM WAGE was the second great goal of industrial reformers. Where there was an oversupply of labor, competition often pulled wages down below the level of a decent standard of living. Other nations, notably Australia and New Zealand, had solved this problem by putting a legal floor under wages, and without any injury to their national productivity. Now we were reinforced by another example. Under the dynamic leadership of David Lloyd George and young Winston Churchill, in 1910–11 Great Britain finally repudiated the market theory of wages and set up its own legal minimum standard.

The National Consumers' League, under Florence Kelley, took the lead in advocating both minimum wages for women and ceilings on the hours they could normally work. The AFL, under Samuel Gompers, was at first opposed to any such action by the government and wanted to have these matters handled by collective bargaining between unions and employers. The unions, however, were then extremely weak, having a membership of only 2½ million, and were primarily confined to the building and printing trades, mining, and railroading. They scarcely touched the women and the unskilled, who, of course, were also the lowest paid.

A tacit agreement was finally worked out between the Consumers' League and the AFL. The League would work for protective legislation for women only. The AFL, in turn, would not oppose the efforts of the League, and, in fact, would permit individual leaders and officials to support its proposals. Since nearly everyone believed that a national minimum-wage law would be declared unconstitutional by the Supreme Court, the League confined itself to pushing a series of state laws.

Back in 1918 when I was teaching in Oregon, I had testified to the need for a higher minimum wage. This had been set years earlier at eighteen cents an hour, or $8.64 for a forty-eight-hour week. Living costs certainly justified the raise, but the war had turned the formerly progressive state into a conservative one. The retail merchants demanded that I be fired or muzzled, and I know they were greatly relieved when I left Reed College in the fall.

I was also active in Illinois on behalf of the minimum wage, and spoke for it in 1924 before the legislature. Illinois did not have such a law, and my statement roused the opposition of the employers, who besieged the university to stop me.

My investigations in Oregon had revealed that the vast majority of workers earned less than the $8.64 a week that was presumably their minimum. This was due to "short time." So my attention was drawn to "unemployment within employment," an important and neglected subject. To compensate for the higher hourly rates set by the act, many employers decreased working hours. This was especially true of laundries.

The varying state laws caused competition between the states. This did not apply in the case of services, but it most certainly did in manufacturing. On the Pacific Coast there was an effort to fix a regional minimum. But this was not possible in the East and Middle West, while in the South the very idea of state protection for women was rank heresy. Southern chivalry did not go that far.

In 1923 the Supreme Court used, in *Adkins* v. *Children's Hospital,* the "due process" clause of the Fourteenth Amendment to declare a minimum-wage law unconstitutional. After Roosevelt's sweeping victory in 1936, the New Deal determined, therefore, to come to grips with the Court. When FDR's effort to enlarge it was defeated, the moderates felt it wise to compromise. With changes in its composition, the administration was eventually assured of a friendly Supreme Court. Then, not only the state minimum-wage laws passed the gauntlet, but also the Wagner Act and the Social Security Act.

In 1938 the administration introduced a federal Wages and Hours bill with five main purposes.

1. It would outlaw child labor under the age of sixteen in industries engaged in or affecting interstate commerce. The defeat of the 1920's, with its attempt to outlaw employment in urban industry of children under fourteen, would be retrieved, and by an even higher age for entry. Setting the employable age at sixteen not only was in accord with realistic views of child development, but also would help to assuage the fears of adults about competition for jobs in periods of high unemployment. The act would therefore protect grownups as well as children.

2. It would fix the normal hours of work in a week at forty-eight for both men and women. Where an employer kept his employees longer, he had to pay them time and a half.

3. It would set the minimum wage at twenty-five cents an hour, which would rise to forty cents after five years. Beyond that it was to be raised only by act of Congress, not, as in Australia and New Zealand, by quasi-administrative-judicial tribunals. Congress was by now suspicious of the powers it had given to various commissions, and wanted in the future to keep its hand on the vital question of wages.

4. It would have jurisdiction primarily over industries affecting the flow of interstate commerce, of which manufacturing was the chief. Mining, lumbering, and interstate transportation would also be included. Agriculture and the service trades would be exempt.

5. It would end the old distinction between the sexes; the act would apply to men as well as to women. Much of the opposition of the extreme feminists was thereby removed.

Despite the bitter opposition of most employers, the bill was extremely popular. The Rules Committee of the House, however, refused to let it come before that body, and for a time action seemed to be stymied. Two primary elections, in Florida and Alabama, broke the jam. Claude Pepper was running for the Senate in the former state, and Lister Hill in the latter. Both campaigned on behalf of the Wages and Hours bill, and both won smashing victories. The rules of the House permitted a majority of the members, upon signing a petition, to bring up a bill for action even if the Rules Committee refused. Immediately after the results of the Florida and Alabama primaries became known, there was a stampede to sign the petition, and the necessary 218 signatures were quickly obtained. Soon after, both houses passed the bill into law, and Florence Kelley was finally vindicated.

After the passage of this act, the advocates of the minimum wage paused, and there was no further legislation for a decade. The grossly depressed industries did have to increase their wage scales, leading, in many cases, to the introduction of machinery and increased automation as a means of reducing production costs.

In 1939 the war enormously increased both production and employment. Women were hired in great numbers. After the entrance of the U.S. into the war, unemployment virtually disappeared. No real effort was made to increase the forty-cent minimum, which went into effect in 1944. Although the Democrats held the Presidency and, hence, the administrative apparatus, the Republicans increased their strength in Congress, and in 1946 actually took control of both houses. With their allies from the South, they made it impossible to increase the minimum.

Victory in 1948 changed the picture, and Taft, as I have said, determined to compromise, rather than resist. The forty-cent minimum was hopelessly obsolete in view of the war and postwar increases in both wages and the cost of living. The groups behind Taft were reluctantly ready to yield some ground in the light of what had happened, both economically and politically.

I sat in on the committee that ratified the treaty of peace in this fight. Being a newcomer, I did not fully grasp the tactics of either side. Pepper, the Democratic spokesman and chief negotiator, and Taft alternately attacked each other for their past and then blandly sugared each other with mutual pledges about the future. I am sure an agreement had already been reached off stage. When the Democrats recommended an increase to seventy-five cents an hour, there was almost no objection. We wanted to conciliate the South and to prevent a breakaway, so we agreed not to expand coverage, and, indeed, slightly curtailed it, notably in the field of cotton presses.

The years passed, and both the cost of living and the productivity of labor increased. Wages and fringe benefits rose markedly. It was inevitable that the minimum wage would rise with them. With the Republican victory in 1952, however, this was delayed. But when the Democrats took back control of Congress in 1954, it became a reality. The real question was whether the increase should be to ninety cents or a dollar an hour. The more cautious approach would have been to the former, which, with its increase of 20 per cent, would have covered the increase in both living costs and per-capita productivity. The employers objected loudly that the increase to a dollar would cause a large amount of unemployment and many business failures. I was the swing man on this issue, and I hesitated for many days while anxious labor leaders paced the outside corridors. An able former socialist who had advocated the minimum wage when it was unpopular but who had become a labor manager for a large clothing firm called to warn me that the dollar minimum would throw tens of thousands out of work in the needle trades.

Yet I decided to take the risk. The rate of a dollar an hour would mean only a full-time yearly wage of $2,000 under the prevailing forty-hour week. This was far below the minimum needed for a four-member family. Moreover, the general profits of business were high. My committee raised the minimum to one dollar. We provided, however, for an impartial review of the situation by the Labor Department, so that if it turned out we had made a mistake, Congress would have the chance to rectify it. In order to get the increase we again had to agree not to expand the coverage. I was unhappy about this, and took a pledge that I would give expansion of coverage priority when the next revision of the scale was proposed.

The Department of Labor made what seemed to be an impartial inquiry into the alleged increase of unemployment and found that in most industries it was either nonexistent or minute. The strongest objection to the minimum wage proved, therefore, to be ill-founded up to the one-dollar level.

During our hearings, I made the acquaintance of Luis Muñoz Marín, the elected governor of Puerto Rico and the leader of the Popular Democratic party. He came to Washington to try to persuade us not to fix too high a wage for his island. He was trying, successfully, to lure industry to Puerto Rico by offering tax exemptions and other favors. He wanted a wide differential in the wage rate, a very different policy from that he had advocated when he made his historic campaign for power in a jeep a decade before. The clothing unions, fearful of a flood of cheap Puerto Rican goods, did not want this differential. At first hand, I saw some of the practical problems that even humane imperialism creates for a country with a vastly lower standard of life. I was impressed by Muñoz' sincerity, his desire to help his people, and his realism in scrapping his natural predilection for high wage rates in favor of a high volume of employment, and I finally worked out a reconciliation under which we granted Puerto Rico a differential that was expected to decrease with time as the workers became more skilled.

But I was glad that we did not have another country of that size to which we would have to act as elder brother. Certainly we were most generous to Puerto Rico. We had quietly returned to them the internal tax on rum, which largely financed their Operation Bootstrap, and their citizens and industries did not have to pay American individual or corporate income taxes. This was the work of Rex Tugwell when he was governor of the island. We did not do this in any boastful manner, and few Puerto Ricans or Americans are aware of it. I know of no other country that has been so generous, and I marvel at the strength of the Puerto Rican statehood party, which wants to assume the full burdens of American citizenship. As our "dominion," the Puerto Rican people have had the full advantages of citizenship without any of the accompanying costs. I regret that the full story is still not known, and wish some Puerto Rican would publicly acknowledge it.

After I was transferred to the Finance Committee, in 1956, my direct connection with minimum-wage legislation ceased. As a member of the Senate, however, I voted for the later increases to $1.25 in 1963 and $1.60 in 1966. These were full-time, yearly rates of $2,500 and $3,200. The country was rapidly becoming more prosperous. There was no possibility of quickly converting Congress and the country to the family-allowance system, which I had advocated a generation before, and in the meantime I did not want to deprive the unskilled of the chance to share in some of the gains of a more affluent society. Moreover, coverage was extended for the first time since 1938. In 1963, the larger retail stores and chains were included, and in 1966, hotels and restaurants. The so-called "papa and mama" stores were still excluded, as they should have been. But even the large farms were included in the latter year, with an initial wage of one dollar an hour, which was to increase by ten cents with each year until the general minimum of $1.60 was reached in 1972.

Claims continued that the higher wages were creating unemployment, but again in 1963 were shown to be greatly exaggerated. However, by 1965 a new and puzzling element had entered the picture. Granted that the increased wage did not result in throwing out of work any large number of those already employed, did it bar from employment many of those coming from the farms into the towns and cities, as well as those reaching maturity as a result of the high birth rates of the period from 1945 to 1961? This was not clear from the unemployment statistics, which covered only those "able to work, willing to work, but unable to find suitable employment." Men and women without industrial experience were apparently not included in the eligible working force; nor were those who were so demoralized by past unemployment that they no longer seriously sought a job.

I suspected that many of these "nonpersons" were living uncounted and unprovided for on the fringes of society, and that consequently things were not as rosy as they seemed. The development of street-corner gangs and their turn toward violence increased my suspicions. They were apparently not part of the official labor force, but they were human beings. Where had they come from? Were they part of the 20 million who had been squeezed off the soil during the last quarter of a century and yet had not gained a foothold in industry? Or were they the children of the displaced? By any reckoning, those who were "out of work" were a larger number than those "unemployed." But how much larger? And how could they be brought into the "work force"? I did not know, but my views were confirmed when three trusted employees of the Census Bureau reported in 1967 that the official count of the population of the country was at least 5.7 million less than the real number. And I was not convinced that those not included were merely absent from home when the enumerators called. Rather, it seemed that some of them were Gorkiesque denizens of the lower depths who slept in stations, streets and alleys, hallways, all-night movies, automobiles, and abandoned houses. They were part of the faceless army of nonpersons.

I was preparing to go into these questions in my fourth term and, if the numbers involved proved significant, to seek remedies. One possible way out that I intended to probe was the relatively slight use of the "learner" device, which permitted a newcomer to be paid 15 per cent less than the minimum for six months. This hourly rate of $1.36, rather than $1.60, combined with Joe Clark's grants for training on the job might bring the excluded into the effective labor force. If this was not enough, I was willing to consider public work on useful projects.

Friends told me that my fears were imaginary—the product of an unduly reformist temperament. Perhaps so, but as the history of the criminal class unfolds and resulting costs multiply, I may be proved right, and my remedies the most economical. In any event, my defeat in 1966 put an end to my efforts along this line.

If the structure of the minimum wage could be recast, I think it would be desirable to transfer the wage-fixing powers from Congress to an appointed board. This would permit close oversight and a speedier adjustment to changed conditions than the present spasmodic action. But perhaps there should be at the same time some consolidation of the different regulatory agencies in order to get a greater degree of uniformity between them. The last word on this has certainly not been spoken.

Welfare and Pension Funds

IN 1954 there were rumors of abuses in the investment and management of welfare and pension funds. This type of fringe benefit had greatly increased during the Korean War. Wage rates had been stabilized and largely frozen as a means of keeping prices down, but there were no such restrictions upon fringe benefits. In practice, they were widely adopted to compensate for the increase in the cost of living and in response to the increased power of labor. By 1954 the reserves of these funds amounted to nearly $50 billion. Most of these were built for future pension payments and death benefits. The welfare funds set up to pay sickness and hospital benefits, being annually financed, did not require large reserves and were smaller in size.

Both management and unions were involved in the operation of the pension funds, the former much more than the latter. While abuses were alleged by both sides, those practiced by labor were cruder than those of management. The Republicans began an investigation in 1954, designating Senator Irving Ives to conduct it. They concentrated their inquiries on labor, and had amassed much material by the time they lost control of Congress in November of that year. Lister Hill, the liberal Southerner who was chairman of the Labor and Public Welfare Committee, then appointed me to carry on the study. It would have been wrong to have discontinued Ives's inquiries or to have dropped his staff, which was both honest and competent, so I continued both the investigations and the staff, one of whom, Paul Cotter, a former FBI agent, was exceptionally able and honorable.

We opened up grave abuses in the handling of pension funds of various small unions, including the Allied Industrial Workers and the Laundry Workers', and, while we could not find definite proof of abuses in the funds of the Teamsters, we found suspicious circumstances. It became apparent that the criminal syndicate had taken over control of some of the small unions. It was discouraging to find that employers in these industries had co-operated with the underworld, and that some insurance companies had made pay-offs to get business.

While we did not have time to go into the management of the employer-directed funds, which were the vast majority, it was obvious that there were many weaknesses and possible abuses connected with them, also. For example, few firms provided for a transferable funding of benefits. If a worker left a company by layoff, discharge, or voluntary separation before he became eligible for benefits, he commonly lost all his rights to a pension or retirement benefit. To get these benefits, it was usually required that the worker be sixty-five years of age and that he had been employed by the company for at least fifteen to twenty years. Workers in the upper age brackets were, therefore, heavily penalized. It was even charged that layoffs were staged just before retirement age in order to free the funds from future charges. Huge reserves were being accumulated, sometimes with the open, and sometimes indirect, contributions of the workers, from which only a comparatively small minority would ever have the right to benefit. These funds have continued to grow and are one of the submerged sources of corporate investment. They are primarily under the control and direction of the employers.

I became convinced that in the future we should work along the lines suggested forty years before by Luther Conant in his book *A Critical Analysis of Industrial Pension Systems;* namely, that each year of work should carry with it a slice of future protection at, say, age sixty-five, which the worker would carry with him even though he moved from job to job. One could see why an individual firm would not wish to adopt such a plan, since it would mean added expense without insuring continuity of service, but from an over-all social point of view it was the fairest arrangement. Time prevented us from exploring this possibility in the depth it deserved, although it was later treated in some detail by Morse's former assistant Merton C. Bernstein, in a book, *The Future of Private Pensions,* for which I wrote the introduction.

Both time and the complexity of the issues also kept us from fully probing the problems connected with the investment of these reserves. The employers were generally given much leeway in this matter and commonly turned the funds over to the trust department of a given bank. There the funds were handled with almost uniform dollar honesty, but with grave issues about their effects left unsettled. For example, should there be any limitation upon the funds to be invested in the company making the contributions? Despite the favorable record of Sears, Roebuck's profit-sharing plan, I felt there should be. A man's financial future should not be dependent on the fortunes of the same company where his present job was. It was desirable to have a distribution, rather than a further concentration of risk. Should the worker be cut off if his company was sold or should he carry his pension rights with him? And what about transfers from one plant to another within the same company?

In view of the restrictions upon benefits, these voluntary pension and retirement plans seemed to be overinsured. Evidence of this is seen in the fact that the reserves by 1967 had mounted to something over $130 billions. This has given enormous power to the banks. Some have claimed that these funds have furnished the reserves by which the recent rash of conglomerate mergers has been effected.

Wise answers to these questions are still awaited, but in 1957 we took a first step. This was to require a full disclosure of receipts and expenditures of such reserves to a Labor Reports Branch in the Department of Labor. These reports were to be open for public inspection, and we depended on the newspapers and minority groups within the unions to take full advantage of this opportunity. They could, thus, spade out any abuses and hence provide a self-enforcing means of preventing improper use of the funds.

We defeated a Republican effort in the Senate to exempt employer-financed and -controlled funds from this requirement, and we added a criminal-penalties section to provide punishment for misappropriation of funds by trustees. We had originally supposed that such acts were punishable offenses under existing criminal statutes. But a federal court, for reasons I have never understood, had ruled otherwise, and we tried to fill that gap with direct legislation. We passed this legislation through the Senate with the help of the AFL-CIO, which was most co-operative in the whole matter. At first there was some opposition from a few of the big insurance companies, but this faded away.

In the House the criminal-sanctions section was lost through the efforts of a Tammany Congressman who was also a well-known author and scholar in labor-management relations and a professor at one of New York's universities. His activities in this case helped a rival to defeat him for renomination in the following primary.

The act was, however, still maimed. The Democratic victory in 1960 provided a Congress more bent on reform, and James Roosevelt picked up the cause and carried it through to passage. As the first witness to testify in behalf of his bill, I told the story of what our investigations had revealed and of the need for criminal sanctions.

On the whole, our work had a good influence. The evidence we turned up in the case of Angelo Inciso, an official of the Allied Industrial Workers, led to his indictment, conviction, and imprisonment for several years. The revelation that the head of the Laundry Workers' Union had a previous criminal record and was operating under an assumed name encouraged groups within that union as well as the AFL-CIO largely to clean up its affairs. The publicity also helped within the bakers' union, some of whose officials had been making "sweetheart" contracts with Illinois employers who, in turn, gave them financial benefits. We thus tore loose some of the underworld parasites who had fastened themselves to minor trade unions and helped to turn back the efforts of the criminal syndicate to take over the American labor movement.

In this whole process no one could have been more constructively helpful than George Meany, the president, and William F. Schnitzler, then the secretary-treasurer, of the AFL-CIO. It was a reassurance to find, as I had always believed, that the heart of the labor movement was sound.

Ralph Nader has more recently used these same reports to show abuses in the administration of the pension fund of the coal miners. The reserves of that fund, built upon an assessment of forty cents for every ton mined, came to a total of about $100 million. Half of this, or $50 million (at one time $90 million), was deposited with the National Bank of Washington, which was owned and controlled by the union. There it drew no interest. Only a small fraction of the reserve was needed to pay current benefits and claims, and the remainder could easily have been invested in sound governmental and industrial securities. The fund was, therefore, losing something over $2 million a year at the very time it was curtailing benefits because of an alleged shortage of reserves. I am confident that such an arrangement cannot continue for long, and that the publicity will compel a reform. I believe the principle of disclosure has been vindicated.

Our work was followed by broader investigations by the Senate Government Operations Committee under Chairman John McClellan, and with Bobby Kennedy as chief counsel. They properly zeroed in on the International Brotherhood of Teamsters and its president, James R. Hoffa. Hoffa and his followers were tough customers, and Kennedy used almost equally tough methods in dealing with them. Investigations were started in many places at once, and a wide variety of papers and records were subpoenaed. Kennedy was abusive in cross-examination, and Hoffa was thrown off balance. After a protracted legal struggle, Hoffa was convicted and sent to prison. In the meantime, the AFL-CIO had suspended his union and had further weakened the efforts of dubious operators to convert other unions into their own instrument.

During the long struggle over benefits and pensions, I walked a straight and narrow line, resisting all attempts to soften the investigation and at the same time preventing it from becoming a witch hunt. The men we were investigating operated subtly. Long-time supporters and hitherto-trusted friends came to my office ostensibly on friendly visits, although it soon became evident that their real mission was to hush up my investigation. I was urged to meet with well-known New York lawyers, who soon showered me with offers of entertainment. My established rule against accepting gifts worth more than $2.50 helped me through that set of trials.

There was another and more difficult series of tests. Could we go after the guilty effectively and yet give them a fair trial and the rights of due process? What we did was to sift all the charges in the privacy of executive session and see that there was no publicity given to the testimony. This protected the men affected from a one-sided blast of adverse publicity, which was one of the worst features of the internal-security hearings, where damaging leaks of testimony were sometimes used to discredit a person. If the evidence justified it, we would schedule a public hearing and inform the persons affected of the general nature of the charges against them. This permitted them to prepare a defense. We also allowed witnesses to be represented by a lawyer, who had a limited right of cross-examination and of making a final statement. In many cases, the witnesses did not take advantage of the rights accorded them. I tried to be fair in cross-examination, but on two occasions I probably was not. When I found that some union officials, no doubt members of the criminal syndicate, had spent on themselves huge sums of money collected from the scanty earnings of their members, I gave them a tongue-lashing comparable to those that Bobby Kennedy later administered.

When I originally proposed these rules for the fair conduct of the investigations, I was told that I was condemning my inquiries to ineffectiveness. But, like Wayne Morse, I believed in procedural as well as substantive rights, and I was confident that fairness in the long run would be more effective than the usual methods of prosecutors. This was borne out by the results. The men jailed and thrown out of office were more numerous than in other exposés, and the union cleanups were more thoroughgoing. No counterattack on the methods of inquiry could be effective.

At the same time I gave equal prominence to such unions as the Chicago Brotherhood of Painters, who were managing a pension-and-welfare fund with conspicuous integrity. This prevented the inquiries from smearing the institution of unionism as such. The Decatur, Illinois, local of the Allied Industrial Workers had not been involved in any of the skulduggery of its national officials or in that of the Chicago local. I made this clear in our Washington hearings and went to Decatur to make it plain to the local citizens and the press. The union baiters did not like to see all this care taken, but I felt it vindicated the ability of Congressional investigations to clean up abuses and yet to do so with fairness and compassion.

Social Security

THE SOCIAL SECURITY ACT OF 1935 was one of the great forward steps in American politics. Some of the costs of old age and unemployment were shifted forward to consumers instead of being allowed to rest almost solely upon the victims. The small contributions of the many created far less hardship than the massed losses of those who finally bore the burden. There was strong popular support for both forms of social insurance when they were finally proposed. And when they were attacked by the big financial and industrial interests in 1936, the people repudiated the onslaught. When the reformed Supreme Court rejected the arguments of the prominent attorneys hired by the Liberty League and upheld the constitutionality of the measure, open opposition to the system as a whole virtually ceased. While opposition to it was still nurtured, as was evident in Barry Goldwater's frank comments during the 1964 campaign, it was distinctly a declining force.

The arguments turned, instead, on the degree of coverage, the scale of benefits, and the methods of financing and administration. We Democrats from the North and the West were in favor of liberalizing the provisions of the law and were joined by the handful of our allies from the South and from the Republican party. During Eisenhower's administration we had the good fortune to have two secretaries of Health, Education, and Welfare, Marion B. Folsom and Arthur S. Flemming, who were private believers in social insurance, while the assistant secretary, Elliot L. Richardson, proved most helpful. The official differences, therefore, between the parties in the Senate on these issues lost much of their former bitterness.

It would not be worthwhile to trace the details of the various improvements that were effected. Benefits were extended to the widows and children of deceased workers. The self-employed were included by the early 1950's, but those in domestic service and employed by nonprofit organizations were excluded. Those in federal, state, and local government had to be provided for by their own systems, which, however, came to be almost universal. By 1966 about 68 million people were covered, or almost 90 per cent of those gainfully employed; nearly 15 million were beneficiaries of the system; and the average monthly benefit for retired workers was $84. This was increased to $99 by 1968.

Throughout the years that the system has been in effect, Congress has operated on the theory that the plan was ultimately to be self-supporting and was not to require a public subsidy. The costs of retirement benefits will be extremely heavy, probably running close to 15 per cent of the national payroll. This will be due to the length of the average retirement period during which benefits will have to be paid. It was originally believed that this was too heavy a load to be borne by future generations of workers, who would have to pay for the past services of their elders. Instead of raising enough money to meet the claims as they accumulated, it had been decided by Secretary of the Treasury Henry Morgenthau, Jr., at the origin of the system in 1935, to make current contributions sufficiently high to accumulate a large surplus. This was to be invested in government bonds, which were to furnish about a third of the revenue ultimately needed to keep the system on an even keel. The reserve was originally expected to amount to $36 billion by 1965 and $47 billion by 1980. Those were enormous sums of money for those days. The government interest payments were expected to take the place of the outright subsidies that otherwise would have been necessary. The financial support of the system was, therefore, to be three-sided, rather than dual: employers, employees, and interest on past compulsory savings.

Many thoughtful students of finance were doubtful about the accumulation of such a huge surplus, thinking that it would cause too drastic a curtailment of consumption. Others defended it, on the ground that it was parallel to the methods used by private insurance companies and would at the same time free the government from the constraint of the banks and the financial community in borrowing needed money. It would refund the public debt in public rather than in private hands.

These problems were partially avoided by the practical method of increasing benefits. The cost of living rose rapidly from 1939 on, and the social function of the security program gained wide approval. Originally the benefits were not intended to be enough to provide adequate maintenance for an old person, but merely to furnish a nest egg that would encourage people to make more adequate private savings. This ignored the needs of the poor, who did not have any money to save, and it also ignored the tendency of the insured middle class to want the system to provide them with a basic minimum, to which private savings could be added.

The mounting reserves in the insurance funds gave Congress the resources to pay for an immediate increase in benefits. But the fiscal conservatives on the House Ways and Means Committee and the Senate Finance Committee were able to insure the future "solvency" of the fund and avert the "danger" of public subsidies by increasing the ultimate contributions of the two parties. After some years, the heightened reassurance of the reserves gave further courage to those who wanted once more to increase benefits.

These actuarial computations were not known to the general public, or, indeed, to most members of Congress, but they were the hidden determinants. I well remember the day in 1957 when Elliot Richardson frightened the officials of HEW by conscientiously revealing that the department's schedule called for an ultimate reserve of over $200 billion.

In practice, the costs of the added benefits were met by three devices:

1. Increasing the percentage contributions of the employers and employees and, later, the self-employed. The original taxes were 1 per cent for each, rising to 3 per cent, or a total of 6, by 1949. These were increased in the 1960's to 3.85 per cent for 1966 and to 4.2 per cent by 1969. By 1971 it was to be 4.6 per cent for each, or a total of 9.2 per cent. By 1973 it was to be a flat 5 per cent for each.

2. Increasing the annual maximum earnings that were taxable. For many years this was $3,000. The upward movement of wages and salaries made this limit obsolete, and it was finally increased to $3,600 in 1951, and $4,200 in 1955. During the latter part of the '50's it was raised once more, to $4,800, and in the mid-'60's to $6,600. For 1968 and subsequent years, the taxable limit was lifted to $7,800. On the whole, the earnings of skilled workers and lower-grade professionals had gone up in about the same ratio, from $1.50 to $3.90 an hour for a 2,000-hour year.

3. Scaling down the ultimate reserve. By 1955 this reserve amounted to $21.7 billion, almost identical to the planned $22.1 billion. During the next decade, however, instead of the reserve rising to $36 billion by 1965, as it was supposed to do, it decreased to $18.2 billion. This was a result of the benefit increases. In 1967 and 1968 the reserve went up again, to a total of $25.7 billion. On the whole, I would not expect reserves for old-age and survivors' benefits to increase in the future beyond $35 billion. The presence of these reserves will suggest to all parties the alternative of raising the benefits and postponing the increase in assessments. Whether this is ultimately desirable, I will not say. It is only what I think will happen. The public will not want to have a huge reserve built up from its current income in order to pay interest to itself.

Unemployment Insurance

UNEMPLOYMENT INSURANCE, a second feature of the Social Security Act, had been one of my principal concerns during the decade from 1925 to 1935. But the form in which it was finally passed was very different from what I had advocated.

Instead the theories of Commons and Brandeis were followed. They were good men and sincere reformers, and it was natural that hard-pressed politicians should turn to them for guidance in a complicated and unfamiliar field. The emphasis was placed upon the alleged ability of the employer to prevent unemployment, and he was made the sole contributor to the unemployment funds. This became known as the Wisconsin Plan, and it originally provided that each firm should have its own reserve, from which it was to pay benefits only to its former employees. The Brandeis-Commons followers appealed to the example of workmen's compensation, where lodging a part of the costs of industrial accidents upon the employers had stimulated them to put in safety devices and institute safety campaigns. Unemployment compensation, they insisted, would have a similar effect; since it was in the employer's interest to prevent unemployment, he would do so.

But this thinking ignored the fact that industrial accidents occur inside the work place and can largely be controlled there, while the forces creating unemployment are primarily outside the work place and cannot be controlled from inside. While firms can do much to reduce seasonal unemployment, they are powerless insofar as cyclical unemployment is concerned. Unemployment caused by shifts in demand is also largely outside the control of the individual firm. In a depression, demand melts away to almost nothing in the steel and machinery industries. Production dwindles and unemployment follows.

Since the Wisconsin school recognized that they had to place a maximum limit upon any assessment paid by employers, they fixed it at 3 per cent in the 1935 act. This meant that benefits in those industries hardest hit by a depression would have to be reduced or discontinued. At the same time, firms with a relatively stable demand would be paying full benefits to their few unemployed and would have returned to them their unused surplus as a reward they did not deserve for "good management." I. M. Rubinow, Abraham Epstein, and I made this argument, and George Meany, then of the New York State Federation of Labor, saw it and was convinced. In most states we succeeded in getting the proposal for separate employer reserves defeated, and, instead, got the legislatures to establish pooled funds as the insuring unit. But the employers, as I had foreseen, took up Commons' cause and insisted on so-called "merit-rating," whereby the amount paid into the central reserve would vary according to the relative amount of unemployment benefits they had paid out.

This was a typical legislative compromise, but it created many grave weaknesses. The primary interest of the employers was now to reduce benefits, rather than to reduce unemployment. That was the way they could keep their liabilities down. They therefore organized to resist attempts to increase the maximum payable when wages started to soar upward, and they fought efforts to increase the scale and lengthen the period of benefits. They also fought many individual claims for benefits. The result was that instead of benefits being one-half of earnings, as was originally provided in the various state acts, they fell proportionally, until in 1965 they were only one-third. This did not include the losses of those dropped from the rolls because they had exhausted their claims to benefits.

During the recessions of the 1950's and of 1960–61, we tried, with the backing of the AFL-CIO, to lengthen the benefit periods and to furnish loans to such states as West Virginia and Pennsylvania, whose reserves were dangerously low. We even tried once to replace the cumbersome, unequal, and inadequate state systems with an adequate national system. Some of the early Commons men later came to admit that they had been wrong in supporting an employer-dominated system. But their conversion was too late.

Despite our efforts, and those of the AFL-CIO under George Meany and Nelson H. Cruikshank, we made no progress. Not only were the employers afraid of the increase in benefits, and, hence, in their contributions, which would have followed a national system, but state officialdom was opposed, as well. The combination was too strong. We had to content ourselves with bailing out state operations intended to protect the unemployed and their children. Thoroughgoing reform is needed.

28

Sickness, Health, and Poverty

Early Efforts

As THE SOCIAL-SECURITY SYSTEM began to be accepted, efforts were made to include sickness and health care in the social protections afforded. In 1950 Truman sponsored an all-inclusive system of health care, which Montana's Jim Murray and John Dingell, of Michigan, introduced in Congress. The American Medical Association sprang to arms in opposition and to defend the traditional system of medical care. It raised at least a million and a half dollars and organized a campaign to defeat various Democratic Senators and Congressmen. Scott Lucas was majority leader and, though not enthusiastic about the proposal, could not attack his President's program. He therefore was made a special target by the AMA and found that although he tried to avoid the issue he could not do so. In my trips downstate I found that doctors' offices were overflowing with campaign literature and that most doctors and their assistants were personally campaigning against Lucas. He was defeated by Everett Dirksen, and the AMA claimed the credit. Millard Tydings, of Maryland, was also beaten, and while the Murray-Dingell bill was not the main cause, the AMA claimed that it was. Legislators accepted the conclusion that the voters were opposed to all forms of health insurance and that they should avoid an open conflict with the AMA.

For some years, naturally, there was no revival of the ambitious plans of 1949–50. The most that was proposed were school clinics and health centers and educating more doctors. The first two largely failed because of both Congressional opposition and lack of state and local co-operation. The AMA and the well-established medical schools were successful in killing the last. They did not want to train more doctors in either new or existing medical schools. The doctors thought, although they did not publicly say so, that more rivals would reduce fees. I could make no headway with my suggestion that the last objection could be met by requiring the recipients of federal scholarships to spend at least three years in some underdoctored community, such as an urban slum or a low-income farming area.

A reaction against the AMA eventually began to set in. The public did not like to see doctors opposing measures to lessen the suffering of the sick and disabled. About 1955 some of us thought we saw a limited opportunity for expanding social security, by including partial protection for those suffering from serious and perhaps irremediable disabilities. Impressed by the large number of seriously crippled men and women I met on my trips through Illinois, I first helped to get the efficient and humane Mary E. Switzer put in charge of the rehabilitation work of the federal government. Then, with my friends in the AFL, who had these same hopes before I did, we began to try to get the severely crippled covered by social security. We were making some progress when we were joined by an unexpected and welcome ally, none other than Walter George, the leader, with Dick Russell, of the Southern conservatives.

George was the son of a tenant farmer and had grown up in poverty and deprivation. Being a man of great ability, he had risen rapidly at the bar, and he became accepted by the planter and moneyed Establishment as a safe defender of their interests. Appointed to the Senate in 1922, he had been their faithful ally for a third of a century. In his long Senate career I could find no record of any action to help the poor and disinherited, from whom he had sprung. Instead, his political friends were of the propertied class, and in particular from the Coca-Cola Company, dominated by the Candler family, and the Georgia Power Company. Now, in the twilight of his life, he was being pushed out of politics by Herman Talmadge, the son of the suspender-snapping Gene, the idol of the so-called "rednecks." Even his old supporters were deserting him and going over to Herman. With his political career nearly over, George evidently decided to break with precedent and do something for the class he had neglected for so long.

The proposal I backed was modest and met a real and obvious need. It helped all classes, and not merely wage earners. It went into the farms and rural hamlets and did not confine itself to industrial centers. It made its appeal to Christian compassion, not to the class struggle. It was a natural for George to make his switch, and go out as a humanitarian, rather than as a crusty conservative. But he wanted further safeguards in the bill. Men under fifty were not to receive benefits, and the funds for the new disability section of the social security law were to be isolated, so that it would not invade the reserves set up for survivors and dependents.

With such sponsorship the proposal moved rapidly through Congress.

The Southern conservatives might deplore George's new attitude, but they could not deny him his wish. The Republican leadership was receiving so many favors from him that they could not oppose him. With George in the foreground, the bill sailed through Congress and was signed by Eisenhower. I think George took pleasure in this during his few remaining years. Once, he even smiled when he met me—an unprecedented occurrence.

On the whole, the act has worked out well. The fifty-year eligibility age has been eliminated, and the benefits opened up to those over the age of eighteen. By 1968 nearly a million people were receiving benefits, 63 per cent being over the age of fifty-three. The surplus in the reserve fund was slightly over $3 billion. This breach in the wall helped to pave the way for the Forand bill.

The Forand Bill

IN LATE 1957 Congressman Aime J. Forand, of Rhode Island, quietly introduced a bill to provide sixty days of hospital care for those beyond the age of sixty-five who were sick and needed care and medical attention. He made no effort to publicize his bill, and there were only conventional notices in the union papers. I did not even know of the existence of such a measure until I went home to make my fall round of meetings. I shall never forget my surprise when at a scantily attended meeting at McLeansboro, the seat of Hamilton County, deep in southern Illinois, a bedraggled oldster with many missing teeth asked me about the chances of passing the Forand bill. I had to ask him to tell me what it was. He gave me the rough outlines of the measure. Then he said, "I need that badly," and the little band of aged courthouse loungers nodded gravely, although without much hope.

I immediately telephoned my Washington office to send me a copy of the bill and material about it, and was ready to answer further questions, which came sporadically during the rest of my trip.

The bill was more inclusive in the popular mind than it really was. It was a mild measure, providing only hospital and nursing-home care, but no doctors' services. It was the result of a people's movement, largely self-generated, but backed increasingly by the 18 million people over sixty-five. Meany and Cruikshank gave it skilled leadership, but fundamentally the drive came from below. From 1958 to 1960, popular support increased rapidly, and as it did, the alert AMA redoubled its efforts in opposition. It was still powerful, but not as powerful as it had been ten years before. The general public did not see it now as the representative of beloved family doctors, but, instead, as a trade association seeking to retain undue favors for its members. The increase in medical and hospital costs had helped to replace the earlier and kindlier image. Despite the devotion of a respectable portion of the doctors, they were fast losing their favorable public image. What the AMA did in opposing Medicare was, in fact, the strongest popular argument in support of the program.

The first test of strength came in 1960. Mills and Rayburn prevented action in the House. But Anderson got a modified Forand bill up for a vote in the Finance Committee and then on the Senate floor. The Democrats had just endorsed Medicare at their Chicago convention, but only five of the eleven on the committee voted for this bill. Similarly, it was beaten on the floor, 51 to 44. In both cases nearly all of the Southern and border-state Senators joined the Republicans in voting against the bill. New Jersey's Case was the only Republican who voted for it. Kerr was the leader of the opposition, but Johnson, who had just been nominated for Vice President, now changed sides and voted for it. The Kerr-Mills bill, which was passed instead, proposed financial assistance to the "medically indigent" who passed a means test. In other words, it was welfare, not social insurance. We were not opposed to welfare payments to the needy who were sick, but we did not believe this should be all.

When the vote on the Anderson amendment was being taken, John Kennedy and I happened to be standing together watching the response of the Senators and the expressions on their faces. Afterward he turned to me and remarked bitterly that the Southerners would not support the national needs and declarations of our party, but would demand their full share of the perquisites and patronage should we be successful in the coming Presidential election. I thought this was a healthy reaction. During the campaign, however, Kennedy concentrated his fire upon the almost solid Republican vote against Medicare and was silent about the almost equal opposition of the Southern Democrats.

Both sides used the next two years, 1961 and 1962, to intensify their propaganda. In the next vote on it in the Senate, we Democrats lost Jennings Randolph, of West Virginia, and Carl Hayden, but we gained three Republicans—Cooper, Keating, and Kuchel. The vote was 52 to 48. When the unrecorded votes of 1960 are taken into account, the Democrats had gained only one vote.

Kerr had forced Randolph to vote against Medicare by granting relief to West Virginia on welfare payments only on condition that he switch from his 1960 favorable vote. With Kerr's death in December, 1962, Randolph was relieved of his commitment. Hayden, nearing the end of his fifty-eight years of service in Congress, also switched. The next score was 50 to 50.

Medicare

IT WAS the election of 1964 that finally turned the tide in this as well as in so many other fields. Goldwater took a highly conservative stand, and even went so far as to advocate the elimination of social security. Johnson not only won with a huge majority, but his party gained thirty-seven seats in the House and made numerous conversions to Medicare, which suddenly became popular. Mills yielded to the change in public opinion and became a supporter.

The Republicans now adopted a completely new strategy. They attacked Medicare not, as formerly, because it did too much, but because it did too little. It now met most hospital costs. The Republicans insisted that it should also provide for doctors' fees and for drugs. From being opponents, they now posed as the true friends of Medicare. So did the AMA. Mills met this shift by proposing a voluntary supplement to the bill. He added doctors' fees after the first $50 paid for by a $3 contribution monthly by the aged and a $500-million contribution by the federal government. Drugs were not covered.

The liberal Republican amendment was narrowly defeated in the House, 236 to 191, and had it not been for the sixty-five freshman Democrats, it would have carried. They voted 58 to 7 against it. The amendment was an apparent reversal of all the old positions, and no one could figure out what were the motives of the Republicans and Southern Democrats. They obviously wanted to escape the opprobrium of being branded as confirmed opponents of Medicare, but some suggested that they had a desire to load the system down with benefits for which the public would not want to pay. The class of 1964 Democrats deserves great credit for resisting the temptation of the Republican amendment; there was never a truer illustration of the old saying "I fear the Greeks even when they bring us gifts." Once the amendment was disposed of, the Medicare bill was passed, with only 115 negative votes. Of these, seventy-three were Republican, over half the total number in the House. Forty were Southern Democrats, and only two were non-Southern Democrats.

The bill next came to the Senate, and the Finance Committee started hearings. I then made the second big mistake of my senatorial career. I had supported Russell Long for whip, or deputy leader, both because I liked him and because he had pledged himself to back Medicare and repeal of Section 14 (b) of the Taft-Hartley Act. Some said my support was the decisive factor in his winning. He technically lived up to his promise and vigorously defended Medicare throughout the hearings. But as we started to vote on amendments, he made an equally passionate plea for eliminating the terminal date on the length of hospital care. Ribicoff joined him, and they made a strong, humanitarian case, emphasizing the sick old people who would have to be evicted from the hospital at the end of sixty days. I voted with Long, but was disconcerted to find former opponents of Medicare voting with me. Some of them were incautious enough to smile broadly as they did so. I went to my office confused and distrustful. Had I done wrong? What were Long's real motives? I worked out the arithmetic and saw that the lifting of the limit would increase the costs enormously and fill the hospitals permanently with the old.

The next day, Nelson Cruikshank, whose sincerity could not be questioned, called on me before the committee met. His face was sorrowful as he told me that this was another effort to load the bill down with excessive benefits. If we took the ceiling off hospital care, we would have to eliminate the doctors' services. I hurriedly checked his suspicions. Knowledgeable people told me he was correct and that Long's motion was another device of the AMA.

I hurried to the committee and told them I had made a mistake and was changing my vote. Some of the newspapermen said that it was the first time they had seen a Senator admit he had been wrong. As on the McCarran bill fifteen years before, I was now given a chance to redeem myself. When the new vote was taken, the Long proposal was defeated, and the bill went to the floor.

We were in despair as the Senate vote neared. Anderson was sick and could not lead us. Mansfield thought we were surely beaten and virtually gave up. Gore and I were striving to hold the line, but it looked as if we would lose by a big margin. We telephoned to Wilbur Cohen, of HEW, for help, and he and Cruikshank came over and told the doubters that labor and the President were both opposed to the Long-Ribicoff amendment, as was being rumored. It was finally defeated, 43 to 39. We then extended the period of hospital care from sixty to ninety days. We also provided for a big slice of nursing-home care for the elderly who were disabled by stroke and shock, subject to a $10-a-day payment by the patient. We did not provide adequate safeguards, however, against overcharges by doctors, hospitals, and nursing homes. And we gave Blue Cross and Blue Shield a large share in the administration of the act.

In this form the bill was passed, 68 to 21. Eight of the supporters of the Long-Ribicoff amendment turned up as last-ditch opponents of Medicare. Cruikshank had been proved right. Russell Long and I continued to be friends, but, reluctantly, I no longer trusted him in such matters. Shortly afterward, in the Finance Committee I defeated an attempt by him and Dirksen to free some of the utility industry from federal regulation.

Johnson took those of us who had worked for the bill out to Kansas

City in his plane to sign it in the presence of Harry Truman. After fifteen years, Truman's proposal had partially come to pass.*

We had spent so much time arguing over the general need for Medicare that two important features were neglected. One was fixing upper limits to the fees charged by doctors and hospitals. The second was taking Title XIX for granted. This provided "Medicaid," or welfare payments, to the sick of all ages who were medically indigent.

Medicaid

IN A FINAL SPEECH after the bill was passed, when many doctors were threatening to boycott both Medicare and Medicaid, I tried to decrease the antagonisms that had grown up. Pointing to the many concessions we had made to the doctors, I appealed for their co-operation. Success or failure, I said, rested with them. We had given them a "sacred trust," and I hoped that they would recognize this fact. Most critics treated this appeal as insincere "hogwash," but I meant it.

At the same time I tried to include the costs of the services of salaried specialists with the hospital charges paid by the special section of the social-security fund. But Mills was intent upon cutting as much off this fund as possible, and I failed utterly. Instead, the bills for these services— anesthetist, psychiatrist, therapist, and others—were to be individually rendered, which had not usually been the case before. These specialists liked this concession and almost immediately raised their rates. The charges created administrative confusion.

I also failed in my effort to include drugs among the services provided. I had become acquainted with the big price markups in this field as a result of Kefauver's investigations. So had the rest of the Senate, but their reform ardor had cooled after including hospital care on a compulsory and doctors' services on a voluntary basis. Mills did not want to take the big drug companies into battle, and the majority in Congress had the same inhibitions. I knew that I had multiplied opposition from many quarters—from doctors, insurance companies and agents, specialists, and drug companies. While the aged were far more numerous, once they had obtained their immediate objective their gratitude would slacken rapidly, and the natural conservative tendencies of old age would more and more become predominant. The times were, however, too crucial to allow those considerations to prevail. The mistakes made in passing the Social Security Act of 1935 were still with us after thirty years of experience. I feared the mistakes of 1965 would still be present in 1995.

But one misgiving proved erroneous. I had been afraid that the volun-

* The best account of the half-century of struggle for Medicare, from 1915 to 1965, is Richard Harris' *A Sacred Trust,* New York: New American Library, 1966.

tary nature of the insurance for doctors' services, with premiums of $3 a month paid by the insured, would mean that a large proportion of the aged would neglect to take out policies. We had tried to make this easier by providing a flat increase in benefits for old age of $3 a month, so that the aged might come in without loss of income from what they had received before. This was an essential aid, but I was afraid that lack of foresight and a desire for greater present income would cause many to pass up the voluntary plan. I had not counted on Robert Ball, the efficient administrative head of Social Security. He had his staff interview every eligible oldster who was getting social security and point out that they could get doctors' services without any diminution of their income. Congress had, indeed, given them the extra $3 a month for this purpose. So excellent a selling job was done that in 1968 only 1.6 million of the 19.6 million or 8 per cent, who received hospital insurance failed to come under the medical-insurance plan. Those covered received almost $2 billion.

Whether so good a job will be done in the future should we get a less devoted administrator is an open question. There is still danger, and contributions have gone up to over $5 a month.

Many weaknesses began to appear in the act once it went into effect. Despite the restraint and compassion shown by many fine doctors, their fees on the average moved up. Many took far more cases than they could properly handle. Hospitals also increased their rates; charges of $50 to $60 a day were common. In many cases they were even more, going as high as $90 a day. Since the hospitals were dealing with mass demands from their nursing and hospital staffs, hitherto badly underpaid, it is hard to apportion the blame, if any existed. But the states and the federal government had no effective machinery for finding out or for enforcing a ceiling, and in the process costs skyrocketed.

One thing is certain: the medical profession, which had bitterly opposed Medicare, profited enormously from it. A new volume of cases was assembled for treatment. Patients formerly treated as charity could now be charged high rates, because the system and not the individual was paying the bills. I had been telling the doctors for forty years that they would gain, not lose, from a general insurance system against the costs of medical care, but I had not foreseen that the costs would be unregulated. Despite my differences with the AMA, I placed too great a trust in the ethics of the profession.

Similarly, I had not seen the danger of too expansive a definition of "medically indigent." New York led the way in this direction, and at first included many of the middle class, who were given medical care without cost. This was moderated after a year or two.

During the last three years I have spent a considerable amount of time in hospitals and have been treated with great kindness by doctors, hospitals, and union insurance funds. I have come to several conclusions from this experience.

The first is that instead of confining insurance to the aged for disabilities from which they are already suffering, it should be extended to include medical care for all ages. Emphasis should be laid upon keeping a patient in good health and on preventing sickness, instead of merely treating a patient after illness has become evident. Truman was right years ago when he tried to do just that. The failure of the public and of the politicians to consider care for everyone in the 1950's deflected our focus to care for the aged in the '60's. This was appealing emotionally, but less productive for the future than medical care of the young. Emphasis should now be placed on prevention.

My second conclusion is that Medicare should not be asked to provide single rooms for patients. Eight- or four-patient wards are about all that the system should provide. More privacy should be paid for by the individual or from private insurance funds.

Third, while I well know the difficulties, I think that we cannot much longer postpone fixing maximum charges for doctors and hospitals. They will, in general, oppose the very idea. Once the idea is adopted, like other groups they will strive to fix the maximum fees as high as possible. The advocates of a free market will presumably support their opposition.

An investigation by the Senate Finance Committee revealed that in 1968 there were, at a minimum, 4,284 individual practitioners who received more than $25,000 from both Medicare and Medicaid. No fewer than 611 of these received over $50,000, of whom sixty-eight were in receipt of more than $100,000. The committee warned that this was an understatement, and that the real number getting over $25,000 was at least 5,000. In a few illustrations the committee showed the details of how this was done—mostly by mass visits to hospitals and nursing homes for which individual fees were charged. The actual totals may even be double those reported.*

It will be a sad travesty if these abuses are permitted to continue. They will not only cost a great deal of money intended for the less resourceful members of society, but also discredit the many ethical doctors who will not do such things themselves but who find themselves unable to discipline their colleagues.

Medicare and Medicaid should not go the way of our farm program and excite the satirical verdict: "Conceived to help the needy, / Diverted to enrich the greedy."

In the apportionment of blame, some must go to the reformers inside HEW. To conciliate the doctors, they did not interpose sufficient checks to determine what was "reasonable compensation." Some blame must also

* Senate Finance Committee, *Medicare and Medicaid: Problems, Issues and Alternatives,* 1970, pp. 81–82, 83–84, 137–143.

go to those of us who were members of the Finance Committee who, because of fatigue, stopped the battle too soon. There is much work for another generation to do in curing the defects without rejecting the institution.

Welfare

THE SOCIAL SECURITY ACT tried to provide a second line of protection for those whose benefits under the insurance system were inadequate, as well as for certain categories of the needy not covered by social insurance. Those covered by old-age insurance would be certain for some years to receive benefits that would be inadequate for full maintenance. Their benefits would have to be based upon past insured earnings. Since these would have been paid for only a short period of time for those who were about to retire at age sixty-five, the benefits would be grossly inadequate in the early years of the act.

There were, initially, large groups not covered by the old-age-insurance features, most notably the self-employed, those in firms with fewer than eight employees, and those in domestic service, agriculture, and nonprofit-seeking occupations. These numbered about one-half of all employed workers.

For those aged persons who were in need, in the judgment of state, not federal, authorities, pensions were to be provided up to $30 a month, with the federal government meeting half the costs. This was the original "old-age-pension" proposal we had advocated.

In addition, federal aid was to be provided for the needy blind and for mothers who had no male to help them support their children. This latter group had originally been cared for by numerous states under the title of "widows' pensions." The purpose was to enable widows to stay at home and care for their fatherless children instead of sending them into an impersonal orphanage in order to go out to work.

As it was realized that divorces and desertions (the poor man's divorce) not only were numerous, but also plunged families into equal or greater trouble than death, agitation developed to include care for children who had lost a parent through the breakup of the family. There was a corresponding change in nomenclature: "widows' pensions" became known as "mothers' pensions." They were included as such in the 1935 act. We certainly did not anticipate, however, the degree to which these allowances would be used, since in 1933 there were only 280,000 children in 109,000 families who were being assisted in this fashion. Despite the inadequacies of the forty-six state laws then in existence, we did not foresee the increase in numbers in the next two generations.

We knew that the system of insurance took care of only a part of the human problem. Numerous groups were excluded who were in need, and the benefits were all too low. Most people, moreover, hated to take a means test in order to qualify. The hard-core unemployed, who could not establish a prior period of employment to be eligible for insurance benefits, were thus thrown back upon the states. The children of employed workers who did not have enough income were not included. Inadequate state laws were not fully corrected. States could still pay grossly inadequate sums for relief. Congress and the state legislatures could, and generally did, appropriate far too little money. But, pleased with what progress had been made, we depended on the future and on the states to cure the defects that developed.

That was the attitude of the economic liberals during my eighteen years in the Senate. We were gradualists. We sought to make more people eligible and to increase both the grants and the federal share. When cripples were brought into the system, we backed the insurance benefits with welfare grants, and we did the same, after some delay, when large numbers were given benefits for additional periods of unemployment. But in dealing with the states, we suffered several disappointments. The amounts paid for children remained low. In 1966 the average for the country was only $39 a month, and in the next year there were twenty-nine states where the average was less than this. In five states the average was less than $20, and in Mississippi and Alabama it was below $15. In the former state the monthly average was, indeed, only $8.35, or twenty-eight cents a day. Many states, particularly in the South, were also niggardly about the numbers they would provide with aid.

We tried several times to increase the amounts old people received by making additional federal grants of $5 a month, which the states did not have to match. Most states passed it on, but some did not and chose instead to decrease the amounts they paid out by an equal figure. In these cases they treated the increased assistance as an aid to the state, and not to the needy, and so benefited the taxpayers. I was highly indignant at this, only to find on a trip back home that Illinois had just quietly done the same thing. And this was under the governorship of an esteemed and humane man. Russell Long, who was sympathetic to my efforts in the Finance Committee, told me that the poor thus lost about one-third of the additional flat grants we paid to the states. On the whole, the federal government was more liberal than the states, although some states, such as New York, were comparatively generous.

The friends of the children were relatively few in number, disorganized, and ignorant of what was happening. There were few protests from Illinois when the planned increase of $5 a month was intercepted. Legislators were less sympathetic to children who were needy than to needy old people. They could visualize the plight of the old, but not of the young. Moreover, the aged could vote and had some strong organizations. In Louisiana and Oklahoma the aged were particularly strong, due to the efforts on their behalf of Huey Long and Dr. Francis E. Townsend.

I was also troubled by the universal practice of decreasing old-age allowances by the full amount of any outside earnings that a pensioner might make. This removed all financial incentive for the needy aged to do useful work. This practice decreased not only the national income, but also the human satisfaction that comes from doing worthwhile things. For years, I introduced amendments permitting a decrease of only fifty cents in pensions or allowances for every dollar of earnings up to where there was an increase in total income of one-third or one-half. This would have resulted in releasing more labor for the service occupations, in which there was a growing shortage, and it would have made the life of pensioners more endurable. But it would have cost the federal and state governments more money. I could never get it adopted by the Finance Committee. Long encouraged me to offer it on the floor as an amendment to the Social Security bill, which he was managing, and with his backing it was adopted. For a few days my hopes ran high. But then the conference committee, despite Long's help, turned it down. I had no further chance.

Even the Democratic administrations gave no help in any of these efforts, and I think they were quietly opposed.

We made no attempt during my decade on the Finance Committee to deal with the causes of the rapid increase in the numbers of children receiving aid. By 1970 these were 6.1 million or 8½ per cent of the childen under eighteen. Part of the increase was undoubtedly due to a better knowledge of the law among mothers, particularly among the Negroes and Appalachian whites. Some of it, I am afraid, was due to desertion by husbands to get their children qualified for benefits. The act passed to strengthen family ties among those bereft of their male head was in this respect working to weaken them. Nobody could estimate the relative prevalence of the two tendencies. We stirred uneasily, but, not knowing what to do, did nothing.

Poverty

PART OF our trouble came from the fact that in trying to rescue certain groups from hunger and great need, we had to leave behind even larger numbers whose claims were as great or even greater than those we included. The means test was generally so humiliating and disliked that many of the most needy were disbarred by their own scruples. The emphasis upon states' rights and the necessity for some decentralization of administration gave great power to the states and local governments, which they commonly used to cut down grants to the most needy, notably children. The states most sympathetic to distress, such as New York, which did not impose a residence requirement for its welfare recipients and tried to be relatively generous, then suffered by drawing to themselves a larger proportion of the rural exodus.

At times it seemed as though we were trying to mop up a flood of human need with a few face towels. I could only console myself with the fact that the total number of the poor was diminishing rapidly and that human defects beyond the control of society were responsible for much of the poverty that remained. Remembering also how attempts to cure or even improve conditions on a wholesale or universal scale in the past had only resulted in failure, I tried to satisfy myself with taking a series of small steps. Perhaps that was the half-conscious wisdom of a society that wanted to be sure that its steps forward were both needed and sound. Many will, however, reject it.

In 1965 President Johnson became the first chief executive to propose a direct war on poverty. Without having much to do with planning the program, I was its enthusiastic supporter. The cautious Congress granted only a billion and a half dollars in funds, and the cost of operations in Vietnam put even that in jeopardy. What was proposed was to create useful jobs for the unemployed and the statistical nonpersons which could not be paid for out of existing local and state revenues. Preschools, under the popular title "Head Start," were one of the first and most useful ventures. The Job Corps taught marketable skills, and such organizations as the Neighborhood Youth Corps cleaned up streets and vacant lots, created play areas and small parks, and planted trees and flowers. In these respects, the new program was similar to the Works Progress Administration, which had been inaugurated during the days of the New Deal and which, amidst much disparagement, had done much constructive work. It was almost identical with what I had tried to do in the Fifth Ward when I was alderman.

In other respects, the program was distinctly innovative. Under the canopy of the Community Action Agencies, legal-aid bureaus were set up to protect the poor in their dealings with landlords, merchants, and finance agencies, and job-training programs and health centers were established and staffed by people from the neighborhood. Attempts were made in some cities to help with desegregation and provide needed personnel for slum and Indian schools by recruiting middle-class volunteers for VISTA (Volunteers in Service to America). This was really a domestic equivalent of the Peace Corps.

While there were the inevitable mistakes that characterize such ventures, on the whole the work was good. Those who exploited the poor—a more numerous class than we are wont to believe—tried to disparage the efforts. There is also a peculiar group of cynics who always attack attempts to help the poor. All this opposition, together with the high costs of the war in Vietnam, kept appropriations for the OEO (Office of Economic Opportunity) about constant at a billion and a half dollars a year. The war on poverty, for which Johnson sounded the bugles so loudly, turned out to be but a skirmish. We can only say of it, as of so many other ventures, "It is far better than nothing." After I was defeated for re-election, as an act of contrition I explored some of these problems in a book, *In Our Time,* which received the same "benign neglect" as some of the problems with which it dealt.

29

Housing

AFTER THE PASSAGE IN 1949 of the path-breaking Housing Act, we in Congress rested on our oars for several years. Despite all the difficulties, the Truman administration did well in pushing public housing. According to the Commission on Urban Problems' *Building the American City,* in the three years from 1949 to 1952 it started no fewer than 156,000 units, and many more thousands were either signed up and ready to go or on the drawing boards for the future. Though this was far fewer than the 135,000 a year prescribed in the act, we were relatively content.

On the contrary, the Eisenhower administration, which took power in 1953, was hostile to public housing. There was, however, a liberal minority among the Republicans—of whom Ernest Bohn, director of Cleveland's public-housing authority, was the leader—who did not want the Republicans to adopt a completely negative policy. A compromise was finally worked out under which at least 50,000 units started by the Democrats were allowed to come to completion, and around 25,000 more, for which agreements had been made and plans drawn, were started. The Eisenhower administration in its publicity stressed completions rather than starts, and on this basis its record was not bad, amounting to 123,000 for the three years 1953 to 1955. This silenced criticism at the time, although the Republicans were really traveling on the impetus originally given by the Democrats. In 1955 the real policy of the Republicans resulted in a great falling off in starts. Only 13,500 new units were begun during the two years 1955 and 1956. I did not learn about this until 1967, since their stress on completions covered up the decrease in starts.

During its final years, the Eisenhower regime followed a dual program. Public housing was allowed to continue at the slow pace of about 22,000 units a year, and the rehabilitation of existing housing was touted as an alternative to the building of new public housing. Baltimore was chosen as the city to exemplify the new policy. There they first tried out the rehabilitation of individual homes on a scattered basis and found, as we had found in Illinois a quarter of a century before, that this was ineffective. Again, one block proved too small an area to hold off the pressure of blight. Instead of redeeming the slums, the isolated experiments were swallowed up by them, and very shortly were as tawdry as before. Then Baltimore concentrated on renovating an entire neighborhood, and chose a thirty-six-block area. I visited this region with some colleagues a dozen years afterward. As often happens, word of an official's visit gets around beforehand, and in this case somebody in Baltimore's rehabilitation office told one of our staff with pride: "We've got our men out in the area today, and it will be all cleaned up when the Senator comes tomorrow." One noticeable fact was that after all this time the job itself was not finished and a nucleus of unimproved housing remained. While good, it was not a substitute for a program of extensive housing projects plus rehabilitation. The Eisenhower administration did not admit this, and we did not push them enough.

John Sparkman was our chief spokesman on housing matters, though he was primarily interested in promoting better housing for the middle class through the FHA (Federal Housing Administration) and the FNMA ("Fannie May," or the Federal National Mortgage Association). We also promoted veterans' housing in the farm counties and small towns. All these organizations did good work for their clients, but they dealt only with the middle or, at best, the lower middle class. We could not get any effective action to deal with the slums of the cities. Instead of building 810,000 units of public housing in six years, as prescribed in the 1949 act, only 270,000 units were built in twelve years (1949–60) and only 207,000 more in the next eight years, or a total of 477,000 in the twenty years after the act.

I had high hopes for rapid progress when Kennedy was elected and appointed Robert C. Weaver to head the Housing and Home Finance Agency. Johnson later appointed him Secretary of Housing and Urban Development. Weaver, a Negro, had been an executive in various reform groups, and had worked with Governor Harriman in New York. The Southerners organized to prevent his confirmation, and I organized the pro-Weaver group. Though hoping for real achievement, after many years I found little progress. Weaver would come to the Finance Committee almost yearly with some new plan, which he would confidently assert would greatly change things for the better. But in practice we could not see much gain. For four years, from 1961 to 1964, an average of only 25,000 units a year of public housing were built. During the next three years the rate of construction rose by about a third. The Kennedy and Johnson administrations seemed relatively uninterested in what was going on in our cities. Or perhaps they were wary of criticizing the most powerful Negro in the government.

No doubt there were powerful influences opposed to public housing, some emanating from upper-class Negroes. This group was interested in maintaining and improving its own position, but had shown little concern for the poor. On the contrary, they viewed them with distaste, resenting their existence. They did not realize the dangers both to themselves and to the nation in the mass migration of millions of Southern field hands. The results were tragic, and they descended upon the nation in 1965 during the eruption at Watts and in many cities during the later years of the '60's.

But in a larger sense we were all faced with 350 years of history and with deep-rooted emotions. The main mass of whites did not want to have any black people live near them, and the Negro aristocracy and middle class wanted to be distant from the poor blacks. As the displaced Negroes moved into the cities, the whites moved to the suburbs. As the percentage of blacks in the public-housing projects rose, the opposition of the whites to public housing increased. Perhaps Weaver cannot be blamed for not being able to break out of traditional class attitudes, and, like the rest of us, was engulfed. But he could have tried harder, and he should have told the nation what was happening—though he could have said the same thing of us in Congress.

I felt this pressure in Chicago. Discovering that most of the new housing projects were for the elderly—euphoniously termed "senior citizens" —I asked the local authorities why this should be and reminded them that children represent the future, with which they should presumably be most concerned. They replied that there was far less opposition to housing the elderly than there was to giving shelter to vigorous families. The fires of racial dislike, intense during the active years, burned low when men reached their seventies. Facing eternity, men mellowed.

In my own community, Hyde Park, I found the same forces at work. The predominant majority thought they wanted to help the Negroes. They wanted good housing for the poor and were theoretically opposed to any color bar. They had been faithful allies of mine for a full quarter of a century. But they wanted Negroes housed elsewhere and not near them. This inconsistency was quickly noted and used by the aldermen from the slum and near-slum wards and was weakening the general movement for public housing. An idealistic young publisher of a community newspaper in Hyde Park then started a campaign to change this attitude and build some public housing in the ward, and I tried to help him.

I soon found out where the real seat of the opposition lay. It was the university, whose trustees represented the upper financial and social Establishment. Under Hutchins, the university had been uninterested in the community around it, which had disintegrated rapidly and badly.

Then the Slum Clearance and Urban Renewal acts had resulted in widespread improvement. Backed by the university, the fifty-block area showed evidence that it was going "to live." But the university trustees, liberal in so much, could not stand for public housing, particularly since it would be partially Negro housing. I tried to convince them that they were strong enough to withstand this. I added arguments of a practical nature. There would be only 200 or 300 families involved, who would be drawn from the top of the waiting list. Hence they would be predominantly whites who had rejected the chance to enter previous public-housing projects located in all-Negro communities. The blacks would probably not exceed 20 or 25 per cent in the project. This was presumably below the "tipping point" which could turn an area all black, and it was the limit that Morris Milgram, a pioneer in private interracial housing, had placed on his proposed Deerfield experiment. Our liberal community could certainly "absorb" this number. And the mixture would be a valuable one, in which an upper middle class would help the poor. Indeed, we might learn from them. The university had been the first in the country to appoint competent black scholars to chairs in mathematics, psychology, and American history, and it had worked out well. It could acquire even greater prestige by being one of the first to initiate a return to old-time America, where the comfortable and the poor lived together as friends in one community.

I must have done a poor job, for the university authorities were not impressed. No doubt they were genuinely frightened by the outbreak of assaults, rapes, and even occasional murders that had followed the influx of Negroes to the city. This had even threatened the existence of the university at one period, although matters had improved since then. I did not blame them, but I hoped for better behavior by the blacks in the future.

Then my powers of persuasion increased. I had already helped both the University of Chicago and the University of Pennsylvania by getting Congress to recognize their future private expenditures for urban renewal as entitling the city to receive twice as large a federal grant, most of which was to be spent in the Hyde Park and West Philadelphia communities. I had swallowed hard before I did this, because Congress had earlier specified that public expenditures were the only qualifying offsets. But I consoled myself with the thought that, while the form was irregular, the purpose and results were worthy.

Evidently the University of Chicago became emboldened by their first success, because they soon asked that $19.5 million more which they had already expended should be counted retroactively to justify a future federal contribution of twice that sum, or $39 million. They wanted me to help them in committee on this even more irregular proposal. I swallowed twice as I thought this one over. But I agreed, and with the help of the committee's staff expert, I got this accepted.

Then I went to the university representative, and he admitted that I had done it a great favor. I said that I hoped the university would do something for me. He blanched slightly. My request was that it withdraw opposition to a public-housing project in the ward. Nodding approval, we shook hands warmly to seal our agreement. But while the young publisher continued his efforts, nothing happened. The university continued to be hostile. Perhaps the representative was true to his pledge as an individual, but I thought we had agreed on a broader program than merely neutralizing an individual. Later I took the opportunity to tell the president of the university of my disappointment over their opposition. He replied that to agree to the project would have stirred up their people "too much."

Perhaps so—although if so, it is a sad reflection on a liberal community. Equally sad is the flexibility of an academic code of ethics. After getting its $39 million, the university felt no obligation to live up to an informal agreement made in the public interest. Meanwhile, I had to listen to denunciations for being a hypocrite and an exclusionist. I resolved in the future to put all such agreements in writing, and to do this before, rather than after, I gave my help. But events moved too fast.

Weaver no doubt was exposed to even stronger pressures. Furthermore, as the first Negro Cabinet member in a white man's world, he probably did not want to be labeled a militant.

It was not until I had left the Senate and had begun my more intensive study of urban problems that I realized how deep was Weaver's resentment toward anyone who dared to tell the truth about what had been happening. However, the publicity our Presidential commission then focused on the situation helped HUD to increase its public-housing starts to 46,000 in 1968 and to make its FHA policies less discriminatory. These hearings and proddings during the Johnson administration had their impact, but the full package of our findings and recommendations landed in the lap of the Nixon administration. For the first three years their record was not too encouraging.

Rent Control

DURING the early 1950's, the legislative battles over housing largely shifted to the continued existence of rent control. For nearly twenty years there had been almost no building. The Depression from the crash to the blitz, 1929–39, virtually stopped new building for a decade, and then the war hit it a second blow. The total supply of housing actually diminished, while the population increased, at first slowly, but after the war rapidly. To protect families of servicemen, war workers, and civilian employees, rent control was imposed along with other price controls. This kept rents and profits down, but, while new housing was largely exempt, the annual rate of new building decreased at the same time. The Korean War created an added strain from 1950 to 1953. I did not believe in permanent rent control, since I knew that it had been tried in Paris and that it did not work. But because of the extraordinary shortages during the previous twenty years, its continuance for a few years was necessary to prevent poor people from feeling the full strain of an uncontrolled increase in rents and to let the landlords share in the burdens.

The legislative battles over rent control were heated. Sparkman and Maybank, both liberal and highly decent Southerners, understood the plight of Northern workmen and the poor, and were in no sense hostile. But they felt that they could not take the lead in defending rent control in the light of the growing intensity of feeling in the South. This duty, therefore, largely devolved upon me.

There were many complexities to the theory and practice of rent control, and I was so busy with other matters that I did not have the time to prepare thoroughly for the heated thrusts that were forthcoming from the opposition. Philip Stern, my research assistant at that time, was always ready with a sheaf of notes that answered the objectors, and at times turned the tables on them. His answers were commonly so subtle that it was hard to understand his advice. I lived in constant terror lest I make a fool of myself. I was reassured afterward, however, by the *Congressional Record* and committee transcripts. Remarks that had seemed doubtful in the making read with an inner pith and consistency.

After the end of the Korean War, rent control was allowed to die, but before it expired I had an ironic experience. While I wanted to protect the poor and lower middle class against big increases in rents, I saw no reason why wealthy tenants should be similarly protected. They, indeed, were often more prosperous than their landlords. Therefore, I got the Senate to decontrol rents over $5,000 a year, and expected to carry this into the final act. But the House conferees objected strenuously. Gradually it became clear that the center of opposition was a Republican congressman from Westchester County, just north of New York City. I was astounded, for this man was also the most vehement antagonist of rent control in Congress. At that very moment he was sending out 2 million copies of a speech denouncing rent control. During a lull in the conference-committee discussion I asked him quietly the reason for this inconsistency. With a sheepish look, he explained that he had many wealthy constituents who spent their winters in New York and rented expensive apartments. Their rents would be greatly increased if my amendment was adopted, and he had to oppose decontrolling them. I marveled at the civic callousness of the wealthy, but their will prevailed.

When we decontrolled nationally, New York City, with the permission of the state, promptly re-established rent control. The result, after thirty years, has, I think, been highly unsatisfactory. I have often wondered whether the local Establishment has co-operated again in maintaining for themselves a system of which they disapprove so heartily when applied to other people.

Slum Clearance and Urban Renewal

THERE WAS a great deal of opposition to the slum-clearance features of the 1949 act. To spend public funds for tearing down worn-out buildings in order to clear sites for public housing seemed to many an immoral act. In Chicago, however, I soon noticed that new housing seldom went up on the cleared sites. When it did, it was almost never housing for the poor. Upon inquiry, I was told that it was because of aldermanic restrictions. When I asked why the aldermen objected, I was informed that their effort was to obtain more taxable properties. Localities under the formula of the law had to provide one-third of the costs of the projects, but their noncash contributions, in the form of streets and facilities, met at least two-thirds of their payments. Their cash payments were only one-tenth of the total. Public housing at first paid far less than the average rate of taxation, so there was a further loss of revenue. The city fathers therefore sought private enterprise, paying larger taxes, to fill the vacant sites.

With these developments, a change came in the goals of the movement. Slum clearance was no longer stressed. Instead, "urban renewal" became the guiding principle. This was done slowly and cautiously. I think this change first became explicit in 1954–55. The Eisenhower administration, which had hitherto merely administered the 1949 grant of a half billion, now launched legislation adding $400 million more for urban renewal, to be spent in two years. This was twice the former annual rate. The opposition to the general idea of urban renewal gradually ceased, except in some cities, including Houston and Dallas. Public money was now explicitly to be used to stop civic deterioration in and around business districts. The business community was in favor of that, and few had moral scruples against it, particularly since rival business districts were springing up near the boundaries of cities and in the suburbs.

Legal changes began in 1954, with the so-called "skid-row" amendment. This permitted the use of 10 per cent of the urban-renewal funds to redeem areas that neither had been nor would become residential in character. I voted in favor of this amendment because I knew the skid rows of Boston, New York, and Chicago, where, on Scolley Square, the Bowery, and West Madison Street, drifters and wastrels congregated. Flophouses, prostitution flats, and cheap burlesque houses abounded. The regions sheltering these activities were esthetic blights and moral-infection centers. Single men, casually employed, needed decent housing almost as much as families. They were prisoners of their own weakness.

But I soon discovered this was only the entering wedge. In 1959 the percentage of exempted funds was raised to twenty, and in 1961, when Weaver came in, the explicit exemption was lifted once more, to 30 per cent, and in 1965 to 35. There was no longer any talk about clearing up the skid rows. The nation was, instead, going to clean up its cities, and it was predicted that even 35 per cent would not be the ultimate limit. In addition, sympathetic interpretation by the administrators of individual projects could decide any number of doubtful cases. A whole school of interpreters argued that the purpose of the act of 1949 had, despite its title and the reports of the Senate Committee on Banking and Currency, not been "slum clearance," but, rather, civic beautification, which they could call "urban renewal."

New Haven was the prime example of this doctrine. Millions were poured into this moderate-sized city as a result of the skilled urging of its energetic mayor, Richard Lee. But we found that most of the funds had gone to protect Yale University from the encroachment of Negro slums. The Yale yard was saved despite the deterioration of the Hotel Taft. But there was some local dissent that said more attention should have been given to housing for the poor. Later, as in other cities, this broke out in a riot.

The net effect of urban renewal was to decrease the amount of Negro housing, and to substitute for it public facilities and housing for the well-to-do.

I was almost alone on the Banking Committee in opposing these successive increases in the percentage to be exempted. Although I approved the beautification of American cities, I objected to this progressive subordination of the major purpose of the law—housing for poor and low-income families. Perhaps only the future can tell whether I was right or wrong.

In 1966 Weaver brought forward his "model cities" proposal, which tended to stress nonhousing needs. I was at first asked to lead the Senate drive for the bills, but I had to refuse because of my increasingly difficult campaign for re-election. Muskie took over and did it well. But the program has been incredibly slow in getting under way, and many of the projects seemed insubstantial.

In the meantime, under pressure from the liberal bloc, Congress slowly gave several hand-washing directives. In 1965 it provided that the urban-renewal activities of a city should be accompanied by "a substantial number of units of standard housing of low and moderate cost and result in marked progress in serving the poor and disadvantaged people living in slums and blighted areas." I interpreted this as a sign of a guilty conscience. It did not have much effect, and in 1967 HUD itself issued a directive to this effect to govern the approval of future urban-renewal projects. But since the waiting list for projects was so long, it did not offer appreciable help.

Under the influence of Proxmire and others, the Housing Act of 1968 became admirably explicit. While low-income housing no longer had to be built on urban-renewal land, it had to be built in equal ratios within a city, and in amounts to more than replace the units being demolished. This should have been done years before. We will see if the bureaucrats finally do it.

During this period, urban renewal became popular in mercantile, financial, and real-estate circles. Run-down and badly depreciated buildings could be eliminated and then the sites resold to private developers for about one-third of their purchase price. In some cases, as in Boston, the new buildings would also be freed from taxation for a period of years. Men who had objected to doing this for the poor were delighted at this turn of events. It was an upgrading of real estate. The prospects of profits were sweetened by local patriotism. Democratic mayors and aldermen found themselves courted by the business community, which had formerly opposed them. In Chicago, the local Republican businessmen were now ardent supporters of Mayor Daley. But my own persistence in opposing the mounting exemptions made more enemies for me in the business world and at the same time heightened the opposition of Secretary Weaver.

After my several legislative defeats, I did help many Illinois communities secure as much as they could from the urban-renewal funds. I did not carry my opposition to the change to individual projects. Elgin was the strongest Republican city in the state and, perhaps, the center of the most intense anti-Douglas sentiment. This had originally been due to the Elgin Watch Company, which feared Swiss watches and demanded a high tariff to keep them out. The company was failing, and I tried to help the new management. But many hundreds of men were thrown out of work, and the Republican mayor turned to urban renewal as a means of attracting new industry. True to form, he wanted to brighten up the central city. I thought it only proper to help.

I launched one ambitious project that failed completely. That was an attempt to reconstruct the stockyards district. This had been Chicago's chief claim to industrial fame as the "Hog Butcher for the World," and it was the scene of Upton Sinclair's *The Jungle*. But one by one, the Chicago packing plants had been closing and moving to smaller cities farther to the west. With lower-priced real estate, one-story plants with straight-line disassembly of the creatures slaughtered were made possible. These replaced the former Rube Goldberg production lines. Transportation costs were also cut. Finally, the last big Chicago plant closed down. When I went out to see the scene of the disaster, I found it was like a bombed-out city. At least a square mile of buildings was falling into ruin. There was no sign of activity, and only an odor betrayed the yards' former function. The South Side had also been hit by other closings, and, despite the silence of the newspapers, the "Back of the Yards" was in grave trouble. Here, I thought, was an opportunity to utilize fully the 35 per cent of urban-renewal funds marked for exemption. I stressed the importance of building up the area, but there was little or no action. Perhaps the urban-renewal administrators and local financiers did not want a senator to be attracting attention to regions other than the central city and its satellites. Perhaps also the job was too big for the funds available. At any event, my proposals fell flat. But the problem is still there. Even the smaller plants have now closed down.

30

Education

Early Interests

EARLY IN MY CAREER I became convinced of the need for two forward steps in education. There should be federal financial aid, and teachers should join the newly formed union, the American Federation of Teachers. Reading Beatrice and Sidney Webb, I became fascinated with the possibility of federal grants-in-aid. They combined the advantages of centralized finance with decentralized administration. It was a way in which the relatively new income tax could be used for beneficial purposes without creating a top-heavy bureaucracy.

I spent the summer of 1919 in the Haverford library working on the emerging practice of federal aid for county agents, vocational education, and good roads. I think Dr. Seaman Knapp had originated the idea, but it had become, along with the income tax, the most important administrative innovation of Wilson's administration. I wrote two articles on the system for the *Political Science Quarterly,* which I think were the first American writings on the subject. They brought down upon my head the sharp criticism of the fiscal conservatives, led by C. J. Bullock, of Harvard, who resented any fusion of national with state and local finance. Perhaps their opposition sprang also from the realization that a greater use of federal aid would require an increase in the federal income tax, to which they were unalterably opposed.

Federal aid was of especial assistance to states whose average income was low. Money raised in the more affluent states was distributed to a greater degree on the basis of relative need. The per-capita basis for apportionment generally followed was rough, but at least a step forward. There was also an approach to greater geographical equality. The South,

414

Southwest, and upper New England benefited from this transfusion of economic resources into their states. The states also adopted the programs federally aided far more quickly than if they had to pay all the bills.

I became a strong advocate of the device, and wrote articles for some of the educational journals. Conservative educators hastened to attack this projected intrusion of the national government into a field that had been reserved for local action, though more recently for states as well. It was a bottomless sea for argument, and I did not want to be diverted from my study of real wages, the theory of distribution, and concrete forms of protective legislation. When I went from Amherst back to Chicago in 1925, I took with me Henry J. Bittermann, who later wrote an excellent book on state aid, *State and Federal Grants-in-Aid,* and enabled me to drop further participation in the federal-aid dispute. I hoped that the fact that it had become widespread within the states would hasten its adoption by federal action between the states. I went to the Senate, therefore, a strong supporter of the general principle and desirous of modifying the accepted formula to help further the poverty-stricken states. I had a running battle with the conservatives of my state on these issues. I stressed the fact that a large proportion of the youngsters in the less prosperous states moved, when adults, to the higher-income states. By their lack of education they held back developments there. It was not enough to have an educational minimum for Illinois; it was also necessary to have a minimum for the country. But that required a transfusion of income into the poorer states.

My second concern about education was that teachers should band together in self-defense. The dismissal of Scott Nearing by the University of Pennsylvania in 1915 and similar incidents elsewhere aroused in many of us both a desire to protect the freedom of academic inquiry and a realization of its importance. Even at such relatively free institutions as Reed and Chicago, I had felt the hot breath of intolerance. So I quickly joined the American Association of University Professors. This, however, was of no help to the vastly greater number of teachers in the high and elementary schools of the country. To show my sympathy with them, I early joined the American Federation of Teachers, becoming, I believe, the second college teacher, after John Dewey, to do so. Unlike many of the collegiate staff who joined in the mid-1930's, I did not try to influence the policies or politics of the union. That was the concern of the lower-school teachers. All I could do was show my sympathy. Somewhat to my surprise, this was understood by the beleaguered members of the union.

The First Venture

ENCOURAGED by its luck in getting the housing bill through Congress, the Truman administration tried its hand on federal aid for education. It proposed a formula that was especially favorable to the South, because of its poverty. This attracted the liberal Southerners, of whom there were then a respectable number. Taft had also declared in favor of federal aid to the states for education. And we hoped for help from the Republican liberals from northern New England. Our opponents seemed to be only the extreme conservatives of both parties.

No sooner had we started hearings on the bill, however, than difficulties mounted. The Catholic hierarchy was insistent that the act provide direct aid for parochial schools. The National Education Association, the foremost advocate of federal aid, became equally insistent that it should not. It wanted federal aid paid only to the states, which in turn could distribute it only to the school districts for the public schools.

There were ten or twelve Catholics among the Senate Democrats, who, taken as a whole, were far more liberal than the average member. They could not, however, openly oppose the demands of the hierarchy. To keep their support, we devised a compromise under which a supplementary bill on health care would give federal grants for this to private and public schools alike, payable directly to the schools, while the major bill, apparently confined to the public schools, would also make grants for school transportation to private as well as public schools. The Supreme Court had recently ruled this latter practice to be constitutional on the ground that it was a service to the child and was doctrinally neutral. Moreover, we made the fact and scope of the transportation purely a state, and not a federal, matter.

Lister Hill, having quietly worked out this compromise, guided it through committee. The Catholics took it in good part, both because it was in the general interest and because they realized that it was the most they could expect at the moment. The NEA sulked. I have never seen a legislative representative angrier than its secretary when he learned of the supplementary health bill. I told him frankly that this was the concession they had to make in order to get any federal aid for the public schools. If they would not agree to it, they must resign themselves to not having any federal aid, for we needed those Catholic votes in the Senate, and even more in the House. He became almost purple in his indignation. But after checking the realities, he and his associates decided to make the best of our proposal. Taft, who was nursing Presidential aspirations, was helpful not only in committee, but also in dealing with the NEA. Though dependent on liberal Democrats for the bulk of their political support, the leaders of that organization, representing the school superintendents, were dependent on the Republican Establishment for their local support. Emotionally, moreover, most of them were conventional Republicans. They might solicit our help but they were a little ashamed to be seen in our company. Taft, as the national leader of the conservatives, had enabled them to support federal aid even though local chambers of commerce were bitterly opposed. Now he was equally helpful in reconciling them to the compromise.

The federal-aid bill was passed by a good margin, and the school health bill was approved on a voice vote. Our Catholic colleagues were as anxious as we to avoid a roll call. No one wanted to precipitate a religious war, and we thought that health was a service to the child, rather than to the doctrine. The ultimate decision was postponed to some future time and left to the states and the Supreme Court.

The bills then went over to the House, where religious tensions were greater. Instead of both bills being referred to the Labor and Public Welfare Committee, only the federal-aid measure was so referred. The health bill was sent, for no justifiable reason, to the Committee on Interstate Commerce. It was no longer possible to treat the two bills as parts of the same program. The result was that the health bill was not reported at all, while the federal-aid bill for the schools was reported with the proviso that it applied only to the public schools. It thus ruled out the possibility that it might provide money for transportation to and from parochial schools. The Catholics received nothing and felt aggrieved. Francis Cardinal Spellman expressed his anger at the action of the House. Eleanor Roosevelt then made some opposing comments, and the Cardinal rejoined by criticizing her record as a mother as evidenced by the marital difficulties of her children. This was, naturally, resented by the many friends of that noble woman, and a compromise on the House floor became impossible. Attempts to unify the forces that favored some form of federal aid met with disaster.

Disturbing Issues

WE WERE COMPELLED to give up the effort. We left matters largely to the House, and from then on for some years were mere bystanders. It is not worthwhile to recount the tangled history of the next five years. There were now two important side issues that threatened federal aid. One involved parochial schools; the second dealt with desegregation.

The official Catholic position was that added costs should not be heaped on Catholic taxpayers unless aid was also given to the schools their children attended. But if this were done, a crucial number of supporters, largely from the South, would vote against the federal-aid system as such.

The decision of the Supreme Court outlawing segregation helped create a Northern demand that federal aid should be granted only where desegregation was practiced. This drew the support of most Negroes, whose numbers in the North were rapidly increasing. They were joined by many white supporters of civil rights, and by those fearful of alienating the Negro vote.

But this issue threw other groups into opposition. There were demagogues on both sides. One Republican made a passionate appeal for desegregation, only to vote against the bill when it was once included. The result was that nothing happened in the next five years so far as federal aid for the operation of the schools was concerned.

We tried to promote federal aid for school construction, which seemed to create fewer sources of division. Voters in the North might badly underpay teachers, but they were more insistent on imposing school buildings. There was, therefore, more general support for the building program than there had been for the previous bills. This was especially true of the South. The rural school buildings there needed great improvement, and the white population was now anxious to have good schools for the Negroes as long as they were separate. We had hope that we might be successful here. But it was not to be. The hard-core Republican and Southern opposition was still too strong. Combined with party differences over the amounts to be spent, even school construction was defeated.

Sputnik

IT WAS the Russian sputnik in 1957 that broke the deadlock and revived the fight for federal aid to education. The extraordinary feat of sending an unmanned, but guided, satellite around the earth was made possible only by the high level of technical education in the USSR. Studies were now appearing, helped by Bill Benton, that were critical of the low quality of mathematical and scientific instruction in the United States. Determined to catch up with, and surpass, the Russians, Congress passed the National Defense Education Act of 1958. It provided aid for the top of the educational structure—namely, colleges and universities. The old differences were dissolved. Negro students as well as whites were eligible for financial aid. Private institutions, whether secular or religious, were equally eligible with public schools. The stimulus given to scientific education was to be of two kinds: aid to students of science, mathematics, and foreign languages; and teaching equipment for science, not only in colleges and universities, but in secondary schools as well. The Democrats favored modest but nonrepayable scholarships; the conservative coalition proposed loans. The conference adopted the latter. What began as a scholarship program was, therefore, stripped of the scholarships. But despite this, the concern of the federal government for the quality of education was asserted for the first time since the Morrill Act, which set up the state universities, had been passed nearly a century before. I of course supported the measure, which passed the Senate 62 to 26. Interestingly, while a majority of the Senate Republicans favored the bill, a majority of the House Republicans did not.

No further progress was made in 1959–60. The old quarrels over desegregation and aid to religious schools still defeated action. They operated also in 1961 and 1962.

But by 1963 the contestants had learned the facts of political life. If the advocates of aid to church schools insisted on completely equal treatment, they would get nothing. Those who favored federal aid but opposed all assistance to religious schools, if they had their way, would also get nothing. The situation was the same with regard to desegregation and loans versus grants. All sides were, therefore, finally ready to compromise.

The result was a series of special measures whereby everyone got something and no one won a complete victory. The easier measures, for higher education, were taken up first. The National Defense Education Act of 1958 was renewed. It increased student loans until by 1968 they were to amount to $195 million more; a million students had already borrowed a billion dollars. The number of graduate fellowships was raised from 1,500 to 7,500 a year. The instructional equipment could now cover English, reading, history, geography, and civics. Aid was also given to school construction.

The passage of these measures showed that under skilled management, special-purpose legislation could be expanded into large-scale and nearly general aid.

Aid for Elementary and Secondary Education

THE MORE difficult problem of aid for elementary and secondary schools remained. Wayne Morse conceived the idea that the aid should be granted to "poverty impacted" school districts according to the percentage of those unemployed and on welfare. The Johnson administration adopted the idea and raised the sums to be appropriated to $1 billion a year. It was labeled "aid to needy children," not to the religious orders through which some of the aid was to be distributed. The number of children in families whose total income was under $2,000 a year or those classed as the "very poor" was made the basis for distribution. The bill also provided more aid for school construction, 140,000 scholarships, $100 million a year for schoolbooks, and another $100 million for new services. The House Committee on Labor and Public Welfare polished the bill further by providing that the nonreligious books furnished to parochial schools should not be gifts, but "loans," even if given on a permanent basis.

Later, the movement for interreligious co-operation started by Pope John XXIII led to an attempt to get the public and parochial schools to co-operate in giving nonreligious courses. It was provided that work in mathematics, science, geography, history, and social sciences could be given in public school buildings, to which students in parochial schools would be not only eligible, but also welcome.

This was what a liberal faction within the Catholic church, led by Bishop Bernard J. Sheil, had long desired. To be effective, however, it required that the parochial and public schools be located close together, in order to reduce the time required to travel from one to the other. Since this was frequently not the case, the possibility offered more hope for the future than realized co-operation for the present.

Backed by Johnson's sweeping victory in 1964, the federal government finally assumed an active role in education. Many forces led to this result. The Democratic victory furnished the essential political majority. The evident desire of Pope John XXIII for Christian harmony and fellowship reduced fears of Catholic domination. Protestant fundamentalism was decreasing at the same time. The NEA was becoming less ambivalent than formerly, when its national leaders would give lip service to federal aid but its local leaders would do little or nothing to help and were often secret supporters of federal aid's opponents. Now the national leaders at least were more robust and were not ashamed to be our allies. This was partly due to an increase in the importance and self-determination of the classroom teachers. With better protection on tenure, they were no longer as frightened as they had been of the school superintendents. The teachers' union, moreover, was growing rapidly and was a force for greater militancy. The NEA, in order to hold its members and attract others, was becoming more liberal and democratic.

There were practical as well as spiritual reasons for the change in attitude of many Catholics. Their school costs were rapidly mounting, as increasing numbers of young women were unwilling to serve as nuns in the unpaid life of celibacy. The lay teachers recruited to fill their places had to be paid salaries that were only a little less than those in the public schools. The Catholics were, therefore, desirous of getting public aid and were willing to take something, rather than get nothing. They hoped that the precedents being established would lead to far greater public funds in the future.

Our success was due in large part to this tenuous alliance, in which the Catholics were given enough to placate them but not enough to frighten the believers in a rigid separation of church and state. In this way we obtained what I regarded as good legislation, diminished religious bitterness, and helped create a more unified country. But we did not settle the basic issues. It will be a long time before that can be done.

In the meantime, our work may have caused the subject of the relationship between the churches and the state to be considered in a friendlier spirit. The terms of successive future agreements will naturally vary according to the costs of parochial education and the degree of religious liberalism in both groups. Perhaps the ideal solution would be for the public and parochial schools to be on the same quadrangle, with the public schools giving nonreligious subjects, and the parochial those ethical and religious teachings thought necessary by the parochial leaders. The same conditions could also be followed by other religious groups that believe in separate religious instruction, of which the Jews, Lutherans, and Seventh-Day Adventists are perhaps the most important.

Despite these recent changes, the amount of federal aid for education, totaling about $2\frac{1}{4}$ billions for elementary and secondary schools, is still relatively minor. But the way has been opened for change. The addition of federal aid gives further strength to the enforcement provisions of Title VI in the civil-rights acts of 1964–65. That section authorized the federal government to shut off federal aid if a local government did not carry out the provisions of the federal law. This is a more effective method than the federal government formerly possessed. Earlier, it could either do nothing or use federal troops to permit individuals to take advantage of the law; now, it could simply stop the flow of federal funds. This was more impersonal and less provocative of passion and conflict. But frequently even this is not enforced.

The multiplicity of federal-aid measures, each with complicated requirements for compliance, creates a large degree of federal control. If the measures could be simplified without leading to the widespread nullification of basic national policies, it would be highly desirable.

Incidentally, the education bills produced a striking change in the parliamentary procedures and tactics of Wayne Morse. For twenty years he had assumed the role of the Great Dissenter. I thought he was generally right, and I gloried in his spunk. He had always emphasized what separated him from others, and took an almost unvarying attitude of austere and hostile negativism. But seniority had at last made him chairman of the subcommittee in charge of the education bills. His problem was now to unify and keep the shaky alliance for them from falling apart, and, if possible, to win additional converts. Therefore, we saw a new Morse as the debate started on the first bill. No longer glowering with righteous indignation, but smiling with amiability, he was the embodiment of friendliness. He shook hands with the most unlikely members, and at times slapped them warmly on the back. They looked bewildered but pleased at this unexpected turn of events. In debate he was conciliatory and had words of praise for critics. He would make minor concessions if forced, but there were no major changes. The parliamentary situation, and not Morse, he said, compelled that. When it was all over, he had carried his bill without amendment, and he then proceeded to thank everyone, including his opponents.

Seeing him work, I thought how unfortunate it was that he had not been given similar tasks years before. How many other negativists could be won over by similar treatment? But my reflections ceased on the morrow, when he resumed his opposition to the bill to save the Oregon Dunes.

31

The Battle for Tax Reform

The 1950–51 Effort

IN JUNE, 1950, we were again plunged into war. North Korea sent its troops south, with the help and stimulation of its Communist allies, China and Russia. Shortly before this, as a conciliatory gesture, we had withdrawn our troops from South Korea. A courageous President Truman decided to resist this aggression by sending troops from Japan. He asked help of the United Nations. Since Russia's representative had earlier walked out of the U.N., he could not veto the proposal in the Security Council. The U.N. pledged its support, although leaving the overwhelming share of the military effort to the U.S.

Because war costs money as well as lives, we had to raise taxes amounting to many billions of dollars. The Truman administration prepared a bill in July, which, with some changes, was reported out by the Ways and Means Committee of the House and then passed by that body under the so-called "closed" rule. This rule, allowing no amendments, means that a bill must be voted for as a whole. Since it was unprecedented for the House to reject such a bill, it was speedily sent to the Senate, where it was referred to the Finance Committee. There the total sum was cut, but new loopholes for tax escape were ingeniously opened.

Before it came to the floor, Humphrey organized a tax seminar, with experts to coach some of us on both the existing and the projected injustices in the tax structure and the added weaknesses in the bill. For years the tax analysis staff within the Treasury had tried to improve the tax laws, but had always been checked by powerful economic and political forces. They wanted to help us now, and at real risk to themselves some public-spirited members, led by Joseph Pechman, volunteered to conduct

423

the cram course. On the surface the Treasury favored tax reform, but in reality it did not want its experts to give guidance to the newly elected liberals. Moreover, despite their verbal protests, I felt that neither the President nor Treasury Secretary John W. Snyder cared much about the issue. Meeting at night, under closely guarded conditions of security, our group felt much as the early Christians who gathered for counsel in the catacombs of Rome must have.

We were briefed on the complicated tax code with the off-stage aid of Randolph Paul. He was then writing a book on the subject and wanted a floor fight on the worst features of the bill, which he could use as a reference. For this reason he gave Humphrey and me personal coaching. Neither of us was on the Finance Committee, but we meant to fight the measure on the floor.

Herbert Lehman joined us, then Bill Langer, but there were few others who would venture into the arena. Dividing the field, we agreed that Humphrey should lead off, with me assisting on the floor, and that each of us would sponsor specific amendments. Lehman, as one of the biggest taxpayers in the country, pulled a strong supporting oar.

Humphrey and I were both frightened at the prospect, for we faced three of the sharpest-tongued and most knowledgeable members of the Senate: Walter George, Tom Connally, and the ranking Republican on the Finance Committee, Eugene Millikin. George had long lost his popular sympathies and was a close ally of big corporate interests. The formidable Millikin would be roused to witty fury by our opposition. Connally still had a touch of frontier populism in his support of a progressive income tax and levies on wartime excess profits, but he disliked Northern liberals more and terrorized many by his brutal sarcasm. When he went after a fellow Democrat with the bull whip of his tongue, he reminded me of a whipping boss on a slave plantation or of a cowboy breaking in a wild horse on the plains of West Texas.

These men were not only impressive in debate, but from their long service on the Finance Committee they knew the tax code thoroughly and had become glib in justifying even its worst features. Moreover, at their elbows was a staff of experts from the Joint Committee on Internal Taxation. If any difficulties arose, they were also fortified by the attorneys of favored private interests, always at hand in the galleries. In contrast, we would be on our own. The experts from the Treasury had done their best in private, but in public could not show their hands or they would be fired. Our own assistants were new to the problems.

We feared a slaughter of the innocents, and Humphrey and I thought we were leaving the catacombs to enter the Colosseum, with its man-eating lions. Most of the press, reflecting their disgruntlement over the 1948 election, treated us as either exhibitionists or naïve idealists. In the main, our fellow Senators were either hostile or indifferent. But while men were dying in Korea and the poor were paying for collective security with both their money and their lives, we felt it was criminal to allow large incomes to escape taxation.

For days we went through a trial by fire. Learning on our feet, we had to deal with a series of shifting targets, sophisticated and plausible. But somehow from the faces of the Senate employees, we sensed that we were holding our own.*

In their advocacy of an excess-profits tax, we supported O'Mahoney and Connally. We also wanted an increase in the corporate income tax, a reduction in the 27½-per-cent depletion allowance for gas and oil, and a series of amendments limiting the avoidance of taxes on income by the capital-gains device, where the rate was only half that on regular income but never more than 25 per cent. We tried to end other abuses, such as family partnerships, whereby a firm was allowed lower tax rates by having infants and wives as partners, though there was no contribution by them of services or capital. The most notorious case involved a son who was made a partner of a family firm shortly after birth. I aroused the ire of the committee by asking whether it could be maintained that the profession of accountancy was so simple that an infant in arms could master it.

Since it was almost impossible to muster the necessary one-fifth of a quorum for a roll call, we were always snowed under on the voice votes. When we did get a roll call, we were beaten, 42 to 18, on the family-partnership amendment. The biggest uproar came over the depletion allowance for oil and gas. After a furious defense of the practice by the Establishment, we saw the depletion principle extended to a whole series of new products, such as sand and gravel and finally, at Connally's insistence, even to oyster and clam shells, and this despite our plea that there were no "dry holes" in these cases, as in gas and oil.

In 1951 the Ways and Means and Finance committees sponsored another tax bill, again grossly inadequate both in the totals to be raised and in its many loopholes. This time, although better prepared, our group held a refresher course and worked hard on a series of amendments. For a week we subjected the bill to vigorous debate.†

To meet the costs of the war, we tried to raise more money and to distribute the burden more justly. For the tax year 1950–51, the extra costs of the war were estimated at around $17 billion. The tax bill as submitted by the Senate Finance Committee in late August would not

---

* Students of tax history and the give and take of floor debate may be interested in this 1950 struggle. See the *Congressional Record,* 81st Congress, Second Session, Part 10, pp. 13671–13705, 13830–13840, 14054–14060, 14092–14116. For an analysis of the debate, see Randolph Paul, *Taxation in the United States,* Boston: Little, Brown & Co., 1954, pp. 554–571. In a special session called after the 1950 elections, an excess-profits tax was passed. See Paul, *op. cit.,* pp. 626–629.
† For a record of this debate, see the *Congressional Record,* 82nd Congress, 1st Session, Part 9, pp. 11805–12382, and Randolph Paul, *op. cit.,* pp. 607–626.

have provided more than $3½ billion initially, and not more than $4½ billion once it was in full operation. This would result in a big deficit, which would have to be met by borrowing. Ultimately, the banks, creating deposits or checkbook money, would meet most of this deficit. Of course, the result would be a rise in the price level. Instead, we wanted to profit from the experience of both World War I and World War II.

In the first war only about one-third of the cost of the war had been met by taxes; the remaining two-thirds were financed by borrowing, of which a large part came, not from savings, but from bank-created credit. In World War II a slightly better record was made when about three-sevenths of the cost was met by taxes. But in each case the great rise in prices, with all its hardships, was largely due to the failure of Congress to pass adequate tax increases. Our little liberal group tried, though to do so was politically unpopular, to remedy this weakness during the Korean War by seeking to plug as many of the loopholes as we could and by providing that those who made money from the war should bear their share of the burden.

We hoped to increase corporate taxes, the rate on capital gains, provide for the collection of taxes at the source on dividends and interest, and improve the provisions affecting family partnerships. Perhaps most important, we tried to reduce the percentage depletion on oil and gas from 27½ to 15.

We lost every battle, and mustered only nine votes, against 71, on the depletion allowance. The nine were: Benton, Douglas, Green, Humphrey, Kefauver, Lehman, Blair Moody, Pastore, and Williams. But we came out of both struggles knowing we were right.

Without going into the merits of progressive taxation (in which I believe), I will say only that justice demands that people with equal incomes should at least pay equal taxes. I coined the term "horizontal equity" to describe what we were seeking. And yet this principle was flagrantly violated. In response to our questions, the Treasury revealed that there was one man who for a decade had enjoyed an income of over a million dollars a year and had not paid a single dollar in federal taxes. Although I was determined to go on in this matter, friendly Senators, including Matthew Neely, told me that I was committing political suicide.

Our efforts were supported by two professors of tax law, William Carey, formerly of Northwestern, later at Columbia, and Stanley Surrey, then of Harvard. Their articles in law reviews on the erosion of the income tax gave a new respectability to what we had been fighting for. Randolph Paul was immensely helpful with his book and articles. The economists, except for Pechman and a few scattered men, remained completely silent and have remained so during nearly twenty years of controversy.

In 1954 the Republicans controlled both branches of Congress, and they brought in their own tax bill. This embodied the extraordinary principle that income from dividends should be taxed at a lower rate than income from wages and salaries. Although our group of Northern liberals, rallying against this principle, which was sponsored by Secretary of the Treasury George Humphrey, gave it a severe floor battle, the bipartisan coalition was too strong. With my own ears I heard Secretary Humphrey justify this principle on the grounds that it would stimulate equity financing and that it was a relief for low-income families, since it was they, he said, who owned American corporations. I could not determine whether he really believed this.

The tax code was completely rewritten, and in such complex language that it was almost impossible to identify the jokers that we suspected had found their way into the act.*

Because of doubts aroused by the tax bill and because of the year's industrial recession, the Democrats won back control over both houses of Congress in November of 1954; I was re-elected by a comfortable margin. When I became chairman of the Joint Economic Committee, with the staff assistance of an old Chicago student, Norman Ture, we uncovered so much material that I changed the term "loopholes" to "truckholes."

The Finance Committee

For several years I had wanted to be transferred from the Labor to the Finance Committee, where future tax policy was usually determined. But Johnson and the Steering Committee always passed me by. First, Russell Long and Clinton Anderson were put on the committee; then, Barkley. Upon Barkley's death, Johnson assigned himself. Smathers, although two years my junior, was also advanced over me. When, in 1955, another vacancy occurred and I was senior to all the other applicants, I again applied. I got nowhere. The liberal commentator Doris Fleeson then began a series of articles in which she accused Johnson of opposing me at the behest of the Texas oil and gas interests. This was probably true. For months he resisted Miss Fleeson, but he finally gave in and allowed me to take the vacant seat. After all, I would be only one of fifteen members. A few years later, in a burst of sardonic truth, he told me that this was the worst mistake he had ever made in his whole political life.

Thanks to Doris Fleeson, for the next eleven years I served on the Finance Committee. This was my most interesting experience in the Senate. Although not at the center of power, I could watch what was happening at the center and sometimes affect its course. It was a most demanding position, for which I studied hard. While continuing to support most of

* For the efforts of the liberal Democratic group and Senator Williams to plug the tax "loopholes," see the *Congressional Record*, Vol. 100, Part 7, pp. 9301–9319, 9602–9615.

the reforms that Humphrey and I had urged in 1950 and 1951, I soon discovered other abuses needing correction. Happily, Albert Gore, an ideal colleague, soon joined the committee, and we worked closely together in the next years.

The Depletion Allowance

I CONCENTRATED my fire upon the depletion allowance. This exempted from all federal taxation 27½ per cent of all gross income from gas and oil up to 50 per cent of net income. The profits in the industry are shown by the fact that in most cases the 27½ per cent of the gross was nearly equal to 50 per cent of the net. In other words, operating costs were low. Moreover, this exemption was granted without any limitation as to the length of time that the well or field had been in operation or the ratio of the tax benefits to the original cost of the well. Thus, in East Texas, around Beaumont, wells still gushed oil after forty years, and, according to an official study, the allowances for the country as a whole averaged thirteen times the total drilling and developmental costs. Other studies have shown a nineteen to one ratio.

The fifteen leading oil companies paid only 8 per cent of their net income in federal taxes, while the average rate for all corporations was 42 or 43 per cent, or five times as much. Oil was the favored industry.

The depletion principle, moreover, was spreading rapidly to other minerals. Uranium also had an allowance of 27½ per cent. Sulphur was given 23 per cent, and the general rule for the whole range of minerals became 15 per cent. Coal was allowed 10 per cent, while sand and gravel and Connally's clam and oyster shells continued to enjoy their favors. Efforts were made to extend the principle to earth and water, and to the fabrication and processing of oil, gas, and minerals as well as to their extraction.

In the late '50's and early '60's, we got the Treasury to estimate the amount of these exemptions. They then totaled around $3½ billion a year, with a net loss in revenue of $1½ billion.

The 27½-per-cent provision for depletion had been inserted in the tax laws in 1926, when the corporate income tax amounted to only 14 per cent of net profits and when it appeared that the oil supply might soon be exhausted. But it had grown into a poisonous infection as the industry thrived. Until recently, the corporate income tax was levied at 52 per cent. In practice, the depletion allowance amounted to a rebate of about 25 per cent, or nearly one-half of the net profits after taxes.

Tax favors of this size led to a misapplication of resources. This did arouse the opposition of a few young economists. They produced statistics proving that even with the rebate, the *average* net returns on the actual investment in domestic oil and gas did not exceed the general average. The allowance had stimulated overinvestment, which in turn had reduced profits. But the ethical effects were even worse. It was manifestly unfair for millionaires to pay less to the federal government than hardworking manual and clerical employees with low or middle incomes. The extent of this injustice was not at first fully realized, but gradually, as we forced the Treasury to make fuller reports, it became widely known.

Although Hubert Humphrey remained completely faithful on roll calls, his main interests had turned in other directions. Since the burden of the fight had now fallen on me, I kept making inserts in the *Congressional Record* to publicize what was going on. With the profit-and-loss statements of twenty-eight companies of the second grade I showed the small amounts most of them were paying in taxes. Over a short period, one company had made $65 million in net profits but had paid no taxes and had actually received a refund of over $200,000. To shield them from popular anger, I gave letters in place of the names of these companies. I now believe that this was excessively chivalrous.

At last, progressive newspapermen and columnists began to pay attention to the issue, and we gathered support. Gore was most helpful, as was the highly honorable Republican conservative Senator John Williams, from Delaware, the heartland of the Du Pont empire.

Our 1951 failure to rally more than nine votes to cut the depletion rate convinced me that it was futile to insist on the elimination of the 27½-per-cent depletion allowance, or even on a flat 15 per cent. The industry was too strong for that, and if I tried to do away completely with the allowance for gas and oil or even to cut it, I would logically also have to attack the myriad of allowances for the other mineral and earth substances. This I thought would be an assault on too wide a front. It seemed better to concentrate on the worst abuse, gas and oil, as a more moderate goal. Later we could move on. My new proposal was to maintain the 27½-per-cent depletion allowance for all firms and individuals whose gross income from oil and gas was less than $1 million a year. For those whose gross incomes ranged between $1 and $5 million, the allowance was to be cut to 21¼ per cent, and to 15 per cent for all with annual gross incomes in excess of $5 million. This would reduce the rebate to the oil and gas groups to about the same allowance as that for other minerals, while it would save, according to the Treasury, from about $400 million to half a billion a year. Interestingly enough, it developed that the vast majority of the profits came from the big enterprises, so that the lower rates for the smaller did not greatly reduce the total savings that could be made.

These modifications outraged Williams, who believed in ideological purity, especially for Democrats. Every time I introduced my graduated reductions, he countered with another bill reducing the allowance to 15 per cent across the board. When he did so, he grinned sardonically as he looked to see how I was taking it. I justified my graduated scale on the ground that the larger ventures had more drillings and, hence, a better distribution of risk than the small. Like Antonio's shipping ventures in the *Merchant of Venice,* complete failure was improbable. Normally, the successes of a large operation could recoup its losses. The small driller, however, was liable to greater risk, thus justifying a higher rebate and a lower tax.

Mixed with this consideration was the hope that I could split off the vast majority of small drillers from the major companies, thus obtaining their neutrality if not their active support. With the exception of a few stalwart Democrats, I did not, however, win any such support. The small operators, with industrial solidarity, stuck by the giants even though their own tax burden would not have been increased. I discovered moreover that many of them acted as pilot fish for the big companies. The giants let the wildcatters do the experimental drilling and suffer any losses from failure. Where successful, the big companies bought out the wildcatters and negotiated leases with the landowners by which the latter would generally receive a royalty of one-eighth of the total yield. The wildcatters were therefore told that if the profits of the big companies were reduced by the Douglas bill, they would get paid less.

Despite the fact that there were probably only three companies in all of Illinois whose gross incomes exceeded $1 million a year, they set the tone of the industry there, which presented a solid front of opposition.

I discovered two other features of our tax laws that gave great favors to the large oil companies. Nearly all the giants also had rich foreign holdings in either Venezuela or the Persian Gulf area. Since the extensive oil deposits there were close to the surface, yields in these areas were fabulous, with operating costs low and profits enormous. From reliable testimony, it seemed that operating costs on the Persian Gulf did not exceed ten cents a barrel and that oil could be delivered via a pipeline on board tankers in Beirut for not more than twenty-five cents a barrel. Nevertheless, the depletion allowance was granted on foreign drillings, too. This was done despite the fact that under the national laws of those countries, the subsurface deposits belonged to the nation and not to the companies, which were merely given a leasing right of extraction. Therefore they had no property wasting away. And yet they were given their 27½-per-cent allowance just the same.

After World War II the underdeveloped countries began to drive better bargains on royalty charges to the foreign groups holding these leases. Formerly these charges had been low, ranging in certain cases from around 12 to 16 per cent of the gross receipts. At these rates the Western nations made a killing. After the war Venezuela raised its share to 50 per cent. The Persian Gulf countries learned about this and followed suit. More recently Venezuela has raised its share again, which started to escalate the charges made by the sheiks. There is a variation as to what price is used as the base for these percentages, but the underdeveloped countries are gaining a larger share. The elegant Kuwait Embassy in Washington and the scale of its entertainments are a proof of this fact.

For us the significance of these payments was that they were treated as taxes, rather than as royalties. Under the international agreements governing so-called "double taxation," such taxes are counted as a dollar-for-dollar offset against such taxes as the same company may owe in the United States. Within the United States, however, royalties to landowners are treated as an operating expense prior to taxes. For example, an American company in country X which has a total gross revenue of $300 million has operating expenses of $50 million. It pays country X 50 per cent of its gross revenue for the right to drill and extract oil. This comes to $150 million, and it has, therefore, a profit of $100 million. Normally, let us say, it would pay the United States a 40-per-cent tax on its profits, or $40 million. But the full amount of $150 million of royalties, now called "taxes," is credited against the amount due Uncle Sam. Hence the company is free of all taxes. If it is not, then the depletion allowance of $27\frac{1}{2}$ per cent of gross income up to one-half of the net income can be applied.

In a Senate debate, the unchallenged statement was made that an immensely prosperous American company operating near the Persian Gulf for year after year paid no taxes at all. Royalties for the use of land are not transformed into taxes simply because a foreign government, rather than an individual, owns the land and the subsurface deposits. Corporate taxes should be levied on profits, not on current operating expenses for the use of land. This abuse was magnified by the fact that the extra credits on foreign operations were also used as an offset against domestic taxes that otherwise would have been paid. I was moving to correct some of these abuses when I left the Senate.

I never questioned the deduction of the cost of dry holes or unsuccessful drillings from the income of the successful drillings conducted by the same person or company. Friends from the oil states often urged me to attack the writing off of all the intangible drilling and development costs in the first year—the fastest of all depreciation rates. The physical wells themselves and their casings were given a longer life, but the labor and other intangible investments were completely written off in the first year and deducted from any tax otherwise due. On the average these amounted to around 80 per cent or more of the total drilling and development costs. The combined depreciation rate was altogether too fast and was a further encouragement to overinvestment. Nevertheless, I decided not to stress this point. It was too hard for the public to distinguish these expenses from operating costs, which in the oil business, as in any other, are legitimate deductions from gross receipts before net income is found. Nor did I attack the quotas imposed on the imports of oil, which kept up domestic prices and swelled the profits of domestic producers. I did try to prevent the domestic state quotas from boosting prices, but I was thwarted by the continued practice of the Justice Department in reporting that all was well.

In short, my modest proposal aimed only to trim the greatest abuse for the largest operations. It was both economically and ethically sound, but it was politically hazardous to any sponsor.

This issue was especially important in the southeastern part of Illinois, where there was an entire Congressional district largely dependent on the oil industry. Wanting to meet the issue head on, I went into the oil centers at Carmi, Mount Carmel, and Centralia to argue my case. There was no open encouragement, although I had the feeling that the farmers, whose royalties of one-eighth of gross revenue would not have been reduced by a graduated tax on profits and who did not like the oil companies; were secretly pleased to see me carry the battle into the heart of the enemy's country. But local Democratic candidates for Congress were terrified by my argument and tried to make it clear that they did not agree. They wanted my help but hoped I would be silent on oil. The big companies circularized their stockholders and dealers over the state, while large amounts of oil money poured in at election times. For the city folk and general taxpayers, the issue was too remote to attract many voters. As I look back on it, it seems a miracle that I lasted as long as I did.

Periodically I brought up my proposal in committee and whenever an important tax bill was being considered on the floor. Inside the committee, I could always depend on Gore and Williams and a shifting one or two others. On the floor, our small coalition's strength averaged around twenty, although once it soared to thirty-one. That vote really aroused the oil companies to redoubled vigor until our votes again fell off. We divided the field: Proxmire stressed the withholding on dividends and interest, while Clark and Gore took other topics. They were all good comrades under fire, and we developed a strong and abiding fellowship.

I concluded that a qualifying test for membership on the Finance Committee was to support the depletion allowance. This position also helped to raise campaign funds for the member. The senatorial Campaign Committee, with Bobby Baker as its operating head, not only raised money from the groups wanting special favors, but also apportioned funds to those on whom it could depend.

A few members of the committee put their careers on the line to do what was right, but there were many disappointments, including Eugene McCarthy. In the House, where McCarthy had served for ten years before he ran for the Senate, he had made a fine record in the early years. Since he seemed that rare combination of scholar and man of action, I campaigned for him in Minnesota in 1958, likening him to Michelangelo's twin figures in the Medici Chapel in Florence depicting the active and contemplative life. When he was put on the Finance Committee, I optimistically thought that the Steering Committee had changed its policy. The next time I brought my depletion amendment up, I told McCarthy it was coming. He said he was going down to the dining room for lunch, but he somehow allowed me to believe that he would be back in time to vote. He was not, but strolled in carelessly after the vote. On the next test, he voted against us and for the oil group. This was his practice after 1961. I finally decided that he had been put on the committee after he agreed with the party leaders to go along on depletion and other important points. Indeed, he seemed not to regard taxation as an important matter.

Toward the end of the long struggle, I became conscience-stricken over the dangers to which I was exposing my fellow liberals. I had often obtained a roll call on the depletion allowance, and the faithful twenty followed into the battle. We were always beaten, after which my colleagues faced reprisals from the oil industry. Gore, Clark, Proxmire, and I gladly took our chances and, indeed, rather enjoyed the battle of matching wits and will power against the giants. But I hesitated increasingly to send others, less concerned, into great danger. It reminded me of the way Lord Raglan and his fellow British generals in the Crimean War had sent the "noble six hundred" into certain slaughter when they ordered the attack by their crack cavalry battalion against the massed Russian artillery at Balaclava. So in my last two years I presented our case, got some supporting help from the ever-determined Proxmire and Gore, and then, instead of asking for a roll call, contented myself with a voice vote, which somewhat shielded the identity of our supporters. It seemed impossible for flesh and blood to break the hold of the massed billions of economic power.

Collection at the Source

BUT the depletion allowance was not the only abuse in our tax system. There were a myriad of others. One of the most important was the failure of the wartime Ruml tax reforms requiring the current collection at the source of income taxes on wages and salaries to include a similar provision for dividends and interest. The provision eliminated the need for the workers to pay the massed taxes at the end of the year. In turn, the proportion of income from wages and salaries that was not reported did not in fact exceed 3 per cent.

No such discipline was, however, applied to the owners of stocks and bonds, for there was no automatic deduction or reporting of their income. It was up to them voluntarily to declare it and to pay the required taxes. Figures from the Treasury for 1959 showed that a billion dollars a year, or about 8 per cent of the total dividends on stock, were not reported, while no less than 34 per cent, or $3 billion, in interest went unreported and untaxed. Some of this was conscious evasion, and some was unconscious misunderstanding. The failure to collect these sums of course reduced revenues annually by about a billion dollars.

As I had been contending since 1950, it was clear that the withholding method was at once more efficient and more just. When the Kennedy administration submitted its tax bill for 1962, it accordingly provided for collection at the source for the basic income tax on dividends and interest. The Treasury experts, under Donald Lubig, came up with a simple and efficient plan modeled on the methods already used for wages and salaries. The institutions paying out dividends and interest were to deduct automatically the basic rate of the income tax (which was then 20 per cent) from all such payments they made. They were to do this without specifying the amounts paid to each individual. Then the recipients could file claims every quarter for any excess payment they had made above that which they owed. This provision was more lenient than the parallel claims made by recipients of wages and salaries, which were made only annually, rather than quarterly. The withholding system, or collection at the source, had worked smoothly and swiftly in the case of wages and salaries, and neutral experts examining the Treasury proposal told us that it would do as well with dividends and interest.

The House Ways and Means Committee adopted the plan, and then the House itself, under its usual closed rule, approved it as part of the tax bill. Gore and I prepared to support it in the Senate.

There had been little or no opposition in the House, and I had almost concluded that this was one reform whose time had come. Never was I more mistaken. Suddenly we were deluged by a letter-writing blitz. Within the space of a month, 65,000 angry letters of protest from Illinois citizens poured into my office. Other Senators received a big volume. When we investigated, we found that the major building and loan associations, whose headquarters were in Chicago, were chiefly responsible for the drive. The banks were also giving vigorous aid. They had held their fire while the House was acting because once the amendment had passed Ways and Means, the closed rule made it impossible to take it out on the floor of the House. The deluge of concentrated opposition we received was even bigger than when Truman fired MacArthur. The letters showed that someone was either misinforming the depositors or at least encouraging such misinformation. A large number of the protestors called the plan the imposition of a "new and discriminatory tax." It was truly astounding to see how these sincere people thought that interest was not income and hence was not subject to taxation. Mixed with this delusion was the recurrent theme that interest and dividends should not be taxed since they were the fruit of saving. No consideration was given to the fact that wages and salaries were also the result of effort and yet were not spared from helping to bear the burdens of society.

My reply was that this was not a new tax, but merely a better method for collecting an existing tax. Furthermore, I gently hinted that the fact that so many were confused on this point was ample proof of the widespread evasion and avoidance of the tax on the part of those who received interest and dividends and of a general failure to report these forms of income. This had no effect.

Another carefully nurtured misconception soon burst upon the scene. In this assault, the letters charged that the tax was a 20-per-cent annual levy on the total capital owned by anyone. Consequently, it was attacked as part of a Communist scheme to confiscate all private capital. A high note of patriotic indignation was thus injected into the discussion, and we were branded as sinister villains seeking to undermine the republic. Our hurried reply was that this was a tax on income, not on capital, and that if a man had invested $1,000 in a building and loan association which bore a 4-per-cent interest rate, then the tax of 20 per cent would be levied on the $40 of interest and not on the principal of $1,000. It would therefore amount at the most to $8 a year and not to $200.

In a final letter of reply we summarized the entire case, showing how widely the income tax on dividends and interest had been evaded and how this had increased the tax burden on others. The remedy was for the savings institutions to forward a fifth of all interest payments to the Treasury and for individuals to file quarterly requests for refund in the event of overwithholding. We pointed out that a similar policy had been followed successfully for twenty years on wages and salaries and asked how the objectors could justify a softer treatment for dividends and interest than for income from effort, although the practice cost the government much and heaped unjustified burdens on other taxpayers. I always inserted my replies into the *Congressional Record* to give them a wider circulation and help offset the stream of propaganda pouring in on us.

It was a vain effort. Nobody seemed convinced. The building and loan associations and most of the banks continued their alliance of opposition. Not only did they brand the new proposal unworkable, but also they deplored the plight of widows and orphans who were dependent on interest. How unjust, how rapacious it was to sweep away these meager savings from threadbare widows! It was never mentioned that the government could not touch their savings unless their income was enough to be taxable. Nor was it mentioned that the elderly received a double exemption from the taxation of their incomes, and a married couple had $2,400 annually exempted from taxation. Another unstressed point was that since dividends and interest were paid mainly to the well-to-do, the amounts ultimately refunded would be a mere fraction of the total, indeed much smaller than in the case of wages and salaries.

Meanwhile, as the tidal wave of mail continued, the big hearing room where we took testimony was full of well-dressed defenders of the widows and orphans. It is a pleasure to record that there were a few dissidents to the general opposition. Arthur Roth, the president of the Franklin National Bank on Long Island, already a maverick in the banking fraternity because of his aggressive tactics, and suspected of planning to invade Manhattan, became even more disliked among his fellow financiers by boldly proclaiming that the plan was both workable and just and that he would be glad to operate under it. I was also proud of a small banker from the northwest side of Chicago, who took the same position, while the highly honorable mutual savings banks of New England and the Northeast abstained from joining in the clamor.

These were the rare, though highly cherished, exceptions, for the tide was irresistible. Almost every Senator was subjected to the same pressures. At the last, the Kennedy administration deserted us. Its concern was chiefly to give a tax rebate on investment as a stimulant to economic growth. If it fought for withholding, it might endanger its whole tax package. Therefore, the administration threw the provision overboard, leaking word to others that there would be no objection to killing the withholding provision. We were not told directly, however, that we were being abandoned.

Although the vote was 11 to 5 against us in the Finance Committee, Gore and I decided to continue the fight on the Senate floor. To the distress of the Democratic leadership, I tried to restore the withholding clause, but was overwhelmingly defeated, mustering only twenty votes.

We felt we had been deserted by those who should have been our allies, and shot down without a hand raised to help us. During the whole discussion, which went on for weeks, I do not remember ever receiving a single letter from an economist supporting our efforts. The tax academicians were so absorbed in promoting dubious economic growth that they were ready to ignore tax injustice.

Senator Harry Byrd, although against compulsory withholding, had been disturbed by our evidence. He abhorred the loss of so much revenue. As a substitute, he proposed that the institutions paying out dividends and interest should also submit a report to the Internal Revenue Service showing the names, addresses, and social security numbers of each recipient, together with the amounts paid to each. The data would be relayed to various regional computer centers. There they would be combined by names and numbers, and the totals paid out would be automatically compared with the amounts reported by the individuals. The IRS could move to collect any amount due. This was done, and is now in effect.

While this eased the conscience of our opponents, it was inferior to the original Treasury proposal. In the first place, it greatly increased the work of the banks, about which they had complained so loudly. Instead of merely transmitting to the IRS a fifth of the total amounts they paid, without identifying the amounts individual recipients received, they now had to report each specific payment, with a complete identification of each recipient. It puzzled me that the financial institutions would accept all this red tape instead of our infinitely simpler alternative.

The second defect in the Byrd plan was that the burden of collecting any unpaid taxes was still imposed on the IRS. The individual continued to take the initiative in reporting his income. While the IRS was furnished with information by which it could check on the accuracy of these statements, this did not automatically collect the amounts due. This required an enormous effort. If all this made sophisticated evaders more careful in filling out their income tax statements, and so diminished evasion, it did not help where people forgot to include interest and dividends or coldly risked detection.

In 1965 I looked into the amounts by which the Byrd proposal had increased collections. The Treasury made a rough and tentative estimate that this would come at that time to about $250 million a year. If this was correct, the government since then would have collected $1½ billion in otherwise unpaid taxes. I have often consoled myself with the thought that this was not a bad achievement in an imperfect world. But I have also been aware that even on the basis of the 1959 figures, the total loss from evasion and avoidance would still be at least three to four times this figure. And with the tremendous increase in deposits in savings and loan associations and banks, the absolute loss may now be still greater than the $900 million a year the Treasury estimated.

I concluded that one way of showing the class nature of the refusal to extend the withholding principle to interest and dividends was to eliminate it from wages and salaries. I moved, therefore, to abolish collection at the source of the tax on all income from effort. Why, I asked, should we be more severe upon the lower-income wage and salaried folk than upon the higher-income recipients of dividends and interest? This would have repealed the Ruml reforms. While knowing that the suggestion would not carry, I wanted to show up the hypocrisy of those who insisted that ownership be exempted but earnings included under the withholding principle. Although I began with a discussion of this inconsistency, the Democratic leadership moved to table in order to shut off any further discussion as soon as I made my formal motion. Of course, the motion to table carried by a big majority. Nevertheless, the leadership had suffered some uncomfortable moments, which we used to practical effect in the many discussions of the issue.

During the heat of the tax struggle I was probably naïve. I could understand why the recipients of interest and dividends would object to collection at the source, but why should savings institutions, such as the building and loan associations, object to such a simple administrative proposal, which would entail less work than the complicated Byrd alternative? It was not until the bill was passed that I began to understand their motives. The probable explanation was that a large proportion of the growth in savings accounts came from the automatic accumulation of redeposited interest. A considerable fraction of depositors did not withdraw their interest, but allowed it to be credited to their accounts. Many of the savers either forgot to report this silent growth in their capital as income or made the naïve assumption that it had happened from spontaneous generation. There was less duplicity on the part of the savers than I had suspected, although there was still a good deal. But there was also more foolishness. It is easy to be foolish when it is profitable. But the savings institutions always knew precisely what was going on. Their resources were growing in part from this very accumulation of compound interest, and they did not want their rate of growth to be slowed down by the amount of the tax. Enjoying the use of funds of which the federal government was deprived, they wanted to hold on to them. The market economists did not protest.

As the struggle ended, I thought the added bookkeeping might soon induce industrial concerns to consent to withholding on dividends. Companies with bond issues and even building and loan associations and the savings departments of commercial banks might do the same. To date this has not occurred.

32

Other Tax Abuses

As WE CONTINUED the battle for tax reform into the 1960's, the research staff of the Treasury exposed many loopholes in existing tax laws and dug up many cases of abuse in the exemptions of Americans living abroad and in the deductions for travel and entertainment claimed as business expenses. Secretary Douglas Dillon deserves credit for making them a part of the record.

Expense Accounts

ELABORATE and costly parties had been treated as legitimate business outlays. Indeed, the expensive restaurants, hotels, and theaters of the big cities had been largely maintained by the expense-account style of life fostered by these deductions. Some of the instances were nauseating; others were hilarious. One businessman maintained a yacht in the Caribbean for the entertainment of prospective customers and those who could send him business. Under questioning about his line of business, this generous host said that he was an undertaker. I could imagine the ghoulish smile with which he greeted his prospective customers.

Once, when visiting President Kennedy at West Palm Beach, I saw the harbor at Fort Lauderdale crowded with expensive yachts. When I asked why there were so many, I was answered by the simple words "Expense accounts." At hotels in Washington, New York, London, and Paris there were, I was told, suites reserved but seldom used by wealthy executives, and occasionally I was offered the hospitality of such accommodations.

In the early 1950's I had made an effort to check this by setting an upper limit on the amount of tax deduction permitted for room and meals. Originally I fixed this at twice the amount allowed public officials. In the early '60's this would have been $32 a day. One could live well on that. Immediately I was deluged by a flood of technical objections. The ceiling would unduly limit commercial travelers showing their wares, and it did not make allowance for board meetings requiring large quarters. I asked for help to work out these technical problems, but it was more convenient for the majority to retain them as an excuse for preserving their expense-account way of life.

Even the lofty American Bar Association obtained exemption for most of its travel for a summer meeting in England on the ground that it was subsidizing a more intimate knowledge of English judicial procedure. Wintertime in the Caribbean was attractive for trade conventions, either on board ship or on land.

Curiously, the Internal Revenue Service, which had not been vigorous in questioning the expense accounts of affluent industrialists, now developed a righteous passion for checking the expenses of union officials, especially those who had supported Truman or Stevenson. But they came to disaster with Walter Reuther when they discovered that he never paid more than $8 for a hotel room or $1.50 for a meal, and that when on tour he always paid his own laundry and valet charges. This so impressed a former FBI agent, Carmine Bellino, that when a highly conservative Senate committee was investigating Reuther, Robert Kennedy, who was counsel for the committee, suggested that he take the stand. The hearing room was crowded because of the anticipated exposure. Then Bellino in a straightforward manner testified to Reuther's Spartan habits, along with the upright finances of the United Automobile Workers. The projected smear collapsed, and when I went into the hearing room a few days later to insist that Reuther be treated fairly, I found the expected inquisitors quite restrained in their questioning. The Bellino testimony helped to modify some easy generalizations about the character of FBI agents.

In exposing another bias of the IRS, John Williams told us how it had approved as a tax-deductible expense a big bribe given to a foreign dictator by an American company doing business in his country. The excuse was that, there, bribery was the accepted practice, without which a company could not operate. So the American taxpayers paid half the cost of corrupting a foreign government.

Damages paid under antitrust suits are treated by the IRS as operating costs. This means that 48 per cent of these costs are met by reduced corporate taxes. The government and the people pay about half the penalties imposed on a corporation when it breaks the law.

One practice that partially surfaced was that of suppliers giving lavish gifts to purchasing agents and company officials. Like the gifts originally offered me, these were ostensibly expressions of friendship. I recalled the widespread pilfering by the manager of a faculty club at Chicago. He finally confessed that, in common with the managers of other private clubs, he had accepted large kickbacks from suppliers and that they in turn had artificially inflated prices. The *Reporter* had once summarized the results of a business-school study showing that the cost of business Christmas presents amounted annually to many hundred of millions. Uncle Sam was footing half the bill. Alongside this came a book, in 1960, from a reputable efficiency expert who, on the basis of wide experience, made similar estimates of white-collar embezzlement by insiders.

On the whole, business seemed far more corrupt than government, and, through the leniency of our tax laws and their administration, public funds were being indirectly used to help promote this corruption. In comparison with the general run of big business, politicians began to look better.

But so great were the pressures by favored groups, as well as the indifference of the general public, that neither administrators nor legislators felt free to act. Our proposals to limit the tax deductibility of travel and entertainment expenses met with the determined opposition not only of business, but also of hotels, restaurants, and theaters, and of the unions in related trades. New York, Chicago, New Orleans, and Miami, which had a large tourist trade, felt especially aggrieved, while vacation areas such as Florida, Arizona, and southern California were also involved. How pleasant it was to have Uncle Sam the unacknowledged but privately paying host for dinner at Antoine's and for evenings at the Stork Club. Uncle Sam also helped the theater, from Shakespeare to burlesque.

We tried to appeal to the suburban wives who were left at home when their husbands traveled, but the only result was to encourage business firms to invite wives to come along with their husbands to conventions. By widening the area of the privileged, family discord was quieted and a possible group of objectors pacified. And we were no nearer to our main objective.

One concession we did wring from the majority was to limit the privilege of tax exemption for presents from one person to another to $25 a year. Gone were the delightful days when diamonds could be given as casual tokens of esteem and affection.

Foreign Residence

AMERICANS living abroad were not tax innocents either. In 1962 we found that those claiming permanent residence in a foreign country were totally exempt from American taxation, and that, if only temporary residents, then a considerable fraction of their income was immune. A well-known movie actor and his wife, each with an income of over a million and a quarter dollars a year, paid Uncle Sam not a penny, because they were listed as permanent residents abroad. This was a favorite device of movie actors, who spent some of the proceeds of past successes under foreign flags or on making new movies on foreign locations while taking full advantage of the tax truckholes. I told Eric Johnston, who was representing that industry, that their record was particularly bad and that while I did not want to pillory any group as such and did not want to single out the movie industry, since there were industrialists and financiers who were as bad or worse, nevertheless, they should clean house and not oppose our reforms. To the best of my knowledge, they did make some improvements.

Corporations and businessmen took more than full advantage of overseas residence. The little principality of Liechtenstein was full of signs showing the headquarters of international holding companies. The capital, Vaduz, played the part Wilmington, Delaware, had a few decades earlier. Some wealthy shipping and oil tycoons shunned residence in their native lands as resolutely as did the fragile expatriates in the novels of Henry James.

Some legitimate reasons were given by international concerns whose American managers had to live abroad. Inevitably this created family problems and caused added expense for education, travel, and double residences. There were also international problems caused by double taxation. We wound up by exempting only the first $35,000 of the income of those living abroad, but I thought we needed a new international convention to deal with the problem. Believing the allowance still too high, I supported Senator Gore in his efforts to reduce it.

Split Incomes

OTHER LOOPHOLES in the tax laws were zealously and effectively defended. Among them were the split-income provisions under which a husband might divide his income equally with his wife for tax purposes and thus avoid the higher rates on the upper brackets of his real income. While women have a right to their own income, I do not think wives should be used as stalking horses to enable their husbands to avoid taxes. Although it is true that the wife of a well-to-do man costs her husband far more than the $600 that is allowed as a personal exemption, it is also true that her addition to the family does not double the expenses. Since the tax saving increases with income, marriage is more blessed financially for the millionaire than for those of the middle and lower economic stations. Wives of the wealthy are scarcely that much better than the wives of the less affluent. But once this favoritism was put into the tax laws in 1946, it seemed that it could not be deleted.

The Taxation of Homes and Buildings

ANOTHER DISPARITY is that people who own their homes are not taxed on the imputed net income this gives them. The renter, on the other hand, receives no credit for the amount that he pays for shelter. X and Y may live in identical houses across the street from each other and each have a cash income of $10,000 a year. X owns his $20,000 house, on which he pays no rent. If he did not own it, he would have to pay a rent of at least $2,500. His real income is, therefore, $12,500 minus local property taxes and maintenance costs. If these total $1,000, his real income is $11,500, but he pays income tax on only $10,000. Y pays $2,500 rent. His real income, exclusive of housing, is thus only $7,500, but he is taxed on the full $10,000 of cash income. This is manifestly unfair, especially since the local property taxes that X pays and the interest paid on any mortgage he owes are also deductible from taxable income.

Thus there are provisions that favor not only the married over the single taxpayer and the suburbanite over the dwellers in the inner city, but also the wealthy over the less affluent and the poor. Indeed, the larger a man's income, the more his federal taxes will be reduced by home ownership and the higher his incentive to enjoy costly and multiple homes. There is no limit to the number of homes whose services are exempted. This subject is now discussed among recondite tax theorists, but it has never really surfaced in public discussions. The desirability of promoting home ownership, which is real, has increased the tax favors to the wealthy estate owner and to those who have three or more homes.

Some have urged as a compensatory device that the amounts paid out in rent should be deductible from net taxable income. But this would further exempt the successive ways in which income is spent. It would still further riddle the tax laws. From a practical standpoint, getting this feature adopted, like getting rid of the split-income provision, now seems a closed issue.

It was not until 1962 that I had the chance to probe the intricacies of the federal taxation of income from buildings, and it was really not until I had been defeated that I could go into it thoroughly. I then learned enough to convince me that there were many things wrong. In the first place, accelerated depreciation at double the ordinary rate was granted on buildings for the first five to seven years. Instead of a 2½-per-cent yearly rate based on an expected life of forty years, the rate of deduction could be speeded up to 5 per cent. It was applied not to the depreciated book value of the building, but to the purchase price to the current owner. Thus, if a new building had cost its owner $5 million, a depreciation credit was allowed amounting to $250,000 a year, or $1,250,000 over the full five years. In fact, the actual depreciation was almost always far less, and often there was an actual appreciation due to correcting the defects that almost invariably show up in new buildings. The owner could then take his $1,250,000 depreciation credit and apply it to his consolidated income account. Thus, if his net income from the building amounted to $200,000 a year, he would get this tax free, with an additional $50,000 a year or $250,000 for five years to credit against other income. The owner might sell the building for the same or an even greater amount than its purchase price. The book value would be $3.5 million. If the new sales price was $5 million, then the difference of $1.5 million would be taxed as a capital gain at half the ordinary income tax rate but never would exceed 25 per cent. Had the federal tax been levied on income, the amounts previously withdrawn from taxation would have been taxed at ordinary rates. The transaction benefited the tax operator but injured the community.

Furthermore, this process could be endlessly repeated. Thus B, the new purchaser, could also claim 5 per cent yearly on his purchase price of $5 million and would be freed from taxation on $250,000 a year for five years. If he sold the building for $4½ million, it would still have been a paying project.

Such tax provisions have led to a rapid turnover in the ownership of buildings—residential as well as commercial. This has discouraged owners from maintaining their buildings. Buildings have been something for owners to buy and sell rather than conserve and cherish. They have not been guarded against deterioration.

Another weakness in the tax law is that the owner is not required to make any expenditures for repairs to arrest physical depreciation. The allowance was merely a financial device, ostensibly designed to protect owners against financial loss; in practice it overprotected them. There were many cases where the book value of the building after the depreciation deduction was almost zero but the building, though badly run down, still had a high commercial value.

If the federal tax laws offered no stimulus for the owner to keep his building up to standard, the local general property tax actually penalized him if he did so. The owner received no credit for major repairs. While minor improvements such as painting and papering could be charged off as operating costs, this was not true of major repairs and improvements, such as putting in new staircases or furnaces, better plumbing and electrical fixtures, air conditioning, and siding to strengthen and beautify the outside of houses. Instead, what commonly happened was that local tax authorities raised the assessed value of the house and, hence, the taxes that the owner paid. Whether the occupant was the owner or a tenant, the former was the one who ultimately was out of pocket, because improvements were penalized. Small wonder, then, that slum housing owned by absentee landlords is allowed to deteriorate. The moral is to get as much as one can out of the building, put nothing back in, and get out quickly.

Along the way, I became convinced that differential rates of depreciation should be applied to different parts of a house. Foundations and walls could last for much longer than the allowed forty years. In England, I had even seen thatch-roofed cottages that dated back to the days of Milton, while in Old Deerfield, in the Connecticut Valley, the frame houses were still strong after three centuries. But floors, stairways, and lighting were another matter, and commonly needed rapid replacement. Later, when I inspected the old-law tenements built in New York in the 1890's and the ugly red-brick row houses of Philadelphia and Baltimore of the 1870's and '80's, I found that their walls and foundations were still strong and adequate.

But we in the Senate had neither the time nor the backing to revise these depreciation rules. Nor could we deal with sale and leaseback practices, whereby a company or a person sold a building to an intermediary and then rented it back. In this way, the rental could be charged off as an operating cost while any profits were taxed at capital-gains rates.

The Single Tax

As GORE AND I made our onslaughts on the tax truckholes, I occasionally received letters accusing me of merely "showing off" while ignoring the worst abuse of all—namely, the failure to tax the "unearned increments" on bare-land values. I was not ignorant of this problem. As a college student I had read Henry George's *Progress and Poverty*. He, and Ricardo before him, had convinced me that the economic rent on bare land, exclusive of improvements in and on the soil, had been largely created by society, by the increase in population and the heightened productivity per capita. At Harvard, the highly conservative Thomas Nixon Carver had once divided incomes into three classes: "earnings, findings, and stealings." Economic rent was not a stealing, but neither was it an earning. It was a finding almost pure and simple. Although the owners did not create the increases in land values, they appropriated them.

I was not a "single" taxer, since I did not believe that such a tax would yield enough revenue to meet all the expenses of the modern state and since there were other forms of unearned income. However, I accepted the general proposition that the community should at least share in the increased values it created. On the walls of my study at home, in fact, I had hung a photograph of Henry George, alongside those of Ricardo, John Stuart Mill, W. S. Jevons, J. H. von Thünen, and Alfred Marshall.

By the time I was in the Senate, the single-tax movement had slumped since the days of its great advocates, Tom Johnson, Samuel M. ("Golden Rule") Jones, and Brand Whitlock. Many economists, by their captious criticisms, had contributed to this debacle. Because of this, and the fact that the issue involved local and state governments, rather than national, I did not take up this reform. I could not set the whole world aright, and in trying to do too much I might imperil what I could do. At any rate, this was my justification for keeping silent on this question while in the Senate. But I am grateful that as chairman of the Commission on Urban Problems I later had the chance to draft a supplementary statement on this subject and was supported by three of my colleagues. Perhaps the most impressive statement was the estimate by Allen Manvel, of the commission's staff, that in the decade between 1956 and 1966, the value of bare land in the country increased from $270 to $520 billions. This was a doubling, and if a share of the increase had been used for the improvement of our cities, we would now be a better society in every way; perhaps not so much blood would have run in the streets.

When I pass before the Great Judgment seat, I hope Saint Peter may forgive my silence as a senator on the increase in land values and accept my later efforts as at least partial atonement.

"Christmas Trees"

NEAR THE END of almost every Congressional session, the House Ways and Means Committee sent over to the Senate a special bill providing for a series of exemptions from the provisions of the tax laws. These could not be legally justified if specifically labeled as benefiting given individuals, corporations, or associations, so identities were disguised by general language. The amendments had been sponsored by influential members of Ways and Means and had commonly been adopted without a public hearing. Moreover, under the closed rule, the bill as a whole had not been scrutinized by the House.

Since the members of the Senate Finance Committee naturally claimed the same privilege of helping their own protégés and favorites, our committee loaded down the bill with further exemptions. Such bills were called "Christmas trees." At almost the last day of the session, when everyone was anxious to go home, the bill would be brought out on the floor. Some of the exemptions were thoroughly justified, but others were not. Everyone on the committee felt entitled to at least one favor, which reminded me of the common-law principle that "every dog is entitled to one bite."

Both in committee and on the floor I opposed those features of the bills that seemed especially unjust. One example concerned a big downstate Illinois company, and another the street-railway system of the Minnesota Twin Cities, which had formerly been in the control of the underworld. I got nowhere. Then I proposed that we should hold public hearings on these exemptions so that they would have to be explained and justified before the general public. This, I argued, would expose the worst and automatically improve the remainder. This proposal was also rejected. In the meantime, I was being hammered in business and political circles at home for not fighting for Illinois companies. Once again, there was the cry of "impractical professor."

I finally compromised to help a few mutual pension funds that had not met the dates required for eligibility. I was then reminded that I, too, had a stake in the "Christmas" favors that I had deplored. At least, I answered, I was ready to hold public hearings on my bills.

In retrospect, I regard this favoritism as one of the worst evils of our tax system. It not only fosters injustice, but also has made our tax laws unintelligible to all but a few initiates, who are highly paid for their knowledge and influence. Some Washington attorneys have grown rich by engineering such legislation.

Sleepers

SOMETIMES new abuses sprouted unrecognized under our very eyes. Once when we were considering a major tax bill, Kerr insisted on inserting what seemed to be an innocent provision, but which turned out to be a Trojan horse. This was to exempt from federal taxation all charitable contributions if in eight of the past ten years 90 per cent of a man's taxable income had been given to charity or paid in taxes. To encourage private charity seemed good, and I missed the booby traps concealed in the language. The proposal was presented only in general form, but there were at least three "jokers."

First, it was 90 per cent of a person's *taxable* income that was the basis —not 90 per cent of real income. Since the amounts exempted under the capital-gains and depletion-allowance provisions are not counted by the Treasury as income, but disappear from sight in their accounting, the proportion actually given away may be only a small fraction of a man's actual income. But the exemption would be on all gifts and not, as usual, limited to 30 per cent of the tax. This provision is especially popular among some of the oil barons of the Southwest.

The second joker is that by creating personal foundations, the donor can retain control of the properties that he is apparently giving away. The income may be spent only according to his wishes and often to his actual profit. Congressman Wright Patman has unearthed many abuses of these foundations. The Rockefellers, Fords, and Curriers have done splendid work through their foundations, but that cannot be said of some others.

The third joker is the right to hold back earnings and income and concentrate most of the payments into two of the ten years and so pay no taxes for the whole period.

I should have been on my guard against the plausible presentation of this bill, but it was first introduced only orally, and I always disliked questioning the motives of my colleagues. Indeed, I wanted to believe in them. But since Patman has exposed some of the weaknesses in these charitable deductions, I have often regretted that I did not insist on a closer examination.

The unlimited charitable deduction now ranks alongside the depletion allowance, the fast write-off of drilling and developmental costs, and the capital-gains privileges as a major reason why so many with huge incomes pay small taxes or none at all. It is also probable that too much local property of churches and charities for other than religious purposes is exempted from the general property tax. Some of the worst abuses of the Middle Ages have begun to reappear.

The Over-all Picture

IN FIGHTING these malpractices, I realized that I might misinterpret the over-all picture. Like a front-line soldier, I was absorbed in the immediate fire fight. But the research of my assistants Howard Shuman and Philip Stern gave me a perspective. They computed that the taxable incomes reported by the Treasury were only about one-half the personal incomes revealed by the Council of Economic Advisers. The other half escaped taxation. The basic exemption of $600 a year per person ($1,200 for those over sixty-five) could account for only a fraction of the difference. The remainder was largely income that most people believed was taxable but that in fact was exempted by a series of little-known devices.

In 1963 Stern estimated that a total of $115 billion of income was escaping federal taxation. The tax base was, therefore, shrunk by that amount, and $40 billion in potential tax revenue was lost. By 1968 the highly conservative Treasury staff estimated the revenue loss from these exemptions at $53 billion, while it was probably closer to $60 billion.*

In elegant satire in *The Great Treasury Raid,* Stern presents an annual massive assault on the Treasury by the groups which, in fact, defraud the taxpayers of these billions.

---

* *Tax Reform Studies and Proposals of U.S. Treasury Department,* 91st Congress, 1st Session, 4 vols., 474 pp., 1969, Joint Publication Committee on Ways and Means of the U.S. House of Representatives and Committee on Finance of the U.S. Senate. We also had reliable verbal assurances on some of these points.

For a raid of its magnitude, the time (high noon) and setting (the United States Treasury, a stone's throw from the White House) showed a breath-taking boldness of design and planning. From out of nowhere, it seemed, they appeared —old people and young, rich and poor, an oil millionaire here, a factory worker there, a real estate tycoon, a working mother, several well-known movie stars, some corporation presidents, even the chairman of a powerful Congressional committee. It was a mixed lot, all right, that converged on the Treasury Building that high noon. Into the building they strolled, gloriously nonchalant. No one stopped them; not a guard looked up to question them. Quickly and quietly they found their way to the vaults; opened them noiselessly with the special passkeys each had brought with him. Like clockwork, with split-second timing, each went to his appointed spot, picked up a bag and walked out as calmly as he had entered. At the exits the guards sat motionless. At precisely 12:04 it was all over. Each of the "visitors" had vanished into thin air.

*So had forty billion dollars from the United States Treasury.**

I kept making insertions in the *Congressional Record* about individuals who apparently escaped taxation and also about the low rates paid by oil and gas corporations. My staff computed from corporate reports, for instance, the taxes of twenty-eight middle-sized companies over a five-year period and showed how they paid only a fraction of the nominal corporate income tax. One company had $65 million in net profits and not only paid no taxes, but actually received a $265,000 rebate.

For years we made no popular headway with general statistics. More convincing to the public were specific instances. While the Treasury, of course, could not, and should not, betray the identity of those who escaped paying taxes, they could specify the numbers in the various income groups who did. Early in the struggle, as I have said, we got hold of the case of a man who for successive years had an income in excess of a million dollars but who during that time had never paid a dollar in federal taxes. The Treasury also told us of one man who had an economic income of $26 million one year and yet paid no taxes. We asked from time to time how certain oil-rich millionaires, reputedly among the wealthiest in the world, could either live continuously abroad in lavish splendor or exercise enormous power at home and yet be popularly believed to be nontaxpayers.

In 1963 the Treasury gave us more precise figures. In that year at least 197 persons with reported incomes of over $100,000 paid no taxes. Of this number, thirty-two had incomes of over $500,000, while twenty had incomes over $1 million. Seldom were there fewer than thirty with reported incomes of over half a million who were nontaxpayers. After I left the Senate, the Treasury reported that in 1965 the number in this group was thirty-five. Had all capital gains and other income been counted, this number would probably have been trebled. Yet these were only the tips

* *The Great Treasury Raid,* New York: Random House, 1964.

of the iceberg. Thousands of others paid scarcely more than a token tax. One scion of a famous family with high personal standards of ethics told the Ways and Means Committee that, while he could arrange his tax statements so that he could avoid all federal payments, as a matter of ethics he paid from 5 to 10 per cent of his income in those taxes. A member of the committee who interviewed a number of stenographers and secretaries found that they paid a much higher rate.

Gore and I thus learned that the "effective" rate of taxation was far less than the stated scale. We had often been told of the supposedly confiscatory rates of 91 and later of 72 per cent for huge incomes. But in fact these were seldom paid. The average payment by groups with incomes over $50,000 was a fraction of the scheduled rate—namely, around 25 per cent. Those with incomes over $250,000, who had been presumed to pay nearly 90 per cent, actually paid, on the average, somewhat less than 25 per cent. There was, therefore, a slight average regression in the effective rates for those in the topmost income classes.

In the spring of 1969 the *Wall Street Journal* published the taxes and tax rates paid in 1967 by the country's fifteen largest oil refiners. This showed an average rate of only 8 per cent on total net profits of over $7 billion, as compared with a basic rate of 48 per cent on the corporate profits of other companies after the first $25,000. These oil companies were therefore getting by with only one-sixth the normal rate of taxation for corporations as a whole. The record was as follows:

Company	Net Income before Taxes (in millions of $)	Federal Tax Paid (in millions of $)	Per Cent
Standard (N.J.)	$2,098.3	$166.0	7.9
Gulf	956.0	74.1	7.8
Texaco	893.0	17.5	1.9
Mobil	594.6	26.9	4.5
Standard (Cal.)	513.1	6.0	1.2
Standard (Ind.)	366.8	74.0	20.2
Shell	342.0	44.9	13.1
Phillips	227.8	52.3	22.9
Conoco	241.4	30.0	12.4
Cities Service	165.3	32.3	19.6
Union	163.8	10.4	6.3
Sun	146.9	24.7	16.8
Atlantic	145.3	None	0
Marathon	138.5	3.7	2.7
Getty	132.8	3.7	2.8
TOTAL	$7,125.5	$566.6	8.0

While those with moderate incomes received a fraction of the tax breaks, most of the exemptions went to the wealthy. On depletion allowances, in 1958, 71 per cent went to corporations with over $100 million in assets, 77 per cent to corporations with over $50 million in assets, and 88 per cent to those with over $10 million. Only 4.4 per cent of the allowances were received by corporations with assets of less than a million. The allowance was for the big boys with a growing percentage of the net income as the size of the corporation increased. Indeed, in the oil industries the deductions for depletion came to 94 per cent of the net income.* In short, our tax system had lost most of its "progressive" character. Furthermore, the burden fell unequally on people with equal incomes.

The starkest contrast was between those members of the wealthy class who paid little or nothing and the poor and moderate-income families who paid a great deal. A family of four living on $3,500, the upper limit of poverty, would be exempted on only $2,750 of its income ($600 per member plus 10 per cent of the total as a standard deduction). On the remaining $750 they paid 14 per cent, or $105.

Gore and I tried to make it clear that if the worst exemptions were eliminated, we would favor a reduction in the general tax rates. We pointed out that any added total receipts could also be used to finance much-needed social progress in housing, health, education, and employment. Some of the industrial unions, notably the United Automobile Workers, joined our fight. But few others paid any attention. In my final campaign in 1966 I probably lost far more votes on this issue than I gained.

A General Summary

IN THE EFFORT to get something, we tried for minor gains and got nothing. We did not advance by trying to be moderate. The extractive industries made no concessions. Even the Kennedy administration yielded at critical moments. Almost no economists, except Pechman, came forward to help us. We lacked a technical staff. We made our fight alone and, while we brought out some of the facts, we might have done better if from the outset we had questioned the sharp differentiation between capital gains and income. Perhaps then the public would have risen more fully in our support to insist on a better solution.

I cannot blame those who are now working for the limited objectives I sought, but as a private citizen I am bolder than I felt I could be as a

---

* See *Statistics of Income, Corporate Income Tax,* published by the Internal Revenue Service. I introduced these statistics into the *Congressional Record* for September 5, 1962.

politician striving for what seemed at the time to be the possible, but which turned out later to be the impossible.

I ask only that those safe in the grandstand who are now critical of my past moderation should themselves step into the battle to help the hard-pressed politicians working today for a more just tax system. The technical details can be worked out. Gains can be spread over a period of years to avoid bunching, and devices can be developed to prevent investments from being "locked in." And in the case of depletion allowances, operators could be allowed up to several times their original investment.

In the winter of 1967, when I gave some lectures on this subject at the New School for Social Research, I doubted whether public opinion would ever focus sufficiently on these evils to insure reforms. I said that, though we in Congress had saved the public a few billions of dollars, in the main we had failed. Was it our fault? Or was it part of the structure of life in which the powerful few, equipped with funds to hire lawyers, lobbyists, economists, and publicity men to protect and increase their privileges, ride roughshod over the low-income groups? In some ways, democracy itself was on trial, I said, and I could sympathize with the youngsters denouncing the "Establishment." One remedy was to make the tax structure conform to accepted ethical and economic principles.

Three years later, there were gleams of hope. My Congressional friends told me of a tremendous wave of public indignation against people of wealth escaping taxation. Some demanded action. A group of progressive legislators organized for that purpose. The final results were, however, relatively disappointing. The depletion allowance was reduced to 24 per cent, and abuses in accelerated depreciation were diminished. But most of the old abuses were retained, and the defenders of the citadel of privilege were not threatened. Popular indignation has subsided, and those who profit from the tax laws breathe easily once more.

Personal Experiences

THE BYPLAY within the Finance Committee was interesting. Byrd was always outwardly bland and courteous, Gore always helpful, Long personally friendly, Williams always upright. After a few years, however, I noticed that whenever I started to speak, two or three members on the other side of the table immediately began to discuss a different subject. Once in a while a fellow Democrat joined them. At first, thinking this was only a matter of bad manners, I let them have the floor, hoping to regain it after they had finished. But when I tried to resume my statement, either the time was up or the interruptions recommenced. After about a year more, I realized that there must be a planned strategy, either to blanket my arguments or to make me lose my temper. A fellow member of the committee and a staff member later confirmed these suspicions. Thereafter I had to give up effective criticism within the committee. Instead, I appealed to the Senate as a whole, and the nation, through speeches on the floor and insertions in the *Record*.

On the House side, Charles Vanik, of Ohio, led a similar crusade against the 27½-per-cent depletion allowance, and he met with similar discourtesy. Indeed, when he took the floor, Speaker Rayburn habitually showed his irritation by wheeling his chair around to face the flag, rather than look at Vanik. Everyone caught the point, although this intrepid young Congressman continued to brave the open contempt of Rayburn.

Taxation and Economic Stabilization

AT BEST, the reduction in truckholes was only the first step in tax reform. We also needed to co-ordinate the economic policies of the government so that we might attain a high and constant rate of economic growth and at the same time prevent recessions and depressions.

I had been one of the first American economists to call for a big public-works program as a counterforce to a depression, and this was before Keynes. It meant throwing more publicly created purchasing power into the economy by bank-financed bond issues. Its purpose was to offset the slump in private investment and the cumulative business decline. Although imperfectly carried out, this program was adopted by the New Deal. At the least, government expenditures for relief and public works prevented the Great Depression from worsening.

Gradually, the compensatory theory of public finance began to be accepted by economists and politicians as well as by such progressive-minded businessmen as those on the Committee for Economic Development. A die-hard group still clung to the idea of annually balanced budgets even in depression years. Senator Byrd held to this theory. But in practice few dared risk these classic solutions in the face of a depression. Increased taxes and curtailed expenditures would decrease effective demand and, hence, increase both unemployment and idle capacity. In this sense, we, as well as Keynes, may have helped to produce a revolution in fiscal thinking. Surprisingly enough, this theory was adopted by President Nixon.

When I went to the Senate in 1949, I began to consider a second method of reversing a cumulative downswing of orders, production, employment, and purchasing power. This was a temporary cut in taxes. It would create a bigger deficit and could be used to encourage the banking and credit systems to create more monetary purchasing power with which to buy government bonds or to use savings that otherwise would not be invested. If, in the process, tax reforms could be accomplished, so much the better.

A tax cut had some advantages over a public-works program. In the first place, it would have an immediate effect, while public works involved a long process of drawing up plans, obtaining legislative authorizations and appropriations, letting contracts, and starting work. Meanwhile, the recession or depression might have come and gone before the prescribed stimulant was given. At a time of business expansion, the delayed expenditures would increase prices, making the next slump even sharper. Furthermore, the personnel of both House and Senate committees made it likely that public-works programs would be favored for sparsely settled areas, rather than for the industrial centers where unemployment was highest.

I had two chances to test a tax cut as a means of reducing a recession. In 1954, when the first Eisenhower recession came, I proposed a reduction of $500 million in the excise taxes on durable consumer goods as a means of stimulating demand. There were three roll calls on this. One proposal carried in a modified form, but two others were lost, by votes of 63 to 25 and 64 to 23.

The second chance came with the sharper recession of 1958. Over the opposition of the brilliant Kenneth Galbraith, who wanted an increase in expenditures, I proposed a tax cut. In order to improve the relative distribution of the tax burden, I suggested this be done by ending federal sales taxes on commodities other than liquor and tobacco. The chief cuts would have been on gasoline, telephone service, and widely used durable consumer goods. These taxes had weighed most heavily on those with low incomes. By removing them, we would create a sharper contrast between the fields of national and state finance, and would turn over the area of sales taxes to the states and localities. The retention of the federal taxes on liquor and tobacco I justified on other grounds. It is a physiological fact that these articles are harmful to consumers, and it was likely that if we removed the federal tax on cigarettes and liquor, profits would be greatly increased by the quasi monopolies maintaining their prices. That had been precisely what happened after the Spanish-American War when the war-imposed tobacco taxes were removed. I later learned that Vice President Nixon was urging a similar plan inside the Eisenhower administration. However, the Treasury blocked such a tax cut and persuaded Johnson to oppose it in the Senate.

Notwithstanding, I pushed my proposal to a vote, and found a respectable number of supporters. Among gains that year was a cut, first, and then the ultimate removal of the federal tax on washing machines.

An obvious weakness developed in all the plans for compensatory spending in a depression. After some years, government deficits became so much a way of life that both the economists and the Congress lost their fear of them. On the basis of crude accounting standards, the deficits continued from the Depression through World War II. Under Eisenhower the budget was balanced in only one year; then deficits continued under Kennedy and Johnson. They became the fiscal rule, not merely a device for hard times. The brain trusters did not object. Some of these deficits, however, were more apparent than real, because capital expenditures, which were income-yielding, were charged to operating expenses, instead of being segregated into a capital budget, as they are in well-conducted private business. Nevertheless, we had not developed a fiscal method that would taper down public expenditures during prosperity.

A school of thought now came to the fore based on Keynes's *General Theory of Employment, Interest, and Money.* This held that there was always a tendency within capitalistic society for the economy to operate at less than its potential. The Keynesians developed mathematical equations to prove why this was so. They did not convince me. A simpler explanation was that the rate of interest was higher than the marginal productivity of capital. The result was that savings temporarily exceeded investment, and there was an accumulation of idle capital. In turn, this created unemployment and idle capacity. The younger economists and a number of financial writers were, however, strongly influenced by Keynes. They favored a continuous injection of publicly created purchasing power to build up production and employment. This meant continuing government deficits. Financial conservatives were appalled by this proposal, but I saw certain advantages, if it were provided with two safeguards. First, public investments should be in socially productive lines, such as the TVA and atomic energy, or indirectly beneficial expenditures for health and education; they should never be used wastefully, as had been the custom under the Rivers and Harbors bills or in financing some of our military expenditures. Second, the public outlays should not absorb an excessive proportion of the national income. While I did not attach any mystic significance to my friend Colin Clarke's figure of 25 per cent as the outer limit for all levels of government expenditure, I wanted the private sector to carry out the major economic activities. I opposed the all-encompassing state employer. The experience of Russia showed how an inner group of experts and politicians could tyrannize over the mass of mankind. Under the shibboleth of workers' control, the bureaucrats, in fact, ruled.

Until the Vietnamese war came along, the outright expenditures of the federal government (excluding insurance benefits and other transfer payments) showed no significant increase in the proportion of the national income or gross national product, but remained constant at from 17 to 18 per cent of the total. In the fields of state and local government, such increases as did occur were caused by the greater concentration of population, requiring more communal services—education, transportation, health, housing, welfare, police protection, and so on.

As long as the debt did not increase faster than the gross national product, I was not disturbed. But the new economics carried to excess might lead to a higher ratio of debt, especially when prices increased. If the gross national product went up by 4 per cent a year, neither the national debt nor the amount of bank-created purchasing power should normally increase at a faster rate. The Federal Reserve and Congress needed to co-operate on such a policy. I did not believe that competitive capitalism contained within itself the seeds of its own destruction, as the Marxists had earlier contended; nor did I regard public expenditures, as such, as either good or bad. It was the task of Congress to make them socially and economically beneficial.

To my mind, the failure to achieve full employment had been due primarily to elements of monopoly and quasi monopoly that in many fields have kept prices above what they would be under perfect competition. This of necessity has dampened demand and employment. These lines of industry could not absorb their full quota of new workers. The latter had to seek work in competitive lines, depressing conditions there, or else float at large as part of a pool of surplus labor. At the same time, the monopolists and their banking partners were reluctant to reinvest their high profits in their own lines of business, since this would inevitably expand their output and cause their prices and profits to be cut. Destructive economic forces were at work, but these were chiefly caused by monopoly and imperfect competition, rather than by capitalism as such. I agreed with Robert R. Young, the crusading railroad magnate, that capitalism had to be saved from the current breed of capitalists.

State and Local Bonds

EARLY in our 1955 study of the tax structure, the exemption from federal taxation of the interest on the bonds of state and local governments loomed as an important truckhole. Originally, this exemption had been justified on two grounds. The first was that since, in John Marshall's words, "the power to tax involves the power to destroy," the courts might hold such a tax to be unconstitutional because it could be used to threaten state sovereignty. The second was the desire to help state and local governments float bond issues for capital improvements.

The second purpose was so well fulfilled that in March, 1967, the average interest rate on municipals was 3½ per cent, as compared with an average of 4½ per cent on long-term federal issues. This difference occurred despite the fact that the local issues were much less safe and would normally have carried a higher, rather than a lower, rate of interest.

Without the tax exemption, the average interest rate on state and local bonds would probably have been at least from 4¾ to 5 per cent, and perhaps higher. Since the total indebtedness of the state and local governments then amounted to nearly $100 billion, it is apparent that the exemption saved them at that time the taxes on from $1¼ to $1½ billion a year. Today the difference in the interest rates is still a full percentage point, with the total state and local issues amounting to $120 billion. The exemption probably saves the owners of these bonds the taxes on at least $1½ billion, and possibly as much as $2 billion a year.

Furthermore, it has provided a convenient tax shelter for the very rich. This was demonstrated some years ago when Mrs. Horace Dodge inherited $56 million from the estate of her husband. She immediately invested all of it in state and municipal bonds, and thus removed the income of her entire fortune from federal taxation. I believe she did not even have to file an income tax return. Tax counselors tell me that when federal taxation reaches around 30 per cent of income, the exemption of interest on state and municipal issues is of more advantage to the taxpayer than their loss from the lower rate of interest. Those in the upper income brackets who do not want to be active in business or take the attendant risks find these tax-exempt securities most attractive. It is estimated that if only the existing income from these bond issues were taxed, the average rate of taxation would be at least 50 per cent on the exempt amounts. Today this would net at least $2 billion. Even if the federal government had compensated the local authorities for the interest subsidy of $1¼ billion, or the difference between the federal and local rates, the net savings would have been at least three-quarters of a billion.

While I believe that the federal government should subsidize the local governments, particularly for welfare, educational, and housing costs, this should be by direct grants, rather than by tax loopholes that subsidize the affluent more than they aid the hard-pressed localities. The law of the jungle in taxation is apparently that before the poor can have a bite, the rich must have a banquet.

We in the North were especially opposed to the Southern practice of issuing so-called "developmental bonds," which were also tax-free. These were used to attract industry by offering free factory sites and buildings. They have provided a haven for runaway industry from the North and West, as well as channeling new investment to the South. This has weakened the unions and labor standards in the North, shrunk the tax base, and increased welfare costs as Northern families have lost their wage earners. The exemption of the local bonds was injuring the North and West grievously at the very time that we had to make good the revenue lost to the nation by these subsidies. In self-defense, John Kennedy and I tried to remove at least this type of exemption, but the South quietly sprang to arms and, by its control over the Ways and Means Committee and the Senate Finance Committee, softly stifled our efforts. Despite our argument that if the South wanted to subsidize such industry, it should do so at its own expense instead of presenting part of the bill to the nation, whose major taxpayers came from outside the South, we could not marshal enough strength from the injured regions of the North and the West.

Finally, after some years, many Northern communities decided to play the same game. They also issued development bonds to attract new industry, a practice that is now widespread. It results in an unhealthy competition between localities, with those states that are opposed to the union shop chiefly profiting. It is another bad effect of tax exemption. To date, the regional and economic defenders of these tax shelters have overpowering political strength in the Senate.

Capital Gains

DURING our study of the tax system, we early faced the question of capital gains. Investments held for more than six months that when sold yielded a surplus over cost were taxed on that surplus, or "capital gain," when realized at only one-half the rate on corresponding incomes. Moreover, the rate was never to exceed 25 per cent. The result was incongruous. Cattle and horses were eligible partly because of their long period of gestation. Senator Edward J. Thye, of Minnesota, tried to extend this privilege to turkeys, holding chickens in the offing. But he was repulsed by the wealthy chicken farmer John Williams, who knew the precise length of the generative cycle of fowl. One could laugh at such absurdities and at the obvious encouragement given the pink-coated horsy set that likes to ride to hounds in British fashion. But the real evils lay deeper. In most cases the capital gains were really income, and yet those who received them were paying much less than the people who received steady income from effort or ownership. This loophole was a direct encouragement to speculation. While speculation has its uses, it is hardly wise to give it precedence over the more solid virtues of work and investment. Although willing to spread these capital gains over a period of years, so that nonrecurring windfalls would not be hit unduly in the year when they occurred, I questioned the advantage given them. Yet such questioning was not only futile; it was made to seem almost as impious as casting doubt on the Ten Commandments.

In *The Great Treasury Raid,* Philip Stern threw new light on the extent and nature of the losses caused by the capital-gains tax. He made a careful estimate that the lower rates decreased the tax base by nearly $6 billion a year, thus costing about $2.4 billion. In 1969 the Treasury estimated the revenue loss at $5 to $7 billion.

Even worse was the failure to apply any capital-gains tax to increases in the value of a decedent's property during his lifetime. If X bought property for $100,000 that upon his death was worth $1 million, the $900,000 increase in capital worth would be completely exempt from taxation when his heirs sold the property. They would be taxed only on the increases enjoyed since the death of X. If they sold the property for $1.1 million, the tax would be on the accretion since death of $100,000 and not on the total increase of $1 million since the original acquisition. Stern estimated in 1963 that from $12 to $13 billion of increment thus escaped taxation in every year, and that the annual revenue loss to the federal government was about $2.9 billion. The Treasury's present estimates, which seem excessively conservative, put this loss at $2 billion. From the standpoint of strict accounting, the fact that part of the capital gain is attributable to a rise in the general price level ought to be taken into consideration. This is seldom done in private industry, and would be difficult to compute, including the question of the proper price index. But it ought to be considered in making a general appraisal of the institution. Some apparent capital gains are due to inflation and its attendant decrease in the value of a dollar.

Stern also pointed out that the amounts of the capital gains not taxed, like the depletion allowances, were not statistically counted and, hence, disappeared from sight. I likened this to a practice of the criminal syndicate, which disposes of the bodies of its victims by giving them an anonymous and hidden burial.

When the Kennedy administration at first supported the idea of taxing inherited capital gains, our hopes ran high. To soften the opposition, we offered to deduct, on a dollar-for-dollar basis, any inheritance tax paid on the amounts inherited. If an inheritance tax of $50,000 had been paid, the capital-gains tax would be that much less. Since then, tax purists have said that I was wrong, although they did not condemn at the time the exemption of the capital gains themselves.

I was also willing to spread the capital-gains tax over a period of years to avoid the high rates caused by bunched income. But all these efforts at conciliation were rejected. The overwhelming majority was determined not to allow society to recapture any of the previously accumulated capital gains. The administration rather quickly gave up the idea in order to put through its investment-credit plans, and again Gore and I were left alone. Once more the economists were eloquently silent. The result was inevitable.

Looking back, I can see that I erred in not giving the device of capital gains closer scrutiny. At first we tried only to curb some of the incidental forms of favoritism. We hoped to raise the rate of taxation from 25 to 28 per cent, to lengthen the holding period of stock from six to nine months, or possibly even a year, and to restrict stock options. But we did not question why realized capital gains should be taxed at a much lower rate than income, even though this fact accounted for much of the complexity of the laws as well as for the loss in revenue. Sometimes the boldest policies may be the most effective. But to those of us who were hard pressed in battle and without strong allies, any such attempt seemed impossible.

Du Pont

I HAD a lurid experience in 1961 in connection with the capital gains made by the Du Pont company on the forced sale of General Motors stock. This divestiture, ordered by the Supreme Court under the antitrust laws, reversed a Chicago district judge. The question then arose as to how the huge capital gains were to be taxed. Du Pont had originally bought 100 million shares of General Motors stock in 1916 when the market price was $2.16 a share. It was at this time worth about $43, with a consequent capital gain of over $41 a share, or a total in excess of $4 billion. The influential head of Du Pont came to Washington to lobby for a proposal that the company should pay taxes of only 7½ per cent on the original purchase price, or 16 cents a share. In other words, they should not pay ordinary corporate income or capital-gains taxes on the $4 billion. I saw no reason why they should not pay the capital-gains tax of 25 per cent. This would have been a little over $10 a share, or about a billion dollars in all. Gore and I urged that companies should not be rewarded for complying with a court order to discontinue a practice in restraint of trade.

We knew that the Democratic Senator from Delaware, J. Allen Frear, had the Du Pont amendment in his pocket, but we could not find out when he intended to present it. When we met he would look anxiously around the committee room to see if he had a majority, and sometimes indirectly raised the General Motors issue by citing the similar case of the Hilton Hotels. Finally, one morning, with a triumphant smile, he brought out his amendment. Gore and I protested that it was an unforgiveable give-away. Then the roll was called. This time we were not surprised that Eugene McCarthy voted for Du Pont. The first vote was a tie, 8 to 8, with Williams withholding his vote. He broke the tie by voting "No." For a conservative Republican from the Du Pont barony of Delaware, that showed courage. I told him afterward that I had heard him likened to a board—long, narrow, and wooden. "But, by God," I said, "you are also upright."

Stock Options

GORE MADE a powerful indictment of the abuses connected with stock options. Many corporations, including those controlled by Morgan and Insull, had in past times given favored executives and others the right to buy stocks at less than market price. When the stock was later sold at a higher price, the gains were taxed as capital gains and not as income. If the stock fell while the option was open, the beneficiary was commonly freed from any obligation to purchase.

The defense given for this practice was that it increased the managers' incentive by giving them a greater stake in the company's prosperity. Obviously it also diluted the equities of the existing stockholders by creating additional claimants for the profits of the companies. It focused executive concern on the price of the stock rather than on the costs and profits of the company. While these two are often interlocked, this is not always the case. From the standpoint of the companies, it would have been better to have made the added payments in cash bonuses or to have granted a liberal share in profits rather than to give stock options. There the incentive would be direct. But in that event the added income would have been taxed at the full rates instead of at the half rate and 25-per-cent maximum of capital gains. The purpose was to enable favored ones to enrich themselves rapidly. It was also said to help young executives climb the ladder of affluence. From reading the financial pages, it seemed, however, that the major rewards went, instead, to those who were in the late afternoon of their business careers and who, as members of the boards of directors, had often voted themselves large tax-free bonuses. The granting of the privilege to outsiders had no justification.

Gore was successful in wringing some concessions from the majority, but we were never sure that they were substantial. Some knowledgeable critics called them minor.

Those Who Were Silent

As I HAVE SAID, during our long fight to reform the tax system most professional economists were silent. It was as though they were either indifferent or afraid. Except for Stern and Pechman, Gore and I had to make our fight alone. Recently, however, the economists have shown distinct signs of improvement and some 500 have formed a loose association to promote testimony in the public interest. The hitherto dead have begun to stir.

33

Further Battles with the Big Gas and Oil Interests

ALTHOUGH our chief battles with the gas and oil interests focused on the depletion allowance, there were other struggles as well.

Federal Regulation of the Price of Interstate Gas

SOON AFTER taking his Senate seat in 1949, Bob Kerr introduced his bill to free from federal regulation the nontransporting producers and gatherers who sold their gas to pipelines for interstate shipment. The conservatives in both parties flocked to his support. On the surface, the issues seemed to be complex, but as I worked through them in early 1950, with the aid of Mel Van Scoyoc and Frank McCulloch, they became relatively clear. I decided that I must oppose the measure when it came up.

Natural gas, with almost twice the heat content of manufactured gas, was rapidly displacing both it and coal. In price, it was far superior to coal, as it was also better in fuel content, ease of handling, and the quantity of smoke emitted by its use. No doubt it was a godsend to the households of the country, and it was gaining ground in industry, too.

Since it was almost invariably found along with oil, Texas, Louisiana, Oklahoma, and Kansas now supplanted West Virginia as the centers of the gas industry. The new oil and gas millionaires tolerated no restraint. They and their companies already owned or controlled from 80 to 86 per cent of the reserves of gas in the Southwest. These nontransporting producers, who would be freed from any regulation under the Kerr bill and who controlled these reserves, were not "small independents in overalls," as had been the case in West Virginia. Instead, the ten biggest companies held 57 per cent of the gas, and the biggest fifteen, no less than 68 per cent. The control within some of the fields was even greater. Thus, in Louisiana nine fields were completely ruled by one company. A few companies controlled most of the reserves in the Texas Panhandle and Hugoton, Kansas, fields, which were the largest.

They were confident that if they could prevent the Federal Power Commission from fixing a ceiling on the price of this gas as it entered the pipelines, they could boost its price by at least ten cents for each 1,000 cubic feet. That would net them, at a minimum, $600 million a year, a sum that, of course, would increase as consumption rose, as it has. They were playing for big stakes, and Kerr was their natural leader. Through the Kerr-McGee Company, which manufactured drilling equipment, he knew the industry, and he possessed large gas and oil interests of his own.

The courts had denied both exporting and importing states the right of regulating the price of interstate shipments as gas entered the pipeline. It had to be, therefore, federal regulation or nothing. At first, the Federal Power Commission had relied on competition to regulate the price, but by late 1948 the current ratios of holdings and the terms of the contracts between the nontransporting producers and the pipelines had convinced it that the only protection for the ultimate consumer lay in federal regulation.

At that time, the chairman of the FPC was Leland Olds, who had been appointed by Roosevelt. Along with two other commissioners, Thomas Buchanan and Claude L. Draper, he wanted to protect the consumers, who lived chiefly in the cities and towns of the East and Middle West. Olds, the son of the beloved George D. Olds, the former president of Amherst, under whom I had served, was an able and devoted public servant. He was a protégé of Frank P. Walsh, who had headed Wilson's Commission on Industrial Relations and, later, Roosevelt's New York Power Authority. But despite Olds's competence and public spirit, he had an Achilles' heel. During the early 1920's he had been, as industrial editor for the Federated Press, sharply critical of our capitalistic system. He had long since outgrown such general views, and now believed in public regulation, rather than public ownership, of those utilities that were private monopolies. But Kerr and the oil and gas crowd had got hold of his early statements and were ready to use them. Aware of this, Olds must have been under severe strain to go along with them. If he let Kerr have his way by interpreting the law in Kerr's fashion, he could continue as chairman. Instead, with his colleagues he bravely insisted on the correct interpretation of the law. Truman, standing by him in 1949, sent his name to the Senate for reappointment. At the hearing, Kerr kept Lyndon Johnson by his side as he struck his threatened blow. The two read into the record Olds's writings of a quarter of a century previous. The committee then voted against confirmation, and, though his name went to the floor, his reappointment seemed doomed. Truman did not openly desert him, but he let him shift for himself.

No one would take up Olds's defense; as the hour for the vote approached, a number of liberals suddenly discovered out-of-town engagements. In the afternoon I made a canvass, found that there was literally no one to speak for Olds, and I determined to do so. For years Olds had been an outstanding and incorruptible public servant who had tried to make the regulatory system work. Even conservatives gave verbal adherence to regulation. Kerr and Johnson were not punishing him for his youthful statements, but, rather, for standing up for the public against the special interests. If Olds was turned down, it would be a warning to all the regulatory bodies not to enforce the laws to protect the public. So I made my plea for mercy. Since the backers of Kerr and Johnson were implacable, when the roll was called only sixteen of us voted for confirmation. Olds was crushed by the experience, and I do not think that he and his family ever recovered from the blow. Later, Buchanan, with no skeleton in his closet and with an impeccable private and public life, but who also favored regulation, was denied reappointment.

I tried to help confirm M. A. Hutchinson, an excellent appointee of Truman for the FTC, who as a reform Democrat had run afoul of Harry Byrd's Virginia machine. But the same crowd defeated him when the showdown came. Those of us who supported him had been shaken, too, by the popular opposition to liberals, by the defeat of Claude Pepper at the hands of his erstwhile protégé, George Smathers, and by the loss of Frank Graham. I knew that Truman, like a good company commander, used to thank those who fought on his side, and I waited with interest to see if he would call me. He never did. Like Kerr and Johnson, with whom he fraternized, he was implacable. But I refused to let this throw me off balance. Supporting him when I thought he was right—which was most of the time—I voted against him when I thought him wrong. I did not intend to fall into the error of Burton K. Wheeler, of Montana, whose reaction to Roosevelt's bad treatment of him on appointments led him to oppose most of Roosevelt's later policies.

In March of 1950, having disposed of Olds, Kerr got the Commerce Committee to bring his bill to the floor of the Senate. Supremely confident of victory, he boasted that we could not muster more than twenty votes against it. Friends of mine reported from the cloakrooms that he was also threatening to attack me. The bill was brought forward in a perfunctory manner by Ed Johnson, who made no real argument for it. At first, Kerr and Lyndon Johnson claimed that they merely wanted to clear up the confusion as to whether the federal government had jurisdiction.

They would have done this, however, by denying it. I welcomed the test, but believed Congress should support both the original act and the decision of the Supreme Court in the Interstate Gas case.

Obviously, the proponents, relying on their strength, wanted to avoid debate. After Kerr had spoken briefly, I took the floor in opposition and held it for three days. Kerr turned all his batteries on me, and was helped occasionally by Lyndon Johnson and the Democratic whip, McFarland.

I felt inadequately matched against Kerr, who had a detailed knowledge of the industry and a unique capacity for brutal and casuistical argument. But I was joined by an expert on the subject in the person of Mel Van Scoyoc, who specialized in gas rates for the FPC. The Philadelphia Gas Company, which was municipally owned, also joined us and gave added support. With McCulloch and Bob Wallace, we gathered basic information, which had an increasing impact on both my fellow Senators and the press. We showed not only the concentration of ownership of the reserves, but also that as demand increased the producers and gatherers, not the pipelines, were in the driver's seat. We analyzed 100 important contracts. Ninety-five provided for an automatic increase in rates at stated intervals, while sixty-five also granted automatic increases if new contracts at higher rates were signed with another producer in the field. Forty-five specifically provided for periodic renegotiations.

I pointed out that once gas lines were laid, their cost was such that their owners would not move them. The pipelines were tied to the producers and gatherers and, as demand increased, were granting price increases to the producers right and left. The distributing companies in the consuming centers were also tied to the pipelines. Once the homeowners had put in gas connections, at a cost of several hundred dollars, they could not and would not shift to another company or another fuel. All were tied together; none could break away. It was an indissoluble natural monopoly.

The average costs for the producers seemed to range from 1.6 to 4.4 cents per 1,000 cubic feet. On their combined operations, after taxes twenty-four of the biggest companies were making 24 per cent on their common stock and surplus. These were the ones who would profit by large additional gains if regulations were removed. And increases in the price of gas as it entered the pipeline would, of course, be passed along, until they would ultimately be paid by the householder at the end.

As the debate went on for two weeks, our strength increased. When the roll was called, there were thirty-eight negative votes, or twice what Kerr and the pollsters had predicted. Those in favor of the Kerr bill got forty-four votes, or only a narrow majority. The debate had served a purpose and had swayed votes.

The bill went to Truman, who, in view of the close vote and the debate, began to have second thoughts about signing it. Kerr boasted that

Truman had given him a promise to sign. But the debate had aroused widespread popular opposition. The increase of ten cents per 1,000 cubic feet that was probably at stake would cost the consumers at first nearly $600 million a year. Even though this might not amount to more than $20 a year on a per-family basis, it was a huge total, and it would increase.

Frank Edwards, then the radio commentator for the AFL, put me on the air every night. There I attacked the Kerr bill and asked Truman to veto it. As the heat rose, letters poured into the White House. Finally, Truman could stand it no longer and vetoed the bill. We had won by a strange route. In view of his slender majority, Kerr knew he could not get the two-thirds required to override the veto.

But the battle was not over. The President may have gone back on his promise to Kerr, but the ties between them were not broken. Truman now appointed Monrad C. Wallgren, the former governor of Washington, chairman of the FPC. The commission in due time reversed the Olds opinion and denied that it had jurisdiction over the price of interstate gas as it entered the pipeline. Then, it was Kerr and the gas and oil men who seemed to have won. Kerr's warm sentiments toward Truman led him to defend the President's dismissal of MacArthur. Some said it was his repayment.

But the minuet was not over. Milwaukee and Detroit did not see why their citizens should pay more for their gas because of the increase charged by the Phillips Company. Therefore, they brought suit to compel the FPC to assume jurisdiction under the existing law. The case was carried all the way to the Supreme Court, which gave final victory to the cities and states.

Kerr's advocacy was by now getting a little shopworn. Fresh faces were needed. So in 1956 Fulbright and Congressman Oren Harris were induced to step into the breach to revive the Kerr bill. Since public opinion against the proposal had subsided, it looked like an easy victory for the gas companies. But a lobbyist for a large private company made the mistake of offering a big gift of money to Francis H. Case, of South Dakota. Case, a highly honorable man, not only refused the implicit bribe, but also reported it to the Senate. A Senate investigating committee under Walter George started out by putting Case, and not the lobbyist, on trial and tried to discredit him. But it turned out that the money for Case was not an isolated gift. It was part of a general pattern. Though Congress passed the Fulbright-Harris bill, President Eisenhower felt compelled to veto it because our second fight had again aroused the public. Once more we were saved, as in the old movie on the perils of Pauline.

When Kennedy was elected President, he appointed as chairman of the Federal Power Commission my former attorney in Chicago, Joe Swidler, now thirty years older than when we had fought Insull together. Swidler finally secured a set of rules giving basic rates for the field, but freeing from regulation the very small producers who had no monopoly position. I had long advocated this change, since it made administration manageable. I hope the long struggle is over, but one can never be sure.

Although estimates are not precise, I believe our fight has already saved consumers many billions of dollars and will in the end save more. It has slowed down the increase in rates that would otherwise have taken place. While the public has long forgotten both the struggle and its contenders, some on the side of the gas companies may have kept track. One thing is certain: Bob Kerr did.

Offshore Oil

A SECOND big battle was over offshore oil and gas. Large quantities of these had been found in land washed by the tides, and in the immediate zone seaward from the low-water mark off the coasts of California, Texas, and Louisiana. In cases from 1947 to 1950 involving these three states, the Supreme Court had ruled that, in accordance with many previous decisions, the tidal lands *landward* from the low-water mark belonged to the adjacent states, as did the submerged lands under bays, estuaries, rivers, and inland lakes, but that *seaward* from the low-water mark the submerged lands belonged to the nation. It was the federal government that had assumed the burden of defense.

Historically, the United States had always claimed federal jurisdiction out to the three-mile limit and had insisted that other nations should not claim more. California, however, had asked for state ownership out to its three-mile limit. Texas claimed state ownership out to three leagues (ten and a half miles). Louisiana had made variable claims, ranging from three to twenty-seven miles, while Senator Holland said that he claimed for Florida only three miles on its east coast, but three leagues on its west.

In his election campaign, Eisenhower had pledged himself to support the state claims, and the overwhelming proportion of the Republicans agreed. So did the conservative Democrats.

Lister Hill split with most of his Southern colleagues to take the lead in proposing that the title to the submerged land seaward from the low-water mark should be specifically vested in the national government, and the revenues from royalties and leases be used for aid to elementary, secondary, and higher education. To promote his bill he coined the happy phrase "oil for the lamps of learning." Our group rallied to support him and kept the discussion going for a month. As in the previous oil struggles, we had arrayed against us the cream of the nation's legal talent. Price Daniel, the favorite of the oil industry, had, as state attorney general, represented Texas all the way up through the federal courts. Although he had finally lost in the highest of courts, he knew every detail of his case and argued it superbly. I think the Texas oil men had wanted him to displace Tom Connally, whose age and lack of technical knowledge made him far less qualified to handle the offshore-oil case.

In any event, Connally went out with a sigh in the sizzling heat of summer, wrote his autobiography, *My Name Is Tom Connally,* and died. Price Daniel appeared in the Senate in his stead and, supremely confident, began his campaign to overturn the Supreme Court. I felt ill-matched in comparison.

Taking the floor early in the debate, I held it for two days and a total of about twelve hours. The atmosphere was intense, although the members were in better temper than they were over the Kerr bill of three years before—probably because Daniel was essentially a gentleman, which could not be said of Kerr. I brought out several important facts about the new bill. The public, I said, had been sold a false bill of goods. This was not a "tidelands" bill, or one to confirm state ownership of submerged lands under bays, harbors, internal waterways, rivers, or lakes. Those were already under state, and not federal, ownership. Neither the Supreme Court nor we questioned this. The issue was simply whether the national government would part with title to the submerged lands *seaward* from the low-water mark. The bill granted these submerged lands to the states without making clear where the coast began or the "historical boundaries" ended. So loose was the language, it might have given the states ownership and control of the submerged lands to the outer edge of the continental shelf, or, roughly, to where the depth of the water was supposed at the time to be 600 feet. This would probably not have been more than twenty miles off the shoreline of California, but it could have been 150 miles or more in the Gulf of Mexico. As I explained, the outer limits for the shelf were not fixed at any definite point, but could be extended to what a state had claimed prior to admission to the union and where it had been "heretofore or is hereafter approved by Congress." This opened wide the door.

I pointed out that while the original treaty with Texas had provided it with a marginal sea of ten and a half miles, or three leagues, this treaty had never been ratified by the Senate. Texas, however, was not admitted to the union under this treaty, but, instead, by a Congressional resolution that specifically provided that the new state was to be on an "equal footing" with all other states. Texas could not, therefore, claim any special privileges; nor could Florida.

From the estimates of competent geologists, it seemed that there were at least $100 to $300 billion worth of oil and gas off the coasts of California and in the Gulf of Mexico. At a minimum royalty of 12½ per cent, the public loss under this bill would have been between $12 and $37 billion. In addition, there would be the loss of what would have been obtained under leasing bids that might have been much more.

I argued that since the federal government had the obligation of defending the offshore zone of three miles, it was recognized under international law as being national, and not state, property. We should not alienate the property of all the citizens for the benefit of those of a few states.

There was no arguable case, I said, for state ownership of land beyond the three-mile (or three-league) limit. To claim it was completely indefensible. Other countries might enter claims for the internationalization of these lands out to the edge of the continental shelf, but in the absence of any such claims these areas should under all circumstances be the property of the nation. The lands out to the sharp drop had been built up for millions of years by the deposits of soil washed down from the continental land mass of which we, the people of the United States, were now the heirs.

Those who offered the bill protested that they did not want to have the states take over the continental shelf, but in committee they had defeated Anderson's proposal to vest the title to this land specifically in the United States. When I introduced the Anderson amendment on the floor, it was defeated by a vote of 50 to 26. This showed that the majority did not favor a definite commitment for national ownership of the continental shelf.

The Daniel measure was passed in early May, 1953, by the substantial majority of 56 to 35. Its opponents were attacked for promoting a filibuster before the vote. I stoutly maintained that this was not the case. We were not trying to prevent a vote, but, rather, to delay it so that both the Senate and the country could become acquainted with the issue.

In this we were ultimately successful. Informed newspaper opposition rose, and my mail ran at the rate of fifty to one against the bill. After its passage, many who had supported the claim of the states to the three-mile and three-league offshore zones could not stomach the idea that the states could also go out to the edge of the continental shelf. The Interior Committee soon offered a supplementary bill almost identical with the amendment that Anderson and I had proposed. It was speedily adopted and became the law of the land. At the time, this was treated as unimportant, but in the end the outer part of the shelf beyond the three-mile limit was found to be where the overwhelming proportion of the oil actually lies. Improved methods of drilling have now made it possible to tap these deposits, and up to 1970 the federal government had realized no less than $4.8 billion from them. There will be more in the future. Since it is highly improbable that these payments would have been made had we not forced the later adoption of the amendment, our fight will already have saved the people a minimum of several billion dollars. This was worth the month of debate that some legislative purists and the big oil interests had deplored.

We also tried to regulate the discharge of gas and oil from the wells, but we did not realize the importance of the issue, because very inadequate safeguards against fire and pollution were provided.

The big oil and gas interests were certainly behind the attempted oil giveaway in the Senate. Through political activity, they were partially responsible for the support of the measure by the conservative coalition. It was at first puzzling to me why this should be so. Huey Long had put through a high state severance tax in Louisiana, which was actually above the 12½-per-cent minimum prescribed by federal law. This had, indeed, been one of the reasons why the oil interests in Louisiana had fought him so bitterly. The Texas severance tax was not as high, but it was still above the federal minimum. The California tax was in fact lower than the federal royalty, but the big opposition came from the Gulf area. Why?

The answer was twofold. The 12½-per-cent federal royalty charge was only the minimum or the qualifying fee. Above this, there was to be competitive bidding on the amount of the "bonus" that was to be paid. In practice, therefore, the ultimate payments under federal ownership might be much more than the minimum of one-eighth, and this has been the case. Furthermore, since competitive bidding under national auspices is subjected to close scrutiny, there is less likelihood for favoritism than in the more diffused and less examined state awards. I have always believed that there were practical economic reasons for the opposition of big oil to federal control. But since I had no proof of this, I was careful not to charge it at the time, and to center argument on the superior claims of the people of the nation as a whole as compared with those of states contiguous to the oil resources of the seas.

Incidentally, after the final disposition of the offshore-oil issue, Price Daniel claimed and received as his reward the governorship of Texas. By Texas oil standards he was not a bad governor. But he was in no sense a progressive.

Oil Shale

THE THIRD BATTLE with the big gas and oil interests over the control of basic resources came at the end of my service in the Senate. It shifted from the Southwest and offshore in the oceans to the western slopes of the Rockies, and from liquid and gaseous pools to oil-saturated rocks.

For years, Senator O'Mahoney had talked to me about the rich oil-shale deposits in the Green and Grand river valleys in northwestern Colorado, southeastern Utah, and southwestern Wyoming. His figures on the quantities involved were so gigantic that I am afraid I discounted them as being largely the product of Western optimism. I was put on guard, however, by the early decision of the Eisenhower administration to close down the experimental plants at Louisiana, Missouri, and Rifle, Colorado. The former was designed to try out methods of extracting oil from coal, and I was definitely interested in this as a possibility for southern Illinois. The latter was experimenting with crushing oil from the western shale or marl. Once in a while, a mountain-state Senator would whisper to me that the oil interests had closed these plants down because they did not want new sources of supply to come on the market and thus threaten their control. The idea that the big oil companies could reach out to control alternative sources of fuel and power seemed then too fantastic to be believed. It is not too fantastic today.

So the matter rested for years. Kennedy restarted the experimental plants, and an advisory board was appointed to recommend a policy for oil shale. It made a detailed report in February, 1965, which attracted little attention. Then I got a letter one day from Ken Galbraith, who had been a member of the board, asking me if I would read the report. Though overburdened with many problems, I could not refuse his request. I took the report home one weekend, read it carefully, and could scarcely sleep.

The Geological Survey had estimated that the total amount of oil in the shale amounted to from 2 trillion to 2 trillion 600 billion barrels. I rubbed my eyes at these figures and at first could not believe them. It must be a typographical error, I thought. But the other figures were consistent. This was six times the total known recoverable oil in the entire world, and also about 600 times U.S. yearly consumption and twenty-five times the total extraction of oil in the whole history of the country. I looked up the price of oil in the field and found it to be around $2.77 a barrel. Thus the total value was from $5½ to $7 trillion.

Almost equally striking, the board estimated that 80 per cent of the oil was located in land to which the people of the United States still had title. Perhaps I was unduly suspicious, but I recalled an old desert saying, "Where the carrion lies, there the vultures flock to feast." With all this potential wealth legally in the hands of the people, I imagined that the human vultures must be getting ready to despoil it. Sections of the report showed that this was true.

The next day I wrote a speech outlining the facts. In order to get popular support for my position, I proposed that the royalties, which were to be a minimum of 12½ per cent plus bonuses under competitive bidding, should be earmarked for the retirement of the national debt. I hoped that this would gain support similar to that Hill had mustered for his "oil for the lamps of learning." Although I knew that budget experts disapproved of earmarked revenues, I also knew that they underestimated the difficulties of passing measures for the benefit of the people, and, as technicians, downgraded the issues. To overcome powerful opposition, one needed mass support. One way to gain this support was to give specific groups, as well as the public, a collective stake in the general interest. Education had been the interest that Hill had tapped. Getting rid of the debt was another such interest. Later, I included housing, education, and health as co-ordinate beneficiaries.

One night session, I waited until the floor was relatively vacant. Then I made my speech. Lee Metcalf, the liberal Senator from Montana, was in the chair, resting after a tumultuous day, but as I swung into my proposal, he listened intently. At the end he asked if he might cosponsor the bill. And so the Douglas-Metcalf bill was born, but the news spread slowly.

The public found the figures, as I had found them a dozen years before, too huge to assimilate. Only in La Salle County in my state did I arouse any enthusiasm. In general, the fuse was wet, and I could not stir any popular support.

Since my senatorial days, there has been an aftermath on this subject. When I was in Denver in July, 1967, for hearings on housing, I took a look at the oil-shale situation. I conferred with representatives of both the private and the public interests. I went up into the oil-shale country itself in the western Rockies and walked over some of the area. It was startling to see oil shale thousands of feet in the air within the mountains, and to realize that it also ran at least a quarter of a mile below the ground. I was alarmed to find that the federal ownership of the field was already under heavy attack. First, there was a legal revival of claims that had been filed from 1917 to February, 1920, and that I had mistakenly assumed had been allowed to lapse. Second, there had been a rash of new filings by speculators between 1965 and January, 1967. It was then that Interior Secretary Udall, using powers granted under the 1920 Mineral Leasing Act, finally stopped the filings, but possibly did so too late.

I found that many of the pre-1920 claims were being revived after they were purchased by agents of big oil companies. I also found that 264 million acres of this land in Colorado alone had already been alienated in the forty years between 1920 and 1961, as had about 80 million acres in Utah and Wyoming. Most of these alienations had occurred under Interior Secretary Albert Fall and Assistant Secretary E. C. Finney, of Teapot Dome fame. There had also, however, been quite a rush of approvals of claims in the latter part of the 1940's, and again from 1953 to 1956. None had been given final approval during the tenure of Udall.*

Even more important, however, was a case hanging over the head of

* For a more detailed description of the oil-shale situation, see my book *In Our Time*, New York: Harcourt, Brace & World, 1968, pp. 29–69, and on this point pp. 39–43.

the government that threatened to grant all of the 1918–19 claims. In a test case in 1966, a district court had approved a large private claim purchased in the 1950's, despite the fact that no development of that claim had been carried out during the intervening forty-six years. The government case had been miserably argued by the Interior and Justice departments, whether by accident or design, and the circuit court in late 1968 felt compelled to affirm the decision of the lower court. This was a bad blow. The government had ignored the fact that there had been no genuine discovery, and that the claimants had slept on their rights for so many years and had made no effort to maintain and develop their claims. I thought all was lost, but the Solicitor General picked up the case and asked the Supreme Court to review it. The Court accepted jurisdiction, and Peter Straus made an exceptionally able argument for the government. In December, 1970, the Court, by a vote of 4 to 2 (three members not voting), upheld the government's contention that the speculators had lost their claim through a failure to maintain and develop the properties after filing.*

The Nixon administration, it must be said, has made, so far, a much better record on oil-shale claims than the two preceding Democratic administrations. There is, however, a striking case of injustice that should be remedied. Fred S. March, a local official in the Interior Department's Bureau of Land Management, argued vigorously for presenting a strong case against the claims of the speculators in the original suit. His superiors attempted to dismiss him from the service but were foiled by a 2 to 1 vote of the Civil Service Commission. He was then transferred to the Pacific Northwest, far removed from oil-shale disputes. We all are much indebted to him, as to others who have fought to defend the rights of the people throughout the tangled history of this struggle.

In the main, the 1918–19 filings had been on the outer rims of the prehistoric oil pool, but from 1964 to February, 1966, other groups had struck at the rich center of the pool. They did so under the Mineral Act of 1872, and under the claim that they were filing for dawsonite and other minerals, not for oil—although it was obvious that in order to extract the dawsonite it would also be necessary to extract the oil. I personally inspected the records of filings in the two richest oil-shale counties of Colorado, Garfield and Rio Blanco, and was startled to find that in Garfield an oil prospector by the name of Merle Zweifel had filed 338 claims, totaling over 26,000 acres, in a little over a year. But even more amazing were his filings in Rio Blanco. There he had entered no fewer than 2,578 placer claims. Each was for a quarter section of 160 acres, or a total of over

* *Hickel, Secretary of the Interior* v. *The Oil Shale Co.*, Case No. 25. See also the government's briefs in this case, and especially the factual history given in the supplementary brief (p. 183). A man by the name of Tell Ertl had bought these long-stagnant claims for a pittance and sold them to Tosco for millions. In two cases he got $1,536,000 and $48,000 a year (*ibid.*, p. 103).

400,000 acres. The mere indexing of these claims filled seventy-nine pages of the master record book. Zweifel indeed stated in a letter to J. R. Freeman, a public-spirited local editor who was trying to fight the private appropriation of these lands, that he had recently filed no fewer than "20,000 claims" covering "4,000,000 acres."

The law of 1872, passed in the days of the small-scale operator, did not place any limit upon the number of claims a man could file. It was certainly never a part of the original intention to legitimize wholesale filings. I tried to get the Interior Department to make a mass attack on these filings on the ground that they obviously failed to satisfy at least two of the requirements laid down in the 1872 act. There could not have been genuine "discoveries" each day on thirty or more claims of from 80 to 160 acres apiece, as was asserted, and it was also impossible to have staked out the four sides of each of these many quarter sections in a day, especially since most of them were in the Rockies and many were alleged to have been staked in the winter, when snow was on the ground. At first, the Solicitor's office refused to make such an attack. Finally, the Bureau of Land Management tried to invalidate the Zweifel claims. But it will take determination to push these efforts to a successful conclusion.

While it is not certain what the Nixon administration will do, there is great danger that we may still lose not only the 1918–19 claims, but also those of 1964–66. If we do, many billions of potential dollars will in all probability be lost.

This matter of the vast oil-shale deposits is one of the many pieces of unfinished business I am compelled to leave on the doorstep of posterity. It may sleep for a few years as Alaskan oil is developed. But there is danger that as the public slumbers, the big private interests will be hard at work.

34

Tariffs, International Trade,
and the Monetary System

It is sometimes said that if all economists were laid end to end,
they would not reach a conclusion. But in the case of protective tariffs,
they would. Almost unanimously, from Adam Smith on, they have favored free trade between localities and nations.

They have done this because freedom of trade permits each nation to
specialize in what it does best. The larger the total market, the more
minute the subdivision of labor and the more economies of scale can be
realized both inside and outside a plant. These result in a greater total
product for all, with the relative gains determined by the terms of trade
established in a free market. To those who urge tariffs as a means of insuring national self-sufficiency in a war-dominated world, economists reply
that freedom of trade, by making all countries interdependent, lessens the
danger of war.

American economists, like the British, have held to these doctrines.
But during the three-quarters of a century from 1860 to 1933, while the
Republican party was in office, our actual practice was highly protectionist. The Republicans passed two successive tariff acts that raised our
duties to the highest level in the world, or, on an average, to about 52 per
cent. The last of these, the Smoot-Hawley Tariff Act of 1930, played its
part in deepening the world depression and in causing other countries to
impose higher duties in retaliation.

With the return of Democrats to power in 1933 and the appointment
of the free trader Cordell Hull as secretary of State, the protectionist policy was reversed. Hull's Reciprocal Trade Act became the strongest force
for expanded international trade. But for over a decade the world had

moved rapidly in the other direction. The Eastern international finance section of the Republican party was finally compelled by the logic of the situation to change its position, although it did so in a somewhat shame-faced fashion. However, the dominant legislative wing of the party, based on textiles, steel, and chemicals, was still strongly protectionist and sought to reverse the Hull policy. In the main, the Democratic party continued to be loyal to its historic position, although as manufacturing moved south-ward there was some weakening. The export of raw cotton and tobacco still served as a low-tariff force in the South.

Hull's bland policy of making initial concessions only to countries that acted reciprocally was but the opening wedge in his program. He followed this with his version of the most-favored-nation clause, which had been given a limited endorsement by the Harding administration. Hull went much further. He extended the reductions first offered to a na-tion granting reciprocal favors to all those countries that did not actually discriminate against the United States. They did not have to lower their tariffs. It was enough if they did not increase them against our products or did not otherwise discriminate against them. Few caught this subtlety. Thus the shrewd, hillbilly free trader and militia captain from the Ten-nessee mountains outwitted for beneficent ends the high-priced protec-tionist lawyers and lobbyists of Pittsburgh and Wall Street.

Since these negotiations, carried out country by country, were time-consuming and complicated, Hull and the State Department proposed to shorten them by setting up two international organizations. The first was the General Agreement on Tariffs and Trade (GATT), which was de-signed to put the reciprocal-tariff agreements on a multilateral basis. All the member nations were to reach agreements for the reduction of trade barriers. The second was the International Trade Organization (ITO), which had similar, though broader, functions, along with some inconsis-tencies.* But with the postwar reaction leading to the Republican Con-gressional victories of 1946, the State Department and Truman hurriedly dropped the idea of the ITO, allowing it to wither on the vine. They also decided not to submit our entrance into GATT by treaty, which under the Constitution would require ratification by a two-thirds vote of the Senate. Instead, they chose to enter by an executive agreement. When asked to define the difference between such an agreement and a treaty, the State Department casuistically replied that the difference was that an agreement, unlike a treaty, did not have to be ratified by the Senate.

The way in which the State Department constantly bypassed the Sen-ate by negotiating executive agreements with foreign powers, rather than by making treaties, naturally excited the opposition both of the economic and political conservatives and of the strict constructionists of the Consti-

---

* I have treated these matters at greater length in my book *America in the Market Place*, pp. 88–97.

tution. A bureaucracy of foreign-service officers, it was alleged, was displacing the representatives of the people in making the decisions that might lead to war or peace, discord or amity. Such resentment was especially strong when the two tariff and trade agreements setting up GATT and ITO were proposed. This, combined with the advocacy of the administrative state by numerous writers, made it seem to many that popular government was on its way out.

When I came to the Senate, I did not take this contention too seriously. I approved much more of the foreign policy of the State Department than I did that of the Senate and the Congress. The memory of what the Senate had done to Woodrow Wilson and the League of Nations burned like a hot coal within me. And I remembered how Congress had passed the 1930 tariff act that launched a deadly international trade war. Believing as I did in collective security and a strong United Nations, I knew that Truman and the State Department were more trustworthy supporters than the bipartisan coalition, which, in its opposition to liberal Presidents, had shown itself to be almost as rancorous as in the days of Wilson.

So I was opposed to the constitutional amendment giving Congress and the Senate, rather than the President and his representatives, the power to ratify or reject international agreements. This proposed amendment was being sponsored by Senator John Bricker, who had been the Republican candidate for Vice President in 1944. It was being supported by the American Bar Association and other highly prestigious organizations.

This did not influence me, for I well knew the built-in bias of all such organizations against measures promoted by the Democratic party. But I was disillusioned and repelled by what seemed to be the relatively low intellectual level of the ranking State Department personnel. Unjustifiable charges were being made against them by Senator McCarthy, and I did not want to add to their troubles. But the more I dealt with the department, the more dispirited I became. While there were many fine and devoted people there, the general average was not such as to make me want to have them as guardians of the republic.

The volume of work that would be transferred from the State Department to the Senate was so huge as to be impossible. This conclusion emerged from a long study that I had an able young lawyer, Larry Carp, of Saint Louis, make for me. It enabled me to ask two brief questions, the answers to which revealed the basic weakness of the Bricker amendment. I inquired whether the regulation and protection of commerce was not primarily a matter for local and state concern in the United States but of national concern in virtually every other civilized country in the world. The answer was that this was so. Then did it not follow, I asked as my second question, that each one of the forty-eight states would be compelled, under the Bricker amendment, to negotiate separate treaties with each one of the rapidly swelling list of nations? The answer to this question was clearly in the affirmative. It was obvious that this would mean that the negotiations would run into the thousands.

Walter George then came forward with a substitute for the amendment that virtually canceled the two provisions and substituted some face-saving language in their stead. I thought this might be a rebuke to the State Department without doing any harm, and I told George I probably would support his language. As the roll was called I realized, however, that the vote was symbolic and that a vote for the George amendment, even though it meant nothing in reality, would be interpreted as a vote for the opponents of the State Department and a victory for the Senate. Since this seemed to me a bad result, I went to George and told him I must withdraw my tentative promise and vote against his substitute. An instant later I had my last chance to vote and voted against it. The amendment was then defeated by one vote.

When the Republicans renewed the Hull program in 1947, they did so for only two years, adding a peril-point amendment that made it hard to go below a point set by the Tariff Commission. They also granted an escape clause if industries were to be severely crippled by a proposed cut.

Stronger in 1949, the liberal group removed the first restriction, to restore the original language. After the elections of 1950, though we still had a slight numerical majority in both houses, it was so shaky that the leadership thought it better to compromise. So we allowed the Republicans to restore the peril-point restriction while we tightened the escape clause. I felt that the leadership had conceded too much to get a two-year extension, but as a junior member who was fast earning a reputation of overactivity, I did not make a stand.

With the Eisenhower victory of 1952, the Republicans, for the first time since 1930, controlled both the executive and the legislative branches. With the help of their Southern allies, they could do what they wanted. But they did not know what that was. They were divided between their internationalists from the East and their economic and political nationalists of the Middle West and mountain states.

Eisenhower met the dilemma by a method typical of harried administrators: he appointed a commission to study and report. He was buying time on the tariff question, as he was on housing and local government.

Although the Randall Commission in 1954 favored a further moderate reduction in tariffs, the Republican Congress began to balk. But the elections that fall resulted in a small Democratic majority, and it was, in fact, the Democrats who made it possible for the Eisenhower program, modest though it was, to be carried out. There was to be no decrease of more than 5 per cent in any one year and no accumulation in cuts. Since the average effective tariff was then about 13 per cent, and it took two or three years to negotiate a reduction at GATT, there would be a cut of less than 1 per cent.

Now it was the Southerners from the Piedmont region who balked at freer trade. They wanted more, not less, protection for their textiles. Johnson was just starting his Senate leadership. Hoping to avoid an open fight with either the Republicans or his own protectionists, he seemed strangely disturbed. I told him that I could not go along with a betrayal of the historic Democratic position. I meant to denounce the bill from the floor and move that the cuts could be cumulative. My move would mean a reduction, not of one-twentieth, but of one-sixth. For some reason, he did not want that issue raised, although I suspected that both he and Rayburn, as old Rooseveltians, were in secret sympathy with what I was trying to do. He asked if I would be satisfied if Byrd, Kerr, and a leading Republican assured me privately that they would agree to my proposal in conference with the House. Would I then refrain from pushing the issue on the floor? I answered that I would. But I wanted to hear with my own ears whether they meant to keep their word. If they did not, then I must have the right to tell the whole story on the floor. I was accepting a private surrender by the Senate power structure, but one that saved their face.

Kerr, the Republican, and I met the next noon in the marble room off the Senate floor, where they both gave me their promise. We shook hands on the agreement, which was solemnly repeated by each of us. Byrd was absent. An aide implied that a Virginia gentleman could not humiliate himself before a Northern liberal. But I was told that I might rely on his acceptance of the plan.

In this roundabout way, we later got a fair-sized reduction at Geneva from GATT. I felt I had done something of which Adam Smith and John Bright would have been proud.

My involvement in tariffs and trade naturally increased when I became a member of the Finance Committee. Kennedy, as President, decided to make the general reduction of tariffs and co-operation with the European Common Market his major legislative concern. Although I thought this overly cautious, while other domestic issues needed equal stress, he had won by a narrow margin and his legislative majority was small. He hoped to conciliate liberal Republicans by appointing Douglas Dillon secretary of the Treasury. Dillon was a free trader, and he served Kennedy loyally in this role as well as in matters of taxation.

One of the most peculiar members of the Finance Committee was George ("Molly") Malone, of Nevada. A mining engineer, a protectionist, and a supernationalist, he arose periodically in the Senate to make much the same speech, always taking at least three hours. After hearing this a few times, members sought refuge in their offices to work on correspondence or joined colleagues over "bourbon and branch water" in the secretary's room. Harry Byrd, though, always heard him through with impeccable Southern courtesy, nodding his head gravely as other members fled. Molly soon became known as "the man who empties the Senate." For four hours, until midnight, at one evening session of the Finance Committee, he kept a hapless advocate of free trade on the stand. His repertoire being limited, he kept repeating the same questions, accusing his poor victim of inconsistency if he faltered in his answers. I often thought that Lewis Carroll might have had here material for an incredible "Molly in Wonderland." Most academicians thought Molly had a low intelligence, but it was not so. Occasionally, if one listened closely or read the *Record* the next morning, one found gleams of practical shrewdness. He was, I think, the first to point out that the introduction of Western technology to Africa and the Orient, where farm incomes are minimal, would result in very low labor costs per unit of manufacturing output. Notwithstanding the predictions of my old teacher Taussig, who was thinking of Europe, this situation could endure for decades.

Newspapermen who followed Finance Committee hearings said that I was both the strongest defender of the administration's policy and the sharpest critic of the State Department. Kennedy was proposing that he be given power in negotiations with GATT and the Common Market to cut tariffs in half or to an absolute average of between 5 and 6 per cent, and also to eliminate tariffs if 75 per cent of the foreign trade in a group of commodities was exported by the U.S. and the Common Market or if the tariff on a commodity amounted to less than 5 per cent. This would have included autos and many types of machinery, thus helping our exports. Since this was a great forward step, I threw my energies into winning approval for the general program. There were, however, two points upon which I ran afoul of the State Department.

We had discovered that although the United States had reduced tariffs since 1934 by three-quarters, or from 53 to 13 per cent,* the European nations whom we had helped so generously were continuing to apply nontariff discriminations against us. For a decade after the war, France had subjected our exports to rigid quotas and arbitrary administrative regulations. Germany, which we had aided in an unprecedented way, limited the free import of American coal to 5 million tons. Above that amount, it charged the prohibitive tariff of $5 a ton. Having taken up this grievance with Finance Minister Ludwig Erhard on a trip to Germany during the summer of 1961, I had found that the Germans had no intention of changing their restrictive policies. The financial support of the dominant Christian Democratic party came from the coal, steel, and chem-

---

* Half of this reduction came from the increase in the prices of commodities where there was a specific tariff of so much a yard or per pound or bushel. The remainder was due to explicit reductions in the tariff schedules.

ical magnates of the Rhineland, and they did not want to have their Ruhr coal put out of business by low-cost American coal mined from our thick seams. At about the same time, the Common Market decided to prohibit imports of our frozen chickens.

There were many other acts of discrimination, about which the State Department blandly professed ignorance. The farm groups rightly complained that the department ignored the obvious plans of Germany and France to cut the importation of low-cost American wheat and of soybeans, which hitherto Europe had not produced. I could understand the anger of the protectionists and their later demand for retaliatory action. But the mention of these matters triggered the European makers of public opinion into harangues of criticism. They said that we were going back on our commitments, and could not be trusted as a future ally. They never admitted their own countries were already discriminating against us. Their complaints were echoed by the most extreme of our own internationalists, whose motto seemed to be "America is never right." I asked the State Department for instances of trade discrimination against us, but although I was fighting its battle in the Finance Committee, it never helped. I could not make up my mind whether its employees were devout Christians, like my fellow Quakers, who would have America suffer all things in the cause of international peace, or masochists who actually took pleasure in being insulted by cultivated foreigners. In fact, they were probably neither, but were in many cases deracinated by residence abroad and by international marriages. They dreaded a conflict of wills with those nations they regarded as both their protégés and our cultural superiors. When their guard was down, Howard Shuman and I were shocked to hear them often refer to these other countries as their "clients." International alliances seemed more important than the mutual benefits of two-way economic co-operation.

In addition, the State Department neglected to inform the Finance Committee how the powerful American chemical industry had maintained a tariff rate of over 100 per cent by using the monopoly American selling price (ASP) as the base price for computing tariffs on coal-tar chemicals instead of the competitive foreign selling price, which was the usual standard for the fixing of rates. The department functionaries were playing it safe, never wanting to offend either the economically or the socially powerful. They were miserable allies; there were few crusaders among them.

With some pain I finally concluded that the State Department could not be trusted to represent the Congress in economic matters. Therefore, I proposed that our representative at trade talks be appointed directly by the President, instead of by the department. This won almost universal approval. So did my proposal that the U.S. should have greater power to retaliate if discriminated against, by going back to the old Smoot-Hawley rates or beyond. I hoped that we would never have to use this weapon, but in view of the European treatment of us, I felt that we needed a stick as well as the carrot. I told the foreign diplomats and reporters that unless there was co-operation, there would be a reaction in the United States, with a setback for all we had been striving for during the last three decades.

The more intelligent understood this, but most of the foreign groups treated this warning with stony hostility. The State Department representatives were scarcely more sympathetic. As late as the spring of 1968, members of the department still denied knowledge of any serious discriminations, although this was the very time that the Commerce Department and our trade representative, William Roth, were at last assembling a mass of conclusive evidence in Japan and Asia as well as in Europe.

My second conflict with the State Department came over the degree of pressure we should put on Europe to broaden the Common Market. That organization had been formed in 1957 by the Treaty of Rome, with its original members consisting of France, West Germany, Italy, Belgium, Holland, and Luxembourg. All tariffs between these countries were to be progressively reduced and ultimately eliminated. For all nations, there was to be a common external tariff, with promised reductions. It was clearly desirable that Great Britain, the three Scandinavian countries, Austria, Portugal, and possibly some others be admitted as soon as possible.

If Britain had moved quickly, this might have happened. But since the reactionary element among the British Tories controlled the government in 1956 and 1957, in accordance with old Tory policy they did not want such cohesion among the continental powers. They organized a rival grouping, the European Free Trade Association (EFTA), including, along with themselves, the smaller countries left out of the Common Market. Under EFTA the member countries were to abolish tariff duties between themselves at about the same rate of speed as their larger rival, but each country was to maintain its own tariff against the rest of the world instead of developing one external tariff.

I favored this progressive reduction of tariff barriers, whether under the Common Market or EFTA. It provided broader markets, within which a greater division of labor was possible. It brought nations closer together, and in the case of France and Germany seemed to reverse the age-old hatreds that three times within a century had plunged Europe into wars, ever more bloody and which on the last two occasions had involved us. In the narrow and immediate sense, such a tariff union seemed to be against our economic interest, since it allowed its members to abolish tariffs, while our goods still faced barriers. These would, however, be less than previously. Nevertheless, the political advantages of a united Western Europe were obvious, and the greater economic prosperity of this area would increase its ability to buy American goods. This might also offset the inward-looking limitations of the European Customs Union.

Therefore I had supported the mild encouragement given to the Common Market by the Eisenhower administration and the still-greater help given by the Kennedy administration. When George Ball, the former United States counsel for the Common Market, became under secretary of State for economic affairs, he wanted to do everything possible to promote that organization and was apparently the author of the clause in the Kennedy proposal that provided for the elimination of all tariffs on goods in a group where 75 per cent had originated in either the United States or in Common Market countries. If Britain entered the Common Market, there would be some thirty-five such groups of commodities almost free of tariffs. Meanwhile, the attraction of the American market would put other countries into the economic union of the democracies, thus widening the area of free trade.

The question was whether Great Britain wanted to join or would be permitted to do so if it applied. Ball would not consider the possibility of rejection. He thought that the only difficulty might arise from Britain's refusal to join. One of the secret purposes of the 75-per-cent provision was, indeed, to induce Britain to enter the Common Market, so that it could get a better chance at the American market. I, too, wanted Britain to join, as well as all the other members of EFTA. A market of 275 million people would be stronger and more effective than two separate ones of 185 and 90 million respectively. But I wanted Britain to make this choice of its own free will. If it wanted to stay out, it should have the advantages of our trade anyway.

I saw dangers in France that Ball, despite his close knowledge of Europe, curiously enough would not admit. He had been persuaded by Jean Monnet that France favored the broadest possible economic union. On a trip to France in 1957, I had had a long talk with Paul Reynaud, by then the leader of the responsible French right. The Common Market was proving a success, and British conservatives were attracted toward it. However, I found Reynaud not only suspicious of Britain's motives, but also quite bitter in his attitude. In 1961 I visited France again, and read the Parisian press quite closely. Charles de Gaulle was in power. Since no one knew what he would do if Britain sought entry to the Common Market, I did not want to prophesy, but in many ways De Gaulle seemed an extreme nationalist, and he had hated Churchill almost as much as he had hated Roosevelt. If he vetoed the admission of Britain, would the other members of the Common Market dare to force the issue? If Britain was not a member, then in only one group of commodities—airplanes—would we and the Common Market have 75 per cent of the world's trade. This would make the provision for the removal of tariffs a complete dead letter.

In order to guard against this danger, Congressman Henry Reuss, of Wisconsin, and I proposed to widen the terms of the Ball plan by discarding tariffs on groups of commodities in which the countries in EFTA, along with those in the Common Market, made up the required 75 per cent. Since this would include Britain, the three Scandinavian nations, and several other small ones, the goods on which tariffs would be removed would rise to far more than the thirty-five groups Ball had so proudly claimed. Free trade would be extended to an economic alliance, including ourselves, of close to 500 million people. This would soon sweep into our ranks a large number of additional countries and create a true economic union of the democracies.

Reuss and I, enthusiastic about this prospect, hoped that Ball and the State Department would welcome it. After all, they were professed free traders, and this would greatly widen the free-trade world. But not at all. With a curious leap of logic, unusual in so shrewd and successful an international lawyer, Ball accused me of applying political pressure on Britain to stay out of the Common Market. This, of course, was patently absurd. Ball and the State Department were the ones who were pressuring Great Britain to join the Common Market by denying added access to the American market if it stayed with an independent EFTA. We would have freed it from this requirement, so that it could decide the issue on its own relative political and economic merits. We would also be able to outflank De Gaulle if he were to turn restrictionist and keep Britain out of the Common Market. In that case, he would not be able to hurt Britain. We would be allies of both the Common Market and EFTA. Furthermore, we would not be accused of trying to sway British decisions, and hence would not arouse more anti-Americanism either in Britain or on the Continent.

Ball fought to the last against our proposal. On the eve of the Senate vote, he reluctantly agreed to take our language in order to avert defeat on the floor. However, I knew that he would probably triumph in the darkness of the conference committee, as he did. Since the protectionists had also taken fright at the proposal to expand, rather than contract, the free-trade area, they joined the State Department in removing the offending language. The State Department and Ball were thus successful in preventing an economic union of all the Western democracies. It reminded me of the experience more than a decade before when the State Department defeated the Thomas-Douglas plan for strengthening the enforcement provisions of the United Nations.

Ball and the officials at State felt vindicated. They had beaten back the efforts of two Midwestern legislators who lacked their knowledge and experience. But history proved us right. Britain did not need their inducement to apply for membership. First the Conservatives and then the Labourites sought membership, on grounds that bore little or no relation to the bait of the Ball amendment. As we had feared, it was De Gaulle who killed the admission of Great Britain. Turning Ball's arguments against him, he accused the United States of trying to force Britain's admission and came out against continental Europe being dominated by the English-speaking countries. Despite the efforts of Senator Javits to revive our proposal, the iron tongue of midnight has apparently tolled upon it.

I became further convinced by this that in foreign, as in domestic, matters we needed more frankness with the public. The State Department has acted as though afraid that if the public knew about the discriminations that foreign governments practice against us, it would again turn isolationist. I have a greater faith in the good sense of the voters. Sometimes the experts are led astray by their own prejudices. But it is not sound strategy to have even correct policies rest upon the ignorance of the public. Fortunately, we are a free society with a fairly independent and inquisitive press. Officialdom, despite its efforts, cannot keep the truth covered for long.

In 1965 De Gaulle showed his hand. The U.S. had been running a big adverse balance of payments ever since 1958. This was mainly caused by our heavy expenditures on military aid and economic assistance to other countries. France had shared in our generosity—which I believed was also justified by our ultimate self-interest. In the process, foreign banks had accumulated billions of dollars of claims against us. If they chose, the countries and their state-controlled banks were entitled to claim payment in gold. Some of this gold had already been sent to them, bringing down our reserve from $21 billion in 1958 to $14 billion in 1965. But there were in addition $27 billion of outstanding claims, of which several billions were in the hands of France. In delivering his broadside against the "Anglo-Saxons," De Gaulle announced that he would call in $300 million worth of French claims on us for gold. Thereafter all of our accumulating debts to France must be settled in gold.

Legally, De Gaulle had the right to do this. Under the international gold-exchange standard, as ratified at Bretton Woods, a nation or national bank might demand that its claims on another country be redeemed in gold. But when the claims had risen to where they were appreciably greater than the gold behind them, then if these rights were fully exercised they would bring down the international monetary system. There was not enough gold to meet the claims. The United States and Great Britain had fractional, not 100-per-cent, reserves. Our obligations were twice the amount of our gold, and the ratio for Britain was at least four to one, and perhaps more. By selling securities and converting them into foreign balances, speculators could stage an additional raid on the currency of both nations.

Before March of 1933, the depositors in our own banks could have prostrated our banking system by demanding that their deposits be redeemed in gold. De Gaulle was apparently ready to do the same thing internationally. He wanted France to accumulate gold so that it could ride out any financial storm by obtaining security for itself at whatever cost to its neighbors. The currency speculators would follow in his wake, believing that the United States would then be forced to devalue, so that a dollar would ultimately command less gold.

The result would be that an owner of an ounce of gold could command more dollars than the thirty-five that had been agreed upon at Bretton Woods. The depreciation of the dollar in terms of gold would actually mean the appreciation of gold in terms of the dollar. De Gaulle seemed to embrace the doctrines of his financial adviser, Jacques Rueff, who wanted to have the world go back to the old-fashioned gold standard, but one by which an ounce of gold would be worth approximately $70, instead of $35. When France and its allies had milked us of our gold, they would then profit from the increase in its price.

I had no doctrinal faith in the gold-exchange system, for I believed it had an inner source of insecurity. Fixed exchange rates could not forever contain changing costs, increasing international claims, and decreasing balances. Instead, I hoped that we might develop an international currency that would be based on something different from either the 100-per-cent-gold or the fractional-gold-exchange standard. As alternate chairman of the Joint Economic Committee, I had given my former colleague Milton Friedman a forum from which he could expound his doctrines of flexible exchange rates. I was personally ready to accept a modified version of this under which currencies could fluctuate within 5 or 7 per cent of the internationally agreed-upon par ratio. Normally this would be enough to re-establish any equilibrium that was disturbed. Along with Reuss, I thought that we might also adopt the principle of the "variable peg," under which par would not be a fixed figure but an average of the market quotations for the past three to five years. This, in combination with the previous zone of tolerance, would introduce an element of flexibility.

I did not want to see us stripped of gold and put at the financial mercy of France, and I thought it unethical of that country to make such an attempt after all that we had done for it. For years I had been urging that we scrap two internal claims on gold: the 25-per-cent gold reserve required on the deposits of commercial banks in the Federal Reserve System, and the 25-per-cent reserve on the currency issued by that system.

When taken together, these locked up about $13 billion of gold for no good purpose. In January, 1965, President Johnson at last asked for the removal of the first requirement. This released nearly $5 billion of gold. Robertson, the chairman of the Banking and Currency Committee, who had primitive views on a metallic currency, was at first much opposed to this, but the Federal Reserve finally persuaded him to support it. I urged that we should go the whole way and remove the second requirement, but this was not done until some years later.

While we were battening down the ship to resist the coming storm, I wanted us to launch a counteroffensive against De Gaulle's tactics. On the floor of the Senate I proposed that we should quietly discourage further travel in France and on French liners and airplanes until De Gaulle changed his policy. Furthermore, since most of the former French colonies in Africa still had their banking facilities in France, we should throw the financial burden for their support upon France and discontinue our aid. The unofficial reply of the State Department was twofold: first, this might weaken our ties with France and, second, we were no longer giving any such aid. I further recommended that since South Vietnam was still doing its banking with the Bank of Indo-China, we should try to cut off or lessen the flow of American exchange into that institution. Years before, on a trip to Paris I had walked into the financial district and, from the mere size of this bank, I could see its importance. As I studied the financial news in the French press and remembered the Stavisky scandal, I realized how strong were its political ties, especially those with the Radical Social-ist party. While France was now militarily out of South Vietnam, the Bank of Indo-China was still in. Claims on the dollar that they acquired ultimately came under the control of De Gaulle.

I urged the Treasury to get Saigon to license American banks to handle as much of our direct business as possible and for us to make many of our payments in currency that could be redeemed only by the military, by the Treasury, or by U.S. banks. Seeing the point immediately, Secre-tary Henry H. Fowler put the suggestions into effect. While he may have been contemplating such a move himself, my efforts gave him the added impetus to overcome the State Department. From conversations with the President, I saw that these suggestions were not distasteful to him.

My final suggestion was a brutal one, to be used only if De Gaulle persisted in his anti-American policies. This was to raise the question of the World War I debt that France still owed us. In 1930 President Hoover had indefinitely postponed further payments, on both the principal and the interest. But we did not legally forgive it; it was still an obligation. Since France was taking advantage of the letter of the law in demanding gold for the obligations we owed, it could hardly object if we asked for payment of its legal obligation to us, although this had slumbered for a third of a century. Rather slyly I suggested that a compromise might be worked out under which France would receive in canceled debt what it demanded on the current balances.

This proposal really drew blood. The State Department was horrified, while the French press and French sympathizers fulminated. However, De Gaulle had been shown that we also had weapons, and were not as soft as he had believed. In a few weeks I received a telephone call from the French Ambassador, who said that Monsieur Rueff was in Washington and would like to talk with me. Would I come to the embassy for lunch with him? My wife and I had often enjoyed being entertained at the French Embassy in the past and had taken delight in the cuisine, the conversation, the hospitality, and the paintings. I told the Ambassador this. But, I added, De Gaulle had virtually proclaimed himself the enemy of the United States, and the embassy was French soil. Until he changed his attitude, I could not discuss matters with his emissary anywhere but under the American flag. I therefore extended a counterinvitation, for him to have lunch or an afternoon sherry with me in my office.

When Rueff appeared the next afternoon, I greeted him warmly. Against a patriotic background worthy of De Gaulle and perhaps of Cyrano de Bergerac, I seated him at the head of the table beneath the flag of the United States and the colors of the Marine Corps. Then I explained that while my New York sherry might not equal his French wines, it came with hospitality as warm as that which his country had always displayed toward Americans. He smiled appreciatively at this sally. Much abler than his critics said, he criticized the international gold-exchange standard as making it possible to expand domestic credit on an international paper reserve that was itself composed of credit. This, as in the late 1920's, he thought, would lead to inflation and ultimate collapse. However, his own remedy was faulty. If immediately carried out, with no changes, it would have meant shrinking the total volume of international currency from $65 to $42 billion. This would have caused a catastrophic fall in prices. Although he did not openly say so, Rueff clearly implied that the price of gold should be raised so that the total volume of international monetary purchasing power would be maintained. Assuming no increase in the quantity of monetized gold, this would have meant an increase to $54 an ounce. He evidently thought that the rise in the price of gold would also bring into circulation large hoardings of gold from family stockings, deposits in the earth, and safe-deposit boxes. Even so, there was no reliable estimate of the amount or the price necessary to attract the gold out from hiding. Moreover, the mere rumor of such a plan would start an international run on our gold, leading to its transferral to Europe as the speculators sought to gain from the proposed increase in price. The gamble was an intolerable risk.

There was no assurance that the production and reserves of gold would meet the needs of international trade. From 1873 to 1896, the demonetization of silver and the slowdown in the rate of production of gold had caused a world-wide fall in the price level, which in turn intensified depressions and led to high rates of unemployment. The later increase in gold production in South Africa, from 1896 to 1914, resulting from the cyanide process, had reversed the price level, introducing the opposite evils of inflation.

Furthermore, an increase in the price of gold would chiefly help the two big gold-producing countries, Russia and South Africa. The first of these was seeking to overthrow and undermine the Free World. The second, with its practice of apartheid, was the exemplar of all that was wrong in race relations.

There was no change in De Gaulle's policy, but gradually there was a shrinkage in American travel in France and in our purchases from that country. As De Gaulle's power over us weakened, so did his economic advantage. At last, in 1968, to solidify his political position, he had to raise wages after the paralyzing student and labor strikes. Then the money speculators moved in on the franc, as they had on the pound, and as they had tried to do on the dollar. The roles were now reversed. De Gaulle was receiving his own medicine, which could lead only to a devaluation of the franc. With a characteristic display of courage, he refused the inevitable.

Under these circumstances we might have felt justified in letting France wrestle alone with the problem. Instead, we came to its aid with an international loan, thus doing what De Gaulle had refused to do in 1965 for hard-pressed Britain. By then I was retired from politics and had no share in the decision. But as a citizen, I was proud that under President Johnson our country displayed magnanimity. After we had rebuked De Gaulle, the United States helped France. It was the kind of friendly firmness in which I believed.

Had I still been in the Senate, I would have supported Friedman's proposal for flexible or freely floating exchange rates had I not feared inflation, against which there can be short-term, but not long-term, hedging. To avoid being tied to fixed exchange rates, we may yet be forced to Friedman's policy, but I would prefer regulation of the currency whereby the International Monetary Fund would allow a long-time expansion rate of around 3 to 4 per cent a year in the paper volume of international currency. This would be apportioned between countries according to the relative amount of their reserves in gold, dollars, and pounds, with some allowance for the needs of the underdeveloped and less-developed countries, plus variations according to the relative rate of production and the business cycle.

The movement toward free trade within the democracies will require some international control of the general price level if we are to avoid both the rigidities of fixed exchange rates and the possible anarchy of widely fluctuating and rising national price levels, such as those from which the continent of Europe suffered in the early 1920's. While the Johnson administration did not fully show its hand, it seemed in 1967–68 to be moving in this direction. In 1971 the Nixon administration took drastic steps to compel foreign countries to stop their discriminations against us, letting the exchange rate fluctuate and imposing an additional 10-per-cent rate on foreign goods. But this was an increase of 10 per cent in the cost of the goods, not a 10-per-cent increase in tariffs. In effect, it amounted to doubling the average tariff rate. It is at least possible that if the State Department had followed our advice in 1962, we might gradually and more amicably have improved our trade relationships without taking this backward step.

As this book goes to press, the administration has agreed to devalue the dollar by about 8 per cent and to rescind the import surcharge, which had predictably damaged severely our relations with Canada, Japan, and our other trading partners. These concessions appear to have made possible a major and long overdue currency realignment.

35

Foreign Relations

My General Purposes and the Attitude
of the State Department

I ENTERED THE SENATE as a firm supporter of collective security and of the United Nations as the only tangible embodiment of that principle. If the Allies would only co-operate in peace as they had in war, they would be able to prevent aggression, and behind this shield they could work together for humanitarian purposes. I thought the history of the thirty years from 1918 to 1948 confirmed these ideas. I had campaigned for them, and I wanted the United States to play its full part. I recognized that during the immediate postwar period Russia had been a disruptive force all over the world. But I hoped that it could be won over to co-operation by our firmness in resisting aggression and by our friendliness if it chose to co-operate. So I supported Truman's policies in Iran, the Near East, and in the defense of Berlin, Austria, and Italy. Emily had supported UNRRA to the limit when in Congress, and I backed the Marshall Plan, which did magnificent work in the economic reconstruction of Western Europe.

With J. William Fulbright, I tried to provide an extra bonus for firms that would deal only with non-Communist unions, and for countries that would work for the economic integration of Western Europe. The State Department bitterly opposed both proposals on the ground that we should not try to influence either the domestic or the foreign policies of the countries we aided.

I was never sure that this was the real reason, for in a few years it was openly co-operating in the creation of the European Common Market, which aimed at doing precisely what Fulbright and I had advocated. I was left with the feeling that this was one more instance of the refusal of the State Department to accept any proposal coming from Congress and to insist that all foreign-policy projects be initiated by itself.

My suspicion was confirmed by another experience. Arthur Holcombe, of Harvard, and Quincy Wright, of Chicago, two veterans in international co-operation, had devised a plan for strengthening the resistance of democratic nations to aggression. This was to create a mutual-security federation inside the United Nations. This group would furnish troops and military aid to any nation adjudged the victim of aggression by a vote of two-thirds of the Security Council and the Assembly. This device would avoid the stalemate created by the charter whereby one member of the big five powers could veto any action by the others. Those nations that did not want to furnish or accept aid could refuse to sign such a supplementary pact and still remain within the United Nations, but those who did sign would implement the will of the two-thirds majority. Despite Russia, the U.N. could still be made an effective agency for peace.

Since this proposal might overcome the paralyzing effects of the veto, I said that I would support it. However, believing that the sponsor should be a senator with more seniority, I suggested Elbert Thomas. A former professor of political science at the University of Utah, he was finishing his third term. He agreed to be the senior sponsor of the proposal, and so the Thomas-Douglas resolution was introduced and referred to the Foreign Relations Committee, of which Thomas was also a member. This insured a hearing, and I hoped that the State Department would at least consider the proposal. Instead, the department brushed it aside as superfluous. The U.N., strengthened by NATO, was said to be all-sufficient. It was implied that the creation of an inner core of collective security would somehow weaken the outer ring of the U.N., although our purpose was the exact opposite.

The department's traditional obtuseness toward Congressional suggestions explains some of its difficulties. The secretary at the time, Dean Acheson, was a man of great ability. An anti-Communist and economic conservative, he had been unfairly attacked by the extreme right wing, which he naturally resented. And yet the Department of State was vulnerable because of some of its past personnel. Alger Hiss, a top official, had been retained despite the protests of the knowledgeable Adolf Berle, who thought that he had firm evidence of Hiss's subversive connections. In his second trial, Hiss was convicted on the ground of perjury in testimony before a grand jury. The evidence, as presented in the New York *Times,* convinced me that I would have joined in the verdict. Acheson's widely quoted statement after the verdict that he would not turn his back on Alger Hiss sounded like misplaced loyalty, and his enemies improperly took his words to mean that he had Communist sympathies.

The department was also vulnerable because of its early naïve error of considering the Chinese Communists only "agrarian radicals." I was always skeptical about this, because during my 1927 visit to Moscow I had seen the Chinese Institute, where large numbers of young Chinese were in training for leadership. One of these was Chiang Kai-shek's son. By 1949 Mao Tse-tung had in fact established a second Communist police state, as anti-American as the Soviets'. Chiang Kai-shek had been driven to Formosa because of the disaffection of his people, not by an American sell-out. However, the right wing blamed this on our foreign policy, and attacked especially the State Department and Acheson. It wanted to "unleash" Chiang Kai-shek to invade the mainland of China. Some of the Far Eastern experts wanted, instead, to recognize the Communist regime, but the official policy was to "let the dust settle."

Since neither of these policies seemed wise, I joined the Committee of One Million, which, during the next decade, opposed recognition of the Chinese Communists. This was a reversal of my stand toward the Soviet Union following my trip to Russia. I justified it because in the meantime both Russia and China had not only adopted a hostile policy toward the United States, but were governing their countries by force and terror. While the members of the Committee of One Million were chiefly domestic conservatives, I saw no harm in co-operating with them as long as they were loyal Americans. I insisted, though, that they accept no money from Chiang Kai-shek or his agents. We were mutually uneasy in this alliance, but they treated me decently. Perhaps my contribution was to impart a saner view about the motives of most of those who differed with us on China, and I rejoiced at preventing more attacks on the leaders of the National Council of Churches.

The public opposition to the country's China policy weakened the position of Acheson. Suffering under constant assaults, he took his reprisal on all legislators by his attitude of lofty superiority. He had been brought up in the tradition of the English class structure. His father was a bishop of the Episcopal church, the most Anglified of American institutions, while his mother was a Canadian heiress. With a towering stature and a formidable mustache, he was the very model of an officer in the Buckingham Palace guards. His elaborate and frozen courtesy did not endear him to those who wanted to defend him. Yet his loyalty to President Truman surpassed that of the rest of the Cabinet when they believed that Truman would be defeated. The latter never forgot that Acheson alone of the Cabinet had greeted him at Union Station on his return from an early, unsuccessful speaking tour. With his sense of personal loyalty, Truman ever afterward stood staunchly behind Acheson. The more vicious the attack, the firmer was Truman's support.

In trying to improve his relations with Congress, Acheson's advisers arranged a series of informal bipartisan receptions in his home. Unfortunately, he himself did little to soften his "image." Always impersonal, he seemed remote in his greetings. He treated Congressman Walter H. Judd, a former medical missionary in China and a good man, although a right-wing critic of Acheson's policies, with ill-concealed hauteur, which of course deepened Judd's dislike. While Acheson might have shone during the question period of the House of Commons or as a member of the House of Lords, he could not unbend enough to win the support of American legislators, despite his great talents and devotion to his country.

During this time, not only was China lost, but NATO was born and the North Koreans attacked South Korea.

NATO

IN SUPPORT of the NATO treaty, I made a major speech in the Senate, to which *Time* gave cover-story (as written by Frank McNaughton) prominence. The opposition to the treaty was led by Taft, still an isolationist. Curiously, those at the other end of the political spectrum, the friends of the Soviet Union, joined him in hostility to the treaty. Taft feared that NATO would draw us into future wars over matters in which we were not vitally concerned. Conversely, the others did not want an alliance that would resist Russia.

In view of Russia's acts of aggression, as well as its blockade of Berlin in 1948–49, I felt that we needed a concert of powers to check any take-over of Western Europe by Russian Communism. For a brief time the U.S. had a monopoly of nuclear power. We had offered to give this up if Russia would promise to do the same. Russia refused, clearly preferring that both sides should have the power of destruction rather than that all should forgo it. For this reason, I urged that we keep our right to produce and, if necessary, to use atomic power as a deterrent.

Within a few months this discussion was made obsolete by the news of Russia's atomic bomb. Physicists had known that this was inevitable, but the pace of development had been hastened by the activities of the British atomic scientists Klaus Fuchs and Alan Nunn May. During the war, and with English letters of clearance, they had come to Los Alamos, where they had learned all our secrets, which, in turn, they passed on to the Russians. This betrayal had not only shortened the Soviets' time in catching up in technical knowledge, but had greatly added to our own sense of insecurity, already triggered by Alger Hiss and the Rosenbergs. There was reason for continued suspicion, although the world did not learn until 1963 that Kim Philby, former head of the British Counter-Intelligence, had been the "third man" for the English Communist agents planted in Washington. Guy Burgess and Donald MacLean, high-ranking members of the British Foreign Service, had defected back in 1951, but few realized at that time that MacLean had not only shared all the secrets of the

Combined Policy Commission, which dealt with atomic power, but had repeatedly used his pass for after-hours visits to the AEC building.*

While opposing any hysterical reaction to the Soviet Union, I thought we should strengthen our defenses against a possible hostile move, and that an alliance with the relatively democratic nations of Western Europe was inherent to our national defense. I also suggested the partial and guarded rearmament of West Germany as a means of strengthening the potential manpower of the democratic alliance.

There was one safeguard, however, that I wanted to attach to our ratification of the NATO treaty. That was to make our dispatch of troops conditional upon a reciprocal pledge by the other members. Like every combat soldier in World War II, I was aware that we had furnished the overwhelming mass of troops for the liberation of Western Europe and Asia. Britain and to some extent France, having been greatly weakened by the long war, were disposed to let the United States bear the major burden, although they retained an equal or predominant share in the making of policy. I was afraid this might continue. From published accounts, it became evident that NATO was counting on a defensive army of twenty-five divisions. As a means of requiring true mutuality, I suggested that we should not commit more than five divisions at a maximum, or one for every four furnished by Western Europe, and, secondly, that this ratio should be followed if Europe did not furnish its quota of twenty. Thus, if Europe stopped at twelve divisions, we would furnish only three, and if they went to sixteen, we would furnish four. We should not commit five full divisions unless Europe provided twenty. To use technical language, I proposed that our expansion of forces should be parallel and proportional to the European contribution, but should not be unconditional. This suggestion seemed sensible and won the support of Arthur Krock, the conservative Washington correspondent of the New York *Times*.

It might have carried had the State Department not opposed it. It insisted on our unconditional pledge, arguing that otherwise we would show a lack of faith in our allies that they would bitterly resent. The department wanted a straight up-or-down vote on NATO. At last, deferring to their supposedly greater knowledge, I did not press my proposed amendment.

Events have shown that my original proposal was right, while the State Department was wrong. France, the nation most immediately protected, never made an adequate contribution, and finally, under De Gaulle, withdrew all its troops from the control and direction of NATO. Great Britain felt so financially insecure that it cut its contribution. The smaller European nations have made inadequate additions. Just as they had de-

* See *The Philby Conspiracy* by Bruce Page, Phillip Knightley, and David Leitch, New York: Doubleday & Company, 1968.

pended on Great Britain before both the world wars, so now they depended on the United States. We have had to bear a major share of the load, and after the Berlin crisis of 1961, as an evidence of our good faith, we dispatched a sixth division to West Germany. The result was that we bore most of the ground defense of West Germany.

Our possession of nuclear power was, of course, the ultimate deterrent to Russian aggression. It has been disappointing that Western Europeans have not admitted this fact. They and the world may pay dearly for the failure to understand where the real danger lies, or the need for cohesion among former allies.

Korea

SOON AFTER the ratification of NATO came the North Korean invasion of South Korea, in June of 1950. This was carried out, with Russian help, by uniformed troops of the armed forces, and created none of the subtleties of guerrilla warfare that later complicated the struggle in Indochina and South Vietnam. By this move the Korean Communists had broken the agreement negotiated with Stalin that we were to occupy the country south of the thirty-eighth parallel. They had moved into the military vacuum created by our withdrawal of troops from South Korea. In a policy speech made during the winter of 1950, Acheson had omitted mentioning Korea south of the thirty-eighth parallel as a territory we would defend. His critics charged him with giving the go-ahead signal to the Communists, although he had added that there was also territory which it was the primary obligation of the United Nations to defend and in which we would join.

Truman did not bother to draw such subtle distinctions. He made a fateful decision—the hardest in his life, he later said. He ordered American divisions to move from Japan to Pusan, on the southernmost coast of Korea, to drive back the Communists. Then he went to the United Nations for confirmation, and, by a lucky chance, Russia could not interpose a veto because it had withdrawn from the Security Council in a fit of pique. We were, therefore, not only able to get our defense confirmed by the U.N., but also all the member nations were called upon to help. Turkey did the best; Britain did little, as did France. India sent an ambulance. On the whole, the United States bore the overwhelming burden, although the U.N. gave our efforts its stamp of approval.

When Truman sent down to the Senate his initial message describing his action, Taft sprang to his feet demanding to know if the President was not arrogating to himself the right to declare war, a function vested in Congress by the Constitution. This led me to study Madison's record of the debates in the Constitutional Convention. I found that the framers of the Constitution had differentiated between the use of force and a formal declaration of war. Where speedy action was required, the President, as commander in chief of the armed forces, was free to use them in defense of national interests. I argued that the unexpected nature of the Communist attack and the need for a quick response if it were to be effective justified the President in moving quickly instead of going through the time-consuming process of first seeking Congressional approval. Lincoln's provisioning of Fort Sumter and his authorization of its defense, as well as his assembling of troops upon Presidential order, were early examples of this use of the latent war powers of the President. Mine was the only constitutional defense of Truman's action at this time, and it influenced me in our discussion of Vietnam policy fifteen to twenty years later.

Throughout the Korean War, I continued to support American policies. In a debate with Taft before a group of newspaper editors in April of 1951, he again referred to the struggle as "Truman's war." I replied that it was an American war, and the use of force by our nation had been approved by the U.N.

In September, 1950, we made a successful landing behind the enemy lines at Inchon, near the capital, Seoul, forcing the Communists to retreat. General MacArthur excelled in the planning and execution of this invasion, which was carried out with precision in spite of the perilous high tides of the harbor. The North Korean forces reeled back in disorder. In trying to follow north of the thirty-eighth parallel, MacArthur made a crucial mistake. The two divisions he sent were separated by the central mountain range; between them there could be no communication or control.

Then the Chinese Communists used this as an excuse to send their troops into Korea. They claimed that our movement north was only a prelude to MacArthur's crossing the Yalu River to invade Chinese territory. This probably was not MacArthur's intention, although he did want to bomb the Chinese positions north of the Yalu. I was urging that we should not go to the Yalu, but only as far north as the "Neck," or the line running roughly from Wonsan to Pyongyang. This would not only have brought us victory, but would also have established the more southern and democratic Koreans as the dominant force in Korea, with a larger share of the population and industry. At the same time it would have created a buffer zone between Korea and China, giving assurance that we did not intend to threaten China itself.

Many others held the same view. But MacArthur, flushed with victory, could not be restrained. He moved far north of the Neck, and in some places close to the Yalu itself. Overwhelming forces of Chinese crossed the river in November and December and drove back our troops in a humiliating series of defeats. My old First Marine Division was engulfed and had to fight its way out southward to the sea, where it was evacuated by ship.

In speeches in Illinois, upstate New York, and before the National League of Cities in Washington, I urged that we should not yield. Indeed, we might consider the use of tactical atomic power against armed and uniformed Chinese forces inside Korea, though I would have banned its use against the civilian population of North Korea and China itself. But I argued that when a soldier entered the armed forces he could not object if his opponents used new weapons that were not forbidden by the rules of modern warfare. There were no such prohibitions in the case of the atomic bomb. Looking back, I do not know whether this proposal was wise. Others held it—at one time, Truman himself. It was strongly criticized by my opponent in the 1966 election, and was finally rejected by Truman after British Prime Minister Clement Attlee made a trip to Washington to dissuade him. It must be remembered, however, that during this period the two chief advisers on American relations in the British Embassy were secret Russian agents.

In April, 1951, Truman came to the end of the road with MacArthur. The latter wanted to bomb beyond the Yalu. Truman was afraid that this would bring Russia directly into the war, creating a nuclear struggle resulting in great loss of life. Because MacArthur defied Truman, the President finally relieved him of his command.

MacArthur's ouster caused a tremendous storm of opposition. In three days I received nearly 10,000 protests in letters and telegrams. These were mostly from Republicans. Truman was within his rights as commander in chief, and I supported him. The Senate leader in defending the dismissal was Robert Kerr, which cemented his alliance with Truman.

Our forces and those of our allies rallied, and, in May, 1951, an effective counterattack was staged that drove back both the Chinese and the Korean Communists. When they were in full flight, Russia proposed a mutual cease-fire and a meeting to discuss peace terms. Truman, anxious to terminate the war and prevent a global conflict, agreed to meet with our opponents at Panmunjom, near the thirty-eighth parallel.

I made a special trip to the White House shortly before this agreement to point out that the white flag of truce that we would carry into Panmunjom would be interpreted in Asia as a symbol of surrender. I urged a different locality and procedure. Truman listened courteously and then brushed me aside by saying he was trying to prevent another world war. I think he was also disgruntled because of our disagreement over the appointment of the two Chicago judges, which I have described.

It seems obvious to me, in looking back, that Truman by his generosity unwittingly put us at a competitive disadvantage. We called off our advance while we were winning. The Communists spun out the negotiations for two full years while regrouping and rearming and carrying on incessant guerrilla warfare. They finally became predominant in troops and armaments. It might have been better if Truman, although agreeing to talk peace, had pushed north to the Neck while we had the Communists off balance, and only then begun genuine negotiations.

Somewhat to my surprise, I was asked by Clayton Fritchey, presumably with the knowledge and approval of the White House, to make the opening speech at the Democratic convention in 1952 in support of the Korean War. In it I pointed out that if we allowed the Communists to take over South Korea, they would be right across the straits from Japan. The latter would then almost inevitably be drawn into the Chinese or Russian Communist sphere of influence.

Underneath the surface, the war had suddenly become unpopular. As the casualty lists mounted and the bodies of our young men came back for burial, the human costs were brought home to thousands of families and to nearly every community in the nation. Photographs of American boys dying on foreign beaches appeared as Republican advertisements in many of the newspapers in smaller cities and towns. Although the Republicans did not openly repudiate the war and, indeed, criticized the Truman administration for not "rolling back" Communism in Europe or "unleashing Chiang Kai-shek" in Asia, they took full advantage of the antiwar sentiment.

After his victory, Eisenhower made an inspection trip to Korea. He thought that a second invasion up the coast would be too costly, since the Communists had taken advantage of time to create an almost impregnable defense. His administration therefore consented to an agreement in July, 1953, giving the Communists all of the territory north of the American battle line, which was nearly identical with the original division at the thirty-eighth parallel. This meant that while the Communist attempt to take over all of Korea had been defeated, the industrial North had been allowed to remain in Communist hands and could be used as a base for future attacks. There had been no "rolling back" of Communism in Korea, or, indeed, in any of Asia or Europe. Had the Eisenhower peace been made by Truman, the Republican criticism would have been violent and overwhelming. Joe McCarthy would have had another field day. Yet the Republicans felt able to make concessions to the Communists to obtain peace that they would never have permitted the Democrats.

Indochina and Vietnam

THE CESSATION of open hostilities in Korea in the summer of 1953 enabled Russia and China to transfer their energies to Vietnam, then, to Laos and Cambodia, called French Indochina. Restored to power there after the defeat of Japan in 1945, the French were maintaining an uneasy rule in the face of a nationwide Communist revolution led by Ho Chi Minh. Just as an effort had been made to convince Americans that Mao Tse-tung was a nationalistic agrarian reformer in China, so now the same elements argued that Ho Chi Minh was only a nationalistic patriot, solely bent on overthrowing France's playboy emperor, Bao Dai, and establishing native rule. Without question, Ho was a nationalist, but for over thirty-five years he had also been a dedicated and disciplined Communist, trained for action in both France and Asia.

I did not like French rule and believed that European imperialism should be eliminated in Asia as soon as practicable. But I wanted it followed by true democracy, not by a police state on the Communist model. Furthermore, I believed that a Communist takeover in Indochina would be followed by a similar movement in the rest of the Malay peninsula. Then what would happen to India?

I posed this question one evening to Madame Pandit, who was then the Indian ambassador to the United States. She admired my wife, and on occasion showed us friendly courtesies. After dinner at the Indian Embassy one evening, I summoned up my courage to ask whether she thought India could stay neutral if Southeast Asia went Communist. Since both she and her brother, Prime Minister Jawaharlal Nehru, were neutralists, I thought she would surely reply, "Of course we can." Instead, her instant reply was, "No, we could not keep India neutral for more than a year. We would inevitably go Communist."

This testimony from such a source has always weighed heavily with me. The French, who had suffered heavy losses in the previous years, retreated into fortified enclaves, later advocated here at home, but which enabled the Communists to concentrate their strength in attacking any one. They chose Dienbienphu. In the winter of 1954, they closed in, and the French were obviously doomed to lose. There was a strong movement for the United States to aid France. While I did not like French rule, I thought the alternative was worse. So, like Richard Nixon, I favored intervention and made a speech to that effect one evening in the Senate. I hoped we would be joined by Australia, New Zealand, and Great Britain, as well as by India and the independent states of Southeast Asia.

It was not to be. General Matthew B. Ridgway, Army Chief of Staff, objected, on sound military grounds, to a land war on the continent of Asia. We would be swallowed up, he reasoned, by space and population. Australia and New Zealand balked at making any substantial contribution. So did Great Britain. France was tired of the continuing sacrifice of men and money and wanted to get out. Public opinion in the U.S. was opposed. So Eisenhower, despite his belief in the domino theory, decided not to move. Instead, that summer a conference was arranged in Geneva.

There the Communists under Ho Chi Minh were given North Vietnam. A non-Communist government was to be set up at Saigon for South Vietnam, and there was to be a plebiscite in 1956 in both North and South on whether the two nations were to be united. The neighboring countries of Laos and Cambodia, which had been part of French Indochina, were recognized as independent nations. The situation seemed parallel to that which had prevailed in Korea, and it was moving toward a similar conclusion.

I supported Secretary of State Dulles in his efforts to build the Southeast Asia Treaty Organization (SEATO), hoping that pooled resistance would at least stop the onward drive of the Communist police states. Poor France, meanwhile, won no respite. Though it had withdrawn from Indochina, it now faced in Algeria the same alliance of nationalists and Communists. The losses there were as great as in Indochina, and lasted until De Gaulle came to power with the support of the Army and took France out of Algeria, and also Africa.

Our involvement in Indochina in the 1960's is discussed in Chapter 43.

Israel

IN 1951 Robert Taft and I were asked to sponsor jointly a resolution earmarking $95 million for economic aid to Israel provided that an equal sum was also set aside for the Arab states. In connection with this bill I had the opportunity to meet the fiery David Ben-Gurion, the prime minister of Israel, Moshe Sharett, the political moderate, Levi Eshkol, the successor to Ben-Gurion, and Abba Eban, Israel's representative at the United Nations as well as its ambassador to the United States. I was greatly taken with all these men and with the devotion of the Jews to their new state. It might have been better had it been established in Kenya, where it would not have aroused the opposition of the Arabs, but the terrible persecutions to which the Jews had been subjected made them yearn not only for a home of their own, but also for their ancient home, in which they had dwelt before they had been forcibly scattered to all parts of the earth.

Zionism had triumphed; the program of Judah Magnes for a tripartite government in Palestine of Jews, Arabs, and Christians went by the board. Thanks to Truman, and over the opposition of the professionals in the State Department, the United States recognized the new state of Israel, and France and Great Britain had to follow suit. When all the surrounding states—Egypt, Jordan, Syria, and Lebanon—mobilized to invade the new country, it seemed impossible that it could successfully resist. The numbers against it were overwhelming. Furthermore, as a nation the Jews had no military experience. But they astonished the world, and in a few days defeated all of the armies marshaled against them. The Egyptians made an especially poor showing.

In the process, nearly a million Palestinian Arabs left their homes and moved into the surrounding states, notably Jordan and the Gaza Strip, which was under Egyptian control. Some had left voluntarily, expecting to return victorious. Others had probably been driven out. All were refugees, and were cared for during the next two decades by the United Nations, on a most inadequate scale.

I sympathized with Israel, and never believed the charge that it would create dual citizenship for American Jews and weaken their loyalty to this country. The two countries were so similar in their basic ideals that I did not believe they would come into conflict. If they did, I relied upon the patriotism of the American Jews. However, in my own dealings I was careful to put our interests first. I refused to accept fees for speaking before Jewish organizations concerned with foreign policy. I turned down many requests to make a subsidized inspection trip to Israel. When the Zionists asked me to introduce a resolution pledging support and guaranteeing the then existing frontiers of Israel, I replied that I would do so only if Great Britain and France would join in this guarantee, but that I could not agree that the U.S. should do so alone. That would be too great a risk. It is a pleasure to record that after my refusal I was never again importuned by the Zionists, although I continued to have pleasant relations with them.

In mid-November of 1956, Bob Wallace and I made a brief trip to the Near East to see the problems at first hand. It was just after Israel had again defeated the Egyptian Army and driven it across the Sinai desert, and after France and Britain had attacked Egypt jointly at Port Said, the Mediterranean entrance to the Suez Canal, and had pushed rapidly southward along both sides of the canal until the United Nations, under severe pressure, ordered all three of the aggressors to desist. We went to Suez, at the southern end, and drove all the way up to Port Said along the canal. In it were at least sixty ships, sunk by the Egyptians in order to put the canal out of business.

They had seized the canal a couple of months earlier, obviously deciding that if the French and British were going to deny them its use, they, in turn, would prevent the two big powers from using it. After a brief resistance, the Egyptian armies had made a miserable showing, fleeing from both the Israelis and the allies. If the U.N. had not acted so quickly, the British and French armies in another day or two would not only have retaken the canal, but would probably have reached Cairo as well. President Gamal Abdel Nasser would have been ousted, and a more conciliatory leader, possibly Mohammed Naguib, would have taken his place.

Relations between Israel and the Arab states would certainly have improved.

But the attacks by Britain, France, and Israel were acts of aggression. Dulles, as a legalist, had felt he could not condone them and had insisted on a hurried night session of the U.N., which resulted in the condemnation of the aggressors. Russia, as an ally of Egypt and an enemy of Israel, had threatened to rocket-bomb Paris if France and Britain did not withdraw. This, according to Douglas Dillon, then our ambassador in Paris, had been more influential in causing France to give in than the action by the U.N. Britain's Anthony Eden had increased the cleavage by concealing his intentions from us. Winthrop Aldrich, our ambassador in London, told me that he had tried for days to get a definite statement from Eden and the British Foreign Office about their plans, but was given a continuous run-around. Aldrich first learned the facts, after the British landing, when Eden was making his statement in the House of Commons. This had so angered Dulles and Eisenhower that when Eden tried to talk to them by transatlantic telephone, they refused to receive his call.

Repudiated by his strongest ally, deserted by Canada, and forced to reverse himself by the U.N., in which he professed to believe, Eden was in a pitiable condition. From the visitors' gallery in the House of Commons I witnessed his further humiliation when the former Welsh miner Aneurin Bevan shook him in debate as a terrier would shake a rat and then flung him verbally aside. The defense of the Tories then fell upon R. A. Butler, who offered a smoothly casuistical denial that there had been any agreement between France, Britain, and Israel to attack Egypt.

The whole affair was a triumph of mismanagement. Nasser might never have taken the canal had the U.S. not refused to help finance the Aswan Dam and the irrigation system that would have brought water and fertility to many millions of acres in Egypt. Believing from afar in the development of the water resources of the Near East, I had favored either a grant or a loan. Standing expectantly outside the room of the Foreign Relations Committee of the Senate, I had seen Dulles emerge crushed and beaten from a session in which he had been turned down on this proposal. I later learned that, among other reasons for opposing the loan, that Southern-dominated group had feared that the dam would increase the production of Egyptian long-staple cotton, which would have competed with the long-staple cotton of the South.

In a sense, then, we drove Nasser into the arms of the Russians, who agreed to finance the dam. At the same time, we were incredibly stupid in our personal dealings with Nasser. On a visit, Dulles had presented him with a pearl-handled pistol, which to the symbolists of the East suggested that we approved his future use of force. Nasser revealed in a speech at Alexandria that a high-ranking American had told him to pay no attention to another American diplomat, who was trying to deter Nasser. If he pushed hard, Nasser should "kick him down the stairs"! This incredible conversation was never denied by the American Embassy in Cairo or by the State Department in Washington.

These would have been mistakes enough, but unfortunately they were only the start. No alternative offers were made to Nasser to stop his seizure of the Suez Canal. The Anglo-French consortium that had legal title to it was encouraged to sit tight. Then when Nasser acted, Eden thought he was dealing with another Hitler, perhaps because Nasser had published a book in which he paraphrased Pirandello: two continents, he claimed, were in search of a hero—himself. Eden, having resolved that the fading glories of the British Empire should not disappear, then laid plans for the joint attack upon Egypt.

At Port Said I saw acres of slums that had been leveled by British naval gunfire. I estimated, from answers to my questions, that not far from 2,500 men, women, and children had been killed and many more wounded. The reason was that the Egyptians had planted their portable shore batteries in the midst of the slum, which they then used as a shield while they fired upon the British transports and cruisers. In reality, they were inviting a return fire so that they could use the dead and wounded for propaganda against the British and the Christian West. Those who waged war were again treating women and children as fodder for their own purposes.

Outside Port Said, I saw the British troops marching northward in good order and then boarding the transports that would take them back to Britain. Relieved to be out of it, they looked happy. I also saw U.N. troops taking over territory as fast as it was being vacated by the British. I thought, too hopefully, that here were the seed pods of a new international order.

Driving through Egypt and, later, through the countryside of Israel and Jordan made it clear that the great economic need in the area was water. The land was an arid desert. With only four to six inches of rain a year, little could be grown except in the few patches that were irrigable. With water, the land could blossom; with it there would be enough for Arabs and Jews alike.

The most pressing human and political problem was the plight of the Palestinian refugees, of whom there were nearly a million huddled in miserable tent camps in the burning sands of Jordan and the Gaza Strip. With subsistence food rations and with no physical cruelties practiced upon them, they were nevertheless desolate after eight years of confinement. Now, after two decades, their condition is even more hopeless.

I thought that the settlement of the water and refugee issues might be combined by developing the resources of the Jordan, the Tigris, and the Euphrates. On the lands redeemed by irrigation, the major portion of the refugees could be resettled as small farmers. In the days of the Babylonian and Assyrian empires, five millenniums earlier, this land had supported a population of over 10 million. But our diplomats, mostly pro-Arab, could not concern themselves with this proposal; they stressed only the immediate issues: clearing the canal and getting a settlement over the Gaza Strip and the Sinai peninsula, which the Israelis had taken during the brief war. Yet the deep hatreds already aroused made future co-operation seem almost impossible to them.

When I met with Ben-Gurion, I argued that as evidence of good will, Israel should announce its readiness to take back a tenth of the refugees, or from 75,000 to 90,000. I recognized that as a practical matter it could not receive the whole number, since that would create a huge fifth column inside this little country. But if it would help, underpopulated Iraq certainly had room for the others. In turn, we should help by furnishing funds to irrigate the vast area.

But Ben-Gurion was no more helpful than the diplomats. He replied that the Arab states, not wanting a solution to the problem, meant to retain the refugees as a grievance. This was probably true, but if Israel and the United States had co-operated on a constructive proposal, there was always the possibility that Jordan and Lebanon, the most reasonable of the Arab states, could have been won over, and that by a judicious use of American aid, Iraq, Syria, and even Egypt might then have been induced to bury the hatchet. Iraq and Syria, moreover, were not as bellicose as they are now. Incidentally, I found that many leaders of the anti-Western and anti-Israel Baath party were graduates of the Protestant College, now the University of Beirut. The Congregationalists had supported this institution for nearly a century, amongst other reasons, to promote good relations between the people of Asia Minor and the United States. I have often wanted to find out why these generous plans miscarried.

At the Weizmann Institute I found scientists working on the desalinization of sea water by a different process from that at our experimental stations. Back home, I urged that we help this research, which ultimately might reduce costs for practical irrigation purposes. Israel and the United States would then make a joint pledge that the results would be made available to all. Then the desert would indeed bloom, and Arab and Jew could both live in plenty.

Perhaps it was foolish for a U.S. senator to think that he could help solve the Arab-Israeli conflict. On my return to the United States, therefore, I busied myself with two lesser problems. I kept stressing that whatever the final settlement, Egypt and the U.N. should permit the free movement of shipping through the Strait of Tiran into and out of the Gulf of Aqaba and the Red Sea, and that Egypt should open the Suez Canal to Israeli ships and goods. With the help of Javits and John Kennedy, I would periodically get resolutions to this effect passed by the Senate as a rider to aid bills. Our opponent in these efforts was no less than Senator Fulbright. Friends continually asked me if, in addition to being anti-Negro, Fulbright was not also anti-Semitic. I replied that I did not believe so, but that he was anti-Israel and, like many of his State Department confreres, strongly pro-Arab. In fact, it is striking how British maiden ladies, such as Lady Hester Stanhope and Gertrude Bell, and American diplomats seem unable to resist Arabic charms.

While at first there was in the United States a small contingent of wealthy Jews on the East Coast who were quite bitter opponents of Zionism and of Israel, because of their fear that this would lead to a dual loyalty, the large majority of the Jewish community was unstinting in its support of Israel. Tens of millions of dollars' worth of Israeli bonds have been bought every year in the U.S., and more millions contributed for the charitable, health, and educational needs of the country. I am continually impressed by this outpouring of devotion, which has now gone on for a quarter of a century and shows no sign of abating. But as Veblen predicted and Ben-Gurion lamented, few American Jews have given up their citizenship to become Israelis.

Berlin and West Germany

IN 1957 and again in 1961 I visited Berlin and West Germany. No sharper contrast could be found in those years than that presented by East and West Berlin. In the Communist city the people were poorly dressed and somewhat emaciated. They walked alone, unsmiling and without animation. The once famous Hotel Adlon looked as seedy as a third-class country inn. Formerly splendid museums were cavernous and deserted. On the western side all was bustle and activity, and the Kurfürstendamm resembled the main street of a big American city. The museums were crowded, the Free University vigorous, and the political rivalry between the center and the dominant Social Democrats was spirited but in good taste. In West Berlin the newspapers were alert and interesting, while in the East the press only echoed the party line. There was no stronger argument for the superiority of our way of life than this visible contrast between adjoining streets. This was the more striking in that Berlin was, itself, 110 miles inside East Germany. West Berlin was therefore quite separated from its economic base, while East Berlin was supposedly the trading and cultural center for Communist Germany.

For years the Communists threatened to take over all of Berlin, or to pinch off its access routes, which, by some incredible military and diplomatic blunder, had been left in Soviet hands. Only the fear of American reaction had prevented them from going through with these plans. In 1957, during one of these recurring crises, I saw them close off some of the access routes, but American firmness finally staved off further action.

The result of the contrast between the two parts of the city was inevitable. Large numbers of East Germans came to their section of Berlin, went over to West Berlin, and then were flown out to West Germany. Several million East Germans had thus voted with their feet, while almost no West Germans had gone east. This was intolerable to the Communists.

In the early summer of 1961 they caught the allies completely off guard. Overnight they erected a barbed-wire wall on the exact line between the two cities and stationed armed guards to prevent any East Berliners from going west. Our Intelligence was, as usual, taken by surprise, with no plans for dealing with the new situation. In desperation many East Berliners used the upper-story windows of tenements on the border to jump to the western side. Sometimes they were caught in safety nets; sometimes they were killed or severely crippled by crashing on the pavement.

Earlier, the Communists had built electrically charged fences between East and West Germany, with wide cleared and mined areas in front of them. There were evenly spaced towers equipped with searchlights and squads of machine gunners to shoot down any refugees who had escaped the land mines. Nevertheless, West Berlin remained for years the Achilles' heel of Communist Germany. Once there, a refugee could be flown over East Germany to a new life in the West.

I had hoped that we would use bulldozers to push away the wall as it was being erected. But we and our allies, the French and British, hesitated. There were long delays, and finally it was decided not to do anything. We did reinforce our brigade of troops, and first Vice President Johnson and then President Kennedy went to the city to reassure the Berliners that we would stand behind them.

The Russians had twenty divisions stationed in East Germany. We had less than one Allied division in West Berlin, so at any time the Russians could have taken over the western city. All that detained them was the fear of what might follow. If we responded with nuclear power, not only Germany, but Russia itself might be destroyed. No one knew for certain whether, despite our pledges, we would in fact do this. But the fear that we might helped prevent an attack, as did the visits of Johnson and Kennedy. The warm and determined speech of the latter steadied the courage of the Westerners and stayed the hand of the Communists.

When I again went into the city in 1961, the crisis had been slightly abated. The Communists were strengthening their wall and sealing the windows of buildings adjoining the western city. I concluded that it would be extremely difficult to amalgamate East and West Germany. In any such plebiscite the Communists knew that West Germany, with its 50 million inhabitants, would outvote East Germany, which had only a third of that number. Therefore they would never agree to a vote, even though they demanded it in Vietnam. Attempts by right-wing German groups to restore the prewar boundaries, which would involve taking a large slice of land from Breslau east, were, however, not in the interests of world peace. West Germany was doing extremely well economically and did not need the East, and West Berlin had confounded the pessimists.

As we drove west on the autobahn, we saw the retarded state of East German agriculture, then still in the horse- and human-power stage of development. Near the border we were depressed by the mine fields to left and right and by the menacing wall and its towers, intended to keep refugees from Communism from fleeing. Held up by armed Communist guards at successive checkpoints, I realized how fragile were the means of access to Berlin and how at any time the Communists might isolate that city. They had tried this in 1948 by a series of successive blockades in the hope that public opinion in the West would not regard these as serious enough to risk a world war. Here freedom did seem to hang by the proverbial thread.

Costa Rica and Nicaragua

MY TRIP to Haiti in 1926 had made me opposed to American imperialism and armed intervention in the Caribbean and in Central America. As I have mentioned, the protests of a number of us helped to cause the pacifically minded Herbert Hoover to pull the Marines out of Haiti, Santo Domingo, and Nicaragua and restore self-government to those countries.

In the early 1950's my former statistical assistant at Chicago, Stanley Posner, began to frequent my office. He had quit academic life and had gone into the laundry and dry-cleaning business, where he had made a fortune. He had a strong streak of idealism, combined with his practicality, and had looked around for an uplifting venture to make his life well balanced. He had found it in one of the most unlikely of places—Central America. There were five little countries whose combined population was then only a little over 10 million. Although they had once been united, in the years before our Civil War, they were now fragmented, race-torn, and mutually hostile. The situation cried aloud for a common market, which could begin with a customs union. But a common country was the goal of reformers.

As Stanley dug deeper into Central American life, he found a massive barrier against his work—anti-Americanism. A series of acts, beginning with the Mexican War in 1846, the Spanish War in 1898, and our wresting of Panama away from Colombia in 1902, had made public opinion in Latin-American countries at best suspicious of our motives and at worst hostile. Then the rapid series of interventions by the Marines, in Haiti in 1914, in Santo Domingo in 1915, and intermittently in Nicaragua, culminating in 1927, sealed the judgment that the United States was imperialistic in both sentiment and deed. Latin-American pride resented it. The good we had done was forgotten; only the evil remained. Nor would the Latin Americans believe that we had changed as a result of the efforts of those of us who were anti-imperialist. Poor Stanley, therefore, had met with ill-concealed hostility. Who was this crazy American with pockets bulging with money who was telling them what was in their interest? Was this a move by the United States to unify in order to control?

In one country, however, Stanley had found a friendly welcome—Costa Rica. His eyes sparkled as he told me of it. Unlike the other Central American states, it was relatively unified racially. Instead of being sharply divided between people of Spanish stock on the one hand and Indians and Negroes on the other, the population was nearly all mestizo. The land was more evenly divided, too, and there were few big coffee plantations. There was no army and only a small force of policemen. The money usually spent on the military was expended instead upon education. Elections took the place of revolutions, and two parties somewhat comparable to our Democrats and Republicans contested for supremacy. The head of the former group, José ("Pepe") Figueres, was a friend of the United States, having graduated from the University of Pennsylvania. He had put down a Communist revolt and had given shelter and welcome to Social Democratic leaders who were refugees from the dictatorships of other countries, including Rómulo Betancourt, of Venezuela, and Juan Bosch, of Santo Domingo. The Costa Ricans worked closely with Muñoz Marín, the president of the Commonwealth of Puerto Rico, and were building up a democratic pro-American coalition. Figueres was coming to Washington soon, Stanley concluded; would I like to meet him? "Of course," I replied, and I sent out to see if the authors of the authentic works on Central America agreed with Stanley. They did.

When Stanley and Figueres appeared in a few days, they both looked worried. After the introductory pleasantries were over, they told me what immediately concerned them. The Nicaraguan army was on the march and was about to invade Costa Rica. Nicaragua was the largest of the five Central American republics. The Somoza family had installed itself there as dictators. They did not relish having a truly democratic republic as a neighbor and had been stirring up trouble for some months. Now, according to Figueres, they intended to take over the country. Costa Rica could not resist. A call to the press services confirmed his story. Stanley then asked me to help, and I inquired what a Democrat could do with a Republican administration. Stanley said if I would ask the State Department and the Pentagon to send some airplanes to the border to hover over the Nicaraguan army with the message that we wanted no trouble, it would help. I agreed to try.

I called the Assistant Secretary of State for Inter-American Affairs, told him the story, and made the request. He, as I expected, treated me coldly. He first feigned ignorance, and then asked sarcastically how as an anti-imperialist I could countenance American interference in Central American affairs. I said that the two policies were not inconsistent; anti-imperialism opposed our interference in the domestic affairs of a country, but what I was asking for was to discourage war in the external affairs of the little countries. I then reminded him that we had not criticized him for his obvious friendship with General Anastasio Somoza, the Nicaraguan President, and his family. I went on to say that I had also not criticized him for his obvious part in forcibly ousting the Arbenz government in Guatemala, because I myself thought Arbenz might well have been pro-Communist. But it *would* be inconsistent if, having done this, the government refused to discourage the invasion of a peace-loving and progressive state, which had turned down the Communists, by a militaristic and reactionary one. I and others would have to protest publicly about that. This made more of an impression, and the conversation ended with my warning that a decision must be made within hours. No promises were given, but I had hopes that the logic of the situation would cause the department to act, particularly since Figueres had been defeated for re-election and was obviously not speaking from personal motives.

Stanley, Figueres, and I met again at ten o'clock the next morning, and soon word came that there were three American P-51's apparently dropping messages on the Nicaraguan troops. Later, the news was that the Nicaraguan troops were no longer advancing, and, finally, that the army was in full retreat. The immediate danger was over. We shook hands joyfully and telephoned our thanks to the State Department, which received them grumpily.

Stanley let matters settle for a few months and then continued his campaign for a customs union and common market for Central America. Figueres helped, and for once the State Department was an active supporter. An agreement was at last signed in 1960 and went into operation three years later. This ended tariffs between the states and created a common external tariff for all five countries. It has been a conspicuous success, by which all the countries have benefited, El Salvador most of all. Whether it will lead to political union is uncertain, because border disputes continue to break out between the members. Most recently the conflict was between the most overpopulated country, El Salvador, and the most retarded, Honduras. In the meantime, Stanley Posner has died, but his ally Figueres has once again become president of Costa Rica. Stanley may now be forgotten, but I regard him as one of the most practical idealists of his time. His constructive example, if continued, should help to change the stereotyped Latin-American view of Americans as being exclusively composed of brutal and selfish moneygrubbers. But the great trouble in Central America (except Costa Rica) is the contrast between the impoverished masses and the small group of wealthy landowners. This is the case, save for rare exceptions, in all Latin America. Unless remedied, it may, however illogically, prove to be our ultimate undoing. Chile, under Salvador Allende, is but an example of what might happen elsewhere.

36

The Depressed Areas

IN 1954, I spent the Lincoln's Birthday recess in southern Illinois. Because of its clay soil, this had always been the poorest, as well as the proudest, part of the state. Its big industry had been coal mining, and the thick veins stretching from Springfield to Herrin had employed at their peak from 80,000 to 100,000 men. But with the recession that February, the bottom fell out of mining. Every day brought news of the closing of some new mine. The worst blow came when the obsolete freight-car works in Mount Vernon, which had employed 1,400 men, and which had been struggling to stay alive, finally shut its doors.

Unemployment was thus high. The men at the public employment offices told me that it was over 20 per cent in the region south of Route 40, or the old national highway from Marshall to Saint Louis. Unemployment insurance protected the former workers in the car factory for a few weeks, but there was nothing for the hardscrabble tenant farmers who were being forced off the soil by the consolidation of the farms. Only a big farm would justify the use of costly farm machinery.

When I returned from Illinois I angered the administration by saying that we were in a "recession." Experts in Washington had not detected the economic downturn and failed to do so for many months.* Moreover, they were still disputing the use of monetary and fiscal policy to avert depressions. I was called a prophet of gloom. But their denials could not brush away what was happening in Illinois. Salesrooms all over the state were stuffed with unsold automobiles, but there were relatively few cars parked outside the factories of the Quad cities. Not only was the recession hurting the region, but there were specific local causes as well. Nat-

* A year later at the annual Gridiron dinner, I was said to be the only man injured by the 1954 "recession." The publishers laughed heartily at this witticism.

ural gas was replacing coal for heating and as industrial fuel. This and the mechanization of the mines were displacing thousands of men. Shaky factories were being boarded up. Whatever one's theories about the business cycle or the so-called "reserve army of the unemployed," the fact of structural unemployment was a harsh reality.

After visiting and speaking throughout the area, I promised that I would try to secure federal help. From my 1928 trip to England, I remembered how the British Tory government had responded when the export trade in coal, steel, and textiles had collapsed, and when unemployment was especially high in South Wales, Lancashire, and Durham. I had always supported foreign aid, which the Eisenhower administration was continuing, but should such concern be only for other countries?

When I went back to Washington, I talked with Senators and Congressmen from regions that I suspected were in similar trouble. I found out that unemployment was high in the cutover timber regions of northern Michigan and Wisconsin, that the iron mines north of Duluth in Minnesota were being exhausted and work was scarce, that both the anthracite and bituminous coal mines in Pennsylvania were suffering as natural gas increasingly displaced coal as the fuel for both home and industry. Up in New England, textile mills were closed as dresses became shorter and new fabrics came on the market. Northern capital moreover was building new mills in the South. Perhaps, also, people were substituting automobiles for clothes as objects of display. On speaking trips, I had verified these facts for myself. I had driven through Manchester and Nashua in New Hampshire in the summer of 1953 and had seen the huge mills, now largely vacant, that lined the river, and friends told me what was happening to Biddeford, in my old state of Maine. The plight of the Upper Peninsula of Michigan and of the Iron Range became vivid after trips to Marquette and Duluth, and Emily and I saw the abject poverty of the earliest Americans when we visited Indian villages in Arizona.

I tried to make the issue vivid in my successful campaign for reelection in 1954. On returning to Washington, I asked Frank McCulloch to organize a task force to help frame a bill for aid to depressed areas. He got the co-operation of Solomon Barkin, of the ILGWU, along with William Batt, who was doing similar work in Pennsylvania. Prentiss Brown, formerly a senator from Michigan and now head of Detroit Edison, also joined the group. By the early midsummer of 1955, I was able to introduce, with many Democratic cosponsors, a depressed-areas bill. It was referred to the Labor Committee, of which I was then a member. Lister Hill kindly made me the chairman of the subcommittee, and we held a series of hearings and finally reported the bill out in the middle of 1956.

Conservatives, of course, opposed the measure. Believing in the ultimate economic adjustment of the market, they did not like the government to help the poor. They insisted that the unemployed should leave the depressed areas for the cities and prosperous regions. We should let nature take its course, for water, they insisted, would find its level.

But in southern Illinois, I had seen for years the attachment of the newly unemployed to their homes and communities. They would stay for months looking for work and hoping, like Micawber, that something would "turn up." Some would get jobs in Saint Louis or Evansville and either commute daily in order to be with their families or visit them on weekends. It was not a satisfactory way of life. To classical economists deprecating our efforts, I quoted the words of Adam Smith himself, who in 1776 had sagely remarked that man "is of all commodities the most difficult to be transported."

I also pointed out that the workers in these decaying towns and villages already had a large amount of "social capital" available for their use, which would have to be duplicated at great expense if they went to Saint Louis, Detroit, or Chicago. They had their homes on paved and lighted streets, with connections for sewers, water, and electricity. In the coal-mining towns, which had been greatly improved over the last two decades, they commonly had gardens. There were stores on the main streets, and churches. Doctors and dentists had their offices there, and elementary and high schools were available for their children. The lodge rooms for the Masons, the Elks, the Moose, and the other totemistic societies then so dear to most Americans, which provided fellowship and security to their members, were already there. So were fire and police departments. No added capital was needed to keep all these facilities functioning. But in the cities into which the sturdy advocates of *laissez faire* were advising the displaced workers to move immediately, such facilities would in the long run have to be duplicated for them. I believed that the amount of "social capital" in all its forms required for the average worker and his family was in fact far greater than the amount of capital required inside the work place. I tried once or twice to prove this from statistics of wealth, but I never had the time to complete the elaborate enumerations. I still believe it, and hope that some young scholar will take up this task. In any event, the necessary facilities, already in existence, were being underused in these communities whose lifeblood was ebbing away. To arrest some of this decay by bringing in new industry, instead of requiring huge new investments in the areas to which the population was being forced, seemed good economics. Besides, how did we know that there would be jobs for them in the cities?

As we worked at the problem, certain requirements became evident. In order to attract new industry, a community had to have an ample supply of industrial water. This sometimes required the construction of dams and the creation of lakes to conserve water that otherwise would run to waste. There was a greater plausibility for the construction of such projects at this time than in the early days when flood control and navigation on the major rivers were used as the justifying arguments. But the level of these new lakes could not fluctuate much. There must be an adequate minimum level, or possibly a constant level, instead of the roller-coaster fluctuations that had characterized the earlier designs of the Army Engineers, who were intent on flood control and navigation but oblivious to the need for industrial development and recreation.

Before my eyes was a prime example of the value of such projects. Kent Keller, the imaginative Democratic congressman from Little Egypt, had managed from various sources to build a big constant-level lake between Carbondale and Marion. He had been fought viciously by most of the local Republicans, particularly those from Marion. They had been successful in holding up expenditures for two supplementary lakes, Little Grassy and Devil's Kitchen. I had managed finally to get both developed for recreational purposes and as supplementary water reserves.

Keller's original lake, officially termed "Crab Orchard" but derisively called "Keller's Folly" or "Keller's Mud Pond," had proved to be a life-saver for such communities as Carbondale, Herrin, and Marion. Formerly suffering from lack of water, which on occasion was even shipped in by train, now these towns had enough to attract industry, which gave employment to many hundreds of men. The lake had also enabled Keller to persuade the War Department to locate an ordnance plant nearby. When this was closed down in the early 1950's, a series of small industries moved into the vacant quarters. This was an obvious second function that government could provide—namely, an industrial park with access roads, buildings, telephone, water, sewage, and electrical connections. I found that at least 1,500 men were employed at the old ordnance works, and if the added employment within the towns was included, the total was well over 3,000. These men, with money in their pockets, naturally bought more than they had. In turn, this gave employment to still more of the unemployed, who by their added purchases put still others to work. We did not claim to have discovered perpetual motion, since we knew there was wastage in the process, but we did contend that there was a multiplier of at least two and possibly more. Taken as a whole, the venture had more than paid for itself.

In return for all these good works, the voters, after ten years of fine service by Keller, had crushingly defeated him in 1942. The community that he had helped most, Marion, led the way in piling up a big majority against him. He was succeeded by an amiable fellow who virtually never made a speech or introduced a bill, but who nearly always voted as his leaders told him to. Poor Keller ran five times more for his old seat, only to be defeated each time. The communities he had helped the most were now the most vehement against him.

I thought Keller's lake was a good precedent. Public and recreational water and industrial parks could provide the external economies that industries needed. American economists had largely forgotten what Alfred Marshall had taught on this subject in his classic *Principles of Economics.* Where industrial parks were not practicable, there were often vacant warehouses and garages that could be used to house new industry. Money could be lent to help new firms acquire fixed and primarily working capital. In this process, the firms and the local banks were expected to make adequate contributions, as was the local government. By a combined effort, new jobs could be created, which would have a multiplied effect.

As all these points were being worked out for the depressed-areas bill, McCulloch, Batt, and Barkin told me that an industrial firm could not be expected to take men right out of the coal mines or from the farms, that there must be some provisions for training them for the new jobs they were expected to perform. Reluctantly, I agreed, aware that each new provision we added would make it harder to get the bill passed. Yet obviously we had to add a provision, too, that those being trained should receive a wage at least equal to the unemployment-insurance benefits. We provided that a community, to be eligible, must have an unemployment ratio greatly in excess of the average for the country as a whole, and this must have existed for a period of from six months to two years.

Later, a friendly former student then a high official in the Labor Department advised me that the department expected high unemployment in the 1960's as the baby boom of the '40's came onto the labor market. She suggested that in order to keep the system from being swamped, I add a further provision that the unemployment in a community must amount to at least 6 per cent before it could be eligible. In the hope of winning the support of the Eisenhower administration, I agreed.

We did not, as it turned out, gain the support of Eisenhower, and the standard set may have been too high. Five per cent might have been better.

The Republicans in the Senate did not stage an all-out war on the bill, and it was passed in the latter days of the 1956 session. I had moved from the Labor to the Finance Committee by then, and John Kennedy had shepherded it through. But the House Republicans refused to allow it to be brought up in the closing days of the session, and we ended with the bill a hope, rather than a reality.

When the new Congress convened in 1957, I immediately reintroduced the bill. We got the Parliamentarian to refer it to the Banking and Currency Committee so that I might steer it, and it went naturally to the Stabilization Subcommittee, of which I was the chairman. Perhaps it should have gone there in the first place. But Fulbright, who by now was chairman of the full committee, was resolute in opposition. He packed the subcommittee with opponents drawn from the Republicans and the

Southern ranks and put himself on it to see that the lid was fastened down.

During our hearings, the able and immensely likable Congressman Brooks Hays criticized the bill because it provided aid to the unemployed of the towns but made no provision for the underemployed and poverty-stricken families of the countryside. This was true. I had not thought I could deal with everything, and trying to help preserve the towns had seemed enough. But I was told that the bill would never pass the House unless the farming counties were included. At first I tried to limit this to the 100 poorest counties, but I was later forced to broaden its scope.

If I had hoped to win over Fulbright by this tactic, I was grievously mistaken. He continued to be implacable in his opposition, and it was obvious that I would never get the bill out of the subcommittee. I then executed a flanking maneuver. Frederick Payne, the former governor of Maine, who had succeeded Owen Brewster, was also on the committee. He was facing re-election in 1958 against the new and popular Democratic governor, Ed Muskie. Maine needed help just as southern Illinois did, so Payne and I joined forces, and at a meeting of the full committee I moved to take the bill from the subcommittee and have it passed on by the committee as a whole. Payne and I knew we had a majority. Fulbright tried to rule my motion out of order. Defying him, I got it put to a vote, which we carried. We then moved to have it favorably reported, and this was ultimately done.

During the discussion, Fulbright and I became very angry with each other, and both of us used rough language. Some reporters said that our epithets were unprecedented. Those interested can find them, unmodified, in the record of the hearings. I remember that I called him "a deep freeze artist," while he made scathing references to my origins and beliefs. This encounter colored our relationship ever afterward. From time to time, we would meet, shake hands, and agree to bury the hatchet, but neither of us could forget what had happened, and our subsequent dealings with each other were governed by wary neutrality. Perhaps his courage in voting against the confirmation of Judge G. Harrold Carswell for the Supreme Court in 1970 may bring us together again. I hope so.

Payne and I became even better friends. He had saved the bill, and I was grateful. I gave him his due praise publicly and on every available occasion. Naturally, this did not sit well with Muskie, who was in a life-and-death struggle with Payne back in Maine. I suspect that this may have tinged our relationship. Finally, after we had not only passed the bill through the Senate, but also had it accepted by the House, Eisenhower gave it a pocket veto. Poor Fred had already been hit hard by his innocent acceptance of favors from Bernard Goldfine, who by his presents had also brought down the icy and aloof Sherman Adams. But this veto by his own President of the Douglas-Payne bill was more than Fred could stand in the face of Muskie's excellent record and attractive ways. On defeat, Payne went back to Waldoboro. He was one of the most decent men with whom I served in the Senate.

The elections of 1958, conducted in the midst of another severe recession, were a landslide for the Democrats. I promptly reintroduced the depressed-areas bill, for the third time. With our increased strength from the North and the West, its opponents were not able to stop it. Over in the House, a group of Republicans led by William W. Scranton, from the anthracite city in Pennsylvania named after his family, swung in behind it, and it was sent to Eisenhower once again. This time he gave it a direct veto, which was not helpful to the Republicans in the 1960 elections. I readied myself for a fourth try. This time I thought we would have better luck.

John Kennedy had been for the bill ever since he had helped with it in 1956, and his decisive primary campaign in West Virginia had made him see poverty in a coal-mining state more vividly than he could ever have understood it from books. He made the depressed areas an issue in his campaign, although he was thinking primarily about West Virginia.

After the election, he appointed me chairman of a task force, which was otherwise almost entirely composed of West Virginians, to draw up plans for West Virginia. I protested that the problem was national in scope and that there were many other areas almost as hard pressed. He agreed to broaden our terms of reference. With the help of Milton Semer, the able expert assigned to the liberal Democratic members of the Banking and Currency Committee, we conducted hearings in Washington and in Charlestown, West Virginia. After we agreed upon a program, Semer and I presented it, on New Year's Day, to the President-elect at Palm Beach. It called for:

1. The immediate increase in both variety and quantity of the food rations given to the hungry.

2. The re-establishment of the food-stamp plan on an experimental basis in a number of depressed counties to see if its previous success could be repeated. If it could, then we looked forward to its wide extension, because it was more self-respecting than the distribution of food commodities. We intended to start the war on hunger by an executive order.

3. The passage of a depressed-areas bill that would help a wide variety of communities and labor-market areas. For semantic reasons, we had re-christened this "industrial development." Localities that needed aid did not want to be labeled "depressed." After all, the poor were now referred to as the "underprivileged" and the "disadvantaged"; the hungry had become the "malnourished"; and slum clearance had been transformed into "urban renewal." My bill, accordingly, had to be called "industrial development and area redevelopment."

4. Special treatment for the Appalachian highlands, where the poverty of the old Anglo-Saxon stock was appalling. I had been able to beat off an explicit recommendation for a costly system of mountain highways. I feared this might degenerate into another pork-barrel measure, although I could see advantages in opening the mountains to tourism and stimulating the latent handicrafts of weaving, pottery, and furniture-making by bringing them closer to market outlets.

Kennedy immediately announced his general support of the program and gave instructions that our bill should be made the first order of Congressional business. On the stormy inauguration night, he returned to the White House in white tie and tails from the inaugural balls and signed an executive order making the distribution of commodities to the needy more adequate. He also directed the Department of Agriculture to start the food-stamp system in a number of hard-pressed and co-operative counties. I got Franklin County, the depressed coal-mining county in southern Illinois, made the experimental county for my state.

As soon as Congress opened, I introduced the bill, S. 1—now backed by a host of sponsors. It went through both houses with almost no opposition. I had originally meant it to be administered by an independent agency under the President, but Luther Hodges, the new secretary of Commerce, demanded, and the President, on the advice of the Budget Bureau, agreed, to have it placed under the general direction of the Department of Commerce. Then the various bureaucracies put in similar claims for jurisdiction. Agriculture obtained control over the farming part, with Rural Electrification putting in its oar. Small Business insisted on taking over a large portion of the industrial loans. Each of these bureaucracies had its own clientele in the country, and each had its favored group in Congress. As we soon found out, the bureaucracies were in fact a fourth branch of government—more powerful in many respects than either the President or Congress. They may have been right in their desire to avoid duplication of staff and quarters. But we did not get the unified administration for which I had hoped, and with which Franklin Roosevelt at the start of the New Deal had been able to endow the TVA. Those days were over. The bureaucrats may still have been idealistic, but they were also power-hungry, and, like the soldiers at the foot of the cross, they wanted any garments that became available for distribution.

During the discussion, we had been forced to drop a provision that McCulloch and I had hoped to retain. We knew that it was too big a job for us to redevelop a great metropolis like Detroit. Instead, we thought that our work should at first be confined to the small towns, and under the Hays proposal also to the countryside. But we knew that labor was not fully mobile within the great cities. I was not sufficiently conscious at the time of the race barriers in the North, but I was aware of the transportation difficulties, and I knew that there were enclaves of high unemployment within cities that seemed externally prosperous. I wanted the redevelopment agency to have power to make experimental probings into some of the worst of these situations as a precedent for redeveloping a section of a city with high local unemployment. But this section of the bill was eliminated. This has been unfortunate. As an example, East Saint Louis, Illinois, with a 65-per-cent Negro population and with high unemployment and weakened tax resources, is statistically part of the Greater Saint Louis labor-market area, whose average unemployment was for years below 6 per cent. East Saint Louis, with its great needs, was therefore ineligible for help because the general average for the labor-market area was raised by the prosperous areas. But the Negro workers of East Saint Louis were prevented from getting work elsewhere by both transportation difficulties and race prejudice. The area as a whole was not a freely mobile labor market, and yet we could not help East Saint Louis because of the high employment in other parts of the area into which the blacks could not penetrate. I finally secured a partial correction of this fault in the law on the very eve of my defeat in 1966. I have often wondered if we might not have headed off some of the recent race riots if we had moved into the ghettos under this act and furnished more employment to those who were shut up within them.

In any event, the act was passed with the essential features of the original bill intact. The members of my staff then told me that this proved that the gestation period for Douglas-sponsored legislation between proposal and enactment was that of elephants—namely, from seven to ten years. This estimate turned out to be amazingly accurate. It was a long-enough period so that many could claim that they had originated the plan and for the vast majority to forget that I had played any part in its early stages. Considering the fact that the bureaucracy had opposed the plan until the last months, it was probably as rapid action as I could have expected. In fact, it was extraordinary that we won at all, and it would not have happened without Kennedy's victory.

Hodges started out well by putting Bill Batt, who had worked so effectively on our informal task force, in charge of the program. Then the Commerce Department announced the granting of the first redevelopment loan, to a company in Arkansas. With a pleased mien, Fulbright, who had worked so vigorously to defeat the bill, announced the happy news, and the majority of his constituents doubtless felt a warm glow of satisfaction over the way their Senator unceasingly worked for their interests.

It has been hard to make a balanced appraisal of the actual results of this act. We never represented it as a cure for unemployment; we merely said it would help. The agencies have made mistakes. They have frequently credited as local contributions the construction of facilities that seem to make no real contribution to industrial rehabilitation. I have often questioned their approval of motels in the mountain regions, for the investment required for each job created is heavy. But sometimes this seems the only alternative, and the secondary and tertiary effects on the demand for food and services may be greater than is evident at first.

I would like to see an actual field study made of the various projects, so that a comparative record could be made. The experience in southern Illinois has been good. A new enterprise, Technical Tape Corporation, was located in Carbondale. The city gave it the use of a vacant building previously used as a warehouse and garage. The federal government subsidized the training of the several hundred workers needed, both black and white, men and women, and made loans of modest amounts to provide the capital. For eleven years the company has been operating successfully at comparatively low costs. The total payroll for the jobs created amounts to well over a million dollars a year. This has provided direct support for a total, including members of families, of over 1,500 persons. The added income has, of course, increased the demand for food, clothing, shelter, and so on, and increased the tax revenues of local government, and presumably those of the national government as well. The workers have been given hope and incentive, which has reduced the social problems of the community and the area.

In the nearby town of Metropolis, in the midst of wide unemployment and underemployment, a glove factory expanded. This has brought more employment and greater earnings, and the company has been able to justify its effort and dispose of its increased output. In Sparta, a few miles to the west, a big printing plant, which was about to move away, has been enabled to stay by the provision of community facilities such as adequate water and parking space. These are going ventures that now stand on their own feet. Indeed, I do not know of any failures in these Illinois projects.

Doubtless there have been failures elsewhere, but my information is that they have been far outweighed by the successes. I cannot prophesy how they will continue, but I believe the system has proved its worth in lessening hardships caused by the depletion of natural resources, shifts in demand, and technical improvements. Just as scientific discoveries have productive "spin-offs" into other fields, so does constructive legislation. Our ventures into subsidizing the training of the new employees enabled Senator Joseph Clark, who was one of the strongest supporters of the depressed-areas legislation, to propose and carry through a much bigger program for training those displaced by technological shifts. In turn, this program has found its greatest usefulness in training unemployed youngsters for entrance into useful occupations. Thus far, this has been the most constructive effort by government in dealing with the difficulties of poverty-stricken youth. The legislation does not have the grand sweep that characterizes monetary and credit policies. But it has reduced structural unemployment and has been a useful device in turning idleness into productive effort.

37

Truth in Lending

As 1960 APPROACHED, my mind went back a quarter of a century to the time when I had given up the struggle for a reform in stating the terms on consumer loans. William T. Foster had died, but his memory was alive in my mind. In the meantime, the volume of this form of credit had increased enormously, to a total of $56 billion. At the same time, the old slogan "Let the buyer beware" was falling into disrepute and was slowly being replaced by the motto for which we on the Consumers' Advisory Board had so unavailingly contended in 1933–34: "The consumer is entitled to the truth."

I thought that we should again pick up the cause and seek to establish at least two simple principles: the real interest rates on consumer debt should be quoted in yearly, and not solely in monthly, terms; and interest should be computed on the amounts actually owed by the debtor and not on the amounts he had originally borrowed. I asked Milton Semer to take charge of the drafting, and he soon prepared a bill. An able legislative craftsman, he has always been a stalwart and yet tactful defender of the general public. I introduced the bill, with five liberal Democrats as co-sponsors. We enlisted the support of many organizations, including the industrial unions, the rapidly growing credit unions, and other consumer groups. Meeting periodically together for lunch, we rapidly developed a fellowship of mutual trust. When Semer resigned to become general counsel of the Housing and Home Finance Agency, I got Robertson, the chairman of the Banking and Currency Committee, to replace him with Jonathan Lindley. Young Lindley was already versed in the practices of consumer credit, since he had been the Washington representative of the credit unions. Although Willis Robertson and I seldom agreed, as a believer in the patronage system, he was willing to let me have one staff member whom I could trust.

We began hearings in 1961 with ample evidence of abuses. First, we verified the facts that the personal finance companies were charging by the month and that many borrowers did not realize that 3½ per cent a month was the equivalent of 42 per cent a year. We found that the prevailing interest rate tended to be the maximum rate permitted under state law. We found, too, that where the debt was repayable on the installment plan, interest was being charged throughout on the original amount borrowed, and not on the amount due. In effect, therefore, borrowers were being asked to pay interest on amounts they had already repaid. This meant that the real rate of interest was about twice what was quoted. An apparent rate of 6 per cent was really approximately 12 per cent. When a bank advertised that its rate was only 4½ per cent, to give the impression of an extremely low rate, in reality it was charging about 9 per cent. As Leonard Wiener, of the Chicago *Daily News,* later said, "It's a lot like renting a 12 room apartment for a year but losing the use of one room each month. Toward the end of the year you're paying a lot more for what you are getting than you were at the beginning of the year."

There were two ways in which this doubling of the rate was effected. The first was by the so-called "add-on" method, where the borrower received the full amount of the credit, and the interest was added periodically. Here the real rate was slightly less than double what was quoted. The other was the discount method, under which the quoted rate and amount of interest was deducted at the time of the loan from the amount being borrowed. Thus, where the loan was ostensibly $1,000 and the interest quoted was 6 per cent, payable in twelve monthly installments over a year's time, the total interest charge of $60 was deducted at the very start. Here the borrower would be credited with only $940, and the $60 in interest charges would amount to more than 12 per cent on the amounts actually owed.

As we went on, we discovered that many borrowers found that, unknown to them, they had also signed up for credit life insurance to indemnify the creditor from any loss caused by their death prior to full repayment. The Better Business Bureaus testified that these insurance rates were exceptionally high. We suspected, but were not able to prove, that the lenders sometimes received kickbacks from the insurance companies. At any event, this was a hidden cost that previously had not been unearthed.

Then it became evident, from both newspaper advertisements and visits to stores and used-car lots, that a considerable fraction of sellers were omitting any statement of either the cash purchase price of the article or the rate of interest, and were, instead, shifting their stated terms merely to the number of dollars the consumer was expected to pay each week or month. Buyers were not encouraged to pay cash. Quite the contrary, they were only told how much they were to pay each month, X dollars for Y months. Sometimes even the number of months was not specified in discussing the charges. This practice was common in the sale of used cars and was widely applied to other durable goods, such as radio and television sets, washing machines, and furniture. It was even being carried into the field of "soft," nondurable, goods, such as clothing. The practice was eloquently defended by officials of "consumer-credit" organizations, which were controlled by lenders. They insisted that buyers were only interested in dollar costs in relation to their monthly or weekly income and not in interest rates. Even juveniles, in the name of "practicality," were encouraged to think and buy on these terms. It seemed strange for children to be encouraged to go into debt for objects that gave only transient satisfaction. But I was informed that my ideas on this point were hopelessly old-fashioned. To get into debt was to get into the swing of things. It was what the market was requiring in many fields.

And yet there were always hidden interest charges levied on the credit that was thus extended. The failure to pay cash upon purchase meant that the subsequent payments were payments not only on the article, but also on the credit that had been granted. The price of the credit was, in reality, a rate, but what this amounted to was not told. As in most cases where the price was not known, it was high. In one of our hearings we found that a woman who had bought some beds on the monthly payment plan was paying a concealed interest rate of nearly 150 per cent. There were many similar cases. Sometimes the concealed rate was even higher.

My proposals aroused heated opposition. I had expected this from the personal finance companies, which operate on monthly, not yearly, rates. I also knew the concealed markup of the used-car dealers was high, commonly from 26 to 30 per cent, and they would protest. But I was not prepared for the deluge of protest that developed from most merchants, and especially from the big department stores and mail-order houses. These had developed a system of "revolving" or open-end credit. Here the purchaser was allowed to buy on credit and then was charged with interest on the amount due from a given monthly billing date. This was generally 1½ per cent a month. This was equivalent to an 18-per-cent yearly rate, but the merchants hotly denied this. Senator Wallace F. Bennett, of Utah, the ranking Republican on the committee, was especially vehement in opposing this arithmetic. In an effort to avoid complications, I did not point out that where the interest on one month's due debt was carried over to the next and succeeding months, the actual rate was compounded and that interest was charged on unpaid interest.

All these groups, and others as well, were vigorous in their opposition. They drew to themselves powerful trade organs, such as the American Retail Association, the U.S. Chamber of Commerce, the National Association of Manufacturers, the American Bankers Association, and the American Bar Association. With the exception of Clifford Case, all of the Republican members of the committee were against the proposed bill. The opponents also made heavy inroads into Democratic ranks. Willis Robertson was even more vehement in his opposition than was Bennett, and he was followed by nearly all his Southern colleagues. A Democrat from a border state, Edward V. Long, who was himself in the small-loan business, had been placed by the Democratic leadership on this committee, and he was a very determined opponent. I could not believe that his designation was accidental. The various mercantile and financial groups also retained a number of law firms composed of influential Democrats who had been active in the days of the New and Fair Deals. Some of these had formerly been my allies and supporters. I was told that the fees they charged were quite ample and that they were well rewarded. Against my will, I was apparently enriching them.

But we also acquired good allies. Father Robert McEwen, a Jesuit priest from Boston College, had early enlisted in the movement and was stirring up intelligent interest in Massachusetts. Professor Richard Morse, of Kansas, was doing the same thing in the Middle West. The credit unions were invaluable. They had fixed 1 per cent on the unpaid balance as their maximum monthly rate, and, in addition, threw in insurance. Some charged less. They were all anxious to have the rates quoted in yearly, rather than monthly, terms, but felt they could not do so alone. If they quoted 12 per cent a year on the unpaid balance, a finance company charging 3 or 3½ per cent a month might seem to the untutored to be making much lower charges. And a bank charging 6 per cent a year on the original amount of the loan would surely seem to be undercutting them. The credit unions wanted the whole relationship between buyers and borrowers, on the one hand, and sellers and creditors, on the other, put on the basis of complete frankness and truth. They were willing to live and be judged by it.

The mutual savings banks of the Northeast were especially helpful. They publicly supported the principle of our bill, and the largest, the Bowery Savings Bank of New York, took advertisements to explain what was involved.

One courageous banker, Herbert Cheever, of South Dakota, was so indignant at the practices in the field of consumer credit that he braved the wrath of his fellow bankers by coming to Washington, where he not only testified for the bill, but also told us privately about some of the current unsavory practices. He, along with Jonathan Garst, the great corn grower of Iowa, and the Amalgamated Banks of Chicago and New York were honorable exceptions to the general rule of bitter bank opposition.

I might have been discouraged by the hostility of the banks had I not known their past record. They had been the chief opponents of the Federal Reserve System when Woodrow Wilson and Carter Glass set it up in 1913. Now they had become its chief defenders and apparently believed that they had originated it. History was even rewritten in some cases to prove that this was true. Furthermore, they had denounced the guarantee of bank deposits when Oklahoma had experimented with it in 1908, and when Bryan had made it a plank in his Presidential platform of that year. Now they would not repeal it. It had in fact saved them in 1933–34. They had joined the brokerage houses in opposing the truth-in-securities act that Roosevelt had forced through during the Depression, but that they now admitted was necessary and beneficial. Once we passed a truth-in-lending bill, I thought they might ultimately claim to have been its sponsors.

But for years passage did not seem possible, because Robertson and Bennett had the committee under firm control. The only staunch supporters were Maurine Neuberger, of Oregon, Joe Clark, and Bill Proxmire. Sometimes there was a fifth vote when the chips were down. But except for one brief day, I was never able to get the bill out of the subcommittee. Conveniently forgetting how I had passed the depressed-areas bill and was finally winning in the field of civil rights, my political critics again took up the cry that I was an "ineffectual knee-jerk liberal," and the banks and business interests in Illinois became even more embittered. Chicago was the main home of the mail-order industry, and there were finance companies at almost every traffic intersection.

I was especially puzzled by the strong opposition of the commercial banks. While they misquoted their actual rates, which were around 12 to 14 per cent, they did not charge as high rates as the finance companies, the lenders of revolving credit, and those who refused to quote any rate at all. Certainly they would not only survive, but also flourish, if the real rates were made available to borrowers.

Finally I learned that the commercial banks were the main source of credit for the finance companies, auto dealers, and others. They did not themselves charge usurious rates, but they wholesaled credit to those who did. One witness testified that they also profited from "under the table" payments made to them by these retailers of credit. I would not conduct a lynching bee, although we had information of personal kickbacks made to many individual bankers by those who charged borrowers high rates. By confining ourselves to consumer credit, we also avoided going into the common practice of requiring commercial borrowers to keep on deposit a large unused balance of the original loan, commonly 20 per cent. This meant that the borrowers had the use of only eighty cents out of every dollar borrowed and that the real commercial interest rate was one-quarter higher than the ostensible rate. But this was another story, and we kept it out of the discussion.

For years the struggle went on. We accumulated evidence, but we were always outvoted. The battle was fought on at least three interconnected levels: the intellectual, the popular, and the political.

On the intellectual level, we stressed the need for the consumer to know how much he was paying for credit. Once this was known, there would be competition among lenders, resulting in lowered rates. Since the amount of consumer credit grew during the period of discussion to over $100 billion,* an average reduction of only 1 per cent in the rates would save borrowers at least a billion dollars a year. I personally believed that the real savings would be much more. What we were trying to do was to extend competitive free enterprise. Although lack of information hurt nearly everyone, the poor suffered most.

I had hoped for support from the market economists, who presumably believed that both sides to a bargaining contract should be informed They never helped, and those who were advisers to the Republicans were relentless in their opposition. Apparently they did not believe that the weak should be well informed if this meant a lessening of the power and income of the strong. In their view the government certainly should not compel lenders to inform borrowers.

The two main arguments of our opponents were that the real rate of interest on the diminishing outstanding balance could not be computed, and that to do so, or even to approximate it, would be disastrous to business.

We pointed out that the rate was already computed and charged in the fixing of the monthly payments. There were four interrelated variables: the original cash purchase price, the number of months over which the payments were to be made, the annual rate of interest, and the amount in dollars to be paid each month. Given three of these variables, the fourth could be easily computed. Under their tables, the lenders actually had rate books showing what the monthly charges would be under varying principals, over-all times, and interest rates. Interest rates were, therefore, already implicitly computed, but this fact was kept from borrowers. The banks were not successful in keeping it from us, however. We got the real rate books from two reputable concerns; and not only used but also quoted them.

There was strong evidence that many sellers and lenders shifted the interest rate between buyers and borrowers according to their bargaining ability as well as their credit rating. The one-price system was not extended into the field of consumer credit.

It would be equally possible to compute the interest rate from the principal, the over-all period of time, and the amount of the monthly payments. Two reputable commercial concerns, in Boston and Balti-

---

* The total amount of consumer credit in 1966 was $97.5 billion. By 1968 it had risen to $113 billion, and by May, 1970, it was $121.3 billion. See *Economic Indicators*, May, 1969, p. 32 and July, 1970, p. 32.

more, concluding that our proposal was the wave of the future, prepared and published rate books that did precisely that. To the distress of our opponents, we publicized that fact. Then the Bowery Savings Bank produced a vest-pocket slide rule to enable borrowers to tell the approximate annual rate they were being charged. The cost of this slide rule was only a cent and a half. The credit unions produced a much larger, circular, slide rule designed for lenders, which enabled them to tell what their annual rates were down to a tenth of a per cent. In the face of all this it became absurd for the lenders and their representatives to maintain that it was impossible to compute the rate. They now shifted their argument. Perhaps, they grudgingly admitted, it could be done, after all, if the payments were regular and uniform. But it could not, they confidently asserted, if the payments were irregular and differed from month to month. They were still defiant, even if forced to retreat to exceptional, rather than normal, circumstances. Although not knowing enough mathematics to disprove them, I thought that even if payments were not spread evenly, the rates could be found. So we proposed that in these cases the main administrative agency, which would be the Federal Reserve Board, should make the computations and decide what the rate was to be. This was obviously not satisfactory to the objectors, whose opposition increased as the intellectual ground began to slip from under their feet. It was not until I had left the Senate that the Treasury actuary, Cedric Kroll, disposed of this final objection by showing that irregular payments could also be reduced to comparable rates.

Although the second argument of our opponents was seldom stated, it was the main intellectual source of their opposition. They thought that if the real rates of interest being charged were known to buyers and borrowers, many would stop buying. A body blow would, therefore, be struck at the beneficent institution of consumer credit.

With all its faults, consumer credit was, on the whole, serving Americans well. It enabled the current enjoyment of durable goods while the consumer paid for them gradually, as they were being used. The buyers did not have to save large sums in advance. And yet it was feared that an exposé of the real rates might create such an irrational dislike of the whole system that people might stop buying or, by postponing consumption until cash could be paid, would not be able to get the goods when they were most needed.

My first reply to this was to quote Stephen Leacock's short essay on "Homer and Humbug, an Academic Discussion." Here Leacock wrote, "My friend the professor of Greek tells me that he truly believes the classics have made him what he is. This is a very grave statement, if well founded." I would then remark that if the truth would grievously hurt American business, this was a very grave charge against business—if true. But I refused to believe that business really depended on either confusion or concealment. I had, in fact, an apparently stronger faith in competition and in the power of truth under free enterprise than its supposed supporters, who in behalf of the free market were opposing truth in lending.

I tried to make it clear that I did not hold to the usury doctrine on the statute books of many states, which provided that the rate of interest on consumer loans should not exceed 6 per cent. This doctrine had been inherited from the Middle Ages, when it was established as a result of the worthy efforts of the Catholic church to protect the needy from the exactions of usurers. It was honored in the breach, rather than the observance, and it had led to the development of the false time-price doctrine, under which the added payments by the debtor were not called "interest," but a price paid for the "use of time."

I recognized that the added risk and detailed paperwork on consumer loans would generally require a higher rate than 6 per cent. I also acknowledged that some borrowers were poor credit risks, although the percentage of losses was relatively low. But I wanted the real rate of interest to be established in the competition of the market by borrowers and lenders who knew what they were doing and who were informed about the real price. I had greater faith in this process than in most outright maximums fixed by the state. If these were out of line with the market, they would generally be violated. But for the bargain to be fair, both parties must be informed. If what the borrowers paid was not known, how could they strike a fair bargain? Thoughtful defenders of *laissez faire* had always insisted on both parties having adequate information. Our principle was, therefore, quite conservative. Of course, we also favored the extension of co-operative credit through the credit unions, and I personally would not have defended loans with an interest rate above 36 per cent. But regardless of these issues, we were trying to provide an equal basis of truth about what the rates actually were.

This requirement of a true annual rate would lead many consumers to shop around for better credit terms and would provide a simple yardstick for comparison shopping. It would permit the immediate recognition of some bad buys. It would also afford a direct comparison with the alternative of using liquid assets rather than borrowing.

Finally, to those who said that shoppers did not care about interest rates, we replied that to the degree that this was true, it was largely due to the fact that the consumers had been deceived for so long a time by so many. Once the facts were known, greater interest and concern would be aroused. This had been found to be true in the pricing of commodities. It would also be true in the pricing of credit.

We pointed out that if, even after education, most consumers still ignored rates, the minority of price-conscious shoppers could still police the market and force sellers to compete on price—for credit as well as for commodities. This greater competition would distribute the economies of lower interest rates more evenly than was currently the case, and in doing so would help the poor, who suffered most from their lack of knowledge.

We were more successful in our popular appeal for truth in lending than we were with our pleas for tax reform. It was not something abstract and far away. Most people had gone through some experience with consumer credit which had left a sour taste. They did not want to admit this publicly, but it was there. The industrial unions and the consumers' organizations were splendid. I entertained their members at periodic luncheons, thus reversing the usual lobbyist-legislative relationship and forming warm personal friendships.

We had two unplanned reinforcements. Hillel Black published his excellent book *Buy Now, Pay Later,* which had a wide circulation in paperback, and a study made in Harlem justified its title, *The Poor Pay More.* After a rough internal struggle, Robertson finally allowed our subcommittee to go on tour, in 1963, and we held hearings in New York. Pittsburgh, Louisville, and Boston. In the last three cities the press was helpful, but there was so much going on in New York that our press notices were overlooked. The testimony, however, was good, and two prominent New York Republicans, Attorney General Louis Lefkowitz and Congressman Seymour Halpern, came out in support of our bill.

One of my decisions slowed its passage but helped to sweeten its final acceptance. During the McCarthy era I had been struck by the fact that many decent people had blundered into false positions from which they could not escape. In my 1955–56 investigations into pension-fund abuses I had also seen how some insurance companies and agents had been caught in similar binds. They had accepted the practice of kickbacks because they thought it was the accepted way, but, upon exposure, repented and dreaded the effect of the publicity upon their wives and children. Although I had pitied these poor fellows, I saw no way of concealing their identity, since the testimony, after private sifting, had to be given in public hearings.

I was more merciful with the usurers. I had the printed testimony revised so that it did not mention the names of those who charged excessive rates, but referred to them as X, Y, Z, and so on. At the same time, our opponents on the committee were given the full details, so they could not charge that these were fictitious examples. This provision for privacy, I was told, would ruin the investigation. While the American public could become indignant at the misdeeds of human beings, it would be indifferent to bloodless abstractions such as X, Y, and Z. To effect any reform, I was told, we must offer some human sacrifices to public opinion. There must be the blood of villains and victims on the altar to make the public believe the issue was serious.

Yet we tried to avoid any sacrifices, and proceeded in a humane way.

Most of the usurers were only following the accepted practices of their industry, and to embarrass them and their families because of the switch in public ethics seemed cruel. We hoped to get reform without pillorying individuals.

We allowed one high official in a big automobile company to get off the hook by not bringing up his earlier statements, made as a professor, criticizing the methods of consumer financing. We spared him embarrassment—and possibly his job. We protected the names of some personal-finance companies and installment sellers. I discovered that liberal financial and business practices did not always accompany liberal political beliefs.

I saw no evidence that any of this mercy ever softened the opposition of the consumer-finance industry, which continued to play rough. But it may have produced less bitterness after the bill was finally passed.

I do not say that this practice of shielding the unethical is possible under all circumstances. We had to disregard it when we reprinted advertisements illustrating some of the practices. Certain actions, moreover, were so grave that names could not be suppressed. But I feel that the precedent was a healthy one, and is capable of some extension.

I was confident that if we could ever get the bill out of committee, we could pass it in the Senate. Few would dare to vote against it. The key to the committee lay with two New England Democrats: Muskie and McIntyre. Both were fine men and excellent senators. But Muskie had taken a subtle but determined opposition to the whole proposal for truth in lending, the nature of which I could never clearly understand. I could not determine whether he was influenced by the arguments of the merchants and finance companies or had independent scruples. I did not feel that I was justified in making a personal appeal to him because I knew that I had once inadvertently made it politically difficult for him, by my praise in 1958 of his Republican opponent, Fred Payne. Although we came from the same state, he owed me nothing. As I struggled to get the bill reported out, Ed, with smiling good humor, always spiked my wheels. I never blamed him. McIntyre followed his lead.

In 1966 the political difficulties inside the committee increased. Joe Clark, who had been a stalwart supporter of this as of other progressive measures, transferred to the Foreign Relations Committee, and Maurine Neuberger decided not to run for re-election. Outside, the tides were turning in our favor, but this had no effect on either the committee or the Senate leadership. Then a ray of hope appeared. Robertson was defeated in the Virginia primaries after the exposure of heavy contributions by bankers to his support.

Sparkman was next in line for the chairmanship. As a liberal Southerner, he seemed in danger from the racist movement led by his fellow

Alabamian, George Wallace. If he was forced out (which neither I nor the bankers wanted) and I was re-elected, I would become chairman, and Proxmire would be the next-ranking member. The banking community paled at the thought of this, and started to work with redoubled energy for Sparkman and against me. Wallace then decided not to oppose him. John was renominated without opposition, and the way was cleared for his re-election. As I went into my own campaign, friends warned of increased opposition from the banks and finance companies. Two of their number were allowed to go on my campaign committee, but most of them were much opposed.

Although I tried to make truth in lending an issue in the campaign, few voters would listen. Their minds were on the Vietnamese war and the Negroes. Suburbanites did not like to hear the matter even mentioned. It reminded them of their financial worries, which had increased as they moved to their new suburban havens. The smiles of the opponents began to widen.

When it was all over, I thought truth in lending was dead and buried for some years. In this I was too egocentric. Proxmire stepped into my shoes and courageously picked up the banner. William B. Spong, the successor to Robertson from Virginia, came out in favor of the bill. Sparkman had supported Robertson out of regional loyalty, but now felt free to switch. Brooke, the new Republican senator from Massachusetts, as attorney general had helped draft the recently passed Massachusetts act and was in favor of the measure. Republican opposition lessened, although Bennett was still implacable and Muskie continued in his former role. My successor, Charles H. Percy, who was in no sense illiberal, was not really opposed to the principle.

Proxmire invited me to be the lead-off witness, and I was treated most courteously by my former colleagues. Cedric Kroll, the Treasury actuary, gave very pointed and helpful testimony that even the rates on "irregular" loans could be computed. The main issue was that of revolving, or "open-end," credit. The mail-order houses and the department stores wanted to have provisions regulating this removed from the bill. Proxmire finally forced a compromise under which the long-term revolving loans were still included but the shorter-term ones were not. This and Proxmire's pledge not to try to strengthen the bill on the floor melted enough opposition so that the bill was reported out of committee. Once on the floor, it was passed unanimously. Long-time opponents, when challenged by critics, could then truthfully say that they had voted for it at the first test.

Some perfectionists have criticized Proxmire for his compromise. I did not and, indeed, paid him high and deserved tribute. I would have done the same thing. He had faced a committee that was still basically hostile and had persuaded it to report out a good bill. The concessions were the minimum price he had to pay for getting any bill at all; and they were later retrieved, with his help.

We were now on our way. The public had certainly not wanted me to continue in the Senate, but, by one of those strange quirks in public opinion, it was now in favor of truth in lending, as well as some of my other measures. Mrs. Leonor K. Sullivan, of Missouri, chairman of the appropriate subcommittee of the House Banking and Currency Committee, had been studying the situation for some years with the help of her able assistant, Charles Helstein. She had felt that the Senate should act first, but now moved into the parliamentary situation under full sail, introducing a much stronger bill than that the Senate had passed. Restoring all of the original revolving-credit sections, she made advertisers, not newspapers, responsible for misleading statements which avoided the basic terms of interest. Lest I lose all newspaper support, I had never dared to propose such a thing. She also outlawed the so-called "juice" loans of the underworld, when the interest rate ran over 45 per cent, and limited the garnishment of wages.

Rather than take chances with the Sullivan bill, the Republicans decided to help pass the Senate one. Nevertheless, Halpern, an early supporter of truth in lending, announced his support of the Sullivan bill. Along with Congressmen Patman and Reuss, he helped to break the back of the opposition.

The Republicans, together with the Establishment Democrats, defeated the Sullivan bill in committee, but the Congresswoman carried her fight to the floor. There she did an unprecedented thing. With the aid of Patman, she reversed her committee and, by an eloquent speech, literally drove most of the opponents off the floor. From the gallery one could see them moving toward the exits. Only twenty-nine dared to stand up against her. Joan of Arc could not have done better.

The bills then went to conference. There the opponents prevented a decision for many days. Proxmire made common cause with Mrs. Sullivan. After a slight face-saving concession, the opposition and Muskie gave way, and a strong law emerged. The Federal Reserve was to lay down the specific rules, and the administration was farmed out to appropriate supervisory agencies.

A few days later, I walked over to the White House to see President Johnson sign the bill. As I went into the historic East Room, old opponents of the measure and representatives of the American Bankers Association welcomed me effusively and with beaming faces. Already they had cast themselves in the role of long-time supporters of truth in lending, and if history pays any attention, that may be how the story will be recorded. I get many letters based on that assumption.

There were at least two unique features of the long struggle. It was a

Congressional, not an administration, bill. The administration under Johnson was extremely helpful during the last year, and probably the bill could not have been passed without its aid. Esther Peterson and Betty Furness, the later consumer representatives, had given unstinting support. But the act was drafted in Congress, fostered in Congress, and altered by Congress. It followed, in short, the type of legislative procedure envisaged by the founders of the republic, which for one reason or another has now been so largely superseded by Presidential responsibility and initiative. Contrary also to all legislative practice, the act that finally emerged was stronger than the bill originally proposed. To conciliate separate groups in our pluralistic society, a bill is usually weakened by successive compromises. Due to Mrs. Sullivan's bold strategy, the act was stronger and better than I had ever dared to contemplate. It had taken the familiar span of eight years, but public opinion had moved far and fast during those last months.* Had the financial community not fought the bill so bitterly, it would have been a milder one. This thought may not yet have dawned upon them. In the official histories that may later be written, I am confident they will be made to appear as the heroic pioneers whose statesmanship was marred by the self-seeking intrusion of Congressional politicians.

As I sat near the President, watching him sign the bill, I must admit that a few tears came to my eyes. A small group of the common people without money or much political influence had finally and at least temporarily prevailed over the massed power of the financial, industrial, legal, and political Establishment. Furthermore, they had done it without recrimination or divisiveness. It was a vindication of early hopes that the truth would, indeed, make men free. Perhaps even the walls of tax privilege might fall if only the trumpets of the people could be made to give forth a more certain sound. I was a retired and defeated senator, but in the afterglow it was the happiest moment of my political life. Much will depend on the alertness of the public and the devotion and energy of the administrators. But the latter are now better equipped to protect borrowers and buyers. If the greater degree of informed competition leads only to a decrease of 1 per cent in the interest rate, it will save over a billion dollars a year. It might lead to much more. But here, as elsewhere, much depends on enforcement. To date the actual experience has not proved encouraging.

* If we go back to the Foster proposals, the time was between thirty-five and forty years.

38

Saving the Dunes

ONE EVENING in the spring of 1957 the telephone rang. It was Mrs. J. H. Buell, from Ogden Dunes, Indiana, near where we had passed so many happy summers. She was president of the Save the Dunes Council, which had voted to ask me to introduce a bill creating an Indiana Dunes national park. Without such protection, Bethlehem and National Steel would destroy the remainder of the shore line. Our friend Donald Peattie, the naturalist, had suggested the possibility of my help.

I answered that of course I was sympathetic, but there was an obstacle. While Chicagoans were the chief users of the Dunes, the area was located in Indiana, not Illinois. It would be bad form for me to introduce the bill, and Mrs. Buell should address herself to one of her own Senators.

Mrs. Buell's reply was that the Save the Dunes Council had tried both of the Indiana Senators, but was rejected. That being the case, I agreed to see what I could do. I could not approach one of the Republican Senators, who obviously had no use for me, but I would talk to Capehart. Although we had differed on most issues, he was a rough-and-ready sort who just might go for the project. If he took the initiative, I would stand behind him, giving him the full credit. Mrs. Buell brightened at the idea and suggested that Mrs. Capehart, who had been her pupil, might also help.

The next day, having arranged an appointment, I told the Senator that I had a proposal that would make him a popular hero. His first reaction was skeptical as he tried to understand why a Democrat should want such an outcome. I gave him a full explanation of the matter and said that the preservation of this remarkable area would be a great thing for Indiana, as well as the whole Midwest. I myself would speak for him in Gary and Michigan City, where the Republicans were weak. The people should have access to the lake front and not be shut off as they had been from 78th Street in Chicago to the outer limits of Gary.

Capehart, warming toward the project, agreed that it would be a shame to industrialize the remaining lake front. If it became a national park, I tactfully insinuated, it should be named after its savior. The suggestion was not repugnant to the Senator, but he cautiously postponed an answer until he had consulted the "boys" in Indianapolis.

After seeing them, he failed to get in touch with me, and I finally called on him a second time. "I can't do it," he told me with evident regret. "They have other plans." Refraining from asking who "they" were, I expressed my regrets and told him that I would then have to introduce the bill myself. In any case, I suggested, if he could not be for us, at least he would not oppose us. "Oh, I can't promise that," he said with an amiable smile. "Probably we shall have to tear the hide off you."

After I introduced a bill to save nearly 4,000 acres and four miles of beautiful shore line, the Indiana politicians, press, and industries at once opened fire. I was, it was said, "interfering" in something that was none of my business and was merely "the representative of corrupt and greedy Chicago," which was trying to prevent Indiana "from developing further as a shipping port and steel center." Not wanting to reflect on Capehart, I was not free to tell the whole story. In justice to him, I have to say he was moderate in his personal criticism. Others made up for his restraint. While the Indiana Democrats behaved much better, some of their leaders made political hay at the expense of Illinois and labeled me the "third Senator from Indiana." Some of them were also close to the steel companies. At this stage, no Indiana elected official dared to support the park.

If there was ever a case where the state approach to a regional need was grossly inadequate, this was it. Aside from the little Indiana state park of 2,300 acres that had been purchased forty years before by generous contributions from Chicagoans, including Julius Rosenwald, the people of the Midwest were about to be shut off from access to Lake Michigan, and the beautiful Dunes would be despoiled into a jungle of steel and asphalt. Indiana, one of the most nativist of states, where the Ku Klux Klan had once swept all before it, regarded its northern lake shore, with its large foreign population, as alien territory. In trying to save the most beautiful region left, I was competing directly with Bethlehem and National Steel and the New York Central Railroad, which had been promised a big volume of freight.

Sometime later, Emily was seated at a dinner next to Charles Halleck, the Republican leader of the House and congressman from the district that included the area we wanted for the park. Furious at my interference, he told her that there would never be a park, except over his dead body. What he wanted was to ring the lake front from Gary to Michigan City with steel, cement, and chemical factories and electrical plants. Behind these factories, another Gary would be built.

We had reports, later confirmed, that leading Indiana Republicans were busy buying options on farmland in the hope of a big increase in population and in land values. A vice syndicate had even offered to give $100,000 to a county political organization for the right to control a chain of brothels in the area.

The worst features of our civilization threatened to invade what had been an earthly paradise. The gross national product from the area, as measured in dollars, would probably increase. But so would smoke, polluted water, crime, and sexual license. Ugliness would replace beauty. There would be more jobs, but a larger proportion of nervous breakdowns and more inmates of mental institutions. Could this be regarded as progress? Rather, it seemed a clear case of the unmeasured "illth," in Ruskin's terminology, exceeding the measured "wealth."

Fortunately, the land around the Dunes was peopled by nature lovers. They abounded in the Chicago area and in the Indiana cities as well, and they sprang to its defense. They made a movie of the Dunes as they were then and as they would be when degraded by more mills. This they circulated in northern Indiana, and they sent me a copy for use in Washington and Chicago. I began to give luncheons to which I invited representatives of conservation societies and a sprinkling of the press. Once or twice a year, with the help of my daughter Helen, I would give a similar lunch in Chicago. Gradually we built up a large group of informed supporters. The hitherto hopeless began to take heart. In a public debate with the Republican Governor of Indiana, I did not do badly. The New York Times, under John Oakes, the Washington Post, the Milwaukee Journal, the Saint Louis Post-Dispatch, and the Louisville Courier-Journal, under Barry Bingham, became strong advocates. But the Indiana press, dominated by the Pulliam interests, opposed us. Chicago's Len O'Connor, of NBC, helped, as did Leo Lerner's suburban papers. The Herald-American, both before and after its acquisition by the Tribune, was our only Chicago champion. I felt it hopeless to approach the Tribune itself, but I did try to enlist the support of the Chicago Sun-Times and the News. Although most of their editors were long-time friends, they told me that my proposal was "contrary to their policy."

Despite all this, we began to make headway in the country, and Laurance Rockefeller, as chairman of the Outdoor Resources Committee, now sponsored a report that strengthened us. He pointed out that while the existing national parks were beautiful, they were nearly all located far from centers of population and, so, were inaccessible to most people. What we needed were beautiful areas close to the big metropolitan centers.

This prescription exactly fitted the Dunes, as it did historic Cape Cod and Fire Island, outside New York. Jack Kennedy and Leverett Saltonstall were establishing a national park, or "seashore," on Cape Cod, and we felt strengthened by their success. Why should the Middle West always be left out? I got my friends Ernest Gruening and Ted Moss, who were on the Interior Committee, to take a trip to the Dunes to see for themselves. As we drove by Gary, we were saturated by clouds of acrid smoke from the steel mills. That, I said, is what would happen to the Dunes if Halleck and Bethlehem got their way. Their nostrils and lungs registered the point. We drove into the quiet and beautiful Dunes country, where next morning Ernest and Ted slipped down to the lake to take a swim before breakfast. They came back ecstatic. It seemed incredible that they were only forty miles from Chicago. Thus we acquired two powerful supporters, and the testimony before one of the subcommittees that they later took strengthened their instinctive judgment. Barratt O'Hara and Melvin Price helped in the House and John P. Saylor, of Pennsylvania, the ranking Republican on the House Interior Committee, defied his powerful constituent Bethlehem Steel to support us with strong and steady aid.

The United Steelworkers now joined us, as did the Democratic organization of Lake County, Indiana. That organization was accused of being in league with the county vice groups. Whether or not true, I never had more public-spirited allies in a good cause. The mayor of Gary, George Chacharis, took to the stump to defend the people's right of access to the lake, and on a summer's outing we walked into the lake together bearing "Save the Dunes" signs. Newsmen had a field day snapping photographs and making movies. Of course I received a shower of letters denouncing me for consorting with so disreputable a character. But since George would not run out on the Dunes question, I would not run out on George. A citizens' reform group, headed by the local representative of one of the marauding steel companies, however, dug up some damaging evidence against him. George might perhaps have bought safety by switching on the park question, but he would not do so, and in due course the Justice Department, under Robert Kennedy, convicted him and sent him to prison.

In Washington one noon when I was entertaining the mayor of Chicago, Dick Daley, Jane Enger announced that there was a suspicious-looking man in the hall. He kept opening the door, sticking his head in, and then hastily retreating. I went out to investigate. There was George, healthier and thirty pounds lighter than he had been, but shame-faced and teary-eyed lest he embarrass me. I insisted that he come in, and we rejoined Dick, who, despite a relatively good record, was also disapproved by many of the conventionally good. The three of us sat down to a good talk over coffee. When George left, I recalled John Hay's closing lines about Jim Bludso, the Pike County steamboat captain.

He were n't no saint, — but at jedgment
I'd run my chance with Jim,
'Longside of some pious gentlemen
That would n't shook hands with him.

Unlike George, under fire others did desert the Dunes. The Eisenhower-appointed head of the Bureau of Parks, Conrad Wirth, who had endorsed the Dunes proposal, reversed himself in public before the opposition of Capehart and his merry men. He is regarded as a great conservationist.

Try as we might, we could never get the warm support of the Kennedy administration, and without it, we could do nothing. I invited Kenneth O'Donnell, Kennedy's confidential representative, to lunch and showed him photographs and the movie of the Dunes. He was tolerant, but, in true Eastern fashion, could not believe the Middle West had anything worth preserving. I suspected that the White House had made a tentative agreement with the new Democratic governor of Indiana that the state would get some choice land on the lake for a harbor, near which National and Bethlehem Steel would put up both blast furnaces and finishing mills.

There was only one recourse left—a direct appeal to the chief. The President was sitting in his familiar rocking chair as I entered the White House office. Since he was friendly and knew my mission, we got down to business at once. I had a folio of photographs, which obviously impressed him. I told him that this was the Midwest equivalent of Cape Cod. "You saved that," I said. "Now help us save this." I left with the feeling that at least he would not oppose us.

The Save the Dunes Council worked hard to get the bill passed and hold back the projected harbor. So did the Steelworkers. They pointed out that the new mills would be automated, which would force the other companies to follow suit, thereby decreasing the total number of jobs available in the area. At a huge Democratic dinner in Chicago, union leader Joseph Germano half shouted at President Kennedy, "I want you to help Paul Douglas to save the Dunes."

The park bill was enlarged to include unsold land inside Dune Acres, and a big acreage west of Ogden Dunes, owned by Inland Steel, the best of the steel companies, which we planned to open up as a bathing beach to relieve the overcrowding of the park itself. The council agreed to this. We did not then oppose the authorization of the harbor and the pledging of the funds to complete it. The Kennedy administration agreed to the compromise, too, fulfilling its part of the bargain, although the Interior Department objected that the big blast furnaces would badly pollute both air and water despite the clauses insisting that these two blights should be eliminated. It was a decimated park, to be sure, that we had obtained. Furthermore, to lessen the opposition of the residents, we had agreed to their right to keep private holdings, fencing them in if they so decided. That was what Interior had been forced to concede on Cape Cod, and we could not demand better terms.

But with all the weakness of the new bill, the way was opened for a bigger park. With the passage of time, the private holders at the eastern end might sell to the government. Some would do so at once. Moreover, the holdouts would seldom extend beyond one generation. Many in Dune Acres and in Ogden Dunes would want to sell as well. With determination on the part of Congress and the nation, we would have a 12,000-acre park within twenty or thirty years. And under the promptings of special groups of conservationists, I had also obtained the inclusion of many hundreds of acres of interior marshlands, which were the nesting and breeding place for the rare blue heron.

With the help of Alan Bible, the friendly head of the Senate Interior Committee, the new bill was passed by the Senate in the 1965 session and went over to the House. There our supposed bargain disintegrated. Bethlehem, National, and Halleck said they had not been parties to any bargain, and I could not produce any tangible evidence to the contrary.

Then Inland Steel broke out in violent opposition. It had not joined the early obstructionists, but this was partly because it did not want rival companies to enter the Midwestern market, as they would if mills, rather than a park, occupied the area, and partly because it was a socially minded company and had a platonic sympathy with our cause. But now it was angry and said I had agreed to let its rivals, National and Bethlehem, have a harbor and mills, while at the same time I was trying to take over its thousand acres to the west and south of Ogden Dunes, though it did not intend to use this land. Moreover, Inland was disliked by the other companies for stopping U.S. Steel and the others from raising the price of steel in the spring of 1962. It had then bailed out the Kennedy administration, and now this was to be its reward. One vice president said, in the words of Leo Durocher, that the good guys always finish last. Thinking to retaliate by defeating the Senator who had opened the doors to its competitors, Inland's Washington attorney and lobbyist, J. Edward Day, was given ample material means of persuasion.

Day had been postmaster general for a brief time at the opening of the Kennedy administration and was a close friend and ally of Adlai Stevenson. He had been a member of the same law firm as Stevenson and had served him as commissioner of insurance and as the head of his kitchen cabinet. He began an intensive lobbying campaign with calls on members of the Interior Committee of the House. Halleck and his friends welcomed Day. Inland was a powerful reinforcement, furnishing a respectable shield behind which the old coalition could continue to operate.

It was up to the House, and after eight years our time was running out. If we failed this time, it would all be over. We could not revive the bill, and bulldozers would roam over the Dunes. First, of course, we had to get the bill reported favorably out of the Interior Committee, and then get it passed on the floor. As the new session opened in 1966, I called upon the leading members of the committee—Chairman Wayne Aspinall, of Colorado, Ralph Rivers, of Alaska, Morris Udall, of Arizona, Leo O'Brien, of New York, and Saylor. Since senators are thought by the House to be haughty and "superior," this helped. Udall and O'Brien pledged their assistance in a typically warmhearted way, and I knew that Saylor, as a sincere and tested conservationist, was on our side.

In the meantime, the two Indiana Democratic Senators and I had agreed on a final compromise. We would give up the 4,000 beautiful acres we had originally wanted, but would get the land between Dune Acres and Michigan City—minus some real-estate developments. Toward the end of the session, Morris Udall, in a superb burst of strategy, got the bill favorably reported, with many of the difficulties ironed out.

I was fighting a losing battle for re-election and had to leave the final direction of the struggle to Kenneth Gray, who had handled it ever since 1960. He did splendidly.

The Democratic leadership felt the bill was dead even if we could get it through the Rules Committee. But a number of old friends, despite heavy responsibilities for other legislation so late in the session, rallied to help. Humphrey, now Vice President and himself campaigning for Democratic candidates throughout the country, called Speaker John W. McCormack and members of the Rules Committee. President Johnson also indicated his support to the Speaker. Members of the liberal, civil-rights, and labor lobbying groups, with whom I had worked so often on other battles, put in extra hours with the Rules Committee and later lobbied with every possibly helpful House member, dividing the list of members as they would for major legislation.

I had never done anything for John McCormack; he owed me nothing, but he knew that I was in deep trouble in Illinois and that of all my legislative work the Dunes park was closest to my heart. He wanted to help. First, he brought the bill through the Rules Committee, with assistance from White House lobbyists and Ray Madden. He then scheduled consideration on the floor despite competing demands for time from supporters of many other bills likely to die because time was running out in the session.

Only a few days remained when McCormack brought the bill up for consideration in the Committee of the Whole, on October 11. Many of the liberal and moderate Congressmen were in their districts campaigning for re-election, and the Speaker was worried. He left the speaker's chair to solicit and count votes for the Dunes in the cloakrooms and on the floor. Within an hour he had determined that the liberal absences were too great, and the bill would be lost, unless . . .

Approaching Halleck, who was relaxed, confident that his forces were slightly superior, McCormack suggested that under pressure of other business he would like to postpone the Dunes bill until later in the week. Halleck jumped at the chance. As the end of the session and Election Day were nearing, even more of the city Congressmen and conservationists would be absent. Halleck felt that the fate of the Dunes had just been settled. McCormack quickly interrupted the proceedings to propose a unanimous-consent request. Final votes on the Dunes would be taken Friday at noon. Halleck agreed, and the order was entered.

What Halleck had failed to recall was that earlier the House had scheduled consideration on Friday of the Demonstration Cities and Metropolitan Development Act (Model Cities). This bill, which, ironically, I had introduced in the Senate some months earlier at the request of the administration, was one of the most important Great Society proposals of the year. The President personally had ordered every effort, threat, or promise to get the liberal Congessmen back to Washington for this vote, and nearly full House attendance was assured.

The Speaker had persuaded Halleck to have the vote on the Indiana Dunes National Lakeshore at the time most likely to guarantee passage. Later Halleck sought to change the unanimous-consent agreement, but McCormack refused. Even with victory pinned down, the Speaker still lobbied for the bill. I am told that his appeal was simple. In the professional's terms of loyalty he merely said, "Paul is in trouble. We have to help."

We won in the House, and on the following Tuesday the Senate accepted the House amendments and sent the bill to the President. Eight and a half years had passed since I introduced the first bill to save the heart of the Dunes. Now we had as law the authorization for $28 million that would assemble the 8,100 additional acres to form the new park. If we could get the money in time, we would save the Dunes for the people. And I have never ceased to bless John McCormack.

Inland Steel accepted the final verdict with good sportsmanship and promptly agreed to sell its land; so this portion of the park will probably be secure. But the remaining industries and Halleck, though retired from Congress, are still opposed. My old friends Morris Udall and Abner Mikva are still helping with rare devotion.

The long struggle over the Dunes quickened my interest in preserving all places of natural beauty. So I supported the creation of national parks on Cape Cod, along the Allagash in Maine, Fire Island, up the Delaware River, at Point Regis in Texas, in southern Utah, and north of San Francisco in and near the redwoods where I had spent a sleepless night in the open forty years before. Every time one of these acts was passed, I felt a thrill of pleasure and gratitude to those who had made it possible but who seldom received credit.

One of the most effective and self-effacing of these was Laurance Rockefeller. Shy and modest, he always took great pains to cover his tracks, but from time to time I learned where his money and influence had helped to turn the tide. The country owes him and his father, John D. Rockefeller, Jr., a great debt. John D., Jr., created the splendid parks in the Grand Tetons, the Great Smokies, and on Mount Desert Island, where in the early twenties I had spent summers, and, in addition, had restored Colonial Williamsburg with impeccable taste. In fact, for a quarter of a century he was almost alone in his efforts to save the environment. Stewart Udall did more in this direction than any previous secretary of the Interior. But, as always, it was dedicated but anonymous people who were the unsung heroes and heroines.

Those who felt as I did were not content with merely preserving natural beauty. We wanted to create some. The lakes at Springfield and Decatur started by my friend Willis Spaulding and by Frank Lindsay had taught me a double lesson. I pushed for Rend Lake, in southern Illinois, not only for reasons of economics, but also to make boating, swimming, and camping available to the folks in dry and dusty towns. Another small lake was created in the deepest section of Little Egypt, and the way was cleared for similar developments south of Danville, in Coles County; near Pittsfield, in Pike County; and for the strongly Republican town of Macomb. I tried to have the state take over some excess and unused land the Army had bought outside of Joliet, but after Congressional difficulties were overcome, the Democratic administration in Springfield, insensitive to the need for recreation, failed to follow up adequately. The word "ecology" had not entered the general public's vocabulary, but that is what I was trying to further for a full decade.

Unsuccessfully, I tried, with my own money, to get more shrubs, trees, and flowers planted and cared for in my own Hyde Park–Kenwood section of Chicago. I reread Bacon's essay on gardens and planted a few more bulbs and trees around my house in Washington. One of the most gracious acts of any First Lady was that of Mrs. Lyndon Johnson in sparking the nation's beautification program. I tried to help by sponsoring measures to remove, by one means or another, the hideous dumps of abandoned autos from public view. Mrs. Mary Lasker has been a marvelously effective aid in this, but the auto dumps remain.

To live close to the beauties of nature does not insure nobility of character. The experience of Nazi Germany proves that in abundance, for Hitler loved the Bavarian Alps, and in Nuremburg, the stronghold of the storm troopers, roses bloomed everywhere. But certainly it is one element in the good life. We should clean up our cities, so that trees, grass, and flowers may come back to urban life, as they were planned by William Penn for his City of Brotherly Love and by General James Oglethorpe for Savannah. Trees and grass are literally purifying agents, extracting carbon from the poisonous gases of carbon monoxide and dioxide. They transmute the carbon into healthy growth and release the purifying oxygen back to the atmosphere. They are, with the plankton of the seas, the manufacturers of oxygen. How malignly ignorant Le Corbusier was in wanting to eliminate trees from the modern city. And how mistaken the sophisticates who try to follow in his wake.

39

Reapportionment

WHEN I FIRST WENT TO CHICAGO, I was impressed by the fact that in violation of the Illinois Constitution of 1871, which required that the legislature be reapportioned after every decennial census, the seats in the state legislature had not in fact been reapportioned since 1900. Chicago's population had been increasing much more rapidly than that of the rest of the state, but the downstate and rural legislators had always refused to raise its proportionate strength in the legislature. Suits to compel the legislature to act in conformity with the constitution were uniformly turned down by the Illinois Supreme Court, on which by law sat only one judge from Cook County. The court ruled that only the legislature could act and that the court had no power to compel it to do so.

The 1930 and 1940 censuses came and went. Chicago's population increased from 2 to 3½ million. Still the legislature would not reapportion. Cook County, with about one-half the state's population, had only one-third of the members of the state legislature. This fact not only thwarted home rule, but also favored certain groups, such as employers over employees, the utility companies over consumers, and, not by chance, Republicans over Democrats. The small-town and farm legislators would not diminish their own power by reapportioning. I found this was true of nearly every state in the union.

Since the legislatures also laid out the Congressional districts, their malapportionment reached into the U.S. House of Representatives. The cities were underrepresented, resulting in an anti-city bias in legislation. Malapportioned Congressional districts cost the cities and the Democrats from fifteen to twenty seats that were decisive on many roll calls.

Following a suggestion by the prescient J. Allen Smith, of the University of Washington, the first to notice what was happening, I had started to write a book on this subject when I was at Amherst, but due to the rush of other work I could not finish it. The material rested in my files for some years and then was made obsolete by the censuses of 1930 and 1940. Unknown to me, my son John worked on the same subject at Oxford, but could not finish his study because of the census of 1950.

After the war, while I was in the Naval Hospital going through a series of operations on my arm, my friend Urban Lavery, then the editor of the *American Law Review,* called on me. He was bringing suit in the name of Professor Kenneth Colegrove to compel the Illinois legislature to reapportion the Congressional seats. I asked on what ground the United States Supreme Court could intervene on representational matters when the state courts had refused to act. Urban replied that the Constitution, in Article IV, Section 4, gave Congress the power to guarantee a republican form of government in the states. The failure to reapportion had, in his judgment, violated that right, and the court had the duty to compel the State of Illinois to act. "How can I help?" I asked.

While Urban had not come for money, and was giving his own services, they did need $800 to print the brief. In an expansive mood, since I knew I was destined for a long spell in the hospital and as a war casualty paid no fees for board and room, I said that I would give half of this. I thus became a silent partner in *Colegrove* v. *Green,* and when the case was argued a few weeks later I was in the courtroom listening closely. Urban argued well, but I could tell from Justice Felix Frankfurter's questions that he was very hostile. He had always favored giving the legislatures full jurisdiction, unhampered by a court's version of their constitutional powers. On this point he could not shake himself loose from a rigid application of the old Brandeis doctrine. Finally, by a close vote, the Supreme Court refused to take jurisdiction, or, in the legal phrase, to grant a writ of certiorari. Frankfurter insisted that the question was political, not constitutional, and that to take it up would plunge the court into a controversial thicket.

Illinois thus reached an impasse. Its constitution of 1871 seemed impossible to amend, because this required a majority of the total votes cast at an election, and not a majority of those directly cast on the amending proposition. Those who did not vote were counted as voting in the negative. They were always such a decisive fraction that all proposed amendments were defeated. Now that the U.S. Supreme Court had refused to act, was help for cities impossible?

Colegrove v. *Green* had, however, stirred up a great deal of interest. State after state found that it was caught in the same trap. Illinois was by no means the worst. In fact, after great pressure we were able to achieve a minor modification in Illinois. The state constitution was made slightly easier to amend by substituting a two-thirds vote of those specifically voting on an amendment for a majority of all those voting in an election.

Under this pressure the employers, the utilities, the Farm Bureau, and the Republicans finally agreed to reapportion the lower house on the basis of population. But they refused to budge on the Senate.

While this made it harder for some interested groups to pass new legislation, they still retained the power of veto. Since their strategy was now defensive, they did not have to control both houses. They had what they wanted. Their only desire was to keep it. As long as they dominated the Senate and the state Supreme Court they could halt further legislative action. And yet there were senatorial districts downstate with only one-sixth the population of some of the Cook County districts.

Meanwhile, facts on representation in Vermont, Rhode Island, Connecticut, California, the Southern states, and others were being collected. Malapportionment was the invariable rule, with change all but impossible. The Supreme Court stiffened its back in the case that Helen Douglas Mankin and Morris Abrams brought against the Georgia unit system of voting, under which small counties were given the same weight as the largest, Atlanta. I also contributed to their struggle. The court refused to reverse *Colegrove* v. *Green,* although not all of its justices liked the position in which Frankfurter had placed them. When he retired, the internal support for the refusal to hear the case rapidly crumbled.

Finally Nashville, Tennessee, under its able mayor Ben West, started a new attack. Like the other big cities of the state, Nashville suffered from gross underrepresentation in the Tennessee legislature, where, despite a direct constitutional mandate, the seats had not been reapportioned since 1901. This time the able city attorneys struck a new note in support of their petition. They relied on the same provision in the Fourteenth Amendment that the Supreme Court had used in the *Brown* case to strike down segregated schools, namely, no state shall "deny to any person within its jurisdiction the equal protection of the laws."

"How can it be said," argued the Nashville attorneys, "that the citizens of Nashville are granted the equal protection of the laws when they are denied equal representation in both houses of the legislature and are, in fact, greatly under-represented?" To throw them, under the Frankfurter doctrine, back upon the tender mercies of the legislature was to deny the citizens of Nashville and other cities their constitutional rights to the equal protection of the laws. Since the lower federal courts would not reverse *Colegrove* v. *Green,* they refused to approve the Nashville plea. So the city carried its case to the Supreme Court, although in both the Illinois and Atlanta cases that body had hitherto disposed of the issue by refusing to take jurisdiction. Now it allowed the case to be presented. After fifteen years, the court was going to hear arguments on apportionment. We hoped that the logic of "equal protection of the laws" would lead to equal representation in the bodies that made the laws.

In early 1962 the Court more than lived up to our expectations. It declared in *Baker* v. *Carr* that unequal representation in the Tennessee House was a violation of the "equal protection of the laws" clause and that the State of Tennessee should reapportion the seats in the lower house. The case had been restricted to representation in that body.

The question was then open as to whether the Fourteenth Amendment also required substantially equal representation in both the legislative branches. The forces that had dominated the various state legislatures were by now apprehensive, but they still controlled the situation. As long as they could control one house by gerrymandered districts, they were not in serious danger. They renewed their attacks on the Court; "Impeach Earl Warren" signs appeared on public highways.

We feared that perhaps they could intimidate the court. Because of its rulings on school desegregation and other controversial matters, the storm against it had been gathering for some years. Though we had narrowly defeated the effort to rebuke and reverse the Court in 1957, by the '60's resentment had grown in conservative circles because of the Court's decisions providing the accused with the right of counsel not only at the time of trial, but also earlier in the judicial process. Dissent had been increased by decisions that protected the accused from police pressure to extract confessions. The economic and political Establishment, always alert to its own rights of due process, had never taken seriously the requirement of the Sixth Amendment that the "accused shall enjoy the right . . . to have the assistance of counsel for his defense," in cases involving the poor, the weak, the racial minorities, and, indeed, most criminals outside the syndicate.

The question of reapportionment was further stretched to involve the constitutional provision regarding a state's representation in the U.S. Senate. Because the states were originally both sovereign and independent, and to avert the probable refusal of Delaware, Maryland, and possibly other states to join the union, the Great Compromise of the Constitutional Convention of 1787 had been adopted. It provided that each state should have two senators. Little Delaware has to have as much representation in the Senate as the more populous states of Pennsylvania, New York, or Virginia. When I came to the Senate in 1949, the twenty-five smallest states, which together elected fifty senators, or a majority, had only 19 per cent, or a little less than one-fifth, of the country's population. It took four people in the larger states to have as much representation in the Senate as was possessed by one in the smaller states. By 1960 this situation had worsened. The eight largest states had slightly over 87 million people, or virtually one-half the total population of 180 million, but they elected only sixteen, or one-sixth, of the 100 senators. The eight smallest states had only 4.2 million, or only a little over 2 per cent, of the population. They also elected sixteen senators, and thus had equality of representation, or one-sixth, with the eight biggest states. One person in the smallest states had as much representation as twenty-one in the most populous. The same relative proportions applied roughly in 1966.* We could not change this because of Article V of the Constitution (". . . no state, without its consent, shall be deprived of its equal suffrage in the Senate"), and we would not try to do so, but it was used as an argument against reapportioning the upper houses of the state legislatures, to which it did not apply.

Incensed by the decision of the court in *Baker* v. *Carr* and apprehensive of further setbacks when the court passed upon similar principles for the apportionment of seats in the upper houses of several states, the legislatures now moved into the national struggle. They wanted to reverse the Supreme Court and restore the old conditions of rural and small-town supremacy. They did so subtly and with great quietness, through the Council of State Governments. Meeting in Phoenix in September as a legislative conference, with more than 750 members attending, and in Chicago in December of 1962, they finally adopted a series of three proposed amendments to the Constitution: to create a super supreme court of the union composed of the chief justices of the fifty state supreme courts to decide whether the federal government had jurisdiction in any case; to deny to the federal Supreme Court any jurisdiction over the system of representation followed in the election of the state legislatures; to set up

---

* From *Statistical Abstract of the United States*, 1969, p. 12:

POPULATION BY STATES (Millions)

A. *Eight Largest States*	*1960*	*1966*
New York	16.9	18.1
California	15.9	18.7
Pennsylvania	11.3	11.7
Illinois	10.1	10.8
Ohio	9.7	10.4
Texas	9.6	10.7
Michigan	7.8	8.5
New Jersey	6.1	6.9
TOTAL	87.4	95.8
Percent of National Population	48.6	48.6
B. *Eight Smallest States*	*1960*	*1966*
New Hampshire	.6	.7
Vermont	.4	.4
Delaware	.4	.5
South Dakota	.7	.7
North Dakota	.6	.6
Wyoming	.3	.3
Nevada	.3	.4
Idaho	.7	.7
Alaska	.2	.3
TOTAL	4.2	4.6
Percent of National Population	2.3	2.3

procedures for the calling of a constitutional convention by the states.*
These proposals were not to be presented by Congress to the states for
ratification, but, by a little noticed and never used alternative provision
in Article V of the Constitution, they were to be submitted to the states by
a separate constitutional convention upon application of the legislatures of
two-thirds of the states. This method was chosen because the legislatures
did not believe they could get the popularly elected House of Representatives to submit any such amendments to the state legislatures. In the
House the big states were by force of numbers largely the controlling
influence. The move was, therefore, to bypass the Congress as well as to
reverse the Supreme Court. The liberal Frank Bane was no longer executive director of the council, and the legislative old-timers, led by those
from such states as Florida, were in full control.

It was provided that if Congress submitted the amendments to the
states, then the device of using a constitutional convention would be
withdrawn. This was equivalent to leveling a loaded pistol at the head of
Congress to obtain acquiescence. It was not clear whether the constitutional convention, once called, was to be compelled to confine itself to
apportionment. It could conceivably go on to other subjects, such as civil
rights and criminal processes. The prospects for mischief were indeed unlimited.

In the states these proposals were quietly introduced, and attempts
were made to pass them through the legislatures hurriedly, with a minimum of public discussion. In this attempt the leaders of the legislatures
were all too successful. The sitting members in malapportioned states did
not want their right to sit in the legislature threatened, and generally the
members from overrepresented districts, having seniority, had more than
average influence. Frequently the leaders of the minority and underrepresented party also came from overrepresented districts and, hence, had a
personal interest in continuing a practice so generally unfavorable to
their party. Paul Simon, a liberal Democrat, was almost alone in the Illinois legislature in opposing the reapportionment resolution, and he was
steamrollered. Except for a few papers, including the Saint Louis *Post-
Dispatch,* the press was on the whole inattentive to what was going on,
and the bar associations were relatively uninterested. This, of course, was
just what the private utilities and most of the state political parties
desired.

---

* See the little-known pamphlet issued by the Council of State Governments called
Amending the United States Constitution to Strengthen the States in the Federal System,
sixteen pages. This records action taken on December 6, 1962, but which was not published until June, 1963. The vote on the three proposed amendments was as follows:
number one, 21 for, 20 against, 5 abstentions; number two, 26 for, 10 against, 10 abstentions; number three, 37 for, 4 against, 4 abstentions. It was the second of these proposals
that received the largest number of ratifications by the states. The first proposal received
the fewest.

Only one citizen, so far as I know, sounded the alarm and broke the conspiracy of silence. A public-spirited and conservative Saint Louis attorney, Arthur J. Freund, exposed the resolutions in a series of letters to the local newspapers, chiefly the *Post-Dispatch,* and recorded their speedy enactment. I had these letters reprinted in the *Congressional Record,* with comments of my own. James Monroe, Jr., and Paul Simon supplied me with additional fuel, which Howard Shuman prepared for printing. We tried to talk to public-spirited members of the press and with labor men. The United Steelworkers and the National Municipal League were among the most alert of the popular bodies, and they took all the action available.

But these stirrings of interest and some fifteen suits to compel both houses of the state legislatures to be elected on the principle of "one man–one vote," while indicative of a swelling public interest, were overshadowed by the growing menace of the malapportioned state legislatures submitting the amendments directly to themselves for action. The number of states passing these resolutions speedily rose into the middle twenties. Only thirty-four was the required goal of two-thirds. All through 1963 and 1964 it seemed as though we would be too late, and reapportionment would lose.

The Supreme Court under Earl Warren then came to our aid. It took jurisdiction in the representation cases for the second house, which had come up through the federal courts. The cases were argued in the fall of 1963. On June 15, 1964, just as the Court was recessing for the summer, it handed down a decision in the Alabama case, *Reynolds* v. *Sims.* Written by Chief Justice Earl Warren himself, with only John M. Harlan dissenting, it applied the *Baker* v. *Carr* principles to both houses of the legislature and rejected the so-called federalist doctrines. In Warren's words:

Legislators represent people, not trees or acres. Legislators are elected by voters, not farms or cities or economic interests. . . . It would appear extraordinary to suggest that a state could be constitutionally permitted to enact a law providing that certain of the state's voters could vote two, five, or ten times for their legislative representatives while voters living elsewhere could vote only once. And it is inconceivable that a state law to the effect that in counting votes for legislators, the votes of citizens in one part of the state would be multiplied by two, five, or ten while the voters in another area would be counted only at face value, could be constitutionally sustainable. . . . The weight of a citizen's vote cannot be made to depend on where he lives. Population is of necessity the starting point for consideration and the controlling criterion for judgment in legislative apportionment controversies. . . . Since we find the so-called federal analogy inapposite to a consideration of the constitutional validity of state legislative apportionment schemes, we necessarily hold that the Equal Protection Clause requires both houses of a state legislature to be apportioned on a population basis.

The Court went on to say that the will of the majority might be as effectively frustrated if one house were apportioned on some basis other than
population as if both were. Thus was the "one man–one vote" principle
finally approved for both houses of the state legislatures.

This decision sent the opponents of popular rule into a veritable
frenzy. It struck at the very centers of their political power. If the conservative groups could keep control of the legislatures of the various states
and then shift power back to them from the federal government, they
would control the country for a long time to come. Even if they were not
themselves racists or opposed to the extension of civil liberties (as they
frequently were), they were naturally pleased at having such new allies to
their cause. The opposition to the Court and its decisions became ever
more formidable. In the state legislatures, those who would lose by reapportionment pressed Congress for action, and it was clear that if a constitutional amendment were then submitted to them, the necessary three-
quarters of the malapportioned legislatures would ratify it in a hurry.
One prong of the conservative attack was to continue on the state level,
where the petitions of two-thirds of the generally malapportioned legislatures were to make mandatory the constitutional convention, with all its
possibilities for evil.

Into this situation my formidable colleague Everett Dirksen injected
himself with a blare of trumpets. He launched a second prong of the
attack whereby Congress by a two-thirds vote of each house would submit
an amendment to the states providing that at least one house of a state
legislature was to be apportioned on some basis other than population.
The threat of a convention with unlimited subject matter was to be used
as a club to induce Congressmen from the big industrial states to accept
the Dirksen amendment as the lesser of the two evils.

Our forces were disorganized. Mansfield, from malapportioned Montana, our party leader, would not lead. Under the influence of the Southern hierarchy, he actually became a cosponsor of the Dirksen amendment.
This muffled much potential opposition, and made both party organizations zealous defenders of malapportionment. The Democrats from the
Rocky Mountain states were mostly afraid of estranging their state party
leaders, many of whom benefited from malapportionment. With the exception of Gore and Yarborough, the Southerners agreed with Dirksen
and Mansfield. They were pushing for quick action, and there was every
probability that they would get it. Although exhausted after a grueling
session and many trips back home, I had to try to prevent Dirksen's
amendment from being adopted.

Fortified by the books John and I had written but never published
and by my part in *Colegrove* v. *Green* and the Georgia case, I took the
floor to oppose the amendment and to tell why. Shuman and Gray in

their invaluable way brought files to the Senate chamber and dug up much current information to feed me as I talked. I described how the pre-1800 constitution of Vermont, providing for equal representation of the towns in the lower house, put the little villages in legislative control over the burgeoning industrial cities; how the same situation existed in Connecticut to an even greater degree; and how in Rhode Island, where Dorr's Rebellion had been a continuing issue, the cities of Providence, Woonsocket, and Pawtucket, where the state's population was concentrated, were dominated by thirty-eight small towns in the Senate. In the Empire State a cleverly worded passage in the constitution of 1894 had bound New York City and Buffalo to perpetual subjection to "upstate" and had enthroned the Republicans as the continued legislative rulers. I showed how the scantily populated counties of seaboard South Jersey controlled the New Jersey Senate and held the great industrial centers of Newark, Jersey City, Camden, and Trenton in subjection. In Maryland, the meager and pro-Southern population of the Eastern Shore exerted a similar influence over suburban Baltimore and the Washington suburbs in Montgomery and Prince Georges counties. Virginia, Georgia, Tennessee, and Alabama were in the same category. In Florida, 15 per cent of the total state population from the northern counties had elected a majority of the Senate.

Illinois, Indiana, and other Midwestern states were notorious examples. I had personally seen how the private utilities profited from this underrepresentation of the cities. Out in the Southwest and the mountain states, the sagebrush counties swamped the cities in the legislatures. In California, where one state senator to a county was the general rule, some 50,000 people in a mountain district of the Sierras had equal representation with the 6 million in Los Angeles County. It was this overrepresentation of the small districts that had permitted Arthur Samish, the liquor and corporation lobbyist, to dominate the legislature and to defy Earl Warren when the latter was governor. Incidentally, it helped Warren understand the real nature of the issue.

In regard to state legislatures, the United States was in nearly the same condition as Great Britain before the Reform Act. The legislatures had failed to adjust to the country's transition after 1900 from a farming to an urban society. The democratic principle of "one man–one vote," I said, for which we had contended and which the Court had at last upheld, needed to be retained and extended, not revoked.

At last newspapers and columnists were paying attention, and, though few of my colleagues were on the floor, I knew from the comments of their assistants that they were reading the *Congressional Record*. But my strength was ebbing. Barely able to stand, I did not know how much longer I could hold the floor. A vote might be called at any moment, and I knew we would be beaten. To my great relief, Bill Proxmire bravely stepped forward in the nick of time. He argued ably and at length, giving me a chance to catch my breath. It was evident that the two of us, with an occasional assist from Birch Bayh, could delay the vote until the Senate and the country were fully informed. When Lee Metcalf finally joined us, we had enough men to keep the discussion going and to organize outside support. The representatives of labor did splendidly, as did the national League of Women Voters, always alert to the public interest. Every morning we all caucused to decide on tactics for the day.

The supporters of the Dirksen amendment were furious at this delay. While many had tolerated protracted Southern filibusters to defeat civil-rights bills, they could not forgive lengthy but germane debate on a crucial subject that hitherto had been more or less shielded from public scrutiny and which they had thought they could rush through. Dirksen moved for cloture on September 8.

The test would come on the second day, or September 10, and the press gallery predicted that we would be crushed. Proxmire acted as our whip and began to organize delegations to call on doubtful Senators. We gained strength during the intervening afternoon and evening, and I then issued a statement saying that we might have more than the necessary third and, hence, be able to continue our debate.

The next morning the deluge began. The middle third of the Senate was making up its mind. Since it did not want to reverse the Supreme Court, it was moving away from Dirksen. In the last hour before the vote, many pledged us their support. When the roll was called, two-thirds of the Senators voted *against,* rather than for, cloture.* We were saved—temporarily.

Dirksen, however, returned to the attack in 1965, following the election. He first introduced in the Judiciary Committee the draft of a constitutional amendment that would have permitted the states to apportion seats in one house of the legislature on some basis other than population. He could not get a majority of the committee to approve this, so, with the continuing aid of his ally Mansfield, he sought to bypass the Judiciary Committee. The device chosen was for him to make the pending business a bill to create an American Legion Junior Baseball Week and then to displace it by substituting his constitutional amendment. Fortunately, I had been informed of his tactics and, by a series of questions when he was making the Junior Baseball Week the pending business, forced him to admit his projected plans.

Once these were exposed, our group decided not to oppose the buffoonery, but to fight the issue itself, on the floor of the Senate. With full mutual trust now developed, our caucus was even more effective than in 1964. Proxmire and Joseph Tydings, who had just come to the Senate,

* The vote was 63 to 30. But about a dozen of the nay votes were from Southerners opposed to cloture, rather than for "one man–one vote."

were effective as whips, and Bayh and Clark were invaluable. The industrial unions, especially in steel, and the consumers' groups were also helpful.

We prepared data showing in more detail than in 1964 how unrepresentative were the state senates. The following table lists those twenty-one states in which less than 40 per cent of the population elected a majority of the senates. In nine states control was in the hands of less than 20 per cent of the population, and in five of these 15 per cent controlled.

State	Per Cent of State Population That Could Elect a Majority of the State Senate
Nevada	8
California	11
Arizona	13
New Mexico	14
Maryland	14
Florida	15
Montana	16
Rhode Island	18
New Jersey	19
Utah	21
South Carolina	23
Wyoming	24
Alabama	28
Illinois	28
Texas	30
Connecticut	32
North Dakota	32
Louisiana	33
Washington	34
Mississippi	37
South Dakota	38

There were many other states where only a little over 40 per cent of the population lived in districts electing a majority of the senate.

The malapportionment was almost as bad in the case of the lower houses of the legislatures. There were twelve states where less than 40 per cent of the population and five where less than 20 per cent elected a majority of the representatives. (See list on opposite page.)

I urged that the right to approximate equality of representation was inalienable and could not be given away even in a popular referendum. The Supreme Court had affirmed this in its decision in the case of *Lucas* v. *Colorado General Assembly*. One generation could not sacrifice its successors or even itself.

On the final vote on Dirksen's amendment, a two-thirds majority, or

State	Per Cent of State Population That Could Elect a Majority of Lower House
Vermont	12
Connecticut	12
Delaware	19
Kansas	19
Missouri	20
Nevada	29
Ohio	29
Florida	30
Louisiana	33
Arkansas	33
Utah	33
Minnesota	35

66 of the 98 votes cast, was required for passage. Dirksen obtained only 59. We had, therefore, been successful a second time in turning back the attempt to reverse the Supreme Court. Neutral observers gave the credit to our little group, which had organized the resistance to the amendment. The official leadership of our party had been the strong allies of Dirksen, and only one Republican, Clifford Case, had voted with us.

I felt that our action would be vindicated by time, if the historians paid any attention to the matter. But the number of my immediate opponents and the intensity of their feelings were increased.

The advocates of minority rule had too much to lose and would not give up. Beaten twice in Congress, they turned back to the states. Hiring the celebrated public-relations firm of Whitaker and Baxter, they staged a vigorous, expensive, yet quiet campaign. Additional states fell into line, until, with thirty-three states demanding a convention by the summer of 1969, the goal of thirty-four was on the point of being reached. In numerous states the lower house passed a resolution withdrawing their action, but in each case the state senate refused to act, so that legally the ranks were unbroken. The campaign was seemingly successful until its leader, Senator Dirksen, died.*

Though it still seemed probable to me that the necessary additional state would be found, luckily it did not turn out that way. Instead, both houses of the Kansas legislature in the spring of 1970 revoked their previous call. This removed the immediate danger. And permanent relief was forthcoming, for a large number of states had specified that if two-thirds

* I am happy to record that during the last days of his life, in the summer of 1969, I saw the warmhearted side of Senator Dirksen. At the time, I was in a hospital recovering from a disabling stroke. Dirksen sent me flowers and generously telephoned his regards. I told him that he was a better man than I, since I did not think I would have acted similarly had the roles been reversed. Two days afterward he went to the hospital, and died almost immediately. I think he knew what was coming.

of the states did not act similarly within seven years, their own request would be canceled. Three states had acted on March 31, 1963. They had led the procession in. Now they joined Kansas in leading the procession out, and others of the class of 1963 soon joined them.

A series of political miracles had happened. A relatively indifferent public had been saved from itself, and now has forgotten all about its salvation. I confess, however, that I can give little praise to most of the press, the bar, and the academicians during the final struggles. The unions, a few concerned organizations, including the League of Women Voters, and a handful of legislators made the fight and won.

On the whole, the reapportionment rulings have worked well, removing some of the grosser inequities. The principle is now being extended to county boards of supervisors and commissioners, where it is giving more representation to the central cities.

But since 1950, the great population growth has been in the suburbs, which both Proxmire and I predicted. As a result, the Republicans have not lost as much as they feared, and may, indeed, ultimately stand to gain. Furthermore, the suburbs, in their dislike for the cities and the blacks, have in most states joined with the rural legislators in anti-city blocs. In consequence, the states have been slow to aid the cities in dealing with their pressing problems of poverty, race, housing, education, and jobs. The domestic future of the country now depends largely on whether the suburbs will recognize and carry out a common program for dealing with metropolitan problems, both urban and suburban. Reapportionment has helped, but not solved matters. Democracy cannot rise higher than its source—the people. An enlightened people will keep up with the problems of their times, but a biased and inflamed people will seldom act either wisely or humanely.*

Earl Warren regards his reapportionment decisions as his most important ones on the Supreme Court. In my whole senatorial career nothing gave me more pleasure than upholding the "one man–one vote" principle. I am grateful to my comrades in arms, Proxmire, Tydings, Clark, and Bayh, and to the host of devoted citizens who made the victory possible, and whose continuing efforts will be needed to maintain the principle.

* Some writers on reapportionment overemphasize the legal and statistical complexities and slight the practical indifference of the rural-dominated legislatures to the needs of the larger communities in the fields of utility reform, labor legislation, welfare, housing, taxation, et cetera. They could not adjust to the movements of the twentieth century. Nor can some of the legal theorists. See Robert G. Dixon, Jr., *Democratic Representation: Reapportionment in Law and Politics,* New York: Oxford University Press, 1968.

PART FOUR

Political Battles
1950–1966

40

The Campaigns from 1950 to 1954

1950

MY COLLEAGUE SCOTT LUCAS, who had been elected Senate majority leader in 1949 to succeed Alben Barkley on the latter's accession to the Vice Presidency, came up for his third term in 1950. He had been generous in his support of me in 1948 and had placed me on important committees. Faced with the geographical cleavages in our party, he had been, on the whole, a good majority leader. I therefore felt it my duty to bend every effort to help him, especially since Congress was late in adjourning that year because of the McCarran Act fight. With the help of Spike McAdams I got hold of a sound-equipped station wagon and, with faithful Joseph Tierney, Ted's brother, as driver and aide, plunged into the campaign. For two weeks I covered the streets of Chicago, speaking from twelve to fifteen times a day, and during the final three weeks carried out a high-pressure downstate tour.

Early in that period I entered Springfield, where I found Governor Stevenson holding aloof from the campaign. When he invited me to spend the night in the Executive Mansion, I urged him to take to the hustings. Perhaps it was presumptuous of me to advise him, but I pointed out that if Lucas was defeated, the Republicans would also take over both houses of the legislature. This would stymie his legislative program.

Stevenson countered with several reasons for not participating in the campaign. By midnight the discussion had grown quite heated. He declared that since his large 1948 majority was due to his Republican support, he should not estrange them. I reminded him untactfully that his big majority did not spring wholly from enthusiasm for him, but from the shocking disclosures about the incumbent, Governor Dwight Green. I thought that it was in his own interest, as well as his duty, to build up the Democratic party in every legitimate way, and the crucial time was in the upcoming election. Years later Lucas himself suggested that another reason for the Governor's refusal to help him was that had Lucas been re-elected he would inevitably have become Illinois' candidate for the Democratic Presidential nomination in 1952. Scott Lucas had grown up alongside the Illinois River, where his ancestors had settled on coming from the South. His Southern blood had made him acceptable to the Southern leaders. This plus the fact that he was a personal friend of both Truman and Barkley might have won him the nomination.

In the last few days of the campaign the roof fell in on us. First, the Red Chinese armies crossed the Yalu River, and thereby endangered the success of the Korean operation, which, only two months before, with the capture of Inchon, had seemed victorious. On the local front, Marshall Field IV, who had just taken over the *Sun-Times* from his father, aided the Democrats' downfall. One of his star reporters, Ray Brennan, stole a copy of the secret testimony of Dan Gilbert before Kefauver's crime committee. Gilbert was the Democratic candidate for sheriff of Cook County. He was a captain on the Chicago police force who had worked under Thomas J. Courtney and had the somewhat dubious reputation of being the "richest cop in the world." The party leaders, for some unknown reason, had insisted on nominating him. His testimony showed that he did have an enormous income for which he could not satisfactorily account.

In the double debacle, the whole Democratic ticket went down to disaster. Lucas was beaten by Everett Dirksen by 285,000 votes, most of the Republican candidates in Cook County were elected, and the Democrats lost control of the legislature. The Republicans promptly stalled Stevenson's excellent legislative program. They rendered the balance of his administration largely sterile, except for the higher level of integrity he tried to instill among the state employees and the improvements he effected in the fields of state welfare and aid to education.

Our rout was so complete that all Democrats knew that in 1952 we would face worse trouble unless we improved both our party structure and our candidates. The crisis brought Stevenson and me together for a conference at the home of Clifton Utley in the Indiana Dunes. Our purpose was to arrange collaborative action to prevent some undesirable elements from taking over the party. We agreed to run a joint slate of downstate delegates for the 1952 convention. The delegates would choose the national committeeman, a position I wanted Jack Arvey to retain. Stevenson promised that he would try to run the gangsters out of the Chicago wards as well as improve the legislature. Promptly fulfilling my part of the pact, I submitted a slate of one-half of the total number of downstate delegates, which the Stevenson aides said they would try to nominate. They would add the other half. This was the end of the collaboration.

The agreement had been verbal, and I am aware that misunderstandings often develop in such situations. Furthermore, my later experience taught me that seldom can two political leaders of the same party in the same state co-operate for long. In the competitive world of politics, even the best men, with similar programs, are thrust apart by pressures from their followers and suspicions of each other's motives. That is apparently what happened in this case. Stevenson's advisers may have doubted my sincerity in rejecting the temptation of Presidential aspirations and thought that I was seeking delegates to vote for my nomination. When I learned that he had filed his own slate of delegates, ignoring all of my suggestions, I was deeply hurt. When I had the chance to confer with him in Washington about the matter, he seemed disingenuous, first contending that he had fulfilled his part of the agreement, which was clearly untrue, and then saying that he had no obligation to do so anyhow.

Stevenson had many personal worries at the time, and probably did not yet know his own mind about the future. In any case, I regret that our abortive alliance mushroomed into permanent estrangement.

1952

IN THE preconvention maneuverings for the Presidential nomination, Estes Kefauver, after announcing his candidacy, proceeded to defeat President Truman in the New Hampshire primary. This was a body blow to Truman's candidacy, and won for Estes his eternal hatred. Kefauver then asked me to support him. At first I declined. Although disappointed with Stevenson, I did not feel it right to come out for someone else as long as he was a possible candidate.

In late March, at the Jefferson-Jackson Day dinner in Washington, Truman announced that he would not be a candidate and that he favored Stevenson as his successor. Stevenson at once issued a statement saying that he was not a candidate, that his duty was to finish his job and run for re-election as governor, and that he could not consider accepting the nomination for the Presidency. The statement seemed conclusive, but to make doubly sure I telephoned several of the Illinois leaders who were close to the Governor to ask if in their opinion the refusal was definite. They agreed that it was.

Feeling that I was under no further obligation to Stevenson, I came out for Kefauver, much against the advice of my wife. In retrospect, I see that I acted hastily because of my unhappy experience, which had made me distrust Stevenson. Yet Estes was not only a fine public servant, who had proved fearless in his conduct of the crime committee, but also the only Southerner to take a national point of view on the question of civil rights and the rules of the Senate protecting the filibuster. Such courage, in my judgment, deserved encouragement. I felt that we Northerners would do well to support able Southerners who rose above sectionalism and the doctrine of white supremacy.

Therefore, I took to the stump for Kefauver in a number of states, including Florida and Maryland. Without doubt, he was the favorite among the rank-and-file Democrats, and he carried primary after primary. But he had three formidable enemies, who were determined to defeat him at any cost. The first of these were the professional Southern politicians, who, instead of being proud that a fellow Southerner had the chance to be nominated, were outraged that he had dared to take so advanced a position on racial and procedural matters. If Kefauver was rewarded for his boldness, it would encourage young Southerners to do the same. Since the political position of the white hierarchy would then be threatened, the Southerners presented a solid front against him. He went to the Chicago convention with his Tennessee delegation, under Gordon Browning, as the only Southern group in his camp.

Most of the big-city organizations also opposed him. While crime and gambling knew no party lines and were as prevalent in then Republican Philadelphia as in Democratic New York, and in Saratoga Springs as in New Orleans, there were, nevertheless, strong elements inside our party that deeply resented Kefauver's exposures of the close connection existing between gambling and urban politics. They were determined to prevent him from going higher.

His final enemy was Harry Truman. Truman had never been friendly toward him, and after the New Hampshire primary his anger rose to white heat. Of course, the President controlled the National Committee, which chose Sam Rayburn as the permanent chairman. Since Rayburn's dislike of Kefauver equaled Truman's, we knew that his gavel and the power of recognition would hurt on the floor of the convention. We were then unacquainted with the precise details of how the delegates were selected, but we knew that Truman's opposition was formidable.

In the meantime, all kinds of pressures were exerted upon Stevenson to reverse himself and become a candidate. While he refused to do so openly, his friends passed the word along that at the proper moment he would be ready. The financial Establishment, which had just helped to nominate Eisenhower over Taft at the Republican convention, also let it be known that Stevenson would be acceptable to them. A knowledgeable but suspicious friend of mine declared that Wall Street nominated both candidates.

Stevenson's friends then suggested that I reverse myself, quit Kefauver, and come out for the Governor. My reply was that I had pledged myself to Kefauver only after Stevenson had publicly declared he would not accept the nomination. Having given my word, I could not leave Kefauver.

In the week before the convention, Estes again asked me to make his nominating speech, but since I felt that this would be an open affront to Stevenson, I contented myself with quiet support. I was able to get three votes for him in the Illinois delegation; three others, who refused to vote for either Stevenson or Kefauver, announced that they were going to vote for me.

The Northerners, led by Senator Moody, of Michigan, then tried to commit the convention to seating only those delegates who agreed to try to have the party candidates appear on the ballot in their states. In this way we would prevent a reoccurrence of the 1948 experience in Alabama and South Carolina. On the first ballot, the Illinois delegation voted 48 to 12 in favor of this position. Most of the other big states did the same. Then Stevenson's supporters, led by Arvey, contended that if our Illinois vote stood, the South would not turn to Stevenson on the second ballot. Pennsylvania, under Arvey's friend Dave Lawrence, had already reversed itself, and, over my protests, Illinois did the same. Moody's motion was shelved, and the convention recessed.

The next day we were in continuous session from noon until the following morning. Frank McKinney, of Indiana, Truman's national chairman, told Kefauver and me that he meant to keep the convention in continuous session until we had nominated a President. This culminating act would follow Truman's Presidential address, and it would mean a session of thirty-six to forty-eight hours. With the gavel in the hands of Rayburn and the pressures from all sides against the Kefauver forces, we decided to play for time and try to adjourn the convention for a few hours so that we could regroup our forces.

At about one o'clock in the morning, I informed Rayburn that I meant to move for a recess until noon. He replied that he hoped I would not do that. I argued that it was cruel to keep the delegates in session in stifling heat for what promised to be a marathon session. With all due deference, I reminded him that a motion to recess was always in order.

"It is in order, Paul," rejoined Rayburn, with a snap of his jaw, "only if the mover is recognized by the chair."

The Illinois delegation was seated in the very front of the hall, directly under the speaker's podium. As the number-two man in the delegation, I was only one space away from the center aisle and the delegation microphone. As I rose, one of the leaders of the delegation told me that I was not to have the use of the microphone and that I would have to depend on my own voice in seeking recognition. The convention was in an uproar as I shouted "Mr. Chairman, Mr. Chairman, Mr. Chairman." I was not ten feet from Rayburn, but he blandly ignored me. From time to time the convention band drowned me out with its music. This kept up for nearly two hours, during which I wore myself almost to a frazzle shouting my motion that we adjourn until noon. The Illinois delegation was furious that I should defy Rayburn in this fashion and poured a constant stream of epithets on me. One man attempted to knock me from the chair on which I was standing, but I parried his blow. Finally, Rayburn took me completely by surprise by recognizing me. Then, to my consternation, I found that under the strain I had lost my voice and could not utter a word. Someone pushed the microphone toward me, and, disheveled from the long struggle, with both hands pushed against my chest, I managed to croak out the motion to adjourn. This was immediately carried, but the movie cameras had caught the whole chaotic scene, and it was rumored that for years the Republicans considered using the movie against me.

Our Northern liberal bloc left the hall with the feeling that we had been abused, but candid friends also informed me that I had cut a most undignified figure in my long struggle with Rayburn and had gone altogether too far.

In retrospect, my performance was quixotic. It doubtless would have been better to have allowed Rayburn's plan to go through and collapse with its own weight. Yet, having been unfairly ignored and in the heat of the contest, there seemed no turning point at the time.

When the balloting began that afternoon, Kefauver was way out in front. He gained only slightly on the second ballot, however, while Stevenson came up fast. Truman, who had arrived from Washington, went to work for Stevenson. Harriman, who had at first co-operated with us in trying to get a strong civil-rights plank, now left us without notice to support Stevenson. This was the final straw.

As the third ballot started and the swing to Stevenson began, Kefauver came to my room in the nearby Stockyards Inn for advice. After canvassing the situation and counting the possible shifts and defections, I told him that he was beaten. In that event we agreed that he would ask his delegates to vote for me and I would immediately ask that they vote for Stevenson. Looking back, I see that this was both foolish and improperly self-regarding. I am glad that it was not carried out.

I offered to go with him to the floor, so that he would not have to make the journey alone. We tried to enter from the back and go to the nearby rostrum from the rear, but that door was locked. So, apparently, were all other entrances around the building. We could hear the periodic roars as delegations began casting their votes, and we wondered if we could get there in time. When we finally discovered an open entrance, we found, to our consternation, that we had emerged in the center aisle leading directly to the platform. People were now aware of our entrance and set up a mingled roar of surprise, approval, and boos.

It was too late to turn back, and Kefauver and I walked side by side in as dignified a manner as possible down the center aisle for what seemed that last interminable mile. It was now clear that what Kefauver had meant as a co-operative act was to be distorted into one that seemed defiant and exhibitionist. At the platform the cohorts of the Democratic Establishment formed a phalanx to prevent our coming onto the platform. Two of my friends sprang to our support and, with their fists and bodies, cleared the way. I faced our formidable chairman. "Mr. Speaker," I said, "in the interests of party harmony, Senator Kefauver is going to withdraw in favor of Governor Stevenson. May I ask that you recognize him for the purpose?"

Rayburn snapped out, "We can't interrupt a roll call. Let Kefauver sit here and wait until we come to Tennessee, and then I will recognize him." In order to humiliate him, Rayburn kept Kefauver in full view not only of the convention, but also of the nationwide television audience while he watched the nomination slip away from him.

This experience gave me an allergy to national conventions that has continued to this day. And yet, with all their crudeness and exaggeration, they move with a certain inexorable logic, generally responding to the various forces in the nation and the party like an equation in vector analysis.

After the convention Emily and I went to Switzerland for a meeting of the Inter-Parliamentary Union. Later, under the shadow of the Jungfrau and in Florence, I licked my wounds before returning to campaign vigorously for Stevenson, not only in Illinois, but in many other states as well. Stevenson conducted an extraordinarily high-level campaign and covered himself with distinction. For the first time, he aligned himself as a liberal Democrat, and grew steadily throughout the campaign. But it was futile. After two wars and twenty years of Democratic rule, the country wanted a change. It was also enthralled by the father image of Eisenhower. Stevenson lost Illinois by over 400,000 votes, and the whole state ticket went down to defeat. We were almost wiped out downstate, and things looked gloomy for the future, especially for my own campaign coming up in 1954.

While Stevenson made an excellent campaign, appealing above all to the intellectuals, the great masses of people had not taken to him as they had to Roosevelt and Truman. Eleanor Roosevelt, his great admirer, said that he never learned to communicate with working people. Shielded, from childhood, by wealth and social position, he had never worked with his hands or known what it was to be physically tired from work, hungry, unemployed, or in danger. Since his nerve ends did not touch those of the masses, he could not really feel with or for them. They sensed this, and he knew they did. For all his brilliance and high ideals of service, he left most people somewhat cold. In 1956 this lack of communication was worse than in 1952. Franklin Roosevelt might have had the same experience had not the crippling attack of polio made him know hardship, pain, danger of death, and a lifetime of disability. He also had Eleanor Roosevelt, who introduced him to New York's slums.

1954

TOWARD the end of 1953, although I had kept in touch with the voters by frequent trips to all quarters of Illinois and had built up a considerable personal following, the prospects for my re-election looked extremely poor. National as well as state patronage, and some in Cook County, was now in the hands of the Republicans. The *Tribune* redoubled its efforts to defeat me. The *Daily News* was still hostile, while the *Sun-Times,* under its new owner, Marshall Field IV, would give me only reluctant endorsement.

Furthermore, McCarthyism was at its height, and I was picked by his followers for slaughter. A number of the Chicago organization leaders, feeling that I would be a loser, would have opposed me in the primary had it not been for the intercession of John S. Clark, the county assessor. Disaffected until the very end, one of them was reputed to have given large sums to my opponent. Again there was no money, and the end of the Congressional session found me curiously exhausted. I was forced to rest for a couple of weeks with Clifton Utley in the Indiana Dunes before I could go on.

As the campaign progressed, an unutterable weariness crept over me. I walked with difficulty, and it was torture to go through the day, let alone to appear full of vitality, in the accepted image of a candidate. Not until many months later did my skilled and beloved doctor, Walter Meyer, find my ailment to be undulant fever, from which he had suffered for years. The diagnosis was difficult, since I had no fever, but a blood analysis finally disclosed the malady. It took a long and nauseating treatment and more than a year and a half of time to restore my health.

Meanwhile, I went ahead with my usual type of campaign, speaking hundreds of times in every section of the state. Joe Tierney was my faithful and efficient companion. Emily traveled with me, making daily forays into the smaller Republican counties. Gradually we began to make some headway, although the usual flood of defamatory pamphlets was circulated through the state, and the *Tribune* ran a vicious series of articles in the last two weeks. In one of these the state auditor, Orville Hodge, declared that I was "morally unfit" for office. Two years later it was disclosed that the same Hodge had stolen $2½ million from the state, and after a hasty trial, meant to hush up the details, he was sent to prison. After that, his abuse of me seemed an amusing accolade of honor, but at the time, it was serious.

There were also encouraging developments. Hosts of friends, both new and old, rallied to my support. Small contributions flowed in. Stevenson repaid my campaigning in 1952 by generously taking to the stump in my behalf. Stuart List, the publisher of Hearst's *American,* was so incensed at a speech by my opponent, Joseph Meek, in which the latter virtually called me a Communist, that he not only closed his news columns to such slander, but also served notice that if it continued he would shut Meek out of the paper. A reaction to McCarthyism was setting in. My opponent was a lobbyist for the big retail merchants. This had strengthened him inside the Republican party, but it weakened him in the general election.

The Republicans were also hurt by the industrial recession. In the preceding fall I had foreseen this when I found the parking lots at the farm-implement factories in Rock Island–Moline relatively empty but the employment-insurance lines long. At the same time, the downstate auto dealers were surfeited with unsold cars. Pointing out these facts, I had urged early remedial action. This had aroused the opposition of the Republicans, the business community, and most of the newspapers, who tried to deny the facts and labeled me "a prophet of doom and gloom." But it was hard to deceive the people when they knew that their neighbors had been laid off. I could feel an undertow moving in my favor.

On the Sunday before Election Day I faced Joe Meek on the national television program "Meet the Press." The reaction was almost unanimously in my favor.

We waited for the returns Tuesday night with my daughters Helen and Jean. When they were all in, I had won by 237,000 votes. My percentage of the total vote was 53.6, one full percentage point down from 1948, but in view of the difficulties a somewhat extraordinary result. For a second time I had beaten the moneyed Establishment.

41

The Campaigns from
1956 to 1964

1956–1958

STEVENSON again defeated Kefauver for the Presidential nomination in 1956, although Estes beat him badly in the Minnesota primary. As a consolation prize, the convention nominated Estes for Vice President. Both men campaigned worthily, although it was impossible for Stevenson to maintain the extraordinary brilliance of his first campaign. Since the Eisenhower spell was still strong, the President won a decisive victory. Stevenson lost Illinois by over 800,000 votes, although our candidate for governor lost by only 37,000. Around the country the Democrats did better in the state, Congressional, and county elections than they did in the Presidential race. Congress remained safely Democratic, although this was a rather empty possession because the Southerners continued to join with the Republicans to maintain the dominance of the conservative coalition.

In 1958, however, the Democrats made some decided gains, especially in the Senate. A half-dozen new senators were elected, sending the Democratic total up to sixty-seven, or twice that of the Republicans. This shift resulted not only from a severe second Republican recession, but also from fear that the defense of the faraway islands of Quemoy and Matsu might lead us into a third world war.

1960

IN 1959 I was once again doubtful of the outcome of the forth-coming elections. For eight years the Republicans had controlled federal, state, and, largely, county patronage. It was obvious, too, that Marshall Field IV had become a conservative Republican and would oppose me. Then, to everyone's surprise, he bought the *Daily News*. This was like Jonah swallowing the whale. But it was no help to me.

The former opposition of some of the party leaders lessened before the meeting of the state Central Committee. Those still hostile realized that although they could beat me in the primary, this would lose them so many votes in the election that their state and, especially, their county candidates would probably be defeated. This would be a heavy blow to the Cook County organization. So I was at last accepted by them as the man who not only came to dinner, but also persisted in staying. Once the decision was made, Democrats all over the state went loyally to work.

The Republicans nominated a personally decent lawyer, Samuel Witwer, who had been active in judicial reform, and who made a vigorous campaign. But various forces were unexpectedly working for me and against him. Many of Eisenhower's former supporters had lost patience because of eight years of lethargy. Republican Governor William G. Stratton had a badly spotted record and, like Green in 1948, was trying for an unprecedented third term. The third recession under the Eisenhower administration was developing, and it was clear that the country's yearly per-capita growth rate was low, probably not exceeding three-quarters of 1 per cent. Street-corner polls showed me to be personally popular, and Republican friends reinforced this sounding with the news that the Governor had decided not to run for the Senate, because his advisers had told him that in a direct contest I would beat him badly.

After a rough primary fight, the Democrats nominated Otto Kerner for governor over Stephen Mitchell, Stevenson's friend and campaign manager, and Joseph Lohman, the state treasurer. Kerner was considered an honorable county judge who would strengthen the ticket. Unfortunately, Mitchell and Lohman soon felt compelled to leave the state.

My favorite national candidate was my old friend Humphrey, but he was eliminated in West Virginia by Kennedy after an excessively rough contest. During the previous two years, Kennedy had grown rapidly, showing new sympathy for poor people and manual workers. Johnson, because of his ties with the oil and gas interests and his past record on civil rights, was impossible as a candidate in the North. Stevenson's friends again hoped that he might be nominated, while he, as usual, demurred. In order to cut down Kennedy's vote, Johnson's financial backers were trying to keep both Stevenson and Humphrey in the race.

Again I was exhausted from the long Congressional session, and, recalling 1952, cautiously decided to stay out of this contest. After Kennedy was nominated, the campaign began slowly in Illinois. Moving downstate with Joe Tierney, I found considerable opposition to Kennedy because of his Catholicism. I therefore increased my support for him, and as my own margin widened I concentrated my efforts during the last six weeks on him and not on me. After his first debate with Nixon, his stock went up markedly, and he made a splendid, vigorous campaign. Back in Chicago I took to the streets in his support, speaking many times a day in the Negro and Jewish districts where the outcome at first was doubtful, and helping also with the Poles and Czechs. It was a great source of satisfaction to work shoulder to shoulder with the Catholic young people, who were stirred to enthusiasm by their handsome and able co-religionist. We carried the battle also into the suburbs.

Meanwhile, I began to pull far out in front. On the Sunday before Election Day the *Sun-Times* poll showed me winning by a half-million votes, and Kennedy by a hundred thousand. But there was a last-minute swing away from us, chiefly on account of the religious issue. The Bishop of Puerto Rico swelled this feeling when he said that those who voted for the Popular Democratic party of Muñoz Marín might lose the fellowship of the church.

When the votes were counted on Tuesday night, I had won by 420,000. Kennedy's margin was only 8,000. The Republicans immediately challenged the vote, alleging that "boss-ridden" Chicago had stolen the election. But when their complaints were investigated, they were shown to be ill-founded. For example, the former voters of one precinct that had been bulldozed for urban renewal could not be blamed for returning to their old precinct on Election Day to cast their ballots. The sealed ballot boxes of another precinct were lost for a time, but when they turned up, the ballots confirmed the count given on election night.

In a sense, Illinois was the crucial state. If we had lost there, then some of the Southern electors would probably have voted either for Nixon or, as a Virginia elector did, for Harry Byrd. Kennedy might not have been elected.

1962

THE CHIEF Illinois election in 1962 was that for United States senator. Everett Dirksen, having served two terms since he had defeated Lucas, was a candidate for a third. He had won a national reputation and was well liked by the voters. Since he was a downstater and the historic division was to have one senator from that section, I thought the Democrats should nominate someone from outside the Chicago area. This was especially desirable because our Democratic governor, Otto Kerner, was a Cook County man. Like Al Smith, I have always favored a balanced ticket racially, religiously, and geographically, if other considerations are approximately equal.

First I tried to persuade Mel Price, the congressman from East Saint Louis, to let his name be advanced. But since he did not want to give up his safe House seat and eighteen years of seniority, I tried to bring forward two other downstate possibilities. One was Irving Dilliard, formerly the fine editor of the Saint Louis *Post-Dispatch*. The other was Paul Simon, a brilliant, honorable, and young state legislator. However, since neither was then widely known, the Democratic leaders finally selected Congressman Sidney Yates, of Chicago. A graduate of the University of Chicago, Yates had made a splendid record as one of the ablest and most respected members of the House. So Emily and I supported him vigorously, she touring the state with Mrs. Yates while I carried on my usual station-wagon campaign with Joe Tierney through most of the downstate counties as well as in and around Chicago.

Early in the year I became aware that the White House and the Democratic leadership in the Senate apparently wanted to appease, rather than oppose, Dirksen. Kennedy had told me in 1960 that Dirksen was about the best Republican Senate leader that we could expect, far superior to his rival, Bourke Hickenlooper. Early in the winter of 1962 I was startled to learn by the grapevine that the President had just signed an appointment to the northern Illinois federal court for Bernard Decker, a Republican judge from Lake County. This appointment, which had never been mentioned to me, made it look as though the White House was in alliance with the Republican Minority Leader. Later it developed that it was. I immediately telephoned Kenneth O'Donnell and said that the appointment was highly irregular and would be interpreted in Illinois as sure proof that the administration wanted Dirksen, and not Yates, to be elected. I told him that I would oppose Decker. After Mayor Daley had reinforced me, O'Donnell agreed not to send the nomination up until after the election. That was all the White House would do. Nothing, however, can be long concealed in Washington. Soon the fact of Decker's pending appointment became widely known, and it eroded much of Yates's support.

Our troubles increased when Vice President Johnson was scheduled to be the main speaker at our big Chicago fund-raising dinner. We had to deal with him through his press secretary, George Reedy, and when we finally got a draft of his projected speech, it was highly unsatisfactory. Its tepid reference to Yates contained no real endorsement. Both Daley and I protested, and, indeed, the Mayor authorized me to tell Johnson that unless he gave Yates a strong endorsement he would not be welcome at the dinner and could tell the press that engine trouble had canceled his flight to Chicago. That persuaded Johnson to draft a new paragraph, endorsing Yates. Since it turned out to be only lukewarm, however, it did not really strengthen Yates.

A third blow came from Senate Majority Leader Mansfield. On the floor of the Senate he helped to organize an afternoon of fulsome tributes to Dirksen, in which he himself went overboard in praise. Humphrey joined in this paean of tributes. Widely reported in Illinois, this still further weakened Yates.

The next blow came the week before the election. Kennedy, bravely facing the Cuban missile crisis, had informed Russia that the fall of any missile on the United States would be treated as coming from Russia and would be met with full-scale reprisals. Meanwhile, Russian reinforcing vessels might not land in Cuba, and the missiles and their launching apparatus must be taken back to Russia. In the fateful week before Russia gave in, I spent most of my time speaking throughout downstate Illinois in support of the President's position. I realized that it was perfectly proper for the President to send his private plane to bring Dirksen back to Washington and to thank him for his help. But according to Dirksen and his press representatives, Kennedy went further, saying that Dirksen had the election in the bag. This claim, which further demoralized our workers, was not denied.

On the night before the election, Mansfield administered the final blow. He announced over a nationwide television program that the President would lend the Presidential plane for a trip he and Dirksen were to take to the crisis areas of the world. This was widely interpreted as another sign of Presidential approval of Dirksen's candidacy.

In spite of all this, Yates made a good showing and was beaten by only about 235,000 votes. Nevertheless, I was dispirited that the administration should treat so shabbily a good candidate who supported the forward-looking policies of our Democratic party. How can we expect the troops to be loyal if the leadership is not?

After the election the White House sent to the Senate the name of Judge Decker for the federal bench. They had made their trade, and obviously received something in return. Dirksen voted for the nuclear test ban treaty and for one or two other administration policies, both foreign and domestic. The believers in *Realpolitik* can, therefore, justify their action.

The undercover alliance between Kennedy and Johnson, on the one hand, and Dirksen on the other was one of the political realities of the 1960's. It was also one of the obstructions the party faced in Illinois, and I believe it continued into the 1968 election. At that time our strongest candidate for the Senate would have been either Paul Simon or Adlai

Stevenson III, the state treasurer. The Democratic leadership refused to nominate either of these men, shunting Simon into the lieutenant-governorship. Instead, they nominated William Clark, the son of my old friend John S. Clark, and a fine young man, but not then a spirited campaigner. He was defeated, while Dirksen was elected for a fourth term. Although we also lost the governorship, Simon was elected lieutenant governor and is a growing force for the future.

Ultimately, the nomination of Decker had far-reaching consequences. In 1971, his court took jurisdiction for reapportioning Congressional districts away from the state legislature. As Decker and his Republican colleague redrew the map, the districts were so gerrymandered as to oust three Democratic congressmen. So the Kennedy-Dirksen alliance gave a final large bonus to the Republicans.

1964

IN 1964 the national Republican party, having been captured by its extreme right wing, nominated Barry Goldwater, of Arizona, for President. In the process they deliberately humiliated Nelson Rockefeller, Governor of New York, and, by their treatment of Rockefeller, by their platform, and by Goldwater's speeches, they abandoned hope of attracting even the moderate group of voters. They wanted a "voice but not an echo."

Since taking office, Johnson, as I have pointed out, had followed a liberal domestic policy and had helped to push through the Civil Rights Act of 1964, which Goldwater as a senator had opposed. Johnson had made a splendid record on domestic issues, including the antipoverty program and education, and on foreign policy seemed much more peace-minded than Goldwater. I forgot old differences to campaign vigorously for him and for our governor, Otto Kerner, who was facing an attractive opponent in the person of Charles Percy.

It soon became apparent that Goldwater was reckless in his foreign policy and highly conservative in his domestic program. Not only had he voted against the 1964 Civil Rights bill, but he had also expressed his doubts about social security. He advocated an all-out war in Vietnam to crush Viet Cong resistance and implied that he favored dropping nuclear bombs. These were ostensibly to defoliate the trees of the jungle, but they would, of course, have killed many troops and civilians. Nearly all Asians would have been estranged by this third use of nuclear energy against Asiatic people. I now realized the full strength of Truman's final decision not to use the atomic bomb against the invading Chinese armies in Korea.

In ending my speeches that fall, I simply asked the audience whose hand they would prefer to have on the fateful button that could start a nuclear war, Barry Goldwater's or Lyndon Johnson's. The reply was always emphatic: Johnson's.

And so was the vote in November.

Like Woodrow Wilson, Johnson has been charged with reversing his campaign pledges. Let me say that in the many times I heard him speak in 1964 I never heard him pledge an end to land warfare. There may have been incautious statements in other states, but not in Illinois, where his campaigners simply argued that Johnson, while not a pacifist, was more pacifically inclined than Goldwater. And so, I believe, he was.

42

My Last Campaign—1966

As 1965 OPENED, I realized that I must soon decide whether I would run for a fourth term. My original intention had been to retire, for I would have been a senator for eighteen years and I knew that many voters weary of a public official when he has been around "too long."

The exception, of course, is in the South, where old senators are valued like old wine, or as the French value old music-hall favorites. In the South the voters realize the value of seniority in furthering their local, racial, and class interests. Indeed, seniority is one of the chief ways by which the South has been able to magnify its influence in Congress. Provided the official has made clear his loyalty to white supremacy, he can probably stay on, once elected, until death. If he does not keep this loyalty, he is likely to go the way of Claude Pepper. It was only a cosmopolitan electorate in Miami that made possible Pepper's later return to office in the lower house.

Another reason why opposition to a Northern senator increases with time is that he is constantly compelled to take a public stand on issues and in so doing offends additional segments of the voting public. Since voters are more often estranged from a public servant by differences than united by agreements, it was inevitable that some of my earlier supporters were either losing interest or going over to the opposition. Moreover, while I had not had much federal patronage at my disposal, except postmasters in Republican Congressional districts, I well knew that half or more of these had lost all interest in me once they had obtained what they wanted, and I had made many enemies among the unsuccessful aspirants. In short, enemies multiply with time, while friends retire, die, become indifferent, or are estranged. One cannot make enough new friends to offset the losses.

By the mid-1960's there had also been three important domestic shifts, which I knew were operating against me. The first was the flight to the suburbs of hundreds of thousands of white families, with the consequent drift toward conservatism and Republicanism. The second was an increase in the number of white-collar jobs in manufacturing, as well as in trade, communications, and advertising. Finally, there was the unprecedented power of youth, as the war and postwar babies came to voting age. Their values stressed the "image" of a candidate, not his record or experience.

As I considered these forces, the outlook became darker. In 1940, when I was an alderman, the population of the Cook County suburbs amounted to less than a million. By 1960 the number had risen to a million and a half. In 1965 there were probably close to 2 million outside the city but inside the county. During this time the population of Chicago itself had remained almost stationary at 3½ million. In twenty-five years the population of the Cook County suburbs had increased from less than one-sixth to over one-third of the county total. The same movement was taking place in the suburban counties outside of Cook. The population of Du Page County, to the immediate west, had soared by 1960 to over 400,000, and continued to increase in the next five years. Its leaders boasted that it was the strongest Republican county in the nation. McHenry County, to the northwest, and the residential areas of Lake County, to the north, were experiencing a like growth. Two-thirds of the state's population was now within a radius of fifty miles of downtown Chicago, and a full half of this was in the residential suburbs outside the city.

Although I had tried to strengthen the party in these areas, as well as to build a personal following, I was swimming against the tide. Those who had moved to the suburbs found the Republicans as strongly entrenched there as were the Democrats in the inner city. Like chameleons, many people take on the color of their surroundings, and here there were practical reasons for doing so. The Republican precinct captains helped with garbage removal, connection with the utility services, and the assessment of property. They might also hush up the derelictions of one's children and perform all the other offices that zealous politicians use to build up their followings. Along with their practical help, they ladled out their political philosophy, damning Chicago's leadership and making the Democrats the villains on the state scene. Democrats who remained faithful to their party were a shrinking proportion.

Furthermore, as a family prospered, its outlook changed. Men and women began to feel like Republicans and did not want to be singled out for jokes at club meetings, in church groups, or on the morning train. It was commonly said that when a Democrat got a driveway and acquired Venetian blinds, he began to split his ticket. With membership in the country club and a new tuxedo, he blossomed into a full-fledged Republican. Even the members of the public-spirited League of Women Voters were not immune to mass and family psychology. I had always worked closely with the League and rejoiced when, after full study, they came to endorse positions for which I had pioneered years before. However, when state and national elections came, the precincts in which they were strongest (as in Winnetka, where in two precincts only two Democratic votes were cast) voted overwhelmingly for the Republicans. This was directly against most of their legislative program.

This tendency was reinforced by the rise in the number of nonmanual workers, in clerical, technical, executive, and managerial jobs. They not only furnished the major portion of the new migration to the suburbs, but, being closer to top management during their working hours, also became predominantly attached to the possessors of economic power and, hence, to the Republicans. Even the political ardor of the skilled workers diminished.

Although most of the suburbanites still worked in the city, the majority soon became indifferent to its welfare. Having found greater material comfort in their new homes, they found it easy to let the city stew in its own juice. Furthermore, the city had become an alien place to many as large numbers of unskilled Negroes, Mexicans, and Puerto Ricans continued to settle there. It was, in fact, the arrival of these dark-skinned peoples that had caused the flight of many thousands to the suburbs. In their new homes they did not want to face the problems from which they had fled.

This tide of antiblack prejudice was shown in various ways. When liberal white groups tried to promote a little racial integration in Deerfield, their efforts were frustrated by bitter opposition. The rich community of Kenilworth, on the North Shore, was one of the most tightly segregated in the nation, since Jews as well as Negroes were, in effect, barred.

The final new factor in this campaign would be the accent on youth. Self-conscious about their power, alienated by a generation gap, the young were not impressed by age or experience. Although the very word "Senate," with the same prefix as "senior," had from Roman days meant a council of elders, supposedly the wisest, the new voters preferred a council of juniors.

It was a curious reflection on myself that, although seventy-four, I was shocked to learn from the press that I was "old." I still worked twelve hours a day and was in good physical health—indeed much stronger than in 1954, when I had suffered from undulant fever. I welcomed every sunrise, but I could not quarrel with my birth certificate. If re-elected, I would be eighty on completing my six-year term. This was not unusual in the Senate, where my colleague Theodore Green had recently retired at ninety.

The opening passage of Frazer's *Golden Bough* was often in my thoughts. There the priest-king of the forest near Lake Nemi, below Castel Gandolfo, paced restlessly in full armor as he awaited the young challenger who someday would emerge from the forest to kill and displace him. This struggle and replacement were part of the life process, from the antlered deer and moose, leading their herds, to the occupants of the executive suites on Wall Street. Many of my colleagues had already succumbed to this fate, and I realized that the end of most politicians, like that of every wild animal, was a tragedy.

In 1965 I even foresaw who the Republicans would nominate as my opponent—if I ran. The nominal choice was one of two men who had also been rivals for the Republican nomination for governor in 1964, Charles H. Percy, of Kenilworth, and State Treasurer William J. Scott. The latter represented the highly conservative Republican county organizations of the state, but he had been defeated in 1964 for the gubernatorial nomination by Percy, who wore a becoming air of moderation. Although Percy had supported Goldwater, and had run much better than the latter, he had been defeated for governor, by 185,000 votes, by the incumbent, Otto Kerner. Many believed that Percy's real goal was the Presidency, and that right quickly. But to attain this goal he must be elected either senator in 1966 or governor in 1968. A second defeat would permanently finish him. The conservatives might prevent him from again getting the gubernatorial nomination, since this would mean their loss of the party machinery, but I thought that they would back him for the Senate. This did not carry with it any patronage or internal political power. Furthermore, many of his Republican opponents believed that I would swamp him and thus rid them forever of a troublesome outsider. They felt toward him in 1966 much as many Democratic leaders had felt toward me in 1948.

But I knew better. Percy was handsome, immaculately groomed, relatively young, and looked even younger. He had risen rapidly to the presidency of his company, Bell & Howell, by a combination of fortunate circumstances. Largely through the medium of stock options, he had become many times a millionaire. Pleasant in his personal manners and very persistent, he had shown himself a master of the selling arts of public relations. He was, in fact, just the candidate for suburbia and middle-class youth: a kind of Horatio Alger hero in a Brooks Brothers suit. From chance remarks he had made to me, I also knew he was acquainted with Stephen Potter's "gamesmanship" and "one-upsmanship," or how, within the borders of outer civility, one could put an adversary at a disadvantage. Potterism, it is said, is the Establishment's substitute for barroom fighting.

Percy would, of course, be backed financially by the large corporations, by the wealthy Eastern Establishment, and by the oil and gas interests. Moreover, he would have the enthusiastic support of Marshall Field IV, who, in reaction against his liberal father and seeking the approval of his fellow millionaires, heartily disapproved of me. Field now owned the *Daily News* as well as the *Sun-Times,* with a combined circulation of about a million. In the final clutches of the campaign these papers and the power of the big corporations and banks would be thrown into the battle on Percy's side. With enormous amounts of money, they would also swamp the airwaves.

If I ran, it would be hard to win against Percy, despite my big victory in 1960. This was confirmed by an extensive statewide street-corner poll that I had taken in the late spring and early summer of 1965. The poll showed that while I would defeat Scott by a 70–30 percentage, my margin over Percy would be much less, only 58 to 42. With Percy's latent resources, I knew I was in for trouble.

Why, then, did I make the decision to run?

A major reason was that I feared my unfinished business might otherwise never get passed. Foremost on my personal agenda were the Dunes and the truth-in-lending bills. Beyond that, if I withdrew, the Republicans would probably pick up my senatorial seat and thereby weaken attempts to end poverty, restore the cities, and improve the nation's schools.

On the hopeful side was the fact that for the first time all branches of government—federal, state, Cook County, and Chicago—were in the hands of my fellow Democrats, which might offer resources I had never before been able to tap. The polls showed I was personally popular, and I never relished running away from a fight.

So in August, 1965, when Mayor Daley urged me to run, I was in a receptive mood. Although it would be a hard fight, we both thought another Democrat would have even more trouble. Before I made a final decision, however, I needed reassurance on three points: that all segments of the party, from the top down, really wanted me as their candidate and would vigorously support me (I did not want halfhearted support again, as in 1954); I must be able to rely on adequate funds for a decent campaign, costing at a minimum $450,000, with a third of that sum on hand before I made my formal announcement; the doctors must find me in sound health and able to carry on the duties of the office for the full six years with complete efficiency.

To test the first of these conditions, as soon as Congress adjourned I spent six weeks going over the state, covering sixty counties in addition to the twenty-five I had visited earlier in the year. During this tour I discussed both national issues and the needs of the localities and the state in relation to them. I never mentioned my own possible candidacy. In short, I gave every opportunity for other candidates to present themselves and did not ask for personal support. The response was overwhelming and hearty. In nearly every county the Democrats voluntarily passed resolutions asking me to run. There was a ring of sincerity to these pledges, sometimes backed with money, which convinced me that perhaps for the first time I would have the support of a united party. Volunteer groups came forward to raise an initial nest egg for the campaign by means of a series of five dinners to be held over the state, beginning in early January with one in Chicago. Nearly 2,000 tickets at $100 were sold for this first dinner, and the advance sales for the others were high.

Meanwhile, my health had been improving as I dieted, exercised, and swam at least half an hour daily. A thorough physical examination showed my blood pressure to be that of a man of thirty, namely 120/70, while my heartbeat, threatening in 1964, was now completely regular. I finished the manuscript of my book *America in the Market Place* during a December vacation in Mexico, and found that I could still work long hours without strain.

So, at the Chicago dinner in January I announced that if the party chose me for its candidate in the June primary, I would give my very best to the campaign. From then until the primary, I spent at least two long weekends a month (Thursday night to Tuesday morning) campaigning back home, specializing in the downstate counties. But I answered over 93 per cent of the Senate roll calls.

The Republicans quickly agreed on Percy, who carried on a skillful and costly public-relations campaign from three floors of offices in Chicago's Loop. He was well packaged and sold to the public as the advertisers would sell toothpaste or a new breakfast food. Handsome pictures of him appeared discreetly everywhere.

I began the campaign by stressing the achievements of the Kennedy-Johnson administrations, together with my own record and program for the future. In six years, I pointed out, the physical production of goods and services had increased by 33 per cent, or a cumulative growth rate of about 4½ per cent a year. This was nearly twice the 2.4-per-cent annual growth rate during the eight years of the Eisenhower administration, while the per-capita increase since 1961 was about 2.9 per cent a year, or four times the rate during the eight Republican years. I suggested that part of this growth was due to the adoption of the principles I had advocated in 1958 and in the 1959–60 study, namely, the use of fiscal as well as monetary policy to stimulate employment and production. I also stressed that this had resulted in the gain of 25 per cent in weekly money earnings for factory workers in Illinois and of about 15 per cent in their real earnings. As for the farmers, their average net income in Illinois had gone up by 60 per cent, from $3,700 in 1960 to $5,900 in 1965. It would be still higher in 1966. In view of all this, I asked, why should we change?

Instead of denying these facts, my opponent disregarded them. He stressed the 8-per-cent increase in the cost of living, of which a full 3 per cent had occurred during the previous year, and emphasized the casualties in Vietnam. To my perhaps prejudiced eye, he was marshaling all the separate and often conflicting grievances of the moment without offering any constructive remedies.

The appeal to prosperity was, of course, only half of my story. The Democrats had also passed, with my assistance, an extraordinary amount of advanced legislation. Foremost among these measures were Medicare for the aged, wholesale and generous aid to education, civil rights, and at least the beginnings of a war on poverty. I not only had supported every one of these measures, but also had taken the lead in many of them during the earlier years when they were unpopular. In contrast to my record, my Illinois Republican colleague, Senator Dirksen, had vigorously opposed nearly all of them.

But merely pointing to the past was not enough. I always discussed my future program, stressing improvement not merely in the material aspects of life, but in its quality as well. We must, I said, clean up our slums and improve the housing of people in both the cities and the countryside. We should reduce poverty, provide more parks and recreational areas for the people of Illinois, clean the pollution from our rivers and lakes, and purify the air of metropolitan Chicago, East Saint Louis, and Granite City. I urged the passage of my truth-in-lending bill, the closing of tax loopholes, the improvement of Medicare by the inclusion of drugs with their generic and not brand names, the promotion of greater good will among people of all races, and, above all, an honorable but durable peace in Southeast Asia. I had the feeling, however, that while the majority of the voters were intellectually in agreement with these programs, they were not emotionally stirred. The drive that had characterized the early days of the New Deal and the 1960 Kennedy campaign was absent. Many had forgotten their blessings and thought only of their grievances. Moreover, Johnson, however excellent his domestic program, was not an inspiring national leader.

The two chief grievances stressed by the opposition during the spring and early summer were the human and economic casualties of the Vietnam war and the increase in the cost of living. Without openly attacking the war as such, my opponent dwelt on the lengthening casualty lists and the hardships experienced by our soldiers. As Senators Fulbright and Morse attacked our Vietnam policy in the worst vitriolic terms, I knew that they were gathering support. Several prominent rabbis, hitherto friendly to me, now came out in open opposition. They wanted aid for Israel, but not for South Vietnam.

For decades I had supported resistance to aggression through a system of collective security, and to this day I see no alternative for the maintenance of international peace. During the 1930's we had seen the fatal weakness of a go-it-alone policy in which nations ignored aggression until they were themselves attacked. This lack of co-operation had allowed the swift rise of the police-state empires of Hitler, Mussolini, and Tojo.

The answer of the democracies had been the United Nations, which was meant to keep the peace through an international force. A built-in weakness, however, was the veto, available to any major member of the Security Council and used at once by the Soviet Union to prevent even the establishment of the international force. In the first test, Korea, the accident of Russia's absence from the council meeting allowed a half-hearted U.N. effort to fulfill the police function by co-operating with American troops already on the spot.

In Vietnam the United States again took the initiative, but this time only a few Pacific nations even pretended to co-operate. I had to admit that there was precious little collective security. Yet aggression needed to be stopped, even though it took the more subtle and puzzling form of guerrilla warfare.

Opposition to the Vietnam war naturally intensified as casualty lists mounted and boys were brought home for burial. Percy's Vietnam proposals were confused, but embodied opposition to the war. As a Quaker and long-time supporter of collective security, I was astonished, baffled, and hurt to find the label of "hawk" pinned on me by his followers.

Toward the end of the campaign, Percy tried to inject another foreign-policy issue into the campaign when he proposed that ultimately the United Nations be given police jurisdiction over the Western Hemisphere. He never seemed to realize that this carried with it the Russian veto. Had this been in effect in 1962, for example, the Russians would have prevented President Kennedy from dealing with the planting of Soviet missiles on Cuban launching pads. But, however basically unsound these trial balloons were, and however sensible my proposals for a direct conference of belligerents to provide for a schedule of mutual de-escalation might be, the exchange had the effect of creating the impression that my opponent was for peace, even if in a bumbling way, while I was regarded as a "hard-liner." The emotional desires of the peace group attached themselves to him and not to me. A man I had saved from a mental breakdown, had partially financed when he was in need, and for whom I had found a much-needed job now circulated letters that attacked me as a cruel politician, bereft of human sympathy. Yet few of the real "hard-liners" came over to me. Disliking my domestic liberalism and being primarily Republicans, they did not allow foreign-policy differences to interfere with their desire for victory and the preservation of their tax benefits and of favorable public policy.

Despite all difficulties, by the Fourth of July our polls showed that Percy and I were running on approximately even terms. Then came two catastrophes. In July, during a long heat wave, several hundred young Negroes went berserk on Chicago's near West Side. Angered because the fire department had shut off the water from hydrants formerly used by them to cool off, the youngsters took to the streets, breaking storefronts, looting, and beating up many whites. To reinforce the police, the National Guard was called out, and order was speedily restored. But the turn to violence deepened the fears and resentments of the neighboring whites. Negro extremists led by Stokely Carmichael, who had taken over James Meredith's march from Memphis to Montgomery, and in so doing had captured SNCC, now systematically exploited those fears. Calling the leadership of the NAACP and the Urban League "Uncle Toms" and urging "black-power" tactics and a break with white liberals, Carmichael apparently wanted a physical confrontation between the whites and the blacks. His support came largely from students and the field hands from the South who were looking for trouble. It was not hard to find it.

Many men and women of good will who had formerly supported the civil-rights cause now became either neutral or hostile. Those who had already been hostile redoubled their efforts to fight civil rights. In this climate and in the heat of August, Dr. Martin Luther King, Jr., who had set up headquarters in Chicago the previous winter, leaving a staff and somewhat obscure plans, started a series of marches into all-white territories. The ostensible purpose was to protest residential segregation and its accompanying schools, which were segregated in fact, although not in law. King's marches, of only a few hundred people, mostly sincere idealists, were always peacefully conducted, but no one knew why he had singled out Chicago, or the source of his now ample funds.

It was soon apparent that one of the purposes of some of his lieutenants, including his chief of staff, the Reverend James Bevel, was to stir up resentment among both blacks and whites against the Democratic party and all its candidates, including the senior Senator. In helping to organize a march in the Gage Park (Thirteenth Ward) community, Bevel declared, "We will march until every white man in the area votes—Republican." King did not disavow Bevel's statement until three months later, and Bevel always remained one of his right-hand men. Nor was the Gage Park quotation an isolated instance of Bevel's espousal of the Republican ticket, for on other occasions when he was asked his preference in the senatorial campaign, he chose "the younger man."

That the influence of the Martin Luther King group should be used to aid my opponent was one of the baffling turns in the campaign. We had understood that my civil-rights record had assured his support. Furthermore, during the second march at Selma, my wife and her friends Mrs. Charles Tobey and Mrs. Harold Ickes went down on their own initiative and joined the protest at great risk to themselves. At that time, in front of the thousands at the bridge, Dr. King had hailed Emily in extravagant terms as the wife of "the greatest of all senators." That his statement was not just idle talk seemed indicated by my later contacts with him and the fact that his wife appeared in Chicago in April at a meeting called by the Automobile Workers. Her tributes were equally warm, and she voluntarily promised that they would do all possible to aid me. Now, however, the forces of their movement were not only undermining my support among the Negroes, but, more potently, frightening the whites against me for my civil-rights leadership.

Mayor Daley followed the correct policy of protecting the right of the protestants to march peacefully. But in doing so he did not win any support from the radical Negro leaders, who continued their vitriolic opposition, while he created deep resentment against the Democrats among the whites—not only in the communities immediately affected, but also in those within a rather wide radius. This resentment was rapidly harnessed by the local Republican leaders into opposition to all Democratic candidates. Meanwhile, young Negro leaders attacked me for not having marched with King. They urged my defeat as a necessary rebuke to the Democratic party and especially to Mayor Daley. They, too, seemed to be well financed from unknown sources.

Finally, King threatened a march into Cicero on the Sunday before Labor Day. Cicero, a separately incorporated Slavic city completely enclosed within Chicago, had the reputation of being one of the most anti-Negro communities in the state. In 1950 when a Negro couple had tried to rent an apartment there, a riot had been provoked in which thousands took part and which turned the town into a Republican stronghold. Since Cicero was outside Chicago, Daley could not protect the marchers, and the Cicero officials lacked the means and probably the will to do so. The then sheriff of the county, a Republican now governor of the state, not only did not have enough deputies to keep order, but had never shown much sympathy for the civil-rights movement. Because widespread bloodshed seemed inevitable, Governor Kerner again ordered out the National Guard.

Daley, with religious, business, and labor leaders, then started a prolonged series of conferences with the King group, and on the Friday before Labor Day announced a statesmanlike agreement. The city promised to give its Commission on Human Relations more power over the open-occupancy ordinance and agreed not to build public-housing units of over eight stories. In these, only the first two stories were to be used for families; the remaining six were to be reserved for the elderly, who, in general, liked the high-rise apartment buildings. The real-estate groups, although still opposed to open-housing legislation, reluctantly agreed to abide by the ordinance. Finally, machinery was to be set up to enforce the peace treaty. In return for all this, Dr. King agreed to call off his march into Cicero.

His left wing did not agree. Furious at what he termed a betrayal, a young leader announced his own march on Cicero, and this time there was no claim of nonviolence. Luckily, the fights were not numerous, and no widespread trouble occurred. Nevertheless, bitter feelings were again aroused, new marches were threatened, and everywhere fear and hatred spread.

This was the background when I began my formal campaign on Labor Day. Our private polls now showed me running slightly behind, with losses in both Negro and white wards, and in the suburbs as well. The question of open occupancy, or, as I preferred to call it, "freedom of residence," had become the underlying issue of the campaign, far outweighing Vietnam, my age, prosperity, or social reform in its popular importance. When age was given by people as a reason for voting against me, it often seemed merely the surface excuse. The real reason was that they were opposed to open occupancy and therefore wanted to defeat me. Age was a convenient excuse. It was not used against Dirksen in 1968, although he was not only in my age group, but also was known to be seriously ailing.

My position was well known. I had tried to make it clear that freedom of residence did not mean that an owner or real-estate agent had to rent or sell to a Negro merely because he was a Negro. If a man was of bad moral character or slovenly, then, whether he was white or black, there was no such obligation. But if otherwise qualified, he should not be discriminated against just because of race. Having been the chief sponsor for proposed national civil-rights legislation and having testified in its support before the Judiciary Committee, I refused to withdraw from it. In speaking before somewhat hostile business and white residential audiences, I defended my position on the ground that both ethics and religion demanded it; that it was the logical corollary of the statement in the Declaration of Independence that "all men are created equal." I argued that such action was justified on a national level under both the Fourteenth Amendment to the Constitution, which guaranteed equal rights to all citizens, and the commerce clause, and on the state and local levels by the police powers of the community. I stressed, furthermore, that if discrimination continued to be practiced on racial grounds, it would ultimately split our multiracial nation apart; we must, instead, all learn to get along together. About one-sixth of both state and national populations was nonwhite, including Puerto Ricans and Mexican-Americans.

My opponent's position was ambiguous. He had campaigned for governor in 1964 on the basis of violent opposition to an open-occupancy law, which he had declared to be "bad legislation," and he had promised that if the legislature were to pass such a bill, he would veto it. As a result, and with widely distributed advertisements and party propaganda, he had picked up a big vote in the residential wards and suburbs. Thus, although Otto Kerner was of Czech stock, Percy had carried the Slavic cities of Cicero and Berwyn by huge majorities. But despite an endorsement by Dick Gregory, the radical Negro comedian, he had utterly failed in the Negro wards.

Sometime after the 1964 election, Percy came to the conclusion that he must try to regain a foothold among the Negroes. He then came out for open occupancy. Indeed, he claimed that he had always been for it but had believed in "voluntary compliance" on the part of the real-estate brokers. He ignored the fact that it was the Republican state Senate that, in 1965, had defeated an open-occupancy bill passed by the Democratic House and that he had not made any real effort to get his fellow party members to alter their position. Nor had he protested when the Republican Senate refused to reconfirm his own employment director at Bell & Howell, Charles W. Gray, as the head of the state Fair Employment Practices Commission. Gray had run afoul of one of Percy's chief financial backers, Robert Galvin, and, upon being turned down by the Republicans and deserted by his employer, had left the state.

When the administration's original open-occupancy bill, applying even to individual homes, was introduced by me in the Senate, Percy had announced his support of it. He set up nearly twenty independent storefront headquarters in the Negro districts, where were distributed large quantities of a pamphlet bearing a photograph of him among Negroes and declaring without qualification his support of open occupancy, and saying that in 1964 he had worked for open occupancy by means of "voluntary compliance." As the campaign wore on and it became apparent that open occupancy was extremely unpopular, not only in the white wards and suburbs, but indeed throughout the state, he again hedged. According to a local report, he brought a big group of businessmen "to their feet" by saying that Paul Douglas wanted to go "too far and too fast," while he himself was for open occupancy only for those buildings that had five or more apartments. This exemption of individual homes and smaller apartment buildings meant, in effect, that his plan for open occupancy would not apply to the residential suburbs, communities, and wards, and would, instead, be confined to the inner city. For this reason it could not reduce the pressure on the Negro ghetto.

The Republican ward organizations then opened a leaflet and word-of-mouth campaign saying that the Democrats were for open occupancy, which they opposed. While there is no evidence that their senatorial candidate was a party to this effective strategy, he never spoke out against it. On the contrary, his personal literature was still segregated and his open-occupancy pledge was confined strictly to the Negro wards.

In early October, the Democratic mayor of Waukegan, Robert Sabonjean, came out as a write-in candidate for senator, focusing his attack on me for my support of open occupancy and friendliness to the Negroes. This man was from an Armenian family which had been forced to come to America because of Turkish persecution. An ironic twist to the situation was the fact that I had lifted Bob from obscurity by making him the Waukegan postmaster, in spite of strong racial opposition to him. He developed sizable support in Lake County, and his vote in November was almost precisely the measure of my county losses. Although without personal means, he spent a great deal of money, and the source of his funds was a mystery. His appeal was to Democrats who resented the Negroes but hesitated to vote Republican. He probably cost me at least 35,000 votes.

The second major blow to the campaign was as unprecedented as it was terrible. I was in East Saint Louis on September 18, after a successful two weeks of campaigning outside Chicago. The momentum was mounting. In spite of all difficulties, my team agreed with some of the reporters that as my record and plans for the future emerged, my support was rising. For the first time I was optimistic. Shortly after seven that Sunday morning, my wife burst into my motel room to say that Percy's daughter had been murdered. Only a few hours earlier, in her own house in Kenilworth, she had been stabbed and beaten to death.

Within a few minutes I drafted a telegram to the Percys expressing my sympathy and announcing that for the present I would suspend my campaign. I canceled my immediate engagements and flew back to Washington to resume my Senate work. After a memorial service, the Percy family left for an undisclosed retreat in California, where they remained for two weeks.

There were mysteries about the murder which have never been explained. Since the investigation was being conducted by the Democratic county officials, I made a special trip to Chicago to urge the leadership not to exploit the situation in any way that would add further grief to the Percy family. The next day the investigation was turned over in an unprecedented move to the local Republican officials. They put a quietus upon any future probing. In the following days, when bombarded with questions as to the effect of the tragedy on the campaign, I merely said that it was too great for anyone to consider political repercussions. In our hearts, my supporters and I knew from the first that it would help the victim's father. By my own action in suspending the campaign we lost the momentum we had achieved, and had to start again from scratch, with less time, so that I was forced to neglect the southern half of the state, where I was strongest.

Most important, my opponent now dominated all news—press, radio, and television. As Stewart Alsop later put it, the public came to think of Percy not as a rich and ambitious young man, but as one suffering from great and unmerited losses. It was true that his first wife had died, that he had been deeply hurt when he lost his gubernatorial race in 1964, and now a beloved daughter had been brutally killed. A huge sympathy vote was inevitable. As one lifelong Democrat later said, "To vote for Percy seemed the least one could do."

From then on I handled him gently, although stressing the issues that divided us: my truth-in-lending bill, Medicare and its further improvements, the closing of the outrageous tax loopholes, the battle for the Dunes and for other parks and recreational areas, the effective cleaning up of rivers, lakes, and air from pollution, constructive steps to improve housing, the antipoverty program, and others. My opponent took no stand on these issues, only making bland statements of general support, with broad escape hatches. He and his managers were trying to minimize any differences with me and to rely on the sympathy vote, opposition to the war in Vietnam, the white backlash, and my age to carry him to victory.

As the tide began to turn against me, the publishers of the three big Republican papers moved in for the kill. So did one of the big television chains. Every news story contrasted my age, seventy-four, with Percy's forty-seven. My worst pictures and those of my wife appeared side by side with shots of my highly photogenic opponent. One photographer later told us ruefully that his paper always rejected better shots of us. Percy invariably was given more space, in more favorable locations. Most of the political reporters were constantly trying to force me on the defensive by demanding that I tell them whether or not the backlash was hurting me, whether my age was not a handicap, and whether I was not losing votes because of the Vietnamese war and sympathy because of the murder. If I remained silent on the backlash, some implied that I was afraid to deal with the issue. When I went into backlash areas and took my stand in favor of equal rights regardless of race, the same papers were silent. They always minimized the constructive issues on which we differed.

In contrast, when the political reporters questioned Percy, they asked easy questions or, in baseball language, "floaters," which he would knock over the fence. I began to feel like the bull in Spanish countries when exposed to the thrusts and darts of the picadors. But at least two of the reporters who followed me around were conspicuously fair in their treatment.

Three weeks before the election, the *Sun-Times* began to publish its poll. On the first day it included Du Page County, which, as I have said, is the strongest Republican area in the country. I polled only 26 per cent of the vote there, lowering my combined percentage to 40. This, of course, discouraged my supporters and helped the band-wagon psychology for Percy. The initial polls also seemed defective because they were often taken in front of the more expensive stores and apartments and at those times of day when few blue-collar workers were present. While the final poll was only 2 per cent below my actual vote, it is also true that the publication of the early polls helped to create the final results. Du Page County had never been typical, and its use in the early polls pulled my vote down unduly and, by doing so, decreased the number who finally cast their ballots for me.

As the bad news continued, Emily and I redoubled our efforts. We had started out by making from seven to eight stops and speeches a day, but in the final ten days I raised this to sixteen or eighteen. In addition to speeches, I shook hands daily with from 2,000 to 4,000 persons. We specialized in going into the backlash wards and suburbs and meeting the voters face to face. Uniformly, we were greeted courteously, and often with personal warmth and cordiality. We began to think perhaps the tide was turning after all. But we felt behind the courteous receptions a basic determination to keep those of alien color away, and we glimpsed what Robert Ardrey has called the instinct for "territorial integrity." We were, perhaps, encountering a basic animal instinct, with which it was impossible to deal by rational argument or ethical appeal.

An interesting case of the smear in reverse developed during the last few days of the campaign. As I have mentioned, in the Negro wards Percy was using a pamphlet that pledged his support for open occupancy and that had photographs of him surrounded by Negroes. This material was kept exclusively in the Negro wards. Elsewhere, the Republicans carried on a campaign against open occupancy. My managers faithfully reproduced this pamphlet, printed a million copies, and had them distributed through the suburbs and white wards. This threw the Percy forces into a near panic. They did not want their contradictory campaign to be exposed. The Percy leaders first threatened the distributors with prosecution on the strange pretext that the pamphlet was being used outside of the areas they wanted it to go. This, they claimed, was foul play. In other words, they insisted that the *exposure* of their segregated campaign was the crime.

At the same time, they falsely accused me of smearing Percy by calling him anti-Catholic and a racist. Of course, I had never done any such thing. Percy had come out against certain features of the recently passed education bill permitting joint classes for public- and private-school students if held in public or nonsectarian buildings. I merely remarked that opposition to such a proposal was a blow at the Catholic parochial schools and to ecumenical harmony, and I thought we should, instead, seek ways of bridging the gap between the two types of education. This, Percy said, was a personal smear. And after Percy's statement about limiting open occupancy, I had said, "Percy is not a racist, but he is blowing kisses to the racists!" Despite this, Percy now claimed that I had improperly "smeared" him. And so it went. Finally, he got big headlines on the weekend before the election by announcing that his representatives would file charges against me before Charles Taft's Committee on Fair Campaign Practices. The charges were withdrawn on the appearance of my attorney, but new and equally unsubstantiated accusations were made. So for a third day Percy dominated the news in his pose of persecuted hero.

He had used this same tactic during the summer, by charging that I

was "a deliberate liar" in circulating pamphlets in La Salle County showing him in 1964 crossing a union picket line at a Chicago television station. This was exactly what he had done, and it had been used against
him with great effect by the Kerner forces in the gubernatorial race of
1964. However, I had given orders not to use the pamphlet in my campaign, because I wanted the contest to be waged on constructive lines. We
had men go all over La Salle County to see if they could find the alleged
pamphlet, and they said it was nonexistent. We then asked Percy's office if
it could produce copies. The staff stalled, but finally admitted they had
not seen any. He had made the charge without any basis, but the Republican press refused to print this fact. The Committee on Fair Campaign
Practices had allowed itself to be used as a magnified sounding board for
false charges, and it did not reply to my later requests that it make a
factual statement about the full circumstances of the case.

This recital shows how subtle operators can "smear" opponents by
falsely charging that it is they themselves who have been smeared. It also
illustrates how agencies originally designed to raise the level of campaigning can be so manipulated as to make them passive accomplices in the
process.

On the Sunday before the election, I shook hands with thousands in
the peddlers' ghetto on Maxwell Street and then hurried to meet additional thousands at the Bears' football game. Finishing in Chicago with a
series of afternoon meetings, I took a plane for downstate. That night and
the following day I had airport press conferences in seven strategic cities.
On my return I held a final press conference and then went into a handshaking tour of the Negro wards. The SNCC and CORE workers followed
me closely, distributing anti-Douglas literature urging a boycott of the
election. Someone from the East had given them nearly $2,000 for this
purpose. I wound up the campaign with a heart-warming rally of a
thousand friends and neighbors in our beloved home community of Hyde
Park.

Election Day dawned with a drizzle. After Emily and I had voted
early, I embarked on my usual tour to the South and Southwest Side
wards and visited, in the course of the day, a dozen ward headquarters
and nearly fifty precincts. The Negro Democratic leaders were doing their
very best, but were faced with much apathy. I could understand this, for
it was only natural for Negroes from the South to ask, "What is the difference between one white man and another?" However, the Negroes did
not desert me, as some have said; while their vote was low, I polled
between 75 and 80 per cent of the total in their wards. If the white fringes
of these wards are omitted, my vote in the black sectors was slightly over
80 per cent.

On the other hand, in the white residential wards the backlash ran
deep and strong. The voting was unusually heavy in the white suburbs,

and the backlash even reached into downstate counties where there were only small handfuls of Negroes. The suburbs of East Saint Louis voted in large numbers, and the Democratic leaders there were pessimistic. Even the ten university precincts in the Fifth Ward, which I had always carried by huge majorities, swung to Percy or were evenly divided.

On the way home as the polls were closing, I told Emily that I was going to be defeated. Then I went to sleep for three hours. When I awoke, the bulletins confirmed my prediction. It looked as though I would be beaten by 420,000 votes and that there had been a shift of about 10 per cent of the vote since 1960, bringing my vote down to only 45 per cent of the total. I would be one of the worst-defeated candidates in the state's history. So I began to prepare a concession statement, with the aid of my son John. At ten o'clock, with Helen and Jean, Emily and I went to the Hilton Hotel, where we met privately with a group of intimate friends and supporters. I told them that if it was to be a wake, it must be a cheerful one. At one o'clock in the morning we entered the crowded basement room where a couple of hundred devoted and sorrowful friends were still gathered. Pushing my way through the crowd, I repeated to myself the advice of Marcus Aurelius, "So live as on a mountain," and I then made the following concession statement:

It appears that I have been defeated by a substantial margin and I have extended my congratulations along with my best wishes to my opponent.

I want to thank the thousands of men and women who, against heavy odds, worked on my behalf and for that of my party.

Finally, I want to thank the voters of Illinois for the privilege of representing them for eighteen years and of fighting for the causes in which I believe. Some of these causes have triumphed; others, I believe, will ultimately prevail.

Let us remember that ours is one country and one state. Let us purge ourselves of any trace of bitterness or divisiveness. Let us start with ourselves—for no one of us is perfect or free from fault.

Then let us try to heal divisions, to erase bitterness and to seek common grounds of agreement with all segments of society regardless of race, religion or political affiliation. It is important to remember that far beyond election day all of us will be living in this country; that what unites us is more important than what divides us; and that we must move forward as a united people to achieve greater justice, dignity and purpose in our society while striving for an honorable and durable peace abroad.

Let me say, finally, that nobody could have had more loyal, devoted support than I have received from you, from the listening audience and from the Democratic Party during the last eighteen years. I shall always be grateful to you for it.

I leave public life with no regrets. I would not change a vote or a position. I shall continue to work on behalf of those causes in which I believe, and I shall always remain your friend, just as you have remained mine.

I went out to pay a final visit of thanks to the Democratic leaders who, despite all our differences, had worked hard for me. I was afraid that the tornado of anti-Douglas votes would carry Adlai Stevenson III down to defeat and snuff out his promising political career. Fortunately this did not happen. Stevenson was elected state treasurer by a majority of about 50,000, and he made a splendid record in that office.

As we drove home, I heard the voice of my opponent, which thirty-six hours before had been accusing me of every foul tactic in the book, saying I had given magnificent service to the state and nation, and that he would be happy if he could be half as good a senator as I was. It should be said that no one could have been more considerate to a defeated rival than Percy has been since that election.

I repeated to myself the closing line of *Pagliacci*, "La commedia è finita!" The job of reconditioning myself for civilian life had begun. There would be new struggles ahead, but they would be of a different nature. Another phase of my life had certainly ended.

PART FIVE

Once More
a Private Citizen

43

After the Election—Reflections

I WOKE UP at noon on the day after the election to find a tidal wave of condolences pouring in upon me. In the next two weeks, as I received some 3,000 such letters, Emily and I wondered where all those negative votes had come from. After drafting several form replies, I spent two hours a day dictating personal letters of thanks and appreciation to close friends and supporters who had stayed with me through the years. But my chief concern was my staff. My defeat had brought them down as well. So I telephoned around the country helping to find openings, and by New Year's all but one had been placed. She found work shortly afterward.

Scattered through local, state, and national governments, and in private business, are, today, a sprinkling of men and women who formerly worked with me. Some of them say that I am responsible for their careers, and this may turn out to be my best contribution.

I was too busy to worry about my own future, which was good, since a defeated candidate can be overcome by self-pity. I resolved to accept what had happened, bear no animosities, look forward rather than back, and know that I could still be useful and happy as a private citizen. Many flattering invitations to teach or lecture helped buoy my spirits. However, since there was none of a substantial nature from Illinois, I somewhat sorrowfully realized that I could not go home again.

Before Emily and I went to the Caribbean for our month of sunshine and study, I received two important telephone calls. The first was from Harry Gideonse, an old friend from Chicago who, after a distinguished career as president of Brooklyn College, had become chancellor of the New School for Social Research, in New York, and also the chairman of the board of Freedom House, a liberal antitotalitarian organization. He in-

597

vited me to teach at the New School and to become the unpaid president of Freedom House. Those two jobs, which would take about two days a week, would enable me to participate in the intellectual life of the times. My salary at the New School plus an NBC television series and other lectures soon brought me an income larger than my senatorial salary, and I began once more to save.

My relations with the New School during the next three years were most pleasant. I liked the students and my associates, although the beards were longer and the skirts shorter than I had ever seen. As a by-product of the lectures, I wrote another book, *In Our Time,* which was published in November of 1968.

The second call, from the White House, asked me to serve as chairman of the Commission on Urban Problems, which had been authorized by Congress, along with an appropriation of $1.5 million. The commission, I was told, need not confine itself to housing, but could consider the broad context of all the difficulties facing our cities. President Johnson assured me that he did not want a whitewash and that we would have a free hand in our studies and recommendations. Under those conditions, I accepted.

The Commission on Urban Problems

THE MEMBERS of the commission, appointed by the President and including four eminent architects, were drawn from across the country and turned out to be a splendid group. From the start, nevertheless, it was apparent that we would have to fight for our promised independence. Robert Weaver, secretary of Housing and Urban Development, asked for a veto over our budget, which we declined. To conciliate him, we allowed one of his representatives to attend all of our meetings. This was a mistake and opened a source of mutual suspicion. Until this time, Weaver and I had enjoyed a cordial relationship, and I had helped to organize the Senate support for his confirmation. But no doubt his position was frustrating, and he was very sensitive to our criticism.

Believing that there is no substitute for the human eye, I proposed that we conduct a series of hearings in cities across the country. Although HUD at first raised objections, over the next seven months we held hearings in twenty-two cities, ranging geographically from Boston and New Haven to Houston, Denver, San Francisco, and Los Angeles, and architecturally from the many-storied tenements of Harlem to the small, single homes of Watts. The cities included most of the chief urban centers, and we personally inspected the slums of each. We saw how false was the current wisecrack: "If you have seen one slum, you have seen them all." At the same time, we took testimony and tried to provide a chance for dissidents, as well as public officials, to speak. Sometimes we preceded the violent riots that took place during the long hot summer of 1967, and at other times we followed them.

While this was going on, research continued by the experts we had engaged to prepare special studies. The more we probed, the more disillusioned we became with the actual progress of both housing and urban renewal. We were dismayed by the complacent ineffectiveness of HUD itself. Naturally, our program did not sit well with either Secretary Weaver or his associates, and as their opposition grew, they bombarded the White House with criticisms of our work.

Howard Shuman, whom I brought to the commission as its executive director, has well summarized some of our findings,* and I cannot do better than to report them, with certain additions of my own:

1. Though the 1949 Housing Act authorized 810,000 units of public housing to be built in six years, only two-thirds of that number had been completed in almost twenty years.

2. In 1967 only 30,000 public-housing units were being built. Of these, more than half were efficiency and one-bedroom apartments for the elderly. Many of the remainder were in the smaller cities. In other words, virtually no housing was being constructed for large families in the ghettos. The lack was the greatest for those who needed it most—namely, poor Negro families. There were relatively few three-bedroom apartments being built for the poor, and still fewer four-bedroom apartments.

3. While the so-called moderate-income housing program, known as 221(d)(3), had authorized 45,000 units a year since its beginning, in reality it took six years to build the number of units authorized for a single year.

4. Urban renewal had destroyed about 400,000 units of housing for poor people. But on the sites that had been bulldozed, the program planned to build only 20,000 public-housing units, or one-twentieth of the number of units destroyed.

5. HUD claimed that the major reason for the low production of all forms of subsidized housing was the lack of sites. Our commission established that well over half of the land in the urban-renewal program had not yet been "committed" to any building whatever. There were sites in abundance. There was also no imaginative use of water fronts, junk yards, and other such locations.

In Detroit and Cleveland, for example, we found vast acreages lying idle when those cities blew up. As Shuman wrote, hundreds of sites in Detroit had been bulldozed, resulting in terrible crowding in the riot sections, although the urban-renewal land was empty of new housing. Nor did the plans for the future provide any. Instead, they called for a medi-

* See "Behind the Scenes and Under the Rug," *The Washington Monthly*, July, 1969, pp. 13–22.

cal center, luxury housing, and athletic facilities for Wayne State University.

6. Taken as a whole, the government programs had destroyed far more housing units for the poor than they had built. While well over a million units had been destroyed by urban renewal, highway programs, demolitions for public housing, code enforcement, and other actions, fewer than 1 million units of all forms of subsidized housing had been created. In the strict sense, it was even less. Based on the existing pace of construction, our projections showed that this pattern would continue.

7. The processing time for all major programs was incredibly slow. One-third of the completed urban-renewal projects had taken longer than nine years. Generally, public housing took three to four years. The same was true for the moderate-income program.

8. Up until the 1967 riots, the FHA had refused to guarantee housing loans in what were called "red-lined" areas. These were the areas shown by actual or mythical red lines on confidential city maps by banks, savings-and-loan institutions, and the FHA. They embraced ghetto areas, where the banks automatically refused to grant loans and the FHA refused to insure. Each then proceeded to blame the other. Thus the official policy was against insuring where it was needed most.

Our criticism of this policy led to some improvement in 1968, but was bitterly resented by the top officials in HUD.

9. In the 1960's the value of the indirect government housing subsidies for the upper 20 per cent of income groups, through the deduction of property taxes and of interest paid on mortgages, was twice that of housing subsidies and welfare payments to the poor. While ignoring the poor, and especially the Negro poor, HUD and the FHA had helped to provide vast housing opportunities for the white middle and upper classes. To reform these policies we brought them into the open. HUD wanted to sweep them under the rug. Yet as we worked, cities were blowing up, and lack of housing was a major cause.

In addition to the growing opposition of HUD, we experienced some major disappointments with our own staff. Most of them did good work. Some did superlatively well. But there were a few who either could not bring themselves to criticize HUD's job or were unable to prepare a coherent analysis of what was happening. They were in strategic sections of our staff, and in the late winter of 1968 it looked as though they would stymie the production of any report worthy of the name. For this reason I myself undertook the first draft of the housing and urban-renewal sections. For five months I worked night and day, seven days a week, preparing this draft. Shuman did the same. Finally, just a half hour before I went out to the Democratic convention in Chicago, I completed my chapters and turned them over to Shuman, Walter Rybeck, and Erwin Knoll for final editing.

When I came back from that racking convention, I was exhausted and suffered a series of intestinal attacks. Nevertheless, I spent a great deal of October working on the report and campaigning for my friend Hubert Humphrey. Immediately after the election we buckled down to finish the report, and in this many of the staff and all members of the commission did themselves proud.

After four revisions we had a report that was unanimously approved by the commission, many of whose members had written key sections. It consisted of 500 pages of closely packed data, with over 200 specific recommendations. It was accompanied by twenty-two detailed research reports and five volumes of hearings. Coleman Woodbury, of the University of Wisconsin, and Richard O'Neill, editor of *House and Home,* did especially valuable work, and of the staff, Walter Rybeck, Allen Manvel, and Stanley Heckman made important contributions. Two young women, Hope Marinden and Sone Takahara, detected a vital omission and prepared several excellent chapters to fill the gap. Neutral sources have called the report "a landmark in the history of urban studies," and have agreed with most of our recommendations. John Fischer, former editor of *Harper's,* called it the best of the urban studies and so basic that it should lead to a revision of our thinking comparable to that effected by the *Federalist* papers.

Among the best sections of the report was the analysis of prefabricated housing, manufactured in separate parts and assembled at the site. After a visit to the National Homes Company in Lafayette, Indiana, I was impressed with the possibilities for large-scale production. Later I was delighted with the agreement between National Homes and Mayor Daley under which 200 four-bedroom houses were to be erected on vacant city-owned and scattered sites in Chicago. Each of these houses had over 1,000 square feet of space, wall-to-wall carpeting, one and a half bathrooms, a well-equipped kitchen, a good living room, decent furniture, plus air conditioning and interior heat. Outside, there were hedges, trees, lawns, and a recreation space with a pool for every eight houses. Each was priced at $13,500, and this included a modest profit for National Homes. Since the city donated the land, under the terms of the legislation, with low interest subsidies for middle-income housing, the units could be rented for $76 a month or $912 a year. They would be used, on a self-supporting basis, for those on the fringes of poverty. The poorest would need additional subsidies—which our commission favored.

Still further economies in the National Homes venture would be made if a duplicate plant is built, as originally planned, in or near the Chicago ghetto. The Chicago building unions, although reputedly tough in bargaining, co-operated in all arrangements, and even volunteered to pay a third or more of the costs of the new factory. But because of many complications, the early hopes may not be realized.

For large apartment buildings we found that S. W. Shelley, of Puerto Rico, had created a cost-reducing innovation. He had whole rooms factory-built, furnished, and hoisted into place, thus saving time and labor. The ceilings provided the floor of the rooms above. The sides of adjoining rooms served also as the sides of the center rooms. Only the front and back of the center room had to be built in the form of panels, also constructed in the factory. Special materials in the ceilings, sides, and panels muffled vibration and noise. In all, nearly 40 per cent of the usual construction work was cut, and the remaining 60 per cent was done in the factory and not on the site. In Puerto Rico, Shelley had already completed a 500-unit apartment building, successfully demonstrating his methods.

However, the economics of prefabricated housing will not be attained unless there is also a mass demand, and this is almost impossible for individuals to achieve. Only the government can act as catalyst. Our report suggested that HUD should select five promising experimental designs for new methods and materials and underwrite the yearly construction of 1,000 units of each for five years, or five times 5,000 units, making a total of 25,000 units. This would not only pay for the overhead but also yield a profit. The results should then be appraised in terms of both cost and quality. I was confident of the results. Senator Proxmire and Congressman Reuss were successful in getting this provision into the 1968 Housing Act (as Section 108) over the opposition of HUD. Full authority for a vigorous public-housing program of more than 100,000 units annually was also given HUD for a two-year period, from 1968 to 1970. Unfortunately, HUD did not take advantage of this opportunity. Under Weaver, the housing experiments never exceeded fifteen units and usually were far less. In spite of the early efforts of Secretary George Romney, the housing bureaucracy still seems reluctant to move. Romney's Operation Breakthrough is a small one, with no really large projects and most of them less than a hundred units. He has claimed a big advance in public housing, from 48,000 in 1968 to 94,000 in 1971. But 17,000 of these are leasings of already constructed buildings, not new ones. Furthermore, 39,000 of the remaining 77,000 are one-bedroom or "efficiency" apartments, leaving only 38,000 others, with few three-bedroom apartments being built. This is a very modest advance over the past.

Experiments have shown that the technical problems of prefabrication and construction can be solved. But, with the exception of National Homes, Shelley, Levitt, and a few others, they have not produced any significant reduction in costs over conventional methods and materials. The success of the new methods, I repeat, hangs upon the development of mass production and this in turn hinges upon the creation of a mass demand. For the lack of these requirements many promising experiments have failed. With them, there would be a chance of success. But how can we make the housing bureaucracy move in a more vigorous fashion? Congress, industry, and the unions all seem to be far ahead of it.

If costs can be significantly reduced, the lower economic middle class can be housed on a self-respecting, self-supporting basis. An attendant cut in housing costs for the poor will also make it possible to provide for more families with the same amount of money. Our commission tried to open the door, hitherto barred, for this solution, which is one of the great challenges of the future. It is the challenge of ridding ourselves of ghettos and their evils. It is the challenge of giving decent housing and a healthy environment to all our people. To me, this is more urgent than spending $30 billion to explore the moon.

Revenue Sharing

THANKS TO the able studies of Allen Manvel, the commission also recommended a form of revenue-sharing of the national income with local governments of 50,000 people or more. This was to be doubled on a per-capita basis when the local governments exceeded 100,000 in population. It would not only bypass the anti-big-city legislatures dominated by the rural regions and the bedroom suburbs, but also help to consolidate the multitudinous small suburban units, reducing them to a manageable number. On the basis of the 1960 population, there were only 700 cities and counties of over 50,000, but they included 122 million people, or two-thirds of the nation's population.

Furthermore, we recommended a reform of the general property tax, which is the chief source of local revenues. The common practice is to tax improvements in the form of buildings at a higher proportion of their market value than is followed in the case of vacant land. This discourages improvements and encourages the withdrawal of land from development. We reached an almost unanimous agreement that both land and buildings should be assessed at their market value.

I went further. Land and natural resources were the gifts of nature and in themselves did not increase. Their owners could and did levy tribute upon what was produced. As population and capital increased, the nearly fixed amount of land became relatively more scarce, and its value accordingly rose. As I have mentioned, I asked Manvel to find the difference between the bare-land values of the nation in 1966 and what they had been ten years previous. Manvel, an able former section chief in the Census Bureau, was very careful about his conclusions. In the summer of 1968, in addition to magnificent work in many areas, he submitted the first draft of his study of bare-land values, which were independent of improvements on or in the soil. He found that they had increased from about $270 billion in 1956 to $520 billion in 1966. This was an increase of $250 billion over the ten years, and an average yearly increase of $25 billion.

We took the results both to private students of America's wealth and to the research staff of the Treasury, which had been making the same type of studies. They pronounced Manvel's results "not unreasonable." The more I examined them, the more I was convinced that they were not only reasonable, but suggested the best source for the added revenues needed by urban areas for housing, recreation, and anti-pollution campaigns.

The increase in land values had occurred independently of any effort by the owners. The price of land had gone up because the supply of it was relatively fixed at a time when there had been an increase in population and in the real national product. The increase had therefore been a "finding." I believed that at least a slice of this increase, say one-fifth, should go to those who had created it. This $50 billion could have accomplished great improvements in the society that had multiplied these values. If the taxes came to two-fifths of the increment, the amount accruing to society would have been $100 billion.

Furthermore, this increase in values had been obtained by a population growth of only 28 million. It has been estimated that by 1985 the population may increase by slightly over 50 million. Production per capita will also rise. A large share of future progress should rightfully go to the general public.

I proposed that the community should take at least a fifth of this "unearned increment," but the commission turned this down by a two-to-one vote. With three colleagues—Coleman Woodbury, Jeh Johnson, and Ezra Ehrenkrantz—I prepared, not a minority report, but a supplementary opinion, which was published in the report.

Perhaps it is too much to hope that this proposal will soon be adopted. Yet land income should certainly be taxed more fully. The American public has avoided this decision in the past by labeling all such proposals as "Henry George's single tax." But to classify a position does not refute it.

The Commission's Experience
with the White House

IN EARLY NOVEMBER, I sent copies of the third draft of the commission's final report to both Secretary Weaver and the White House. In addition, I wrote Joseph Califano, the President's assistant, asking for an appointment for the commission. At this time the report would be formally presented to the President and the group could receive the usual expression of thanks. The members had worked hard, donating a large share of their private lives. There had been seventy-one meetings in twenty-one months, with additional assignments for several.

After waiting a few days, I tried to telephone Califano, but whenever I called his office he was at home, and when I called his home he was "taking a shower." When I finally reached this well-bathed young man, he said he would meet me at the White House at a specified time. He did not. After I had waited an hour and a quarter, an assistant to the assistant appeared and asked how many had signed the report. I said it was unanimous. After another wait, Califano came to repeat the question and looked disappointed at my reply.

He informed me that the President was angry at the report's criticism of HUD's failure to provide housing for the poor. I said that the report was truthful and should help to correct the failure and to fulfill the President's program for such housing.

Califano then proposed that the commission should submit its report to President-elect Nixon. I explained that this was impossible because our legislative mandate required that the President receive the report by December 31, 1968. Since Califano discouraged an appointment and since a personal letter to the President brought no reply, the commission unanimously backed my release of the material to the press by December 15. This we did, although HUD tried twice to stop us. Finally, having delivered the report, the commission, unthanked by anyone, went out of business.

Our experience was not unique that year. The White House had also given the silent treatment to the much publicized Report on the Causes and Prevention of Violence by Governor Otto Kerner's commission, and to the useful report of the President's National Advisory Commission on Rural Poverty. Since all three studies had criticized current conditions, the President ignored them.

And yet the Congress would not have set up the commissions, or financed them, had all been rosy. It was no pleasure for any of the President's appointees to publicize mistakes. But our assignment was to make a faithful study of urban problems, and we had done the best we could.

Looking back, I can see that the President's frustration over Vietnam and his loss of popularity in the opinion polls made him increasingly resentful of all criticism. While he wanted the poor to be well housed, he did not want it said that after five years of his administration they were still not cared for, and that some of his agents had really not tried hard enough to remedy matters. During his last sixty days in office, his memory of old antagonisms blotted out many current goals. He reverted to the Johnson of his Senate period, 1949–60.

As we tried to make clear in our report, the obstacle was greater than HUD: it was the ambivalence of the American people. Although no one wanted to maintain slums, few of the middle class wished to be neighbors of either the white or Negro poor. When public housing was suggested for moderate-income neighborhoods, there was an outcry against it. On the other hand, by confining all of the poor to inadequate space, already decaying and desolate, slums are perpetuated, and the children who live in them must follow the ghetto pattern. Dispersion is important, and yet mayors and aldermen yield to popular pressure and draw the noose tighter around the slums. If we would all take a stand together, we might overcome the prejudices. We will never do so if government yields to racism and snobbery and then denies that it has done so.

The Democratic Convention

I WENT TO CHICAGO as a delegate-at-large to the disastrous Democratic convention of 1968. For a month, the Chicago newspapers had been full of statements from the leaders of the SDS showing that they were determined to create incidents that would cause the police to strike back. Had the police managed to keep discipline, this might have been avoided. But they could not withstand the combined stress of fatigue, fear, and extreme provocation. Large numbers of protestors, angered at the ban against camping in the parks, filled the streets near the hotels and around the convention hall. Police efforts to restrict the movement of the crowd were thwarted by the protest leaders shouting directions over bullhorns and pushing girls and "innocents" up to the front. Though most of the crowd wanted a peaceful protest, the behavior of a few, showering abuse, refuse, and even excrement, inevitably provoked violence. As the police overreacted, the SDS leaders accomplished their objective. Fortunately, no one was killed, but many were hurt, and the Democratic party was so wounded that it could not win. Leftist critics of Humphrey broke up his meetings in Philadelphia and Boston, and, along with their actions in Chicago, placed an unjust stamp on his campaign. Humphrey, contrary to Johnson's later interpretation, gained rapidly after his Salt Lake City speech, in which he showed a willingness to go the second mile to gain an honorable peace. But he had too far to travel.

Although ill, I did my best to help Humphrey. I campaigned in Illinois and the Middle West, and gave far more than I could afford both to his campaign and to those of progressive Democratic Senators and Congressmen. But the curse of the convention sent Hubert down to defeat by almost as narrow a margin as that by which Nixon had lost in 1960. I think this was a loss to the country, although Nixon has done better than I had expected.

As a Democrat, along with George McGovern and others, I helped raise money for deserving Democratic Senators who needed funds for the

1970 elections. We distributed more than $600,000 for their campaigns, contributing more than the impoverished national party did and with lower administrative costs than those of other widely advertised private committees.

Taxes and Tariffs Again

OVER THE YEARS my abiding concerns have been domestic, and after my defeat I renewed activities in behalf of two of these. With Walter Reuther and other tax reformers, I tried from 1966 to 1969 to remove the injustices rampant in our tax system. We did not succeed, and, with the exception of Phil Stern, the wealthy liberals would not join our committee. They profited too much from the existing order.

In the fall of 1970, forty years after I had helped to draft the protest against the Smoot-Hawley tariff, I took up a similar task in connection with a tariff bill the House Ways and Means Committee had reported. This bill was based on quotas, rather than on increased duties, and was in fact worse than Smoot-Hawley. That act, by imposing a higher tax on goods coming into the country, discouraged imports. By cutting production costs and trading margins, however, foreign goods could still compete with both American and other foreign goods. No such safety provision exists in the case of quotas. No one knows the total to be admitted or the prices to be charged. Many abuses could result.

In a letter to economists I repeated the 1930 arguments, pointing out that those prophecies had then been fulfilled, and the mutual shutting off of both exports and imports had led to a trade war that was one of the causes of the rise of the Nazis and the breakup of the democracies. Trade wars could not be combined with peaceful alliances. And yet the blame for the nontariff discriminations was not now as great in the case of the United States as in that of other nations. They had been shielded from legitimate criticism by our State Department, while the Tariff Commission denied all legitimate relief to our injured producers. Such acts have only strengthened the demand for retaliatory action by us. This move, however, would only make matters worse.

I urged that the U.S. should call an international conference, at which each nation would confess its sins and lay out a mutual program for getting rid of the nontariff discriminations under a specific timetable. The U.S. would do the same, beginning with the abolition of the American selling price (ASP), which had imposed an excessively high duty on chemicals by changing the application of the tariff from the foreign competitive price to the domestic monopolized price.

In 1930 we had felt abundantly vindicated when 1,028 economists signed our petition. While it had no immediate result, it had an ultimate effect in strengthening Cordell Hull's hand in getting his reciprocal-trade program adopted. In 1970, with the co-operation of the Committee for a Fair Trade Policy, which worked closely with us, we obtained no fewer than 5,025 signatures. May this petition ultimately have five times the influence of the former one!

Vietnam and the Committee for Peace with Freedom

IN 1967 I served as the organizing chairman of the Committee for Peace with Freedom in Vietnam, which supported resistance to Communist aggression in that country. We began with a distinguished group of about 140 Americans, including former President Eisenhower and General Omar Bradley. Our membership rose to over 1,500. Hoping for mutual de-escalation of the war, we opposed a one-sided U.S. withdrawal. We worked especially for land reform, so appropriate in a rice-producing economy. This had been successful in Japan, Korea, and Formosa, where Wolf Ladejinsky had taken the lead.

Meanwhile, even the smallest towns and streets of our country saw boys brought home in aluminum boxes, killed in a faraway war, dimly understood, and in support of a corrupt local government. Sentiment against the Vietnam war mounted rapidly. Other nations that had wanted our help and protection not only refused to help us, but also joined in a torrent of denunciation. Totally absent was the sense of collective security that we had helped to create during World War II, and that was tenuously kept alive during the Korean War. The other nations considered only their short-term interests and expected us to bear the full burden. Our people, while preferring a mutual withdrawal, were moving toward a one-sided exit. Aware of this, the Communists made complete American withdrawal the prior condition even for discussions of peace. In turn, this blocked all effective approaches between the United States, China, and North Vietnam.

Because he had lost public support, Lyndon Johnson finally withdrew from the Presidential race. His later broadcast conveyed a more palatable interpretation, but seemed an attempt to falsify history. The truth was that Eugene McCarthy's vote in New Hampshire, which amounted to 43 per cent, was, in itself, almost enough to cause the withdrawal, but this was not all. Private polls in Wisconsin showed that in that state's primary, coming in two days, McCarthy would defeat Johnson by more than two to one. This was the final blow.

With the passage of time, great weaknesses have appeared in the American position in Southeast Asia. They were highlighted by the publication of the hitherto secret Pentagon papers, plus the private studies of two competent scholars, E. G. Windchy and Anthony Austin.* These have centered on the Gulf of Tonkin incident in August, 1964. North Vietnamese torpedo boats were represented as having made unprovoked attacks at that time, one on the American destroyer *Maddox* and one on the *C. Turner Joy.* This was the assigned reason for the administration-sponsored resolution legitimizing our extensive use of force in Vietnam. It was a virtual declaration of war.

The resolution was passed unanimously by the House; there were only two dissenters, Wayne Morse and my heroic friend Ernest Gruening, in the Senate. I could not bring myself to doubt the testimony of Secretary McNamara before Congressional committees and the assurances of Senator Fulbright, and so I voted with the majority. This resolution was then used by the administration to justify wide-scale aerial bombardment of many North Vietnamese positions.

The 1967–68 study of our involvement in Vietnam made by members of McNamara's staff, now known as the Pentagon papers, in the version released by Daniel Ellsberg, together with the books of Windchy and Austin, shows that while the firing of torpedoes at the *Maddox* on August 2 certainly occurred, we had provoked it. South Vietnamese gunboats flying no flag, but American-bought and directed and probably under control of the CIA, had previously attacked Communist installations on islands in the Gulf of Tonkin and given them a severe shelling. The Communist launching of torpedoes was, therefore, in response to this attack, rather than an unprovoked assault. Furthermore, there are reasons to doubt the peaceful mission of the *Maddox,* as represented by McNamara. It seems to have strayed into North Vietnamese waters, which had been set by that government at twelve miles from shore.

From the start there was confusion about the alleged attack on the *C. Turner Joy* on August 4. The officer in charge cabled that there had been one, but a few hours later expressed doubts. Although both the Navy and the Defense Department finally confirmed the attack, there is no evidence that it actually occurred. After a three-year study, Anthony

* See *The Pentagon Papers,* as published by *The New York Times,* New York: Bantam Books, 1971, especially pages 259–68. This document is a summary of an original study courageously made under Secretary McNamara by the Defense Department.

The Beacon Press published a four-volume, 3-million-word version provided by Senator Mike Gravel (hard-cover, $50; paperback, $20). This was said to include all but 5 per cent of the original study. The rejoinder of the Defense Department was to publish all but five sections of the original report.

See also Windchy's *Tonkin Gulf,* New York: Doubleday, 1971, and Austin's *The President's War,* Philadelphia: J. B. Lippincott, 1971. For a good analysis of the news as seen from the media point of view prior to the publication of the Pentagon papers, see Marvin Kalb and Elie Abel, *Roots of Involvement,* New York: W. W. Norton, 1971.

Austin maintains that the rumor derived from a wrong decoding of North Vietnamese messages that referred to August 2, but were thought by the U.S. to read August 4.

In any event, great decisions were built on a faulty base. Wayne Morse deserves much credit for presenting to the Senate facts that had apparently been leaked to him from a high source. Because he could give no source for his information, his fellow Senators failed to believe him. Along with my colleagues, I erred in believing McNamara instead of Morse. The Secretary did not tell the whole truth when he testified before the Senate Foreign Relations Committee. He corroborated the false impression of American innocence. The deception of the administration is clear when the text of the Tonkin Gulf resolution is compared with one drafted some months before the alleged assaults. Moreover, an official "scenario," showing the necessary steps to arouse public opinion before and after the occurrence marked "D-Day," suggests a willingness on the part of the administration to manipulate events and perhaps trigger a D day.

These are the facts about the legal opening of hostilities. Whatever the responsibilities of President Johnson and Secretary McNamara, it is to their credit that for some months they resisted an effort by the military to commit our ground forces to open war in Vietnam. That came early in April, 1965, long after Johnson's triumphant re-election and inauguration. After the bombing of the American embassy in Saigon, the administration not only started further bombing in the north, but also ordered the Marines to take the offensive and sent more ground troops. The escalation of the war steadily continued until we had 700,000 ground troops in South Vietnam by the winter of 1968.

The Communists then openly attacked most South Vietnamese cities. From a military standpoint, they finally failed; but from a propaganda standpoint, they succeeded. Clearly they remained a very effective foe. It seemed to most Americans that, after years of heavy outlays in men and money, we had not gained enough support to justify a continuance of the war. When the military asked for another 206,000 troops, it was the last straw. Johnson said "No," and soon withdrew from the Presidential race. Against a similar background, Nixon later chose a partial withdrawal from Vietnam.

These facts do not exonerate the North Vietnamese. As shown by investigations in Hue and Cambodian cities, their policy has been both vengeful and bloody. The facts do not alter the probable attempts by the Communists to dominate Southeast Asia. They do raise profound questions about American involvement, as well as about the relations between Congress and the executive, and the attitude of the military and diplomatic bureaucracy toward both Congress and the public. Neither the diplomats nor the military gave Congress the full facts, apparently not trusting its members with the truth.

Granted that a nation of 200 million people of diverse backgrounds does not readily arrive at a wise consensus, it nevertheless is reckless for any administration to treat the members of Congress as dupes to be fed false information in order to gain their acquiescence. The degree to which the military and diplomatic leaders should share the truth with those whom the nation has chosen as its representatives is a grave problem for the future.

We must also face the consequences of the war upon our own people. If the Vietnamese have been cruel in reprisals, a growing number of young Americans have also developed callous and bloody ways, as revealed at My Lai and in other "incidents." Also, in the sterile boredom of their lives, many in the armed forces have become drug addicts. Furthermore, because of the financial burden of the war, this prosperous nation lacks the wherewithal to deal with its own domestic problems, to remake the ghettos and to spend enough on health and education for coming generations. We must weigh these needs to establish our national priorities.

Going back further, the Pentagon documents remove any romanticism about our relation with Ngo Dinh Diem. We were responsible for installing him as ruler in South Vietnam, and we made a most unfortunate choice. Instead of trying to unify the country, he deliberately estranged the Buddhists. Instead of trying to help distribute the land more equitably, he moved in exactly the opposite direction. Such land reform as had been introduced was canceled, with the result that the ownership of land became more concentrated. Instead of introducing more self-government, he helped destroy such local self-government as did exist. His was a bad administration.

In the end we deserted him, and allowed him to be seized and assassinated without lifting a finger in his defense. Our initial good intentions had been completely misplaced, and we had given a poor account of ourselves and of the democracy we supposedly were trying to install.

Most disillusioning was the memorandum by Assistant Secretary of Defense John T. McNaughton in which he ascribed the aims of the Pentagon as: "70%—To avoid a humiliating U.S. defeat (to our reputation as a guarantor). 20%—To keep SVN [South Vietnam] (and the adjacent) territory from Chinese hands. 10%—To permit the people of SVN to enjoy a better, freer way of life." This is a direct contradiction of our country's official claims.

44

Reflections on the Future

DURING THESE LAST YEARS several experiences have deepened my encounter with life. The first, beginning in December, 1968, has been sickness. The day after we sent our Urban Commission report to the President, I succumbed to Asiatic flu with heart and lung complications. Extreme fatigue and frustration had sapped my resistance, but I was grateful that my health had held out until our work was done.

Twice the old gentleman with a scythe advanced toward me wearing his most winning smile. Then he retreated, and the doctors said I could go home. Emily and I finally went to Puerto Rico to swim, walk on the beach, and add some chapters to this autobiography. During the spring of 1969 I worked on the more impersonal sections, trying them out in lectures at the New School. Then in late May and June I took up the college lecture and commencement circuit, but noticed that I tired easily and that my once-excellent memory was becoming hazy.

On August 11, when I went to my office downtown, I found myself walking and talking confusedly, and I went to see my doctor. He telephoned Emily to come and take me home. I could see that she was distressed, while I was vacuously happy. Stepping out of the car, I fell flat on my face and, to my surprise, found that I could not move or speak. I heard an occasional car pass, although it was as in a dream. In falling, I had dragged Emily down, but she extricated herself and managed to move me into the house. How she did this, I shall never know, since she weighs a hundred pounds less and is a full foot shorter than I. Trying to stand, I fell again, and then inched along to my bed, where I stayed until the next noon. Then for the third time in eight months I made the journey to the hospital by ambulance. There I stayed for three weeks.

All my children were attentive, and their visits, as well as Emily's constant presence, were consoling. It became apparent that my mind was not affected and that the stroke was confined to the right side. I was grateful to Medicare for the help it gave with doctors' fees and hospital charges, and for the generosity of AFTRA (American Federation of Television and Radio Artists), which I had joined for my NBC television series. After coming out of the hospital there were months of physical therapy— swimming, walking, hand and leg exercises—and valuable experiences with the therapists. Emily and our good doctor, Bretney Miller, encouraged my reviving interest in things intellectual. So in October, with Emily's invaluable help, I went back slowly to work on this book. With the coming of the New Year I began to draft missing chapters.

My second experience was with youth. In the spring of 1970, the chancellor of the Chicago Circle of the University of Illinois wrote that his institution wanted to confer an honorary degree upon me. Since I was then badly crippled, I hesitated to accept. But the degree was a gesture of conciliation that I could not decline.

The Chicago branch of the university had been built on the site of Hull House, where Jane Addams had lived for half a century. The original plan had been to bulldoze the whole area, destroying not only an old Greek community, but all of the settlement buildings. This idea shocked me into action; I organized and spoke at several protest meetings. Since public disapproval rose rapidly, the university was caught in a bind. The whole project was threatened, but fortunately Irving Dilliard, who had just been elected to the board, provided statesmanship. In the end, the board reversed itself to save the central building.

Once having decided to preserve rather than destroy, the university did a remarkable work of restoration. Today the fine old mansion embodies the living tradition of a great period in Chicago's history. Filled with the furniture and photographs of the extraordinary group who once worked there, Hull House adds rare distinction to the new brick-and-mortar campus. This was the background of the offer of an honorary degree.

Shortly before the convocation, I received an unsigned letter from a group of "concerned" students and faculty members, demanding to know my current views on Vietnam. If they were not satisfied with my answer, they threatened some form of action. A petition of some ninety names accompanied the letter. The Chicago press reported that these people planned a demonstration.

Not wishing to embarrass the university, I offered to let the chancellor announce that bad health prevented my coming. But the university had already suffered a series of harassments by the group and refused to capitulate. Against my doctor's advice, I offered to appear at an open meeting with the protestors. This proved "unacceptable" to the group. They would come only to a closed meeting, in which they would control the attendance and release the publicity. As this news spread, public opinion turned against them.

The *Sun-Times* ran an editorial explaining that I was being recognized for my general record, which it commended. Kenneth Galbraith, who was to be the commencement speaker, not only declined to attack my Vietnam position, but gave me heart-warming praise and laid down sensible limits to the practices of dissent. This was of tremendous help. Finally, my gallant Emily played a part. She had been invited to join in a popular television colloquium to discuss her new biography of Margaret Sanger. However, on arrival at the studio she found the very articulate leader of the protestors, a young philosophy teacher. In perfect good temper, Emily defended not only me, but also academic freedom.

I kept out of the battle, but before the convocation I told a group of reporters that the young people had a right to dissent and that their horror at the war casualties was also right. Then I waited with interest for the walkout against my degree. About fifty protestors out of an attendance of 15,000 rose quietly and left the hall. The press said that thirty of these were young faculty members.

While the experience was trying, it was constructive. If the planners had hoped for either a surrender or a violent confrontation, they were defeated. The dissenters were treated in a friendly and civilized way—as dissenters were not in my day. When exposed to this treatment, their numbers melted away. But they could still keep their dignity as citizens. The university administration had been both humane and wise.

At this period I received a surprising gift from my earlier years. As I cleaned out a stack of economics books and papers in the basement, I became aware of a change of emphasis in my old concerns with the function and the theory of production, to which I had given so much thought in middle life. Discouraged by the cold reception of my views, I had not kept up with current trends after I had plunged into politics. I was now astonished by the extent to which the Cobb-Douglas function had been accepted. Economists had taken it up in Europe, Japan, and Australia. Paul Samuelson, Nobel Prize winner, had included a favorable reference in his authoritative text, *Economics*.

Most gratifying was its acceptance by the Economics Department of the University of Chicago. The work had never received a favorable word from my old colleagues, whose criticisms had, indeed, been severe. Now the faculty had called to a professorship Marc Nerlove, leading productivity theorist in the country. He was, incidentally, the son of my colleague Sam, and had grown up in an apartment directly below ours.

A seedling that I had planted long ago, but left untended, had been cared for by younger men and in the fullness of time has become a sturdy tree. All this was heady news for an ailing and retired politician. I thereupon decided to return to economics to carry my studies a step further. In this I was most fortunate in renewing my scholastic alliance with Grace Gunn, who had recently retired after twenty years of service with the Senate Finance Committee. Since Australian labor statistics were superior, we began with studies from the 1950's and '60's, with observations from 160 industries in each of four years. The results were strikingly like those of thirty years earlier. An increase of 1 per cent in labor, with capital constant, brought an increase of .6 to .65 per cent in product or net value added. An increase of 1 per cent in the quantity of capital, with labor constant, brought an increase in product of from .35 to .4 per cent. An increase of 1 per cent in the quantity of both labor and capital brought an increase of nearly 1 per cent in product. Perhaps most important, the share that labor received of the net value added by manufacturing corresponded closely with labor's exponent in the production function.

Our first studies persuaded Joseph Pechman, of the Brookings Institution, to come to our aid. He arranged for a more extensive analysis, through a half-million-dollar computer lying idle some hours each day. Moreover, Mrs. William Hook, Research Associate of the Economic Studies Program at Brookings, agreed to become a co-worker. We are extending the Australian study to cover the period from 1912 to 1970, and also refining our measurement of production. Progress so far has been exhilarating and has confirmed the work that Cobb and I had undertaken at Amherst forty-five years earlier.

I have another project. It is an adventure in the arts, somewhat brashly conceived perhaps, by an economist-politician, but one that has increasingly filled my thoughts. It may develop into an essay or a small book on the "Last Phase of Genius." For some years I have been gathering materials and otherwise preparing myself. It has seemed to me that there are common principles of reconciliation as well as innovation underlying such disparate works as Micheiangelo's last *Pietà*s, the last five quartets of Beethoven, and the strange fantasies of Shakespeare's last plays. When I am tired of computers and statistics, this is something on which to stretch my mind.

Meanwhile, Emily, who has borne the burden of my convalescence, has managed to continue her own creative work. She had learned years earlier to salvage a quiet time for writing by rising very early in the morning. In this way she had written a book that she wanted to call *Women in a Man's World,* but which came out as *Remember the Ladies: The Story of the Women Who Helped Shape America.* Before Women's Lib, she wrote with insight on the feminist movement. In 1970, after extended research, she brought out *Margaret Sanger, Pioneer of the Future,* the first full-length biography of that remarkable woman. Currently, she has finished a lively story of Illinois to be used as a supplemental high-school reader.

During my afternoon walks in our peaceful middle-class community I sometimes caught glimpses of the tragedies that underlie so much of life. There is an imposing stone mansion of mystery, with tightly curtained windows, where two years ago I saw a man in a bathrobe walking on the lawn with the stiff-legged gait of a cripple. He disappeared within, and I have never seen him since. Then one afternoon a bearded and unkempt youth stepped out of the house, into an expensive car that suddenly appeared, and was rapidly driven away. About this time I also saw a couple of young people, with all the external marks of alienated hippies, enter another nearby home, to be seen no more. "For Sale" signs have appeared on four of the most impressive houses that sit high above the street, one vacant since the owner committed suicide two years ago. Changing my usual stroll one day, I inspected a house the police had just raided, taking a half-million dollars' worth of heroin and its black owner into custody. I wonder at the mixture of individual sin and social disintegration in all this, and whether it represents the normal flux of individual families or the flight of timorous whites as Washington becomes increasingly a black city.

More than ever I now enjoy my large family. Since the John Douglases live near Washington, I have seen their Katie and Peter develop from charming children to maturity. In my convalescence I became better acquainted with Paul's four youngsters: Philip, at Princeton; the twins, dark-haired Carolyn and blonde Chrissie, both entering college; and young Paul, who is avid for science books. Their visits and purposeful idealism help give me a confidence in the oncoming generation that most of my contemporaries lack. Meanwhile, my eldest daughter, Helen, has enhanced our lives by moving nearby, and we cherish the visits of my dear Dorothea and Amanda, her athletic ten-year-old.

The happiness of Jean with her husband, Ned Bandler, and their two small sons is a bright light that never fails us. Ned has been the best of counselors and a perfect son-in-law. We also rely on old friends, again neighbors, such as the Greenebaums and the Engers. Jane, now executive secretary for Senator Eagleton, has given me a part-time secretarial replacement in her sister, Virginia De Simone. These two young couples, along with several others, add much to our happiness.

And we have patio companions, starting with a pair of cardinals whom we feed throughout the year. If we forget, they remind us with indignant calls. The male is our chief ornament, glowing like a giant ruby when he perches on our evergreens. There is also a tiny, timid chipmunk who rarely ventures from his walled retreat, where he keeps his family, if any, in safe obscurity. Occasionally we are cheered by the visits of a female raccoon from nearby Rock Creek Park. Once, at dawn, she paraded across the patio with her family following in single file, her small burly mate and the two young ones. Although we don't exactly communicate, when "Scampy" comes, we offer food. This she always washes in our pool, not, I am told, for hygienic reasons, but for lack of salivation.

On spring and autumn evenings a pair of squirrels, predators on our bird seed, put on a high leaping act which dwarfs the efforts of any daring young man on a flying trapeze. Traveling in a circuit in the upper reaches of our white oaks, they perform their dangerous jumps apparently for no other reason than pure sport. They follow this exhibit with a run along the points of the picket fence that surrounds our swimming pool. Sometimes one of them gives us a baleful look, as though to say, "We know we are not your favorites, but we surpass all others." A friend who has watched us through the years, as we watch the squirrels, says that our feelings have mellowed not only for squirrels but also for right-wing Tories.

Occasionally at night I rehearse the names of former comrades in my struggles of the last half-century. I feel like Susan B. Anthony, the valiant old war horse of the woman-suffrage movement, who almost in a trance two days before she died recited the names of her comrades in her half-century crusade.

I cannot always agree with Browning's cheery lines in "Rabbi Ben Ezra." Old age brings losses of dear ones as well as physical afflictions, and also perhaps a darkening of the horizon. Certainly there is much wrong with the world today. Nevertheless, I see bright spots. The caliber of those in the Senate is higher than when I entered it, as is the politics of Illinois, both Republican and Democratic. I am enthusiastic about the new breed of young statesmen, including, among others, Adlai Stevenson III, Paul Simon, Anthony Scariano, and Abner Mikva.

On the personal level I have the happiness of congenial work, congenial friends, and my home with Emily. And so my spirit rallies to recite:

> *Grow old along with me!*
> *The best is yet to be,*
> *The last of life, for which the first was made.*

Index

Index